AIDŌS

AIDŌS

*The Psychology and Ethics
of Honour and Shame in
Ancient Greek Literature*

DOUGLAS L. CAIRNS

Learning Resources
Centre

CLARENDON PRESS · OXFORD
1993

Oxford University Press, Walton Street, Oxford OX2 6DP

Oxford New York Toronto
Delhi Bombay Calcutta Madras Karachi
Kuala Lumpur Singapore Hong Kong Tokyo
Nairobi Dar es Salaam Cape Town
Melbourne Auckland Madrid

and associated companies in
Berlin Ibadan

Oxford is a trade mark of Oxford University Press

Published in the United States
by Oxford University Press Inc., New York

© Douglas Cairns 1993

British Library Cataloguing in Publication Data
Data available
ISBN 0-19-814684-1

Library of Congress Cataloging in Publication Data
Cairns, Douglas L.
Aidōs: the psychology and ethics of honour and shame in ancient
Greek literature / Douglas L. Cairns.
Includes bibliographical references and index.
1. Greek literature—history and criticism. 2. Psychology in
literature. 3. Aidōs (The Greek word) 4. Ethics in literature.
5. Honor in literature. 6. Shame in literature. I. Title.
PA3015.P78C35 1993
880.9'353—dc20
ISBN 0-19-814684-1

1 3 5 7 9 10 8 6 4 2

Typeset by Joshua Associates Ltd, Oxford
Printed in Great Britain
on acid-free paper by
Bookcraft (Bath) Ltd
Midsomer Norton, Avon

FOR OWEN

οὐδένα θησαυρὸν παισὶν καταθήσῃ ἀμείνω
αἰδοῦς

PREFACE

THERE is clearly a great need for a comprehensive study of the concept of *aidōs* in Greek literature; the importance of the concept is apparent to anyone who has read at all widely in epic or tragedy, yet understanding of its essence is hindered, even among specialists, by the complexity which emerges once one appreciates the range of situations in which the relevant terms occur and the range of attitudes and responses which they are able to convey. While there does exist a number of limited studies, particularly of *aidōs* in Homer and of its meaning in crucial passages of Hesiod and Euripides, which are often very useful, the only comprehensive study made in the present century is that of von Erffa (1937), and, in spite of the merits of this work in many of its interpretations of individual passages, its overall approach is too disjointed to be helpful.

My aim, then, has been to provide the comprehensive overview which would assist as many as possible of those who might wish to gain some understanding of this important concept. In the absence of any other full and detailed modern study, I felt it best not just to concentrate on the isolation of generic characteristics of *aidōs*, but to investigate in detail the work of the concept in individual passages of individual works by individual authors, both in order that the work should be of use as a work of reference to students and scholars of Classics, who might wish to discover what I have to say about *aidōs* in some important passage or in some work in which it plays a significant role, and in order that a work which, I hope, will lay the groundwork for future studies of *aidōs* could not be accused of over-simplification or of glossing over the details. The book, however, is not solely or even principally intended as a work of reference, but as a contribution to the major areas of study in which an understanding of *aidōs* is important, and so I have tried, as far as possible, to keep in mind the interests of students and scholars in the fields of Greek intellectual history, Greek popular morality or values, Greek literature, and Greek philosophy. Accordingly, while the work as a whole addresses questions of interest to those Greek scholars of an intellectual-historical, social anthropological bent, it is to be hoped that its parts may be useful in more diverse ways, as limited contributions to, say, literary interpretation of Homer or tragedy, or philosophical interpretation of Plato and Aristotle.

Something should be said about the scope of the work. Chronologically, we cover the period from the beginning of Greek literature to the death of Aristotle, and it was never my intention to pursue the study beyond the end of the classical period, but within that period far from every work by every author who uses *aidōs* and its relatives is considered. Some readers may miss extensive discussion of Aristophanes, or the historians, or, perhaps most conspicuously, the orators. Certainly, any study of Athenian society and values will glean valuable material from the speeches of the orators, as from Aristophanic comedy; but these authors are omitted here, mainly because, once a chronological framework is adopted, and it is thus determined that Homeric, archaic, and tragic poetry will precede treatment of the orators, most of what the latter could tell us about *aidōs* has already been established. Initial researches, moreover, into Herodotus, Thucydides, Aristophanes, and the orators revealed to my satisfaction that no case could be made for the kind of prominence in the thought-world or artistic fabric of their works that is enjoyed by *aidōs* in the works which are considered in detail below. Broadly, these fall into two categories. First, there are those literary works in which we have the opportunity to observe the operation of *aidōs* as a dynamic force in human motivation, in which judgements as to the role and character of *aidōs* in individual passages can be set in the context of the characterization of the human agents involved and of the moral and intellectual outlook manifested by the work as a whole. In general, our best information on *aidōs* as a social and a psychological entity comes from those works, namely the Homeric and tragic poems, in which the opportunity to gather information as to the explicit and implicit values and evaluative categories which are operative in the text is combined with that of observing *aidōs* as a considerable emotional and motivating force in literary representations of human agency. In comparison with what can be gleaned from Homer and tragedy, the bald statements of the orators about *aidōs*—its typical presence in themselves and their clients and its typical absence in their opponents, its great value as a trait of character, and so on—are one-dimensional and unremarkable.

Secondly, we have the texts and authors who are considered in the final chapter, principally Plato and Aristotle, whose pronouncements on *aidōs* are of particular value in so far as they represent the reactions of two great moral and political philosophers to the phenomena of Greek psychological, ethical, and social experience as they appeared to them. These authors, in fact, may be seen as the early practitioners of an inquiry into the nature of *aidōs* and of the moral and social values which it promotes of which the present work is a continuation, and their observations are all the more valuable by virtue of their first-hand experience of the conditions of Greek moral and social life. Generally, then, the present study focuses on those who have, through artistic representation, something to *show* us about *aidōs* and those whose moral and political doctrines have something to *tell* us about *aidōs*. (Those who are reading this preface after a reading of the book will notice that neither of these categories covers the archaic poets considered in Chapter 2; they are included largely because their uses of *aidōs*-terms enable us to address the question of how far social and moral attitudes relevant to *aidōs* changed and developed in the period from the presumed date of the composition of the Homeric poems to the fifth century, but also because the paraenetic poets in particular provide valuable information on more general aspects of traditional values.)

Given the width of the audience for which this book is intended, it has seemed better to translate all extensive quotations from the Greek and to transliterate important Greek terms. There remains a certain amount of untranslated Greek in a few, very specialized contexts (such as notes on readings or emendations in the Greek text chosen for translation), but Greekless readers can rest assured that they are not being deprived of any information that is essential for their purposes. The translations are usually my own, and have no pretensions to literary merit. Transliteration is generally confined to single words in their lexicon form, except where transliteration of more than one word, sometimes in inflected form, is necessary to demonstrate to the Greekless the presence of terms derived from roots which they already know. Long *e* and *o* are marked as such (*ē*, *ō*), but otherwise quantities are unmarked.

In the matter of the rendering of Greek names, it was originally my intention to transliterate directly wherever this practice produced forms with which I felt reasonably comfortable. Gradually, however, so many inconsistencies developed that I decided to opt for those (usually Latinized) forms in more general use. The punctilious will detect inconsistencies in this, too (*Glaucon* and *Adeimantus*, not *Glauco* and *Adimantus*), but non-specialists may be relieved to find forms with which they are more familiar.

The greater part of this book developed from a doctoral thesis submitted to the University of Glasgow in 1987, and accordingly the greatest debts which I have incurred in the writing of both book and thesis are owed to my supervisors, Professor D. M. MacDowell and Mr A. F. Garvie, whose example of generous, fair-minded, and dedicated scholarship I have tried always to keep before me. I should also like to thank my external examiner, Professor W. G. Arnott, for his constructive and detailed criticisms, and his encouragement to pursue the project further. In developing my thoughts on *aidōs*, in extending my research to cover Plato and Aristotle, and in beginning the revision of the work for publication I was fortunate to be aided by the award of a Study Abroad Studentship by the Leverhulme Trust, which allowed me to spend an enjoyable and fruitful year (1987–8) at the Georg-August Universität, Göttingen; to the Research Awards Advisory Committee, its Secretary, and to Professor Dr C. J. Classen and all those who made me feel welcome in the Seminar für klassische Philologie, I am very grateful. At this stage, too, an anonymous reader for the Oxford University Press made valuable suggestions which helped consolidate my plans for the future shape of the work. Further research, revision, and, finally, the writing of the book itself were carried out in New Zealand, where generous research grants from the University of Otago allowed me to obtain many of the books and photocopies I needed from abroad. In these final stages I was assisted by several friends and colleagues: Professor Agathe Thornton read a version of the chapter on Homer and gave me the benefit of her great experience, Robert Hannah, of the University of Otago, advised me on a point of art history and iconography, and Dr Dougal Blyth, of the University of Auckland, saved me from serious error and pointed me firmly in the right direction by commenting on a draft of the section on Aristotle. (I should say that my concept of the right direction is not necessarily endorsed by him, and I may, in any case, have strayed since he first showed me the way.) Of all those who helped me at this stage, however, I owe most to my friend and Otago colleague, Robin Hankey, who read the entire final draft of the book with a meticulous eye for detail and a constant concern for the clarity, articulation, and consistency of the work as a whole. I quickly realized that a polite expression of objection or doubt from Robin usually pointed to a real deficiency of substance, structure, or approach, and I have tried to follow his advice to the best of my ability. Both I and my readers have much to thank him for. Finally, I extend my thanks to the Delegates of the Press for giving me the opportunity to publish this work, and to the Classics Editor, Hilary O'Shea, for her advice and patience during the long period of its composition.

Books are both like and unlike offspring: one is reluctant to bid farewell to that which one has nurtured, but a book has no natural gestation period, nor is there any fixed stage at which it may be said to have come of age; hence the tendency is to hold on, to update, and to revise for as long as possible. I know that if I were to work further on this project I should learn a great deal more and change my mind on many issues; but, as it is, having said what I have to say in some shape or form, I commit this study, provisional, incomplete, and flawed though it may be, to the wider world, accepting, as an author must, full responsibility for its shortcomings.

D.L.C.

Dunedin
February 1991

CONTENTS

Abbreviations   xv

Introduction   1
   0.1. General
   0.2. *Aidōs* and Emotion
   0.3. Shame and Guilt
   0.4. Shame-Culture and Guilt-Culture

1. *Aidōs* in Homer   48
   1.1. How Things Look and What People Say
   1.2. *Aidōs* in Battle
   1.3. *Aidōs* towards Others: The Cement of Homeric Society
   1.4. *Aidōs*, Women, and Sex
   1.5. *Aidōs*, 'Intelligence', and Excess
   1.6. Other Terms
   1.7. Conclusion

2. From Hesiod to the Fifth Century   147
   2.1. Hesiod
   2.2. The Homeric Hymns
   2.3. Elegiac and Iambic Poets
   2.4. Pindar

3. Aeschylus   178
   3.1. General
   3.2. Crucial Passages
   3.3. The Rejection of *Aidōs*
   3.4. *Aidōs* and *Sebas*

4. Sophocles   215
   4.1. General
   4.2. *Ajax, Electra, Philoctetes*

5. Euripides   265
   5.1. Personal Honour and Status
   5.2. Friends, Suppliants, and Guests
   5.3. Honour, Reputation, Retrospective Shame, and Guilt
   5.4. Sexuality and the Sexes
   5.5. The Importance of *Aidōs*

6. The Sophists, Plato, and Aristotle   343
    6.1. Conscience and the Ordinary Athenian
    6.2. Protagoras and Moral Education
    6.3. Doing Wrong in Secret: Or Shame-Culture versus Guilt-Culture
    6.4. Plato
    6.5. Aristotle

Epilogue   432

References   435
Glossary   455
Index of Principal Passages   459
General Index   472

ABBREVIATIONS

The following list contains those abbreviations used in the notes. For abbreviations of periodicals etc., see References. Abbreviations for ancient authors and works should be self-explanatory, but where there might be a possibility of doubt, I have expanded the customary form. Names of scholars cited (without dates in parentheses) in discussing textual matters are those whose proposals are to be found in the apparatus criticus of the relevant OCT or other (named) edition.

*ARV*²	J. D. Beazley, *Athenian Red-Figure Vase Painters*² (Oxford, 1963).
Bonitz	H. Bonitz, *Index Aristotelicus* (Berlin, 1870).
Bond	Euripides, *Hypsipyle*, ed. G. W. Bond (Oxford, 1963).
Bruns	I. Bruns (ed.), *Supplementum Aristotelicum*, ii. 2 (Berlin, 1892).
Davies	M. Davies (ed.), *Epicorum Graecorum Fragmenta* (Göttingen, 1988).
DK	H. Diels and W. Kranz (edd.), *Die Fragmente der Vorsokratiker*⁶ (Berlin, 1951).
FGH	F. Jacoby (ed.), *Die Fragmente der griechischen Historiker* (Berlin and Leiden, 1923–58).
Gigon	O. Gigon (ed.), *Aristotelis Opera*², iii. *Librorum Deperditorum Fragmenta* (Berlin, 1987).
Guthrie	W. K. C. Guthrie, *A History of Greek Philosophy* (Cambridge, 1962–81).
IG	*Inscriptiones Graecae.*
Italie	G. Italie, *Index Aeschyleus*² (Leiden, 1974).
Kaibel	G. Kaibel (ed.), *Comicorum Graecorum Fragmenta* (Berlin, 1899).
LIMC	H. C. Ackerman, J.-R. Gisler, *et al.* (edd.), *Lexicon Iconographicum Mythologiae Classicae* (Zurich, 1981–).
LP	E. Lobel and D. L. Page (edd.), *Poetarum Lesbiorum Fragmenta* (Oxford, 1955).
LSJ	H. G. Liddell, R. Scott, and H. Stuart Jones, *A Greek-English Lexicon*⁹ (with Suppl.) (Oxford, 1968).
Maehler	H. Maehler (ed.), *Pindari Carmina cum Fragmentis*, ii. *Fragmenta. Indices* (Leipzig, 1989).

Mette	H.-J. Mette (ed.), *Die Fragmente der Tragödien des Aischylos* (Berlin, 1959).
ML	R. Meiggs and D. M. Lewis, *A Selection of Greek Historical Inscriptions* (Oxford, 1969).
MW	R. Merkelbach and M. L. West, *Fragmenta Hesiodea* (Oxford, 1967).
Nickau	Ammonius, *Qui dicitur liber de adfinium vocabulorum differentia*, ed. K. Nickau (Leipzig, 1966).
N²	A. Nauck (ed.), *Tragicorum Graecorum Fragmenta*² (Leipzig, 1899); repr., with Suppl. by B. Snell, Hildesheim, 1964).
OCT	Oxford Classical Texts.
PMG	D. L. Page (ed.), *Poetae Melici Graeci* (Oxford, 1962).
Radt	S. Radt (ed.), *Tragicorum Graecorum Fragmenta*, iii (Aeschylus), iv (Sophocles) (Göttingen, 1985 and 1977).
RE	A. Pauly, G. Wissowa, W. Kroll, *et al.* (edd.), *Real-Encyclopädie der klassischen Altertumswissenschaft* (Stuttgart and Munich, 1894–1980).
Schmid–Stählin	W. Schmid and O. Stählin, *Geschichte der griechischen Literatur*, i. 1. *Handbuch der Altertumswissenschaft*, vii. 1. 1 (Munich, 1929).
Snell–Maehler	B. Snell and H. Maehler (edd.), *Bacchylidis Carmina cum Fragmentis* (Leipzig, 1970).
SVF	H. von Arnim (ed.), *Stoicorum Veterum Fragmenta* (Leipzig, 1903–24).
Wehrli	F. R. Wehrli (ed.), *Die Schule des Aristoteles* (Basle, 1944–59).
West	M. L. West (ed.), *Iambi et Elegi Graeci ante Alexandrum Cantati* (Oxford, i², 1989; ii, 1972).

Introduction

0.1. GENERAL

This study takes as its starting-point an examination of the usage in Greek authors of the cluster of terms centred on *aidōs*, notoriously one of the most difficult of Greek words to translate. Von Erffa rightly insists that *aidōs* is 'eine eigene Kraft, für die uns das Wort fehlt',[1] yet the significance of this observation is all but ignored in the remainder of his account, in which he is constantly concerned to identify separate meanings and persists in the separate treatment of nouns, verbs, compound verbs, adjectives, and adverbs which are derived from the same root and which obviously operate in the same general area, as if there were some methodological advantage in regarding data on (say) *aidoios* as of a different order from that offered by the usage of *aideomai*. In what follows, by contrast, I treat the concept of *aidōs* as a whole, and I have no qualms about using instances of the various cognate terms as evidence for the significance of the central concept to which they refer. Thus, while a certain amount of attention is accorded the usage of the various individual lexical items, far more time is spent on the attempt to identify the essence of *aidōs* by the delineation of the linguistic, psychological, social, and ethical contexts in which it operates. Throughout, *aidōs* is used as shorthand for the concept under investigation, and while this usually, though not always, indicates that some term belonging to the *aidōs*-group occurs in the passages under discussion, it should not be assumed that the reader will necessarily find the noun itself in the text. Such a procedure, it seems to me, avoids the dangers of dividing the inseparable that are inherent in the 'separate meanings' approach,[2] but it will no doubt disappoint anyone in search of a neat classification of senses.

To consider the concept of *aidōs* as a whole, however, is not to hold a priori that *aidōs*-terms cannot be used in different, more or less distinct senses, or that, because the Greeks used one word, *aidōs*, for which we have to use several, they therefore could not distinguish between these different senses. Even the most conceptually unified set of terms can manifest a range of distinguishable senses through its

---

[1] (1937), 9.
[2] On the dangers of this approach, cf. Adkins (1970), 2–6; Scott (1980), 13.

application in various specific contexts, and even monolinguals with no access to the ways in which speakers of other languages conceptualize experience in terms which are not coextensive with their own can be perfectly aware that they use words in different senses. Most ordinary users of language can detect equivocation in those cases in which it is possible, and if monolinguals could not distinguish different senses of their words, monolingual dictionaries (with whose approach we might compare the pseudo-Platonic *Definitions* and the relatively developed concepts of homonymy and synonymy in Aristotle) would be impossible. And, in fact, it is apparent that *aidōs* and its verb, *aideomai*, do have distinct senses. Not only do the terms take on specific connotations from their application in specific contexts (such as the use of *aideomai* in the context of supplication, where it can be a virtual act-description meaning 'I accept your supplication'), but there is also a more fundamental distinction in sense arising from two forms of basic usage. If I may anticipate: the verb *aideomai*, when it occurs with an accusative referring to another person or persons, is used in two more or less distinct ways, either to convey inhibition before a generalized group of other people in whose eyes one feels one's self-image to be vulnerable, or to express positive recognition of the status of a significant other person; the two stock English translations, 'I feel shame before' and 'I respect', thus succeed in isolating distinct senses of the Greek term. Yet there is unity in this distinctness;[3] for the purposes of this illustration, let *aidōs* be an inhibitory emotion based on sensitivity to and protectiveness of one's self-image, and let the verb *aideomai* convey a recognition that one's self-image is vulnerable in some way, a reaction in which one focuses on the conspicuousness of the self. (These are provisional definitions, which, I hope, are substantiated in what follows.) This established, we might agree that an informative, if rough and ready, translation of *aideomai* might be 'I am abashed'. (I mean not that this translation will suffice in every instance of the verb, but that it captures, roughly, features common to most instances.) If we then consider the person or persons designated in the accusative as the focus of this sense, we can see the connection between the two usages—in both cases one is driven to focus on oneself and one's own status or self-image as a

---

[3] Both the distinction and the unity are perceptively recognized, with reference to the Homeric poems, by Riedinger (1980), a fine article to which I would have referred more often in Ch. 1, had I known of its existence earlier.

result of a certain focus on a significant other, before whom one is 'abashed'.[4] Yet the other differs in nature between the two usages; in the 'I feel shame before' usage the status of the other is irrelevant, the 'other people' may be, in one's own eyes, worthless or indifferent, and, although one 'takes them seriously' because they may criticize, one does not in any way recognize any special status of theirs. In the case of the 'I respect' usage, however, one does precisely that; the feeling of *aidōs*, entailing concentration on the self and one's own status, is prompted by and focuses on consideration of the status of another, a person of special status in one's own eyes. The content of the focus on the other is thus different in the two cases: in the former the other is significant simply as a possible source of criticism, while in the latter the possibility of criticism from the other is either absent or deeply buried, and recognition of some special status *vis-à-vis* oneself is to the fore. Obviously, there may be some overlap between the two cases— one may actually respect those whose criticism one fears, and one may actually fear the criticism of those one respects, but there remains a difference of emphasis, and many instances are sufficiently clear cut to demonstrate that the two categories do exist.

One might object that the notion of positive recognition of another's status in the 'I respect' usage is only secondary to that of self-directed inhibition, and that, if the locution can be taken as conveying respect, this is only because its primary reference is to one's own inferiority *vis-à-vis* another. This approach, however, does not meet the demands of the evidence; Theognis can complain that he 'gets no *aidōs*' from his beloved, and clearly the situation he would like to see is not one in which the latter shows particular inhibition with regard to

---

[4] Assuming some such sense as 'I am abashed' (conveying the idea of concentration on the self and consideration of its status), we can account for the unity in all the ways in which the sense of the verb *aideomai* may be completed. These are: *aideomai* + acc., where the acc. denotes a person or persons (in the two senses identified above); *aideomai* + non-personal acc. (referring to actions or states of affairs); + inf. (where the inf. refers to the action inhibited); + part. (usually present, of an action already begun); + conditional clause; + noun clause. In all these cases the terms which complete the sense constitute the focus of the feeling of inhibition or self-consciousness, that *in respect of which* one is 'abashed'. (This formulation is not intended to rule out the possibility that the accusatives which often occur with the verb might be felt as direct objects, as opposed to 'accusatives of respect'; indeed, in this case, the distinction between the two forms of accusative would not amount to much (both limit the sphere of action of the verb). Thus, in what follows I occasionally speak of 'personal' and 'non-personal' objects. That personal accusatives of the 'I respect' type, at least, were felt as objects might be suggested by locutions such as 'receiving *aidōs*' (see n. 5 below) and the use of the noun + gen. ('*aidōs* for . . .'), which is analogous to that verb + direct object.)

his lover's opinion of him, nor is it primarily one in which the beloved would recognize Theognis' status indirectly by demonstrating a sense of his own inferiority; quite straightforwardly, the poet is complaining that the boy shows no positive regard for him as one who should enjoy special status in view of the benefits he has conferred.[5] It is by no means impossible that ordinary users of Greek should have been intuitively aware of these different senses, but whether they were or not, the differences of connotation and application do exist, and there would be no point in our ignoring them.

Aidōs and its direct derivatives, however, are not the only terms we shall consider; the (probably cognate) set of terms centred on the adjective *aischros* (ugly) are also relevant, as are numerous others which have a similar reference to 'appearances', as well as those which designate critical responses to actions and situations that 'look ugly' (such as *nemesis, oneidos,* etc.). There also exist other clusters, notably that based on *sebas,* which, while etymologically unrelated to *aidōs,* can operate within the same field of usage, and so points of similarity or difference between these and *aidōs* are noted and discussed. Yet, while the most important category of data has been furnished by the examination of the instances of the relevant terms in the texts of the authors considered, it has never been my intention to conduct an entirely lexicographical study, and, accordingly, I also consider passages in which none of the basic terms occurs, but which seem to me to merit discussion, usually on the grounds that they manifest some element typically constitutive of the *aidōs*-situation or reveal the operation of similar standards. Finally, due cognizance is taken of contexts which illustrate or might be thought to illustrate the operation of standards other than *aidōs,* in order that we might go some way towards discovering what *aidōs* is not, as well as what it is.

---

[5] Thgn. 253; cf. *Od.* 8. 480 (bards 'have a share in honour and *aidōs*', this *aidōs* consisting in others' recognition of their special status); also Tyrt. 12. 40 West—no one cheats the warrior who has won honour in battle of *aidōs* (= due recognition of his honour and status). It is not necessary that the recipient of *aidōs qua* respect should actually be of superior status, but he or she must enjoy a special claim to status or consideration in some respect, usually by virtue of some specific relationship such as supplication, guest-friendship, or *philia* (friendship).

0.2. *AIDŌS* AND EMOTION

That *aidōs* is an emotion is, I take it, uncontroversial; Aristotle regards it as more like a *pathos*, an affect, than anything else,[6] and the numerous passages to be considered below which illustrate its emotional character give us no reason to doubt him. This is not the place to give a detailed account of the nature of emotion, or even to decide categorically what an emotion is and what should and should not count as one; nevertheless, some general observations which might help us focus on the parameters of the task that lies ahead are clearly in order.[7] First, I am convinced that no approach to emotion can ignore the cognitive aspect, and therefore that those who make some form of evaluation or appraisal essential to and constitutive of the emotion are correct.[8] For all the straightforward examples of emotion that we shall consider, and certainly for *aidōs* and its nearest analogues in English, an evaluation is essential for and constitutive of the emotion; to be afraid, it is necessary to evaluate some object, action, experience, or state of affairs as threateningly dangerous. Even if one can be afraid of something (such as spiders) which one can rationally appreciate as harmless, and thus experience an episode of fear without the belief that x is threateningly dangerous, nevertheless, such an irrational and pathological form of the emotion must have its roots in an original evaluation that spiders are, in fact, dangerous.[9] Similarly, to experience shame is to place an action, experience, or state of affairs in the category of the shameful, the criteria of the shameful being supplied by subjective attitudes and cultural conditioning. Emotion-words like *aidōs*, then, are not simply names for bodily sensations; an occurrence of fear, shame, anger, or *aidōs* relates to some perceived attribute of the world 'out there', and such emotions are thus ways of seeing and

[6] *EN* 1128[b]10-15, etc.; see 6.5 below.

[7] The literature on emotion and emotion-theory is vast: for comprehensive surveys, covering both philosophical and psychological viewpoints, see Lyons (1980) and de Sousa (1987); also the collections of essays by Arnold (1970), Rorty (1980a), and Plutchik and Kellerman (1980). Other studies I have found useful include Bedford (1956-7); Ewing (1957); Warnock (1957); Kenny (1963), 1-75; Thalberg (1964); Pitcher (1965); Izard (1977); Kemper (1978); G. Taylor (1985), 1-16; Ortony, Clore, and Collins (1988).

[8] For the view that (all, most, or many) emotions are specified by their element of appraisal, see Peters (1970), 188 etc.; Lazarus, Averill, and Opton (1970), 217-21 etc.; Averill (1980a and b); Lazarus, Kanner, and Folkman (1980), esp. 192-4, 198; Lyons (1980), chs. 3-4; Solomon (1980), 258-9, 274-6; G. Taylor (1985), 1-5. This view is also implicit in many other studies which stress the element of evaluation in emotion, e.g. those by Bedford and Pitcher cited in n. 7 above.

[9] See Lyons (1980), 76-7; cf. G. Taylor (1985), 2-5.

responding to the world; to experience such an emotion in response to a particular stimulus is to construe the situation, cognitively, in a particular way.

Aidōs is most readily identified as an emotion by the fact that it is regularly described as having physical or physiological symptoms (typically blushing) and as involving characteristic behavioural responses (such as averting one's gaze, bowing or veiling the head, etc.). That we are inclined to take such factors as indicative of the emotional nature of *aidōs* tends to suggest that, even if we do recognize that emotions are not simply 'feelings', but do involve beliefs or appraisals, we none the less see the occurrent emotion, in which the appraisal of the situation leads to certain physiological changes and characteristic behaviour patterns, as the central and paradigm case.[10] This intuition, I am sure, is right; most people, I imagine, asked to define 'fear', would think of occurrent before non-occurrent senses, and if it is not the fact of perceptible physiological change which gives the emotions their specifically emotional character, it is difficult to imagine what else does. The occurrent sense of most, if not all, emotion-words, therefore, will be the primary one (to which others, presumably, are focally related), and thus the paradigm case of an emotion will involve both an evaluation of the situation and occurrent physiological changes. Yet it remains the evaluative aspect that specifies and differentiates the emotion. The case against physiological specificity of the emotions may have been overstated, and science may one day be able to prove that every emotion is distinguished by its own set of neurophysiological and visceral changes,[11] but such scientific progress, surely, will prove neither that emotions are distinguished by the perceived feelings which we regard as the typical manifestations of each, nor that the emotion-words of our language or any other are names for distinct syndromes of physiological change. The emotions of

[10] This is the view of Lyons (1980), 56–7; cf. Ewing (1957), 59, and contrast Bedford (1956–7), 300–1.

[11] I am thinking of the well-known experiments of Schachter and Singer, in which subjects in whom a state of arousal had been induced (by the injection of a stimulant of the sympathetic nervous system) identified their states in terms of different emotions according to their appraisals of their immediate context. For discussion, see Kemper (1978), 166–87; Lyons (1980), 119–23, 132–5; de Sousa (1987), 53–5. De Sousa points out (and Lyons recognizes, p. 132) that Schachter and Singer may simply have considered too limited a range of physiological changes; perhaps even the cognitions that they supplied to supervene upon the undifferentiated state of arousal brought with them physiological changes that might be discovered to be subtly different in the case of different emotions. (On the possibility that each emotion might constitute a specific neurophysiological event, see Kemper, 146–65; de Sousa, 47–76.)

shame and embarrassment illustrate the point. It would be difficult, or, I should say, impossible, to argue that these two emotions differ by virtue of the bodily changes experienced by their subjects or observed by others; if, therefore, they are to differ physiologically, their physiological differences will be deep, not accessible. Users of English, therefore, will regard these two emotions as distinct not because they are somehow dimly aware of the putative specificity of the deep physiological changes involved, but (it is more plausible to believe) because they possess implicit knowledge that 'shame' and 'embarrassment' differ as a result of their belonging, broadly if not categorically, to different 'scenarios', constituting slightly different appraisals of slightly different situations.[12] (Embarrassment is generally taken to be less intense, more trivial than shame, and to apply to rather different types of situation, although obviously the two do overlap.[13])

This is one reason why it is unlikely that all emotions should be differentiated by their attendant physiological changes. There is also, however, the point that cultures differ in the emotions they identify in language—the emotion-words of one culture are not always immediately convertible into the language of another. This, of course, is notoriously the case with *aidōs*, and one of the ways in which *aidōs* cannot simply be equated with 'shame' (a regular candidate as a translation) is that *aidōs* quite patently covers the emotions of both shame and embarrassment. Unless the Greeks experienced only one set of physiological changes when experiencing both shame and embarrassment whereas English speakers experience two distinct sets, this again suggests that emotion-words in a given language are not applied on the basis of some dim awareness of the specificity of the physiological processes involved. It is much more likely that English

[12] Cf. Bedford (1956-7), 281-2, on 'annoyance' and 'indignation'.

[13] The overlap seems to lie in the fact that, although shame can relate to moral failings while embarrassment seems to be restricted in application to merely social situations (Ortony, Clore, and Collins (1988), 142), shame can also refer to social shortcomings, failures, or awkwardnesses. Lyons (1980), 113-14, argues that embarrassment always involves a real audience, whereas shame does not, but G. Taylor (1985), 69-70, is right to argue that embarrassment can occur in private. She would claim that, in this case, the audience must be present in fantasy, and cannot simply be constituted by the self's judging the self (as she allows may be the case in shame; see 0.3 below), but I am not so sure. Taylor also argues that the simple perception of being exposed can in itself be sufficient for embarrassment, but not for shame (70), which requires a negative judgement of the self. This seems correct: one can be embarrassed to speak in public, and one's embarrassment may be adequately explained by the public nature of the action; but if one were ashamed to speak in public, people would naturally wish to discover the reasons for one's shame, what it was one was ashamed *of.*

differentiates shame and embarrassment where ancient Greek did not, because the values of English speakers suggest a difference between two closely related scenarios which is, in terms of Greek values, not significant enough to warrant the development of distinct labels. If scientists one day identify all the various physiological changes involved in emotion and succeed in separating each 'emotion' from the others in physiological terms alone, what they will have distinguished will not necessarily correspond to the emotional word-tokens of English or any other language.

Several studies recognize this, yet take the view that emotions as such can be distinguished from the emotional concepts expressed in emotion-words, and try to characterize emotions in terms that are not linguistically tied to one specific culture.[14] It is impossible not to have some sympathy for this approach, for it accounts for the fact that features of emotional experience can often plausibly be shown to be culturally universal,[15] even though emotional concepts may be culturally relative. But there is also much to be said for the stronger view of Averill,[16] that emotions are social or cultural constructs, and the concepts of emotion embedded in language *are* the emotions for the particular culture. The two approaches differ in that Wierzbicka and others regard the cognitive-evaluative component of the emotion as somehow separable from the culturally relative values encapsulated in emotion-concepts, and thus hold that the emotions are 'there' and the emotional concepts of any given language are simply mapped on to them, whereas Averill points out that, although emotions do incorporate universal biological 'givens', an emotion as such does not come into being until its evaluative component has been supplied by development in a particular socio-cultural environment. The truth, it seems to me, is likely to be more complex and to lie somewhere between the two extremes. It certainly seems plausible to argue that we experience more emotions than we have words for, and that not every emotion needs to be labelled.[17] The great novelists are adept at portraying emotion in their characters, adumbrating the context to

[14] See Wierzbicka (1986) and Ortony, Clore, and Collins (1988), 8-9, 172-6; cf. Kemper (1978), 85-8.

[15] See (e.g.) Ausubel (1955) on shame and guilt; Izard (1977), 5-7, 18, and *passim*, esp. 411 on sexual shyness, 422-3 on guilt; Ekman (1980) on universality and culture-specificity in facial expressions.

[16] (1980*a* and *b*); cf. Lazarus, Averill, and Opton (1970), 215-17; also the unpublished views of Robert Kraut presented in de Sousa (1987), 250-1.

[17] Cf. Warnock (1957), 51; Kemper (1978), 86.

convey the characteristic feeling-tone to the reader, and not every emotion portrayed need be named to be recognizable.[18] It is equally possible that members of two distinct cultures may be capable of more or less identical emotions (including the necessary evaluative content), even though the emotion has been labelled in one culture and not in the other.[19] Similarly, the evaluative belief that identifies the emotion may remain relatively constant between cultures, and the emotion-words used, though different, cover a similar range of experience. Thus Averill seems to me to be wrong to suggest that the guilt of the Jew is different from the guilt of the Christian simply because each form of guilt rests on values and attitudes specific to a particular religion and culture,[20] since it seems clear that the *structure* of guilt need not differ as a direct result of difference in the values which establish its proper eliciting conditions. In some cases, however, it will be impossible to specify the evaluative element of the emotion without relating that emotion specifically to the values of one culture (such will be the case with *aidōs*, and with Averill's example, the Japanese *amae*).[21] Thus

---

[18] Cf. Wierzbicka (1986), 587; Ortony, Clore, and Collins (1988), 3, 8.

[19] Ger. *Schadenfreude* seems to me an excellent example.

[20] (1980a), 50–1.

[21] Wierzbicka (1986) claims that emotions identified by terms specific to a particular language are experienced by users of other languages which have no equivalent token, and that these can be made explicable to users of other languages by analysing the evaluative/situational determinants of the emotion into smaller descriptive units, using 'culturally universal' concepts such as 'say', 'want', 'good', and 'bad'. Such a procedure, however, may enable us to identify experiences of our own which are similar to a complex, culturally dependent emotion such as *aidōs*, or to understand the range of experience covered by *aidōs*, but it could never convince us that we have experienced *aidōs* as such. This one will only do when one sees, for example, the emotion of inhibitory shame as relevantly similar to the emotion of respect for another (see 0.1 above; also below, this section) and *when this perception of similarity influences the evaluative belief that is constitutive of one's emotion*. To recognize that we feel respect where a Greek might feel *aidōs* provides no warrant for the claim that we experience *aidōs*, since shame, embarrassment, shyness, and respect are many, their associations and their identificatory beliefs different, whereas *aidōs* is one, with one closely related set of identificatory beliefs. Ortony, Clore, and Collins (1988) similarly seek to classify emotions using (supposedly non-culture-specific) classifications which distinguish positive and negative reactions to various categories of elicitors. Thus reactions to agents (as opposed to events or objects) are distinguished according to whether they focus on self or other as agent (see their table on p. 19). In applying this framework to *aidōs* one would distinguish two emotions, since *aidōs* focuses on both self and other (see below, this section), and, indeed, the authors are perfectly willing to claim that several common emotions (such as remorse) are in fact compounds of more than one emotion-type. Yet if *aidōs* depends on its own broad unity of evaluation, and not on a combination of distinct identificatory beliefs, there is no reason to regard it as a compound, and if it cannot simply be analysed into subsidiary parts which happen to correspond to emotions familiar to users of English, then in experiencing shame etc. users of English are not experiencing 'aspects' of *aidōs*.

different cultures will most probably have some or even many emotions in common, but where they differ widely in their conceptualization of the aspects of emotional experience perceived as salient, it is reasonable to regard their distinct emotional concepts as distinct emotions.

Accordingly, the labelling of emotion in a given culture can make all the difference to what the emotion actually is, and so, when infant members of a culture acquire their emotional repertoire and vocabulary, what they learn is not (or not solely) how to label discrete physiological experiences, but how to recognize the situations which their culture considers appropriate to particular concatenations of evaluation, feeling, and behaviour.[22] That the ways in which these situations are constructed and conceptualized may be culturally relative is obvious, and the fact that the values and ideology of a culture can give rise to significantly different ways of construing human emotional experience provides further evidence that the cognitive aspect of the emotion, the evaluation in terms of one's own society's world-view, is sufficient for the differentiation of the emotions.

This is not to say that there may not be constants in the emotional experience of all human beings, simply that it is the conceptualization in a particular cognitive pattern of whatever responses (innate or learned, phylogenetic or ontogenetic) and physiological changes there may be that effectively makes the emotion: *aidōs* is not simply 'shame' plus 'embarrassment' plus . . ., but a unique way of looking at the world in its own right; and this is true even though the physical symptoms and behaviour patterns typical of *aidōs* may be found in their entirety under the heading of different emotion-terms in other cultures. Nor do I mean to disparage the physiological symptoms of *aidōs*; on the contrary, they constitute an important part of the phenomenology of *aidōs* which will help us pin the concept down. The point is that *aidōs* is more than just its symptoms and it is not study of its symptoms that will lead to greatest success in discovering its essence.

Far from every use of an emotion-word refers to an occurrence. Obviously, there are dispositional senses: 'I am afraid of the dark'

Neither as a whole nor in part, then, is the experience of *aidōs* as such available to those who do not conceptualize emotional experience in the same way as did native speakers of ancient Greek.

[22] For fuller discussion of the ways in which a repertoire of emotions might be acquired, see Kenny (1963), 65–9; Averill (1980*b*); de Sousa (1980*a*), 142–3; (1980*b*), 285–6; (1987), 181–4.

informs you not about an occurrence of fear at this very moment, but about a disposition of mine to experience fear, a disposition which can itself be described as fear. Fairly obviously, I think, the occurrent sense of the emotion is prior to such dispositional senses; although I may, as a matter of fact, never or almost never experience an occurrence of fear, because my fear of the dark leads me to avoid dark places,[23] the locution would be inexplicable unless it implied a previous occurrence of fear and a tendency towards future occurrences. I can be angry at the government's education policies without jumping up and down, raising my voice, and going red in the face, but equally my dispositional anger must, given the right stimuli, be liable to boil over into occurrence for it to make sense. Beside these dispositions there exist dispositions of a second order, not those in terms of which we are said to be 'angry' or 'afraid', but those in accordance with which we might be said to be 'irascible' or 'timid'.[24] These examples, in English, are less explicitly emotional—we are less likely to describe them as emotions than as dispositions towards particular emotions. Yet even a second-order disposition can be described in the same terms as an occurrent emotion; we still hear it said that 'so-and-so has no shame', and the 'shame' whose absence is thus decried is a second-order disposition regarded as a desirable character trait. Although we no longer talk much about shame in these terms in English (the positive locution that is the converse of that quoted above is no longer found), the analogous terms are still so used in modern Mediterranean languages, and most students of ancient Greek will immediately recognize that *aidōs* is often used in precisely this way. Greek, then, will use the same word, *aidōs*, for the occurrent emotion (cf. 'feeling afraid'), the first-order dispositional sense of the emotion (cf. being afraid without the occurrence of fear), and the second-order disposition (cf. 'timidity').

This, however, is not all. Emotion-words may also be used in a number of ways which indicate neither the occurrence of the emotion nor the possession of a disposition. For example, the statement 'The accused is deeply ashamed of what he has done' is not intended to attribute an occurrence of shame at the time at which it is uttered, although perhaps it does imply a disposition towards shame over the crime; much more obviously, it attributes an attitude of repentance and repudiation which might be felt to deserve a more lenient attitude on the part of those with the power to pass judgement and sentence.[25]

[23] Cf. Kenny (1963), 68.   [24] Cf. Lyons (1980), 56.
[25] Cf. Pitcher (1965), 344; also Lyons (1980), 159.

Equally, if I tell a student, 'I'm afraid I'm too busy to see you now,' I am not describing myself as either a patient of fear or the possessor of a disposition towards fear; and similarly the plea, 'Have pity,' is usually uttered not as an injunction to undergo an occurrent emotion, but as a tactic to change the mind of its addressee and elicit some substantive form of help. Yet, although such locutions may be parasitic on those which refer to occurrences or dispositions, they make sense and remain legitimate uses of the emotion-words. This is because, even though their function is not to report or interpret emotional occurrences, states, or dispositions, they none the less make use of the evaluative categories which constitute and differentiate the emotion. When the agent for the defence observes, in mitigation of his client's offence, that the latter is ashamed of what he has done, he represents him as placing his own action in the category of the shameful, as evaluating it exactly as would someone who was subject to shame; when I say, 'I'm afraid I'm too busy to see you now,' I am representing myself as evaluating a future (imminent) situation as bad and (normally) to be avoided; and the plea, 'Have pity,' draws on the concept of pity as an evaluative response which places its recipient in the category of 'victim of undeserved suffering'; whence its power—even if the recipient of the appeal does not actually experience pity, he may for some other reason feel it right to help the undeservedly suffering. Accordingly, once the evaluation that is constitutive of the emotion is identified, all or almost all uses of the emotion-words will fit.[26]

Thus some uses of *aidōs*-words will not describe or refer to an occurrence of *aidōs* as an affect, and others will have only an etiolated connection with occurrent *aidōs*, yet all must still, as legitimate instances of *aidōs*-terms, be comprehensible in terms of the view of the world, the evaluative categories, which *aidōs* represents. It is, therefore, these evaluative categories that we need to study, and so the study

[26] Thus it does not much matter whether we consider that every instance of an emotion-word is an instance of the emotion or not. If we believe (as do, for example, Aristotle (see 6.5.1. below) and Lyons (1980), 56–8) that only an occurrent emotion qualifies as an emotion *sensu stricto*, we shall still have to pay attention to legitimate uses of emotion-words, in our case *aidōs*-words, that do not immediately refer to an occurrent emotion as such, precisely because such locutions operate under the same evaluative categories as do the occurrent uses; but if we believe that *aidōs* as an emotion may also encompass non-occurrent aspects, or even that all uses of emotion-words give primary data on the relevant emotion (as appears to be the claim of Bedford (1956–7), 300–3, and Pitcher (1965), 346), then our procedure in evaluating the data on the concept of *aidōs* will not be very different.

of *aidōs* becomes a study in Greek values. And (if I may present without argument what I think becomes abundantly clear in the sequel) the study of *aidōs* becomes a study in Greek values of honour, for the notion of honour is never far away from the evaluation that is constitutive of *aidōs*.[27] It is the concept of honour, indeed, which explains possibly the most unusual feature of the usage of *aidōs* and its verb, *aideomai*, to which we have already alluded. That *aidōs* covers both shame and embarrassment is easily explained; even in English we see the similarity between the two emotions, and they may even, in some contexts, be interchangeable. Less readily explicable to the ordinary reader of early Greek is the fact that there exist two stock translations of *aidōs*, two uses of the verb *aideomai* governing the accusative case: 'I feel shame before . . .' and 'I respect'. Clearly, though, the notions of shame and respect are not totally unrelated; to feel inhibitory shame (*aidōs* is always prospective and inhibitory in the earliest authors) is to picture oneself as losing honour, while to show respect is to recognize the honour of another. The combination of the two in one concept, however, is unfamiliar. Yet it is also entirely logical; as will emerge below, to be concerned with one's own honour is to envisage oneself as one among others, also bearers of honour; thus to limit one's own claim to honour is to accept one's status *vis-à-vis* others, to inhibit self-assertion is to recognize how such conduct would impinge upon the honour of others, and to experience inhibition before the audience whose disapproval might lead to impairment of one's honour is clearly akin to the inhibitory self-consciousness one might feel in a situation in which one was forced to consider one's own status in relation to that of another person. Sociologically, of course, these observations are not surprising; but it is not often recognized that in the concept of *aidōs* we have an implicit recognition of the ways in which the honour of self is inextricably bound up with that of others.[28] One essential unity across the range of usage of *aidōs* and its

[27] This statement should be read with the qualification that the values of 'honour' in ancient Greek are intimately connected with quasi-aesthetic standards of appropriateness which classify actions or states of affairs as 'beautiful', 'ugly', 'unseemly', etc. Thus *aidōs* may be seen as a response to a state of affairs in which honour is at stake, or as a sense that an action or situation is 'ugly', 'not nice'.

[28] Less often recognized, that is, by classical scholars; H. B. Lewis (1971: 41) well points out that even in English shame is close to the sense of awe before a significant 'other', while the continuum between concern for one's own honour and acknowledgement of the honour one owes others has been recognized in the linguistic habits of other cultures; e.g. Benedict (1947: 104–7) notes that expressions of respect for those to whom one owes a debt of gratitude in Japanese literally stress the shame or dishonour (sense of

verb *aideomai* thus lies in their focus on the balance which exists between honour of self and honour of others. Accordingly, in what follows we shall concentrate to a great degree on the values of honour which constitute the sphere in which *aidōs* operates and which give rise to the evaluative judgements which are constitutive of the emotion, and we shall have occasion to note that the inclusivity of *aidōs* as a response to the honour of self and others is mirrored in the inclusivity of the code of honour itself, a code which integrates self-regarding and other-regarding, competitive and co-operative stand-ards into a remarkably unified whole.

0.3. SHAME AND GUILT

The uniqueness of *aidōs* is one, very strong indication of the crucial importance of cultural factors in constituting the essence of an emotion. Even if many or all of the feelings and responses that make up *aidōs* can be paralleled in other cultures, even if some of them are cross-cultural universals, the overall conceptualization of *aidōs* by means of its orientation into a specific set of values in effect sets it apart as a distinct and separate way of seeing the world. Thus, although aspects of *aidōs* may be familiar, the whole is *sui generis*, and it would be wrong to assimilate the concept as a whole to anything in our own language or experience. Yet this is not to say that there is nothing in our experience to assist us in making contact with the experience of *aidōs*; on the contrary there is much. In particular, there is shame, a stock translation of *aidōs* in English and an obvious candidate for partial equivalence. *Aidōs* is not shame (the two are very far from coextensive, and *aidōs*-words in Greek will bear a set of connotations different from those of shame in English),[29] but the two concepts share many features in their phenomenology and associ-ations. The notion of the 'other' or the audience is common to both,

inferiority) of the speaker *vis-à-vis* the other (in a somewhat similar way the *aidōs* which is respect for another may also encompass one's own comparative lack of worth, one's bashful feeling of inferiority). A particularly intriguing analogue to *aidōs* is found in the Bedouin *Hasham*; see Abu-Lughod (1986), 103–17 and index s.v.; emotion-terms which unite the responses of shame and respect are also found in Australian aboriginal languages, according to Wierzbicka (1986: 591–2).

[29] In particular, since *aidōs* relates to others as well as to oneself, it is commonly more positive than shame; it is recommended as a virtue, and is valued for its maintenance of propriety in reciprocal arrangements in which one's own honour is bound up with one's obligations to others.

both are associated with the eyes and visibility, they share the characteristic symptom of blushing, and both may be attended by typical behaviour patterns such as averting the gaze or seeking to hide oneself.[30]

For many, a distinction between shame and guilt is a given, and this intuition is often given substance by the analysis of professional psychologists, anthropologists, and philosophers. Indeed, the popular intuition and the theoretical construct often go hand in hand, the one lending credence, in different ways at different stages, to the other. One very basic distinction, found both at the popular level and in the works of the 'shame-culture' theorists to be discussed in the next section, rests on a distinction between internal and external sanctions: guilt relies on the internal sanctions provided by the individual conscience, one's own disapproval of oneself, and shame is caused by fear of external sanctions, specifically the disapproval of others.

Now, it is clear that shame bears a frequent, and some would say an essential, reference to the concept of an audience, and in many cases this audience will be a real one. One feels shame before those who witness one's actions, and focuses on what the members of that audience may say or think of one. Even this kind of response, however, is not a simple fear of disapproval or a straightforward response to purely external stimuli. The internalized component is to be found both in the categorization of one's own situation as one which can be viewed as shameful and in the negative judgement of oneself that is caused by the sense of being under public scrutiny. Gabriele Taylor's account of shame is very good on this point. In her view, the function of the audience, even a real audience, in shame is to bring the individual who is subject to the emotion to focus on the self; the critical judgement of oneself which is constitutive of shame is never formally identical with any critical judgement of the audience.[31] The assessment of the audience may be positive, neutral, or negative, and where it is negative, the subject of shame may endorse it or reject it, but even where a critical judgement on the part of the audience is

---

[30] As features of *aidōs* these are documented below; on the phenomenology of shame, see in particular Piers and Singer (1953), 19 (blushing and instinctive behaviour) etc.; Tomkins (1970), 107 (inhibits eye-contact); H. B. Lewis (1971), esp. 37 (visual imagery), 38 (related to desire to hide); Izard (1977), 385–419, esp. 386 (averting gaze and bowing head), 387–9 (blushing), 394–5 (originates in aborted infantile attempts to establish eye-contact with strangers (?)), 412–14 (inhibits eye-contact, intimacy); G. Taylor (1985), 64–7 (notion of audience and 'other' in shame-imagery).

[31] G. Taylor (1985), 64–8; cf. (with less precision) Lynd (1958), 34–43 etc.

endorsed by the self, it is not identical with the negative self-judgement that is constitutive of shame.[32] To be viewed with approval by certain people, for example, may occasion a sudden revision of one's self-image leading to a loss of self-esteem, if those people are such that one would not wish to draw their approval, or if their approval implied that they were placing one on a lower level than that to which one aspired. Equally, the audience may be indifferent, and one might feel shame that one had gone to such lengths to impress them, judging oneself negatively as too dependent on others' appreciation or not good enough to warrant it. Thirdly, the audience may strongly disapprove of one's actions, and one may reject their interpretation, and yet still feel shame, because, having been brought to realize that one's conduct can be seen in a poor light, one feels that one has let oneself down, or placed oneself in a position of weakness, or because one regards it as a failure to secure the approval of (certain) others or ignominious to be the recipient of any form of criticism. And finally, one may be brought by the audience to see that one's conduct in fact falls short of standards to which one does oneself subscribe, and thus one may endorse the critical view of the audience, but, as in all the other cases, the judgement that is constitutive of the emotion depends on oneself, even though it may be facilitated by the reaction of others. Thus, even where a real audience is present, it is far too simple to say that shame is a response to external sanctions; in every case shame is a matter of the self's judging the self in terms of some ideal that is one's own.

It is, however, true that in all the cases so far considered shame has been elicited by the presence of a real audience, and so one might think it possible to argue that shame requires such an audience. Clearly, however, this is not the case—shame in English and *aidōs* in Greek often (perhaps more often than not) anticipate the judgements of others in the absence of any real audience or any actual criticism. Nevertheless, one might say, shame still depends upon the idea of an external audience to bring it about, and the notion of the external audience is the main catalyst of the emotion.[33] Yet if we allow that an individual's anticipation of others' disapproval may be wildly wide of the mark (as, I think, we must), then we must recognize that shame of this type, where the audience is present only in fantasy, depends less

[32] G. Taylor (1985), 64.

[33] See Ausubel (1955), 382: a fantasy audience is necessary for shame, and (383) shame rests on external sanctions alone (this despite the acknowledgement of 'internalized' moral shame on p. 382). Such seems also to be the opinion of Rorty (1980a: 498–9), and is the view taken of *aidōs* in Homer by Scott (1980: 15).

on input from the hypothetical judgements of others than on the sensitivity of the self to the ideal or standard in question.[34] If I anticipate criticism of my actions or situation where none is likely to be forthcoming, or anticipate more severe criticism than is likely, and feel shame on that account, then the roots of my shame are to be sought in my character, my own standards or ideals.

Such shame, however, still bears a reference to other people as audience, and so it still might be possible to claim that, in requiring the notion of an external audience, shame differs fundamentally from guilt, which can relate exclusively to the self and the conscience of the individual.[35] Yet in both scenarios already discussed, that in which an audience is present in fact and that in which it is present in fantasy, we have seen that, in spite of the explicit reference to the concept of an audience, internalized standards do come into play, and the proximate source of shame is the self's judgement of the self. The second scenario, moreover, shows that shame can occur even in private, in the absence of any real audience, and that its occurrence can be determined by the sensitivity of the individual. Should it not be possible to dispense with the external audience altogether, and for shame to occur with no reference to any judgement but one's own?

It should be clear that particular occurrences of shame need give no place in their ideational content to an external audience, that agent-reports of shame do not always refer to 'other people', and that imaginative representations of shame in literature often portray shame before the self.[36] That shame can occur in one's own eyes is not surprising, given the role of internalized standards even in shame referring explicitly to others, and given the fact that explicit reference to an external audience may be nothing more than a projection of this internal standard. Taylor's view of the role of the audience as catalyst again provides the best explanation of shame before oneself; even an actual, external audience is only a means to bring a previously unconsidered interpretation of the agent's action or situation to his or her attention; to consider the hypothetical judgements of a fantasy audience is to see oneself in a different light, to step back from

[34] Cf. Isenberg (1980), 367. On the fantasized audience as an internalized ('generalized' or 'eidetic') other, see Piers and Singer (1953), 67; cf. H. B. Lewis (1971), 23, 39.

[35] Guilt can, of course, be prompted by a real or a fantasy audience too, and it is by no means necessary that the ideation of guilt should be entirely free of reference to the reactions of other people. See Piers and Singer (1953), 67; Rawls (1973), 465, 483-4; cf. Wicker, Payne, and Morgan (1983), 36.

[36] A copious collection of examples in Lynd (1958), 27-71.

self-absorption and take a detached view; thus, in Taylor's opinion, it is the detached view of one's own actions or situation that is necessary for shame, the appreciation of a possible observer-description of one's actions or situation, not the concept of an external audience. One can be one's own audience, provided one comes to take up the position of a detached observer *vis-à-vis* oneself. References to the audience, then, and metaphors of 'eyes' and 'being seen' indicate the essential role of the detached observer in shame; thus shame does require the concept of an 'other', but the 'other' may be wholly internalized, such that one can be an observer to oneself.[37] This formulation may seem rather like having one's cake and eating it (shame requires the concept of the detached observer but not a real or hypothetical external observer, so that the notion of the observer may be at once essential and metaphorical), but it has the great merit of demonstrating how the structure of shame is the same in all cases—where there is a real audience, where an audience is present in fantasy, and where the role of the audience is played by oneself.

In all cases of shame, then, one is brought to a negative evaluation of oneself in respect of some ideal, and the catalyst may come from within as well as from without. In respect of reference to internal versus external sanctions, then, shame will not differ from guilt. For theories of how shame can rest on internal standards just as much as guilt and yet still be distinct from that concept, we turn to the psychoanalysts.

A succinct psychoanalytical distinction is given by Piers:[38]

1. Shame arises out of a tension between the ego and the ego-ideal, not between ego and superego as in guilt.
2. Whereas guilt is generated whenever a boundary (set by the superego) is touched or transgressed, shame occurs when a goal (presented by the ego ideal) is not being reached. It thus indicates a real 'shortcoming'. Guilt anxiety accompanies transgression; shame, failure.
3. The unconscious, irrational threat implied in shame anxiety is abandonment, and not mutilation (castration) as in guilt.
4. The Law of Talion does not obtain in the development of shame, as it generally does in guilt.

---

[37] See G. Taylor (1985), 57–68; cf. Piers and Singer (1953), 67; Isenberg (1980), 366. H. B. Lewis (1971) insists frequently on the necessity of internalized standards for shame (e.g. 115), but in referring to the 'other' she never seems explicitly to acknowledge that this role can be played by the self, although on occasion the fantasized other seems to be a function of the self (e.g. 23, 37, 39).
[38] Piers and Singer (1953), 23–4.

We can ignore the typical psychoanalyst's assumption that conscious emotions are based on hypothetical unconscious anxieties (point 3), since, even if it were true, it would be of no help to us in distinguishing conscious occurrences of shame and guilt. Equally, the remark about the Law of Talion is simply a reflection of the intuition that guilt has to do with punishment in a way that shame does not; this point may be useful, but we can disregard it for the moment.[39] The crux of Piers's observations lies in his first two points, concerning superego and ego-ideal, transgression and failure.

Piers himself points out that psychoanalysts differ in regarding the ego-ideal as a construct distinct from the superego or as an aspect of it; Freud himself could use both terms interchangeably,[40] but on occasion clearly regards the superego as the more inclusive term,[41] and thus we find Lewis (1971) following the procedure rejected by Piers, of regarding the ego-ideal as an aspect of superego functioning. In this scheme both shame and guilt are superego functions, the former relating to that aspect of the superego called the ego-ideal, the latter to an aspect of the superego to be identified (tautologously in either case) either as 'sense of guilt' or as 'superego'. It will be seen that the difference of approach is a trivial one, given that those who regard the ego-ideal as an aspect of the superego and those who regard the two constructs as distinct subdivisions of a larger entity agree on the role of the two elements to which they relate shame and guilt.[42]

To say that shame and guilt are both superego functions (or that they belong in the ego-ideal and superego respectively, which comes to the same thing) is to say that they involve evaluations of the ego, or, more loosely, of the self.[43] This much is not surprising. That they are

[39] The relationship between guilt (i.e. guilty feelings, guilt as a state of mind rather than a state of affairs) and punishment might be used (as it is by G. Taylor (1985: 89)) to support the view that guilt, like punishment, is about what we do, not what we are (see below).

[40] In *The Ego and the Id* (= Freud (1961*a*)), pt. iii. Here Freud seems to regard the two terms as coterminous, and thus there is less scope for distinguishing the punitive from the ideal element; both seem to go closely together at p. 34 of the essay. On the history of Freud's use of the terms 'super-ego' and 'ego ideal' or 'ideal ego' (the latter concept is the first to occur, but the former eventually takes over), see the editor's introduction in Freud (1961*a*), 9–10.

[41] In the *New Introductory Lectures on Psychoanalysis* (Freud (1964), esp. 64–7).

[42] Freud's initial practice of treating superego and ego-ideal as interchangeable may, however, reflect a sense that the superego construct does not admit of a neat division between the aspect which deals with prohibitions and that which represents ideals (see n. 40 above); but this is a different view from that taken by Piers and Lewis.

[43] Cf. H. B. Lewis (1971), 25.

different sorts of self-evaluation, different kinds of self-regulation, is the burden of their location in distinct aspects of the superego, or in ego-ideal and superego. Both Piers and Lewis agree that the ego-ideal is formed by the internalization of the ideals of loving parents and reinforced by identification with the sibling and peer groups, while its counterpart, which we shall for convenience call the superego, is formed by a similar internalization of the prohibitions of punitive parents.[44] Hence the distinction between failure and transgression, the second of Piers's criteria for the differentiation of shame from guilt.

It is thus apparent that Piers's first two criteria are so interrelated as to collapse into one: shame accompanies failure because it is concerned with goals and ideals, and for it to be concerned with goals and ideals is for it to be a function of the ego-ideal. This is not in itself reprehensible, but it does mean that the location of shame in the ego-ideal is of no independent value for distinguishing that emotion from the superego function called guilt. 'Ego-ideal' and 'superego' are abstract constructs which group together classes of phenomena felt to be distinct and which therefore have no explanatory force in demonstrating that the phenomena are, in fact, distinct.[45] Thus the location of shame and guilt in ego-ideal and superego respectively presupposes their distinctness as psychic phenomena, and so the essence of Piers's distinction between shame and guilt is to be found in his statement that shame concerns failure to achieve a goal or to match an ideal, guilt transgression of an internalized prohibition.

It would be wrong to focus too closely on the supposed distinction between failure and transgression; any transgression of a boundary is a failure to observe it, and a failure to achieve a goal can be a transgression of an interdiction. Thus, in dealing with agent-reports of shame or guilt, we cannot simply decide that any reference to transgression indicates guilt and any reference to failure, shame. A more serious objection to Piers's formulation lies in the fact that parental punishment may take the form of humiliation, or of unfavourable comparison with an admired ideal, while parental encouragement to achieve goals, to be like the admired ideal, may take the form of injunctions or prohibitions.[46] Already the distinctions between the contents of the superego and those of the ego-ideal begin to seem blurred, and we begin to wonder if Freud was not right originally to

[44] See Piers and Singer (1953), 25–30 etc.; H. B. Lewis (1971), 18–29.
[45] Cf. Lynd (1958), 81–2.
[46] Just so Glaucus' father told him 'not to disgrace the race of [our] fathers' (*Il.* 6. 209).

regard the terms as interchangeable; but presumably Piers would argue that the important thing is the attitude of the individual—if one sees one's act or omission primarily as a transgression of a rule, then one can legitimately be said to be subject to guilt, while if one sees the act, omission, or state of affairs primarily as a failure to reach an admired goal, then one can be described as subject to shame. And if one sees a given act or omission as both a transgression of an internalized prohibition and a failure to match an internalized ideal, then one is presumably suffering from both guilt and shame, the two remaining conceptually distinct.

This is very much the approach of Lewis (1971), but she goes beyond Piers in drawing from the distinction between goals and prohibitions, failure and transgression, a further important distinction which seems to me to be the most hopeful criterion for a broad, though not an absolute, differentiation of shame from guilt. In failing to achieve a goal or to meet an ideal one is failing to *be* what one would like to be; in transgressing a prohibition one is *doing* what one should not. From the distinctions already postulated by Piers, therefore, there follows another, that shame is concerned with the self as a whole, with what kind of person one is and would like to be, and that guilt is concerned with one's actions as an agent, with what one does.[47]

This distinction explains a lot; it explains why shame tends to be assuaged by restoration or increase of self-respect, guilt by making amends,[48] why causal responsibility is necessary for guilt, but not for

---

[47] H. B. Lewis (1971), 27, 30, 34–6, 43, 89, 197, etc.; cf. Lynd (1958), 23, 49–56, 207–8. The same distinction is found, without the jargon, in both Rawls (1973), 440–6, 482–4 (shame concerned with 'excellences', both moral and non-moral, guilt related to acts violating the moral code and infringing rights of others), and G. Taylor (1985), 89–107, 130–41. Taylor also draws a distinction between guilt and remorse, such that guilt focuses on the agent as doer of the deed (or as responsible for the omission), where the act or omission is felt to leave a stain on the self, while remorse focuses on the act itself, as an action which one would like to undo if one could. Taylor's scheme is thus: shame— whole self, concerned with self-respect; guilt—concerned with self as agent of specific acts felt to leave a stain on the self; remorse—concerned with acts and their effects on others, not with the self.

[48] See H. B. Lewis (1971), 27, 45, 89; Rawls (1973), 484; also G. Taylor (1985: 90 etc.), who argues (97–8, 104) that the aim in repayment motivated by guilt is to discharge the burden on oneself, not to right the wrong, the latter objective being part of the concept of remorse. Taylor recognizes that real people often use the terms guilt and remorse interchangeably, but argues that this is because both can involve the idea of reparation (104); such reparation, however, is necessary for remorse, but not for guilt—where the agent sees reparation as a means to rehabilitation of the self, it is guilt that is involved; where the focus is on the wish that an action harmful to others might be undone, we

shame,[49] why shame can be felt with reference not just to one's own actions and omissions, but also to wishes, desires, character traits, physical characteristics, passive experiences, and those actions of others which somehow reflect on oneself.[50] These are the most important phenomenal criteria which establish that shame and guilt are indeed distinct concepts, therefore the fact that the shame/self versus guilt/agent distinction accounts for them must indicate its cogency.

I doubt, however, whether even this distinction can eliminate grey areas altogether. Shame may not, unlike guilt, be specifically linked to actions or omissions which violate one's own moral standards, but, crucially, it can operate in that context. Proponents of the distinction between shame as focusing on the self and guilt as focusing on the self as agent of acts will argue that the distinction remains even when shame is elicited by violation of moral standards with which the agent identifies: when one feels shame at one's moral conduct one focuses on the kind of person one is, on the whole self, on one's failure to match one's self-image or to manifest a prized moral excellence; guilt, on the other hand, focuses on the specific transgression of an internalized injunction, dealing not with the whole self but with the discrepancy between one's moral self and one's (immoral) act.[51] Thus, they argue, although shame and guilt can be elicited by precisely the same sort of

have remorse. Thus it is conscious difference of focus between the two concepts that serves to distinguish them; yet Taylor also argues that 'There are ... occasions when ... it may be impossible for anyone, including the person herself, to tell whether she is prompted by feelings of guilt or by remorse.' This can only be true if the distinction which Taylor based on the conscious attitude of the individual is not in fact reflected in the consciousness of the person concerned. Here I am inclined to pay more attention to the popular fusion of guilt and remorse than to Taylor's attempt to separate them.

[49] One often finds the contrary opinion (e.g. Bedford (1956-7), 290-1; Solomon (1980), 254; Ortony, Clore, and Collins (1988), 135), but it is wrong. One can be ashamed of one's baldness, one's illegitimacy, the behaviour of one's compatriots abroad, etc. See Lewis (1971), 43; Rawls (1973), 444; G. Taylor (1985), 90-1; Morris (1987), 238. Normally, guilt involves moral responsibility, but cases do occur in which guilt is experienced even though the individual is quite aware that s/he was not morally culpable. Taylor (loc. cit.) suggests that in these cases causal responsibility is enough—the agent knows s/he is not to blame, but guilt attaches to the fact of having been the cause of some unfortunate occurrence. This explanation does seem to cover most cases of even irrational guilt, and perhaps those few cases in which guilt might occur in the absence of even causal responsibility are parasitic on the standard case; see Morris (1987).

[50] See Lynd (1958), 53-6 (shame over one's parents); H. B. Lewis (1971), 29 (one would feel shame, but not guilt at competitive failure or sexual rebuff), 66; Rawls (1973), 442-5; G. Taylor (1985), 76-84.

[51] See Lynd (1958), 49-50, 207-8; H. B. Lewis (1971), 35-7, 87; Rawls (1973), 445-6, G. Taylor (1985), 92, 134-6.

situation, although both can concern violation of internalized moral standards, in every case they differ in emphasis; even where the individual experiences regret both at having failed to live up to a valued self-image and at having violated an internalized prohibition, the strands of shame and guilt can be conceptually distinguished.[52]

There are, however, two problems with this. First of all, it is very doubtful that such a fine-tuned distinction between focus on self *simpliciter* and focus on self as agent of specific acts can be maintained in practice. It is clear, for example, from the accounts of Lewis and Taylor that they believe that both shame and guilt judge the self and direct anger at the self. The difference is supposed to be that in shame, but not in guilt, the self is the direct focus of the emotion. Shame, however, is not simply generalized dissatisfaction with the self, but rather involves a negative evaluation of the self in the light of some specific shortcoming; where a shortcoming is highlighted by a specific action contrary to one's moral standards, it is impossible that shame should not have a reference to the discrepancy between conduct and ideal self-image. Thus even a straightforward case of shame (in the terms of the theory under discussion) might focus on both specific action and ideal self-image.[53] Equally, the guilt that is caused by specific acts is caused by specific acts that set up a discrepancy between self-image and conduct, and thus guilt will always involve reference to both ideal self and conduct.[54] Lynd and Taylor argue that a positive self-image is maintained in guilt, but destroyed in shame, guilt involving the discrepancy between positive ideal and specific transgression, shame involving a feeling of general unworthiness,[55] but I doubt very much whether shame must involve the kind of complete

[52] H. B. Lewis (1971), 35, 96; Rawls (1973), 482; G. Taylor (1985), 136. Lynd (1958: 23, 208) goes rather further towards acknowledging that, although shame and guilt generally do differ in focus and emphasis, they may overlap in such a way that sharp distinction is impossible.

[53] Thus one can see why Ortony, Clore, and Collins (1988: 136–7) characterize shame in precisely the same terms as (e.g.) G. Taylor (1985) uses to characterize guilt (shame involving disapproval of the self as agent, i.e. disapproval of agent's actions, not agent alone or actions alone; emphasis on agent as cause). This clearly is an adequate account of that shame which refers to one's own actions or omissions; but the authors ignore the fact that shame need not focus on events of which the agent is cause, or on the notion of agency at all.

[54] See Izard (1977: 444) on the internalized standards that, he claims, come into play in the functioning of guilt, but not in that of shame: 'Internalized standards . . . have both an inhibiting (should not) component and positively valued ideal-goal (ought to) component.' This seems to acknowledge how hard it is to separate totally prohibitions from ideal goals.

[55] Lynd (1958), 50, 208; G. Taylor (1985), 92, 134–5.

denigration of the self that they demand. In this respect, shame and guilt seem to me rather to resemble each other in that they can centre on dissatisfaction with aspects of self and behaviour. It may be tidy to claim that shame involves thoughts like 'What a terrible person I am!' and guilt thoughts like 'What a terrible thing to do!' and to argue that 'What a terrible person I am to do such a terrible thing!' indicates a concurrence of shame and guilt, but it is unlikely that the real world can admit such a sharp conceptual distinction, particularly when even the 'pure' case of shame *qua* evaluation of the whole self will frequently contain an integral reference to some action perpetrated by the self as agent, and the 'pure' case of guilt will inevitably encompass a reference to an overall ideal of the self. Quite simply, self-image will constantly be called into question by specific acts, and in such situations the sharp distinction between shame and guilt will begin to disappear.

Thus the opposite extremes of the polarity bear a strong resemblance to each other, and this suggests that, even without invoking the idea of the fusion of shame and guilt, the two may not be entirely distinguishable in practice. This brings us to our second objection: neither the distinction in focus between self *simpliciter* and self-as-agent nor the notion of fusion of shame and guilt in functioning is respected by popular usage or reflected in the intuitions of ordinary users of language about the nature of the concepts to which the words refer;[56] and yet such usage and such intuitions constitute the starting-

[56] Reports of individuals asked to categorize their experience and understanding of guilt and shame in accordance with the criteria advanced by emotion theorists for their differentiation are presented with commentary in Wicker, Payne, and Morgan (1983). It seems to me particularly significant that the responses of the participants in the two experiments recorded in this study show no effective distinction between shame and guilt in their rating of the two on the following scales: (*a*) I was more concerned with how *others viewed me* (vs. *I viewed myself*); (*b*) I wanted to *hide* (vs. *make restitution*); (*c*) I felt *extremely* I had done an unjust thing (vs. *not at all*); (*d*) I felt I was *not at all* living up to my ideal self (vs. *extremely*); (*e*) I was unhappy *with myself in general* (vs. *only with my behaviour*). Other differences are slight, and tend to be differences of degree, rather than indications that shame and guilt are mutual antagonists (see the comments of the authors on p. 38). The subjects whose responses are given by Izard (1977: 397–9) show a similar tendency to disregard the differentiae proposed by the theorists. H. B. Lewis (1971: 173) argues that her survey of indicators of shame and guilt in patients of psychoanalysis indicates that 'shame and guilt seem to be mutually exclusive reactions, in the sense that they are not very likely to occur together', i.e. within the same 500-word unit (this despite Lewis's own assertion that shame and guilt 'fuse' and 'co-occur', pp. 35, 96, 197). But this experiment is worthless, since it scores shame and guilt not in accordance with the participants' reports of those emotions but on their use of locutions which Lewis interprets as indicators of shame and guilt, and the establishment of these (170) begs several questions: I leave the reader to ponder the opportunities for misclassification of guilt and shame inherent in the statement that 'Guilt anxiety is scored whenever a

point for the distinction. It is perfectly clear that users of English often use shame-words to describe reactions to specific acts, without reference to character-type, ideal image, or particular excellences, and equally clear that when they reproach themselves as bad people for having committed specific bad acts they sometimes describe their experience as shame and sometimes as guilt (but very rarely as shame plus guilt). Usage suggests, then, that in connection with one's own acts as a moral agent, shame is more or less interchangeable with guilt. It is not at all clear to me that it is better to impose an abstract conceptual distinction on the empirical data than to accept at face value the evidence of those data to the effect that shame and guilt overlap.[57]

To sum up: even if a distinction between self-evaluations which focus on what we are and those which focus on what we do is tenable in the abstract, this distinction will not furnish an absolute criterion for the separation of shame from guilt in ordinary usage. It is best to assume that, although in English shame and guilt can often be distinguished phenomenologically by virtue of their different associations and connotations, the fact that popular usage fails to provide an adequate distinction in certain contexts indicates an area in which no effective difference between the two concepts exists. But even if one were to disagree with this, and uphold the Lewis–Rawls–Taylor approach, one should be clear how slight a difference of emphasis this postulates between the two concepts. In the sphere of the evaluation of one's own conduct in moral terms the difference involves little more than a shift in ideation from '*I* should not have done that,' to 'I should not have done *that*.' Such a shift clearly does not amount to much; it certainly does not amount to a distinction between a concept that is fundamentally non-moral and one that is, or between one that is solely

phrase (clause) contained a reference to "adverse criticism, abuse, condemnation, moral disapproval, guilt or threat of such experience".'

[57] The overlap is accounted for by Ortony, Clore, and Collins (1988: 142–3) with reference to the thesis that guilt is not properly an emotion in its own right (see Ortony (1987)), but rather a name for the emotion (a compound of shame and remorse?) experienced when the criteria for objective ('socio-legal') guilt are satisfied (i.e. when one is morally or at least causally responsible for a specific crime or misdeed). This is an intriguing approach, which helps bear out my contention that overlap exists, but I see no real reason to discount the identification of guilt as an emotion in ordinary language, and doubt that Ortony's linguistic criterion as to what constitutes a genuine emotion (that the locutions 'being x' and 'feeling x' should both refer to an emotion, so that 'guilty', 'abandoned', etc. do not qualify) constitutes an adequate test (since, e.g., 'embarrassed' has a sense in which 'being embarrassed' does not imply 'feeling embarrassed').

concerned with external sanctions and one that is based on individual conscience.

This discussion of shame and guilt, of course, is subordinate to our study of *aidōs*, a concept from a language which has no words covering exactly the same range as either shame or guilt. Yet *aidōs* is continually characterized by classical scholars in terms of shame, and in terms which presuppose a sharp and self-explanatory distinction between shame and guilt. Thus the foregoing analysis seems to me worth-while—first of all because it indicates that even if we do choose to characterize *aidōs* in terms of shame, this does not commit us to the view that *aidōs* involves mere observance of external sanctions and has nothing to do with any sort of internalized standard. Secondly, since there is no distinction to be made between shame and guilt in terms of internal versus external sanctions, and since guilt and shame can, in certain circumstances, overlap (or, if you prefer, co-occur), we should be ready to admit that a characterization of a given instance of *aidōs* in terms of shame need not rule out a characterization in terms of guilt. And finally, if we keep in mind the distinctions employed by Lynd, Lewis, Rawls, and Taylor to differentiate shame from guilt, we shall be able to apply them to instances of *aidōs* in such a way as to demon-strate that, if guilt involves reference to specific actions of the self as agent rather than the whole self, then *aidōs* is, in these terms, quite often closer to guilt than shame.[58] The purpose of my discussion of shame and guilt, therefore, was partly to demonstrate the elusiveness of an absolute distinction, in order that no simple assumption of such a distinction should cloud the reader's understanding of what follows, and partly to achieve a better understanding of the issues involved in the attempt to differentiate shame from guilt, in order that this under-standing may later be used to arrive at a more balanced appreciation of *aidōs* than has hitherto been achieved. A further purpose, however, was to lay the groundwork for a re-examination of the antithesis between shame-cultures and guilt-cultures, to which we now proceed.

---

[58] Those familiar with the operation of *aidōs* in Greek literature might be interested to note, for example, that, according to Rawls (1973: 446, 483–4 (cf. H. B. Lewis (1971), 170)), guilt focuses on the prospect of resentment and indignation on the part of others, especially those one has harmed (this sounds very much like the situation sometimes covered by *aidōs* and *nemesis* in Homer: see 1.1.2 below), and that, according to G. Taylor (1985: 100), guilt focuses on a 'disfigurement' of the self (elsewhere a 'stain'). This notion of 'disfigurement' is especially relevant to *aidōs* (1.1.3–4 etc. below).

0.4. SHAME-CULTURE AND GUILT-CULTURE

A classic and straightforward statement of the shame-culture versus guilt-culture antithesis, the very one to which E. R. Dodds referred when he first applied the antithesis to classical Greece,[59] is offered by Ruth Benedict:

True shame cultures rely on external sanctions for good behavior, not, as true guilt cultures do, on an internalized conviction of sin. Shame is a reaction to other people's criticism. A man is shamed either by being openly ridiculed and rejected or by fantasying to himself that he has been made ridiculous. In either case it is a potent sanction. But it requires an audience or at least a man's fantasy of an audience. Guilt does not. In a nation where honor means living up to one's own picture of oneself, a man may suffer from guilt though no man knows of his misdeed and a man's feelings of guilt may actually be relieved by confessing his sin.[60]

Thus the basic distinction is between shame as a response to external sanctions and guilt as a response, uniquely, to internal sanctions. As I argued above, such a conception of shame and guilt is untenable, since at all stages both shame and guilt possess an internalized component, and neither is differentiated from the other by the fact that it may occur before a real audience, before a fantasy audience, or before oneself.[61] The application of an inadequate conception of shame and guilt is manifest at several points in the above extract: guilt is first of all narrowly and ethnocentrically conceived with reference to the Judaeo-Christian concept of 'sin', and then linked with 'honor' and 'living up to one's own picture of oneself' in a way which indicates a readiness to represent in terms of guilt any form of shame which has reference to

[59] See Dodds (1951), 17–18, 26 n. 106, and ch. 2 ('From Shame-Culture to Guilt-Culture') in general. For other applications of the antithesis with reference to ancient Greece, see, e.g., Adkins (1960*a*), 48–9, 154–6, 170 n. 10, 312 n. 5, 353 n. 12; Lloyd-Jones (1971), 2, 15, 24–7, 55–6, 171 n. 102; (1987), 1–2. This last reference indicates the currency of the antithesis in classical studies, and, indeed, the status as a shame-culture of either Homeric society or classical Greek society as a whole (Dodds and Lloyd-Jones differ on this point) is commonly regarded as uncontroversial (e.g. Carter (1986), 2 n. 2); cf. G. Taylor (1985: 54–7), whose application of the hypothesis that Homeric society is a shame-culture coexists with a sophisticated appreciation of the nature of shame which undermines the very basis of that hypothesis.

[60] Benedict (1947), 223; see 222–4 as a whole and cf. 195, 273, 287–8, 293, etc.

[61] See Singer in Piers and Singer (1953), 51, 76–7; and cf. Rawls (1973: 446, 483–4) on the external sanctions frequently encompassed by guilt which nevertheless do not negate its reference to internalized ideas of 'right'.

internalized standards. This fixation on external sanctions as the focus of shame leads Benedict, when she acknowledges the presence of internalized standards and 'conscience' in Japanese society, to describe the phenomena in terms of guilt.[62] The rigidity with which the criterion in terms of external and internal sanctions is applied thus prevents the recognition that the presence of internalized standards of behaviour may be all of a piece with those phenomena which are classified in terms of shame; instead, Japan is categorized not as a 'true shame culture', but as a shame-culture with an admixture of guilt. Taking Benedict's survey of Japanese society as a whole, however, one can readily see how both acute concern for the opinion of one's fellows and the capacity to act on the basis of internalized standards are instilled by that nation's emphasis on honour, status, and reciprocal obligation; in many cases, no doubt, Japanese do what is expected of them as a result of social pressure, but many of the obligations they feel compelled to meet are perceived as unconditional, and it is impossible to imagine that in these cases the sense of duty does not become internalized.[63]

The position is very similar in another early formulation of the antithesis. According to Leighton and Kluckhohn (1948), the Navaho 'have not internalized the standards of their parents and other elders, but, rather, accept these standards as part of the external environment to which an adjustment must be made'; this is because '"Shame" ("I would feel very uncomfortable if anyone saw me deviating from accepted norms") plays the psychological role which "conscience" or "guilt" ("I am unworthy for I am not living up to the high standards represented by my parents") has in the Christian tradition.'[64] Accordingly, the Navaho are free of the emotions of remorse and self-reproach, and experience no misgivings over misdeeds which remain undetected.[65]

[62] Benedict (1947), 2–3, 222.

[63] Benedict (1947: chs. 5–8) discusses obligations which Japanese are strongly conditioned to accept and strive consistently to fulfil; Benedict's own description of, e.g., the enormous stress placed on repaying one's debt to one's parents (101–2, etc.) and the degree to which Japanese feel bound to honour their 'moral indebtedness' (103) offers no hint whatever that they do not themselves endorse the requirements involved in performing their duties. As Ausubel comments (1955: 386), 'Few other cultures lay greater stress upon the sanctity of moral obligations.'

[64] Leighton and Kluckhohn (1948), 106; see 104–7 in general.

[65] Leighton and Kluckhohn (1948), 106; cf. 171. Again, these aprioristic general-izations are undercut by other data which their authors present; Ausubel (1955: 386) well characterizes the process of early childhood education outlined by Leighton and Kluck-hohn (13–43) as 'one of acceptance and intrinsic valuation of the child, leading to the first or implicit stage of moral responsibility based on personal loyalty.'

The theoretical basis on which these formulations rest goes back to Margaret Mead's 1937 collection, *Cooperation and Competition among Primitive Peoples*. Cultures are classified according to their reliance on external or internal sanctions, examples of the former being 'ridicule', 'abuse', and 'execution by royal decree', and of the latter 'obeying a tabu for fear of death and disease' and 'abstaining from illicit sex activities for fear of punishment by the ghosts'; the essence of the distinction is that external sanctions 'must be set in motion by others' while internal sanctions, once they are established within the character of the individual 'operate automatically'.[66] At first sight, it appears that this distinction mirrors that between shame and guilt, for Mead immediately follows up these remarks by observing that the only two cultures included in the study which display a character structure comparable to 'our own Western European forms' rely on guilt as an internal control, and that 'in societies in which the individual is controlled by fear of being shamed, he is safe if no one knows of his misdeed; he can dismiss his misbehavior from his mind', whereas 'the individual who feels guilt must repent and *atone* for his *sin*'.[67] Shame, she continues, is a principal external sanction in North American Indian cultures.

This initial impression, however, is deceptive, for Mead's conception of internal and external sanctions accommodates more than the simple contrast between conscience and fear of external pressure. In the initial description of internal sanctions, for example, we notice the presence of 'obeying a tabu' and 'fear of punishment by the ghosts'; if these responses do indicate the operation of internal sanctions, they nevertheless do not, in Mead's view, betoken guilt or conscience, as she makes clear when she points out that 'In societies which are regulated by tabu, the individual who breaks a tabu is safe if he can invoke a stronger magical force.' Fear of surpernatural consequences, Mead believes, can operate automatically within the character of the individual, but need not indicate internalization of principles of behaviour.[68] There exist internal or quasi-internal sanctions which need have nothing to do with guilt or conscience.

[66] Mead (1937), 493.
[67] (1937), 494 (original emphasis).
[68] The position of the divine sanction in any culture, in fact, is ambiguous; as a character in the satyr-play *Sisyphus*, attributed by some to Critias (B 25 DK), makes clear, fear of the gods is fear of an external sanction which nevertheless has power to deter where other external sanctions give out—it can deter doing wrong in secret. Such fear may simply be fear of an external agency, with no implication that the individual has made the standard his own, or it may be a facet of the response to a standard which has been internalized, albeit with initial reference to the threat of divine punishment.

Mead's view of shame and the sanctions to which it refers runs parallel to her view of fear of supernatural unpleasantness. She is prepared to recognize that shame can be a 'relatively internal sanction', at least 'when it is very strongly developed',[69] and, in the subsequent 'tabular summary of character formation', items such as 'fear of being shamed by *any* failure', 'fear of loss of status', 'fear of shame, loss of position in others' eyes', and 'extreme fear of being shamed before others' occur as internal sanctions.[70] The appearance of 'fear of shame' in this list indicates an initial failing, the failure to distinguish between shame as a state of mind (subjective) and shame as a state of affairs (objective)—'fear of shame' can only mean 'fear of disgrace', 'fear of *being shamed*'. This confusion suggests that in her initial description of shame as an external sanction Mead meant only that *disgrace* is an external sanction, and so there need be no implication that shame as a state of mind is an external sanction, even though it may rest on such a sanction. Thus when we read on it might appear that Mead simply takes the view that, although disgrace is an external sanction, fear of disgrace is an internal sanction. Such a view, presumably, would have to accept that fear of punishment is also an internal sanction; but if any focus on an external sanction is itself an internal sanction, Mead's whole antithesis collapses, and so, although her exposition does lend itself to the above interpretation, it must be rejected.

So the presence of 'fear of being shamed by *any* failure' etc. in the list of internal sanctions can only be explained with reference to the statement that shame may become a 'relatively internal' sanction when it is strongly developed. Accordingly, since an internal sanction is defined as one which operates automatically without having to be set in motion by others, Mead acknowledges that shame can operate in the absence of an audience, and that even fantasy of an audience need not be immediately related to a process that must be set in motion by others. Shame involving fantasy of an audience would then be exactly parallel to fear of supernatural agency—once conditioned to experience such anxiety, one will do so automatically wherever the eliciting conditions are right, but even so one will not possess a conscience which maintains that certain sorts of behaviour are wrong in themselves (for we remember that the individual who is 'controlled by fear of being shamed . . . can dismiss his misbehavior from his mind').

Such a conception quite apart from its inadequacy as an account of

[69] (1937), 494.   [70] (1937), 487–505.

shame, raises problems for Mead's own argument. Shame, she believes, can rest on an internal sanction but does not involve internalized standards of behaviour, for those who are typically subject to
shame possess no mechanism which would prevent them contraven-
ing the standards of their society if they felt they could do so with
impunity. In the immediate context, however, concern for internal
versus external sanctions is illustrated as follows:

So the devout Catholic who alone on a desert island would still abstain from
meat on Friday may be said to be responding to an *internal* sanction, which we
customarily call conscience; whereas the businessman from a middlewestern
city who regards a visit to New York as a suitable occasion for a debauch in
which he would never indulge at home conducts his exemplary home behavior
in response to an *external* sanction.[71]

Concern for popular disapproval is clearly the motivation behind the
normal behaviour of the businessman, and he acts in breach of the standards normally imposed upon him when he feels he can get away with it;
this, according to Mead, indicates response to external sanctions. Yet we
have seen that Mead believes that fear of being shamed, even though it
can constitute a relatively internal sanction, entails no mechanism which
would rule out doing wrong in secret; clearly, if a readiness to do wrong
in secret betokens response to external sanctions, then shame, on
Mead's thesis, must always be a response to such sanctions. If, on the
other hand, shame may invoke internal sanctions, then someone in
whom such sanctions are operative should not be quite so able to dismiss
his misbehaviour from his mind, even if no one knows of his misdeed.

Mead's account, therefore, singularly fails to distinguish between
shame- and guilt-cultures in terms of the sanctions employed, and the
distinction between internal and external sanctions breaks down in
confusion; what looks like greater subtlety with regard to the internalized component of shame than is manifested in the later studies already
discussed turns out to be a muddle, since precisely the same sort of
behaviour may be described as a response to both internal and external
sanctions.[72] If one observes the conventions even in the absence of an

[71] (1937), 493 (original emphasis).
[72] Mead's argument is justly criticized by Singer in Piers and Singer (1953: 63–7). In
reply, Mead (in the preface to the 1961 reprint of her 1937 collection) berates Singer for
'trying to mix the first tentative gropings of 1935 with the sophistication of 1953' (!); she
herself, however, continues to make use of the theoretical categories and sociological data
of the earlier study, with little explicit modification or correction, in works as late as Mead
(1950).

audience because of the strength of one's sense of shame, then one is responding to an internal sanction; but the only way in which Mead can differentiate such internalized shame from guilt or conscience is to argue that shame implies no internalized standard of behaviour which could deter one from doing wrong in secret or give rise to anxiety over a transgression which remained undetected; and this is as much as to claim that shame rests on external sanctions. Response to internal sanctions, in Mead's definition, demands that one should conform even where one might transgress with impunity; to conform in this way should, or at least could, mean that one has accepted and internalized the relevant standard, but Mead refuses to allow that this could be the case except in those few societies which exhibit Western European forms of character structure supposedly based on the development of guilt and conscience.

It is clear, then, that the distinction between shame- and guilt-cultures, despite its essential reference to external versus internal sanctions, is supported not by consideration of the operation of such sanctions alone, but by certain a priori assumptions relating to the uniqueness of Western society. The observant, in fact, will already have noticed the presence of such assumptions in the exposition of Leighton and Kluckhohn quoted above, for in their formulation some of the subsidiary criteria on which the shame- and guilt-culture antithesis is based are more apparent than in the passage cited from Benedict. The Navaho, we remember, do not internalize the standards of their parents (and other elders), and are controlled by shame rather than the Christian 'conscience' and 'guilt' which rest fundamentally on the standards represented by one's parents. Possession of a conscience or a sense of guilt, therefore, is being related to a specific pattern of development in a specific form of parent–child relationship. '"Shame"', we are told, 'is the agony of being found wanting and exposed to the disapproval of others, as opposed to the fear that some single superior person will use his power to deprive one of rewards and privileges'; thus shame is found in societies, like the Navaho, in which sanctions are imposed 'laterally' rather than from above.[73] The implicit contrast, therefore, is between the forms of socialization and personality development displayed in Navaho society and the pattern of parent–child relationship which dominated white, middle-class, Protestant America in the period in which the authors wrote; and this contrast is supported with reference to the Protestant conception of an omni-

[73] Leighton and Kluckhohn (1948), 105–6.

scient, punitive, paternalist Deity which is felt to underlie and reinforce the practices of white American parents.[74]

Thus the concealed props of the antithesis are laid bare; it still rests on a dichotomy between external and internal sanctions, but supervenient on this criterion is the further thesis that guilt and conscience, and therefore truly internal sanctions, can exist only in societies in which the child is socialized by parents who stress the kind of imperatives, the absolute Good and Evil, which are hypostatized in the figure of a fatherly Deity. The shame-culture–guilt-culture antithesis, then, stands in a direct line of descent from Weber's Protestant ethic (hence the attribution of the lack of the drive for 'progress' in the Navaho to the status of their society as a shame-culture).[75]

The basis of the antithesis is therefore more complicated than appears from Benedict's formulation (although Benedict is certainly employing the same underlying assumptions as are evident in Leighton and Kluckhohn).[76] It is not simply reliance on external as opposed to internal sanctions that differentiates a shame-culture from a guilt-culture; rather the latter is a product of a particular (and rare) method of socialization. The tendency in the works cited, however, is to read the distinction in terms of methods of parenting and socialization back into the society under discussion in such a way that only a society which relies on Protestant, Anglo-American methods of parenting can be said to place much emphasis on internal sanctions.[77] Hence the impression that the two criteria (the one in terms of external or internal sanctions and the other in terms of methods of parenting) are wholly coterminous. The truth, however, is that use of the second of these criteria, to a large extent, determines the application of the first; evidence for internal sanctions and even for guilt-like behaviour is being ignored because these sanctions are not set up by the methods applied in white, middle-class America.

This primacy of criteria other than that based on the nature of the sanction is explicitly acknowledged in the later Margaret Mead.[78] In

---

[74] '"Conscience" is related to the belief in an omnipotent God who knows all' (Leighton and Kluckhohn (1948), 106).

[75] Ibid. Cf. the hypothesis of Mead (1950: 370–1) that the development of a character-type analogous to that of 19th-cent. Europe among the Manus of the Admiralty Islands facilitates their ability to participate in the 'machine civilization of the Europeans'.

[76] Benedict (1947), for example, is at pains to demonstrate that the Japanese child is brought up to refer standards of behaviour not to parental authority but to 'other people'; see her ch. 12, 'The Child Learns'.

[77] Cf. Ausubel (1955), 389–90.

[78] See Mead (1948*a* and *b*); (1950).

these later studies guilt-cultures are still rare, the distinction between external and internal sanctions is still employed, and societies whose values are promoted and protected by shame still belong to a different order from those in which guilt is prominent; but now the emphasis is much more on the unique conditions for the development of conscience which are supposed to exist (or to have existed) in America, Great Britain, Northern Europe, and scarcely anywhere else.

These studies make explicit and give theoretical support to the view taken by Benedict and by Leighton and Kluckhohn that the development of conscience is a function of a particular form of character development in a particular parent–child relationship. The starting point is the Freudian construct of the superego (in a guise which refuses explicitly to acknowledge the role of the ego-ideal and shame in superego functioning) as the mechanism by which individuals internalize the prohibitions and ideals of parents who adopt a pose of absolute authority over the child; Freud and his immediate followers, Mead points out, had regarded the model of superego formation found in their well-to-do European and American patients as a universal feature of character formation, and certain (unnamed) social anthropologists had followed them in regarding development of the superego as equivalent to the acquisition of culture.[79] Mead, however, wishes to go to the other extreme; the superego formation which allows us to speak of guilt and conscience depends on conditions which are realized in very few societies, and thus few societies produce individuals who manifest the phenomena of guilt and conscience.[80]

The criteria for the development of guilt and conscience under this hypothesis are relatively clear, and broadly speaking, they are those which guided Benedict and Leighton and Kluckhohn in distinguishing guilt-cultures from shame-cultures. The conditions for guilt arise in 'systems in which the parents are executors and interpreters of the sanction', '... in which the referent [*sic*] is the parents themselves as the approving and disapproving figures', and in which the sanction employed by the parents is 'I, your father, or your mother, will punish and reward you in terms of your behavior'.[81] The parents, that is, 'must

[79] (1948*a*), 513. It is worth observing that Freud was less impressed than are the guilt-culture theorists with the possibility that his model of superego formation might dominate the morality of an entire culture: 'as regards conscience God has done an uneven and careless piece of work, for a large majority of men have brought along with them only a modest amount of it or scarcely enough to be worth mentioning' (Freud (1964), 61).

[80] (1948*a*), 513–18; (1948*b*), 525; (1950), 366–71.   [81] Mead (1950), 366–7.

think of the child as qualitatively different from themselves'[82] (or, as Leighton and Kluckhohn put it, they pose as omnipotent or omniscient),[83] and their word is law, to be accepted absolutely and without further justification.[84] Such a pattern, moreover, belongs with 'a conception of the Deity which sees Him as primarily concerned, like the parent, with moral behavior, and as backing up the parent in dealing with the potentially immoral child'.[85]

Such are the criteria for guilt and conscience, and guilt and conscience, straightforwardly enough, rest on internal sanctions. For Benedict as for Leighton and Kluckhohn the application of such criteria, albeit with less explicit acknowledgement, was sufficient also to distinguish cultures which relied on internal sanctions from those which relied on external sanctions. Concern for the former was guilt, and shame involved nothing but the latter.[86] The situation in the writings of Mead, once again, is less straightforward. Shame, it now appears, may relate (always relates ?) to sanctions which are internalized, but there are degrees of internalization. When parents are the 'executors and interpreters' of the sanction, but refer to others rather than themselves as figures of approval or disapproval, and when the sanction is not 'I, the parent, will punish you or reward you', but 'people will gossip about you', internalization will occur, but will vary in accordance with the degree of 'focus' on the parent as the custodian of the values invoked. Thus:

Among American Indians it is possible to find the whole gamut of degrees of internalization, from the high internalization among the Ojibway, who may commit suicide from the shame engendered by an unwitnessed event, where

[82] Mead (1948*a*), 514.
[83] Leighton and Kluckhohn (1948), 106.
[84] Leighton and Kluckhohn (1948), 53: white parents typically control their children with such injunctions as: 'Do it because I say it is right', 'do it because I say so', and 'do it because I am your father and children must obey their parents.' Such an approach is constantly contrasted with the Navaho practice of pointing to the consequences (supernatural, in terms of 'what people will say', or purely practical) of the undesirable action; see 34, 48–9, 50–4, 170–1. The idea is that white children learn abstract and absolute standards, whereas Navaho children are simply alerted to the unpleasant consequences contingent upon certain courses of action, with no implication that they are to regard such actions as wrong in themselves (53–4, 170–1). Cf. Benedict (1947), 273, 287–8; Mead (1948*a*), 514–18; (1950), 367–70.
[85] Mead (1948*a*), 514; cf. Leighton and Kluckhohn (1948), 106.
[86] So also Ausubel (1955), who disputes the conclusions of Benedict etc., but accepts their basic premise that shame and guilt relate to external and internal sanctions respectively.

despite the verbal reference to the whole group, the child spends a great deal of time in the small family, and the much lower degree of internalization in the Zuñi, where children live in a crowded multifamilial existence where the 'people' referred to are actually present and parents invoke masked supernaturals to punish their children while themselves miming the position of being the children's defenders.[87]

The argument, then, though it is far from clear in the original, is that references by parents to other people as sources of disapproval can none the less be perceived by the child as highlighting standards to which the parent expects the child to aspire, provided they occur in circumstances in which the parents themselves are the focus for the transmission of the values concerned; the contrast is presumably between one situation in which the child forms the idea that the parent wishes him to adopt a particular standard and does so as a result of a desire to live up to the parental ideal, and another in which the child focuses more on the externality of the agency of disapproval, with little appreciation that a parental standard is being invoked.

To go this far already destroys the shame- and guilt-culture antithesis in its original and crudest form, because shame-cultures now resemble guilt-cultures in their reliance, to different degrees, on internal sanctions. In place of the original formulation we now have two antitheses, one between shame- and guilt-cultures and one between cultures which do and do not rely on internal sanctions.

The second of these is based on focus on the role of the parent as the means to internalization; internalization is low where the child tends not to regard approved and disapproved behaviour in terms of the parent's values, and high where it does. It is Mead's contention, however, that societies exist in which the child internalizes no standards or sanctions at all, because in these societies parents do not convey to the child any fear of disapproval, either their own or that of others.

The new distinction between shame- and guilt-cultures implied by Mead's theory resembles the old, in that it rests both on the manner in which cultural standards are conveyed to the child and on the content of the injunctions by which those standards are conveyed, but it differs from it in abandoning the view that the poles of the antithesis differ in

---

[87] See Mead (1950), 366–8. The position in this later work is a clear modification of that in Mead (1937), as discussed above, and of that in Mead (1948a), 518, in which reference by the parent to 'what people will say' is straightforwardly taken as a sign that 'the parents do not set themselves up as punishing and rewarding surrogates of the culture'.

respect of their reliance on external versus internal sanctions. It is no longer assumed, that is, that the guilt or conscience produced by socialization after the American pattern constitutes the only possible model of internalization of values, and accordingly the guilt-culture, though defined in precisely the same terms, no longer has a monopoly on the use of internal sanctions; but the guilt-culture is still sharply differentiated from the shame-culture as that which produces autonomous moral agents with a desire to live up to personal moral principles, and it is only in the guilt-culture that the phenomena of guilt and conscience can occur. If there is to be any difference at all in the internalization that takes place in (say) Ojibway society and that which takes place in white, middle-class America, that difference must lie in the ability of members of the latter society to recognize moral obligation in terms of right and wrong, and to accept and internalize the kind of generalized moral principles which can operate with no reference to other people at all. The new position thus clarifies and deepens somewhat that adopted in Mead (1937) (the assumptions as to the rarity of the conditions for guilt are, at least, now out in the open), but the overall criteria and approach retain an essential similarity.

The two antitheses produce three categories of society: those in which the sanctions of guilt and conscience can operate because the child is brought to accept and internalize the values of parents who adopt a pose of absolute moral superiority, those in which guilt is absent, but in which standards may be internalized according to the degree of focus on the parents as custodians of culturally approved standards, and those in which the individual internalizes no standards of behaviour whatever, but conforms out of fear or expediency. The criteria used to establish these categories, however, are arbitrary. No explanation is forthcoming as to why focus on the parent as cultural surrogate should determine the degree of internalization of values, and no argument is given to discount the prima facie plausible thesis that individuals may just as well internalize the values of their peers or of other significant and admired figures outside the family unit.[88]

The hypothesis of a successful, functioning, and complex society in which the individual does not internalize and subscribe to at least

---

[88] Again, the presumed conditions for conscience and internalization in a particular society at a particular time are being taken as universal criteria, so that their absence in other societies necessarily indicates the absence of the phenomena of conscience and internalization themselves.

some cultural norms is extremely doubtful. As examples, Mead offers the Samoans, the Balinese, and the Iatmul of New Guinea;[89] in all these societies the parent is certainly a less commanding presence in the upbringing of the child, and responsibility for children may be widely shared, but the case for non-internalization of values is weak. In Samoa and Bali, in particular, children, even on Mead's account, have to learn and cope with complex forms of ritual and culturally approved behaviour, and are controlled, corrected, rewarded, and punished, until observance of the conventions and etiquette of the society becomes second nature; there is nothing here that rules out internalization, and much, even in the brevity of Mead's descriptions, that positively suggests it. In Samoa, according to Mead, the child or young person is repeatedly expelled from social gatherings when he fails to meet their requirements, and it can hardly be that the adult individual does not come to endorse the forms of behaviour which facilitate his participation in society as the right ones.[90] Mead's statement that 'transgression and non-transgression are matters of expediency' refers to a state of affairs which is no more inevitable in Samoan society than in middle-class America, where it might just as well be a matter of expediency to avoid, from 'omnipotent' parents, punishments which must, given their lack of justification in any terms other than parental fiat, seem to the child totally arbitrary. Bali provides an even better example; the case against internalization rests on two observations: that the child is passively manipulated (sometimes literally) by adults until it comes to be able to assume the correct social posture by itself, and that children are deterred from behaviour deemed undesirable by means of a feigned display of terror on the part of the child-minder, which reinforces a connection between inappropriate behaviour and inhibitory, undifferentiated fear, with the result that the adult's response to the prospect of transgressing a conventional boundary is one of instinctive withdrawal. The activation, however, of this instinctive response in the adult Balinese clearly indicates that transgression of the norms prescribed by ritual and convention is felt to be unthinkable, and this suggests at least the possibility that the individual may subscribe to the standards to which he conforms, even

[89] All three in Mead (1948*a*), 514–18, the latter pair only in (1950), 369–70.
[90] As part of his detailed refutation of Mead's view of Samoan society Freeman (1983: 188–90) adduces evidence of notions of sin and guilt, in opposition to Mead's view that 'transgression and non-transgression are matters of expediency'. Mead also characterized the Samoans as uninhibited by any deep sense of shame, in which she is again refuted with copious evidence by Freeman (see index, s.v. 'shame').

if this conformity is instinctive and unquestioning. Mead, moreover, underplays the significance of the role of adult admiration for the child's correct behaviour in creating a sense of pride which might issue in internalized ideals.[91]

A priori it is extremely doubtful that any society could exist in which no internalization of standards of social and moral appropriateness took place; all societies have a need to produce members who are reliably capable of following the prescribed forms of behaviour, and any which relied wholly on external sanctions to achieve conformity would be caught in a perpetual pattern of offence and reprisal so pervasive, oppressive, and chaotic that its existence would surely be threatened.[92] Even the most anarchic and primitive societies studied, moreover, have conventions and rituals which they regard as absolutely sacrosanct;[93] in every society, surely, there are actions which no member would ever perform, even if they could be performed with impunity. Again, a society in which conformity was a simple matter of expediency, would be one in which enforcement of conventional standards was also a matter of expediency—those who conform not out of obedience to internalized standards but as a simple response to external pressure could scarcely be credited with standards of their own when they set in motion the external sanctions required to discipline others. But this is clearly not the case in those societies in which internalization is supposed not to take place; the Balinese adult does not terrify the child who acts in breach of convention simply for his or her own convenience; rather, as in all societies, adults use external sanctions to produce individuals who have successfully adopted the appropriate cultural norms, norms which the parent or authority-figure accepts, at least implicitly, as the right ones. Equally, those who set in motion the external sanctions of punishment and disgrace against adult transgressors cannot be conceived as simply promoting personal interests or expressing personal, unprincipled

[91] (1948*a*), 516.
[92] Cf. Ausubel (1955: 378–9, 386) and Izard (1977: 422–3), who argue that basic conditions of parenting and socialization demand a degree of internalization of standards in most, if not all, societies.
[93] Thus Ausubel's guarded admission (1955: 379, 386) that the inhabitants of Dobu Island in Melanesia (as described by Benedict (1934), 131) may belong to a society 'so anarchic and unstructured ... that the potentiality for guilt experience [*i.q.* concern for internal sanctions, in Ausubel's formulation] is never realized' is unnecessary. On Benedict's own account, it emerges quite clearly that even the Dobuans have internalized some of the expectations of their society (such as the requirement that one bow one's head on approaching one's father's village, p. 141).

annoyance; if external sanctions are set in motion in maintenance of the norms of a society this implies the existence of a body of people concerned to uphold those norms.[94] The existence of a society in which the group is ready and willing to apply external sanctions in maintenance of norms of socially approved behaviour, but in which, at the same time, no member of the group ever endorses or sees any obligatory force in the standards which are maintained by those sanctions is extremely unlikely.[95]

Ultimately, the procedure in all the societies studied by Mead and the shame-culture theorists is identical—parents or others control the child by external sanctions of reward and punishment, pleasure and pain, until the child can reliably meet the requirements of society on its own; no convincing explanation is given as to why the application of external sanctions in early childhood gives rise to internalized moral standards in one society and not in another. All societies, surely, rely on both external and internal sanctions; to rely on the former alone would, in fact, imply that the society possessed no norms of culturally approved behaviour at all, for it would imply that both the initiators and the recipients of external sanctions saw no intrinsic value in any standard of behaviour whatever; one would have no reason to decry any behaviour in another, except where one felt that one's interests had been damaged by the other's actions or that they might be advanced by criticism of his failings, and there would be no action whose performance one would rule out absolutely. I know of no convincing proof that such an unusual, unsocial society exists.

The distinction between Western guilt-cultures following the Freudian pattern of superego formation and those cultures which base their values in honour and shame is equally arbitrary, for it rests on the assumption that guilt and conscience can only exist where children are told from an early age that certain things are absolutely wrong and certain things absolutely right, with no justification beyond the fact that these statements are made by figures of paramount moral authority. Such a theory attaches almost magical power to the terms right and wrong, good and bad; guilt is supposed to be rare or impossible in societies in which children are not told that they are

---

[94] Cf. Dickie (1978), 94; also Ch. 1 n. 113.

[95] These remarks, moreover, are compatible with (although they do not require or presuppose) the position that elements in the development of internalized standards and conscience may be phylogenetically determined, and thus culturally universal.

'bad' when they do something 'wrong'.[96] Such insistence on un-explained absolutes is supposed to inculcate a concern for the moral status of actions as such, rather than the tendency to focus on the external fact of disapproval.[97] These terms, however, cannot carry such a load; to a child, a parental description of an action as wrong, or of a child who has transgressed as bad, simply imparts parental dis-approval; parental disapproval can be registered in any number of different ways, and, even assuming that focus on the standards of one's parents is necessary for guilt, guilt should be possible in any circum-stance in which the child is able to form an impression of parental values and preferences. The idea that conscience, or a concern for the moral character of one's actions as such, can only arise in a rigidly authoritarian environment demanding unconditional acceptance of absolute imperatives is deeply suspect; in the middle-class American 'guilt-culture' great stress is placed on the role of punishment from the earliest ages, on the introduction of a strict regime under which the child's freedom is severely constrained, and on imparting to the child a sense of its own wickedness; such conditions, which prevailed over a relatively short period in the history of a particular group of societies, and even then not in all milieux or without considerable support from other methods,[98] seem, in fact, less likely to issue in the autonomous moral conscience than an approach which accepts that a child should not be punished until it knows what it is being punished for and which prefers to justify prohibitions in terms that the child can understand.[99] There is no reason why it should be thought that an approach of the latter type leaves no room for the adult actively to adopt and uphold the standards imparted in earlier life; and no basis for the claim that guilt may only occur in circumstances in which the individual feels that

---

[96] See Benedict (1947), 190-2, 197, 287, 293; Leighton and Kluckhohn (1948), 50-4, 171; Mead (1948*a*), 517; (1948*b*), 525-8.

[97] Benedict (1947), 287; Leighton and Kluckhohn (1948), 170-1; Mead (1948*b*), 525, 528.

[98] It is greatly to be doubted whether the American guilt-culture, creating what in 1940 Mead recognized to be an 'increasingly rare type of character' (1948*a*: 521), ever existed. As Ausubel points out ((1955), 387, quoting Benedict (1947), 223), 'The presence of the stock, the pillory, and the ducking stool in the public market place offers eloquent refutation to the statement that "the early Puritans who settled in the United States tried to base their whole morality on guilt".'

[99] Cf. Ausubel (1955), 383-4, 387. One need not turn to specialized works on child-psychology, but only to the plethora of popular babycare handbooks to discover how much more closely modern practices of child-rearing in Western society approximate to the Navaho or Japanese model than to the strict regimes described by Benedict and Leighton and Kluckhohn as prevalent in the 1940s.

he is in breach of a specifically parental injunction; if internalization of values takes place to the extent that one comes to acquire a set of generalized principles accepted as binding on oneself as well as others, and if one is capable of accepting responsibility for breaches of such a code, then it seems to me that the criteria for guilt and conscience are satisfied, regardless of the particular conditions obtaining in the earliest stages of socialization.[100] The unnamed anthropologists whom Mead criticizes for their error in equating superego (conscience) formation with the acquisition of culture were, I should say, entirely correct. Any acculturated human being will possess internalized standards, and anyone who possesses internalized standards possesses a conscience.[101]

These considerations, I should say, leave the antithesis between shame- and guilt-cultures in tatters. There is no justification for the unlikely claim that there are societies in which internalization of social and moral values does not take place, and none for the view that conscience is a phenomenon restricted to a very few cultural contexts. If this is so, then I cannot see much use for the antithesis, since it can no longer serve as a useful tool for a qualitative distinction between societies; neither a 'true' guilt-culture, whether it be one that relies exclusively on internal sanctions or one which tries to base all morality on moral absolutes derived from one's parents, nor a 'true' shame-culture has ever existed—the categories of the antithesis are mere empty sets. If it is objected that the distinction may still be useful as an abstract model, in terms of which the practices of real societies, all of which manifest both kinds of response to different degrees, may be measured, then one might point out, first, that this is neither the use for which the antithesis was intended (there being no such thing as an abstract culture) nor that to which it has traditionally been put. The major objection, however, is that the categories of such a simple bipolar model are two wide and too imprecise; conceived as a distinction between response to internal versus external sanctions, the antithesis is liable to produce only the wholly unremarkable conclusion that all societies rely on a combination of both types of sanction in various

---

[100] For a detailed critique of the cultural determinism which issues in the belief of Mead and others that, since guilt and conscience exist in American society, they must therefore be phenomena which develop only where the conditions pertaining in America are replicated, see Freeman (1983), esp. 3–61, 281–302.

[101] Cf. Ausubel (1955), 380.

different and complex ways,[102] while any other modified form of the antithesis, accommodating the truth that both shame and guilt may involve internal sanctions and 'conscience', is equally unlikely to isolate any criterion which might furnish a sharp distinction between shame- and guilt-cultures.

I have gone into this issue at such length because I believe that the continued currency of the shame-culture and guilt-culture antithesis in classical contexts masks almost total ignorance of its original terms and significance; too often Homeric or classical Athenian society is characterized as a shame-culture simply because evidence makes it quite clear that these societies placed considerable stress on honour, shame, and reputation. Those who apply the antithesis, therefore, are responding to real features of Greek society. The interesting questions, however, concern not the existence of these features, but their significance—what they amount to in terms of differences between the ancient Greek world-view and our own; and therein lies the danger of unreflective application of the shame- and guilt-culture antithesis, for that antithesis most certainly is an attempt to argue for profound psychological differences as a basis for a fundamental distinction between distinct forms of society. To say that classical Greeks placed a greater explicit emphasis on public esteem than do (for example) citizens of modern Britain is true, but to regard this observation as proof that ancient Greece was a shame-culture requires an appreci- ation of the qualities which the latter description isolates; and the fact is that there is no simple correlation between the empirical data on the prominence of notions of honour, reputation, and 'face' in Greek popular morality and either of the two main hypotheses on which the shame- and guilt-culture antithesis stands. Concern for honour, even when it is acute, betokens no simple reliance on external sanctions alone. Homeric society, on account of the centrality of honour in Homeric ethics and etiquette, is frequently regarded as a paradigm shame-culture,[103] but Homeric characters clearly do possess standards of their own; not only are they aware of what is expected of them

---

[102] A model such as L. Kohlberg's moral development theory is more useful, in so far as the more subtle gradation of response over the six stages (from fear of punishment to recognition of universal moral obligation in terms of personal and reflective moral standards) offers a greater plurality of matrices, but even in this case dispute will inevitably arise over the legitimacy of separating the stages themselves and over their application to the complex circumstances of real life. For Kohlberg's theory, see (most conveniently) Kohlberg (1981); his schema is competently applied to the Homeric poems by Stanton (1983).

[103] See (e.g.) Dodds (1951), 17–18, followed (surprisingly) by G. Taylor (1985), 54–7.

by society, they have also internalized many of these expectations to the degree that deviation from them is unthinkable, and may, on occasion, manifest an awareness that the individual can, in a very real sense, make the values of the group his own.[104] If, on the other hand, a guilt-culture is one in which the individual internalizes and seeks to live up to parental standards and in which the parental model looms large as the agency which imparts the lesson that certain forms of behaviour are right and wrong, then ancient Greek society was at all periods and in many respects a guilt-culture.[105] Since the traditional explanations of the differences between shame- and guilt-cultures do not apply, the cash value of any continued designation of a society in terms of one or other of the two categories is unclear; the simple statement that a shame-culture is one in which people talk rather a lot about honour and shame seems to be devoid of much informative content.

This is not to say that there are not significant differences between our society and that of ancient Greece which may be usefully explained in terms of tendencies to emphasize shame rather than guilt. Shame, for example, does belong with a considerable expressed emphasis on the good of reputation, on one's public persona, on one's peers as a major source of moral authority; those societies regularly designated shame-cultures, moreover, are typically small-scale societies which tend to construe obligation in personal rather than abstract terms. Any difference between a 'shame-culture' and a 'guilt-culture' in these terms, however, will be one of degree rather than of

---

[104] See 1.2.3, 1.7 below; also Ch. 1 nn. 107, 113, 150, 190, 225; cf. Cairns (1990).

[105] It is instructive to note that a feature of American society which for Leighton and Kluckhohn (1948: 106) indicates the presence of the rare phenomenon of guilt or conscience (conscience or guilt = 'I am unworthy for not living up to the high standards represented by my parents'; cf. Mead (1948*a*: 520): guilt is 'the fear of not measuring up to the high standard which was represented by the parents') is in the Greek context typically taken to be a feature of a shame-culture (cf. Ausubel (1955: 385), who similarly observes that this alleged guilt-culture feature is part and parcel of the Japanese shame-culture as described by Benedict (1947)). Such concern to live up to ideals may be better referred to shame, but this is a form of shame which is not differentiated from guilt either by reference to external sanctions or by focus on parental standards. In Greek society the paternal model is a constant focus of *aidōs*; see, e.g., the stress on living up to the standard set by one's father in the *Iliad* (6. 206–10, 446, 479–81, 9. 252–9, ll. 783–4) or in the reflections of Sophocles' Ajax (432–40, 463–6, 470–2). Greek literature and mythology, moreover, offer ample evidence for the central role of the strong father, and thus much potential evidence for the kind of character formation allegedly found in guilt-cultures; see Dodds (1951), 45–8. (Dodds is arguing for a distinction between Homeric and later society, but much of his evidence (60–2) either comes from or may be paralleled in Hom.)

kind, for none of the phenomena mentioned is confined to so-called shame-cultures (we all inhabit several small-scale subcultures, and the concept of personal honour plays a significant, if less overt, part in our everyday lives), and none positively rules out internalized standards, conscience, or recognition of moral obligation as such.

Any attempt to maintain a revised antithesis between shame- and guilt-cultures would have to be based on a more sophisticated phenomenological analysis of shame and guilt than was carried out by the proponents of the original antithesis. The discussion carried out in the previous section posited certain important conceptual distinctions between shame and guilt in English, but none of these holds out the promise of a workable distinction between two wholly opposed categories of society. If shame refers to a valued image of the self or to the possession of some prized excellence, and guilt to specific actions incompatible with one's self-image, then a shame-culture could only be one in which the child is exhorted to be a particular kind of person rather than to refrain from a particular type of act; and although there is a certain amount of evidence which suggests that Greek culture actually did place greater emphasis on the excellences of persons and on ideal self-image than we do,[106] the difference is again one of degree, for focus on agents rather than acts can only be a matter of emphasis;[107] any focus on oneself as a certain type of person must take into account the character of one's acts, and any rejection or repudiation of a specific act must encompass a conception of one's selfhood. Nor should we ignore the importance of role-models and the drive to conform to an image of an ideal type in our own development.[108]

The conceptual association of shame with the 'other' and with visual imagery might offer more hope of a broad distinction in character between societies which tend to construe their moral experience in terms which suggest shame and those which do so in terms of guilt; the ability to feel oneself under scrutiny, even the scrutiny of oneself, which is characteristic of shame is presumably developed in situations

[106] In their own ways, the determination of the Homeric hero to be a certain kind of man (to behave like an *esthlos* rather than a *kakos*; see, e.g., Hector at *Il.* 6. 443–6 and Odysseus at 11. 404–10) and the agent-centred moral theories of Plato and Aristotle (see Irwin (1977), 280–6; Annas (1981), 157–69; also Gosling (1973), 41–51, and 6.4.3 below on Pl.'s *thumoeides*) testify to a somewhat greater expressed emphasis on the character of persons than on the character of actions; but even the Homeric hero is concerned with the character of his acts, and the moral theories of Pl. and Arist. do not reproduce exactly the emphases of popular morality.

[107] Cf. Annas (1981), 158.

[108] Gosling (1973), 44; Annas (1981), 159.

in which one actually does become aware of oneself as exposed to the gaze of others and comes to think of oneself as liable to others' judgement, and so it is plausible to suppose that this tendency to see one's actions from another viewpoint is more pronounced where one's own evaluation of oneself actually is, in one's early development and later, brought into frequent and explicit relationship with that of other people. This is as much as to say, once again, that a tendency to construe one's experience in terms of shame rather than guilt may be more common in small-scale, face-to-face societies. It is important, however, to be clear what this statement entails: no absolute dichotomy between two types of society (for even the greater anonymity of modern society leaves considerable room for the development of a concern for one's image in the eyes of others); no distinction in terms of external versus internal sanctions; no exclusion of the phenomenon of conscience; and no denial of the existence of personally endorsed moral standards. A tendency, then, to react to one's moral and social behaviour in terms classifiable as shame rather than guilt may reveal a certain diference of character from someone whose tendency was in the other direction, and replication of such a tendency in a significant number of members of a given society might, if it could be established beyond reasonable doubt, serve roughly to differentiate that society in terms of character of 'flavour' from others; but we should not ignore the fact that such differences of emphasis, differences in the conceptualization of experience, can often be more or less alternative ways of construing the same phenomena.[109] Since this

[109] Since shame and guilt can overlap, they may at times be alternative descriptions of the same experience; and although the absence of a concept of guilt as such in early Greek indicates a conceptual outlook which differs considerably from our own, it would be wrong to imagine that much of the experience which we should describe in terms of guilt or conscience is not covered by concepts which Greek does have. Hence there is a great deal of truth in Dover's view (1974: 220 n. 3) that 'the difference between "guilt-cultures" and "shame-cultures" ... [is] ... a difference more in the way people talk than in the way they feel.' This is subject to the important qualifications: (*a*) that differences in the way people talk can indicate major differences in the way they construe their experience; and (*b*) that shame and guilt are not simply 'feelings', and so there is no purely 'feeling' component that is separable from the cognitive/evaluative; yet Dover is still much closer to the truth than Gould, who claims, in direct response to the above remark, that the difference between guilt and shame is a fundamental one 'between a concern with moral purity or "goodness" and a concern with efficacy and aggressive achievement' (1978*a*: 287). In the end, one must ask oneself how much difference there is between a society which possesses two conceptual clusters, shame (the more extensive) and guilt (which often overlaps with one form of shame), and one which has one main concept resembling shame more than guilt, but not excluding elements of the latter, and which is capable of adumbrating other aspects of guilt in various different ways. In my view Greek and English, in this respect at least, differ more in style and tone than in the psychological facts to which their concepts refer.

is the case, I feel there is little to be gained by the continued application of the shame-culture versus guilt-culture antithesis, and would prefer to see it abandoned in favour of a more detailed appreciation of the differences (as well as the similarities) in the ways in which we and the Greeks construct our experience, and of the structural differences which lie behind them.

I

Aidōs in Homer

In Homer the range over which *aidōs* is employed is at its widest, and to a great extent the subsequent history of the concept is one of refinement of its uses and diminution of its prominence. Syntactically, however, the usage of the verb *aideomai* is at its simplest in Homeric epic: it is followed by only two constructions, either governing an object in the accusative (which is always a personal object)[1] or being followed by a prolative infinitive.

The essential, inhibitory nature of *aidōs* in Homer is immediately indicated by the operation of the verb, *aideomai*, with the infinitive. At *Iliad* 7. 93 the reaction of the Greeks to Hector's challenge to single combat is reported: 'they felt *aidōs* to refuse, but feared to accept.'[2] Similarly, Telemachus explains, speaking of his mother, 'I feel *aidōs* to pursue her against her will from the house under compulsion.'[3] In both these passages *aidōs* is inhibitory, it prevents the performance of the action expressed in the infinitive.[4] *Aidōs* thus involves a check of some kind; it modifies the conduct of those affected.[5] Its restrictive nature is recognized in those few passages in which its abandonment is advised. At *Odyssey* 3. 14, Athena, urging outspokenness on the youthful Telemachus, tells him that he has 'not the slightest need of *aidōs*'; later, at line 96 of the same book (= 4. 326) it is recognized that *aidōs* may cause one to keep back information in order to spare another's feelings.[6] *Aidōs* may also be disadvantageous on certain occasions: its presence in a needy man, such as the beggar Odysseus, is not good,

---

[1] Thus this object never refers to an action; there is thus no possibility that *aideomai* could mean 'I am ashamed of *x*', i.e. of having done *x*; the verb is always used *prospectively* in Hom.

[2] αἴδεσθεν μὲν ἀνήνασθαι, δεῖσαν δ᾽ ὑποδέχθαι.

[3] *Od.* 20. 343–4: αἰδέομαι δ᾽ ἀέκουσαν ἀπὸ μεγάποιο δίεσθαι | μύθῳ ἀναγκαίῳ.

[4] *Il.* 21. 468–9; *Od.* 14. 145–6 are similar.

[5] For the inhibitory force, cf. *Il.* 15. 657–8: the Greek warriors 'did not scatter throughout the army; *aidōs* and fear (*deos*) held them back.' Clearly, then, *aidōs* operates negatively: it inhibits; see Verdenius (1944–5), 47–8, 49 n. 2, 51. Von Erffa's insistence (1937: 5, 40) that *aidōs* is positive arises from a confusion of its effects, usually beneficial, and its mode of operation.

[6] *Aidōs* of this kind is clearly altruistic; see Scott (1980), 25; cf. 1.3.4 and 1.7 below.

Telemachus tells us (*Odyssey* 17. 347). Finally, in *Iliad* 10 (237–8), Agememnon urges Diomedes to ignore any feeling of *aidōs* which may lead him to consider status before merit in choosing an accomplice in nocturnal espionage. In circumstances, then, in which an absence of restraint is desirable, *aidōs* is specifically excluded.[7] I argued in the Introduction that the restraint provided by *aidōs* is an emotional one, and this is borne out by its location in the *thumos* (*Iliad* 15. 561 and 661).[8] If *aidōs* is an emotion, then its occurrence depends on the disposition of the individual and on the particular conditions which have contributed to the development of his or her character, and so we need not be surprised if it is not effective in every individual or on each and every occasion.[9] As an emotion, it is very often coupled with pity or fear.[10] In these cases the very fact that *aidōs* is named together with one of the other emotions shows that they are not identical, yet the combination does suggest that *aidōs* works on the emotional level. Where *aidōs* does occur together with one of these emotions, it is generally true that pity accompanies *aidōs*, or a request for *aidōs*, for the helpless, the less fortunate, or those who assume a position of inferiority, while fear accompanies *aidōs* for one's superiors.[11]

Simple instances of the verb *aideomai* with a personal object indicate that *aidōs* can focus on other people, but the ways in which this is so remain to be established, for *aidōs* focuses on 'others' in different ways and for different reasons. In one significant class of examples the reference to the personal object of the verb is amplified by a clause giving the grounds for *aidōs*. In such cases the personal object of the verb is not the direct recipient of one's actions (as in the 'I respect'

---

[7] On this topic and these passages, see Pearson (1962), 42–3; for a parallel from a modern Greek community, see Campbell (1965), 150.

[8] *Aidōs* is also found in the *phrenes*, *Il.* 13. 121–2; on these passages, see Scott (1980), 14. Neither the *thumos* nor the *phrēn* is exclusively emotional in Hom., in the sense of excluding all rational content (E. L. Harrison (1960), 66–7, 71–2, 74; cf. Halliwell (1990), 39–41), but, as Schmitt well points out (1990: 185–8, 191–211), this accurately reflects the impossibility of a total separation of affect from cognition in specifying the content of an emotional event; the *thumos* and the *phrenes* do think, but they do so in a particular way that is distinct from the exercise of pure intellect. *Nemesis* is more frequently situated in the *thumos*: *Il.* 2. 223, 16. 544, 17. 254; *Od.* 1. 119, 2. 138, 4. 158; Scott (1980), 26.

[9] See Murray (1924), 83, 89.

[10] See von Erffa (1937), 28–31, and the remarks of Redfield (1975), 118; *aidōs* is coupled with pity at *Il.* 21. 74, 22. 123–4, 419, 24. 44, 207–8, 503; *Od.* 14. 388–9, 19. 253–4, 22. 312, 344. On pity in Hom. in general, see Scott (1979), 1–14. For *aidōs* and words connoting fear, see *Il.* 1. 331, 3. 172, 18. 394, 24. 435; *Od.* 8. 22, 17. 188; cf. 1.3.1 below, on *aidoios* in combination with *deinos*.

[11] Pity: e.g. *Il.* 21. 74; fear: e.g. *Il.* 1. 331; *Od.* 17. 188.

usage), but some person or group of persons who will constitute their audience. In *Iliad* 22, for example, Hector explains (105–7): 'I feel *aidōs* before the Trojans and their wives with the trailing dresses, lest someone baser than myself should say, "Hector trusted in his might and destroyed the host."' The 'lest' ($\mu\acute{\eta}$) clause, of the same type as would be used with a verb of fearing, further suggests the affinity of *aidōs* with fear, the warrior's *aidōs* here taking the form of apprehension at what other, even inferior people may say. This fact demonstrates the difference between this use of the verb and that in which its focus is the special status of another person; here the focus of apprehension need enjoy no special claim to consideration, but simply possesses the capacity to criticize. This type of passage thus indicates a fundamental connection in Homer between *aidōs* and popular opinion which we shall now explore in more systematic fashion.

1.1. HOW THINGS LOOK AND WHAT PEOPLE SAY

What follows examines the terms used in the Homeric poems to describe or adumbrate the sanction with which *aidōs* is most fundamentally and explicitly connected in the poems, namely 'what people say'. It will become clear that much of this section is directed against the theories of A. W. H. Adkins; that this should be so, however, is not in any way due to a desire gratuitously to attack Adkins's position, but rather involves a recognition that his work has set the agenda for anyone who wishes to follow him in studying Greek values through the value-terms the Greeks themselves used. There appears to be something of a consensus, unarticulated in print but often voiced in private, that Adkins's work can be disregarded as outdated; but this is unsatisfactory, for his views do deserve to be taken seriously, and, if they are to be shown to be false, the challenges they pose should at least be directly confronted. Accordingly, I examine in fairly close detail below the terms used in Homer to express popular disapproval, both because some of these are integral to Adkins's characterization of Homeric values and because Adkins's views on the behaviour of these terms must be tackled if our account of *aidōs* is to proceed.

With regard to Homer, it is Adkins's basic contention that the sharp distinction which he finds between competitive and co-operative values[12] is rooted both in the values and in the vocabulary of the

[12] See Adkins (1960*a*), ch. 3, *passim*.

poems. This view affects his evaluation of *aidōs*, since, although he recognizes that *aidōs* itself operates in both competitive and co-operative spheres, he claims that the restraint provided by *aidōs* is weak in the co-operative, strong in the competitive, because, of the terms employed in the poems to convey blame and popular disapproval, some (the strong ones) are confined to competitive failure, while others condemn failure in co-operation.

1.1.1. *What People Say*

The thought of popular opinion is a major source of motivation in the Homeric poems; sometimes it is referred to as such, as when Phoenix explains how he was restrained from the murder of his father by 'one of the immortals', 'who placed in my *thumos* the words of the people and many reproaches of men, in order that I should not be called a parricide among the Achaeans' (*Iliad* 9. 459–61).[13] This looking forward to 'what people will say' parallels exactly the reaction of Hector in the passage quoted above, and indeed the placing of 'the words of the people and many reproaches of men' in Phoenix's *thumos* can be seen as a periphrasis for the placing of *aidōs* in his *thumos*.[14] Similar explicit expressions occur at *Odyssey* 16. 75 (= 19. 527)[15] and 21. 323 as the objects of the verbs *aideomai* and *aischunomai* respectively,[16] revealing once more the relevance of our terms to these notions.

1.1.2. Nemesis

The most important expression of popular disapproval for our purposes, however, is *nemesis*.[17] The relationship between *aidōs* and *nemesis* is so close that many instances of the latter will be considered

---

[13] *Il.* 9. 458–61 were athetized by Aristarchus, but Plutarch (see Allen's OCT app. crit.) is probably right to assume that this was on account of their shocking content; the lines certainly seem to belong here. On their content, see von Erffa (1937), 5.

[14] The terms used here to express others' opinions are δήμου φάτις and ὀνείδεα.

[15] Where δήμοιο φῆμις (= popular gossip) occurs as the object of the participle αἰδομένη.

[16] See 1.6.4 below, on the essential synonymy of the two verbs in Hom. Other instances of the phrase δήμοιο φῆμις (*Od.* 15. 468, 14. 239) are less important.

[17] On *nemesis* see von Erffa (1937), 30–5; Redfield (1975), 115–18; Riedinger (1980), 69–75; Scott (1980), 26–30.

individually in the main discussion below; at this point a few remarks on the nature of that relationship and on the operation of *nemesis* will suffice.

Aidōs and *nemesis* frequently occur as a pair; see, for example, *Iliad* 13. 121–2,

ἀλλ' ἐν φρεσὶ θέσθε ἕκαστος
αἰδῶ καὶ νέμεσιν.[18]

and *Odyssey* 2. 64–6,

νεμεσσήθητε καὶ αὐτοί,
ἄλλους τ' αἰδέσθητε περικτίονας ἀνθρώπους,
οἳ περιναιετάουσι.[19]

The nature of the relationship becomes clearer when we examine *Iliad* 17. 91–5: 'Ah me! If I leave behind the fine armour and Patroclus, who lies here for the sake of my honour [*timē*],[20] what if one of the Greeks should see and feel *nemesis*? But if I, alone though I am, fight Hector and the Trojans out of *aidōs*, what if I am outnumbered and surrounded?' Menelaus considers two alternatives; either he can leave behind the arms[21] and body of Patroclus and risk the *nemesis* of his fellows, or he can give in to the *aidōs* which the thought of their disapproval arouses in him and remain where he is, in spite of the danger. *Aidōs*, then, foresees and seeks to forestall *nemesis*.[22] A similar example of the interaction of *aidōs* and *nemesis* is given by von Erffa.[23] At *Odyssey* 20. 343 Telemachus explains his reluctance to send his mother away in terms of *aidōs*, while at 2. 136–7, he refers to the *nemesis* of others as his reason for not doing so.

In the passage from *Iliad* 17 the object of *nemesis* was an action which could be viewed as cowardice, as it was in the other passage quoted above from *Iliad* 13. The term frequently has a similar reference (*Iliad* 6. 351, 13. 117–19, 292–3, 10. 129–30).[24] We shall also

---

[18] 'Each of you set *aidōs* and *nemesis* in your *thumos*.'

[19] 'Do you, too, feel *nemesis*, and feel *aidōs* before those who are your neighbours.'

[20] I use 'honour' for *timē* throughout in the sense of prestige, status, or worth, the dishonourable being that which might diminish these. I do not think this is problematic, especially as these terms are so familiar in the context of Mediterranean anthropology (see Just (1985), 174 with n. 11), but it is as well to point out that any wider connotations of 'honour' should, for the moment, be disregarded.

[21] These would be a valuable trophy for the Trojans, and proof of their success. On the importance of trophies and other means of concrete proof, see Finley (1956), 132–7.

[22] Note, too, the connection between *aidōs* and being seen.

[23] (1937), 30.

[24] On these, see Scott (1980), 26.

encounter passages in which warriors are urged to feel *nemesis* lest the body or arms of a fallen colleague be captured by the enemy.[25] But *nemesis* does not operate entirely within the competitive sphere. In *Odyssey* 2. 136–7 it was imagined as directed at a breach of the loyalty expected in a son towards his mother, while in the previous passage quoted from the same book (64–6) it was invoked against the excessive behaviour of the suitors. There is also a link between *nemesis* and loyalty in those places where Penelope's sensitivity to *nemesis* is given as a reason for her desire to finish Laertes' shroud before choosing one of the suitors as her husband.[26]

In fact, the range of usage of *nemesis* is very wide: it is frequently employed in condemnation of violence or excess,[27] and also in a number of minor social contexts, where it censures infringement of decorum.[28] In some cases it seems to signify little more than anger, although, as Redfield points out,[29] it always connotes anger in which the subject feels himself justified, anger which is directed at some transgression or deficiency on the part of someone else. There is always the possibility, then, that *nemesis* may refer to a breach of *aidōs*, even when the latter is not mentioned, and even in cases in which it does not obviously refer to one of the particular contexts in which *aidōs* regularly occurs.[30]

In a number of passages *nemesis* is explicitly denied or disclaimed (in such expressions as 'I feel no *nemesis*' or 'there is no need for *nemesis*'). The action thus freed from *nemesis* is therefore regarded as justified or understandable.[31] In a similar manner, when a character urges, 'Feel no *nemesis*' (μή νέμεσα, etc.), he is effectively apologizing beforehand for annoying behaviour which he nevertheless feels is demanded on the particular occasion.[32]

---

[25] See 1.2.5 below.

[26] *Od.* 2. 101–2, 19. 146–7, 24. 136–7.

[27] It is frequently directed at the suitors, for example: *Od.* 1. 228–9, 2. 64, 17. 481 (the suitors as a group disapprove of Antinous), 21. 146–7 etc.; the gods in the *Il.* feel *nemesis* when one of their number becomes involved in human strife: *Il.* 5. 757–9, 872; correspondingly, a god who acts in the manner condemned by *nemesis* is said to be without *aidōs*: *Il.* 15. 129 (cf. 115, where Ares tries to forestall *nemesis* at what Athena sees as his lack of *aidōs*); see von Erffa (1937), 33.

[28] e.g. *Od.* 4. 158, 22. 489.

[29] (1975), 117; cf. Scott (1980), 26.

[30] Hence, as Riedinger (1980: 69) points out, von Erffa's list of passages (1937: 35) in which *nemesis* is not the correlate of *aidōs* seems rather over-inclusive.

[31] *Il.* 2. 296, 3. 156, 4. 413; *Od.* 1. 350, 18. 227, 19. 264, 20. 330; cf. Redfield (1975), 117–18; Scott (1980), 27.

[32] *Il.* 10. 145, 15. 115, 16. 22; *Od.* 23. 213; cf. Hohendahl-Zoetelief (1980), 22–4.

The neuter adjective *nemessēton* occurs seven times in the poems in the sense 'occasioning popular disapproval'. In *Iliad* 9. 523 (= *Odyssey* 22. 59) the expression is οὐ νεμεσσητόν ('there is no occasion for *nemesis*'), which corresponds to the former of the two kinds of passage mentioned in the previous paragraph. In the other passages there is an obvious reference to 'how things look', to a quasi-aesthetic concept of appropriateness; in *Iliad* 3. 410 and 14. 336, for example, the term is applied to the performance of the sexual act at a time or place which is felt to be inappropriate. At *Iliad* 19. 182 and 24. 463 the question of the correct conduct for individuals of a certain status is foremost; in the former passage Agamemnon is informed that it will not be *nemessēton* for him to make amends with Achilles since it was he who began the quarrel; apparently the *nemesis* which is here denied is to be imagined as directed at a king who would show himself weak by giving in to his inferiors;[33] in the latter Hermes refuses to accompany Priam into Achilles' presence, on the grounds that to accept a mortal's hospitality would be *nemessēton*, unfitting for a god like himself. Finally, at *Odyssey* 22. 489 Eurycleia tells Odysseus that it would be *nemessēton* for him to remain in his beggar's rags; again physical appearances and the status of the person concerned are stressed. This idea of appropriateness and of appearances in the adjective, together with its connection with popular disapproval, reveals it as clearly comparable with those terms which express more explicitly the notion of 'how things look', namely *aischros* (ugly; neuter *aischron*) and *aeikēs* (unseemly; neuter *aeikes*).[34]

1.1.3. Aischos, Aischros, *etc.*

Crucial to Adkins's thesis is the family of terms of which the adjective *aischron* is a member. We shall consider that term, the neuter singular of the adjective, in a moment, but first we shall examine the usage of some of its relatives. The root meaning of the noun *aischos* is 'ugliness',

---

[33] For an alternative explanation (which seems to me less probable), see Scott (1980), 29.

[34] See von Erffa (1937), 25. There also exists an unparalleled use of *nemesētos* in the masculine at *Il.* 11. 649, where the adjective is coupled with *aidoios* (derived from *aidōs*) and predicated by Patroclus of Achilles; the meaning may be 'liable to feel *nemesis*', or the adjective could be synonymous with *aidoios* here. Whatever the meaning, the passage is evidence of a certain fluidity and multivalence in the use of our terms; on which, see Cheyns (1967), 17.

and this connotation is present throughout the range of its uses. At
Odyssey 11. 433 *aischos* is the legacy left by Clytemnestra to the rest of
her sex, and the context is clearly one of disgrace or infamy. *Aischos*
also has an obvious reference to popular disapproval at *Odyssey*
18. 225, where Penelope tells Telemachus that he will suffer *aischos*
and *lōbē* (disfigurement) among men for allowing a guest under his
protection to be 'disfigured'. Quite clearly, appearances are stressed in
the use of all three of these terms. *Aischos* and *lōbē* occur together
again at *Iliad* 13. 622, and again they appear to be rough synonyms:
Menelaus, exulting over his defeated opponent, Peisander, claims that
the Trojans have no lack of *aischos* and *lōbē*. The context is that of
Paris' breach of guest-friendship in abducting Helen, yet the terms
employed do not refer primarily to the disgrace of the Trojans, for
Menelaus goes on to say that the *lōbē* which the Trojans do not lack is
that which they inflicted on him (ἥν ἐμὲ λωβήσασθε).[35] Although
Menelaus is condemning Paris' conduct, and promising divine
punishment, he decides in this instance to stress the disgraceful nature
of that conduct for himself, the patient, rather than for the agent. It is
Adkins's contention[36] that these terms always operate in this way,
always 'discrediting' the perpetrator, not the sufferer, of the 'disfigurement'. This feature of the usage of such terms, moreover, is central to
Adkins's sharp dichotomy between competitive and co-operative
values, for if these 'strong' terms of disapproval can only condemn
patients, then they can only condemn competitive failure, or weakness.[37]

In the examples just quoted *aischos* was both the state which might
arouse popular disapproval and the state resulting from popular
disapproval. In the plural *aischea* can refer both to the state considered
disgraceful and to the reaction of others to that state. The two uses,
however, should not be sharply distinguished, since 'ugliness' is the
dominant connotation of both and because it is natural that a condition deemed ugly by popular opinion should be designated by the

[35] *Lōbē* also occurs at *Il.* 3. 42, 9. 387, 11. 142 (where it is qualified as 'unseemly',
aeikēs), 19. 208; *Od.* 18. 347, 19. 373 (note *aischea*), 20. 169, 285, 24. 326, 433. Verbal
forms (disgrace, insult) occur at *Il.* 1. 232, 2. 242, 13. 623; *Od.* 23. 15, 26. One whose
situation is disgraceful may be described as a *lōbētēr*, as at *Il.* 2. 275, 11. 385, 24. 239 (with
elenchees, 'disgraces'), or *lōbētos*, as at *Il.* 24. 531.
[36] (1960*a*), 42 and *passim*.
[37] Paris' conduct, it need hardly be said, can be condemned, and is so at *Il.* 3. 46–51
(see Long (1970), 133); but Adkins's thesis would only be obviously false in this case if
Paris' co-operative failure were censured in exactly the same terms as Menelaus'
competitive failure, which it is not.

same term as the words, ugly in themselves, used to comment upon it. At *Odyssey* 1. 229 it is to acts liable to arouse disapproval that *aischea* refers; the disguised Athena offers Telemachus an opinion on the excessive behaviour (note line 227, ὑβρίζοντες ὑπερφιάλως, 'behaving with excessive *hubris*')[38] of the suitors, saying that any sensible onlooker would experience *nemesis* upon witnessing the many *aischea* taking place before him. Adkins[39] believes that this use of *aischea* comments adversely only on Telemachus' failure to be master of his own house, but this can hardly be the case when Athena has been referring to the *hubris* of the suitors, when she is masquerading as a guest in Telemachus' house (as we shall see,[40] strict conventions demand courtesy between guest and host—it is surely incredible that a guest should draw attention to a host's disgrace) and when Tele- machus obviously takes the goddess's words not as criticism but as sympathy.[41] Let it be clear that the conclusion that the conduct of the suitors reflects badly on Telemachus is one which *could* be drawn, but this is surely not Athena's intention here. Here, then, *aischea* does refer to the suitors' dishonouring of another, but it is they, the agents of the dishonour, not Telemachus, its patient, whose situation is regarded as discreditable. The possibility of *nemesis*, moreover, at the suitors' 'uglinesses' and their *hubris* further suggest that these deficiencies entail breaches of *aidōs*.[42] It is, as Adkins would admit, obvious that

---

[38] On *hubris*, see MacDowell (1976), Fisher (1976), (1979), Cantarella (1981), (1982).

[39] (1960*a*), 42.

[40] Below, 1.3.5.

[41] Cf. Long (1970), 130–1.

[42] Fisher (1976 and 1979) (cf. Cantarella (1981) = ead. (1982), on *hubris* in Hom.), is right to stress, to a greater extent than does MacDowell (1976), the connection between *hubris* and the dishonouring of another person. MacDowell may be right to insist that it does not always require a victim, but Fisher and Cantarella do go some way to showing that, even where there is no immediate patient, the arrogant assumption of superiority and contempt for the *timē* of others which *hubris* entails imply the dishonouring of others. In this respect the accounts of MacDowell and Fisher may, to a large extent, be reconciled, although MacDowell would still insist that *hubris* can connote exuberance (the 'original meaning', as Hooker (1975) asserts, wrongly, in my view) or self-indulgence with no reference to the concept of honour; see now MacDowell (1990), 18–23: I am not, however, quite convinced that the *hubris* of animals and plants is to be taken as seriously as he claims. However this may be, there is at least a typical, if not a necessary connection between *hubris* and dishonour. Let it be noted, then, that *hubris*, referring to affronts on the honour of others, is a *pejorative* term; to attempt to dishonour another, even if one is successful, is, at least in the eyes of some, not always to win honour for oneself (cf. Riedinger (1980), 77). Precisely the same point is made in this passage by the designation of the suitors' behaviour as *aischea* as is made by its designation as *hubris*; and since *hubris* involves lack of concern for another's *timē*, it is natural that it should attract *nemesis* and thus involve a breach of *aidōs*.

aidōs is felt, when active, to prevent breaches of the co-operative virtues and that the suitors are without such *aidōs*—they are described as *anaideis* throughout the poem; but the important point here is that lack of *aidōs* in the co-operative sphere can be seen as the perpetration of *aischea*, deeds disgraceful for their agent, which suggests that such conduct may be *aischron* for its agent.[43]

From *aischos* (or *aischros*) is derived the verb *aischunō*, of which the basic meaning is 'make ugly' or 'disfigure', and in five passages of the *Iliad* it is this literal, physical sense that the word bears, being used of the mutilation of dead bodies.[44] In other passages the usage is more figurative, and thus the verb might be translated 'to disgrace' (*Iliad* 23. 571, Menelaus to Antilochus, 'You have disfigured my *aretē* [excellence]', 6. 209, the injunction of Glaucus' father, 'Do not disfigure the race of your fathers'), but these are really no more than transferrals of the physical application of the verb. Similar is *Odyssey* 2. 85–6, where Antinous the suitor reacts angrily to Telemachus' criticism: 'What a thing to say, shaming [αἰσχύνων] us; try to fasten the blame on us, would you?' Antinous thus reacts to a charge of co-operative failure (abuse of hospitality and dishonouring of another) as to an affront to his own honour; although he denies (87) that the suitors are responsible for the dissipation of Telemachus' patrimony, he does not deny that the charge that they are could 'disfigure' them; in fact he says it could. This corroborates our findings in the case of *aischea* at

[43] At *Od.* 19. 373 the reference of *aischea*, together with *lōbē*, is to the insults which cause disgrace, to the reaction of other people, rather than to the behaviour occasioning that reaction. The same is true of *Il.* 3. 242, where the term *oneidos* (reproach) also occurs, 6. 351, where *aischea* is coupled with *nemesis*, and 6. 524. The usage of *aischea* is a good example of the way in which the terms under discussion can shift in their application from the subjective to the objective; similar is the use of *oneidea* at *Od.* 6. 285, where the term refers to the situation which leads to reproach, rather than to the reproaches themselves.

[44] *Il.* 18. 24, 27, 180, 24. 418, 22. 75; in this last passage the verb governs κάρη (head), γένειον (cheek), and αἰδῶ; the first two terms suggest that *aidōs* is also physical here, in the sense of 'genitals', a meaning often conveyed (though only once in Hom.) by the neut. pl. adj. *aidoia* (*Il.* 13. 568); *aidōs* also occurs in this sense at *Il.* 2. 262 (Thersites' *aidōs* covered by his clothes); cf. Ger. *Scham*. Beil (1961), perhaps influenced by the parallel with the concrete meaning of the German term, or by Freud (191b; 99–100 n. 1), sees this physical sense of *aidōs* as in some way the primary one, to which he relates all others by means of the common link of 'fear of exposure (*Entblößung*)'; I cannot, however, see how one can find any evidence for any hypothesis of 'original significance' in the poems (this applies also to the attempt of Hooker (1987) to posit for *aidōs* an original sense of 'religious awe'; not only is this not the original meaning, it is not even a regular meaning). It is interesting, however, that in these two passages of the *Il.* (2. 262, 22. 75) the word *aidōs* denotes not the reaction but its object, that which attracts *aidōs*; again, this is an example of the shift from the subjective to the objective field.

Odyssey 1. 229; in that passage the suitors' conduct was seen to generate *aischea* discreditable to themselves, and now it seems that criticism of that conduct could implicate them in *aischos*, since, it seems difficult to deny, such must be the result when one person *aischunei* another.[45]

There remains the adjective *aischros*. The root meaning is, as we should expect, 'ugly', but there is only one instance of the adjective in a personal application in Homer, when Thersites is described as 'the ugliest man at Troy' (*Iliad* 2. 216). In several passages[46] the expression αἰσχροῖς ἐπέεσσιν ('with ugly words') occurs; in each case the locution refers to the fact that an affront is being offered, and since an affront is an attempt to dishonour its patient, the ugliness of the words clearly could reflect on their recipient. Hesychius' explanation (s.v.) of the force of *aischros* here ('capable of bringing disgrace, *aischunē*') is therefore not wrong.

Similarly, the adverb *aischrōs*, on its only two appearances in the poems, refers to the act of abusing or reproaching someone (*Iliad* 23. 473, *Odyssey* 18. 321). Again, it is clear that a verbal affront is intended to, and often does, humiliate or dishonour its recipient. The flavour of the phrases 'to address with ugly words' and 'to address in an ugly manner' is thus similar to that of the verbs 'to abuse' or 'to insult', although the adjective *aischros* and the adverb *aischrōs* have an aesthetic aspect that 'insulting' and 'insultingly' do not. Accordingly, just as to address another insultingly, while indicating an attempt to discredit, may in fact discredit agent, patient, or neither, depending on the circumstances, so to address another *aischrōs* may admit the same possibility; and since the ultimate reference of the adverb itself is to the 'aesthetic' aspect of the utterance, there thus exists a possibility that the adverb (or the adjective in the analogous locution) should convey a general feeling that ugly words are generally unpleasant and to be avoided. In some cases they will be justified, but in others they will not; Hector's abuse of Paris may plausibly be regarded as belonging to the former category, but the two uses of the adverb occur in passages which suggest the latter.

In *Iliad* 23 the lesser Ajax addresses Idomeneus *aischrōs*, and the

---

[45] See Long (1970), 131; cf. Riedinger (1980), 74, 77.

[46] *Il.* 3. 38, 6. 325, 13. 768; cf. 24. 238. The combination ὀνειδείοις ἐπέεσσιν ('with reproachful words') is comparable, and slightly more common: see *Il.* 1. 519, 2. 277, 16. 628, 21. 480; *Od.* 18. 326; cf. *Il.* 22. 497, where either ὀνειδείοισιν is a neut. subst. or ἐπέεσσιν is to be 'understood'. The combination ὀνείδειον μῦθον (internal acc.) also occurs: *Il.* 21. 393, 471.

latter clearly resents the affront, but when Achilles interposes he regards the very fact that a quarrel is taking place as 'unseemly' (493) and urges the pair not to bandy 'bad' ('unsuitable', *kaka*) words. The adverb, then, qualifies the address as abusive and insulting, and clearly to be abused and insulted can diminish one's honour in the eyes of others; but it is also important that abusive words can be regarded as inappropriate and that the very fact of a quarrel can be condemned in quasi-aesthetic terms whose sense is similar to that of the adverb itself. In the other passage the speech which is delivered *aischrōs* is directed at Odysseus by his unfaithful maidservant, Melantho, and while it is undoubtedly humiliating for the former that he should have to endure such abuse from an inferior, the possibility remains that the poet's auditors are expected to disapprove of Melantho's behaviour, since ill-treatment of guests and abuse of one's master (even if he is incognito) is not the kind of conduct which is commended in the *Odyssey*. Thus, while the essential nature of the affront must entail some attempt to discredit its recipient, the use of the adverb *aischrōs* in such contexts may also refer more generally to the unpleasantness of the utterance itself, and, depending on the circumstances, it may also be discredit-able for the agent, the deliverer of the affront, to address another *aischrōs*. Accordingly, the mere use of these phrases need not in every case entail that the recipient of the affront actually is discredited—to abuse a man is not always to disgrace him; to be addressed in an ugly manner is to be placed in a position that is potentially *aischron* for oneself, a position, too, in which one may well feel that one's honour is at stake, but whether one is or is not actually dishonoured may depend on the situation, the status of agent and patient, and the partiality or otherwise of any potential audience.

The neuter singular, *aischron*, occurs only three times in the poems, all three instances being in the *Iliad*, and all three referring to one very narrow area of activity, that of return from a military enterprise with nothing to show for it. *Iliad* 2. 298 is the most succinct of the three: 'it is *aischron* to remain a long time and return home empty-handed.' Similarly, lines 119–22 of the same book stress the effects on the warriors' reputations and the disgrace of giving up before victory is achieved: 'This is *aischron* even for future generations to hear, that a force of such quality and such numbers as this should wage so ineffect-ively an unsuccessful war against inferior opposition.' The third passage is 21. 436–8, where Poseidon says to Apollo: 'Phoebus, why do we two stand apart? It is unseemly, when others have made a

beginning; yet this is more disgraceful [*aischion*], if we return to
Olympus without a fight.' Again, appearances constitute the main
incentive, and the context is again one of returning home without a
fight.[47]

The term *aischron*, then, describes a situation in which martial
prestige is at stake, and characterizes it as liable to excite the disapproval of others; we shall see from a large number of passages in the
Iliad that *aidōs* is normally the reaction to the disgrace which would be
incurred in such a situation. Yet this is a term of very infrequent
occurrence, and so it is surely unwise to build as much upon it as does
Adkins ('*aischron* . . . is the most powerful word used to denigrate a
man's actions').[48] Admittedly, Adkins is correct in saying that *aischron*
is confined to the competitive sphere in Homer, but, as we have just
seen, this is not true of *aischos* and *aischunō*; nor is there any reason to
assume that the co-operative uses of the latter two terms are in
themselves any less powerful than their competitive cousins. The
adjective *aischros* refers to appearances, whether those of a man, an
action, a state of affairs, or whatever; it is extremely unlikely that such
a term, offering adverse comment on the external aspect of an action
or situation, should have any intrinsic reference to competition or co-
operation independent of its context. The paucity of contexts in
Homer certainly does not allow us to conclude that *aischron* can only
be employed in the competitive sphere; indeed, the usage of other
terms from the same root suggests that it is largely a matter of chance
that the term is exclusively competitive in the three passages in which
it occurs.[49]

1.1.4. Aeikēs *and* Aeikelios

There are, moreover, terms which Adkins depreciates or ignores
which have a similar application to that of *aischros*; we have already
looked at *nemessēton*, now we consider *aeikēs* and *aeikelios*, by far the
most frequent terms expressing unseemliness and unfittingness in
Homer.

[47] It is significant that Apollo strongly resists the invitation to fight; his *aidōs* for his
uncle (21. 468–9) outweighs the *aidōs* at failure which Poseidon's *aischion* in 437 seeks to
arouse. It is also interesting that Apollo implies that his conduct in refusing to fight is
'sensible' (*saophrōn*, 462); cf. Long (1970), 132 n. 37.

[48] (1960*a*), 30; cf. 33.

[49] On the deficiencies of Adkins's treatment of *aischron*, see also Long (1970), 129–32.

In the vast majority of the passages in which the adjective *aeikēs* occurs it is the primary, physical sense which dominates. When qualifying *potmos* or *loigos*, for example, it refers primarily to the unpleasant nature of death by violence.[50] Similarly, the blinding of the Cyclops is *aeikelios* at *Odyssey* 9. 503, and Odysseus would have suffered 'disfiguring pain' (*aeikelion algos*) had he been devoured by Eumaeus' dogs (*Odyssey* 14. 32). At *Iliad* 24. 19 the noun *aeikeiē* refers to the physical disfigurement against which Apollo protects Hector's body.

In a number of passages *aeikēs* and *aeikelios* seem to convey the ideas of meanness and low status. Often, for example, the disguised Odysseus' clothes and accessories are so designated, and the reference seems to be to their humble status and unsuitability for a man of Odysseus' position.[51] Something of the flavour of 'mean' or 'contemptible' seems to be present in the use of *aeikēs* with *noos* (understanding) at *Odyssey* 20. 366, and *aeikelios* of the kind of army that Odysseus feels Agamemnon is better suited to lead at *Iliad* 14. 84.[52] The idea of low status is also present at *Odyssey* 6. 242 and 13. 402, where *aeikelios* is used first of the previous impression of Odysseus held by the Phaeacians and secondly of the appearance lent him by Athena as part of his beggar's disguise. In both passages the idea that people of low status are also of unpleasant appearance may influence the choice of epithet.

The concrete meaning 'disfigure' is also the primary one of the verbs *aeikizō* and *aeikizomai*, which are often used in the *Iliad* of the mutilation of dead bodies.[53] There is only one instance of the verb in which the sense could be considered figurative, at *Odyssey* 18. 222, where Penelope chides Telemachus for allowing the beggar to be *aeikisthēmenai*. Odysseus has suffered no physical disfigurement, but he has been struck by Antinous and was involved in a scuffle with Irus.

---

[50] See *Il.* 1. 341, 398, 456, 4. 396, 9. 495, 16. 32; *Od.* 2. 250, 4. 339, 340, 17. 130, 131, 19. 550, 22. 317, 416. The notion of 'dishonourable' in this use of the adjective is, it seems to me, only secondary, although obviously in many circumstances to die violently will be seen as proof of inferiority. Death in battle is not always dishonourable, however (contrary to the implication of Adkins (1960*a*: 42)); see, e.g., *Il.* 15. 495-6, 22. 110, 24. 214; cf. 13. 275-91, where Idomeneus implies that one's *aretē* is not diminished by wounding or death, provided one's wounds are honourably received (on this passage, see Claus (1974), 16). See further Long (1970), 136; Griffin (1980), 96.

[51] *Od.* 16. 199, 24. 250 (his clothes), 13. 437, 17. 197, 357, 18. 108 (his satchel), and 20. 259, 24. 228 (other items).

[52] Cf. Odysseus' description of the bed on which he spent many sleepless nights as *aeikelios* at *Od.* 19. 341.

[53] *Il.* 16. 545, 559, 19. 26, 22. 404, 24. 22, 54. At 22. 256 the sense of the future ἀεικιῶ is clearly physical (*pace* LSJ, s.v.); Hector says that, if he defeats Achilles, he *will* strip him of his arms (so he will dishonour him), but he will not maltreat his body.

The adjective *aeikēs* is most relevant to our discussion when it occurs in the neuter, whether alone or qualifying *ergon* or *erga* (deeds). Here again, however, we should consider the adjective first of all as descriptive of the *erga* themselves, before assuming that an *ergon aeikes* reflects on either its agent or its patient. In three passages in the *Iliad*[54] the expression 'it is not *aeikes*' describes a situation that is both natural and fitting. The idea of honour is most prominent in the second of these (15. 496), where Hector claims that death in battle is not dishonourable when one is fighting on behalf of one's native land. In these passages the main point is that other people, in viewing the particular situation, will not feel that it merits their disapproval. The neuter *aeikes*, then, has a similar application to that of both *nemessēton* and *aischron* in that it comments on the outward aspect of a situation and categorizes it as one of which people are liable to disapprove.

Adkins claims that 'In all cases where *ergon aeikes* refers to a defeat, military or social, it is the person who "performed" the *ergon aeikes* who is discredited.'[55] There is no need, however, to be so categorical. At *Odyssey* 17. 216, for example, *aeikes* describes the insulting and excessive manner in which the goatherd, Melantheus, addresses Odysseus and Eumaeus. The agent's behaviour is undoubtedly condemned, yet Odysseus is provoked to anger, and it can hardly be that it would not be considered unfitting for him to be insulted by a goatherd. But *aeikes* does not mean 'discreditable'; its primary reference is to the goatherd's words themselves, and it will depend on the circumstances whether an unseemly act damages the reputation of the agent, the patient, or both.

In some passages, however, particularly those in which there is no patient, and where only the status of the agent is involved, actions described as *aeikea* do reflect primarily on the latter.[56] In others, where there is a patient, it often seems clear that in designating the act *aeikes*, the speaker intends to condemn the agent.[57] This need not mean, however, that the honour of the patient could not also suffer, for in a society which cares as deeply about honour as that portrayed in the Homeric poems, there is always the possibility that to suffer the *aeikea erga* of others might be construed as dishonourable. Adkins[58] says as much with regard to *aischea* and *aeikelios*, and there is no good reason

[54] *Il.* 9. 70, 15. 496, 19. 124.
[55] (1960*a*), 43.
[56] e.g. *Il.* 14. 13, 19. 133, 24. 733.
[57] *Od.* 15. 236, 23. 222, 4. 694, 20. 394, 22. 432.
[58] (1960*a*), 41–2.

to assume that an insult designated *aischea* is any more insulting or dishonourable for the patient than one which is described as *aiekes*. Since, as we saw, *aischea* can discredit both agents and patients, it seems entirely arbitrary to deny *aeikes* the same possibility.

Particularly relevant here are those passages which refer to the murder of Agamemnon.[59] In these, the deeds of Clytemnestra and Aegisthus are described as *aeikea*, and the condemnation which the description entails is obviously directed at them; the same is true of *aischos* used of Clytemnestra at *Odyssey* 11. 433.[60] Yet Agamemnon has clearly been dishonoured by his wife's infidelity, and the very bitterness of his complaints in Book 11 indicates that he regards the manner of his death as an impairment of his honour.[61] Disinterested members of society would presumably condemn Aegisthus and Clytemnestra's crime before Agamemnon's failure, but the fact remains that he suffered an ignoble fate, and it is quite possible that people could comment adversely on, for example, his failure to retain the loyalty of his wife, or the unheroic manner of his death, and this could have a detrimental effect on his posthumous fame.

As well as postulating an exclusive reference for *erga aeikea* to the discredit of agents, Adkins also argues for a distinction between *aeikēs* and *aeikelios* on precisely this point, namely the application of the former to the discredit of agents and the latter to that of patients. Given the closeness of the terms themselves, this is prima facie unlikely, and it does not take much effort to show that it is also untenable.

The inconsistency of Adkins's approach in this matter is demonstrated by two passages from the *Odyssey*, the second largely a repetition of the first. At 16. 106–9 (cf. 20. 316–19, where Telemachus is the speaker) Odysseus says: 'I should rather die in my own house than continually be witness to these *aeikea erga*, guests being maltreated and maidservants being dragged *aeikeliōs* [adverb] through the fine rooms.' Now, according to Adkins's schema, *aeikea erga* in 107 refers to the suitors, and it is they who are thereby condemned, while

---

[59] *Od.* 4. 533, 11. 429; cf. 3. 265, where Clyt.'s adultery with Aeg. is also an *ergon aeikes*.

[60] Cf. Long (1970), 130 and n. 30.

[61] e.g. he describes his death as 'most pitiable' at *Od.* 11. 412 (οἰκτίστῳ θανάτῳ). Scott (1979: 6–8) examines the usage of *oiktros* etc. in Hom., and shows that *oiktros* is only once used of the death of a warrior in the poems. She concludes (7): 'It is as if the feeling involved in *oiktros* is aroused only by people placed in a position of peculiar humiliation, of especially shameful failure under Homeric *aretē* standards.' This would support the view that Ag.'s death was also dishonourable for himself; but this last is a point which should, in any case, be obvious.

aeikeliōs in 109 reflects badly on Telemachus,[62] in the sense that it is
disgraceful that the head of the house should be unable to protect his
dependants. There is, however, no basis for this distinction in the text,
which speaks only of unseemly acts of which the treatment of the
serving maids is one. Both *aeikea* and *aeikeliōs* refer to acts which the
speaker, and presumably other people as well, find unpleasant; the
disguised Odysseus has even more sympathy for Telemachus than the
latter knows, and in his mouth both terms condemn the unseemly
conduct of the suitors, but the situation has its implications for both
parties, and the suffering of such unseemliness could easily be taken by
an enemy or a rival as an indication of the weakness of the victim. The
suitors are condemned in this passage, but Odysseus and Telemachus
could be dishonoured by their conduct; thus the terms *aeikea* and
aeikeliōs have no *intrinsic* reference to agents or patients, but rather
describe actions or situations which may reflect on the reputation of
agents and patients alike; any specific reference of such terms to
agents and patients will be a product of the specific context and the
intention of the speaker in that context.[63]

Of the terms so far discussed, then, *nemessēton*, *aischos*, *aischea*,
aischron, and *aeikēs*/*aeikelios* refer to the external aspect of actions or
situations which are liable to excite adverse comment, while *nemesis*,
aischea, and *oneidos* can be used of the reactions of others to those
actions or situations. People may react critically to both competitive
and co-operative failure, and, in cases of affront, even though an
affront necessarily involves an attempt by one person to dishonour
another, the situation may in fact be discreditable for agent or patient
or both, depending on the circumstances. There remains to be
considered the group of terms based on the nouns *elenchos* and
elencheiē.

---

[62] This is explicit at (1960*a*), 41.

[63] The position of the *aeikea erga* which Achilles perpetrated against Hector's corpse is
similar (*Il.* 22. 395, 23. 34). Ach. is condemned for committing them, even by the gods,
and yet his intention is clearly to dishonour his vanquished opponent, and indeed H.'s
body would have suffered mutilation had not this been prevented by supernatural means.
Griffin (1980: 85 n. 9) is in favour of the view that the adjective reflects on the patient,
but his reference to the occurrence of the verb *aeikizō*, used in the passive of the physical
disfigurement of H. at 22. 404, does not prove that *aeikea erga* must reflect on H., any
more than the fact that *kakizō* means 'I harm' proves that *kaka erga* are deeds harmful for
their patient. Segal (1971: 13) sees the words as criticism of Ach. I am sure that this is
right, but it is also necessary to recognize that the situation might have a detrimental
effect on the honour of both parties, regardless of the immediate reference of the phrase
aeikea erga.

1.1.5. Elenchos, *etc.*

The root meaning of *elenchos* appears to be something like 'showing up', and it is this sense which links the Homeric *elenchos* (neuter) with the classical term, which is masculine (usually translated 'proof' or 'refutation'). The plural of the Homeric noun can be used concretely of people who are exposed to the disapproval of others (just as we can say, 'you are a disgrace'). In two passages (*Iliad* 5. 787 and 8. 228) those so described are urged to show *aidōs*, and part of the object of that *aidōs* is the implication of unworthiness contained in the reproachful description, *elenchea*. To describe someone in these terms, then, is to excite their *aidōs* at the slur on their reputation.[64] A similar term, *elenchees*,[65] works in the same way (*Iliad* 4. 242, 24. 239).

The singular *elenchos* occurs at *Iliad* 11. 314-15, where Odysseus tells Diomedes that *elenchos* would be the result were Hector to reach the Greek ships. Similar is *Odyssey* 21. 329, where Eurymachus foresees *elenchea* as the result for the suitors, should the beggar Odysseus succeed where they have failed in drawing the bow. Since these *elenchea* are expressed in terms of what 'some baser person' (τις κακώτερος) will say, the connection between *elenchos* and popular opinion is explicitly made. Penelope reinforces the idea of popular opinion at 331-3, in claiming that the suitors have forfeited their right to *eukleia* (good reputation) by reason of their actions in the house of Odysseus. Adkins[66] calls Penelope's implicit application of *elenchea* to the suitors' co-operative failures a 'persuasive definition' (a use of language in which the prescriptive force of a word is retained while its descriptive reference is altered), and it is indeed clear that she has a different view of the application of the term from that of the suitors; but it is not at all clear that she is using it in a way that others would find novel or impossible.[67] We have already seen that the suitors'

---

[64] Cf. *Il.* 2. 235, 24. 239. On the latter, see Hohendahl-Zoetelief (1980), 62, and on *elenchos* in general, 62-6.

[65] This form may be an adj. (LSJ, s.v.) or an alternative noun form to *elenchea* (Leaf (1900-2) and, apparently, Kirk (1985), on *Il.* 5. 242). The existence of a superlative, albeit irregular (*elenchistos*), perhaps favours the former view.

[66] (1960*a*), 39.

[67] Cf. Long (1970), 134. Adkins's reply (1971: 6-7) does not, it seems to me, answer this point, which rests essentially on the danger of generalizing from such a paucity of evidence. The view taken here is supported by Riedinger (1980: 77 n. 53), who also observes that Pen.'s use of *elenchea* belongs with those other passages which suggest that their dishonouring of others is dishonourable for themselves.

actions could be designated *aischea* and that it was possible for one who criticized these actions to be seen as 'disfiguring' the suitors, and obviously *elenchos* is a word used in similar contexts to these. It is far from impossible in terms of Homeric language for Penelope to use this term in censure of the suitors; other characters in the poem also condemn them and the poem was obviously composed for an audience which would share their condemnation. The fact that the suitors are insensitive to criticism in most places,[68] or that they are more concerned with the *elenchos* of being worsted by a beggar than by that of dishonouring another person, does not mean that criticism of their co-operative failures is not in keeping with the values of their society or that the term *elenchos* cannot be used to convey such criticism.

One has to concede, however, that in most of its uses the root *elench*- does refer to competitive failure. The noun *elencheïe* (disgrace) occurs four times in the context of defeat in battle or failure in some other kind of competition.[69] At *Odyssey* 14. 38, however, Eumaeus says that it would have been a source of *elencheïe* for him had he failed to prevent his dogs attacking the beggar Odysseus, a visitor to his home. Here the word does refer to failure, but it is failure to accord another the protection he deserves, a co-operative, not a competitive failure.[70] The same is true of the usage of the superlative adjective *elenchistos*; in three of the four passages in which it occurs it does refer to disgrace resulting from failure on the field of battle,[71] but in the fourth it has no such reference. At *Odyssey* 10. 72 Aeolus calls Odysseus ἐλέγχιστε ζωόντων ('most despicable of living men')—the reason for his being so lies in the fact that he appears to Aeolus to be hated by the gods, and while the latter's evidence for the gods' hatred comes from Odysseus' failure to reach Ithaca in spite of the gift of the bag of winds, this is not

---

[68] But not all; remember *Od.* 2. 85–6, discussed above (cf. Riedinger (1980), 74).

[69] *Il.* 22. 100, where Hector foresees Polydamas' criticism of his leadership, 23. 342 and 408, where *elencheïe* is envisaged should Antilochus lose the chariot race, and *Od.* 21. 255, where it is the result of Eurymachus' failure to draw the bow.

[70] On this passage, see Adkins (1960*a*), 33 and (1971), 8; Long (1970), 125. Adkins's reply to Long's objections to his remarks in *Merit and Responsibility* is to point out that Eumaeus' failure is described in the same terms as failure in battle, the implication being that the sense of the term employed is intrinsically martial or competitive. Adkins's point, however, proves nothing; use of a word in a given context does not entail that elsewhere it inevitably carries the associations of that context.

[71] *Il.* 2. 285, where Agamemnon would be *elenchistos* if he left Troy without defeating his opponents, i.e. if he were to act in the manner described as *aischron* at 298 (cf. Adkins (1960*a*), 33); 4. 171, where Ag. is concerned at the prospect of criticism of his failure to protect Menelaus (and to win the war); and 17. 26, where Men. is called an ἐλέγχιστος πολεμιστής ('a most contemptible warrior').

obviously a failure in competition. To be *elenchistos*, then, or to be open
to *elenchos* or *elencheiē*, is to be in a position in which one is liable to be
mocked or criticized, and there is nothing inherent in the words which
would exclude their use in non-competitive contexts.[72]

All the terms discussed in this section are connected with 'how
things look' and with 'what people say'; these are the words which
indicate the grounds for *aidōs* and the consequences of ignoring it. The
range of their collective usage is wide, and there is no real reason to
believe that some refer exclusively to any one circumstance or that
some are more powerful than others. Nor is there any reason to
assume that words which span both the co-operative and the
competitive spheres necessarily lose their power in the former. Adkins
makes much of the 'effectiveness' of popular disapproval in the two
spheres,[73] and it is perhaps true that the characters of the Homeric
poems, or some of them at least, are more concerned about criticism of
their competitive than of their co-operative failures. This, however, is a
matter not of the power of the terms employed but of the realities of
the particular situation. A strong individual in any society is able to
ignore others' censure of his breaches of the 'quiet' moral virtues; but
he will have to take notice of any accusation of weakness or inferiority,
because even if the person making the accusation is an inferior, the
charge may encourage an enemy or a competitor to attempt a trial of
strength. It is not the power of words decrying competitive failure
which is more compelling than that of those criticizing failures in co-
operation, but the likely results of ignoring criticism in either sphere.
No word, no matter how 'powerful', constitutes effective restraint;[74]
the only effective restraint in every circumstance is physical force,[75]
and that is the ultimate sanction feared by the hero who is sensitive
about his reputation as a warrior and head of his community. Criticism
of competitive failure is taken seriously because a challenge from a
rival is a likely outcome if it is not so taken. As students of Greek

---

[72] In addition to the forms discussed, the verb *elenchō* occurs twice in the sense 'expose
(to ridicule)', 'put to shame'. At *Il.* 9. 522 Phoenix urges Achilles not to *elenchein* the
mission of the ambassadors; presumably they would be embarrassed to return without
success. At *Od.* 21. 424 Od., having drawn the bow, tells Telemachus that his beggar
guest does not shame (*elenchein*) him. The bond between host and guest creates a tie of
collective honour, a tie which is most often evident in passages in which the host's
honour is said to be committed by failure to protect his guest (see 1.3.5 below), but
apparently the failure of the guest could also implicate the host.
[73] (1960*a*), 39, 46 etc.; similarly Scott (1980), 16, 20, 23, 31.
[74] See Havelock (1978), 22.
[75] Cf. Pitt-Rivers (1965), 29.

society we ought to take note of this and give it its due weight, since
this is part of the reality of Homeric society, but equally, if we wish to
gain an accurate insight into the moral ideology of the poems, we must
recognize that the practical difference in attitude to competitive as
opposed to co-operative failure is not reflected in the usage of the
terms of disapprobation we have considered; rather, competitive and
co-operative failures are condemned in similar, often identical terms.

1.2. *AIDŌS* IN BATTLE

1.2.1. *General*

We have already seen that *nemesis, aischos, aischron, aeikēs,* and *elenchos*
together with their relatives can decry cowardice or shirking in battle;
cowardice is disgraceful, and, accordingly, a major function of *aidōs* is
to remind the soldiers in the field of that fact. Thus in some passages
the simply cry '*Aidōs!*' can be enough to raise the prospect of the
charge of cowardice and to spur the combatants on.[76] In two passages
the simple exhortation is expanded: '*Aidōs*, Argives, useless specimens,
though admirable in appearance.'[77] The warriors are criticized as
elenchea, a 'disgrace'; disapproval has been uttered and more is implied,
with *aidōs* being the response required to dispel the unfavourable
impression.

Used as an appeal, a reminder of the disgrace of defeat or
cowardice, *aidōs* appeals to each individual's concern for his own
honour, but it also works to promote the safety of the entire force
and to achieve the objectives of the army as a whole. In the very
thick of things it often acts to prevent flight, as in *Iliad* 16. 422, or at
5. 529–32,[78] where Agamemnon, alarmed at the lack of vigour in his
men, 'went through the ranks with many exhortations, crying,
"Friends [*philoi*], be men, and strengthen your heart, and show *aidōs*
for each other [ἀλλήλους αἰδεῖσθε] in the rush of battle; when men
show *aidōs* more are saved than slain; but when they flee, there is
neither fame [*kleos*] nor strength."' In this passage the safety and
glory of the individual and the group are inextricably linked, and
aidōs benefits on both levels. In the use of the word ἀλλήλους (each

[76] See *Il.* 13. 95, 15. 502, 16. 422.
[77] αἰδώς, Ἀργεῖοι, κάκ' ἐλέγχεα, εἶδος ἀγητοί, *Il.* 5. 787, 8. 228.
[78] Repeated at 15. 561–4 with a slight change of wording.

other), too, we see how the members of each contingent are the guarantors of their fellows' bravery.

The situation is similar at *Iliad* 15. 655-8; Hector has driven the Greeks back to their ships, and is wreaking havoc amongst the army. The poet goes on: 'The Argives did of necessity withdraw from the foremost ships, but they remained on the spot together by the tents, and did not scatter throughout the encampment; *aidōs* and fear [*deos*] held them back, for they kept reproaching each other.' It is, therefore, the certain knowledge that one's comrades will witness one's actions and one's reluctance to acquire a reputation for cowardice in their eyes that arouses *aidōs*. This does not mean that if an individual felt that he could, he would necessarily take the opportunity to act like a coward; it may, in any case, be unthinkable for him to do so; but the individual is not left to decide for himself whether he should flee, since the presence and exhortations of his fellows remind him of the disgrace of defeat and of the need for *aidōs* at that prospect.

The reproaches of one's fellows, moreover, remind one of the importance of popular opinion; by exhorting each other to stand their ground the warriors present themselves as the audience which would disapprove of any breach of *aidōs*. Thus, in the passage just quoted, *deos* must be taken closely with *aidōs*; the fear which prevents the host scattering cannot be fear of Hector, for that would be more likely to produce the opposite response, but must denote fear of reproach, fear of the consequences of not heeding *aidōs*.[79] That there is, then, a calculative aspect in such passages cannot be doubted.

The poet goes on to tell us (15. 659 ff.) that the chief of those who aroused the *aidōs* and *deos* of the warriors was Nestor, who, in lines 661-6, urges them as follows:

Friends [*philoi*], be men, and set in your *thumos aidōs* for other men [or 'people', *anthrōpoi*], and remember, each of you, your children and wives and property and parents, both those of you whose parents are alive and those whose parents are dead; I beseech you here on their behalf, though they are absent, to stand bravely, and not to turn to flight.

Nestor exhorts his comrades to feel *aidōs* for 'other people', but who these might be is not absolutely clear.[80] The other people could belong

---

[79] Cf. von Erffa (1937), 30.

[80] For von Erffa (1937: 6) the words ἄλλων ἀνθρώπων are *leer* and *nichtssagend*, and so must be interpolated; neither I nor Verdenius (1944-5: 53), however, can understand quite this degree of mystification.

to either of two categories; the corresponding phrase in the Greek is an objective genitive after the noun *aidōs*,[81] and so is analogous to an accusative after the verb *aideomai*. The verb can take two kinds of accusative in Homer, referring either to a generalized group of other people who constitute the audience of one's actions, or to the direct recipient of one's actions. Verdenius[82] suggests that the other people here belong to the former class, and refer to the unspecified witnesses of the warriors' actions, and this might well be right, but equally Nestor does go on to mention specific people for whom the soldiers should have regard, and this further point seems to be prompted by the phrase 'other men' in 662; so perhaps the people named in 663–4 are included under the other people of 662, and the warriors are being urged to show *aidōs* directly for them.[83] But for the overall interpretation of the passage these distinctions do not matter, for the import of Nestor's speech is clear: *aidōs* involves living up to standards of bravery and manhood and having regard for other people. Whether or not the warriors are being asked to show *aidōs* towards their dependants, consideration of their dependants is certainly being urged, and that consideration is not simply requested with regard to the material consequences of defeat for these people, as the reference to those whose parents are dead shows; the plea that the warriors should think of their parents, even though dead, shows that Nestor regards their dependants as sharing in their honour, and so liable to be affected by any disgrace the warrior may suffer. Both the appeal to *aidōs* and the appeal to the memory of children, wives, property, and parents are concerned with the honour and reputation of those addressed. Even in the case of the reference to living dependants, the implication that the warrior has a duty to protect is not separable from the idea that his honour is at stake, for to fail in one's obligations is itself discreditable and diminishes one's reputation for strength.

Behind this passage there clearly lies the idea of a community of honour.[84] Other passages, too, reinforce the idea that others have an interest in the honour of the individual; family honour, for example, is

[81] The only other instance of the noun with an objective genitive occurs at *Od.* 14. 505, where the person designated by the genitive is the direct recipient of the feeling of *aidōs*, of the 'respect' of the agent.

[82] (1944–5), 53.

[83] So Redfield (1975), 120–1.

[84] On the community of honour in modern Mediterranean societies, see the remarks of various authors in Peristiany (1965), 35, 42, 89, 119, 179, 245, 249–50. Dover (1974: 237–8) shows that the notion is widespread and natural, applicable to modern Western society and not confined to 'shame-cultures'.

in the keeping of the warrior, hence the injunction of Glaucus' father, μηδὲ γένος πατέρων αἰσχυνέμεν ('not to disgrace the race of our fathers', *Iliad* 6. 209).[85] The converse, that a father rejoices in the fame of his son, is also found.[86] In *Iliad* 6 Helen expresses the wish that she might be the wife of a better man, one who took notice of the *nemesis* and *aischea* of men (350–1). The context is that of Paris' slacking in battle, and Helen clearly feels that her husband's disgrace reflects upon her. Hector, too, is perturbed by others' criticism of his brother.[87] Other characters, however, are less concerned with the honour of their relatives than with their safety, and the attitude of Helen towards Paris in *Iliad* 6 is in sharp contrast to that of Andromache towards Hector in the same book.[88] Similarly, Hecabe would rather her son avoided Achilles entirely than bow to the demands of honour and face him (22. 82–9).[89] At 22. 482–507 it is the complete dependence of the hero's wife and family on their protector, and his duty to protect, that are stressed, rather than the implication of the dependants in the hero's honour; but this idea is still relevant, in that the pitiful fate which Andromache foresees for herself and her son presumably diminishes their status, and so must have implications for Hector's own honour; it is, of course, too late for Hector to do anything about it, but the passage does perhaps suggest the kind of considerations which Nestor's appeal on behalf of the heroes' dependants would have raised in their minds.

1.2.2. *Defeat, Intentions, and Results*

We saw in section 1.1 above that defeat in battle and cowardice were consistently described in terms which condemn them as unseemly and subject to popular disapproval; in each of the three passages in which the word occurs *aischron* refers to the disgrace of failure in the martial context.[90] The implication in those passages is that the empty-handed return of the warriors will be proof of their failure, and it would seem that such failure is disgraceful regardless of any circumstance which may be adduced in mitigation. This attitude also prevails in *Iliad* 17

[85] Cf. *Od.* 24. 508.
[86] *Il.* 6. 446, 479, 8. 285; cf. Redfield (1975), 33.
[87] *Il.* 6. 523–5.
[88] See esp. 6. 431–2; cf. Farron (1979), 22.
[89] See Farron (1979), 26.
[90] *Il.* 2. 119–22, 298, and (with comparative *aischion*) 21. 437–8; see 1.1.3 above.

(336–7), where Aeneas tells his fellow Trojans, 'This is *aidōs* to go back to Ilion overcome by the battle-loving Achaeans because of our cowardice.'[91] Part of Aeneas' strategy in attempting to arouse the *aidōs* of his comrades is his suggestion that to return to the city at this point will be taken as a sign of cowardice. No doubt many Trojans fought well enough, but this is not envisaged as an adequate excuse.

In Book 8 of the *Iliad* (139–44) Nestor advises Diomedes that since Zeus is manifestly favouring Hector, a prudent withdrawal would be the best policy. Diomedes recognizes the validity of the old man's advice (146), yet cannot bring himself to act upon it (147–50): 'But this thought comes as a sore vexation to my heart and *thumos*; for one day Hector will say as he speaks among the Trojans: "Diomedes was put to flight by me and ran to his ships." That will be his boast, and on that day may the broad earth gape for me.' Nestor answers this anxiety with the claim that no one would believe Hector were he to impugn Diomedes' honour in such a way (152–6). As Adkins points out,[92] Diomedes does not simply rely upon his own opinion of himself, nor does Nestor advise him to do so.

On the other hand, Nestor, the older and wiser of the two, clearly does believe that Diomedes' *aidōs* (for that is surely what his anxiety is) is misplaced, and so Diomedes may be rather more sensitive to unjustified taunts than is thought normal. It is also important to remember that, in spite of the relationship of *aidōs* to the opinion of others, it is not reducible to a cool calculation of consequences; Diomedes' anxiety at future embarrassment is not a wholly rational appraisal of a likely outcome, but an emotional response; it can therefore be criticized as appropriate to the facts or otherwise,[93] but

---

[91] αἰδὼς μὲν νῦν ἥδε γ' ...: von Erffa (1937: 6) sees *aidōs* as a virtual synonym of *aischron* here, and takes the words as meaning, 'This is a disgrace ...'. This is a valid translation (cf. Cheyns (1967), 23), but von Erffa's assumption of a separate meaning is unwarranted; Verdenius (1944–5: 55) points this out, and suggests that the passage, like the others we have been discussing, is an exhortation to *aidōs*, the sense being, 'This is occasion for *aidōs*' or 'let *aidōs* be present'. The usage does, however, illustrate the frequent shift from designation of subjective reaction to that of objective situation, the object of the reaction, in the use of these terms.

[92] (1960*a*), 48–9 = (1970), 31–2. Dover (1983: 40) criticizes Adkins here, but his criticism is of his expression ('Nestor cannot say, "Don't worry, it isn't true"'), rather than of his meaning, which is that D. does not feel himself able to ignore the taunts of his enemy.

[93] Because of the element of evaluation in emotion, and the possibility of the beliefs which are part of the emotion being misplaced or false, or because emotions are a matter of degree, and it makes sense to consider some excessive; see Warnock (1957), 51–8; Ewing (1957), 63–74 (in reply to Warnock); Thalberg (1964), 53–4; Pitcher (1965), 339–40; de Sousa (1987), ch. 7.

need not be dispelled by a rational appreciation of the facts of the situation. Nor need Diomedes' reaction represent an appraisal of the situation with which every member of his society would agree. Diomedes is also a young warrior, and an intense fear of public criticism is a regular feature of the young person in Homer, often persisting even when deprecated or inappropriate.[94] So it would be unwise to build any very sweeping generalizations on this passage. Nevertheless, we are shown here a Homeric hero deeply concerned for what other people, even his enemies, say, and it is certainly true that he is not urged by Nestor to content himself with his own knowledge of his worth; thus the power of what people say is clearly very considerable. This cannot, however, mean, as Adkins claims,[95] that the hero's self 'only has the value which other people put upon it'; Diomedes' concern for what others might say presupposes a high personal image of the self; he has an idea of his own worth which he fervently hopes others will share, and the prospect of the contrary causes him great anxiety. The fact that popular opinion can be of the utmost importance to a Homeric warrior and that his self-image often requires the validation of others does not mean that the hero has *no* idea of his own worth.

Diomedes' reaction is interesting in other ways, too; it is significant, for example, that a hero can be concerned about the opinions of his enemies as well as of his peers—the 'significant other' need enjoy no special status in one's own eyes, but may simply serve as a catalyst for the realization that one's conduct may be construed in a discreditable light.[96] One need not agree with this construction, but still a personal ideal (Diomedes' much cherished image of himself as one who never runs away) is involved. In his wish that the ground would open up (and swallow him), too, Diomedes exhibits a classic shame reaction, the desire to hide oneself from view.[97] Taken as a whole, then, his response presupposes an acute concern for ideal self-image and great self-consciousness, but both the fear of Hector's taunts and the wish for concealment demonstrate that this is a self which is highly vulnerable

[94] Cf. Telemachus in *Od.* 3. 24 (he persists in his *aidōs* even after Athena/Mentor has informed him that such a feeling would be inappropriate) and Nausicaa at *Od.* 6. 275-88 (she is worried lest others criticize her for accompanying Od. to town, a sensitivity which emerges as inappropriate when her father is critical of her failure to bring her guest to the palace herself at 7. 299-301); see Dickie (1978), 94-5, and on this feature of the youthful Nausicaa, see Besslich (1981), 107.

[95] (1960*a*), 49; cf. (1970), 44.

[96] Cf. Verdenius (1944-5), 53.

[97] See Introd. 0.3 above.

to the judgements of others. These aspects of his response are
paralleled in *Iliad* 4: at line 171 Agamemnon tells Menelaus that he,
Agamemnon, would be *elenchistos*, were he to return to Argos without
his brother. At 175 we find the familiar distaste for leaving an
enterprise unfinished, and at 176-81 Agamemnon imagines the taunts
of 'one of the Trojans' as he jumps on Menelaus' grave. At this
prospect he reacts as did Diomedes: 'then may the broad earth gape
for me'.[98] The two brothers are thus closely bound in honour, and the
death of Menelaus would be a disgrace for Agamemnon, not simply
because others would charge him with failing to protect his brother, or
because his death would give their enemies a chance to dishonour
them both, but also because it would negate the whole purpose of his
mission, which was to recover Menelaus' wife and restore his honour.

Again, it appears that the judgement to be feared, whether that of
one's own side or that of one's enemies, is based on results rather than
intentions, and Adkins is therefore right to stress the importance of
results in Homeric society, particularly in the warrior society of the
Iliad, and particularly in the context of the individual's *aidōs* for the
opinions of others. There are a number of reasons for this; above all,
one's enemies are hardly likely to consider anything other than results,
since any action upon which they can place a discreditable interpretation is good for their morale and bad for one's own; the position,
however, with regard to the judgements of one's friends is not quite as
straightforward, and requires rather more consideration.

There does, in fact, exist a number of passages in which characters
do attempt to persuade others to consider intentions (or circumstances) rather than results; but only those which refer to success or
failure in battle need concern us here. Perhaps the most striking of
these is *Iliad* 14. 80-1, where Agamemnon offers the opinion that 'it is
no cause for *nemesis* to flee from danger, not even by night. Better to
run and escape danger than be caught.' This is a clear reversal of the
view found in those passages we have discussed so far (that retreat is
discreditable no matter what the circumstances), and it should be
noted that Agamemnon is urging a consideration of circumstances
(greater advantage) rather than of results. But his attempt to convince
his audience has little chance of success, as indeed one might expect
from the far greater number of passages in which retreat is said to be
disgraceful *simpliciter*.[99] Immediately Agamemnon has spoken the lines

---

[98] Cf. also *Il.* 17. 415-9.
[99] See von Erffa (1937), 33; Scott (1980), 26.

quoted, Odysseus reacts with great vehemence (83 ff.), and expresses the opinion that he is unworthy of his kingship,[100] better suited instead to command of 'some *aeikelios* army' (84).[101]

Other passages are similar; a character claims that there is no cause for criticism in the particular situation, and so wishes to be judged other than on results, but is proved wrong by events. At *Iliad* 13. 222 Idomeneus asserts that none of the Achaeans is responsible for the current reversals, which must be the will of Zeus (226), but, as Poseidon points out (232-4), and as Idomeneus himself is, in any case, well aware (228-30), this does not excuse wilful withdrawal from battle.[102] The tone of *Iliad* 17. 91-105 is somewhat different. There, as we have already seen,[103] Menelaus debates whether he should obey *aidōs* by attempting to defend Patroclus' body or risk the *nemesis* of his fellows by saving himself. At 98-100, however, he seems to change his mind, and expresses the view that it would be unjustified of his comrades to feel *nemesis* against him, since Hector is obviously fighting with the aid of the gods. None the less, he does not follow the implications of this view, and withdraw entirely; another thought occurs to him, and he decides to pursue a different method of rescuing the body, with the help of Ajax (102-5). In spite of his expressed belief, then, that no one could find fault with one who fled in the face of divine intervention, he decides not to do so, and follows, with a slight modification, the course dictated by *aidōs*. So apparently Menelaus does not have complete confidence in his fellows' capacity to take the same reasonable view of the circumstances as he takes himself.

On the other hand, the passages just cited, in which the reference to circumstances and intentions is proved misguided or not acted upon, do at least indicate that there could be a degree of doubt or of difference of opinion as to whether intentions *were* relevant, and this suggests that some did not feel themselves absolutely constrained by such maxims as 'it is disgraceful to retreat'.[104] In general, however, it

---

[100] Cf. Thornton (1984), 127. On Ag.'s inadequacy (the best translation of the term *kakotēs* as applied to him at 13. 96), see Taplin (1990).

[101] Cheyns (1967: 31) ignores the context and takes Ag.'s words as a statement of orthodoxy. Hector incurs *elencheiē* by refusing to retreat (n. 114 below), but retreat only emerges as the honourable course in retrospect, as a result of Hector's failure.

[102] See Adkins (1960a), 14; (1971), 8.

[103] See 1.1.2 above, on *nemesis*.

[104] See Claus (1974), 16, 20; Gaskin (1990: 8-9) similarly notes, *re* Menelaus' conduct in *Il.* 17, that his reflectiveness gives the lie to the position of Snell and Voigt that Homeric man simply confirms his conduct to the external norms which belong with his social role (cf. n. 290 below). It is not, however, quite true to say that Men. 'withstands

does seem that for most the power of popular opinion, which could never be counted on to share, or even to be aware of, one's own interpretation of one's actions, was too strong to ignore. The major exception to this, the main area in which popular opinion does appear to have been willing to consider circumstances and intentions, is that of death in battle, which may be *aeikēs* to the eye, and which is indisputably a failure, but which may, nevertheless, be glorious, depending on circumstances (on, for example, the valour shown by the victim or the status of his killer).[105]

In the context of the power of popular opinion and the relative weakness of the individual's ability to content himself with his own interpretation of his actions, one figure, Paris, seems rather out of step with the others, and this is particularly true in the sixth book of the *Iliad*, where his character emerges in sharp contrast to that of his brother Hector. On three occasions in the poem Hector addresses Paris αἰσχροῖς ἐπέεσσι ('with ugly words'), abusing him for his slackness in battle.[106] The second of these episodes begins at 6. 325, where Hector, having hastened to Paris' house, commences his rebuke; he assumes that Paris has kept himself away from the field out of anger (326), and points out that such anger is inappropriate when people are dying on his behalf; Paris himself would be angry with another whom he saw slacking (329–30); *a fortiori* he, the cause of the conflict, should not hang back.[107] This, like other passages we have discussed, is clearly intended to arouse *aidōs* by the implication of inappropriate behaviour.

the allure' of the norm 'only cowards retreat'; he does not entirely withstand it, but rather adapts to it reflectively.

[105] See n. 50. Schofield (1986: 15–16), points out that, away from the immediate context of the battlefield, a good reputation in the eyes of one's peers is compatible with a certain amount of failure (e.g. Nestor's failure to persuade in *Il.* 1 does not diminish his excellence as a counsellor); clearly, then, the heroes of the *Il.* do not consider only the ultimate success or failure of an enterprise in absolutely every case, therefore a blanket description of their society as a 'results culture' (Adkins's term) is misleading; yet Adkins's observations are based on real features of the society of the poem, and so should be accommodated, even if we think his conclusions too sweeping.

[106] *Il.* 3. 38 ff., 6. 325 ff., 13. 768 ff. H.'s words are only really insulting, however, in the first of these passages.

[107] The phrase σὺ δ' ἂν μαχέσαιο καὶ ἄλλῳ ('you would fight, fall out with another') seems to be a variant of, e.g., καὶ δ' ἄλλῳ νεμεσᾶτον, ὅτις τοιαῦτά γε ῥέζοι (23. 494, 'you two would feel *nemesis* towards anyone else who did these things'). Such expressions suggest that the standard being breached is universal, that the speaker is justified in his complaint, and that his criticism is in accordance with the values of its recipient; see Hohendahl-Zoetelief (1980), 11–13, and cf. *Od.* 6. 286, 15. 69, where the 1st pers. of the verb is used, implying the subject's agreement with the standards of society.

In his reply, however, Paris shows no *aidōs* whatever, and while he does say that he has been thinking of returning to battle (337-9), he reflects merely that to do so 'seemed better', and adds, philosophically, that victory attends now one man, now the other. He acknowledges the validity of what Hector has said (333), but gives no indication that he is moved either by Hector's reference to those to whom he bears a responsibility, or by the threat of disapproval, of *nemesis* at his lack of *aidōs*, that is implicit in 'you would fight with another, if you saw him slacking'.

Paris, indeed, does not seem to be concerned that his reputation might be diminished by his absence from the field of battle, nor does he seem particularly upset at his brother's reproach. This suggests that his susceptibility to *aidōs* is low, and the impression is confirmed by the words of Helen, who continues the attack against Paris when Hector disdains to address him; at 350-1 she wishes that she had been the wife of a better man, one who took heed of others' *nemesis* and *aischea*. Paris, then, is insensitive to others' disapproval, and therefore not susceptible to *aidōs*, even when his reputation as a warrior is at stake.[108] This does not mean, however, that his heterodoxy is legitimate; rather it characterizes him as a poor specimen in terms of the martial values of the other combatants; yet his deviation from the norm does give us a glimpse of a plurality of views on the complex of values centred on honour, a plurality which must surely have been greater in the real world for which the poem, an imaginative and idealizing artistic production, was composed.

Later in Book 6 Paris and Hector meet again, and here the latter is more reflective on the subject of his brother's shirking, addressing him as follows (521-5): 'Look; no man, if he were being reasonable [*enaisimos*], would dishonour your work in battle, since you are brave; but you hold back willingly and do not wish to fight. My heart is pained in my *thumos*, when I hear shameful things [*aischea*] about you from the Trojans, who are undergoing a lot of trouble for your sake.' Hector is no longer trying to incite Paris to action by imputing lack of martial zeal, and concedes him his bravery, claiming that anyone who was *enaisimos* would share his appreciation of it. Hector is therefore modifying his earlier criticism, yet explaining why he felt it necessary to make it. The implicit assumptions in his speech are illuminating. First, the *enaisimos*: reasonable people, Hector implies, do not cast aspersions on the honour of those who are essentially brave; this

[108] Cf. Redfield (1975), 114.

suggests both that one's reputation for valour is not entirely vulnerable to the attacks and reproaches of others, and that there are some people who are prepared to judge one's bravery in battle by taking more than one's immediate conduct into account. The *enaisimos* in this passage is in sharp contrast to the τις κακώτερος ('some baser person') of others,[109] who judges on results alone and who takes delight in criticizing the efforts of his betters, even when their qualities are well known. Thus Paris is essentially brave; but he still holds back, and so criticism is justified; only someone who was unreasonable would call him a coward, yet (it is implied) he can reasonably be criticized, because he slacks of his own accord (*hekōn*). Paris therefore deserves criticism not on the grounds that his behaviour looks like cowardice, but because he is, of his own accord, failing to pull his weight, and this criticism is the more justified, Hector further implies, by virtue of the fact that Paris is the cause of the Trojans' troubles. According to Hector, then, justified criticism of Paris would be based not on results, on the simple fact that he shirks battle, but on appreciation of the discrepancy between his ability and his motivation, and on the legitimate expectation that he should play a full part in the fighting.

Hector thus offers a reflective analysis of Paris' case that is very different from the simple judgement based on results; indeed, the passage suggests some reasons as to how and why intentions may be less important than results in the evaluation of martial prowess. Neutrals and those well-disposed to the subject may be prepared to give him the benefit of the doubt—for them, one who appears to be acting like a coward may still be an essentially brave man; but war is a serious, competitive business, and those involved will not often be prepared either to accept excuses when a loss has been incurred, or to spare one whose conduct has led to defeat and disgrace, however brave he has been in the past. In the same way the individual hero will know quite well that those who might be expected to support him, should he seek to excuse a retreat or some other failure, will be few, and accordingly his own estimation of his bravery and value will not be sufficient to allay his fears regarding the disapproval of the majority.

The hero, it is important to note, is not pleading his case before some impartial body: judgements are made in the society of the *Iliad* on the personal level, and the judges and the judged have a high degree of emotional involvement in the situation; those fearing criticism are not submitting themselves to a system honed by

[109] *Il.* 22. 106; *Od.* 6. 275, 21. 324.

philosophy or jurisprudence, but to the far from impartial judgements of others like themselves. Both the sensitivity to criticism and the criticism itself are expressed in emotional terms, and while the emotional responses may have rational and evaluative aspects, they are not directly equivalent to rational analysis. The fact that results may be more relevant than intentions in such contexts is not the product of some inability of the participants to consider intentions, but a consequence of the personal and emotional character of the situation. In modern contexts, too, analogous emotions are quite capable of producing identical results. There is a type of shame which is very closely concerned with the judgement of others rather than with one's own estimate of oneself, and we are all well aware that other people make judgements about us based solely on appearances; it is not uncommon for us to be concerned at their judgements, even if we know them to be false. One who, as a result, say, of some problem of balance, is forced to walk with a pronounced stagger, may be acutely concerned lest other people think him inebriated, in spite of his own awareness that his gait is the result of circumstances entirely beyond his control. Equally, someone who has her foot trodden on in a crowd will very likely experience an instinctive feeling of resentment (feel *nemesis* at his breach of *aidōs*), even though she does not really believe that the offender has stepped on her foot on purpose.[110] Nor is inability to be content with one's own knowledge of the facts regarding one's merits and worth peculiar to the reaction of shame; guilt can also persist in those who know they have 'done nothing wrong'; we are inclined to regard such cases as irrational, but they do occur.[111] If Homeric society can be a 'results culture', then so, given the same extra-legal, extra-philosophical contexts, can our own.

1.2.3. *The* Aidōs *of Hector*

In the passages which introduced the last section we saw how sensitivity to *aidōs* could result in an individual's modifying his conduct out of concern for criticisms whose validity he did not accept and which were made by people who enjoyed no special claim to consideration in his eyes. Thus the judgement of others which gives rise to *aidōs* in these

---

[110] Cf. Dover (1974), 238.
[111] For an exposition of the position that the experience of guilt in one who is not in the accepted sense culpable is still a genuine case of guilt, see Morris (1987).

cases need not be personally endorsed, and so in some cases *aidōs* depends more on a sensitivity to criticism *per se* than on subjective evaluation of the character of one's own conduct. This is not always the case, however, and we have already seen that the remarks of Hector to Paris invoke a standard to which Paris himself is supposed to subscribe, and that Hector can take considerable trouble to justify his criticism on the basis of norms which he must regard as comprehensible to his addressee. The contrast between Paris and Hector, in fact, is one of the most prominent features of the sixth book of the *Iliad*, and is particularly evident in the susceptibility of the two to *aidōs*. Since Hector is the more admirable of the two, there is thus a strong presumption that we are to see his attitude to *aidōs* as more proper than that of his brother.

In her speech at 6. 407–39 Andromache begs Hector to pity herself and her son, and to carry out the future defence of Troy from within the fortifications. He replies as follows (441–6):

Truly, all these considerations weigh with me, lady; but I feel terrible *aidōs* before the Trojans and their wives of the trailing robes,[112] if I sneak away from the war like a coward [*kakos*]. Nor does my *thumos* bid me, since I have learned to be brave [noble, *esthlos*] and always to fight among the first of the Trojans, winning great fame [*kleos*] for my father and myself.

It is *aidōs*, then, which drives Hector to fight in open battle, in spite of the pity he feels for his wife and child. It is clearly unbearable for him that others should consider him to be acting like a coward. But this is not his only reason for rejecting Andromache's appeal; he knows that there is something else which impels him to risk his life, something within himself not dependent on his fear of what the Trojans might say, and it is to this factor that he refers when he indicates that his *thumos* produces the same result as his *aidōs*. Hector effectively tells us that it is his own wish to face the Greek heroes in battle, and, indeed, that it is unthinkable for him to do otherwise. Neither the commands of his *thumos* nor his 'education' in meeting the standards required of an *esthlos* should be sharply divorced from the *aidōs* which he has just expressed. His *aidōs* is his first expression of his inability to act in a cowardly way, and it is explicitly referred to 'other people'; but the demands of his *thumos*, a product of his 'education', have the same effect, and so Hector's *aidōs* is clearly not the reaction of a person who is solely concerned with the unpleasant consequence of popular

---

[112] ἀλλὰ μάλ' αἰνῶς | αἰδέομαι Τρῶας καὶ Τρῳάδας ἑλκεσιπέπλους.

disapproval. His *aidōs* does not inhibit conduct which he would contemplate, if he were convinced that he could get away with it, but rather reinforces and expresses his rejection of certain behaviour as unthinkable. Hector alludes to an education in the values and expectations of his society, and the sensitivity to custom thus produced will be *aidōs*, a quality which will later figure prominently in Greek theories of education and character development. Hector's education will have taught him how society expects him to behave, and so contributes to the formation of his social role; in as much as his *thumos* and his *aidōs* combine in leading him to pursue this role, he has obviously made the values under which he acts his own, made the expectations of society equivalent to his own expectations of himself. The reference of *aidōs* to other people, therefore, does not necessarily entail simple conformity to others' standards,[113] and, in his attitude to his own behaviour as well as to that of his brother, Hector considers more than just 'how things look' to other people.

Hector is faced with a similar situation in Book 22, when it is his parents who attempt to dissuade him from going into battle. Again he is inexorable (91), and again he sees his choice to remain in the field in terms of *aidōs*. This time, however, his *aidōs* is not directed at the implication of cowardice, but at the charge that he has failed in his duty to protect Troy and its people. He cannot return to the city, he claims, because Polydamas will be the first to set up *elencheiē* (disgrace) for him (100). Polydamas had urged him to lead the host back to the city when Achilles had made his initial return to the fray, and Hector had disregarded his advice;[114] the result was disaster, and now Hector is afraid to return within the walls (104-7): 'But now that I have

[113] My interpretation of this passage agrees with that of Dickie (1978: 94) who compares *Il.* 11. 404-10, where Odysseus, too, finds it unthinkable to behave like a *kakos*. Dickie also points out that the very prominence of popular disapproval as a sanction in Homer presupposes that those who disapprove do so out of their personal ideas of right and wrong; therefore the characters of the poems must possess these standards and not simply react to the external stimulus of others' disapproval. One should, however, be aware that criticism of another's failings is not always disinterested; it may, particularly in a competitive context, be more often a result of a rival's or enemy's exploitation of one's weak spot than genuine outrage at a breach of society's standards; but this cannot always be the case, and to that extent Dickie is right. It is also worth noting in this context that characters sometimes state outright that the values by which they are liable to be criticized correspond with their own ('I too would feel *nemesis* if anyone else were to do such things', *Od.* 6. 286, 15. 69, see n. 107 above).

[114] It is interesting that *elencheiē* may be the result of refusing to retreat, since other passages stress the idea that retreat itself is disgraceful. No doubt, however, H. could have been convinced that retreat afforded the means to avoid dishonour only if it could have been shown that his failure was inevitable.

destroyed the host by my own recklessness [*atasthaliai*], I feel *aidōs* before the Trojans and their wives of the trailing robes, lest some baser person than I should say, "Hector trusted in his might and destroyed the host."' There are two important points here. First, Hector regards it as normal that he should be condemned for failing in his duty to others; that disgrace should be the punishment for such failure shows that the requirement to protect is regarded as a demand of personal honour. Secondly, Hector is clearly aware that he has done something reprehensible. This does not mean that his *aidōs* is retrospective, as von Erffa points out;[115] explicitly, it is still the reproach of others that he fears, and his apprehension is still prospective. Nevertheless, in giving the reason for his *aidōs* in line 104 he clearly expresses his awareness of his own culpability, and awareness of one's misdeed is a prerequisite of conscience, a word which, in its Latin and Greek forms, *conscientia* and *suneidēsis*, refers explicitly to the idea of 'awareness'. Hector knows he is culpable, and he knows this because he is familiar with the standards by which others will judge him; although he articulates his 'conscience' of his past mistake in terms of prospective apprehension, the reproach of the Trojans is still hypothetical; his awareness of his misdeed is thus subjective, and it troubles him in the present; he does not have to await the actual disapproval of the Trojans. Nor is he simply upset or resentful at the prospect of censure, an unpleasant consquence of his mistake, for he is aware that any censure that may be forthcoming is justified; by his own standards, he knows he has failed, and he applies the pejorative word, *atasthaliai*, to his own conduct.[116] The explicit reference to 'other people' is perhaps not what we should associate with a 'pure' case of retrospective conscience, but it would be wrong to deny that the germ of that idea is present in this passage; Hector's awareness of his misdeed coexists with his prospective fear of disapproval.[117]

Hector's *aidōs* thus reveals something of the complexity of the concept in Homer; it is Hector above all others whose *aidōs* manifests this complexity, and it is not without reason that he has been called a hero of *aidōs*.[118] The depth of the emotion in these two passages

[115] (1937), 8.

[116] *Atasthaliē* (the sing. of which the word in the text is the pl.) does not connote simple mistake, but rather 'boldness' or 'excess'; we shall meet the term again in the *Odyssey*, coupled with *hubris* and used of the suitors; on its meaning, see Greene (1944), 18–23.

[117] See also Verdenius (1944–5), 59, on this passage.

[118] See Redfield (1975), 119.

should warn us against generalizing too readily from others; in particular, in neither of these passages is Hector's *aidōs* like the simple fear of (unjustified) abuse manifested by Diomedes in *Iliad* 8. We have also seen that Hector can offer, in conversation with his brother, a more reflective model for the evaluation of a warrior's worth than emerges from those judgements which are uttered in the heat of battle.

1.2.4. *Personal Honour and Co-operation in Battle*

We saw in the last passage how it seemed to be expected of Hector that he should not endanger his men; failure to meet this requirement could bring *elencheïe*, which suggests that the standard might be enforced and upheld in the individual by *aidōs*. In both the passages quoted from *Iliad* 6, moreover, in which Paris was criticized by Hector, reference was made to the former's responsibility to those who were fighting on his behalf (6. 327-30, 525). We also noticed how hortatory appeals to *aidōs* in the thick of battle were intended to have the effect of ensuring discipline in the host and promoting the security of all; to the passages already cited can be added *Iliad* 15. 502-3: 'Aidōs, Argives; now is the time either to perish or to be saved and defend the ships from danger.' In such appeals, then, co-operation among the troops is achieved through the appeal to the individual's concern for his own honour, while in the other passages it seems that the charge of failing one's comrades-in-arms was seen as one which might bring disgrace on the subject and arouse his *aidōs*.

The idea of personal honour thus has its part to play in co-operation as well as in competition, and this is true in two ways: appeals to individual concern for competitive failure may in fact promote co-operation, or co-operation itself may be a requirement of personal honour; co-operation on the field of battle may be promoted by *aidōs* at competitive failure or by *aidōs* at co-operative failure.[119] In dealing with the first of these possibilities we shall be concerned mostly with the responsibility of the heroes to their fallen comrades, for it is in this context that *nemesis* in particular has a considerable role to play.

[119] I should point out that a comprehensive study of co-operation in Homer would be much more extensive than the following few remarks on the role of personal honour in promoting co-operation on the field of battle; more will be said below in 1.3, and, for fuller accounts of the individual's responsibility to his fellows in the *Il.*, see Kakridis (1963), chs. 1-3, and Roisman (1984), *passim*, esp. 6, 9-11, 17-32.

Glaucus' words after the death of Sarpedon (his fellow Lycian) are both typical and instructive. The first point in his speech (*Iliad* 16. 538–40) refers directly to Hector's responsibility to his allies: 'Hector, now you have completely forgotten your allies, who for your sake are perishing far from their own people and their fatherland, and you have no desire to protect them.' In the next line Glaucus informs Hector and the Trojans of Sarpedon's fate; clearly he feels that Hector should have taken steps to prevent it. Now that Sarpedon has fallen, however, Glaucus comes to the more pressing question of the rescue of his body, addressing the general company of Trojans and their allies (544–6): 'Friends, stand by me, and feel *nemesis* in your hearts [νεμεσσήθητε δὲ θυμῷ], lest his arms are taken and the Myrmidons disfigure his corpse. . . .' The Trojans and their allies, Glaucus' *philoi*, are asked to feel *nemesis* lest Sarpedon be stripped of his arms and his body suffer disfigurement. The Lycian leader would be a considerable prize for Patroclus and the Myrmidons, his armour concrete proof of their success. It is therefore a matter of honour, both collective and personal, that his comrades should take steps to retrieve his body and avoid disgrace. The application of the verb *nemesaō* in this passage is worthy of comment: if *nemesis* is always anger in which one feels oneself justified, then there must be an object of the Trojans' *nemesis* here; but obviously the correlation between *nemesis* and *another*'s breach of *aidōs* is not relevant, for in a society in which warfare is a way of life it is scarcely credible that one should be expected to refrain from killing one's opponent out of *aidōs*, or that it was considered occasion for resentment when an enemy kills a friend. Glaucus surely cannot be asking the Trojans to feel *nemesis* towards Patroclus for killing Sarpedon.

The passive form of the verb, νεμεσσήθητε, with middle (quasi-reflexive) sense, is the clue; the *nemesis* of Sarpedon's fellow soldiers is directed not at Patroclus but at themselves; the breach of *aidōs* is their own, or would be. There are two sides to the reaction of shame at the prospect of disgrace: the inhibitory, when the agent suppresses the action which might lead to ignominy; and the angry, resentful aspect, which comes into play when the reprehensible action is abandoned and positive steps are taken to wipe out any suggestion of an insult; this emotion can be covered by *aidōs* (in hortatory appeals especially), but here it is expressed by *nemesis*.[120] That this *nemesis* is self-directed,

---

[120] The verbs *nemesaomai/nemesaō/nemesizomai* and *aideomai* can thus refer to the same type of reaction, namely the rejection and avoidance of discreditable conduct; see

moreover, is a clear sign that Homeric man can possess standards of his own.

In *Iliad* 17 the question of duty to one's fallen comrades arises for both sides, the Greeks striving to rescue the body of Patroclus and the Trojan side still involved in recriminations regarding the body of Sarpedon. We have already noted how Menelaus, at 17. 91-105, debates whether he should attempt to rescue Patroclus' body, giving in to *aidōs*, or consult his own safety, thus risking the *nemesis* of his fellows. The question of Menelaus' obligation to Patroclus arises in line 92, where he mentions that Patroclus has died fighting for his (Menelaus') *timē*; Patroclus has done something for Menelaus, who now finds it difficult to escape doing something for Patroclus. Later in the same episode, after calling on the leaders of the Argives as his *philoi* (248), he appeals to their *nemesis*, much as did Glaucus in the previous book: 'Let someone go of his own accord, and let him feel *nemesis* in his heart [νεμεσίζεσθω δ' ἐνὶ θυμῷ] that Patroclus should become sport for Trojan dogs' (254-5). At line 95 Menelaus saw his responsibility to Patroclus as prompted by *aidōs*, now it is *nemesis* which he imagines will motivate the others to intervene. The force of *nemesis* here seems to lie in a vivid imagining of the discreditable event; the hero is urged to regard the disgrace of losing a comrade's body as a real and present possibility, and *nemesis* will then occur as a response to the failure, the breach of *aidōs* thus envisaged. It will be seen that the heroes' concern for their own, personal honour is invoked to encourage an attitude of responsibility towards other members of their contingent; the honour of each, in fact, is closely bound up with that of

von Erffa (1937), 33. Verdenius agrees with the general interpretation of this usage, but points out that *aidōs* differs from *nemesis* in the manner of its operation (1944-5: 49-50, esp. 49 n. 2). At *Od.* 4. 158-9, however, the present νεμεσσᾶται comes very close to αἰδεῖται in sense (von Erffa, 54; contrast Verdenius, 49 n. 2): νεμεσσᾶται is reflexive once more, and refers to Telemachus' evaluation of a breach of *aidōs* on his own part—'he thinks it wrong, unseemly [West, in Heubeck, West, and Hainsworth (1988), ad loc.] to manifest uninvited speech.' This comes to very much the same thing as would αἰδεῖται ἐπεσβολίας ἀναφαίνειν. Perhaps the difference in sense of the two verbs can be grasped theoretically, but there is very little practical difference in this particular passage. At *Od.* 2. 64 νεμεσσήθητε is probably best taken as reflexive, and so a reproach from Telemachus to the Ithacesians (Verdenius (1944-5), 50; Redfield (1975), 116), although an injunction to them to feel *nemesis* towards the suitors would be equally possible (so West, ad loc.); it seems less likely that the words are addressed to the suitors as an appeal to their *nemesis* with regard to their own conduct (the last two interpretations are also considered by Long (1970: 131 n. 36)). At *Od.* 1. 263 νεμεσίζετο θεούς clearly means 'he feared the anger of the gods', and thus, as a prospective fear of disapproval, the verb comes close to *aideisthai* in this context; αἰδεῖσθαι θεούς, however, is only found in contexts of supplication and guest-friendship in Hom.

the others, and this brings about co-operation rather than a simple
attitude of *sauve qui peut*.

The appeal to personal honour which is implicated in the collective
honour of the group is not, however, the only means of encouraging
the heroes to act in the interest of their fellows, for each hero bears
certain obligations towards the others that are not directly connected
with the fact that the loss of a comrade's body reflects badly on the
whole company. In fact, even in those passages which we have just
considered, where such concerns are invoked by means of the appeal
to *nemesis*, this element of motivation coexists with another. Appeals to
nemesis, for example, can be addressed to the general body of the army
addressed collectively as *philoi* (*Iliad* 16. 544, 17. 248);[121] Glaucus
alludes to Hector's responsibility to his allies (16. 538–40), and
Menelaus, in the context of his reluctance to leave Patroclus' body
behind, mentions the service rendered him by Patroclus (17. 92); so,
too, Paris is reminded by Hector that the Trojans and their allies are
fighting on his behalf (6. 327–30, 525), and Hector feels himself
responsible for the deaths of many of those whom he was supposed to
protect (22. 104–7).

The implications of these passages are brought out more clearly in
another passage of *Iliad* 17, where again the point at issue is Hector's
responsibility to the dead Sarpedon. At 142–7 Glaucus threatens the
withdrawal of the entire Lycian contingent, on the grounds (147–8)
that they receive no gratitude (*charis*) for their efforts in the field.
Hector's lack of *charis*, Glaucus claims, is manifested in his failure to
rescue the body of Sarpedon, his *xeinos* (guest-friend) and *hetairos*
(comrade-in-arms, 150). The fact that Hector has failed to save
Sarpedon, it is suggested, will discourage others from fighting on his
behalf, since they can scarcely expect him to act in their interests when
he has failed one to whom he was bound by such strong ties of guest-
friendship, comradeship, and gratitude. The value of Sarpedon's
services, then, as well as specific ties between him and Hector, put
Hector under an obligation to help him wherever possible, and to
rescue him from ill-treatment and dishonour when dead.[122] Sarpedon
enjoys special status as a result of his pre-eminence as a warrior and
because he is Hector's *xeinos*, but it is clear from Glaucus' words that
the other Lycians also expect *charis* from Hector, and the evidence
suggests both that it was seen as a duty of *hetairoi* to come to each

---

[121] See Kakridis (1963), 8, for further examples of this address.
[122] See Kakridis (1963), 96; Long (1970), 124; Roisman (1984), 17.

others' aid in battle,[123] and that each member of either side, Greek or Trojan, could be considered the *hetairos* of the others.[124] Thus any member of one's own side might be covered by the obligations which exist between *hetairoi*.[125] Our next task is to show how these obligations, and others, are integrated into the system of values based on honour, and to demonstrate how *aidōs* operates in the individual's acknowledgement of the claims of other people.

1.3. *AIDŌS* TOWARDS OTHERS: THE CEMENT OF HOMERIC SOCIETY

1.3.1. Aidoios: Aidoios *and* Deinos

Frequently in the poems we find people described as *aidoios*. Those who deserve this designation, people before whom one feels *aidōs* (the 'I respect' usage, *aidōs* for the direct recipient of one's actions) fall into three broad categories: those before whom one feels inferior, who fill one with a sense of awe; those with whom one has a tie of *philotēs*;[126] and those who are helpless or who throw themselves on one's mercy. In the feminine, however, the adjective is used formulaically of any respectable woman.

---

[123] Copious evidence in Kakridis (1963), 65–70 (on *hetairos* in general, see 47–77; cf. Roisman (1984), 17).

[124] Kakridis (1963), 56–8; *hetairoi* might be members of one's own clan (52–5) or simply the heads of clans among themselves. One's *hetairoi* may also be one's *philoi* (61, 64, etc.).

[125] Thus Adkins's statement (1963: 37; cf. 1971: 4) that 'Diomedes is far more closely bound to a Lycian who is his *philos* [a ref. to *Il.* 6. 119–236] than to a Greek who is not, even during the Trojan War,' deserves the important qualification that, unless an active state of enmity exists between D. and another of the Greek leaders, all the Greeks at Troy are his *hetairoi* and so presumably his *philoi* too. Admittedly disputes can arise, but when they do they are regarded as disputes between *philoi*, and are condemned as such. (See 1.3.2 below.)

[126] *Philotēs*, not *philia*, is the term for the tie between *philoi* in Hom.; *philoi* ('friends' is an inadequate translation) may be bound to one by a blood tie, or by shared membership of some other group, or in virtue of some other bond, such as guest-friendship; there may or may not be an element of personal affection in the use of the term; on *philoi* and on the adjective *philos* (which applies to kin, to those towards whom one feels affection, and, in what is often seen as a possessive sense, to objects and parts of the body (or of the personality—*thumos* etc.)), see Adkins (1963) (followed by his disciple, Scott (1982)); Kakridis (1963), 1–46; Benveniste (1973), 273–88; D. B. Robinson (1990). (For Adkins and Scott the 'possessive' sense is primary, but its very existence is disputed by both Beneviste and Robinson, in the latter case very convincingly.) For a history of *philia*, see Fraisse (1974).

Where *aidoios* is the only adjective employed it most often refers
to those in the third of these categories; in other contexts, however,
it is frequently combined with other adjectives which help define the
precise grounds on which the designation *aidoios* is warranted. One
of these is *deinos*, which is derived from *deos* (fear) and of which the
stock translation is 'terrible'; we might, however, regard it as
approximating to something like 'awesome' or 'imposing'. At *Odyssey*
14. 234, as part of his yarn designed to deceive Eumaeus, Odysseus
tells how, after his family prospered, he became *deinos* and *aidoios*
among the Cretans. At *Iliad* 18. 394 Hephaestus describes Thetis as
a *deinē* and *aidoiē* goddess, and goes on to describe a debt of
gratitude which he owes her. The two examples appear quite
dissimilar, but the common factor seems to lie in the special status of
the person described: Thetis is *deinē* for Hephaestus because he
owes her a favour, and this constitutes a tie between them, while
Odysseys' Cretan is *deinos* because of his wealth and power. In
combination *deinos* and *aidoios* seem to describe a sense of awe or
inhibition which one feels towards one's superiors or those whom
one respects for some other reason.

The relationship between *aidoios* and *deinos* thus operates in much
the same way as does that between *aidōs* and fear, and one feature of
the use of both combinations is their use in portraying the attitude
of inferior towards superior. The two heralds in *Iliad* 1 (331), for
example, feel both dread and *aidōs* for Achilles, not only because he
is their superior but also because he is particularly fearsome in his
present mood. Similarly, Eumaeus experiences both *aidōs* and fear
with respect to his masters, Odysseus and Telemachus. At *Odyssey*
14. 145-6 he tells his disguised master of his feelings towards
Odysseus: 'Even in his absence, stranger, do I feel *aidōs* at naming
him; for he treated me exceptionally well [πέρι γάρ μ' ἐφίλει, 'he
treated me as a *philos*'] and cared for me in his *thumos*.' His *aidōs*
here clearly approximates to a very considerable respect for his
master; his reluctance to name him[127] strikes us as an indication of

---

[127] Von Erffa (1937: 19) is perplexed at the use of καὶ οὐ παρεόντα here; Scott (1980:
47 n. 33) suggests two explanations: Eumaeus is avoiding the pain of naming his long-
lost master, or he is influenced by the superstition that if one divulges a name the
enemies of its owner gain some kind of magic control over him. *Aidōs*, however, is never
used of the avoidance of pain *per se* in Hom.; and the second explanation can hardly be
right, since Eum. pronounces the name at 144. The lines are an exaggerated expression
of Eum.'s respect; he is affecting *aidōs* at taking the liberty of using his master's personal
name, something which he represents as inappropriate for one of inferior status and
which he will not do in his master's absence, much less to his face. In some societies (see

fear, yet the reason for this reluctance is not Odysseus' severity but his kindness; like Hephaestus for Thetis, then, Eumaeus feels some kind of awe for one who had treated him well. At 17. 188–9 the swineherd tells the disguised Odysseus that he will carry out Telemachus' instructions, even though he would rather not, explaining: 'I feel *aidōs* for him and fear him, lest he abuse me in future; the rebukes of one's masters are difficult.' This passage shows that the object of one's *aidōs* in situations like these is the immediate recipient of one's actions; in experiencing fear and *aidōs* towards Telemachus it is Telemachus' own disapproval that Eumaeus fears, not that of other people in general; but as we have seen, not all passages of this kind stress the concern for the dis-approval of the object of *aidōs*, but rather the element of positive recognition of the other's special status.[128]

1.3.2. Aidoios *and* Philos

In addition to finding *aidoios* and *deinos* as a pair, we also meet them in combination with a third adjective, *philos*, as in *Iliad* 3 (172), where Helen tells Priam, her *philos* (dear) father-in-law, that he is *aidoios* and *deinos* in her eyes. There may be any number of reasons why Priam should be *deinos* to Helen; he is a great king, and a reverend old man, and in both these senses may be considered her superior.[129] He is also manifestly her *philos*, as the father of her new husband.[130]

At one point in the *Odyssey* (8. 21–2) Athena covers Odysseus with *charis* (grace) and makes him mightier in aspect, with a view to making him *philos*, *deinos*, and *aidoios* in the eyes of the Phaeacians. Being stouter and taller, Odysseus could obviously expect to appear *deinos*,

---

Benedict (1934), 137, on the inhabitants of Dobu Island) inferiors are not permitted to use the names of their superiors, and, in this passage too, there is a trace of the idea that use of a personal name implies familiarity.

[128] Concern for the other's disapproval: cf. *Il.* 24. 435–6, where Hermes is posing as Achilles' *therapōn*; positive regard: cf. Beil (1961), 60–2.

[129] A king is obviously one's superior: cf. *Il.* 4. 402, where *basileus* is qualified by *aidoios*, and *Od.* 18. 314, where *aidoiē* is used of a queen. That one feels *aidōs* for the old on the grounds of their superiority is the assertion of von Erffa (1937: 11) on *Il.* 22. 419–20, where, he believes, old age attracts *aidōs* because of its authority and pity because of its disabilities; this seems quite likely. The most explicit statement of the claim of the old to *aidōs* comes at *Od.* 3. 24: 'it is a source of *aidōs* for a young man to address an elder.'

[130] This is not to suggest that *philos* is merely a kinship term here; clearly the adjective also has an affective meaning, as is allowed by Adkins (1963: 33), Kakridis (1963: 5–8, 15–17), and Benveniste (1973: 281–2).

and the other two epithets take their force from this fact; looking like a
man of wealth and power, Odysseus will be more likely to find people
who will entertain him, since, *philotēs* being the reciprocal relationship
that it is, one who looks as if he can repay one's hospitality is a better
prospect than one who does not. And if he is both *deinos* and *philos* it is
only natural that he should be *aidoios*, since men feel *aidōs* towards those
whose presence they find imposing and towards those who are their
philoi. The implication that it is only on these grounds that Odysseus can
expect *aidōs* from his prospective host should, however, be rejected. As
we shall see, even those who are neither *deinos* nor the *philoi* of those
they encounter are still entitled to *aidōs*; but it would appear that one
could be more confident of receiving hospitality if one could create the
impression that any kindness would be rewarded; hence Odysseus'
statement (*Odyssey* 11. 360) that he would be more *aidoios* and more
philos to men were he to return to Ithaca 'with a fuller hand'.

There appears to be a certain degree of interchangeability in the
way in which *deinos* and *philos* accompany *aidoios*. We might compare
the last-quoted passage with, for example, *Odyssey* 14. 234, cited in the
previous section; in the former Odysseus expects to become more
aidoios and more *philos* as a result of increased wealth, while in the
latter he becomes *deinos* and *aidoios* by the same process. The *deinoi*, it
would seem, are attractive propositions as *philoi*. In *Iliad* 18 the
question of the relationship between *philos* and *deinos* arises in
connection with the gratitude owed to one who has done one a
kindness. At lines 386 and 425 Thetis is described as *aidoiē* and *philē*,
while at 394, at the beginning of a passage which gives powerful
grounds for Hephaestus' *philotēs* with her, she becomes *deinē* and
aidoiē. At 14. 210, on the other hand, Hera explains to Zeus that she
believes she will be called *philē* and *aidoiē* by Oceanus and Tethys if she
succeeds in bringing about a reconciliation between them. Apparently,
one to whom one owes a debt of gratitude may be both *philos* and
deinos. Quite obviously, then, *deinos* does not immediately refer to the
idea of fear in such contexts; both *deinos* and *philos* may describe one
who has a special status in another's eyes, and it is this special status
that makes one *aidoios*.

Philotēs is a frequent ground for *aidōs* in Homer; in addition to the
passages already quoted and others in which *philos* and *aidoios* are
combined,[131] there also exists a number in which the operation of *aidōs*

---

[131] *Il.* 10. 114; *Od.* 5. 88, 19. 254; cf. von Erffa (1937), 11. On *aidoios* and *philos* and the
association of *aidōs* and *philotēs*, cf. also Benveniste (1973), 277–8.

in *philotēs*-relationships may be observed in more detail. Telemachus (*Odyssey* 20. 343–4) feels *aidōs* at the thought of expelling his mother from the house against her will; in Book 2 (134–7) he gives elaborate reasons for his compunction: his father would punish him were he to do as the suitors ask, his mother herself would set 'hateful Erinyes' against him, and people in general would feel *nemesis* towards him. Clearly, the requirement that one should show *aidōs* towards one's mother is backed up by the strongest of sanctions, and the *aidōs* which responds to the special status of another may be backed up by *aidōs* at popular disapproval of any failure to recognize a legitimate claim to respect; but Telemachus is not simply constrained by fear of punishment or opprobrium, for at line 131 he stresses the debt of gratitude which he owes his mother by acknowledging that it was she who gave him life and nurture. This debt is also felt to be a factor in producing *aidōs*; in the *Iliad* (22. 82–4) Hecabe bares her breast to her son and bids him show *aidōs* (and pity) on account of the nurture she gave him:[132] 'Hector, my child, show *aidōs* for this gesture, and have pity on me, if ever I held up my breast as a solace to you; remember these things, dear [*philos*] child.'[133] What Hecabe does in this passage is to place her son's sense of obligation under stress by means of a dramatic gesture which calls vividly to mind the imperative that a son should honour his mother; the exposure of the breast both demands that Hector should act to restore the honour which his mother has momentarily abandoned by revealing what should be concealed, and focuses his attention on the very basis of Hecabe's claim to special status. It is to this special status, to his mother as a bearer of honour, that Hector's *aidōs* should respond, and while this obligation is backed up by sanctions of popular disapproval at its breach, it is not to the *aidōs* which responds to such sanctions that Hecabe appeals. The *aidōs* which acknowledges the *timē* of others, especially of *philoi*, is thus clearly distinguishable from that which focuses on the opinions of those who witness one's actions.

[132] With reference to this passage, Beil (1961: 61) points out that Hecabe is not urging Hector to consider what people will say of him, but asking him to respond in accordance with a sense of personal duty. See 1.7 below, and, on the ways in which *aidōs* as recognition of others' *timē* conveys Homeric man's sense of moral and social obligation, see Riedinger (1976 and 1980), *passim*.

[133] In urging Hector τάδε αἴδεο, Hecabe is using an emotive feature of the mother–child relationship (her breast) metonymously for the real object of the *aidōs* she wishes to arouse (herself). Similarly, in other passages some feature of the particular relationship in which *aidōs* is felt appropriate is used as the object of the verb in place of a personal object; cf. *Il.* 9. 640; *Od.* 16. 75, 19. 527, 21. 27–8 (and see Scott (1980), 22).

Strife is to be avoided among members of the same family, even if the family is divine: Athena is deterred by *aidōs* from provoking a confrontation with her uncle Poseidon (*Odyssey* 6. 329–30), while in *Iliad* 21 (468) avuncular *philotēs* again gives rise to the *aidōs* which prevents a quarrel between Apollo and the sea-god. In both cases the divine sphere reflects the norm in human family relationships. The tie of *philotēs*, however, is not simply one between members of the same family, but exists in relationships in which no blood tie is involved.[134] As might be expected, *aidōs* is also a feature of this type of *philotēs*. In *Iliad* 24, for example, Zeus informs Thetis that his wish in assigning Achilles *kudos* (glory) is to preserve the *aidōs* and *philotēs* which bind Thetis to him (110–11); a *philotēs*-relationship already exists between the two, but this further favour strengthens it and secures Thetis' *aidōs* for the future.

We have seen already that the heroes of the *Iliad* were each other's *philoi* and that they had certain obligations to each other which it was a matter of honour to uphold; while it is true to say that cohesion in battle is produced to a great extent by the warriors' individual concern for their own honour, we also sensed that there was more to their obligations than that; we can now appreciate that, as a group of *philoi*, they are obliged to accord each other *aidōs*. The sanction against neglect of this *aidōs* may still be popular disapproval, since the belief that *aidōs* is appropriate among *philoi* will be shared by the community in general, but there will also be a direct tie between the *philoi*, as well as a form of *aidōs* directed not primarily towards the reactions of a wider public, but towards the reactions and status of the other party to the relationship.

The issue of the hero's obligations to his *philoi* arises most conspicuously in *Iliad* 9, where the ambassadors attempt to persuade Achilles to return to the fighting.[135] Not much is made of *aidōs* or *philotēs* in this context, but what is said is significant, and indeed the whole purpose of the mission is to persuade Achilles to consult the interests of the rest of the army rather than his own injured *timē*.[136] The appeal to *eleos* (pity) at line 302 is also important, in that it is a clear attempt to exploit an emotional tie that might be expected to

---

[134] The extension of the term *philos* to those outside the kinship group is not a primitive feature; cf. Finley (1956), 116. (Yet Finley still feels able to say (28–9) that the hero's only responsibility was to his family.)

[135] For a full discussion of this episode, see Roisman (1984), 5–22.

[136] Roisman (1984), 5–6.

exist between one hero and his comrades.[137] *Aidōs* makes its first
appearance in this episode at 508, but here the context is not one of
Achilles' responsibility to his comrades, but of the god-given benefits
of giving in to entreaty—'Prayers' (*Litai*) being personified as
daughters of Zeus, and so bearers of a special claim to honour which
may be recognized by *aidōs*. Ajax, however, who speaks after Achilles
has rejected the appeals of the others and whose words have the
greatest effect,[138] does refer explicitly to that responsibility, and to
aidōs and *philotēs*. At 630-2 he charges Achilles with neglect of the
philotēs he enjoys with the rest of the army, and reminds him of its
reciprocal nature; the other Achaeans honour (ἐτίομεν, 'paid *timē* to')
Achilles with their *philotēs*, and it is implied that he should return their
friendship.[139] In conclusion, Ajax asks Achilles to 'feel *aidōs* for his
house' (640), an allusion to the fact that, as well as being Achilles'
philoi, he and his colleagues are guests under his roof, and so deserve
aidōs on that basis. This appeal is not separate from that to *philotēs*, but
part of it; similar conduct is required in both relationships, and, in
practice, once the initial bond between host and guest is forged, *xeinoi*
are treated as *philoi*.[140] Ajax underlines this by concluding his speech,
and his appeal to *aidōs*, with the claim that he and his fellows wish to
be considered Achilles' dearest friends (642).

Ajax and his colleagues, then, consider it worthwhile to attempt to
persuade Achilles by referring to their friendship as members of the
same army (and it is clear that this friendship has affective as well as
formal aspects); they do not, it is true, suggest openly that his refusal to
be persuaded is unseemly or discreditable, or name any sanctions
which may be brought to bear as a result of his neglect of his *philoi*, but
then their purpose is not threatening, but cajoling. And there are
indications enough that they regard his obstinacy as unusual and
excessive; line 523, for example, 'Up to this point your anger has not
been blameworthy (*nemessēton*)', should be read with the emphasis on
its beginning, while the remarks of Phoenix that even the gods are

---

[137] Scott (1979: 1-14) distinguishes *eleos* (a positive feeling of sympathy, often
associated with *aidōs* (11) and appropriate among *philoi* (11-12)) and *oiktos* (pity
combined with revulsion, felt towards the humiliated, etc. (cf. n. 61 above)); Roisman
(1984: 12-13) shows that while *philoi* are not explicitly obliged to accord each other *eleos*,
they do so on a recurrent basis, and concludes that *eleos* constitutes part of the duty one
owes one's *philoi*.

[138] Roisman (1984), 14.

[139] *Philotēs* thus refers not to a state of affairs or a relationship in 630, but to an action,
the act of *philein*.

[140] On *xenia*, see 1.3.5 below.

open to persuasion (497) suggests that Achilles' concern for his *timē*, exceeding even that of the gods, is abnormal. Likewise Ajax's remark that even one whose brother or son had been murdered would accept compensation (632–3) implies that Achilles is going too far in his anger. Clearly, therefore, it is regarded as desirable that one should listen to one's *philoi*, consult their interests, and accord them *aidōs* as part of one's obligations as a member of a reciprocal system of *timē* and *philotēs*; as in any society, however, arguments on one's responsibilities to others may have no power to coerce those who put their own interests first.

The avoidance of strife within the peer group appears to have been an ideal, but so too was the pursuit of honour, and although the opposing forces at Troy may be considered as two groups of *philoi*, each individual within the group also cherishes his own claim to honour; and where honour exists as an acknowledged factor in the motivation of men, there also exists a hierarchy, for if everyone has equal honour, then no one has any; by the same token, honour can be regarded as a commodity, and one man's acquisition of honour will often be another man's loss.[141] Thus a situation could easily arise in which acute concern for one's own honour might be combined with a wariness of one's rivals and a determination that they should not increase their honour at the expense of one's own. In this situation the individual might be subject to competing claims, and *aidōs* might enter

[141] Thus the acquisition of honour in Hom. is often described in terms of a 'zero-sum game', in which any gain must be at the expense of another's loss; see Adkins (1960*b*), 31; Gouldner (1965), 49–51; Pitt-Rivers (1965), 24; Dover (1974), 231; Mackenzie (1981), 75; Carter (1986), 5–6 (these studies are all worth consulting on concepts of honour, in Homer and elsewhere; the best study of *timē* in Hom., however, is by Riedinger (1976)). The zero-sum view, however, can be taken too far; in many straightforward contexts, in which there is a confrontation or challenge between two parties, one side's loss will be the other's gain; but to dishonour another is not always to acquire his honour for oneself; Aegisthus clearly does not emerge with credit from his part in the murder of Agamemnon (e.g. *Od.* 3. 249–50, 258–66; Aeg. killed a much better man (250), but did not himself become much better by doing so), and the suitors' *aischea* against the house of Od. reflect badly on themselves (*Od.* 1. 229 in 1.1.3 above, and cf. n. 42 above, on *hubris*). Again, in cases of affront, much will depend on the status of the parties and the attitude of others: my attempt to dishonour you may be ludicrous or gratuitous, given the gulf in our status; my friends will regard my enemies as dishonoured by my challenges, while my enemies' friends may see my attempts to dishonour as discreditable for me; and the impartial may side with one or other or neither of the two parties, depending on the circumstances. Equally, one man's gain of *timē* need not always be another's loss; at *Od.* 1. 95 it is Athena's purpose that Telemachus should win *kleos* (fame) on his journey to Sparta and Pylos; this acquisition of *kleos* in subsequent books involves his general growth in heroic stature, not just the amassing of guest-gifts, and there is no one who suffers a loss corresponding to Tel.'s gain.

into these claims in more than one sense—concern for one's own honour, which may take in *aidōs* at the prospect of any loss of status, may conflict with the honour of the group, which *aidōs* helps defend, or with the requirement that one's superiors and one's *philoi* be accorded *aidōs*.[142] *Aidōs* responds to *timē*, whether one's own, that of one's *philoi*, or that of one's superiors, in all these different ways, and this indicates both the inclusivity of the concept of *timē* and the way in which the *timē* of each member of a group inevitably exists in close relation to that of the others.

1.3.3. *Conflicts in the Code of Honour*

Although the forces at Troy may be seen as groups of *philoi*, some enjoy greater status than others. We have already seen that *aidōs* is a proper response with regard to one's superiors, and in straightforward situations there is no problem about this; the heralds in *Iliad* 1 (331) are quite obviously Achilles' inferiors, and the *aidōs* they show him recognizes that fact unambiguously. In other situations, however, the position may be more complicated, particularly when two or more of the most prominent heroes are involved, for in such situations the matter of superiority is not always clear, the participants are in any case *philoi*, and one party may decide to push his own claim, either to superiority or to parity; *timē* is important in this, for while one hero may have more *timē* than another, in dealing with his fellow heroes he is never dealing with one who has a negligible claim to *timē* of his own.[143]

An episode in *Iliad* 4 shows how problems might arise; at 370–400 Agamemnon, who is pursuing the task of urging the army on to greater effort with no little enthusiasm, abuses (368) Diomedes, accusing him of slacking and comparing him unfavourably with his father. Diomedes himself does not immediately respond, but his companion, Sthenelus, the son of Capaneus and so, like Diomedes, one of the *epigonoi* (the sons of the Seven against Thebes), reacts angrily to the suggestion that his generation is inferior to the previous. Significantly, he sees the matter in terms of *timē*, arguing that his generation

---

[142] In seeing these conflicting imperatives as part of one large system of values based on honour I concur with the remarks of Schofield (1986: *passim*, esp. 17–18) on the inclusive nature of the heroic code; cf. Riedinger (1976); (1980), 68–9.

[143] See Mackenzie (1981), 71.

was successful where their fathers failed, and that they should therefore enjoy greater *timē* (410). Sthenelus thus takes Agamemnon's words as an affront to his honour, and we can see how a dispute might arise on that basis. Diomedes' response, on the other hand, is totally different—at 401-2 he refrains from making any reply at all, αἰδεσθεὶς βασιλῆος ἐνιπὴν αἰδοίοιο ('out of *aidōs* for the utterance of the reverent [*aidoios*] king'). As leader of the expedition Agamemnon is of paramount status, and Diomedes acknowledges this with *aidōs*. After Sthenelus has spoken, he explains why he has taken no offence: he realizes (412-18) that Agamemnon is attempting to encourage the troops to greater effort, and accepts his right to do so, for, as he points out, both the glory of success and the sorrow of failure rest with him. Diomedes, then, does not resent (οὐ νεμεσῶ, 'I feel no *nemesis*', 413) remarks which another has taken as an affront because he can understand why the remarks were made; he makes allowance for Agamemnon's aims, and so for his intentions, and for his status, together with the pressures and responsibilities which that status entails. Thus, where honour is at stake, circumstances and intentions can be very important.[144]

Sthenelus and Diomedes, therefore, exemplify opposite responses, both of which are envisaged by the values of society; Sthenelus' is the individual response, conscious of personal *timē*, while that of Diomedes takes loyalty to the peer group and respect for one's superiors into account.[145] We see the latter attitude again in Book 10 (237-9), where Agamemnon excuses Diomedes from the need to

[144] This is mainly true of one-to-one situations, however, in which the status and intentions of the person delivering the affront will help determine whether or not the recipient of the affront decides to commit his honour; the individual will have to consider, for example, whether the other person *meant* to diminish his honour, as well as whether it would be a proper decision to regard the affront as a matter of honour at all (i.e. whether other people will consider him dishonoured should he fail to take action); on this, see Pitt-Rivers (1965), 25-8, 33-4. Vlastos (1975a: 16, 98) has two examples of the relevance of intentions in the context of an affront: in *Od.* 22 Phemius is ecluded from Od.'s revenge against the *hubris* of the suitors on the grounds that he was not a willing participant to it (οὔ τι ἑκὼν . . . οὐδὲ χατίζων, 351), and in *Il.* 23 it matters to Menelaus, in considering an affront to his *aretē* (571), whether Antilochus willingly (ἑκών, 585) impeded his chariot. Both these episodes, as Vlastos points out, tell against the utility of a blanket description of Homeric society as a 'results culture', although, as we have seen, outside the one-to-one situation, where a generalized 'other people' is making judgements on the conduct of individuals, intentions often do not matter; cf. Pitt-Rivers (1965), 64.

[145] D. does not forget the affront, however, and lets Ag. know this at 9. 33 ff., when the latter's fortunes are at a low ebb. Yet his patience in biding his time is still strongly contrasted with the less reflective response; see Griffin (1980), 74.

consider *aidōs* for one of superior birth and rank when choosing an accomplice for the mission behind enemy lines: 'Do not, out of *aidōs* in your heart [in your *phrenes*], leave the better man behind, and take the worse as your companion, yielding to *aidōs* or out of regard for birth, even if he is more kingly.' Agamemnon is being disingenuous (trying to ensure that Diomedes does not select Menelaus, 240), but even so his argument must be plausible, and *aidōs* for one's superiors must be a normal response, or one which could be expected in some individuals at least. On the other hand, a response like that of Sthenelus may also be envisaged as normal, as at 10. 129–30, where Nestor's denial that anyone will feel *nemesis* at Menelaus' commands in the present instance implies that such a response might be likely in other instances (cf. 114–15, where Nestor foresees *nemesis* on the part of Agamemnon should he charge Menelaus with dereliction of duty).[146] Where *aidōs* intervenes, then, it helps subdue the *nemesis* which is occasioned by an affront to one's *timē*,[147] while, on the other hand, the very use of the term *nemesis* suggests that the affront, the failure to recognize another's *timē*, is a breach of *aidōs*.

It is suggested by Scott[148] that the absence of the *aidōs* experienced by Diomedes in Sthenelus and others in the same situation reveals the weakness of the restraint which *aidōs* provides. If the fact that some feel *aidōs* in a given situation while others do not means that *aidōs* is weak, then we shall have to accept this argument. In reality, however, this phenomenon tells us nothing about the strength of *aidōs*, but simply demonstrates that it is an emotion to which some are more sensitive than others, or which different individuals, as a result of their upbringing and disposition, tend to experience in different situations.[149] We should not consider fear to be weak simply because some are more prone to it than others, nor pity, nor love; rather we judge the power of these emotions by their power in individual human beings; and we have seen that in some individuals *aidōs* can be powerful to the point of being undesirably so. It should be no surprise that it is not powerful in every individual.

[146] *Nemesis* is the normal reaction of heroes to rebukes which they consider unjustified or insulting (see Hohendahl-Zoetelief (1980), chs. 1–2); hence the precaution, μή νεμέσα ('do not be indignant').

[147] Cf. Redfield (1975), 116.

[148] (1980), 17. Adkins also frequently claims that *aidōs* is weak because it is not effective in every individual on every occasion; see (1960*a*), 45–6; (1960*b*), 31; (1971), 9 etc.

[149] This is the view of G. G. A. Murray (1924), 88–9, and he seems to me to get it exactly right.

At *Iliad* 23. 473 ff. a quarrel breaks out between Ajas, son of Oeleus, and Idomeneus; after a quick burst of invective from both sides (in which the former addresses the latter *aischrōs*, 1.1.3 above), Achilles quickly interposes (492-4): 'Stop this exchange of rough and bad words, Ajax and Idomeneus, since it is not fitting. You two would also feel *nemesis* against anyone else who did such things.' Ajax addresses Idomeneus *aischrōs*, and clearly the latter's honour is subject to an affront, but Achilles reprimands the conduct of both as unseemly and occasion for *nemesis*, and since these terms refer to the same ideas of appropriateness and disapproval as does *aischrōs*, the latter term may also have implications for the conduct of Ajax. This is clearly a minor quarrel, and perhaps that is why it is considered inappropriate, but where *timē* is at stake, the cause of the dispute can be less important than the fact that an affront has taken place, and so it is important that disputes can be deprecated as unseemly, that they can attract *nemesis*, and that the standard by which this is so can be seen as universal; in pointing out that Ajax and Idomeneus would disapprove of their own conduct in another (καὶ δ' ἄλλῳ νεμεσᾶτον), Achilles is urging them to apply their own standards to the present situation, to categorize their own behaviour in terms of values which they share with others.[150] Let it also be noted that Ajax's attempt to dishonour does not automatically succeed; instead, the circumstances are such that challenge and retaliation alike are unseemly, and neither party is dishonoured by backing down.

We have seen that *aidōs* can override resentment at an affront, and that *nemesis* is the reaction of one who feels himself affronted. In an ideal situation, then, *aidōs* should prevent affronts, and forestall *nemesis*; failing that, if an affront has occurred, *aidōs* should prevent an excessive reaction to it, in those cases in which the affront is offered by a superior or a *philos*. But ideal situations are few in any society, and disputes do arise, particularly since the resentful reaction to an affront is also prompted by the system of values based on honour. At this point we can hardly help but be reminded of the quarrel which stands at the centre of the plot of the *Iliad*. When Achilles is insulted by Agamemnon, his reaction is to complain of his opponent's *anaideiē* (lack of *aidōs*),[151] and the grounds for this accusation clearly lie in the

---

[150] Cf. Dickie (1978), 94; cf. also nn. 107, 113 above.

[151] *Il.* 1. 149, 158; cf. 9. 372-3, where Ach. again refers to Ag.'s *anaideiē* and claims that *kuneos* (dog-like = *anaidēs*) as he is, he will not dare look him (Ach.) in the face. Even one as shameless as Ag., it seems, would experience *aidōs* when faced with one he has wronged, since the averted gaze is a sign of *aidōs*, not of *anaideiē*, which is reflected in the

slight he has suffered upon his *timē*. Adkins, in connection with this and other passages, points out that there is a natural tendency to set a higher value on co-operative values in others when one has oneself been wronged,[152] and there is plainly a great deal of truth in this, but this does not mean that Achilles' description of Agamemnon's conduct as *anaideiē* is unwarranted in terms of Homeric values; *aidōs* and *timē* are associated, as we have seen.[153] Besides, others do seem to share Achilles' perception of the situation; certainly all those who express an opinion feel that Achilles was the wronged party; at 19. 86 Agamemnon is abused for his provocation of Achilles, while according to Phoenix at 9. 523, the latter's initial anger against Agamemnon was not *nemessēton*. Even Agamemnon himself admits as early as Book 2 (377) that it was he who started the quarrel. Most importantly, however, Nestor, the first to attempt to calm the two, sees the matter in terms of their *timē*, pointing out that Agamemnon should not deprive Achilles of a prize allotted him by the other Achaeans (visible proof of the *timē* he has won in battle), and that Achilles, although of divine birth and the greater warrior, should bow before the greater *timē* of a king who rules from Zeus (1. 275–84).[154] In

ability to look others straight in the face even when one has grounds for *aidōs*. The dog is particularly associated with shamelessness (a result of its lack of genital inhibition, according to Freud (1961*b*: 99–100 n. 1)), *Il.* 1. 225, 3. 180, 6. 344, 8. 423, 21. 481; *Od.* 4. 145, 8. 319, 11. 424, 19. 91; other passages in which a human being is called 'dog' may be relevant, but the context does not always make it clear that the insult is levelled on the grounds of shamelessness. In connection with Ag.'s *anaideiē*, we should notice that Ach. also charges him with *hubris* (1. 203, 214, 9. 368; cf. von Erffa (1937), 19); *hubris* and *anaideiē* are also combined in the suitors (1.5.2 below).

[152] (1960*a*), 61.   [153] Cf. Lloyd-Jones (1971), 12–13.
[154] Much has been written about this episode: see Adkins (1960*a*), 37–8; (1971), 8–9; (1982*a*), 298–302; Long (1970), 127–8; Lloyd-Jones (1971), 12–13; Riedinger (1976), 260–1; (1980), 73–4; Mackenzie (1981), 72–5; Dover (1983), 37–8; Schofield (1986), 27–9; Gagarin (1987), 285–7, 303–5. Much of this discussion centres on Nestor's phrase at 275, '*agathos* though you be'; see text below. Lloyd-Jones, Riedinger, and Schofield all stress the importance of *timē* in this episode, and specifically N.'s plea that both Ach. and Ag. should consider each other's *timē*. Describing this concern, that each should have his proper *timē*, as a concern for 'justice' Lloyd-Jones is misunderstood by Gagarin, 287; the concern for 'justice' is a concern that legitimate claims to *timē* should be recognized and disputes between *philoi* avoided, and as such belongs within the general scheme of values based on honour; see Riedinger, locc. citt.; Schofield, 28. The notion of justice is not inappropriate, given that there is an obvious feeling that each party bears an entitlement to his own honour which the other should not ignore. There is, however, no reference to a standard of justice as such (no occurrence of any *dikē*-word), and in his later article (1987) Lloyd-Jones underestimates the extent to which other-regarding behaviour is part of an inclusive code of honour in Hom. To claim that N. advances only prudential arguments to each man (Adkins (1982*a*), 325; Mackenzie (1981), 73–4) is to misrepresent the situation. (Discussion of the relationship between *aidōs* and *dikē* is best left until we can examine the evidence furnished by Hesiod's *Works and Days*, see 2.1 below.)

reminding Agamemnon of Achilles' deserved *timē* Nestor is referring
to the same phenomenon as did Achilles with his charge of *anaideiē*,
namely, the failure to respect the *timē* of another; Agamemnon, then,
certainly is *anaidēs* in disregarding Achilles' *timē*,[155] while Achilles
himself is reproached for being without the kind of *aidōs* shown by
Diomedes at 4. 402.

The implications of this aspect of the quarrel for the wider question
of the nature of Homeric values are manifold; we see, for example, that
although Achilles does not act as Diomedes did, or as Nestor urges
him to, nevertheless he is not regarded as in the wrong (9. 523); while
the reflective response, the response with which other-regarding *aidōs*
is associated, may be the ideal, it appears that retaliation for a wrong
suffered is felt to be legitimate. Two kinds of response are thus
envisaged: one of self-control and one of self-assertion—one of regard
for the *timē* of others, one of regard for one's own. *Aidōs* moreover,
may be part of both responses, *aidōs* for one's *philoi* and superiors on
the one hand, and *aidōs* at the prospect of humiliation resulting from
failure to avenge the affront on the other; Achilles is clearly influenced
by the latter at 1. 293-4, where he claims that he would be called *deilos*
(a coward) and *outidanos* (a nobody) were he to yield to Agamemnon in
every matter. Obviously, the two responses conflict, and where they
do, the conflict will be between concern for the *timē* of others and for
the stability of the group and concern for one's own *timē*.[156]

The conflict is also one between co-operative and competitive
standards; Agamemnon pursues his own interests at the expense of
another, and Achilles follows the promptings of competitive rather
than co-operative *aidōs*, and so, for them, at least in this instance,
competitive values outweigh co-operative. That this should be the
case, however, is, as we have seen, not an inevitability of Homeric
language. But is it an inevitability of Homeric values? What exactly are
the values in this situation?[157] First, we have an ideal, which we might

---

[155] As Adkins acknowledges (1960*b*: 31) = (1987*1*: 9); cf. Scott (1980), 16.

[156] Cf. Lloyd-Jones (1971), 26-7.

[157] Before the 1987 general election in Britain there featured in the serious press a
protracted correspondence concerning the desire of the Conservative party for a return
to 'Victorian values'. Contributors, however, differed in their definition of 'values'; pro-
Conservatives cited thrift, self-help, and chastity as Victorian values, while anti-Conser-
vatives pointed to poverty, disease, child labour, and sexual hypocrisy. Clearly, one group
limited 'values' to aspirations and explicit moral ideology, while the other felt able to cite
any and every social circumstance as the result of a value. The truth lies somewhere
between the two; values involve more than explicit moral ideology; they emerge from
events, from choices, from omissions, etc.; but not everything that emerges is a value.

regard as part of the 'moral ideology' of the poems, that quarrels among *philoi* are undesirable, that they are unseemly, and that one should be sensitive to the *timē* of other people as well as to one's own. Then we have an allowance, which is certainly a value, that one who has been insulted may legitimately retaliate. But the crucial question is the place of Agamemnon's behaviour in the scheme of Homeric values. Adkins argues[158] that Agamemnon has a claim to deprive Achilles of Briseis, a claim based on his paramount *aretē* (excellence, including prowess, birth, and status)[159] which is acknowledged by Nestor's exhortation in line 275, 'Do not take this girl, *agathos* [the adjective corresponding to *aretē*] though you be.' Yet the concessive clause does not acknowledge any claim on Agamemnon's part, but rather points out that although an *agathos* is normally entitled to all the privileges that are going, there are some things even an *agathos* should not do, limits which even an *agathos* should not transgress.[160] It is certainly not part of the structure of Homeric values that any and every action of an *agathos* is legitimized by his *aretē*. This is true of Agamemnon, whose behaviour is not condoned, and it is even more true of the suitors in the *Odyssey*, who are certainly *agathoi*, but who are condemned throughout the poem, their *aretē* being largely irrelevant to those who condemn them. The fact that *aretē* is unaffected by breaches of the co-operative virtues does not mean that such breaches are condoned; *aretē* encompasses so many aspects, such as birth and wealth, which could never be affected by anyone's disapproval, that it is difficult to imagine it being affected by anything but the severest material disaster.[161] The conduct of both Agamemnon and Achilles in this episode reveals that *they* prefer to put competitive standards before co-operative, and clearly under Homeric values, based as they are on the one central concept of honour, situations of this sort will tend to arise. But the competitive path is not the only one which might be followed; we have seen both that another approach to disputes, also based on honour, exists (indeed exists as the ideal norm), and that Nestor advises Agamemnon and Achilles to adopt this approach. In

---

[158] (1960*a*), 37.

[159] On *aretē*, see Adkins (1960*a*), ch. 3.

[160] The best explanation of this phrase is still that of Long (1970: 127); for others, see Mackenzie (1981), 73; Dover (1983), 37–8; Gagarin (1987), 303–5.

[161] In the *Od.* both Eumaeus (17. 322–3) and Penelope (19. 124–6) lose some *aretē*: Eum. because he loses the status of a free man (even then he does not lose all his *aretē*) and Pen. because her husband, in whose *aretē* she shares and on whom her *aretē* depends, has gone; see Pearson (1962), 49. Pen., moreover, exaggerates, since her very resistance to the suitors is a manifestation of her *aretē*.

the episode itself, then, the values of the (emotionally involved) antagonists differ from those of the sage repository of conventional wisdom, and Homeric values are clearly not unequivocal on the matter of disputes.

Agamemnon does, it is true, court the charge of *anaideiē* much more sanguinely than he might a charge of cowardice, but this is not a question of the relative power of the two charges, but of the material consequences of ignoring them; the charge, 'you are a coward' challenges Agamemnon's rights, privileges, and status in a way that the charge, 'you are *anaidēs*' does not, simply because it leaves him vulnerable to challenges from rivals and to the disaffection of his followers. Popular disapproval is not effective in itself, whether in the competitive or the co-operative sphere. Clearly, though, Agamemnon's weighting of competitive over co-operative considerations will be understandable in terms of Homeric values, given the pragmatic context in which those values must operate, and it will certainly indicate a tendency in the hero to pay more attention to competitive than to co-operative failures; yet it is worth stressing that his is not the only response envisaged by Homeric values, nor is it regarded as an acceptable response by others. The values of society as a whole cannot simply be read off from the self-interested actions of its most powerful members.

The fact that Agamemnon can apparently seize Briseis and get away with it does, of course, have its implications for the values of Homeric society; the point, however, is not that the *agathos* has a claim to do as he likes, but that disinterested members of the community do not consider it worth challenging the entire system simply in order to register their disapproval of the misdeeds of the strong. (Again, this is in no way a consequence or a reflection of Homeric value terms.) A head of state, even now and even in the democratic West, whose policies are carried out with injustice, lack of consideration, and selfishness is less liable to fall from office than one whose incompetence endangers the interests of his or her subjects or supporters, and the sanctions brought to bear against failures in co-operation are rarely made to match those which follow automatically upon abject inefficiency. This obviously causes some leaders to value competitive success over the co-operative excellences, and it indicates a tendency in their subjects to acquiesce in their doing so. But society's disapproval of the co-operative misdemeanours of the strong is not necessarily negated by the ability of the latter to ride it out, even though this ability depends on the tendency, both of the many and of those whose disapproval might matter, to avoid 'rocking the boat', except when the boat itself is in danger of sinking. If the failure of the Greek chieftains at Troy effectively to coerce Agamemnon into serious consideration of the right of Achilles to honour indicates a preference to 'wait and see' rather than to challenge the head of a hierarchy in which are invested their own hopes of success and security, and if this is a value, then the values in this case do not differ greatly from our own.[162]

Adkins claims that while Agamemnon may be *anaidēs* in refusing to acknowledge Achilles' *timē*, it is not *aischron* for him to do so.[163] The context, however, gives us no clue on this question, and the paucity of evidence for the usage of *aischron* in Homer scarcely equips us to decide one way or the other. Yet we do know that *aischron* refers to the appearance of actions or situations, and that it implies that the situation thus described will be such as to occasion popular disapproval; we have also seen both that Agamemnon shows no concern for popular disapproval and that quarrels can be condemned in terms of their unseemliness. We remember, too, that the suitors do perpetrate *aischea* which reflect badly on themselves, that criticism of this behaviour could 'disfigure' (*aischunein*) them,[164] and that throughout the *Odyssey* they are characterized as *anaideis*. It is interesting, therefore, to find that on two occasions (22. 414–15 and 23. 65–6) they are condemned because 'they did not honour [pay *timē* to] any of the men that dwell upon the earth, whether base or noble, whoever came to them'. The suitors, then, are *anaideis*, commit *aischea* discreditable to themselves, and do not accord others the *timē* they deserve; I should hesitate to say that it is impossible that their conduct could be termed *aischron*, and the same holds of the conduct of Agamemnon.

1.3.4. *Good Manners: Telemachus*

In the *Odyssey* we find that much is made of *aidōs* for others in the context of the youthful Telemachus' dealings with those he meets on

---

[162] Here I concur with Adkins's argument (1982*a*: 323–4) that the values of the Homeric hero in this respect are essentially those of the modern nation-state; but the values of states reflect the values of those who rule them, and the values of those who rule reflect the values of those who acquiesce in their rule (in states in which one is allowed the luxury of acquiescence).

[163] (1960*b*), 31.   [164] See 1.1.3 above.

his travels to gather news about his father. At 3. 24 he experiences *aidōs* at the thought of addressing the aged Nestor,[165] even though Athena has assured him that he has not the slightest need to feel that way (14). Telemachus' instinctive *aidōs*, normal and typical in one of his age, is active even when he is assured that no one will think the worse of him for abandoning it, and the fact that he does not abandon it shows that the emotional reaction that *aidōs* represents is not equivalent to a simple calculation of the responses of others.[166] Rather Telemachus' *aidōs* is deeply rooted in his temperament, which is portrayed as characteristic of one making the transition from boyhood to manhood.[167]

Telemachus is showing similar reticence at 4. 158–60, where, describing his behaviour towards Menelaus, Peisistratus explains: 'He is *saophrōn* [modest, sensible, well-behaved, cf. Fr. *sage*], and he feels *nemesis* in his heart [νεμεσσᾶται δ᾽ ἐνὶ θυμῷ] that he should come here for the first time and break into speech uninvited in your presence, you in whose voice we rejoice as in that of a god.' As we have already noted,[168] νεμεσσᾶται ('he considers it inappropriate') comes very close to the sense of αἰδεῖται here: both verbs would refer to possible breaches of the decorum expected by society. It is therefore interesting to note the association of *aidōs/nemesis* and *saophrosunē* (in classical Greek, *sōphrosunē*), a concept which will later express some of the notions of self-control and self-inhibition present in *aidōs*.[169] At no stage, however, could the two terms be considered completely synonymous; *sōphrosunē* may promote or presuppose certain emotions, but it is not an emotion itself; rather, as here, one who is *sōphrōn* can manifest *aidōs*. In Homer, *saophrōn* works much as do other words which connote 'good sense',[170] and the interaction of these with *aidōs* will be discussed below.[171]

---

[165] See n. 129 above.

[166] Cf. de Sousa (1987), 153: '... once begun, an emotional reaction is difficult to stop, even when the grounds are removed.'

[167] Tel. eventually overcomes his *aidōs* in this episode, and he does so by means of *tharsos* (boldness, 3. 76; cf. θαρσήσας, ibid.). The opposition of boldness and *aidōs* is one we shall meet again, and one which clearly demonstrates the inhibitory nature of the latter; cf. the pseudo-Platonic definition (*Def.* 412c) τολμήσεως ὑποχώρησις ἑκουσία δικαίως ... ('a willing and justifiable withdrawal from boldness'; cf. von Erffa (1937), 41).

[168] Cf. n. 120 above.

[169] On *aidōs* as a forerunner of classical *sōphrosunē*, see North (1966), 6–7; cf. Greene (1944), 20. Of course, *aidōs* and *sōphrosunē* can still be linked, even in the classical period, esp. in contexts like the present one, where the modesty of a youth or woman is involved; see esp. Pl. *Charm.* 155a–161a, where the youthful Charmides' *sōphrosunē* is manifested in his blushing and his *aidōs*.

[170] See North (1966), 3–5.   [171] See I.5.1.

Telemachus' *aidōs*, as we have just seen, could go too far, and interfere with the purpose of his journey; but just as he feels *aidōs* towards his hosts, so he expects that they will respond in kind towards him, and he realizes that this, too, may conflict with his purpose, which is to find out the truth about his father. Hence he entreats Nestor and Menelaus (at 3. 96 and 4. 326, respectively), 'Do not spare me any details out of *aidōs* or pity.' Telemachus imagines that *aidōs*, concern for his feelings, may lead his hosts to withhold unpleasant details regarding his father's fate. *Aidōs* here clearly denotes concern for the recipient of one's actions, its primary reference to an altruistic concern for another's feelings.[172]

1.3.5. *Other* Aidoioi: *Guests and Beggars*

Aidōs, then, of a different kind from that which has regard for the effects of the disapproval of 'other people' for one's own honour, is a powerful influence over the conduct of Homeric man *vis-à-vis* his fellows; it is a desirable quality and helps enforce the norms of society. So far, however, we have seen it in action only with regard to those who have some claim to it arising from their special relationship to the subject, be they his superiors, his family, or his *philoi*. But other categories of people, who cannot demand *aidōs* on the grounds of their power or their *philotēs*, are nevertheless felt to be entitled to it; this group of *aidoioi* consists of those who enter a community from outside (and are thus largely at the mercy of those they encounter), namely strangers, including beggars, and suppliants (considered in next section), all of whom may, to some extent, be subsumed under the heading of *xeinoi* (strangers, guests, hosts, guest-friends).[173] Unlike those groups discussed so far, however—one's *philoi* or one's superiors—these people rely not on their own *timē* to attract the *aidōs* of others, but on that lent them by Zeus, their protector and *epitimētōr* (*Odyssey* 9. 270).[174] Obviously, though, society will only impart this special status to those who enter a community from outside because it

---

[172] Gagarin (1987: 288) tells us that the only example of disinterested behaviour he can find in Hom. is the Phaeacians' conveying Od. home, but Tel.'s plea in these two passages presupposes that disinterested concern for another's feelings is a normal element of Homeric etiquette.

[173] *Xeinoi* are *aidoioi* at *Od.* 8. 544, 9. 271, 19. 191, 316. On the institution of guest-friendship in general, see Kakridis (1963), 86–107; cf. Finley (1956), 109–14.

[174] See Adkins (1960b: 25), who interprets *epitimētōr* as 'he who imparts *timē*'.

regards it as desirable that they should be protected; the impulse to
protect strangers thus arises from within society, and the divine
guarantee of special status does not detract from the importance of the
institution of guest-friendship as a manifestation of Homeric values.[175]

To disguise Odysseus as a beggar on his return to Ithaca is a master-
stroke on the part of the poet of *Odyssey*,[176] for it is only when the
suitors are confronted by the beggar that the full extent of their
anaideiē (as well as their *hubris* and *atasthaliē*), for which they are
criticized throughout the poem, becomes apparent. In *Odyssey* 17 the
beggar Odysseus goes to town, and is encouraged by Telemachus (who
by this time, of course, knows who he is) to make the rounds of the
suitors begging for alms; he is also told that, as a beggar, he is exempt
from the need to show *aidōs* (347, 352); *aidōs* is not good for him,
because as a man in need he has to overcome any inhibition he might
feel at approaching others directly and without the formality of
etiquette.[177] Again, *aidōs* inhibits, and where an absence of inhibition is
desirable, *aidōs* is not. Antinous, however, takes another view of the
matter, and when approached, exclaims (449) 'What a bold
[*tharsaleos*][178] and *anaidēs* beggar you are!' He goes further than this,
indeed, and hurls a stool at Odysseus' back, arousing the censure of
several in the company, most immediately that of the victim himself:
Antinous will be punished, if the gods and the Erinyes protect beggars
(475-6). Antinous is contemptuous of the beggar's complaint, but
his contempt merely excited the disapproval of the others, who

---

[175] Cf. Scott (1980), 19-20. Verdenius (1944-5: 52) believes that strangers are
accorded *aidōs* not because of their weakness as outsiders, but because they are unusual
and mysterious; there may well be something in this, and the *aidōs* which one feels for
them may arise at least partly from an uncertainty about their origins, status, intentions,
or character which could lead to inhibition of any impulse to harm them. Cf. Finley
(1956), 111-12, 134-5, 137 on the ambivalence of the stranger. Equally, however,
uncertainty about the status of another places honour under stress, with implications
both for oneself and for the other person if a wrong move is made; *aidōs*, I should say, also
responds to this aspect of the situation, and not simply to the strange or uncanny.

[176] Cf. Havelock (1978), 161 ff.; on the importance of the theme of guest-friendship in
the poem as a whole, see Thornton (1970), 38-46, etc.

[177] Cf. 17. 578, where Penelope asks Eumaeus whether it is *aidōs* which causes the
beggar's reluctance to enter the house, and opines, 'a beggar who feels *aidōs* is no use' (or:
'... is a poor beggar') (κακὸς δ' αἰδοῖος ἀλήτης). The adjective *aidoios* is active here
(manifesting *aidōs*), while elsewhere it is passive (deserving *aidōs*). On the analogy of this
passage von Erffa (1937: 13) believes that the adverb at *Od.* 19. 243 (the disguised Od.
claims that he sent his guest, the fictitious Od. of his tale, on his way *aidoiōs*) is also active
(i.e. the host accorded the guest *aidōs*); but the sense could just as well be passive/
proleptic ('... so that he should be *aidoios* to others'). Cf. Scott (1980), 33 n. 4.

[178] Again, boldness as an antonym of *aidōs*; cf. n. 167 above.

vehemently express their *nemesis* (οἱ δ᾽ ἄρα πάντες ὑπερφιάλως νεμέσησαν, 481). The standard that beggars deserve *aidōs*, therefore, is so widely acknowledged that even Antinous' fellow suitors disapprove of its breach.

There then follows, delivered by one of the suitors, an empirical and materialistic justification of the advisability of treating beggars with *aidōs*. Antinous, he maintains, did οὐ καλά[179] in striking the beggar, and he is, indeed, doomed, if there is a god in heaven (484), for 'gods in the guise of foreign *xeinoi* frequent communities in every shape and form, viewing the *hubris* and law-abidingness of men.' In harming a stranger, then, one may be harming a god, and so caution is required when dealing with strangers; if this belief, based on the common folk-tale motif of theoxeny, was at all widely held, it is evidence for the uncertainty with which strangers were regarded.[180] The reference to the possibility of divine disapproval or punishment suggests an appeal to external sanctions, but this impression should not be taken at face value. Whatever we may think about our own gods and their commandments, few of us, I imagine, believe that the Homeric gods ever actually imposed their preferences on their mortal subjects; thus, at the cultural level, we are bound to see such invocations of divine power in the cause of social values as indications of the importance invested by a society in its institutions. The standard, therefore, that one should receive strangers kindly is prior to the justification. At the level of the individual, however, the divine sanction may be perceived as a means of securing conformity to a standard to which the individual does not automatically subscribe—may, that is, operate as an external sanction. But this will be the case in any society which believes that its values are upheld by invisible (or, as here, disguised) deities; for some, the threat of divine displeasure may be the only effective sanction; but for others the notion that the gods disapprove of certain conduct is taken as a reinforcement of values which one has already internalized and accepted, and appeal to the divine sanction as a reason for avoiding transgression need indicate nothing more than

[179] 17. 483. *Kalon* means beautiful and *aischron* means ugly, so one might expect οὐ καλά (*i.q.* 'not *kalon*') to be equivalent to *aischron*, but Adkins (1960a: 43-5) denies that this is ever the case in Hom., and argues that *kalon* does not commend success as *aischron* condemns failure; this begs a very large question, since *aischron* is rare and, in any case, has no intrinsic reference to competitive failure. For other passages in which 'not *kalon*' (etc.) may be equivalent to *aischron* (including *Od.* 21. 312-13, also in the context of Ant.'s maltreatment of the beggar), see Long (1970), 128.

[180] Cf. n. 175 above.

the operation of the internalized standard. Thus, in this passage (485–
7), the speaker need not hold that observance of the custom of guest-
friendship is worthwhile only in so far as it ensures that one will never
unwittingly lay oneself open to divine anger; that the reference to the
divine sanction is made indicates that there may be some who need a
justification in these terms, but justification in terms of self-interest
does not imply that self-interest is the only possible motive.

Beggars are only a species of the genus *xeinoi*; their profession
demands that they wander from town to town; other *xeinoi* may have
any number of reasons for leaving the security of their own communities, but, like the beggar, they are *xeinoi* by virtue of their being
outsiders and unprotected, except by the gods. At *Odyssey* 14. 386–9
Eumaeus gives his reasons for affording the beggar Odysseus protection: 'And, old man of many sorrows, since a god [*daimōn*] has brought
you to me, do not try to charm or bewitch me with lies; nor for that
reason will I show you *aidōs* [αἰδέσσομαι] or treat you as a *philos*
[φιλήσω], but because I fear Zeus *xenios* and pity you yourself.'
Eumaeus gives two reasons for showing *aidōs*; fear of the god who
protects *xeinoi* and pity for the beggar himself; showing *aidōs* is not the
same as showing fear or pity, but both help define *aidōs* here. There are
clearly two strands to the *aidōs*-reaction in the context of guest-
friendship, and these, the prudential and the altruistic, the uncertainty
when confronted by an unknown outsider and the positive regard for
another human being, are expressed by Eumaeus' two motives. Both
these aspects can be expressed by the verb *aideomai*, which may have
either the god or gods who underwrite the standard or the stranger
himself as its object.[181] It is difficult precisely to establish the sense of
αἰδέσσομαι in the present passage; the association with the verb
philein, which refers to the concrete acts Eumaeus will perform in the
entertainment of his guest,[182] suggests that it, too, refers to Eumaeus'
conduct, to his acceptance of the beggar as his guest; the verb *aideomai*,
regular in contexts of guest-friendship, seems to have taken on positive
connotations from such contexts, and to have come to describe the

[181] 1: object Zeus or the gods— *Od.* 9. 269 (context of both *xenia* and supplication) and
Il. 24. 503 (context of supplication); 2: personal object— *Od.* 14. 388 (= the present
passage) and *Od.* 22. 312, 344; *Il.* 21. 74 (context of supplication). At *Od.* 21. 28–9 the
opis (anger) of the gods and the table of hospitality are the objects Heracles failed to
aideisthai in killing his guest, Iphitus; cf. *Il.* 9. 640 (*aidōs* for the *melathron*, or house), and
n. 133 above, on the verb governing some central, emotive feature of the *aidōs*-
relationship; for the table as the central feature of *xenia*, cf. *Od.* 14. 158–9, 17. 155–6,
19. 303–4, 20. 231–2 (and Gould (1973), 97).
[182] See Kakridis (1963), 42–3; Adkins (1963), 34.

behaviour involved in the acceptance of a *xeinos*, rather than the occurrence of the emotion which the *xeinos* excites.[183] The verb *aideisthai*, then, appears to be as descriptive and characteristic of the action of receiving a guest as is *philein*.

Eumaeus explains his *aidōs* for his guest in terms of his obedience to divine law (and fear of divine punishment) and his own capacity for pity. There is, however, another sanction against the ill-treatment of guests, one both more immediate than the wrath of Zeus and more compelling than the individual's instinct for pity. It is to this that Eumaeus refers when the beggar Odysseus first stumbles towards his hut, forcing the swineherd to save him from the attack of his dogs. The dogs safely driven away, Eumaeus remarks (14. 37–8): 'Truly, old man, the dogs nearly tore you apart, and you would have poured *elencheiē*[184] on me.' Failure to protect a guest, if it became known, might lead to *elencheiē*, 'showing up', and thus another kind of *aidōs*, different from that one accords the recipient of one's hospitality, but still related, enters the picture. Proper treatment of strangers is an imperative which is supposed to be widely observed; this being the case, popular disapproval will inevitably be the consequence of any breach of the standard. Thus *aidōs* can work in two ways in the attitude of the host: first as a concern for the stranger himself, a withdrawal from the prospect of doing him harm, and secondly as a concern for the opinion of others or for the values of society. It cannot be too strongly emphasized that all these motives, the other-regarding, the fear of punishment, and the fear of opprobrium, coexist, even within the same individual, and therefore should not be considered in isolation; it would be wrong to say that Eumaeus' concern for Odysseus is entirely altruistic, but neither is it entirely self-regarding.[185]

That the honour of the host is diminished by his failure to protect a guest emerges from a number of passages, some of which we have

---

[183] Emotion-words can describe behaviour or attitudes appropriate to, or typically prompted by, an occurrent emotion as well as the occurrent emotion itself, and the statement made by the use of an emotion-word (e.g. 'I am ashamed') need not be a report that an occurrence of the emotion is taking place; cf. Bedford (1956–7), 300–3; Pitcher (1965), 344–5; Lyons (1980), 159.

[184] Cf. 1.1.5 above.

[185] Cf. in general Pearson (1962), 62–3; also on 14. 386–9 and Eumaeus' altruism, Havelock (1978), 164. In that passage Eum.'s active desire to help is important, as it is at 15. 373, where he describes how he reckons part of his income as available to help *aidoioi*; cf. 14. 56–8, where he states his obligation to help *xeinoi* and beggars as *themis* (the right thing to do); cf. Havelock, 163; Hohendahl-Zoetelief (1980), 117.

looked at already.[186] Telemachus, for example, is concerned at his
failure to welcome a guest properly because of the suitors' behaviour,
and feels *nemesis* at himself on that account (*Odyssey* 1. 119–20); his
own *nemesis* at himself mirrors that of others, and again illustrates the
point that one can subscribe to the values under which one stands to
be criticized. The *nemesis* of Penelope at her son's failure to protect his
guest is certainly aroused in Book 18 (220–5):

You have lost your wits and intelligence, as this event which has taken place in
our house shows, where you allowed the *xeinos* to be disfigured/dishonoured
[*aeikisthēmenai*] in this way. What if a *xeinos* sitting in our house should come to
some harm from such terrible mishandling? On you would fall the *aischos* and
lōbē among men.

Penelope chides Telemachus for his failure to act in accordance with
aidōs, yet it is his wits (*phrenes*) and his intelligence (*noēma*) that she
blames. Telemachus agrees that good sense does lead one to act as
custom demands (227–30), but points out that he is prevented by the
suitors, whose 'bad intentions' (232) are opposed to his own sound
grasp of the principles involved. We shall explore this link between
good sense and proper behaviour below;[187] for our immediate
purposes it will suffice to record that *aischos* and *lōbē* are felt to accrue
from any failure to protect a guest.

   Words of seemliness and appearances abound in the last passage,
and we noted in our discussion of these terms how the unseemliness of
the situation could reflect on either the doer or the sufferer of the
action described as unseemly; we have just seen how Telemachus is
affected by the actions of the suitors, but in other passages, as we
saw,[188] their actions seem to reflect as badly on themselves as on
Telemachus, if not more so. Accordingly, abuse of another's hospitality
can be regarded as disgraceful, even if those who act in this way are not
always concerned at disapproval on that account. Certainly both abuse
of hospitality and failure to protect a guest are described as inappropriate and unseemly.[189]

   The courtesy demanded of both parties in the relationship of guest-
friendship is also governed by *aidōs*, and *aidōs* is thus an important

[186] On *Od.* 16. 106–7, 20. 316–19, cf. 1.1.4 above (on *aeikēs* and *aeikeliōs*); in general, see
Kakridis (1963), 95.
[187] See 1.5.1.
[188] Above, 1.1.3, 1.1.4.
[189] At *Od.* 20. 294–5 (= 21. 312–13) it is 'not *kalon*' to abuse another's guests; cf.
17. 483 and n. 179 above.

element in the success of hospitable entertainment. In Book 15 of the *Odyssey* Telemachus is anxious to take his leave of Menelaus, but has no wish to cause his host offence. Menelaus, however, brushes aside his anxiety (probably itself akin to *aidōs*, and certainly further evidence that concern for others' feelings formed part of Homeric etiquette), saying (69–71): 'I feel *nemesis* against any other host who "loves" [or 'entertains', behaves/treats as a *philos*] excessively, but hates excessively too; moderation is better in all things.' This form of expression, in which the speaker rejects a course of action by referring to the *nemesis* he would feel at such conduct in another, suggests both the universality of the standard and the speaker's agreement with it, and indicates that the individual is acting in line with values which he shares with others.[190] Excess is to be the object of Menelaus' *nemesis* here, and the fact that excess can attract *nemesis* indicates that *aidōs* might cause one to reject excessive behaviour. A desire not to overstep the bounds of good manners in the host–guest relationship seems also to explain Odysseus' *aidōs* at *Odyssey* 8. 85–6, where, moved by the bard's song, he hides his face in order that his hosts should not see him weep. Elsewhere in the poems even the greatest heroes do not experience *aidōs* at shedding tears,[191] and at *Odyssey* 4. 195–6 Peisistratus, who had joined the others in a lament for those who did not return from Troy, explains that he feels no *nemesis* at those who weep for the dead.[192] This last passage, however, is an excuse, and implies that weeping on the part of a host or a guest in the context of hospitality could be considered inappropriate if not warranted by circumstances or if the grief of one were not shared by all; probably, then, Odysseus' *aidōs* is not occasioned by weeping *per se*, but by the possibility of discourtesy towards his hosts, in that his tears might indicate less than complete satisfaction with their hospitality or disturb the pleasant atmosphere which all hosts attempt to create.[193]

[190] See nn. 107, 113, 150 above.
[191] See *Il.* 1. 357; cf. Scott (1980), 23; at *Il.* 16. 22, however, weeping is stigmatized as the act of a 'silly girl'.
[192] Cf. 19. 264, of Penelope's tears.
[193] Beil (1961: 55) recognizes this motive, but also feels that Od.'s *aidōs* is a mechanism for the concealment of 'an especially sensitive intimate-sphere of the soul'. This may be right; it is hard to be certain. Od. weeps again at 8. 522–31, prompted by Demodocus' song of the wooden horse; as a result, Alcinous decides to bring the bard's performance to a close, since it is not pleasing to all present (538), and makes it clear that successful hospitality depends on the enjoyment of both guests and hosts (538–43); see Slater (1990), esp. 217–19. Od.'s concern for convivial propriety in the morning banquet is matched by that of Alcinous later, just as, in Book 15, both Telemachus and Menelaus are anxious to avoid giving offence.

The feeling that one should not burden one's hosts with one's troubles certainly occurs in Book 19 (118-21), when Odysseus expresses reluctance to bewail his own misfortunes in another's house, lest one of the household or his hostess herself feel *nemesis*, and there is a similar idea at *Iliad* 24. 90-1, where Thetis' unwillingness to join the other gods seems to be based on reluctance to infect their carefree hilarity with her troubles.

Besides the negative justification of kindness towards strangers (the theoxeny idea) and the negative sanction of ill-repute for those who fail to do so, we also find a positive, but none the less materialistic, justification at *Odyssey* 19. 333-4, where Penelope informs us that the fame of good men (men who are *amumōn*) is spread by *xeinoi*. Thus good reputation is the reward of proper conduct, just as ill-repute is the lot of those who treat guests badly.[194] Yet Penelope does not simply say that *xeinoi* report on the behaviour of their hosts *qua* hosts, but that they carry the fame of anyone who is *amumōn* (noble) and who 'knows *amumona*' to all men; conversely, she remarks (329-31) that 'all mortals' curse those who are 'harsh' and who 'know harsh things'; although she begins her speech from the context of guest-friendship, she seems to believe that society in general shares her abhorrence of moral wickedness and appreciation of moral goodness. This pattern, of the extrapolation from guest-friendship as a paradigm case to the wider sphere of proper behaviour in general, is fundamental to the *Odyssey*; the essential badness of the suitors, their failure to play the game according to the rules of *timē*, is demonstrated in their abuse and perversion of hospitality, while the society of those who practice guest-friendship is sharply contrasted with that of the Cyclopes, who are distinguished from civilized peoples by their lack of social integration and ignorance of *themis* (9. 188-9).[195] When Odysseus first sets out to

[194] Cf. *Od.* 17. 415-18, where the beggar Od. promises to spread Antinous' fame. According to Walcot (1970: 80), Pen.'s remarks indicate only 'the Greek passion for fame and reputation'; but justification of values in terms of self-interest (the fame to be won) does not entail that those values involve nothing more than self-interest. It is undeniably true that Greek justifications of morality, at all periods, tend to be self-interested, or at least self-referential; but the reasons for this are obvious and natural—the justifications, 'do it because it is right' or 'do it because it is in the interests of the community' beg the further questions,'why should I do what is right?' and 'why should I do what is in the interests of the community?' The question, 'why should I do what is in my own interests?' however, is rarely asked.

[195] Cf. von Erffa (1937), 36; Long (1970), 139; Havelock (1978), 159-60. Pearson (1962: 43-4) shows both that *themis* and *dikē* represent custom, 'how things are done' in the *Od.* (cf. Havelock, 179-84), and that Cyclopean society emphasizes the importance of these by contrast. The poet of the *Od.* clearly believed that his society was a civilized one

ascertain the disposition of those who inhabit the Cyclops' island he refers to two alternative types (9. 175-6): 'Are they *hubristai* and savage and not *dikaioi* [just], or are they *philoxenoi* [hospitable] and endowed with a mind that listens to the gods?' Thus the values which promote the observance of the laws of hospitality are precisely those which characterize a community as civilized, and we can see how Penelope's remarks on the conduct of men in general can spring from contemplation of their attitude towards guests in particular; one's attitude to those who enter one's community from outside is indicative of one's sensitivity to justice and propriety in general. This being the case, *aidōs*, which is central to the institution of guest-friendship, obviously has a role of considerable importance in the society of the *Odyssey*.

Protection of strangers was, then, a Homeric ideal, one which is clearly recommended with great emphasis to the poem's audience.[196] We should not, however, be blind to the possibility that the ideal is recommended so strongly precisely because practice often fell short of it; we have seen that materialistic justifications are sometimes felt necessary. Materialism also affects the institution in the form of the exchange of gifts which was the norm among *xeinoi*; Odysseus is constantly concerned to amass booty for his return to Ithaca (his fictitious description of himself doing just that at 19. 272-4 is quite in character), and he even asks the Cyclops for a gift outright (9. 268). In addition, we have seen that at 11. 360 he believes he will be more *aidoios* and more *philos* to all men if he can return to his home with a substantial amount of wealth. He is *aidoios* no matter how much he possesses, but his own experiences as a beggar tend to confirm that while *aidōs* towards all strangers is the theory, ill-treatment of those of them without means might all too often be the practice.

1.3.7. *Supplication*

The institution of guest-friendship is very closely linked, especially in the *Odyssey*, to another code of behaviour, that of supplication, and, indeed, the boundary between suppliant and stranger is difficult to

by virtue of its possession of *themis* and *dikē*, with which *aidōs* is intimately connected as the force which dictates their observance.

[196] See Havelock (1978), 161-76.

define.[197] A suppliant is a 'comer' (*hiketēs*),[198] and we often find strangers, who come unprotected into an alien community, either describing themselves as suppliants or resorting to supplication. On arriving on the Phaeacians' island Odysseus undertakes supplication of the local river-god, referring to the etymology of *hiketēs* and stressing his right to *aidōs* (*Odyssey* 5. 447–50): 'That man is *aidoios* even to the immortal gods who comes [*hikētai*] as a wanderer, as I now come as a suppliant [*hikanō*] to your stream and your knees, after toiling many toils. But have pity, lord; I claim to be your suppliant [*hiketēs*].'[199] The general 'immortal gods' of this passage is particularized in the Zeus *xeinios* of *Odyssey* 9. 269–71, another indication of the closeness of *xenia* and *hiketeia*:[200] 'Show *aidōs* for the gods, my good man; we are *hiketai*. Zeus *xeinios*, who attends reverend [*aidoioi*] *xeinoi*, is the *epitimētōr* of *hiketai* and *xeinoi*.' Zeus *xeinios* protects both strangers and suppliants; at *Odyssey* 13. 213 he is given another cult-title, *hiketēsios*, which is obviously derived from his function as protector of suppliants, but which is used in that passage in a context of his punishment of human crimes in general.

Since one who is a *xeinos* might also decide to style himself a suppliant (although suppliants do not behave exactly as do other *xeinoi*)[201] much of what was said about *xenia* also holds good for *hiketeia*. In a number of contexts, however, the connection between supplication and *xenia* is not prominent, in that those involved are not stranger and prospective host; in these situations, supplication is employed to further a specific request. Like the *xeinos*, the *hiketēs* appeals to *aidōs*, his claim to which seems to rest both on his special

---

[197] On supplication in general, see Gould (1973), 74–103; also Kopperschmidt (1967), 11–53; Stagakis (1975), 94–112; Thornton (1984), *passim* (esp. 119 on the role of *aidōs*); on the closeness of *xeinos* and *hiketēs*, see Gould, 79, 92 n. 94*a*, 93–4; cf. Stagakis, 109–10. For parallels from other cultures, see Abou-Zeid (1965), 254–5; Gould, 98–9, 101; Thornton, 170–1.

[198] Adkins (1963), 35.

[199] Od.'s supplication is 'figurative' here, in that he employs the language of supplication, including a reference to 'knees', but does not make the ritual contact (with the knees and the chin) required for 'full' supplication; on 'full' and 'figurative' supplication, see Gould (1973), 76–7, etc.; cf. Kopperschmidt (1967), 20–1. Full supplication entails that the supplicated must use force if he is to break contact, and so increases the pressure on him to accede to the request; this might also increase his *aidōs*, since denial of the request, involving the use of force where custom and divine sanction deprecate it, entails a more significant and striking breach of convention in these circumstances.

[200] Cf. *Od.* 7. 165.

[201] See Gould (1973), 93–4; not all strangers, it should be added, employ the language and gestures of supplication.

status as a protégé of the gods and on the ritual self-abasement to which he subjects himself;[202] he therefore claims *aidōs* both as one enjoying *timē* (invested in him by the gods) and as one abandoning a claim to *timē* and thus placing relationships based on *timē* under stress.

Supplication does occur in both the *Iliad* and the *Odyssey*, and we have detail enough to be able to understand how the institution works, yet we have no real opportunity to study the operation of *aidōs* in those who accept supplications—to discover, for example, to what extent ritual contact might affect the feeling of *aidōs*. This is because, although *aidōs* is frequently mentioned in appeals and is requested from the supplicated, no character ever states explicitly that he has been moved by *aidōs* to accept another's supplication, or even that he has had to overcome his *aidōs* in rejecting the supplication.

The episode of the supplication of Chryses in Book 1 of the *Iliad* shows that *aidōs* is the proper reaction in such contexts; all the other Greeks, we are told (22–3) wanted to *aideisthai* the priest, but Agamemnon, to whom (with Menelaus) the supplication was princi-pally addressed (16), sent him away *kakōs*.[203] The use of *aideisthai* in this passage indicates both how integral *aidōs* is to the context of supplication and how its links with that context affect its semantic range. In expressing their readiness to *aideisthai* the Greeks were presumably not predicting the future incidence in themselves of an occurrent emotion; in this context *aideisthai* 'means' 'to accept supplication'—it refers to the behaviour of one who receives a suppliant in the proper way. No doubt the word is so used because the occurrence of the emotion of *aidōs* is considered appropriate and normal in this context, and so probably the occurrence of *aidōs* as an emotional event in such contexts is logically prior to the designation of the conduct promoted by such *aidōs* as *aideisthai*, but this passage indicates that the verb is sufficiently established in the context to have taken on positive connotations from it.

In the peacetime contexts of the *Odyssey* the dominant impression given is that the pleas of suppliants should be heeded; Polyphemus' rejection not only of Odysseus' pleas (quoted above) but even of the power of Zeus himself is intended to be shocking; so in the

---

[202] Gould (1973), 94–6.

[203] The use of the adverb *kakōs* in 25 (= 379) *may* be an explicit condemnation by the poet of Ag.'s misconduct (*kakōs* does censure misconduct and reflect badly on agents at *Od.* 2. 266, 4. 766, 17. 394), but the adverb can mean 'in bad case' (cf. *Il.* 2. 253 etc.) and may refer to Chryses' condition rather than Ag.'s conduct. If the word were an explicit authorial comment, it would be a member of a very select group; see Griffin (1986).

supplication of Chryses in *Iliad* 1 Agamemnon's roughness, out of step
with the attitude of all his colleagues as it is, is clearly gratuitous.
However, in situations in which the suppliant is an enemy begging for
his life a common-sense attitude seems to have prevailed. In *Iliad* 22
(123–4) Hector laments that he can expect no mercy from Achilles
even if he lays down his arms as his mother requests, and, such is the
savagery of his opponent at this point in the poem, his prognosis is
clearly correct. In those scenes of supplication which are presented
directly in the narrative of the *Iliad*, in fact, no suppliant is spared.[204] In
the passion for revenge which often motivates those who kill
suppliants there seems to be little room even for the distinction
between real and figurative supplication.[205] At *Odyssey* 22. 310 the
priest, Leodes, takes hold of Odysseus' knees, and in 312 utters the
suppliant's appeal: 'I supplicate you, Odysseus [γουνοῦμαί σ']; show
me *aidōs* and have mercy.' The appeal to *aidōs*, however, and the ritual
clasping of the knees make little impact on Odysseus, who instead
treats Leodes' case on its merits; the priest claims that he never said or
did anything *atasthalon*, but rather attempted to restrain the suitors in
their deeds of *atasthaliē*, but Odysseus considers him implicated in the
suitors' misdeeds and kills him. Although Odysseus kills a suppliant in
the very act of supplication, no condemnation is forthcoming, nor are
any misgivings expressed. Later in the same book, both the bard,
Phemius, who utters a plea for *aidōs* at 344, having already clasped
Odysseus' knees, and the herald, Medon, who supplicates Telemachus
(365–70), are spared, not because Odysseus is noticeably moved by
their appeals, or because he cannot bring himself to break ritual
contact, or because he fears the wrath of Zeus, but simply because he
has been persuaded, largely through the intercession of Telemachus,
that they are innocent of the crimes of the rest of their company.

The case of Lycaon in *Iliad* 21 is interesting; Lycaon was spared by
Achilles on a previous occasion, and it may be that a successful
supplication had something to do with this.[206] At 71 he clasps Achilles'
knees, and at 74 he appeals for *aidōs* and pity, adding (75), 'I am in the
place of a reverend (*aidoios*) suppliant.'[207] Lycaon *has* effected the full
ritual contact of supplication, and yet he claims only to be 'in the place
of a suppliant', 'a sort of suppliant'. This may be significant; while

---

[204] See Griffin (1980), 91; we do, however, hear of suppliants being spared; see text
below on Lycaon in *Il.* 21; cf. Gould (1973), 80 n. 38; Pedrick (1982), 132.

[205] See Pedrick (1982), 139 and *passim*.

[206] *Il.* 21. 35–44, 77–80; cf. Gould (1973), 80 n. 38.

[207] ἀντί τοί εἰμ' ἱκέταο, διοτρεφές, αἰδοίοιο.

supplication of a foe in battle might have been an expedient which was worth the attempt, it could be that rejection of such supplication, perpetrated by one who only moments before had been attempting to kill the recipient of his appeal, was regarded as understandable, if not normal.[208] Achilles has certainly become extremely savage by this time, but still there is no indication that his rejection of Lycaon's appeal, or even of his claim to *philotēs* (which, though technically justified, is nevertheless unquestionably tenuous), is an act which society would find abhorrent; Lycaon himself has little hope that his plea will be successful (92–3), and his description of himself as 'a sort of suppliant' seems to express a similar lack of confidence. He does, as Gould points out,[209] abandon his supplication by relaxing his grip on Achilles' spear and stretching out his hands, and thus he accepts that Achilles' desire for revenge will mean his death, but there can scarcely be any doubt that Achilles would have killed him in any case, and neither the ritual contact nor the appeal to *aidōs* and pity has any effect on him.[210] Indeed, the tone of both the passages in which Odysseus and Achilles kill their suppliants suggests that the desire for vengeance, when such vengeance is justified against an enemy or one who has affronted one's honour, may legitimately override both the sense of *aidōs* and consideration for the rules of supplication.

The position of those who undertake supplication in situations of

[208] Why does Lyc. say he is 'like a suppliant'? Leaf (1900–2: ad loc.) believes that he is referring to his claim to *philotēs* with Ach. (they have broken bread on a previous occasion, 76ff.); he is merely 'a sort of suppliant' because Ach. does not recognize him as a *philos*. But being a quasi-*philos* does not make one a quasi-*hiketēs*; one does not have to be the *philos* of the addressee in order to supplicate, although reference to any tie of *philotēs* or *charis* which may exist will always be a useful argument in making an appeal. Leaf obviously takes Lyc.'s γάρ in 76 as explanation of his use of ἀντί, but it seems more natural to regard it as introducing the grounds on which he hopes Ach. will accept his appeal (their sharing of bread, see Gould (1973), 79 and n. 36, 81; Scott (1979), 11; (1980), 18–19); Ach. acknowledges this claim contemptuously at 106; it does not necessarily follow from this, however, that Lyc. would not be entitled to see himself as a suppliant in the full sense of the word. More likely Lyc.'s use of ἀντί implies some doubt as to whether one in his position may legitimately be regarded as a suppliant, and this doubt more probably arises from the fact that he has been Ach.'s adversary until the commencement of the appeal than from the ambivalence of his claim to *philotēs*. (See Scott (1980: 18), and Parker (1983: 182 and n. 207) who distinguishes between 'help me' and 'save me' supplication; this distinction covers more neatly the differences in response which Pedrick (1982), attributes to artistic differences between the two epics.)

[209] (1973), 81.

[210] This does not, of course, call for the modification of Gould's invaluable remarks (1973: 76–7, etc.) of the 'rules' of supplication, as Pedrick (1982) seems to think; Gould himself recognizes that the theory of the rules and their observance in practice may differ.

conflict, then, appears weak; if there is little at stake in the encounter, or if a ransom is offered which pleases the supplicated, as seems to have been the case on Lycaon's first meeting with Achilles,[211] the supplication may be accepted, but in practice it seems that supplication in such contexts is felt to be resistible. In other contexts, however, where the suppliant is genuinely a 'comer' in that he is unknown to the recipient of his appeal, and where guest-friendship and supplication almost coincide, his position seems to be rather stronger, in so far as one supplicated by a stranger has no legitimate grounds for treating his suppliant with violence, and the impression created is that the use of violence in such situations would deserve the severest condemnation.[212] Thus, although the ritual of supplication does not differ between war- and peacetime contexts, the situation does, and Homeric values make allowances for that difference, so that the defeated warrior who undertakes supplication as a last desperate expedient does not have the same claim to *aidōs*, is not *aidoios*, in the way in which a genuine 'comer' would be. Hence it is not just that Greek values pragmatically admit that a victorious warrior bent on revenge is unlikely to show *aidōs*, although this is certainly true, but rather the unlikelihood of his showing *aidōs* is legitimized, and he is acquitted of an obligation which is otherwise felt to be powerful.

Priam's supplication of Achilles in *Iliad* 24 provides a good indication of the precariousness of the suppliant's position in situations in which there is a great deal at stake. Achilles has been told that it is the will of Zeus that he should heed the old man's plea (24. 133–7), and it is almost unthinkable that he should ignore such a direct command, yet the supplication must still take place, and when it does, it creates a formidable amount of tension.[213] At 503 Priam bids Achilles αἰδεῖο θεούς ('show *aidōs* for the gods'), and since Priam is aware of the will of the gods in this matter, this may be a general usage, 'respect the gods (on account of their power)'; but this would be unparalleled, since in Homer the gods are accorded *aidōs* only as protectors of guests and suppliants, and so it is probably better to take the words in that sense here. The main point of Priam's appeal, however, is not that as a suppliant, he is under divine protection, but that he deserves pity, as an old man in a situation

---

[211] Cf. *Il.* 11. 106, 21. 100–2 (Ach. used to ransom his vanquished opponents).
[212] Cf. perhaps, the poet's condemnation of Heracles' breach of guest-friendship at *Od.* 21. 28.
[213] Cf. Gould (1973), 79–80, 96.

analogous to that of Achilles' own father.[214] And it is this appeal to pity and the reference to Peleus which have the greatest effect on Achilles, as he sees that Hector's fate will be his—and Peleus' even more pitiful than Priam's. Achilles does, then, feel pity, and he is aware of the need to obey Zeus' instructions and to avoid harming a suppliant;[215] yet he does not say that he feels *aidōs*, although his acceptance of the supplication itself may be construed as 'showing *aidōs*'. An indication of how *aidōs* might arise in such a situation, however, is afforded by the description of Achilles' reaction on first seeing Priam at 24. 480-4; he feels *thambos* (astonishment) at his appearance and at his immediate performance of the ritual gestures of supplication, and this reaction is compared to that of those who received an exiled homicide into their presence.[216] Both the homicide in the simile and Priam himself are suppliants, and some kind of awe or astonishment is the reaction they arouse; this is not uniquely a reaction to the shedding of blood, for although the suppliant in the simile has shed blood, Priam has not, and it seems that it is the supplication itself, or perhaps the appearance of one who intends to supplicate in a particularly tense situation, which arouses such an emotion. It does not seem too far-fetched to suggest that this feeling of awe, of uncertainty, towards a suppliant of somewhat ambivalent status might be related at least to one aspect of the *aidōs* which is appropriate to the situation.[217]

[214] At 22. 418-22 it is Pr.'s intention to employ this argument as the main point of his appeal, and he does so at 24. 486-501 and 503-6.

[215] Although when he does refer to these points, it is in the context of the danger of his ignoring them (560-70).

[216] The simile thus inverts the roles of the parties in the narrative, to the extent that it is Ach. who is a killer in the real situation, not Pr. But the homicide is a man affected by *atē* (delusion, disaster), and the point of the comparison may be that it virtually requires *atē* on Pr.'s part to approach Ach. (As Macleod points out (1982*a*: ad loc.), the *atē* of the killer is naturally that which causes him to commit the act of homicide, although the phrasing ('as when dense *atē* takes hold of a man, and he, having killed a man at home, has arrived at the home of others') does perhaps suggest that it is *atē* that drives the homicide to approach strangers. One wonders whether this should be taken at face value, and whether the implication is that all suppliants require *atē*, but more probably the point of the reference is Pr.'s *atē* alone, and the wording of the simile has been influenced by the narrative (see other examples in Fränkel (1921: 95-6)).

[217] This would certainly square with Verdenius's assertion (n. 175 above) that strangers of whatever kind arouse *aidōs* as a result of 'das Ungewöhnliche in ihrer Erscheinung'. (This, perhaps, sounds more like *sebas* than *aidōs*; but the two can be very close; see 1.6.3 below.) Gould (1973: 96 n. 111) suggests that the *thambos* of the spectators in the simile may imply a horror of pollution; Parker (1983: 134-5) believes that the supplication of a prospective protector by a homicide may be an appeal for a minimal sort of purification, but (135 n. 5) is sceptical about the argument that *thambos* is

1.4. *AIDŌS*, WOMEN, AND SEX

A number of passages exists in which *aidōs* occurs in a broadly sexual
context, whether in relationships between the sexes, where it affects
women particularly, or with reference to an individual's own sexuality
or to sexuality in general; in the former category *aidōs* is concerned
with the social role of men and women, while in the latter it relates to a
coyness regarding sex, sexual organs, and bodily functions.[218]

1.4.1. *Women's* Aidōs

Women's *aidōs* differs from that of men in its reference, and women
can also be accorded *aidōs* as a special category on their own. We have
noted instances of women being described as *aidoïe* (deserving *aidōs*) in
connection with some specific relationship; usually *aidoïe* is accompanied by *deinē* or *philē* in these contexts, and the adjective commends
exactly the same qualities as it would when used of a man. Frequently,
however, *aidoïe* is the only adjective employed,[219] and it may describe
a queen of the highest birth[220] or a relatively humble household
servant;[221] rarely are the reasons for the use of the adjective apparent
in any specific activity of the woman so qualified. The explanation of
the apparently indiscriminate application of the epithet, however, lies
in the role of women in society and the nature of women's honour.
Society sets different standards for women from those it sets for
men,[222] the main virtue required of women being faithfulness; men's
honour is vulnerable through women, and men have an interest in
ensuring that the women under their control remain faithful and
sexually pure.[223] Although women, by virtue of their upbringing in

a reaction to pollution. Supplication as described in the simile may also be relevant to
Ajax's assertion (*Il.* 9. 632-3) that the relatives of the victim accept ransom from his
killer; for a parallel from Bedouin society, see Abou-Zeid (1965), 254-5.

[218] On the Greeks' attitude to sex in more general terms, see Dover (1974), 205-13;
Parker (1983), 74-103; cf., more briefly, Henderson (1973), 3-5.

[219] *Il.* 2. 514, 21. 479, 22. 451; *Od.* 3. 381, 451, 8. 420, 10. 11, 17. 152, 18. 314, 19. 165,
202, 336, 583.   [220] *Il.* 22. 451; *Od.* 18. 314.

[221] *Aidoïe tamiē*: *Od.* 1. 139, 7. 175, 15. 138, 17. 94, 259.

[222] This is true of many more societies than the ancient Greek; see Pitt-Rivers (1965),
42. On this phenomenon in Hom., see Adkins (1960*a*), 36-7.

[223] See Adkins, ibid.; cf. Campbell (1965), 146; Pitt-Rivers (1965), 45; Lloyd-Jones
(1987), 6.

society, may subscribe to the standards imposed upon them without question, and be critical of the deficiencies of other women, ultimately the standards to which they adhere are laid down by men.[224] It is in adhering to these standards and in being above any slight on her honour that a woman deserves the title *aidoiē*; thus in maintaining her own honour and that cf her male protector a woman merits honour, which is recognized by *aidōs*, in return.

A woman, then, receives *aidōs* for her observance of her social role, and there is thus a degree of reciprocity in the operation of *aidōs* here, since it is, as we should expect, *aidōs* on the woman's part which helps her remain within the guidelines laid down by society. Such *aidōs* frequently manifests itself as a coyness about dealings with the opposite sex, and is employed to particularly subtle effect in the characterization of Nausicaa in *Odyssey* 6. Nausicaa, promised a husband by prophecy and anxious to meet him, employs an artifice to obtain leave from her father to go out, since, as we are told (66-7), 'she felt *aidōs* to mention fertile marriage to her dear father outright'. The marriage is 'ripe' or 'fertile', like Nausicaa herself, and it is this consciousness of incipient sexuality that produces Nausicaa's *aidōs*.

This *aidōs* colours the subsequent encounter with Odysseus. Once the two have met Nausicaa wishes Odysseus to come to her father's palace, but is unwilling to have him accompany herself and her maidservants. She knows that there are people, *huperphialoi* (excessive, vulgar people) and the familiar τις κακώτερος ('some baser person'), who will comment adversely on her conduct (274-5), and she imagines their reproaches at length (276-84). All this is strongly suggestive of *aidōs*, as are her concluding remarks (285-8): 'That is how they will speak of me, and these things would become reproaches [*oneidea*] for me. I too feel *nemesis* at any other girl who does such things, who, against her parents' wishes, mixes with men before entering openly upon marriage.' At first sight it appears that Nausicaa's concern here is simply to avoid being caught committing an offence which she has been only too willing to commit in secret. Yet she also says that she, too, would experience *nemesis* at anyone who did such things, a locution which indicates one's agreement with the standards under which one is liable to be criticized,[225] and so it seems as though there is a contradiction in this passage; Nausicaa is saying that she has standards of her own, yet it is clear that if these standards proscribe

[224] Pitt-Rivers (1965), 67.
[225] Cf. nn. 107, 113, 150, 190 above.

associating with men before marriage, then she has not acted on them, and appears less concerned with the offence than with its discovery. But this appearance is false; τοιαῦτα (such things) in 286 refers not to Nausicaa's own conduct, but to that censured by 'some baser person' in the speech Nausicaa has just imagined (276–84); and 'mixing with men before marriage' refers not to her own conduct in the poem up to that point, but to that of a girl who behaves in the manner criticized by this 'baser person'; Nausicaa, too, would feel *nemesis* against such a girl, and that is why she has no wish to invite the reproaches which such people normally receive, unjust as they would be in her own case.[226]

But where does this leave Nausicaa's *aidōs*? If we were right in recognizing the signs of *aidōs*, then it appears that in this case the emotion encompasses nothing more than simple fear of disapproval; Nausicaa knows very well how gossip can distort the most innocent of situations, and is thus determined not to give the gossips a chance; if this is *aidōs*, then it is *aidōs* which bears no relation to one's own opinion of the character of one's actions. This, of course, is perfectly possible; Nausicaa is a young person, and exhibits the sensitivity to others' opinions typical of the young in Homer;[227] her fear of what others will say in this instance is, moreover, misplaced, and her father criticizes her for leaving Odysseus to make his own way to the palace (7. 299–301). Yet the tell-tale signs of *aidōs* may hint at rather more than this. Nausicaa's outward behaviour towards Odysseus has been impeccable; but we know that she sees him as a potential husband, and the motif of marriage has already been used in the episode to colour our impressions of the encounter; we know, too, that the thought of marriage occasions *aidōs* in Nausicaa. It seems very likely, therefore, that Nausicaa's fear of unjustified reproach is another means of indicating her underlying sensitivity with regard to the opposite sex; she is sensitive to criticism precisely because the thought of beginning a relationship which will lead to marriage is uppermost in her mind. The signs of *aidōs* in this passage, then, which occur in the context of Nausicaa's emphatic demonstration of her disapproval of girls who go further than she has done, are used to remind us of the *aidōs* she manifested when first taking her leave from her father. Her modesty, it

---

[226] Hainsworth (in Heubeck, West, and Hainsworth (1988: ad loc.)) translates μίσγηται (288) as 'associates with', but this is a verb with distinct sexual connotations, and in this context it bears the same degree of innuendo as does the imagined speech of the rougher elements in the town; Rieu's translation (Harmondsworth, 1945), 'consorts with', has the right flavour; see further Cairns (1990).

[227] Cf. n. 94 and 1.3.4 above.

need hardly be said, is presented as entirely becoming, and rather fetching; her behaviour is, by her own youthful standards, very slightly *risqué*, but her father takes an indulgent view, even though he knows all about her desire to meet a husband, and ensures that the proprieties are observed by seeing to it that she is accompanied by maidservants on her outing (6. 66–70). *Aidōs* thus underlies the characterization of Nausicaa throughout this episode; it represents, behind her remarks to Odysseus, her own sense that she is treading a delicate path, but this very appreciation is used to characterize her as possessing the modesty regarded as desirable and attractive in one of her age and sex.[228]

The modesty towards the opposite sex shown by Nausicaa is not confined to unmarried women. On two occasions we find married women expressing reluctance with regard to sex even with their husbands, and doing so on the grounds that others will disapprove. In *Iliad* 3 (410) Helen refuses to go to her husband's bed—it would be *nemessēton*—and goes on to explain that it is the censure of the Trojan women that she fears (411–12). Clearly, it is simply not the right time for Helen to think of sex; she is troubled by Paris' showing in the duel with Menelaus, and no doubt the sight of them both together has caused her to reflect on her conduct in leaving Sparta. Inappropriateness of place is Hera's (feigned) reason for refusing sex with Zeus at *Iliad* 14. 330–40; if she were to sleep with Zeus in the open on Mount Ida she would be unable to return home afterwards—it would be *nemessēton*; she is, then, feigning *aidōs* at being seen in the act of love and at facing those who might have seen her.

Just as a sensitivity about sex is common to married and unmarried women, so shyness of the other sex persists in women after marriage. Penelope's *aidōs* prevents her facing the suitors alone (*Odyssey* 18. 184), while in *Odyssey* 8 shyness of sex itself and of the company of males combine to ensure that while the gods meet to see Ares and Aphrodite in bed, the goddesses remain at home out of *aidōs* (324).

The shyness towards men and coyness about sex exhibited in these passages are manifestations of women's *aidōs* in a broader sense, in that they indicate the fulfilment of some of the demands of women's honour, which is itself maintained by *aidōs*. In general, a woman's duty is to her husband or father and to the family group of which he is the head. Penelope's loyalty to Odysseus, for example, also entails loyalty

---

[228] The way in which the episode plays off surface decorum against underlying erotic tension is well brought out by Just (1989: 224–5).

to his father, and on three occasions she expresses the conviction that other women will feel *nemesis* against her should she allow Laertes to go to his grave without a shroud.[229] Her primary loyalty, however, is to her husband, and twice we find this duty described as 'feeling *aidōs* for [*aidomenē*] her husband's bed and for popular opinion' (*Odyssey* 16. 75 = 19. 527).[230] The husband's bed receives *aidōs* as a quasi-personified symbol of the marital relationship,[231] while popular opinion is the agency which helps enforce Penelope's duty to her husband and which will condemn any neglect of that duty. It is significant that the participle has these two objects, for Penelope's *aidōs* for her husband and their marriage bed suggests a more personal and internal obligation than does *aidōs* at what other people might say. Obviously, popular opinion establishes and upholds the principle that it is a woman's obligation to remain loyal to her husband, but the fact that Penelope venerates the relationship itself suggests that, for her, the standard laid down by society is also a personal conviction.

Along with Helen and, to a lesser extent, Aphrodite, Clytemnestra is a prime example of a wife who felt no *aidōs* for her husband's bed, and it is she who is contrasted with the faithful Penelope in *Odyssey* 11.[232] Agamemnon tells Odysseus, in lines 432-4 of that book, how Clytemnestra has poured *aischos* on herself and all women to come (even the good ones), and it is clearly *aischos* of this kind that Penelope's *aidōs* forestalls. Clytemnestra's lack of *aidōs*, on the other hand, is expressed in Agamemnon's description of her as 'dog-faced' in line 424.[233] Agamemnon also draws the contrast between his wife and Odysseus', who is described as *pinutē*, *periphrōn*, and as 'knowing good plans in her *phrenes*' (445-6); all these terms refer to ideas of 'good sense', and this good sense promotes exactly the same conduct as *aidōs*; the link between good sense and *aidōs* will be explored below.

The requirement to be loyal to the head of the household, however, extends beyond the kinship group to other members of the *oikos*; at *Odyssey* 22. 424 twelve of Odysseus' maidservants are said to have 'embarked upon *anaideiē*' by consorting with the suitors, and these are marked out for punishment. Their offence is of a sexual nature, but more importantly it is also one of disloyalty to their master; this disloyalty and this *anaideiē*, however, are also manifested in their

---

229 *Od.* 2. 101, 19. 146, 24. 136.
230 εὐνήν τ' αἰδομένη πόσιος δήμοιό τ' φῆμιν.
231 Cf. nn. 133, 181 above.
232 Cf. Roisman (1984), 55-6.
233 Cf. *Od.* 4. 145, 8. 319, and n. 151 above.

disregard of the *timē* of those (their superiors) who attempted to retain the loyalty of the household for Odysseus, since the loyal servant Eurycleia explains her statement about the maids' *anaideiē* with the amplification, 'paying *timē* neither to me nor to Penelope herself' (425). The women's disloyalty, then, also encompasses a failure to accord others the *timē* they deserve, and it is this failure that is designated *anaideiē*, as it is in the case of the suitors and in that of Agamemnon when he fails to observe the *timē* of Achilles.[234] By their conduct they are also said to dishonour Odysseus himself (418) and to have 'poured *oneidea* on' Telemachus and Penelope (463-4); their disloyalty is an insult in itself, entailing as it does disregard for the instructions of their superiors, and, although as *anaideiē* the maids' conduct is discreditable for themselves, it also discredits the head of the household, since failure to secure the loyalty of one's inferiors may be taken as an indication of weakness. The notion of a community of honour is thus also relevant within the household, and particularly relevant with regard to the behaviour of its female members.

1.4.2. *Sexuality*

A certain amount of coyness regarding sex does seem to have been common to both sexes; the use of *aidoia* (neuter plural adjective) in the sense 'genitals' occurs only once in Homer (*Iliad* 13. 568), but a similar sensibility is implied by two instances of the noun *aidōs* in a similar concrete sense.[235] Both these uses are further evidence of the flexibility in the usage of these terms; the *aidoia* are not deserving of *aidōs* in the same way as a suppliant, say, yet they are a cause of *aidōs*, while in the case of the two concrete uses of the noun, *aidōs* is not a subjective reaction, but an object of that reaction; *aidōs* can be used of that which arouses *aidōs*, much as words like 'fear' or 'shame' can describe both subjective reactions and objects of reactions in English.[236]

Propriety in a sexual context might also be the issue at *Odyssey* 6. 221-2, where Odysseus declares that, out of *aidōs*, he will not allow himself to be washed by Nausicaa's female attendants, who would thus see him naked. The commentators point out that men are more than once bathed by women, both slave and free, in the *Odyssey*,[237] and it is

[234] Cf. 1.3.3 above.   [235] *Il.* 2. 262, 22. 75.   [236] Cf. n. 44 above.
[237] See Hainsworth (in Heubeck, West, and Hainsworth (1988)), on 6. 217-22, and cf. Thornton (1970), 40-1; Scott (1980), 25 and n. 52.

suggested that Odysseus' *aidōs* is motivated by his present filthy
condition (mentioned in 220); von Erffa, however, refers to lines 135–
6, where Odysseus' approach to the young women, in spite of his
nakedness, is excused as a matter of necessity, and the natural
implication of these lines is that, in normal circumstances, a man
should not appear naked before young women. In the other passages
in which men are washed by women, the context is either one of *xenia*,
and the guest is washed in the house of his host, or the master of the
house is washed in his own house by one of his own servants; this is
not the case here (Odysseus has not yet been accepted as a *xeinos* in
Alcinous' palace), and it may be that it was considered improper for a
man to be seen naked by women except in certain well-defined
situations.

1.5. AIDŌS, 'INTELLIGENCE', AND EXCESS

1.5.1. *'Intelligence'*

We have already noted a certain difference of moral atmosphere
between the *Iliad* and the *Odyssey*, in which there is, for example, a
greater expressed concern for the co-operative virtues. This is,
however, a difference of degree, not of kind; the *Iliad* is not blind to the
desirability of these qualities, but there is obviously less scope for them
in a society at war than in one at peace, and, indeed, the distinction
between peace and war may go a long way towards explaining many of
the apparent differences of outlook.[238] A more profound difference,
perhaps, lies in the greater degree to which the gods of the *Odyssey*
have an interest in the justice men show in their dealings with each
other, and this will be considered towards the end of this section.

As we have seen, several passages dealing with aspects of proper
behaviour in the *Odyssey* lay great stress on 'good sense'; Agamemnon's commendation of Penelope's loyalty, for example (11. 445–6),
emphasized qualities which are conventionally translated by words
like 'wise' and 'sensible'. This association of apparently intellectual
qualities with proper behaviour, and so with *aidōs*, is not confined to
the *Odyssey*,[239] but is much more evident in that poem, particularly in

---

[238] Cf. Pearson (1962), 48, 219 n. 2.
[239] See *Il.* 15. 128–9, where Ares' lack of restraint is attributed to a lack of both *noos*
(mind, understanding) and *aidōs*. Cf. *Il.* 6. 350–2, where Paris has no regard for *nemesis*

the cases of Penelope and Telemachus, both of whom are virtually types of the good sense and *aidōs* appropriate to those in their respective positions, and both of whom attract words like *pinutos* and *pepnumenos*, etc. In *Odyssey* 4, for example, Telemachus' shyness in facing Menelaus (158–60) is described by his companion Peisistratus as *nemesis* at appearing over-bold, and explained by the fact that he is *saophrōn*.[240] The context is one of emotion, and Telemachus' *saophrosunē* explains his shyness, yet *saophrōn* need not describe an emotional disposition or mean 'bashful' here; the word takes on these connotations from the context, but elsewhere does not imply much more than do other terms which commend good sense. In some way, then, good sense conduces to *aidōs*. Similarly, lack of sense may coexist with lack of *aidōs*, as in *Odyssey* 17 (454), where Antinous, who has shown a flagrant lack of *aidōs* in his words to the beggar, is charged with lack of *phrenes*.

Just as Antinous is condemned for his lack of sense in his treatment of the beggar, so the herdsman, Philoetius, whose reaction is a true manifestation of *aidōs*, is commended for his good sense (*Odyssey* 20. 227–8): 'Herdsman, since you seem to be neither a bad [*kakos*] nor a senseless [*aphrōn*] man, but rather I myself recognize that wisdom [*pinutē*] attends your *phrenes*, . . .' A man who does not treat strangers well is thus not only *aphrōn* but also *kakos*. We might well compare 18. 383, where Odysseus charges Eurymachus, who has just acted without *aidōs*, indeed (381) with *hubris*, with consorting with men who are 'worthless and not *agathoi*'.[241] We are thus confronted with usages of *agathos* and *kakos* which, based as they are on the possession of co-operative moral virtues, differ sharply from those stressed by Adkins, undoubtedly the majority, which commend (or decry the absence of) qualities such as ability in warfare, efficiency, wealth, and noble birth.[242] We could conceivably regard the co-operative uses as 'persuasive definitions', but such an expedient is inadvisable when we have no way of knowing whether or not the society for which the poem was composed would regard such uses as legitimate; if anything, the general tone of the *Odyssey*, which assumes that its audience will condemn the suitors, conventional *aretē* and all, suggests that it would.

and has no *phrenes* (wits, sense, (?) literally, 'diaphragm'). Ares' *phrenes* are also impaired in 15. 128–9. On *noos* and *phrenes* see E. L. Harrison (1960), 71–4, 74–5; Schmitt (1990), 174–221, *passim*.

[240] See 1.3.4 above.
[241] Cf. Long (1970), 126 n. 16, 154.
[242] Adkins (1960*a*), 31–3, etc.

It seems we must simply reckon with two uses, one which is both socially descriptive and evaluative of competitive qualities, the other purely evaluative, referring to co-operative qualities.[243] Given these two uses, and the failure of Odyssean usage to conform to a neat and tidy pattern, it is quite possible for the suitors to remain *agathoi* in the former sense in spite of being called 'not *agathoi*' in the latter, and it is important that the terms *agathos* and *kakos* can be used of alternative criteria of excellence, criteria based on the possession of 'good sense' and *aidōs*.

Certainly, there are not many instances of the co-operative application of *agathos* and *kakos* as qualifications of persons in the poems, but there are non-personal, neuter uses which must be considered. We have already looked at Penelope's statement (*Odyssey* 18. 215–25) that Telemachus' failure to protect his guest revealed his lack of sense and would implicate him in *aischos* and *lōbē*; Telemachus accepts his mother's criticism, but wishes to defend himself against her attack on his *phrenes* and his *noēma* (intelligence); hence (228–32): 'But in my *thumos* I understand and know both good and bad. Previously I was still a foolish infant. Yet I cannot contrive everything that is wise, for these men, with their evil intentions, surrounding me, one from one place, one from another, drive me to distraction, and I have no helpers.' Telemachus, then, also sees the impulse to protect a guest in terms of good sense, and since to protect a guest, and to be aware of the consequences for one's reputation of not doing so, are both reactions with which *aidōs* is concerned, there is once more an obvious link between acting in accordance with *aidōs* and good sense. We should notice, therefore, that Telemachus' knowledge encompasses 'good and bad' (*esthla* and *ta chereia*, terms synonymous with *agatha* and *kaka* (neuter plurals)). Now, Adkins[244] points out that neuter usages of *agathos* (*agathon*) and *kakos* (*kakon*) do not affect his thesis on *aretē* as the most admired quality because, 'to say of an action "it is *agathon* (*kakon*) to do x" is simply to say that it is beneficial (harmful) to do x, without passing any moral judgement on the rightness or wrongness of x'. This may be true as far as it goes, but neuter uses of these adjectives and their synonyms are not confined to uses of this kind, but can take many different forms. In the present passage the suitors are described as 'thinking *kaka*' (κακὰ φρονέοντες), a regular idiom for 'with harmful intent', the *kaka* in this case being intended towards their patient. Similarly, at *Odyssey* 1. 43 'thinking *agatha*' means 'well-

<hr/>

[243] Cf., e.g., the adj. 'noble' in English.   [244] (1960*a*), 31.

disposed'; yet at *Iliad* 6. 161–2 Bellerophon's 'thinking *agatha*' is not a reference to his attitude towards someone else, but either a description of the moral character of his thoughts or an indication that he is consulting his own interest ('thinking advantageously to himself'); at *Odyssey* 2. 67 the *kaka erga* ('bad deeds') of the suitors are mentioned, and the sense is clearly not that these deeds are disadvantageous only to Telemachus or even only to the suitors, but that they are in a much more general sense socially and morally unacceptable.[245] Likewise here it would be to misrepresent the tone of the passage to suggest that Telemachus replies to his mother's criticism merely by pointing out that he knows what is good for him. Telemachus knows what he should do in order to act in the manner expected of him, and it is in that sense that one course of action is *esthlon* and another *kakon*. In criticizing her son's 'intelligence' Penelope is urging him to react both to the fact that he has failed in his duty to his guest and to the possibility that others will see this as grounds for reproach, while Telemachus, in pointing out that he knows *esthla* and *ta chereia*, wishes to impress upon his mother his awareness that it is not *esthlon* that a guest should be treated as the beggar has been, because it violates a norm which is portrayed as universal. If we must translate *esthla* as 'advantageous', we cannot legitimately complete the sense by adding 'for me', since Telemachus is not simply consulting his own interest; if we translate 'advantageous (for society in general)' then we should notice how much closer this comes to 'right'. Telemachus is saying that he knows what the standards of society are and how they affect him.

This is not to say, however, that what is good for society in general cannot coincide with (or be represented as coinciding with) what is good for individuals; we have seen that proper conduct is often justified in terms of expediency, and it is, indeed, an underlying message of the *Odyssey* that self-interest is promoted by proper behaviour.[246] Yet self-interest is not the sole object of the 'good sense' of the characters of the poem,[247] nor is 'good' conduct merely that which promotes one's own good, even though it may be to promote one's own good to behave in the way expected of one.

Telemachus' 'intelligence', then, allows him to perceive what is 'good', and the aim of good sense in general is the recognition and

---

[245] Cf. 8. 329, 9. 477, 14. 284, 16. 380, 17. 158, 20. 16, 24. 199, 326; and see n. 203 above, on the adv. *kakōs*. On *kakos* etc. in the *Od.*, see Hankey (1990), 87–91.

[246] Explicit at 22. 372–4.

[247] Cf. in general, O'Brien (1967), 32–3.

fulfilment of the requirements of society. Thus *aidōs* and intelligence
(loosely defined) conduce to the same ends. This does not, however,
mean that *aidōs* is an intellectual quality, nor does it imply that
Homeric man adopted an intellectualist approach to ethics. It is
salutary to point out[248] that terms like *noos* and *phrenes* cover a wide
range in Homer, from the intellectual to the emotional or dispositional, and that when, for example, such a term covers both intellect
and character, it does not subsume the latter under the former. Good
sense is not necessarily austerely intellectual or calculative in Homer,
and what one 'knows' can describe one's character, especially moral
character, as well as one's intellect; Telemachus' knowledge of good
things is like Polyphemus' knowledge of lawless things (*Odyssey* 9. 189,
428); as Polyphemus acts consistently in a lawless way, is a lawless
person, so Telemachus will act consistently in a 'good' way, will be a
'good' person. Awareness of the standards of one's society is expressed
in terms of this 'knowledge', and is regarded as an ingrained feature of
one's character, a kind of 'knowledge' which is imparted by the process
of socialization and which implies the ability to construe one's
situation properly in accordance with the norms adopted in the course
of that process; *aidōs* is prompted by and relies on this awareness, and
inhibits any impulse to act contrary to it, and thus it is no surprise and
no problem that good sense and *aidōs* produce the same results.

1.5.2. *Appropriateness and Excess*

We saw in section 1.1 above that the terms which place conduct in the
category of that which is liable to arouse popular disapproval refer
fundamentally to appearances. Society's condemnation of inappropriate conduct is thus of a quasi-aesthetic nature, based on 'how things

---

[248] As does O'Brien (1967), ch. 1; cf. E. L. Harrison (1960), 67. O'Brien takes to task
scholars such as Dodds (1951: 17) and Gould (1955: 7), who see Socrates' identification
of morality and knowledge (of one's ultimate self-interest) foreshadowed in Homer.
Dodds himself (ibid.) notes that 'knowing' covers both knowledge and disposition in
Homer, but still tends to assume that the former is prior to the latter. Pearson (1962: 60)
follows Dodds, but is less guilty of the assumption that the overlap indicates that
Homeric Greek sees disposition in terms of knowledge. (In his discussion of *noos* etc. in
general, 52–60, Pearson stresses the importance of good sense in the evaluation of a
person's worth; one might remember that both *aphrōn* and *kakos* are used by Odysseus at
Od. 20. 227 to refer to the disposition to behave improperly.) On *noos* etc. and their place
in the depiction of the psychology and selfhood of Homeric characters, see now the
thorough analysis of Schmitt (1990), 126–228.

look'; one consequence of this is that excess is condemned and moderation, that which conforms most closely to the norm, is approved.[249] As a sensitivity which rejects actions and situations designated 'ugly' or 'unseemly' *aidōs* may thus be operative over a whole range of situations which do not belong to any of the categories to which it is particularly relevant. In *Odyssey* 1. 227-9, by now a familiar passage, excess, appropriateness, and good sense interact with the complex of terms based on *aidōs*; the suitors perpetrate 'uglinesses' (*aischea*, 229), they act 'with excessive *hubris*' (ὑβρίζοντες ὑπερφιάλως, 227), and their conduct is opposed to that of which a sensible man (*pinutos*) would approve; that the *pinutos*' disapproval is described as *nemesis*, moreover, suggests that in other individuals such excess might be inhibited by *aidōs*.

The suitors, it need hardly be said, are cast as *anaideis* throughout the poem, and many people express their *nemesis* at their actions. Apart from their *anaideiē* they are condemned for two other major vices, their *hubris* and their *atasthaliē*, both of which imply going too far.[250] At 20. 169-71 their behaviour is described in terms of all three: 'Eumaeus, I hope the gods punish [or 'extract *timē* for'] the *lōbē* [disfigurement] which these men in their *hubris* and *atasthaliē* [ὑβρίζοντες ἀτάσθαλα] contrive in another man's house; they have no share of *aidōs*.' A lack of *aidōs*, then, may lead to or be accompanied by acts of *hubris* and *atasthaliē*, and, indeed, these two vices, implying lack of inhibition and failure to respect the *timē* of others, operate as rough autonyms of *aidōs*.[251] Since the dangers and undesirability of these vices are stressed in prominent passages at the beginning and end of the poem,[252] the benefits of possessing and showing *aidōs* emerge by contrast as a central theme, a theme which is pursued throughout the work by means of a paradigm *aidōs*-situation, that of guest-friendship.

Abhorrence of excess, however, is not a quality peculiar to the *Odyssey*, although it is perhaps more prominent there than in the *Iliad* (war gives more scope for excess than does peace); we do, in fact, find similar notions in the *Iliad* and, indeed, a case could be made for the proposition that moderation and avoidance of excess are as central to that poem as they are to the *Odyssey*.[253] In particular, the conduct of

[249] On appropriateness, moderation, and excess in Homer, see Pearson (1962), 39-41; Long (1970), 135-9; cf. Greene (1944), 20.

[250] See Greene (1944), 18-23.

[251] Cf. Long (1970), 136.

[252] 1. 32-5, 24. 454-60; on the former, see Dodds (1951), 32.

[253] Cf. Thornton (1984), 142.

Achilles has, by the closing books of the poem, become excessive to the point of savagery; Priam describes him as '*atasthalos* and violent' (*Iliad* 22. 418), and, after his excess has taken the form of dragging Hector's body daily round the walls of Troy, even the gods begin to worry about his conduct. Apollo is the first to voice their concern, and he does so in terms which should be familiar by now, complaining of Achilles' lack of sense (he has no *phrenes enaisimoi* or *noēma*, 24. 40), and of the loss of his senses of *aidōs* and pity (*eleos*, 44);[254] without *aidōs* Achilles has become virtually a beast, and he 'knows wild things, like a lion' (41).[255] Achilles' loss of *aidōs*, his departure from the norms of ordinary and predictable behaviour, begins in Book 9, where he rejects appeals to pity and to *aidōs* (302, 640) and receives a veiled warning about the possibility of *nemesis* (523), but the real increase in savagery and excess comes after the death of Patroclus;[256] the lack of *aidōs* against which Apollo threatens *nemesis* (24. 53) is not only a lack of compunction for Hector, but a lack of regard for the normal limits of human conduct; Achilles' behaviour is not simply inconsiderate, it is unnatural and futile (52–4).

This passage, then, indicates that similar standards with regard to appropriateness and excess obtain in both the *Iliad* and the *Odyssey*. It is also significant that Apollo envisages the *nemesis* of the gods as a direct result of Achilles' conduct;[257] elsewhere in the *Iliad*[258] any *nemesis* the gods feel towards mortals is based on slights they feel themselves to have suffered; but here it seems that the reaction is to be

---

[254] Apollo also comments on the ambivalence of *aidōs* here (45); this line is certainly much more appropriate in the other context in which it occurs (Hes. *WD* 318), but the question of 'interpolation' in Hom. is vexed, and we can hardly be sure that the Hesiodic passage has influenced the present one, that the two do not share a common proverbial origin, or that line 45 did not stand in its present place when the *Iliad* was given the form in which we have it.

[255] Hence von Erffa's statement that '*aidōs* distinguishes man from beast' (1937: 36; cf. Redfield (1975), 211). Similarly, inanimate objects (rocks and boulders) are sometimes described as *anaidēs* (*Il.* 4. 521, 13. 139; *Od.* 11. 598), presumably because they are fixed and unchanging and so bereft of the peculiarly human and social quality of *aidōs* (perhaps with particular reference to the impossibility of bending the will of a rock by entreaty).

[256] Reflected in the prominence of the theme of the mutilation of the corpse; see Segal (1971), esp. 18 ff.

[257] Not all the gods are prepared to share Apollo's *nemesis* (see 24. 56–63), and the dispute between Ap. and Hera as to whether the gods should come to the aid of Hec. is certainly conducted on the terms of which of the two, Hec. or Ach., is more their *philos*; yet it is clear that the *nemesis* which Ap. threatens is to be directed at Ach.'s excess, not at his maltreatment of a *philos* of the gods, even though it is also part of his argument that the gods should honour Hec. because he has honoured them.

[258] e.g. 4. 507, 8. 198.

directed simply at the excessiveness and inappropriateness of Achilles' behaviour. Such a reaction, therefore, does not differ from the *nemesis* a mortal might feel at similar conduct, but it is significant in itself that the gods are seen to be taking an interest in human propriety not unlike that which might be shown by a man.[259] With this we might compare *Odyssey* 14. 284, where Zeus *xeinios* is said to feel *nemesis* at *kaka erga*;[260] in his capacity as protector of guests Zeus already has an interest in human conduct, but only in so far as maltreatment of guests is felt to infringe his prerogative;[261] here, however, the natural implication is that he dislikes *kaka erga* in general. *Nemesis* in these passages therefore stands midway in its development from purely human disapproval to an exclusively divine reaction,[262] a development which seems to take place because the gods were first felt to share human standards, then to impose them.

The feeling that the gods share mortals' disapproval of excess is widespread in the *Odyssey*; at 14. 83-4 Eumaeus expresses his belief that the gods 'dislike'[263] *schetlia erga* (harsh deeds) and prefer *dikē* (justice) and moderation (*aisima erga*).[264] From this there follows a general assumption that the gods will have a hand in the punishment of the suitors;[265] in 22. 413-15 and 23. 63-7 this assumption occurs together with a reference to the suitors' failure to accord others the *timē* they deserve, a failure which indicates their lack of *aidōs*, while in the second of these passages it is said that they have been punished for their *atasthaliē*, which might also imply lack of *aidōs*.[266] Breaches of *aidōs* may thus be reasons for divine punishment.

---

[259] Cf. Redfield (1975), 213.

[260] Cf. n. 245 above.

[261] Cf. Burkert (1985), 248.

[262] In Hesiod *nemesis* is not yet an exclusively divine anger, though this is the dominant idea in the personification at *Th.* 223; in another personification, however, at *WD* 200, *nemesis* is popular disapproval, the correlate of *aidōs* (see Wilamowitz, 1959, i. 350 n. 1; Verdenius (1985), ad loc.). Elsewhere in Hes. the term has the same significance as in Hom.; the gods can resent infringements of their own honour (*WD* 756) and share the *nemesis* of men (*WD* 303-4, fr. 70. 27 MW), but *nemesis* is still mainly human disapproval of other humans (fr. 197. 8, fr. 204. 81-4 MW). At Tyrt. 10. 26 West *nemesēton* implies *nemesis* as popular disapproval, but *nemesis* fairly quickly becomes an exclusively religious concept (Thgn. 118-2; Pind. *Ol.* 8. 86; *Pyth.* 10. 42-4), until its use no longer concerns us.

[263] οὐ φιλέουσιν, the only instance of the verb *philein* (elsewhere 'entertain', 'treat/behave as *philos*') in the sense of approval of an abstract entity. See Kakridis (1963), 40.

[264] On the 'moral' sense of *dikē* here, see Dickie (1978), 96-7. On *dikē* as 'proper behaviour' in the *Od.*, see n. 195 above.

[265] Cf. Burkert (1985), 249.

[266] Cf. 24. 351-2, where Laertes is of the opinion that the suitors have suffered the reward of their *atasthalos hubris*.

This point emerges more clearly from Telemachus' appeal to the Ithacesians at 2. 64–7: 'Feel *nemesis* yourselves, and show *aidōs* for your neighbours. Fear the wrath of the gods, lest they cause some change [or 'change their attitude'] in their resentment at *kaka erga*.' Telemachus asks the people to feel *nemesis* at the destruction of his inheritance, most probably directed at themselves for allowing it to happen, but possibly also at the suitors who are responsible for it.[267] They are also urged to show *aidōs* with regard to the opinions of neighbouring communities (the community would have an interest in the status of its leaders and communities might vie with each other for prestige). If, however, it is occasion for *aidōs* and *nemesis* towards oneself merely to acquiesce in the commission of misdeeds like those of the suitors, it is obviously a major breach of *aidōs* and lack of concern for *nemesis* actually to perpetrate such misdeeds; thus the wrath of the gods at *kaka erga*, which Telemachus mentions as his third point, is clearly directed at offences proceeding from the suitors' lack of *aidōs*, while there appears also to be a hint that, should the Ithacesians be implicated in the punishment to come,[268] they will only have their own lack of *aidōs* and self-directed *nemesis* to blame.

It also emerges from this passage, as from *Odyssey* 14. 284, that the gods dislike *kaka erga* in general;[269] in the latter case it was Zeus *xeinios* who took an interest in such deeds, and one might wish to consider the deeds in question as infringements of his prerogative as protector of guests; at 2. 64–7, however, the connection with guest-friendship is more tenuous, and it seems unlikely that the gods are to be envisaged as regarding the suitors' conduct as an offence against themselves. The same is true of 22. 38–40, where Odysseus charges the suitors, 'You wooed a man's wife while he was alive, neither fearing the gods, who inhabit broad heaven, nor expecting any *nemesis* of men in the future.' Wooing another man's wife while he is still alive is not one of the particular offences against *aidōs* discussed above, nor are the gods *specifically* protectors of the marital relationship as they are of guests and suppliants, yet Odysseus states it as a fact that both the wrath of the gods and the *nemesis* of men would result from the suitors' illicit wooing of Penelope. If the suitors had no regard for the *nemesis* of men

---

[267] Cf. n. 120 above.

[268] West (in Heubeck, West, and Hainsworth (1988), on 67) adduces the suffering of Troy for the misdeeds of Paris, and of the Greek army for Ajax Oeliades' rape of Cassandra as parallels for the punishment of wrongdoers overtaking the whole community; cf. also Hes. *WD* 240–1.

[269] On *kaka erga* (as opposed to *kaka*), cf. Hankey (1990), 89–90.

then they were *anaideis*, and the act of wooing another man's wife is presumably felt to be occasion for *nemesis* not only because it dishonours another, but also because it transgresses the normal order of things and is 'inappropriate'. Anything of which others disapprove, then, may arouse *aidōs* in those who are sensitive to that emotion, and thus *aidōs* might cover a range of situations much wider than consideration of those with which it is chiefly concerned would suggest.

It is also assumed in this passage that the gods share men's disapproval, and so, in theory at least, any breach of *aidōs* may excite divine anger and lead to divine punishment. The gods might therefore enter into any situation in which *aidōs* is relevant; yet it is not true to say that *aidōs* is a religious scruple, for only in a few well-defined situations in the poems (those of guest-friendship and supplication) do characters experience *aidōs* for the gods, and in these cases respect for the gods is both an aspect of respect for the institution in general (in the same way one can feel *aidōs* for some other feature of the relationship, such as the table or the hall where hospitality is offered) and a response to superior power and status that is not qualitatively different from a similar response to a powerful human superior. There are thus no exclusively religious uses of *aidōs* in Homer,[270] and when *aidōs* is urged as an appropriate response, as at *Odyssey* 2. 64-7, its explicit focus is normally other human beings; when consideration of divine resentment of an offence is urged, words of fearing, rather than *aidōs*, are used.

1.6. OTHER TERMS

On pages 23-7 of his study von Erffa considers other terms which approximate to *aidōs* in some of their uses; these, in the main, are terms which express an idea of inhibition together with a reference to respect for another's status; in most cases they are, as *aidōs* is not, operative in the sphere of man's response to the divine.

---

[270] Contrast Hooker (1987), who sees the 'I respect' sense of *aidōs* as prior to the 'I feel shame before' sense, and regards the former as 'religious awe'; there is no basis for this in the poems.

1.6.1. Hazomai

Most examples of the verb *hazomai* are concerned with the proper reaction to the gods[271] or their representatives.[272] In this sense it does resemble *aideomai* in that it is an inhibitory response to the special status of its object, and it inhibits disregard for, and maltreatment of, that object. Its inhibitory force and its connection with the numinous are shown at *Iliad* 6. 266–7, where Hector explains:

> χερσὶ δ᾽ ἀνίπτοισιν Διὶ λείβειν αἴθοπα οἶνον
> ἅζομαι.[273]

Like *aideomai*, therefore, *hazomai* can express inhibition with the infinitive, or respect for another with an object, but the reference to ritual clearly sets it apart. It can, however, be used in a context where aideomai might also occur, provided that context is one of those in which *aidōs* is specifically linked to the divine sphere; hence Odysseus' warning to the Cyclops (*Odyssey* 9. 478–9) that he will be punished by Zeus and the gods because he has no scruples at eating his guests (ἐπεὶ ξείνους οὐχ ἅζεο ... ἐσθέμεναι).

1.6.2. Opizomai

The *opis* of the gods, originally their all-seeing eye, comes to denote their anger.[274] If a connotation of 'seeing' or 'being seen' is retained in the term, then, given the link in Homer between *aidōs* and an audience, it is highly appropriate that one can *aideisthai* the *opis* of the gods (*Odyssey* 21. 28, in the context of guest-friendship). The verb *opizomai*, however, works much as does *hazomai*,[275] although it has no inhibitory use with the infinitive. Thus it may approximate to *aideomai* in those religious contexts in which *aidōs* is appropriate; fearing the wrath of Zeus *xeinios* at *Odyssey* 14. 283–4 might amount to the same thing as feeling *aidōs* towards the same object. The verb has a human object at *Iliad* 22. 332, but this exceptional use presumably has a point;

---

[271] *Il.* 1. 21, 5. 434, 830.
[272] *Od.* 9. 200.
[273] 'I shrink from pouring wine to Zeus with unwashed hands.'
[274] See von Erffa (1937), 25–6.
[275] Ibid.

Achilles reminds Hector, "ἐμὲ δ᾽ οὐδὲν ὀπίζεο νόσφιν ἐόντα",[276] and it seems that Achilles regards his wrath as equivalent to that of a god.[277]

1.6.3. Sebas

Closest to *aidōs* of all those terms considered by von Erffa is *sebas*, a concept which will also demand our attention at later stages of this study.[278] Like *aidōs*, *sebas* can acknowledge the status of others and inhibit action; in Homer the noun seems always to be used of the subjective reaction to some special aspect of another person, of a material object, or of a situation, although in later literature it comes more readily to denote the quality in the other person, etc. which arouses the reaction in others. In the formulaic expression, '*sebas* holds me as I look on',[279] *sebas* seems to be a feeling of wonder or astonishment aroused by the impressive or the unusual, perhaps akin to *aidōs* but not clearly expressing the idea of respect which *aidōs* conveys. At *Iliad* 18. 178–80, however, it appears as a virtual synonym; in urging Achilles to react to the possibility of the mutilation of Patroclus' body Iris exhorts: 'Let *sebas* come to your *thumos* that Patroclus should become a plaything for Trojan dogs; yours is the *lōbē*, if the body goes disfigured.' If *sebas*, then, can be a feeling aroused by the prospect of disgrace, it must be very close to *aidōs*. The usage of the verbs derived from *sebas* confirms the closeness of the two concepts; twice in *Iliad* 6 (167, 416–17) *sebazomai* expresses, as might *aideomai*, inhibition of the impulse to harm another of a particular status; in the former passage Proetus refrains from killing Bellerophon, and in the latter Achilles refrains from stripping his victim, Eëtion, of his arms. At *Iliad* 4. 242 the other verb, *sebomai*, is used in the passage in which *sebas* comes closest to *aidōs*:

Ἀργεῖοι ἰόμωροι, ἐλεγχέες, οὔ νυ σέβεσθε;[280]

---

[276] 'You did not fear my wrath in my absence.'

[277] Cf. the use of *mēnis* of Ach.'s wrath in the poem, otherwise typically of divine anger; cf. Schein (1984), 91, 121 n. 4.

[278] *Sebas* is studied (along with *phobos* (fear) and, occasionally, *aidōs*) in a series of articles by Jäkel: (1972) on Homer and early poetry; (1975) on Aesch.; (1979) on Soph.; (1980) on Eur. These constitute useful collections of evidence, but their observations, analysis, and conclusions are generally pedestrian.

[279] *Od.* 3. 123, 4. 75, 142 (with fem. part), 6. 161, 8. 384.

[280] 'Argive archers [or 'mere boasters'; see Kirk (1985), ad loc.], you disgraces, are you not ashamed?'

The implication of cowardice in *elenchees* clearly marks this exhortation to *sebas* as very similar to the more common exhortation to *aidōs*. *Sebas* and *aidōs* are thus obviously very close; both, I should hazard a guess, are, at bottom, occurrent emotions, and probably only one familiar at first hand with their occurrence and with the kind of situation in which they occur could reliably tell the difference. In Homer both accompany a reluctance to embark on conduct which is instinctively found unacceptable, and both occur at the prospect of disgrace; *sebas*-verbs, however, do not occur with a general 'other people' as their object, and so have not the explicit connection that *aidōs* often has with the judgement of others; nor does *sebas* share quite the specific connotations of *aidōs* as a reaction to suppliants or guests, for example, and it seems to involve less of a positive regard for the status of others *vis-à-vis* one's own. It is interesting to note that while *sebas* shares with *aidōs* an inhibitory aspect and a reference to disgrace in Homer, in later literature it is in the sense of respect for others of a particular status that the two concepts will overlap.

1.6.4. Aischunomai

I have left consideration of the three uses of *aischunomai* till last, in order to consider the question of the degree to which that verb may be seen as synonymous with *aideomai*. In two of these three passages there can be no question but that the verbs are synonymous. The likelihood is that *aideomai* and *aischos/aischros* are cognate, and certainly *aideomai* works as a reaction to the commission of deeds which may be described as *aischron*, *aischea*, or which may involve one in *aischos* (disgrace) or invite the *aischea* (insults) of others; *aischunomai*, on the other hand, is clearly a derivative of *aischos/aischros* and is probably a later formation than *aideomai*; nevertheless, it refers to the same reaction to the prospect of disgrace or humiliation expressed in terms of *aischos* or *aischron*. In *Odyssey* 7 Odysseus explains why he did not accompany Nausicaa to her father's palace; gallantly he represents the decision as his rather than the girl's (305-6): 'But I was unwilling, out of fear and shame [δείσας αἰσχυνόμενός τε], in case your *thumos* should take offence to see us.' Here the familiar connection with fear and the reference to Alcinous' disapproval mark out *aischunomenos* as synonymous with *aido(u)menos*, and the fear of popular criticism to which Odysseus refers (307) is exactly that which Nausicaa articulated earlier (6. 273–88) in terms which were clear indication of her *aidōs*.

At *Odyssey* 21. 323–9 *aischunomai* is even more obviously a synonym of *aideomai*; the participle governs "φάτιν ἀνδρῶν ἠδὲ γυναικῶν" ('what people say'),[281] and the familiar fear of what 'some baser person' may say is expressed, his reproaches summarized by *elenchea* in 329. At 18. 12, however, the situation seems less transparent; Irus tells the beggar Odysseus that he is being urged to drag him away, and goes on, "ἐγὼ δ' αἰσχύνομαι ἔμπης".[282] If *aischunomai* were to be equivalent to *aideomai* here, we should expect the phrase to express Irus' reluctance to treat a beggar with violence, and, indeed, there is nothing in the text to indicate that this is not the meaning, but if Irus really is taunting Odysseus (9), then such compunction might seem out of place, although it might be that feigned scruple is part of the taunt. Von Erffa, however, believes that Irus is saying that he considers it *aischron* for himself to become involved with so menial a task, and thus insults Odysseus by claiming that it is beneath his dignity to expel him.[283] This does seem to fit, but it is not certain, and even if it were, it is not impossible that *aideomai* should convey the same sense. The evaluation which is constitutive of the emotion of *aidōs*, and thus implied by the verb *aideomai*, entails the thought that a given situation or action is *aischron*, or unseemly; every instance of the verb *aideomai* with a following infinitive will entail the placing of the action expressed by the infinitive in the category of the unseemly; and so it is not impossible that *aideomai* could be pushed to bear the sense which von Erffa postulates for *aischunomai* here. I should not, therefore, use this passage as evidence for any fundamental difference in the function and significance of the two verbs.

1.7. CONCLUSION

This chapter has shown, I think, that Homeric society is one in which standards of honour dominate, that these standards are broad and inclusive, and that there is no basis for any hard and fast distinction between competitive and co-operative virtues in the terms used to evaluate conduct in accordance with these inclusive standards of

---

[281] Cf. αἰδομένη . . . δήμοιό τε φῆμιν at 16. 75, 19. 527.
[282] 'I, however, am ashamed to do so.'
[283] (1937), 23.

honour. A wide range of behaviour, both competitive and co-operative, is brought within the compass of the honourable and the dishonourable by the use of words of seemliness and unseemliness in its evaluation. *Aidōs* is intimately connected with this inclusive concept of honour as a concern for one's own honour (in both competitive and co-operative contexts) and for that of others. For reasons already given, I feel the designation of Homeric society as a 'shame-culture' is misleading, but the importance of honour in that society can hardly be overstressed. No doubt many who call the Homeric society a 'shame-culture' are responding to precisely this fact, but such a practice has the disastrous consequence of obscuring what the application of the label is supposed to illuminate, namely the respect in which a 'shame-culture' can be said to differ from a 'guilt-culture'; and if the application of the label brings with it the criteria which were originally advanced as the differentiae of the two categories, then it constitutes nothing less than a travesty of the truth. Better, then, to attend to the phenomena than to slap on glib labels.

Given this close connection with honour, *aidōs* is definitely a concept with a considerable social aspect; the verb *aideomai* can take 'other people' as its object, either on a one-to-one basis, as a concern for the other party to a relationship, or in a general way, as an anxiety focused on one's own position in the eyes of others; in a wider sense, too, *aidōs* is a sensitivity which regulates one's behaviour towards one's society in general. It would be wrong to deduce from this, however, that *aidōs* amounts to a simple calculation of the effects of courting society's disapproval; even where *aidōs* is directed towards a general-ized group of 'other people' whose disapproval is envisaged it is not synonymous with the calculation of the probable consequences of one's actions; rather, the prospect of a given set of consequences produces either the occurrent emotional inhibition which *aidōs* represents or the evaluation which *aidōs*-words entail in their disposi-tional, non-occurrent applications. Since *aidōs* looks forward—inhibits future action—an element of calculation is inevitable, but this is equally true of any prospective check, even that provided by one's personal moral conscience. Calculation may, in many cases, be necessary for *aidōs*, but it is never sufficient; it is not the calculation 'Can I get away with it?' that is constitutive of *aidōs*, but the evaluation 'Is this action disgraceful, unseemly, incompatible with my honour, etc.?'

Nor is it true to say that *aidōs* is always calculative. It will not be so, for example, in all those passages in which it is envisaged as a spontaneous response to some claim to consideration presented by another person; Hecabe, for example, does not, or at least not primarily, ask her son to consider whether he will incur the reproaches of others when she bids him feel *aidōs* for her breast.[284] As an emotion, moreover, *aidōs* can persist when the grounds for it have been dispelled; Telemachus is told (*Odyssey* 3. 14) that no one will think ill of him in his attempts to ascertain his father's fate, yet (24) his *aidōs* remains strong; Telemachus' character is such that he is liable to such *aidōs*, and his *aidōs* is instinctive, rather than calculative. Nor is the self-regarding element always to the fore; the *aidōs* which Telemachus imagines his hosts may show him out of concern for his feelings (*Odyssey* 3. 96 = 4. 326) can hardly be self-regarding, and it would be churlish to suggest that Eumaeus, who saves a portion of his income in order to help *aidoioi* (*Odyssey* 15. 373), does so for reasons of self-interest.

As well as looking towards others in these different ways, however, *aidōs* also looks towards the self, and reflects the individual's own values, character, and ideals; it springs, I should say, from the conscience of the individual, although many will regard this as a controversial assertion. Redfield, for example, who furnishes a subtle and informative account of *aidōs*, writes that *aidōs* is 'nothing like conscience'; yet he goes on, '*Aidōs* is a vulnerability to the expressed ideal norm of the society; the ideal norm is directly experienced within the self, as a man internalizes the anticipated judgements of others on himself.'[285] This is at least an advance on the views of those (mainly German) scholars, who claim that Homeric man possesses no internal standard, is incapable of decisions, and simply adjusts his conduct to suit the external standards of society;[286] it is in this sense that *aidōs* is sometimes called a public form of conscience;[287] no doubt the oxymoron is deliberately paradoxical, but it is unhappy in so far as it suggests complete reliance on external standards, and to rely on external standards is not to manifest a conscience at all. Even where

---

[284] *Il.* 22. 82; cf. Beil (1961), 61.

[285] (1975), 116.

[286] The views of these scholars are largely iterated in their accounts of the inability of Homeric man to reach a personal decision (a result of the absence of a concept of selfhood); see Snell (1928), 24–5; (1930*a*), 141–58; Voigt (1972); Fränkel (1975), 75–85; Snell (1975), chs. 1 and 2; that the Snellian approach is still alive and kicking is demonstrated by its appearance in Scott (1982), 3–4. For detailed criticisms of views of this kind, see Wolff (1929); Sharples (1983); Halliwell (1990), 36–42; and esp. the two recent and authoritative studies by Gaskin (1990) and Schmitt (1990).

[287] Verdenius (1944–5), 50, following Jaeger (1939), i. 8; cf. Scott (1980), 14.

aidōs refers quite straightforwardly to anxiety occasioned by the prospect of others' disapproval, there is no absolute dichotomy between the internal and the external, the personal and the public, since even to recognize that a given action or occurrence will damage one's status in the eyes of others will demand a subjective idea of one's own worth,[288] an ideal self-image which is placed under threat, and an awareness of the standards under which one is liable to be criticized, and each of these elements, even in a response occasioned by external stimuli, must be internal to the individual.

This much, however, need suggest no more than does Redfield, yet I believe that Redfield's position is untenable, for two reasons, the second following from the first. First, the statement that 'a man internalizes the anticipated judgements of others on himself' seems, unless it is a tautology, to conflate two quite separate scenarios; clearly one can anticipate the judgements of others, and one's anticipation will necessarily be internal to oneself; it could not be otherwise, and even to point out that this is so should be unnecessary. If one then adjusts one's conduct in accordance with these anticipated judgements, one is reacting to other people's standards, which *need not* correspond with one's own. If, however, one has 'internalized' the anticipated judgements of others, so that the ideal norm is experienced within the self, in what sense are the judgements those of others, and in what sense are they anticipated? If one's *aidōs* rests on internalized judgements, one is clearly no longer simply anticipating disapproval. Redfield seems to believe that judgements can be internalized and yet remain those of others, but I fail to see how, if this were the case, the reaction of *aidōs* would differ from simple anticipation, or fantasy, of others' judgements; there seems, in this case, to be no need for the reference to 'internalization'. Yet there is a need for this reference, for while *aidōs* obviously can involve the anticipation of an adverse judgement which one does not oneself endorse, it does not *always* work in this way.

Redfield's definition, then, seems to waver between a picture of *aidōs* as based on anticipation of external sanctions, and one as based on internal sanctions which somehow remain the judgements of others. This is incoherent, because it assumes that one can internalize a standard and yet not make it one's own. If, however, one does possess internal standards of conduct, even if they happen to correspond

---

[288] To be sensitive about one's honour entails a claim to honour, which is subjective; see Pitt-Rivers (1965), 21-2, 72.

entirely with the expectations of society, one must, in some sense, possess standards of one's own. And clearly characters in the Homeric poems do possess such standards; Hector reveals this quite clearly in *Iliad* 6, when he tells us how his *thumos* and his understanding of his position as an *esthlos* make it impossible for him to act like a coward. The same point emerges equally clearly from those passages in which (*a*) characters feel, or are urged to feel, *nemesis* at their own conduct; (*b*) it is pointed out that the present recipient of criticism would criticize the same behaviour in another; and (*c*) a character expresses his endorsement of the standards to which he or she must conform by affirming that he or she would feel *nemesis* at such conduct in others.

This brings us to the second point, which is that Redfield denies these standards, which operate on the individual as internal sanctions against inappropriate conduct, the status of 'conscience'. Clearly the problem here lies in our definition of that term. Redfield's own observation, which is correct, that morality in Homer is not distinguished from conformity, seems to suggest that he reserves conscience for those for whom morality *is* distinguished from conformity, for those who are capable, we might say, of becoming 'prisoners of conscience' or 'conscientious objectors'. This, however, appears to me a rather austere conception of conscience, albeit one which does answer to intuitions about the use of that term in English (and German) and which would no doubt find considerable support. A useful distinction between two forms of conscience, however, is made by Jung,[289] who distinguishes between 'ethical conscience', which involves reflection and deliberation, and may be based on a set of moral principles which are personal to the individual, and thus sometimes require opposition to the standards of other members of society, and 'moral conscience', which comes into operation instinctively and automatically, and which is based on the standards assimilated early in life. I do not know that these terms are helpful in themselves, but the distinction does seem a valid one, and one which enables us to allow the characters of the Homeric poems the kind of internal corrective mechanisms, based on awareness of the standards of their society, without which they would not merit the status of socialized human beings at all, and to draw a distinction between this

---

[289] 'Das Gewisssen in psychologischer Sicht', Studien aus dem C. G. Jung Institut 7 (Zurich, 1958), 185ff., cited by Stebler (1971), 14. Jung calls the 'ethical conscience' (*ethisches Gewissen*) 'the true and actual conscience', but his recognition of the other as a type of conscience is none the less valuable.

kind of conscience and that to which we refer when we use terms like 'conscientious objector'.

The assumption that the conscience of Homeric man is of this kind, moreover, allows us to accommodate some of the observations on which those who see him as incapable of decisions and as simply adjusting his conduct to his environment base their arguments. They point out, for example, that the individual's consideration of the requirements of his social role is sufficient to produce an instinctive and unquestioning determination to conform to the ideal; this suggests, however, not that the standards being observed are imposed from outside, but that they have become part and parcel of the individual's character; if, in fact, Homeric characters did simply react to external stimuli and conform to standards which they did not intuitively regard as their own, then we should expect a great deal more of that reflection and deliberation which Snell and others find so conspicuously lacking.[290]

Aidōs, then, is, or perhaps better springs from, an internal state of conscience[291] which is based on internal standards and an awareness of the values of society; these standards will have become internal to the individual precisely because of their uniformity and of the power of popular opinion to enforce them, and will have been imparted early in the process of socialization. To characterize his action as inappropriate the individual requires at least a minimal identification with the standards of society, and in many cases these standards will be in a very real and important sense his own. Yet the observation that morality is not distinguished from conformity in Homer is an important one, even though it does not entail the absence of conscience. A limited amount of disagreement with the values of society can be expressed by simple *anaideiē*, disregard for popular disapproval, as in the case of Paris, or by denying the applicability of popular disapproval in situations in which it generally is applicable, as Agamemnon does at *Iliad* 14. 80-1; but there is no case in the poems in which *aidōs* opposes conformity out of loyalty to a competing, personal standard, or occurs at the prospect of a breach of a standard which is not generally accepted. Characters can deprecate the *aidōs* of

---

[290] Mead (1937: 493) observes that once standards or sanctions are internalized, they operate automatically. For the view criticized here, see Scott (1980), 13 (cf. Fränkel (1975), 84); for further illustration of the point at issue, cf. the very different attitudes to Od.'s conduct in *Il.* 11. 404-10 taken by (on the one hand) Dickie (1978: 94) and Gaskin (1990: 8) and (on the other) by Voigt (1972: 87-9) and Snell (1975: 156).

[291] A tautology, but one I hope I may be allowed for the sake of emphasis.

others, but they do so because it is seen as natural, though unhelpful, in the circumstances, not because the standard on which it rests is different from their own. So *aidōs* does not rise above the 'moral' conscience to the level of the 'ethical' conscience in Homer

Aidōs is also exclusively prospective in usage Homer. Thus if it does relate to a minimal sort of conscience, it does not approximate to our notion of the retrospective 'bad' or guilty conscience. Prospective *aidōs*, however, can be based on a retrospective awareness that one has done something discreditable, and the feeling of anxiety thus occasioned, which the Homeric character articulates in terms of prospective *aidōs* (because his anxiety at having transgressed or failed focuses more prominently on the knowledge that this is humiliating than on the simple fact that it has occurred), may even conceal a similar anxiety to that which we designate 'a bad conscience', provided the individual endorses the negative evaluation of his action which he projects on to others.[292] Explicitly, however, *aidōs* in Homer is always concerned with the present (as respect for another) or the future (referring to future disapproval, or inhibiting future performance of action expressed by a verb in the infinitive). This should not be taken, however, as ruling out the possibility that the characters of the poems are capable of what we call remorse,[293] simply that they do not articulate that idea by means of *aidōs*, or, indeed, by means of any term which would designate it unambiguously as the feeling which we describe in these terms.[294] So while the operation of *aidōs* in Homer does presuppose a minimal sort of conscience, this does not coincide with our concept of conscience in all its applications. Nor *is aidōs* conscience, any more than guilt is conscience for us; rather both these

[292] See 1.2.4 above, on *Il.* 22. 104-7.

[293] Some, for example, believe that Ach. shows remorse at the death of Patroclus (*Il.* 18. 98-126, etc.; so Lloyd-Jones (1971), 22; contrast Redfield (1975), 22) or that Helen's self-reproach at *Il.* 6. 344-8 (cf. 3. 180) shows something of that emotion (so Farron (1979), 17 (cf. 21-2, on 24. 764); contrast Hohendahl-Zoetelief (1980), 30 ff.).

[294] Seel (1953: 302-9) gives examples of the ways in which Homeric characters express ideas close to what we should regard as retrospective conscience, and suggests reasons as to why Homeric language cannot fully express a concept of conscience. He shows, convincingly, I believe, that responses which we should link to that concept are not totally absent from the poems. The concept, however, is ours, not that of Homeric characters; if a culture does not possess the terminology which would isolate the phenomena under the heading of a particular concept, then it seems to me that it does not possess (or recognize) that concept in the proper sense, although it may recognize, and construe in different ways, the phenomena to which the concepts of another culture refer. In expressing myself thus I differ in emphasis (but not, I think, in substance) from Gaskin (1990: 5-7), who argues that Homeric Gk. does possess and recognize concepts for which it has no conceptual term.

emotions, in their respective contexts, spring from and refer to conscience, if conscience is understood as that which encodes the standards and values of the individual.[295]

[295] It should be remembered, however, that *aidōs* bears a dispositional sense, indeed can occur as a trait of character, to a greater extent than does guilt in English.

2

From Hesiod to the Fifth Century

In the literature which survives from the period between *c.*700 BC and the beginning of the fifth century there are certainly instances enough of *aidōs* and its relatives, but these are largely heterogeneous, and many are uninformative, either replicating commonplace uses of the terms which we have met before, employing them in contexts too general to be of any interest, or, because of the fragmentary nature of the context, failing to provide necessary additional information. In general, we shall find that our best evidence for *aidōs* and similar concepts comes from literature in which we have the opportunity to observe fictional representations of human beings whose motives are discoverable from the texts in which they are portrayed; not all the archaic poets are moralists or social commentators, but the majority of the relevant instances of *aidōs*, etc. come from those who are, and all too often these tell us merely that *aidōs* is considered a good thing, or sketch a situation in which it is appropriate. There are, however, a few passages of sufficient interest to warrant our attention, and in these we shall observe a limited number of significant developments and modifications of the standards found in the Homeric poems.

There are several reasons for caution in drawing conclusions about the development of society and of social and moral attitudes from a comparison of Homeric with archaic literature. Most obviously, perhaps, the evidence furnished by the lyric, elegiac, and iambic poets is fragmentary, and pictures of values which emerge from it are scarcely likely to be complete. There are, moreover, differences of genre, and of the criteria of what can and cannot properly be expressed in a given genre—if an archaic poet evinces attitudes different from those which would find approval in Homer this need not be a sign of development, but may be an expression of sentiments considered inappropriate for epic. The poets under consideration in this chapter, too, represent a variety of different voices, and mirror the attitudes of different sections of their communities in different places at different times; their heterogeneity cannot simply be set beside the homogeneity of the Homeric poems. Nor do the Homeric poems themselves give us the last word on the values of the society in which they were given their final form; mere accident may entail that Homer offers us only a fraction of the possible range of a given term, and development need not be invoked wherever a term enjoys a wider range in post-Homeric poetry.[1]

The Homeric poems, moreover, do not represent any one historical society, but rather an amalgam of the old and the new; in this amalgam, however, there is an attempt to preserve an atmosphere of antiquity, and institutions of days long before the poet's own are retained.[2] Together with this archaizing tendency seems also to go an idealizing tendency; alternatives to the values which are paramount in the poems may not be given a full hearing, and there may well have been a far greater plurality of opinion in the society which received the poems than in that which is depicted by them. Perhaps the most significant contrast to be discovered between the Homeric poems and many of the works considered in this chapter is that between the idealism of the former and the realism of the latter.

2.1. HESIOD

Most of the instances of *aidōs* etc. which occur in Hesiod are of minor importance and need no comment.[3] There is, however, one passage which begs discussion, if only because it is so well known, namely that at *Works and Days* 317–19, in which the poet exploits the *topos* of the

---

[1] On the hazards of inferring cultural change from the comparison of Homeric and post-Homeric poetry, see Fowler (1987), 3–13.

[2] According to Fowler (1987: 8), to speak of an archaizing tendency in Hom. is 'to beg a question'; but there can surely be no doubt that the society of the *Od.* embraces many forms that antedate the likely period of the poem's composition, and so evidence of newer social forms in the archaic poets need not imply that a specific social change has taken place since (say) 700 BC. As regards values, however, Fowler's caution is more clearly in place—the antiquity of many of Hom.'s institutions does not prove the antiquity of the poems' values.

[3] We might, perhaps, note the use of *aidoia* as 'genitals' at *WD* 733–4, and the occurrence of *aidōs* as a response towards an especially gifted person of superior status at *Th.* 80–93; this passage offers many parallels with *Od.* 8. 169–73, but in that place *aidōs* is not the response of the admiring audience but a quality of the speech of the gifted individual (whose *aidōs* contrasts with the lack of *aidōs* manifested by Euryalus in the narrative immediately preceding this description, and reflects the *aidōs* he accords others).

ambivalence of *aidōs*.[4] This passage has been much discussed,[5] but to enter into the various points of controversy in detail would be to treat it at a length out of all proportion to its value for this study; on the other hand, misinterpretation of the passage has often entailed mis-apprehension about the nature of *aidōs*, so some attempt at exegesis is obviously desirable.

Using the text of West,[6] I translate: '*Aidōs* is not good at looking after a needy man, *aidōs*, which greatly harms as well as helps mankind; it is true what they say [τοι], *aidōs* to poverty, *tharsos* [boldness] to wealth.' Most probably all three lines are proverbial maxims which Hesiod has adapted to his own purpose;[7] the closely similar lines in the *Odyssey* (17. 347 and 352) also have a proverbial ring, and the sense of 317 is presumably the same as that of those lines, namely that *aidōs* is a hindrance where it inhibits the conduct required to fulfil some desired and legitimate end. Perhaps in other contexts the proverb could be used to justify behaviour which would otherwise appear as *anaideiē*, and perhaps it could even have been used with an element of 'worldly-wise' acknowledgement that there is no room for the niceties of proper social behaviour in those who are seeking to satisfy some great or basic need. Line 318 is a proverbial recognition of

[4] We have met ambivalent *aidōs* before, in passages where it is recognized as obstruc-tive or unhelpful: *Od.* 3. 14, 96, 4. 326, 17. 347 (cf. 352, 578); see Ch. 1, *init.* It is not auto-matically assumed that Hom. is earlier than Hes., though this seems to me the most likely position (see Edwards (1971), 199–206; Havelock (1978), 214–15; against West (1966), 46–7); I have treated the Homeric poems first because the culture they represent is *sui generis* and looks back into the past, and because they offer basic and detailed infor-mation about *aidōs* which could not be gleaned from Hes.

[5] See in particular Cook (1901), 341; Sinclair (1925), 147–8; Hoekstra (1950), 99–106; Verdenius (1962), 141–2; McKay (1963), 17–27; Valgiglio (1969), 169–174; Walcot (1970), 60–5; Claus (1977), 78–83; cf. von Erffa (1937), 48–9.

[6] Thus I read κομίζειν (found in three papyri and one MS of Stob.) and not κομίζει (the reading of the mediaeval MSS) in 317. The acceptance of the paradosis has led to much discussion of 'bad shame', and to the distinction of two kinds of shame, on the analogy of the two kinds of *eris*, 11–26 (see Verdenius (1985), on 317, ἀγαθή; 318, αἰδώς). But the idea of two kinds of *aidōs* does not clearly emerge even with this text; 318 says not that there are two kinds of *aidōs*, but that *aidōs* is now harmful, now helpful; this must be the sense of 317–18 even with the reading κομίζει, and this sense is conveyed much more clearly by West's text, in which ἀγαθή is predicative and has its regular sense of 'good at'. As West himself points out (1978: ad loc.) the predicative use with the infinitive is strongly supported by *Od.* 17. 347 and 352. Possible reminiscences of these lines in Euripides (*Hipp.* 383–7; *Erechth.* fr. 365 N²; see Cook (1901)), even if accepted as such, prove nothing about Hes.'s text (*pace* McKay (1963), 17 and n. 2).

[7] As is agreed by Hoekstra (1950), 99–106; McKay (1963), 21; Claus (1977), 81; West (1978), on 318, 319. Thus it is as likely that *WD* and *Il.* 24. 45 share a common proverbial ancestor as that the latter is an 'interpolation' from the former, although the sentiment is certainly more apposite in its Hesiodic context.

the inefficacy of *aidōs* in some situations, and 319, as McKay plausibly suggests,[8] probably goes back to a proverb by which the poor consoled themselves with the contrast between their superiors' arrogance and their own respect for others and for proper conduct.

The key to the proper interpretation of the passage in its context, however, is to appreciate that Hesiod is not offering us a general homily on the *aidōs* of the poor. The inappropriateness of *aidōs* for a needy man in 317 should not be interpreted generally, that is as a sociological observation that the poor as a class fail to get on as a result of their *aidōs* (for then we run up against insurmountable difficulties in attempting to identify the focus of this sentiment), but as directed at Perses; lines 286–319 of *Works and Days* contain repeated admonitions to Perses, and the specific point of this section is to convince him to work. The recommendation of work as the best means of acquiring wealth and *aretē* is the core of this whole passage, and if 317–19 are to be taken as a general reflection on the state of the poor, we must assume that the *aidōs* of the poor as a class prevents them working; the poet provides no motive for *aidōs* of this kind, but he does motivate *aidōs* on Perses' part. It is Perses to whom the observation that work is not an *oneidos* (reproach, 311) is addressed, and so the *aidōs* which is to be dispelled in 317 will be that of one who considers work to be beneath his dignity.[9] Line 318 simply draws the moral that *aidōs* is not always a good thing before Hesiod cites another proverb in 319. The key to his adaptation of this saying lies in the ambiguity of the expression of the original. The vagueness of the preposition *pros* in this line is best rendered by a non-committal 'to'; in the original positive proverb, '*aidōs* to poverty, *tharsos* to wealth', the sense will have been that poverty conduces to *aidōs* (a good thing) in the poor, wealth to *tharsos* in the rich; but Hesiod cites this proverb ironically; he accepts its truth,[10] but changes its meaning. He has already reminded Perses

---

[8] (1963), 21.

[9] See von Erffa (1937), 48; Hoekstra (1950), 104; Verdenius (1985), on 311, ὄνειδος. This interpretation might be supported by Eur. fr. 285 N², 14, where *aidōs* leads a poor nobleman to reject physical work. G. Nussbaum (1960), however, points out that in Hes. and Hom. work is not felt to be degrading in itself, and contrasts this attitude with the later, classical outlook which presumably explains the Euripidean passage. But Perses clearly does reject work, and does prefer the life of his social superiors; perhaps it is work as performed by those of a status lower than that to which he himself aspires that he finds objectionable. Perses might reject not work *simpliciter*, but the identification of himself with a lower, peasant class and this would not entail either that noblemen are ashamed of the work they do or that peasants are ashamed of that which they do.

[10] The gnomic particle τοι 'forces the general truth upon the consciousness of the individual addressed', Denniston (1954) 542; cf. Verdenius (1985), on 319, 287.

that his idleness and so by implication his shunning of work as an *oneidos*, will mean poverty and hunger (302); now he effectively reverses the sense of the proverbial maxim; *aidōs* is still 'a feature of'[11] poverty, *tharsos* of wealth, but these are the features that make the poor and the wealthy what they are; *aidōs* conduces to poverty, *tharsos* to wealth.[12]

The main point of these lines, then, is Perses' *aidōs*, and remarks about the inhibition or shame of the poor as a class are unwarranted. Perses is asked to abandon a specific form of *aidōs* which, like misplaced *aidōs* in Homer, inhibits the achievement of some desired goal, and it is implied that he should show the *tharsos* needed to overcome this *aidōs*. This positive connotation of *tharsos* is supported by *Odyssey* 3. 76, where it is also opposed to inappropriate *aidōs*,[13] but the word is frequently negative in character,[14] as indeed it probably was in the proverb which Hesiod adapts, and the poet shows his awareness of this negative aspect by adding an injunction against carrying *tharsos* too far in 320—'But wealth is not to be stolen.'[15] This excessive *tharsos* is then equated with forcible robbery (321) and with a desire for gain (*kerdos*) which leads one's understanding (*noos*) astray; these vices are then subsumed in the generic *anaideiē* of 324 which drives away *aidōs*.[16] *Tharsos*, therefore, can be a positive antonym to misplaced *aidōs*, but it can also be taken too far, and thus lead to *anaideiē*, the negative antonym of *aidōs*. There could be no clearer indication than this that the argument about *aidōs* is an integral part of Hesiod's advice to Perses on the proper acquisition of wealth.

Both *aidōs* and *anaideiē* are used of proper behaviour in an economic context here; in the immediate sequel, however, where further examples of *anaideiē* are given (327-32), the focus is on proper

---

[11] West's translation of *pros* (1978: ad loc.).

[12] So Verdenius (1985), on 319, πρός. Verdenius and West are both right about this word; the former gives the sense in Hes.'s ironic adaptation, the latter that in the original proverb.

[13] Cf. Ch. 1 n. 167.

[14] See *Od.* 17. 449, 18. 331; *Il.* 21. 395 (and cf. West (1978), on 319); contrast McKay (1963), 19-20.

[15] So Verdenius (1985), on 320, δέ; cf. Claus (1977), 83.

[16] Cf. 359. *Aidōs* (and *nemesis*) occur in the context of taking by force also at fr. 204. 81-4 MW, but there the reference of the lack of *aidōs* involved is to the breach of an oath; *aidōs* should help maintain oaths because in swearing an oath one commits one's honour to its observance, and because perjury entails manifest contradiction of the statement upon which honour is staked. It also entails flagrant disregard for the superior power in whose name the oath was sworn and for other parties involved, who are denied their right to the truth.

behaviour in a more general sense: harming guests and suppliants is condemned (327), as are breaches of *philotēs* (seducing a brother's wife, 328-9, maltreating an aged parent, 331-2).[17] These offences are punished by Zeus, and they are punished as *erga adika* ('unjust deeds', 334).

This suggests that there is a link between *aidōs* and *dikē* (suit, settlement, custom, justice), the concept which has dominated the first part of the poem, and this link is explicit in the poet's description of the collapse of moral standards in the current, iron age of civilization. The iron-age men, he tells us at 185-8, will be ungrateful to their parents (a breach of *philotēs* and so of *aidōs*, but also a crime which attracts divine anger, 187), the settlement of disputes will be a matter of physical strength (*cheirodikai*, 189), one man will sack the city of another, and there will be no recognition of the man who abides by his oath, who is just (*dikaios*), or who is good (*agathos*); rather the wrongdoer and the man of *hubris* will be honoured (189-92); the settlement of disputes, once again, will be a matter of physical strength, and there will be no *aidōs* (192-3).[18] People will lie and perjure themselves (193-4), and envy of others will rule the day (195-6); the disruption of civilized values, in fact, will be so great that Aidōs and Nemesis, personified, will take themselves from the earth, and men will then have no refuge from troubles (197-201).

The association of *aidōs* and *dikē* is thus apparent, and *aidōs* and *nemesis* are obviously appropriate in the context of these offences which involve lack of regard for the honour and status of others. In the passage under consideration *dikē* occurs twice (189 and 192), and both occurrences refer to the settling of disputes by force rather than by agreement. In an important study of *dikē* in the poem, Gagarin[19] argues that the word refers primarily to the process employed in the

---

[17] The other offence mentioned is that of harming orphan children (330); this is not a specific breach of *aidōs* in Homer, and indeed at *Il.* 22. 484-506 it is assumed that a fatherless child will be harmed; Hes. may be thinking of the obligation to protect orphaned children of a member of one's own family (Verdenius (1985), on 330, ὀρφανά), or it may simply be felt as excessive to maltreat the helpless.

[18] Reading οὐκ ἔσται in 193 rather than West's ἐσσεῖται. With the traditional text ἔσται can be understood with δίκη δ' ἐν χερσί (Verdenius (1985), on 192), whereas with West's text one must either consider ἐν χερσί also to apply to αἰδώς or take αἰδώς ἐσσεῖται absolutely; but while '*dikē* will be a matter of force' makes sense, '*aidōs* will be a matter of force' seems unlikely, and 'there will be *aidōs*' is far too vague. There is no problem in Hes.'s saying that there will be no *aidōs* in 192-3 and proceeding to describe the departure of *aidōs* in 197-200, any more than there is a problem in his following χειροδίκαι in 189 with δίκη δ' ἐν χερσί in 192.

[19] (1973).

peaceful settlement of disputes; this sense of the term is certainly prominent, and this explains the close link between *dikē* and the questions of property and the proper acquisition of wealth which prevail in the contexts in which it occurs. We have seen that *aidōs*, too, is involved in this economic sphere at 320–4, and so, in that sphere, *aidōs* can be the impulse or disposition which leads one to observe *dikē*.[20] *Aidōs*, however, is clearly connected with more than simply economic behaviour; breaches of *philotēs* and offences against suppliants and guests are also offences against *aidōs* in the poem. Gagarin's point, however, is that *dikē* does not enjoy this extension of reference, and is *restricted* to the narrow sense of 'suit', 'arbitration', or 'settlement'.[21]

This, however, cannot be true; there are, indeed, many instances of *dikē* as 'judgement' in the poem, but behind such judgements lies a principle; this is shown most clearly at 225–6 in which the poet speaks of 'those who assign straight *dikai* [judgements] to foreigners and natives and do not depart from *dikaion*', where *dikaion* is the principle of fairness which makes a *dikē* 'straight'. A *dikē* may be straight or crooked and so may be a legal process and nothing more, but Hesiod is quite able to make it clear that, in a wider sense *dikē* refers to more than the process[22] and includes the general righteousness in which

[20] Cf. Fränkel (1975), 121.

[21] Gagarin insists on two separate senses of *dikē*, based on two separate etymologies, and finds that in the Homeric poems one sense, the legalistic one, is confined to the *Il.* and the other, that of 'proper behaviour', to the *Od.* (1973: 82–6), the two meanings being strictly separate. His remarks on Hom. square with the evidence to a certain extent (cf. Havelock (1978), chs. 7–10), but the rigidity of his distinction is unwarranted; in the *Il. dikē* occurs only four times, and three of these occurences do refer narrowly to adjudications (16. 542, 18. 508, 23. 542), but the other (16. 388) refers to the principle of equity required to make adjudications fair; cf. the instances of parts of the adj. *dikaios* (11. 831, 13. 6, 19. 181), and Dickie (1978), 98; equally, in the *Od.* the sense of *dikē* as 'settlement' does occur (9. 215, 11. 570); the case for total separation of these meanings rests only on Gagarin's etymologies, which can scarcely be proved and which in any case have no prescriptive force over usage. (Gagarin in himself, without abandoning his general approach, expresses slight reservations about his strict separation of the 'two senses' in his subsequent article (1974: 188 n. 15), and goes even further towards tacit correction of his earlier view of *dikē* in Hes. in (1986), 46–9, esp. 49.)

[22] At 270–3 Hes. effectively opposes the adj. *dikaios* to the noun *dikē* to indicate that there is more to *dikē* in the wider sense than simply success in a dispute; one may have more *dikē* in that the adjudication has gone one's own way, and yet not be *dikaios* (a state of affairs which cannot, the poet is sure, persist in the long term). This use of *dikaios* points to a wider sense of *dikē*, a sense which Hes. employs freely in the poem; it is impossible that instances of *dikaios* and *adikos* should have nothing to do with *dikē*, as Gagarin (1973: 93) asserts; see Claus (1977), 77; Rodgers (1971), maintains that *dikē* involves nothing more than prudence in one's own interests; but whereas Hes. argues that to act with *dikē* is to act in one's own interest (213–85 in general), Rodgers argues

judgements should be pronounced; it is by means of this principle that Zeus 'straightens judgements' (9),[23] and it is this principle that is personified in much of the poem (213, 217, 220, 256, 275, 283); Hesiod's precise point is that, although Perses and the local noblemen have been party to a legal process, they have not abided by *dikē*.

The principle of proper behaviour in submitting disputes to arbitration, however, is not the only non-procedural sense of *dikē* in the poem; we have already seen that, in 327–34, various offences against propriety, symptoms of the driving out of *aidōs* by *anaideiē*, are described as *erga adika*, and if it is *adikon* to maltreat guests, etc. it must be a demand of *dikē* to protect them; this renders invalid Gagarin's assertion that '. . . no violator of the rights of a suppliant or a guest, no doer of any wrong except that connected with litigation is ever spoken of as violating *dikē*.'[24] *Dikē* must, then, have a reference to proper moral behaviour in the poem,[25] and the close relationship between that concept and *aidōs* is now that much easier to understand; *aidōs*, on the one hand, plays its familiar role as that which renders one sensitive to the general values of society and which inhibits departure from them, while, on the other, it works closely with *dikē* in that both concepts reflect the notion that other people have certain rights, namely to honour (recognized by *aidōs*) and to their possessions (the sphere in which *dikē* is most obviously active). *Dikē*, however, is extended beyond the economic sphere and is associated with *aidōs* in more general areas of respect for others, and thus the possibility arises that *dikē* itself may be regarded as a principle of distribution, not just of economic rights, but also in relationships which involve mutual obligations of honour, answering to the principle, apparent in Homer, that legitimate claims to honour should be recognized. That this is true emerges clearly when we note that Hesiod several times opposes *dikē* to *hubris* (191, 213–18, 238); if it takes *hubris* to violate *dikē*, then violation of *dikē* will involve contempt for the honour of the victim. Nor is it merely the case that every act of theft, misappropriation, or subversion of the legal process inevitably entails lack of *aidōs* for its

that to act in one's own interest is to act with *dikē*, an illegitimate conversion, since Hes. never claims that the category of advantageous actions is coextensive with that of just actions.

[23] See Verdenius (1985), ad loc., and *passim*.

[24] (1973), 91; Gagarin's view that *dikaios* and *adikos* cannot be used as evidence for the application of *dikē* is incredible, and is based only on his strict insistence on disputed etymologies.

[25] See Claus (1977), 78; Dickie (1978), 99; Havelock (1978), 216–17; Garner (1987), 5.

victim, for, as we have seen, standard paradigms of *anaideiē* (in its traditional sense of disregard for the *timē* of others) may also be seen as offences against *dikē*. Not only, then, does 'injustice' encompass lack of regard for the honour of others, but lack of regard for the honour of others may also be viewed as 'injustice'.

A clear indication that *dikē* refers to more than litigation is given at 276–80, where the poet claims that *dikē* separates man from beast; as Claus points out,[26] the beasts are not differentiated from man simply because they do not possess a system for the settlement of disputes, but because they do not have the civilized qualities of the *dikaios*, the just man, qualities which, in the *Odyssey*, served to characterize civilized communities as different from barbarous races like the Cyclopes.[27] Admittedly, Hesiod does argue from the general sense of *dikē* possessed by humans to its application in legal disputes (280–5), but this does not restrict its reference to litigation in 276–80. The separation of man from beast by *dikē* in this passage contrasts with the position in the *Iliad* (24. 40–5), where it was the absence of *aidōs* that rendered Achilles more beast than man.[28] Yet it is Aidōs and Nemesis that depart when *dikē* breaks down, and it is clear that a 'more advanced' Hesiod has not simply replaced *aidōs* with *dikē* as the major force in the promotion of civilized behaviour; *aidōs* and *dikē* go hand in hand, the latter as a description of the behaviour of mankind in a civilized society, and the former as a sensitivity to the norms of such a society.[29] It is, therefore, important to recognize both that *aidōs* can respond to the rights of other persons in connection with property, which is the sphere in which Hesiod most often locates *dikē*, and that *dikē* is associated with the honour-based standards of proper behaviour governed by *aidōs*. Since this is the case, it is sensible to acknowledge that questions of entitlement to property and to honour

---

[26] (1977), 77–8.
[27] Cf. Pearson (1962), 82; also Ch. 1 n. 195.
[28] See von Erffa (1937), 52–3; also Ch. 1 n. 255.
[29] If we need any confirmation that *aidōs* in Hes. 'still' separates man from beast, we need only look at *Th.* 312 and 833, where *anaidēs* is the adj. applied to Cerberus, the 'raw-eater' (311), and to the *thumos* of a lion. Similarly the Calydonian Boar is *anaidomachēs* at Bacch. 5. 104–7 Snell-Maehler, and Death is *anaidēs* at Thgn. 207 and Pind. *Ol.* 10. 105; neither can be persuaded to show quarter. The personification of *aidōs* is also important; clearly, the capacity to feel *aidōs* is valued (its departure is a sign of the destruction of civilized standards), and so *aidōs* emerges as a valued *quality*; this entails a dispositional sense for *aidōs* beyond the occurrent, and indicates that, for Hesiod, the capacity to experience *aidōs* is a positive and beneficial trait of character. (On personification of *aidōs* and other such concepts, see von Erffa (1937), 54–8; Wilamowitz (1959), i. 347; Burkert (1985), 184–6.)

cannot be rigidly separated, and that *dikē* may also be used to adumbrate that notion of equity in the distribution of honour, the idea that some forms of dishonouring another are not legitimate, which we found to obtain in Homer.

2.2. THE *HOMERIC HYMNS*

Most of the instances of our terms in the so-called *Homeric Hymns* are unremarkable, and only a limited number of passages in two of the major hymns, those in honour of Demeter and Hermes, need concern us.[30]

In the *Hymn to Demeter*, *aidōs* occurs chiefly as a response to the special status of another person, its focus in such cases being the other party to a one-to-one confrontation. At 64-5 Demeter asks Helius for help in finding her daughter: 'Helius, show me *aidōs* as one god to another, if ever I have cheered your heart and *thumos* in word or in deed.' For Helius to accede to this request would be to accord Demeter *aidōs*, and so the imperative, 'show me *aidōs*', probably has something of special connotation of 'accept my appeal' that it has in contexts of supplication. As in that context, however, the appeal to *aidōs* presupposes an occurrent sense of the emotion, the *aidōs* which one feels towards a person of a particular status, and the appeal to the inhibitory emotion in such circumstances seems to be an invitation to recognize one's own inability to dismiss the request, to find oneself rejecting all other options as unacceptable. These options may appear unacceptable, and so produce inhibition, because one has a special regard for the other person, because the other person enjoys some special protection, such as that of Zeus in contexts of guest-friendship and supplication, or because the standard which is invoked in the particular circumstance, of loyalty, perhaps, or of gratitude,[31] is one which society in general feels should be upheld. More than one of these motives may be present in any given situation. In this particular case the sun god's reaction to Demeter's appeal is one of recognition of her status as a deity and of sympathy for her suffering, expressed in

---

[30] Although the collection of *Hymns* as a whole may contain material from periods as late as the Hellenistic Age, we may be fairly confident that these two major hymns (*h. Hom. Cer.* and *h. Hom. Merc.*) belong to the period covered by this chapter; see Richardson (1974), 3.

[31] As in this case; we remember that one to whom one owes a debt of gratitude could be described as *aidoios, philos*, and *deinos* (1.3.2. above).

terms of the verbs *hazesthai* and *eleairein* in line 76. Both these responses, recognition of special (particularly divine) status[32] and pity,[33] may convey something of the emotional response of *aidōs* in this case, without either being equivalent to it.[34] Demeter's request for *aidōs* is based on a specific tie which exists between the two deities, a reciprocal tie requiring reciprocity of honour, while Helius' response has other grounds, namely Demeter's status as a goddess and her present pitiable condition.

At line 190 of the same hymn *aidōs* is once more a direct response to Demeter's special status; when Metaneira noticed the goddess, '*aidōs* and *sebas* and pale fear [*deos*] took hold of her'. Metaneira does not yet know that she is in the presence of a goddess, but Demeter's appearance did cast a divine light on the doorway (189), and this no doubt accounts for the fear of line 190. Even though Metaneira's *aidōs* and *sebas* do respond to the stranger's more than mortal appearance, it is unlikely that these terms convey reactions which are specifically linked to the numinous; rather they seem to acknowledge both the superior status of the goddess, even in her guise as a human being, and the element of uncanniness in her appearance. The combination of *aidōs* and *deos* is frequent in Homer,[35] while *sebas*, as we saw, does respond specifically to the uncanny or the unusual in several Homeric passages.[36]

That *aidōs* is not confined to the religious sphere in the hymn is apparent from Metaneira's opening speech to the goddess at 213–15: 'Greetings, lady (for I expect that you are of noble, not mean stock);

[32] On *hazomai*, cf. 1.6.1 above.

[33] For *aidōs* and pity, see Ch. 1 n. 10.

[34] Cf. von Erffa (1937), 23.

[35] See Ch. 1 n. 10; also 1.3.1 above.

[36] 1.6.3 above. As in Hom., *sebas* is subjective here, describing a response to some quality in another which inspires awe; probably the first instance of the word in its objective sense ('that which arouses awe') comes in the 8th of the epigrams preserved in the pseudo-Herodotean life of Hom. (8. 3–4), where the *sebas* of Zeus *xeinios* attracts *aidōs*, and his *opis* is the sanction brought to bear upon those who disregard it. (Schmid-Stählin, I. i. 224, regard the epigrams as genuine archaic poetry.) At *h. Hom. Cer.* 10–11 *sebas* describes the response of gods and men to the narcissus which is to entrap Persephone, but there the term has a slightly extended sense, 'occasion for, cause of *sebas*' (cf. *aidōs* at *Il.* 17. 336–7 and *Od.* 3. 24; Ch. 1 n. 91). We shall see that the objective use of *sebas* becomes more common. That which arouses *sebas* may be described as *semnos*, as at *h. Hom. Cer.* 1 and 478 (note *sebas* in 479 and cf. *h. Hom. Merc.* 552), and Demeter and her daughter are described as both *semnai* and *aidoiai* at *h. Hom. Cer.* 485–6; *semnos* and *aidoios* are clearly analogous, but whereas *aidoios* can be used of gods and men alike with no appreciable difference of meaning, *semnos* tends to be pejorative when used of human beings.

aidōs and *charis* [grace] are apparent in your eyes, as if you were descended from kings who deal in justice.' *Aidōs* is manifest in the eyes because the feeling of shame or inhibition naturally causes one to avert one's gaze, and it is therefore understandable that the location of *aidōs* in the eyes should become proverbial.[37] In this and similar contexts *charis* appears simply to be the general 'attractiveness' of the person which renders her admirable to others,[38] but the ascription of *aidōs* to Demeter is less simple and more interesting. The goddess has given signs that could be interpreted as manifestations of *aidōs*—her head is veiled (182, 197) and her eyes were downcast (194). The narrative makes it clear that this behaviour is motivated by grief at the loss of her daughter, yet, in her grief, she does conduct herself with dignity, respect, and decorum, and it is possible, therefore, that Metaneira conjectures *aidōs* from this restrained and modest behaviour, particularly since the goddess is a guest and, in her humility and restraint, is behaving as a guest should. Metaneira need not, then, be regarding *aidōs* as a quality or disposition unrelated to any specific conduct on the part of the goddess,[39] but since *aidōs* is associated with *charis* as a trait of a particular class, it is very likely that she ascribes to her a disposition towards *aidōs* beyond the experience of the emotion which she believes she has observed, and, indeed, there need be no sharp dividing line between the dispositional and the occurrent senses.

Metaneira also believes that Demeter's *aidōs* indicates royal birth; we have seen that people of superior status attract *aidōs*,[40] but the point of these lines seems to be that they are, typically and as a class, capable of manifesting it.[41] As we have just seen, moreover, *aidōs* was part of Metaneira's reaction to the appearance of the goddess at 190; in that place *aidōs* was a response to Demeter's superior status, while in the present passage it is a manifestation of it. Thus in some situations *aidōs* may be appropriate to both of two parties to a relationship, and the *aidōs* which is apparent in one of a certain status

[37] Cf. Arist. *Rhet.* 1384ª34; also Ch. 1 n. 151 above.
[38] Cf. *Od.* 8. 18–23 where Odysseus becomes *philos*, *deinos*, and *aidoios* as a result of Athena's pouring *charis* on his head and shoulders (1.3.2 above), and 169–77 of the same book, where two types are contrasted, one who has *aidōs* and one who has none, the latter's lack of *aidōs* being matched by an equivalent deficiency in *charis*. By virtue of this association with *charis*, *aidōs* clearly emerges as an attractive and desirable personal attribute, an important social asset.
[39] As Richardson (1974; ad loc.) seems to imply.
[40] Specifically, kings are *aidoioi* at *Il.* 4. 402 (cf. *Od.* 18. 314, of a queen, Ch. 1 n. 129); Hes. *Th.* 80; fr. 43a. 89, fr. 361 MW.
[41] Cf. 2.3.5 below, on *aidōs* as an aristocratic quality in the Theognid corpus.

may be answered by a corresponding feeling of *aidōs* in those they encounter. A proper disposition with regard to the honourable, then, is honoured with *aidōs* in return.

In the *Hymn to Hermes* much is made of the *anaideiē* of the eponymous protagonist. Following his theft of Apollo's cattle, he is addressed by his mother at line 156 as ἀναιδείην ἐπιειμένε ('you who are clothed in *anaideiē*'), the same phrase as is used of Agamemnon by Achilles in *Iliad* 1 (149). Theft involved *anaideiē* also at *Works and Days* 324, and the *anaideiē* in such cases must lie in both the disregard for the consequences of being found out and the lack of concern for the status of the other person involved. It is this proper regard for the status of others that Hermes feigns at 381–2, where, denying the charge of theft, he expresses his *aidōs* for Helios and the other gods, his *philotēs* for Zeus, and his fear of the anger of Apollo.[42] The use of the verb *opizomai* of Hermes' attitude towards Apollo indicates that the proper relationship between the two should be one of respect for the latter's status as a superior and more powerful deity,[43] but it is precisely Hermes' intention to contest that power and status and to assert his own *timē*, with the ultimate view that it be acknowledged by the other gods.[44] Hermes' *anaideiē*, then, which entails the disregarding of the *timē* of another, occurs in the context of his attempt to win *timē* for himself, much as does that of Agamemnon in the *Iliad*. In the hymn, however, this *anaideiē* is not deprecated, but celebrated; even though the god's behaviour is described as *anaideiē*, a pejorative term, it is presented not as reprehensible, but as admirable, and the god is celebrated as patron of the clever trickster. This (paradoxical) valuing of the undesirability quality *anaideiē* in the context of clever wickedness forms an important by-tradition in Greek literature, one which is particularly apparent in Old Comedy.[45]

[42] Ἥλιον δὲ μάλ' αἰδέομαι καὶ δαίμονας ἄλλους, | καί σε φιλῶ καὶ τοῦτον ὀπίζομαι.

[43] See 1.6.2 above, on *opizomai*.

[44] Cf. 172–3: 'As for *timē*, I, too, shall achieve the same divine *timē* as Apollo.' See Walcot (1979), 345; cf. Gagarin (1986), 41.

[45] Detienne and Vernant's study of cunning intelligence (1978) embraces practical cleverness, artifice, and deceit, especially in myth, but, rather disappointingly, does not address the question of the paradoxical valuing of clever wickedness and *anaideiē*; for a good treatment of this theme, see Whitman (1964), esp. 31–4 on *h. Hom. Merc.* The tension between *anaideiē* as an undesirable quality in real life and its celebration as an essential feature of comedy is most apparent in Ar.'s *Knights*, where the *anaideia* of the real-life Cleon is condemned while that of the (even worse) Sausage Seller is celebrated. The Sausage Seller, like Hermes, denies his crimes on oath, and to the face of his victims (*Knights* 298, 1239), and this, as clear disregard both for one's own reputation should the truth become known and for the status/rights of the other, is the essence of *anaideia*. Cf.

2.3. ELEGIAC AND IAMBIC POETS

2.3.1. *Callinus*

The early Ephesian elegist, Callinus, transports us back to the martial atmosphere of the *Iliad*, and gives us further opportunity to observe the operation of *aidōs* in the martial context. Fragment 1 in West's collection begins as follows (1–4): 'How long will you lie there? When will you take a spirit [*thumos*] of courage, young men? Have you no *aidōs* before your neighbours to hold back so? You think you are at peace, but war holds the entire country.' This kind of hortatory appeal to *aidōs* is familiar from the *Iliad*;[46] the poet accuses his fellow citizens of slacking, and seeks to arouse their *aidōs*, urging them to consider what others will say. There is no essential difference in the way *aidōs*

Arist., *Rhet.* 1380ᵃ19–21, where *anaischuntia* (= *anaideia*) consists in denying what is obvious and is described as a sort of contempt for the other person. (Cope (1877: ad loc.) well compares Ar. *Knights*.) *Anaideia* and clever wickedness in comedy are escapist and subversive; thus the practices of the Sausage Seller and his like mirror not admired qualities but impulses and desires suppressed in quotidian society. There may be something of this in the characterization of Hermes as a cheat and a thief, and Hermes the thief is certainly associated with festivals of licence (Burkert (1985), 410 n. 26; perhaps Hipponax 3a and 32 West, cited by Burkert (ibid.) are also to be seen against a ritual background), but Nilsson (1955: 507; cf. Burkert (1985), 158) is no doubt right to suggest that Hermes' theft of Apollo's cattle in the Hymn represents the attribution to a pastoralist god (*h. Hom. Merc.* 567–8, 570–1) of a crime of a kind typically practised by a pastoralist society. Here we should note the use of cattle-theft as an attempt by an initiate to the adult community to establish his claim to honour in competition with a figure of recognized status and prowess; honour is won by the thief not merely because his exploit is daring and cunning (as among the Sarakatsani: see Campbell (1964), 206–12), but at least partly because the theft was perpetrated against a victim of a particular status. This has a remarkable analogue in the practices of the modern Cretan community described by Herzfeld (1985: 162–94); cf. also Plut. *Thes.* 30. 1–2, cited by Walcot (1970), 98 n. 1; (1979), 344. Almost certainly, then, the exploit of Hermes in the Hymn represents a form of behaviour as common among ancient as among modern Greek pastoralists; for other cases of (admirable) theft and cattle-rustling in early poetry, cf. *Il.* 11. 670–762; *Od.* 19. 395–7 (Autolycus' furtive prowess a gift from Hermes); and see further Walcot (1979). Hermes' cattle-theft in the Hymn, however, is much more like the sheep-stealing of Herzfeld's 'Glendiots' than the large-scale and overt acts of robbery described by Nestor in the *Iliad*—deceit, cunning, and skill are as necessary for the Hermetic exploit as for the 'Glendiot'; cf. Brown (1969), 5–7. On the attitude to lies (typically seen as *anaideia* in classical lit.) in early poetry, see n. 84 below.

[46] Cf. Jaeger (1972), 107, on the adaptation of Homeric *Feldherrenreden* by Callinus and Tyrtaeus. That these poets draw on the hortatory tradition apparent in Homeric *Mahnreden*, however, need not be made to imply that their poems were performed immediately before action was joined; on the likelihood of their performance at military symposia, held on campaign, see Bowie (1990).

works in this passage from its operation in various passages of Homer, yet von Erffa[47] contrasts Callinus' expression with that of *Iliad* 5. 529–30, and finds significance in the fact that, whereas the Homeric warriors are asked to *aideisthai* each other, Callinus' fellow citizens are urged to show *aidōs* for the opinions of members of other communities, other city-states; in the one case the warriors are asked to show concern for their own reputations and in the other for that of their community. This is certainly true, and the arguments of the two passages are not identical, but this is not necessarily a reflection of the different social background in either case. The situation of the participants is undoubtedly different; the heroes of the *Iliad* do not live in the same kind of society as does Callinus (although the monumental composer of that poem might have), but even in the *Iliad* the idea of a community of honour in which all the members of one contingent were involved is of considerable importance, and we do find an appeal to *aidōs* with regard to the reputation of one's own community *vis-à-vis* other communities in the *Odyssey* (2. 65–6); such appeals, surely, must always have been possible. It would also be erroneous to imagine that Callinus' warriors are not concerned about their individual reputations in the same way as Homer's; personal and collective honour go hand in hand.

2.3.2. *Tyrtaeus*

Similar exhortations may be found in the fragments of Tyrtaeus.[48] Typical is the substantial fragment 10 West, in lines 15–18 of which the young warriors are exhorted to remain in formation and fight, to make their *thumos* great and strong, not to think of their own safety, and, in short, to avoid flight, which is 'ugly' (*aischrē*), and so brings disgrace. Even in fragmentary form Tyrtaeus is much freer with the adjective *aischros* than is Homer, but, broadly speaking, it is used in contexts similar to those in which it is found in the *Iliad*. Its primary reference is still to physical appearances; at 10. 21 ff. it is *aischron* that an older man should be killed fighting in the front ranks before the younger warriors, and while this situation obviously reflects badly on the young, it is its external appearance which is primarily condemned as 'ugly'. The relationship between ugliness and disgrace is apparent at

---

[47] (1937), 61–2.
[48] On Tyrt.'s date (mid-7th cent.) and historical background, see Podlecki (1984), 92–7.

line 26; the wounds of the older man (to his *aidoia*) are *aischra* to the eyes and *nemeseton* to look upon.[49] The stress on physical appearances here is reinforced by the addition 'to the eyes' after *aischra*; it is this adjective that describes the external aspect of the scene, while the idea that the scene itself is reprehensible is conveyed by *nemeseton*, though the disapproval referred to by *nemeseton* is also directly related to the visual aspect.[50] The ugliness which is occasion for disapproval here reflects primarily upon the young warriors, whose position in front of their older comrades should prevent such eventualities.

Flight, then, is *aischros*,[51] as is any sign of hanging back in battle, and Tyrtaeus makes much of the idea that it is the duty of the *agathos* to be brave in battle and to avoid flight;[52] cowardice means the destruction of *arete*, is equated with 'learning shameful (ugly) things', and brings with it a train of ills (fragment 11. 14-16 West). An indication of the nature of these is given in 10. 1-12, where the fate of a beggar, who has (probably) been exiled for cowardice,[53] is contrasted with that of a warrior who has died fighting in the first rank for his homeland. The former drags his family with him as he wanders, is hateful to everyone he meets, is afflicted with poverty, 'disfigures his *genos*',[54] and is, in short, 'attended by every sort of *atimie* [dishonour] and *kakotes* [baseness]'. As a result neither he nor his family in the future receive any consideration or *aidos*. This person, then, has failed in his duty, and in his present condition is unable to see to the needs of his parents, his wife, and his children; without *time* he is accorded no *aidos*. This reminder of the disgrace which can accrue from cowardice is therefore a clear appeal to the *aidos* of the poem's addressees.

The converse of this scenario is given in fragment 12 West. There, having expressed the view that martial *arete* is the most important variety of excellence,[55] Tyrtaeus goes on to describe the rewards

[49] For the physical sense of *aischros* cf. fr. 11. 19 West.

[50] On the closeness of the 'moral' and the 'aesthetic' here, cf. R. Harder (1972), 164; Fränkel (1975), 156.

[51] Cf. 12. 17 West.   [52] See 10. 1-2, 11. 14, 12. 1-20, 43-4 West.

[53] Although in Tyrt.'s time Sparta was not the harsh militaristic society it became (see R. Harder (1972), 168-173), in his attitude to cowards ('tremblers', 11. 14, came to denote a class of dishonoured Spartiates), at least, Tyrt. foreshadows the outlook of his successors; on the Spartans' severity towards cowards, cf. Hdt. 1. 82. 8, 7. 231-2, 9. 71. 3; MacDowell (1986), 42-6.

[54] αἰσχύνει τε γένος (9), thus failing to meet one of the warrior's fundamental duties, not to disfigure the *genos* of his fathers (*Il.* 6. 209; *Od.* 24. 508; I.2.1 with n. 85 above).

[55] Tyrt., of course, does take a different view of the essentials of *arete* from Homer, preferring martial *arete* to all other kinds (12. 1-20 West; cf. Xenophanes' preference for a different kind of *arete*, 2. 1-12 West/DK). This is not a redefinition of *arete*, even

attendant on those who manifest such *aretē*. The warrior who has died for his city brings fame to it, its people, and his own family (23–4), and the entire city mourns and honours him, and his family after him (27–30); his fame survives (31) and, though dead, he becomes immortal (32). The warrior who is fortunate enough to fight bravely *and* escape death is also honoured by the entire community, and for the rest of his life (37–42): 'Everyone pays him *timē*, young and old alike, and after many pleasant experiences he goes to Hades, and as he grows old he is conspicuous among the townsfolk, nor does anyone wish to deprive him either of *aidōs* or of *dikē*, but all, young and old alike, give up their seats to him.'[56] This individual receives the *aidōs* and *timē* denied to the beggar in fragment 10, and both these acknowledge, as the poem as a whole makes clear, his *aretē*. The fundamental connection between *aidōs* and *timē* is once more apparent, and, as in Homer, *aidōs* is relevant both as a sensitivity towards the shameful or unseemly, as it reflects upon oneself, and as a positive regard for the honour of another.

The values of Tyrtaeus, then, are essentially those of the Homeric poems; but differences do exist, some important, some less so. It need not, for example, surprise us that a beggar is described as being without the *aidōs* of others, in spite of the fact that the beggar is an *aidoios par excellence* in the *Odyssey*. Just as the Odyssean theme that beggars deserve *aidōs* was idealistic, stressed for artistic purposes, and, even in that poem, often ignored in practice, so Tyrtaeus stresses the ignominy of the beggar's life in order to reinforce his warning. Tyrtaeus' beggar, however, does seem to belong more to the real world than that of Homeric fantasy, and perhaps it is a feature of the world he portrays that utter defeat and total loss of *aretē* seem a more present possibility than they do to the heroes of epic; no doubt utter defeat is also possible in Homer, and no doubt a severe loss of reputation could,

though in 11. 14 cowardice is said to destroy all *aretē*; rather 12. 1–20 recognizes different kinds of *aretē* in the same way as do several passages of the *Od.* (4. 725–6, 8. 244–9, 13. 45–6); nor does Tyrt.'s idea of martial *aretē* differ much from that of the *Il.* (although even there *aretē* does not solely consist in bravery in battle); von Erffa (1937: 61) is certainly wrong to say that *aidōs* is linked to *aretē* for the first time in Tyrt. On *aretē* in Tyrt., see Jaeger (1972), with Pearson (1962), 48, 75, 231 n. 8; Adkins (1960a), 70–3; Fowler (1987), 32.

[56] On giving up one's seat as mark of *aidōs*, cf. Ar. *Clouds* 993. Note that, as a result of the respect in which he is held, the great warrior is unlikely to be cheated of his due (probably in a legal context; on *dikē* here, see Gagarin (1974), 190, 197); this suggests that to cheat another in litigation is to disregard his status, and so to manifest *anaideiē*; it also suggests that questions of *dikē* are not entirely separable from questions of *timē*.

in theory, lead to total loss of *aretē*, but these are not eventualities which the heroes themselves actually stress, and although the Homeric characters are acutely concerned for their reputations, none of them ever looks like losing all his *aretē* in the way described by Tyrtaeus.[57] In this sense the fragments of Tyrtaeus seem to reflect a real world in a way that the Homeric poems do not.

Probably the most important differences between the world of the Homeric poems and that of Tyrtaeus lie in the relationship of individual to community. It is not that Tyrtaeus' warriors bear a responsibility to a community which Homer's heroes do not—we saw that the warriors of the *Iliad* were bound by strong ties not only to their kinsmen and followers, but also to the leaders and members of other contingents of the whole force; nor is it the case that warriors in Tyrtaeus are fighting for their families and dependants in a way that Homer's are not—Nestor could appeal to the thought of the dependants whom the heroes had left behind as a means of arousing *aidōs*, and Hector is clearly, in an important sense, fighting for the survival of Troy. Yet in Tyrtaeus it is certainly true, as many scholars point out,[58] that the city-state emerges as a far more concrete entity demanding the loyalty and obedience of the individual than do the communities of Homeric society. In Tyrtaeus it is the *polis* as a whole, not the army, which sees to the distribution of honour, which can control the rewarding of *aretē* with *timē* and *aidōs* (fragment 12), and this association of the concept of fame with the organ of the *polis*, this *Politisierung der Ruhmesidee*, as Jaeger calls it,[59] resembles the classical model of the city-state, with its rewards and punishments for good or bad service, more than it does the Homeric world. The development of the *polis* therefore makes a difference to the operation of the concepts of honour and shame.

The adoption of the hoplite phalanx some time before Tyrtaeus

[57] We remember that Eumaeus loses half his *aretē* on losing his freedom at *Od.* 17. 322–3 (Ch. 1, n. 161), and loss of liberty is exactly the kind of material disaster which might destroy *aretē*; in Hom. disapproval in itself is not sufficient to do so. (Certainly, it is *kakoi* that sneak away from battle (e.g. 6. 443), but this does not mean that an *agathos* becomes *kakos* simply by doing so.) In the world of Tyrt., however, it might be possible to regard one subject to universal opprobrium for his cowardice as without *aretē*, on the one hand because cowardice, apparently, might ultimately reduce one to the status of a beggar, and on the other because Tyrt. affects to see bravery in battle as the only important *aretē*; clearly one's reputation for bravery can be affected by the taunts of others in a way that, e.g., one's wealth or nobility of birth cannot.

[58] Jaeger (1972), 122ff.; Snell (1961), 37–8; (1975), 167; R. Harder (1972), 159–60; O. Murray (1980), 131; Carter (1986), 8–9.

[59] (1972), 124.

wrote his elegies must make a difference, too; although the Homeric hero is a member of a community of honour and is dependent to some extent on the behaviour of the army as a whole, the degree to which each individual depends on his fellows must be greater in the closely packed ranks of the hoplite battle. Such developments as we can discern in Tyrtaeus (and Callinus), however, do not entail a complete transformation of Homeric values; indeed, the core of those values remains in the elegists—it is still disgraceful to flee, it is to the benefit of a wider community if one does not flee, honour is the reward of bravery, the honour of the individual is implicated in that of the group, etc. But the structure in which these central values operate has changed, and if we wish to gauge the measure of this change, we need only compare the conduct demanded by Tyrtaeus with that of the Homeric Hector, torn between the desire to increase his personal honour and the claims of his city and dependants, or ask ourselves how Tyrtaeus might regard a hoplite warrior who decided to behave like an Achilles.[60]

2.3.3. *Solon*

Although much of the surviving poetry of Solon deals with more or less moral topics, there are few instances of *aidōs* and its relatives, and not much that is relevant. One fragment, however, is of particular interest (32 West): 'If I spared my country, and did not defile and disfigure my fame [*kleos*] by undertaking tyranny and brutal violence, I feel no *aidōs*; for in this way I think I shall excel over all men.' This is the first time we have encountered the verb *aideomai* with a conditional clause, and von Erffa[61] regards this passage as the first

---

[60] Even here one must be cautious; in the classical period, too, concern for individual honour can conflict with the duty of loyalty to the *polis* or the army, as in the notorious case of Alcibiades (Thuc. 5. 43. 2, 6. 15. 2, 6. 89); likewise Alcibiades' opponent, Nicias, can jeopardize the interests of his city out of concern for his own honour (7. 48. 4). Even attachment to the collective honour of the *polis* can cause conflict between individual and group: at Hdt. 9. 53 (Plataea) a Spartan company-commander disobeys an order to retreat out of an unwillingness to shame his city; here concern for the honour of the city, as fostered by Tyrt., actually leads to disloyalty to those who implement the city's policies. Similarly, at Thuc. 8. 27. 2-3, the Athenian commander Phrynichus is worried lest fear of reproach cause his men to reject his policy of strategic withdrawal. In both the *polis*, archaic or classical, and the Homeric poems, then, the concern for personal honour which the community fosters for its own protection may give rise to forms of individualism which impair the common good; the differences between the two contexts are therefore of degree rather than kind.   [61] (1937), 62-3.

retrospective use of the verb. In one sense this is correct, in another not. We have, indeed, met *aidōs* with reference to an event in the past before (*Iliad* 22. 104-7)[62] where Hector's *aidōs* at future abuse is based on his awareness that he has done something which others will consider reprehensible. In this case, too, *aidōs* has to do with the reproaches of other people; the context, as given by Plutarch, who quotes this and the following fragment (almost certainly from the same poem), indicates that Solon is arguing against a widespread belief that he has failed to win as much glory as he might have, and it is with reference to these criticisms and taunts (given in fragment 33 West) that Solon feels no *aidōs*. Yet it is important that, as is not the case in the passage from the *Iliad*, Solon appears to be considering taunts which have already been uttered, and so the *aidōs* which he disclaims can no longer be considered wholly prospective; it relates both to past conduct and to past, or at least present, criticism of that conduct. Nevertheless, there remains a reference to the future, for Solon explains his lack of *aidōs* by affirming his confidence of greater glory to come, and this suggests that one aspect of the *aidōs* he rejects might be related to future damage to his reputation.

The real importance of this fragment, however, lies in another direction: Solon is faced with a relatively widely held belief that he has acted in a way that brings him no credit; people are saying unpleasant things about him, yet he feels no *aidōs*, and relies instead on his own interpretation of his actions; he rejects the belief that he has, through lack of initiative, lost an opportunity to increase his honour, and instead relies on his own conception of the honourable, directly controverting the belief that failure to achieve competitive success is dishonourable with a claim that such success, improperly gained, is itself dishonourable. He does imply that ultimately he will be vindicated by the approval and recognition of others, yet he still feels able to ignore present mockery, and this is something which Adkins[63] claims no one does before Socrates. Solon thus opposes a popular standard of the honourable by means of a standard of his own, a fact which is unaffected by his belief that his own evaluation will ultimately be endorsed by others. It is not in itself new that *aidōs* can be inactive in the face of certain reproaches, for numerous characters in Homer feel no *aidōs* when reproached, most notably the suitors. In general, however, they simply ignore reproaches which they know cannot seriously damage their position; they do not disagree with those who

[62] See 1.2.3 above.   [63] (1960*a*), 155 and n. (d).

say that their conduct is dishonourable, they ignore them. Characters like the suitors, or Paris, then, are simply *anaideis*,[64] and no character in Homer is portrayed as relying on his own sense that his conduct is positively honourable in opposition to others' claims that it is dishonourable. This is precisely what Solon does, in contrast to the likes of the Diomedes of *Iliad* 8, who does not find himself able to ignore the taunts of others even though he does not agree with them.[65]

2.3.4. *Theognidea*

In the collection of poems that has come down to us under the name of Theognis we have an opportunity to witness *aidōs* and the other relevant terms in action in a wide range of contexts, and *aidōs* itself enjoys an importance in the corpus comparable with that accorded it in the Homeric poems. It is unlikely that all the excerpts given in our collection are by Theognis, and there is dispute as to the date of that poet himself,[66] but for our purposes it is sufficient that the corpus as a whole should constitute a collection of poetry in which certain basic suppositions and features are common both to disputed passages and to those which can with some certainty be considered genuine, and

---

[64] Here we might compare the unabashed admission of the loss of a shield in Archilochus fr. 5 West, criticized as *anaideia* by the 5th-cent. Critias (fr. B 44 DK). This fr. does not oppose conventional ideas of the honourable with a subjective alternative, as does Solon's, but the freedom from the constraints of 'what people say' which it exhibits is none the less important. Contempt for popular disapproval is also apparent in Arch. fr. 14 West ('no one who pays heed to the censure of the people can enjoy much in the way of pleasures'; it is unlikely that this is a threat to bring down popular approval on the addressee, as Burnett (1983: 58 n. 15) claims); cf. also fr. 133 West, which disputes the opinion, found in Tyrt. 12. 23–34, that those who die bravely in battle receive *aidōs* and are honoured after death (see Gundert (1972), 80–1; Fränkel (1975), 139). For our purposes it is sufficient that these voices of dissent from the more idealistic mainstream (see Whitman (1964), 37–9) should be heard, and it scarcely matters whether or not these opinions are those of the poet himself. (For the dangers of the unreflective assumption of self-expression and autobiography in Arch., see Dover (1964); Tsagarakis (1977), 16–18, etc.; the fact, however, that Critias attributes *anaideia* to Arch. himself at least indicates that the first-person utterance of fr. 5 West was not, as is the case with fr. 19 West (see Arist. *Rhet.* 1418^{b}27–32), given in its original context to another person.) For criticism of conventional ideas of *timē*, we might compare Xenophanes' depreciation of the honour accorded physical strength in athletics, fr. 2 West and DK.

[65] Cf. 1.2.2 above.

[66] West (1974: 65–71) favours an early date, and links the genuine poetry of Theognis with the tyranny of Theagenes in the latter part of the 7th cent.; Podlecki (1984: 143) prefers the mid-6th cent. *floruit* given in the chronographers. Various approaches to Thgn.'s date and the historical background also appear in Figueira and Nagy (1985).

that no excerpt should date from a period later than the early fifth century.[67]

Whatever may be the case with regard to other elegy,[68] it seems virtually certain that the kind of poetry preserved in the Theognid corpus was composed for performance at the aristocratic drinking party, the symposium.[69] Certainly, all the passages which we shall consider emerge in a clearer light when seen against that background; several of the passages in which our terms occur deal directly with behaviour at the symposium, others reflect the political concerns of its aristocratic participants, while others seek to impart the virtues of the aristocracy to younger members of the group, a process which must be seen in the context of the prominence of pederasty in aristocratic circles, with which our terms are also concerned.

Aidōs should govern proper conduct at the symposium; at lines 479–83 the behaviour of one who drinks immoderately is described: 'whoever exceeds the limit in drinking is no longer in control of his tongue or his mind; he says awkward things, which appear *aischra* to the sober, and he has no *aidōs* at doing anything when he is drunk;[70] although he was sensible [*sōphrōn*] before, now he is a fool.' Again *aidōs* is associated with *sōphrosunē*[71] and opposed to excess;[72] its abandonment here under the influence of alcohol and its association with self-control[73] indicate its

[67] As is likely; allusions to the invasion of the Medes (757–64, 773–88) indicate the inclusion of some passages of early 5th-cent. date. There is no passage which can certainly be attributed to any later period.

[68] Bowie (1986) makes a strong case for a sympotic origin for all but extended, narrative elegy; cf. id. (1990) on martial elegy. Contrast West (1974), 10–14; Fowler (1987), 102–3.

[69] See West (1974), 11–12; Patzer (1981), 203–4; a sympotic origin for the Cyrnus poems which some consider the only genuine Thgn. is confirmed by 237–54, and if the remainder of the corpus is not by Thgn., it will presumably have made its way in as a result of similarity of style, origin, and purpose, forming a collection, originally composed for symposia, to be sung at future symposia (Patzer, 203–7). On the symposium in general, see O. Murray (1980), 197–203, (1983*a*); (1982*b*), and now, above all, (1990).

[70] αἰδεῖται δ' ἔρδων οὐδὲν ὅταν μεθύῃ. This is the first example we have encountered of *aideomai* followed by a present participle where the verb does not also govern a direct object (contrast *Od.* 8. 86, and see Verdenius (1944–5), 48 n. 1, against von Erffa (1937), 19; cf. Callinus 1. 2–3 West). We have now met *aideomai* + acc., + inf., + part., and + conditional clause (Solon 32 West). While in all these cases the verb itself tends to look forward (whether to others' disapproval or more generally to a situation which one characterizes as shameful, unseemly, or embarrassing), it is clear that its immediate reference can be to (*a*) future conduct, (*b*) present conduct, or (*c*) past conduct (Solon 32; 22. 104–7).

[71] Cf. 1.3.4 above.　　　　　　　　　　　　　　　　　　　　　[72] Cf. 1.5.2 above.

[73] North (1966): 18, notes that *sōphrōn* takes on positive connotations of self-control from its use in this passage, but that it is still basically in the sphere of 'good sense' (cf. 431, 453–6, 497–8, 655–6). *Aidōs* thus bears the same relation to good sense as in Hom.

essential inhibitory nature. The social character of the concept is also apparent, in that the drunkard without *aidōs* ignores the effects of his conduct on others, who find his words inappropriate or embarrassing. The drinker's *aidōs* should make him sensitive to the 'ugliness' of his behaviour. This idea of ugliness is expressed again at 627-8, where it is *aischron* that a drunken man should be in the company of the sober and that a sober man should remain in the company of inebriates; clearly the experience would be unpleasant for the odd one out, and it is the unpleasantness of the situation itself which is described by the word *aischron*; such a scene simply does not look right.[74] As in Homer, then, *aidōs* in the Theognid corpus is the force which creates and sustains the awareness of and concern for the effects of one's behaviour on others which is necessary for the enjoyment of conviviality by all.[75]

Since the corpus is so closely related to the life of the aristocracy, it is not surprising that the concept of *aretē* looms so large, for *aretē* is the quality which the *aristoi*, the aristocrats, claim to possess. Many of the excerpts which employ the complex of terms based on *aretē* (including the adjectives *agathos*, *kakos*, etc.) relate to a background of social change; in some of these it appears that such change, in which one class gains ascendancy over another, can in itself render the *agathos kakos* and vice versa (55-8, 1109-13, both in passages bearing the Cyrnus tag), and there *agathos* etc. must be socially descriptive rather than morally evaluative. In other places, however, it seems that it is moral qualities that render one *agathos* or *kakos* (most notably 145-8, another Cyrnus passage). Other passages can be read in both social and moral senses, while some seem to combine the two; a case in point is 53 ff. (again, a Cyrnus passage): in 57-8 *agathos*, *esthlos*, and *deilos* (base) refer to social class, but in 59-68 the former *deiloi*, now *agathoi*, are chiefly characterized by their moral failings, cheating, faithlessness, and unreliability as friends (all of which could be seen as involving lack of *aidōs*). In addition, while it sometimes appears that *agathos* is a title conferred by success (165-6, 797-8, not Cyrnus passages), elsewhere success and wealth are irrelevant (315-18, = Solon 15 West).[76] Where *aretē* is not tied to success it may be moral, but in view of the confusion

[74] For this quasi-aesthetic outlook, cf. 502: excessive drinking can *kataischunai* (disfigure) one previously *sophos* (wise). Both the drunkard and his conduct 'look ugly' (a powerful disincentive, given that aristocrats are supposed to be *kalos* in appearance).
[75] On the standards of protocol and the importance of creating the appropriate atmosphere at symposia and banquets, see Slater (1990); cf., with specific reference to Thgn., Levine (1985).
[76] Cf. Pearson (1962), 76-7.

of social and moral *aretē* in 53–68, it is hardly safe to assume this; it seems, in fact, most likely that many of the passages in which these terms occur reflect and promote a belief that the nobility were, as a class, morally good and their inferiors morally bad.[77] The discussion of *aretē* in the corpus will thus reflect a political crisis in which the position of the aristocracy, and their claim to be the 'good men' of the community, came under attack,[78] and will constitute an attempt by those who composed for performance in an aristocratic context to reclaim *aretē* for themselves and their kind as an inclusive concept, not simply acquired by financial and political success, to reinforce their vision of themselves as the true *agathoi*.[79]

The prominence of these themes in the Cyrnus excerpts is clear even from the cursory survey above, and it should be remembered that Cyrnus is a youth, a new initiate to the adult male aristocratic community; although some of what the corpus has to say about *aretē* may simply be general political and social reflection, much of it must be addressed, with didactic intent, to Cyrnus and others like him.[80] Even the pederastic pieces largely concentrated in the so-called 'second book' will be relevant here, since the role of the older aristocrat as educator of his young protégé is only one aspect of his relationship with him as lover to beloved.[81]

The function of the handing down of aristocratic values from older to younger is evident in 27–30: 'With good will towards you, Cyrnus, I impart the precepts I learned from the *agathoi* when I was a boy; be sensible, and do not derive prestige [*timai*], success [*aretai*],[82] or

[77] Not an unparalleled idea; cf. Lloyd-Jones (1971), 47; Ferguson (1979), 39 (a parallel from Chinese wisdom literature).

[78] We have seen that some of our best and most specific evidence for the phenomena under discussion comes from Cyrnus poems, and since these, at least, are generally considered genuine Theognidean excerpts, Thgn. presumably reacted to a real historical situation, but in view of the dispute about his date, we cannot be sure exactly when this situation may have existed. It seems likely, moreover, that the aristocracy could have felt themselves threatened at any time from the 7th cent. to the 5th, and even if the corpus as a whole contains many accretions to the genuine work of Thgn., passages which are not authentic may still indicate similar aims and presuppositions; promotion of aristocratic values, at least, must have been a fairly general feature of the symposium. Cf. (and contrast) Nagy (1985), 41–6.

[79] Here I am much indebted to the discussion of Patzer (1981), *passim*. Cf. Cobb-Stevens (1985).

[80] Cf. Patzer (1981), 201–2.

[81] See Dover (1978), 202–3, and, on pederasty, education, initiation, and the symposium, Bremmer (1990).

[82] I take the plural, *aretai*, to denote concrete examples of excellence, i.e. successful exploits or achievements, but perhaps it might signify the reputation for excellence, i.e. status. 'Skills' is another possible, but less likely translation.

wealth from disgraceful [*aischra*] or unjust deeds.' These lines probably belong with those which follow them in the manuscripts, in which the youth is advised to associate with *agathoi* rather than *kakoi*, to eat and drink with them, and to learn from them. The passage as a whole, then, justifies the process of learning aristocratic virtue in the context of the symposium, and the virtues which it recommends are moral ones. The implication is there, however, and it is brought out more fully in other surrounding passages, that the vices which are decried are those liable to be perpetrated by now ascendant inferior classes.[83] That it is a mark of the *agathoi* to forego desirable ends achieved by unjust or disgraceful means[84] implies that they are led to do so by their *aidōs*, and this is substantiated by passages like 83–6: 'Not even if you searched among all men would you find more than one ship would hold of those who have *aidōs* on their tongues and eyes,[85] whom profit [*kerdos*] does not lead to disgraceful [*aischron*] dealing.'[86]

[83] See 39–52, 53–68 in particular.

[84] Cf. 465–6: 'practise *aretē*, and let what is just [*ta dikaia*] be dear to you; do not let profit [*kerdos*] overcome you when it is *aischron*.' Cf. 1147–50 (unjust (*adikoi*) men disregard the anger of the gods and are always after others' possessions, forming disgraceful (*aischra*) compacts for evil deeds); and 607–10 where profit made from lying is said to be *aischron*, *kakon*, and not *kalon*. This attitude to lying contrasts with that of the *Od.*, where Od. often lies to further his own aims. A distaste for deceit does, however, emerge from 9. 312–13, and from 4. 339 (a criticism of Od.: see Stanford (1968), 17–18); and with Od.'s deceit contrast that of Aegisthus, of whom the adjective 'deceitful' is used pejoratively at *Od.* 3. 250. Od.'s lies are, for the audience of the *Od.*, obviously somehow 'all right', probably by virtue of their skill, wit, audacity, etc. (see Walcot (1977)), but perhaps also because, as Stanford alleges (19–22), they are never maliciously (but only teasingly) intended to deceive one who has a right to the truth, such as a friend, associate, or fellow citizen. The attitude of the Greeks to deceit, however, does harden over the centuries; certainly the idea that it is *aischron* to tell lies becomes common in the 5th cent., and in the 5th and later centuries Od. can be seen as villain rather than hero. The Theognidean passages allude to the ambivalence of *kerdos*, and this is an idea that is present in Hom. (4. 339 again), and in Hes., where it is associated with *anaideiē*. A term expressing the bad side of *kerdos*, *aischrokerdeia*, comes into use in the 5th cent.: Soph. *Ant.* 1056; Hdt. 1. 187, etc. Behind the distaste for improper *kerdos* in the Theognidea there probably lies a distaste for the commercial practices of inferior classes.

[85] On *aidōs* and the eyes, cf. on *h. Hom. Cer.* 113–15, 2. 2 and n. 37 above; on *aidōs* and the tongue, cf. Ar. *Knights* 276–7, 637–8, where *anaideia* is associated with a ready tongue and a loud voice.

[86] That there was a danger that social change, in which the wealth of the *agathos* declined, might lead to the abandonment of aristocratic standards of proper behaviour seems to emerge from passages like 383–92, where a man who is a stranger to *kakon* (ambivalent between 'trouble' and 'wrongdoing'), having fallen into the discreditable condition of poverty and bearing many *aischea* against his will, learns to commit many evil acts, involving lying and cheating and strife (cf. 649–52). The implication of these lines is both that poverty is discreditable in itself (cf. Tyrt. 10. 1–12; Hes. *WD* 717–18 also recognizes this, but urges his audience to forbear reproach; parallels from modern Greece in Walcot (1970), 60–4) and that it leads to dishonesty. Lines 393–400, however,

Elsewhere the rarity of *aidōs* is associated with moral decline, and it is a fairly safe assumption that moral decline in this body of poetry is associated with the ascendancy of the lower classes. Lines 289–92 provide a good example: 'Now the vices of the *agathoi* become the virtues for the *kakoi* among men;[87] they rejoice [? text uncertain] in perverse laws/customs. *Aidōs* has perished, and *anaideiē* and *hubris* have conquered *dikē* and now hold the entire country.'[88] Similarly, at 635–6 *aidōs* and *gnōmē* are said to be qualities that distinguish *agathoi*, of whom there are now few examples.[89] In these passages *aidōs* is seen as a character trait that promotes good conduct in general and is opposed to contrary dispositions such as *anaideiē* and *hubris*;[90] *aidōs* promotes *dikē* both in its general sense of 'righteousness' and in its particular application in the context of the proper acquisition of wealth,[91] and its departure from the world is regarded as a symptom of

whether a continuation of this poem or a new excerpt, provide a corollary; poverty distinguishes the *deilos* from the man who is 'much better', and the latter continues to exercise the aristocratic virtues of justice and loyalty (*aidōs*) towards his *philoi* (cf. Cobb-Stevens (1985), 163).

[87] Or: 'the ills of the *agathoi* become advantageous to the *kakoi*.'

[88] This sentiment is reiterated at 647–8.

[89] The point about the rarity of the *agathos* here might seem to suggest that the term refers only to moral excellence, but it is more likely that *agathos* here, like 'gentleman', refers to both social and moral excellence, the point being that, in the face of infiltration of the aristocracy by the *nouveaux riches* (see 183–92) and possible attraction of aristocrats into non-aristocratic activities, only the man of good birth and good character qualifies as a true 'gentleman'.

[90] At 41, 379, and 1082a the antithesis of *hubris* is *sōphrosunē*, and at 1135–50, a thoroughly Hesiodic excerpt, *sōphrosunē* abandons the world as *aidōs* did in Hes., and her departure entails that men embark on disgraceful compacts to cheat others of their possessions. Clearly *aidōs* and *sōphrosunē* work in much the same way in the corpus: *sōphrosunē*, of course, is a disposition of character, or even a virtue, and the way in which *aidōs* and *sōphrosunē* can express the same ideas here indicates that *aidōs* is also being used in a dispositional, non-occurrent sense as, one might say, the disposition of one who possesses *aidōs*, just as *anaideiē* is the disposition of one who does not. In the passage at 1135–50 it is notable that the state of affairs which is attributed to the departure of *sōphrosunē* is also seen as a result of man's failure to respect the gods; the gods also punish the improper pursuit of wealth which *aidōs* helps prevent (197–208); as in the *Od.* and Hes., then, the gods punish human crimes in a general sense. As a result religious and moral offences converge, and can be designated by the same terms (note *eusebēs* etc. in 1141–4), and one can *aideisthai* the gods in a general way (1181–2). This use, however, remains but a species of the usage 'respect for those of greater status'.

[91] Gagarin (1974: 193–4) concludes that *dikē* etc. are mainly, but not exclusively, concerned with economic behaviour in the corpus. To his one example of a clear exception to the rule (313–14) I would add 27–30, where it is not only the pursuit of wealth, but also of prestige and success by improper means which is *aischron* and *adikon*. Equally, in 292 (cited above) *dikē* is used quite generally (opposed to *anaideiē* and *hubris*), and need not be related to any specific behaviour (cf. 132). Gagarin admits that there are uses of *dikē*, *dikaion*, etc. which are quite general (ibid.), but his inference that these

the decline of civilized values. All this is very similar to Hesiod's picture of moral decline in the fifth age of man, but in the Theognid corpus moral decline cannot be sharply divorced from social change, and the moral qualities which are being abandoned in the present turmoil, like *aidōs*, are promoted in an aristocratic context as virtues which the young aristocrat must adopt.

The didactic purpose of the association of *aidōs* with the *agathoi* emerges most clearly at 409–10: 'You will lay down for your children no treasure better than *aidōs*, which attends good [*agathoi*] men, Cyrnus.'[92] The association of *aidōs* with *aretē* is therefore fundamental in the corpus; this tells us, as we already knew, that *aidōs* is a desirable quality in most circumstances, indeed, a virtue; we have met, too, the idea that *aidōs* is an aristocratic quality,[93] but obviously this would not be accepted by society in general as analytically true.[94] Even in Homer those who were endowed with *aretē* were expected to show *aidōs* in a variety of different ways, but the two did not go as closely together as in the Theognid corpus, and *agathoi* like the suitors could ignore *aidōs* without damaging their *aretē*. The impression we get in the corpus, however, is that *aidōs* and other moral qualities are necessary for *aretē* and, indeed, *aidōs* appears as the most important of these qualities, since it not only implies and promotes specific varieties of proper behaviour in particular spheres, but may also provide the impetus to behave as one's society requires in any sphere. Traditional *agathoi*, presumably, are now no longer necessarily distinguished from other classes by their wealth, success, and status; needing something more with which to identify themselves, they find it by appropriating proper behaviour and civilized values and making these, in combination with noble birth, essential for the title of *agathos*.

should not be credited with moral overtones because, in specific contexts, *dikē* refers to economic behaviour rather than general propriety would only be plausible if the previous steps of his argument, on the twofold etymology of *dikē* and on *dikē* in Hes., had been correct. Clearly, though, improper (*adikon*) behaviour is not confined to the economic sphere, although it may be exercised in that sphere, and the principle of fairness that is observed in keeping one's hands off others' property is not entirely distinct from the requirement that the honour of others be recognized.

[92] In 1161–2, where the language is similar, *aidōs* is still associated with education, but, rather than a quality of *agathoi*, is a reaction to those who are *agathoi*; on the face of it, the poet asks Cyrnus to accord *agathoi aidōs* as a means of acquiring a good character to pass on to his children; this could be seriously meant, but the lines may parody the earlier couplet, and the point of the parody may be a homosexual joke; Cyrnus should show *aidōs* for *agathoi* (i.e. the poet) by returning his favours. See text below.

[93] *h. Hom. Cer.* 213–15; see 2.2 above.

[94] The proverb adapted by Hes. at *WD* 319 suggests the opposite view.

Thus *aidōs* is appropriate for *agathoi* in general as a disposition towards proper behaviour, their behaviour in the symposium being an index of their general moral and social character; it is also recommended in a more specific sense, however, as a central element in the concept of friendship which binds, on the one hand, the aristocratic participants in the symposium and, on the other, the parties to the homosexual relationship.

We saw in Homer that *aidōs* was a proper reaction towards one's *philoi*, and although *aidōs* does not occur in that connection in Hesiod, the concept of *philotēs* and the proper modes of conduct towards ones *philoi* remain the same in all essential aspects in that author. In Hesiod as in Homer *philotēs* is a reciprocal relationship (*Works and Days* 353–6), but it is not necessarily a calculating or materialistic one; there may be an intrinsic pleasure in giving (357–8), and forgiveness and constancy are also stressed (707-16).[95] Nevertheless, reciprocity of friendship is regarded as fundamental,[96] even if this is not all there is to the relationship,[97] and in the Theognid corpus it is frequently with the obligation to return a favour that *aidōs* is concerned.[98]

That it is a basic duty of the *agathos* to accord his *philoi aidōs* is stated explicitly at 399; this contrasts with the behaviour of the (morally and socially) *deiloi* at 58-68, 101-112, who are untrustworthy as friends and who do not return one's favours.[99] The complaint that a favour has not been returned, and that *aidōs* has been ignored, is a frequent one in the corpus; typical is 253-4, where the poet complains that, despite his having presented Cyrnus with the gift of immortality through song, he receives little *aidōs* in return. The context there is clearly amatory, and this is an indication that the advice from older to younger on how to behave as an aristocrat should, which is at the core of much of the corpus, is to be seen against a pederastic background. Hence 'showing *aidōs*' comes to denote the rewarding of kindnesses with sexual favours (1263-6, 1329-34). As aristocratic male society approves of showing *aidōs* in general, so it is represented as approving of the *aidōs* which the

---

[95] On these aspects of *philotēs* in Hes., cf. Fraisse (1974), 47–9 (in general 46–50).

[96] Cf. Pearson (1962), 86, 88.

[97] Pearson (1962), 245 n. 2 (cf. Fraisse (1974), 47–9).

[98] On *philotēs/philiē* in the Theognidea, see Fraisse (1974), 50–6 (esp. 50–1 on its aristocratic nature); cf. Pearson (1962), 85–8.

[99] Great stress is laid in many passages on openness and constancy between *philoi* (79–82, 95–6, 97–100, etc.), but it is recognized that true *philoi* are rare, and so caution towards ordinary *philoi* is also urged (73–4, 75–6, 115–16, 116–17, etc.); the advice to adapt one's character to that of one's *philoi* (213–14, 215–18) probably commends affability rather than duplicity.

beloved should accord his lover; at 1272 a greedy boy is said to have become an *aischunē* (disgrace)[100] to the friends of both parties to the relationship, while at 1297-8 a boy for whom (presumably unrequited) *philotēs* threatens to lead the poet to Hades is urged to 'fear the wrath of the gods and the rumour of men'.[101] Whatever society may really have thought of boys who said yes,[102] the values which are invoked in these passages to induce them to do so are those which govern proper behaviour among *philoi*, and the obligation to show *aidōs* by returning a favour is common to all kinds of *philotēs*.[103] Clearly, the various spheres in which Theognidean *aidōs* is operative are all ultimately related; those who behave properly in the symposium, as a result of *aidōs*, will be disposed to behave properly in general (the symposium being a microcosm of society);[104] they will be appropriate examples to their *philoi*, friendship properly conceived being of the utmost importance to the aristocratic symposiasts; and they will be able to instil a proper sense of *aidōs* in new members of the group, youths who will learn what *aidōs* for one's *philoi* means by their participation in a pederastic relationship. Thus *aidōs* emerges as central to a remarkably coherent moral ideology centred on one particular aristocratic institution.

---

[100] This is the first instance of the noun *aischunē* we have encountered (cf. von Erffa (1937), 73). Here it appears in the objective sense, but later it will also be found in a subjective sense, as the reaction to or mental picture of disgrace and so as equivalent to *aidōs*. In the objective sense it takes on the sense of Homeric *aischos*, although, unlike *aischos*, it normally has no physical sense (*aischos* continues as 'ugliness' after *aischunē* has become common; but see *aischunē* used of embarrassing physical disfigurement at Pl. *Laws* 878c). On the figurative description of a person as an *aischunē*, cf. the Homeric use of *elenchea/elenchees*, 1.1.5 above; also Thuc. 8. 73. 3 (*aischunē*); Ar. *Ach.* 855 (*oneidos*).

[101] θεῶν δ' ἐποπίζεο μῆνιν βάξιν τ' ἀνθρώπων. The verb *epopizomai* properly refers to divine anger, and only governs 'the rumour of men' here by a kind of zeugma; in doing so, however, it comes close in sense to *aideomai*.

[102] At 1329 it is supposed to be *kalon* for the boy to accede to the lover's request, and not *aischron* for the latter to demand the return of a favour; the invocation of the obligations incumbent upon *philoi* thus places a good construction on conduct which might in a wider sense be regarded as discreditable in the youth (see Pl. *Smp.* 183cd; Dover (1978), 81-91).

[103] Von Erffa (1937: 71) is therefore wrong to see the *aidōs* demanded at 253, 1266, and 1331 as derived from the respect one owes one's elders. On the link between pederastic and wider forms of *philotēs/philiē* in the corpus, and for an account of the way in which the qualities recommended and deplored in the beloved mirror those valued and depreciated in the city at large, see J. M. Lewis (1985).

[104] As argued by Levine (1985).

2.4. PINDAR

Aidōs does occur in the extant poetry of Pindar, but it does so in ways which are largely incidental to those ethical attitudes—avoidance of excess, sensitivity to divine resentment[105] and human jealousy—which one regards as characteristically Pindaric. Familiar uses recur; the victor in athletic contests, for example, is *aidoios* (*Isthmian* 2. 37) or possesses a *charis* which attracts *aidōs* (*Olympian* 7. 89), strife within the family involves breach of *aidōs* (*Pythian* 4. 145-6), and *aidōs* towards one's parents is obligatory (*Pythian* 4. 218); *aidōs* also occurs in the context of coyness about sex at *Pythian* 9. 12 and 40-1, and in that of concern for one's status as a warrior at *Nemean* 9. 34-7 and *Pythian* 4. 174.[106]

Three passages are of rather more interest for the way in which they refer to an explicit connection between *aidōs* and foresight. In a difficult passage of *Olympian* 7 (43-7) *aidōs* is associated with that quality (or made a daughter of Prometheus, which is the same thing),[107] and contrasted with the forgetfulness which caused men to omit to light fires to Athena. *Aidōs* is thus seen as that which prevents neglect of one's obligations to the gods, but this is so only because *aidōs* inhibits neglect of obligations in general. The link with foresight and clear-sightedness (*aidōs* is contrasted with the 'cloud of forgetfulness', 45) corresponds to the traditional association of *aidōs* and 'good sense', and indicates that *aidōs*, since it involves an evaluative response, must proceed from an accurate perception of the given situation, and that, as a prospective, inhibitory response, it must involve an appreciation of the possible consequences of one's actions, an anticipation that a given action is unacceptable or disgraceful. Similarly, in *Nemean* 11 (45-6), man's tendency to go too far in the

[105] A notion of which only the germ is present in Hom. (Greene (1944: 20) suggests the following as indications of the concept of divine resentment in minimal form: 5. 440-2; *Od.* 4. 78-81, 22. 287-9; one might also include 7. 446 ff. (cf. Adkins (1970), 36).)

[106] To be wounded in the back is a disgrace (it causes one to be disfigured, *aischunthē-men*) at *Nem.* 9. 27; cf. 13. 288-9; Tyrt. 11. 19-20.

[107] No interpretation of προμαθέος αἰδώς (44) is really satisfactory (see von Erffa (1937), 77-8; von Erffa's translation, 'the *aidōs* of a forethinking man', is best passed over without comment), but unless προμαθέος is (or conceals) a nom. adj., 'foreseeing' or 'forethinking', which might agree with the nom. *aidōs*, then Jebb's solution (1882: 155 (followed by Gildersleeve (1890), ad loc.)), '*aidōs*, daughter of Prometheus', is the best available, even though it is an unparalleled genealogy and a locution which is difficult in the absence of the article or some such word as θυγάτηρ.

pursuit of *kerdos*,[108] is attributed to his ignorance of the plan of Zeus, equated with hope which is without *aidōs*, and contrasted with foresight (*promatheia*). The intelligence, then, which enables one to foresee the consequences of one's actions and properly to characterize one's own conduct is, for Pindar, indispensable to *aidōs* in its prospective sense.[109]

The association of *aidōs* with foresight and good sense allows Pindar to make a subtle joke at *Nemean* 5. 14–18; he expresses his *aidōs* at relating an unsavoury event in the history of the house of Aeacus (the murder of Phocus by his two half-brothers, Telamon and Peleus), and explains his reticence by the observation that 'it is often most prudent for a man to know when to keep silent'. This suggests that the poet's *aidōs* is based on a prudential fear of unpleasant consequences, but this fear can hardly be genuine, since the allusion to the event is quite clear, and, in fact, the poet reveals what he claims to conceal.[110] We have, then, nothing but elegant and witty praise of the victor; Pindar pretends to expel any disreputable elements from his victory ode, and contrasts silence (*to sigan*), which conceals ignoble deeds, with the poet's craft, which makes noble deeds immortal. But he need not have mentioned the episode at all, and it is most probable that his reason for doing so is a literary one, involving both the clever and courteous 'suppression' of unsavoury detail and a sly joke, to the effect that the poet must show prudence in his selection of material, lest his patrons refuse to pay him. The *aidōs* of this passage, therefore, is manifestly not genuine, and so should not be taken as evidence for the prudential nature of the concept. The 'meaning' of the verb *aideomai* in this passage relates not to the description of an emotional state, but to the categorization of an event as unseemly and inappropriate to a laudatory context, and this categorization itself is subordinate to the contrast contrived between noble deeds and their opposite; thus this passage exemplifies the way in which the intention behind the use of an emotion word need have nothing to do with the description of an occurrent emotion.

[108] Here, then, *aidōs* does relate to Pindar's chief moral concerns, the avoidance of excess and the dangers of over-prosperity; similarly, at *Ol.* 13. 115 *aidōs* is required for the proper enjoyment of pleasures, and at *Nem.* 9. 33–4 *aidōs* is opposed to the desire for *kerdos*.

[109] Pearson (1962: 85, on Thgn. 1135–46) expresses the view that *sōphrosunē* is, above all, the ability to foresee the consequences of one's own actions; this might go some way to explaining the frequent association of this term with *aidōs*, though I doubt very much that it would cover all instances of *sōphrosunē*, which is not a purely intellectual kind of 'good sense'; for a further association of *aidōs* with good sense in Pindar, see fr. 52b. 50–1 Maehler (*euboulia*). [110] Cf. *Ol.* 1. 52–3.

3

Aeschylus

Moving from archaic poetry to drama we return to a genre which, like epic, represents the action of human characters in a context in which they possess their own status, function, and motivation, and which involves their interaction both with the events which constitute the plot of the piece and with other characters; we are thus able to observe the operation of *aidōs* and related concepts in beings who, while they are not accorded the multiplicity of traits and idiosyncrasies which may constitute the personalities of real people, are nevertheless presented for the consideration of real people as representations of human agents. Tragedy may be the representation of an action, as Aristotle insists, but action, if it is to be intelligible at all, requires human agency, and intelligible human agency requires motivation, states of mind, character.[1] In Aeschylus and the other tragedians the complex of terms centred on *aidōs* occurs with some frequency; these terms themselves (like a multitude of others) refer to states of mind, to features of personality, to motivation, and thus it should be one of the great mysteries of scholarship that it was ever objected that concepts of this type, or the concept of character *tout court*, should not be imported into the study of Greek tragedy. Given the explicit emphasis of the texts on states of mind and motivation, we cannot do other than take these elements into consideration. To be sure, we cannot approach the characters of Greek tragedy as though they possess personality which extends beyond the play as read or seen in performance, nor can we look for characterization behind or beyond what is

---

[1] As Arist. well knew, at least in so far as he regarded it as normal that tragic action should manifest the ethical character of the agent; see Halliwell (1986: 149–67), who is also correct in pointing out (164–5) that Arist.'s emphasis in his discussion of *ēthos* is on the generic and the normative (very much on the possession of excellence of character and its expression in action), and it may well be that the practice of the tragedians was in this respect more likely to meet his tastes than ours, but it is my impression that the role of character in tragedy itself goes somewhat beyond Arist.'s limits, and in particular that the *personae* of tragedy evaluate each other and set forth their own motives in language which does more than merely illustrate a significant moral choice (*proairesis*); it is this impression that I hope to substantiate below by means of the light that study of *aidōs*, etc. can shed on character and motivation in tragedy.

said and done in the play; but the fact that those who participate in the action of Aeschylean tragedy comment on the states of mind and motives which make themselves and others act as they do indicates that personality is far from irrelevant to action. While we should expect to find the *personae* of tragedy humanly intelligible, for the purposes of interpretation we do not need first to turn to vague concepts of human intelligibility (for naturally I find my interpretation of A's character infinitely more humanly intelligible than yours); rather, we can examine the role of the motives, dispositions, and states of mind which are there in the text, for these explicit indications of character and motive, and the character and motives they adumbrate, are essential to the portrayal of human agents as originators, interpreters, and recipients of the action of the play. Character is thus a function of plot, and reaches its greatest depth in the motivation of important characters to significant actions, not as something added to those actions, but as an essential part of them; as we shall see, motives such as *aidōs* can be absolutely integral to the action of the play, and I therefore have no qualms about investigating the role of *aidōs* in the inner life of Aeschylean characters. To concentrate, indeed, on such motives as *aidōs* may, if we interpret that concept aright, offer some hope of appreciating the characters of tragedy from the perspective of the values of the original audience.[2]

---

[2] For modern discussions of the role of character and tragedy and/or Aesch., see Jones (1962), 30–3, 37–8 (on *ēthos* in Arist. *Poetics*), 77–81 (against characterization in Aesch.); to Jones's strictures Easterling (1973: 3–19 (cf. ead. (1977), 121–9, on characterization in Soph.)), Dover (1973: 58–69, esp. 69), and Winnington-Ingram (1983: 141) oppose the ideas of human intelligibility and the need to make action plausible; Gould (1978*b*) seeks to modify this position, and points to some (formal and rhetorical) features of tragedy which militate against detailed characterization and which should certainly not be used as indications of personal idiosyncrasies; considerations of form, however, do not preclude characterization, though they may limit the ways in which we may look for it (cf. Vickers (1973), 52–6; Easterling (1990), 92–3; see also, on the effects of 'rhetoric' on characterization (with specific reference to Eur.), Conacher (1981)); G. O. Hutchinson (1985; pp. xxxiv–xxxv) sensibly points out that characterization in Aesch. goes beyond that which is necessary simply to make action plausible, and Goldhill (1986: 168–98) has an excellent account of the interdependence of character and action (or, in his terminology, 'discourse', a somewhat wider term) and demonstrates the importance of the references to character and motive which are there in the text; cf. id. (1984), 68–74, 167–8, and now (1990); also Vickers (1973), 424. On character, action, the *Poetics*, and tragedy, see also Heath (1987), 115–23 (cf. Blundell (1989), 16–25); it is encouraging to see that the important new works by Goldhill and Heath, though differing widely in ideology, are in broad agreement on the importance of some conception of character. Students of characterization and individuality in Greek lit. will now also wish to consult the collection of essays by Pelling (1990), of which the studies of both Goldhill and Easterling (1990), cited above, form part. As a theoretical introduction to the issue of characterization in tragedy, Easterling's contribution could scarcely be bettered.

Our study of *aidōs* in Aeschylus, then, will concentrate on those passages in which the concept is central to the motivation of major characters as an integral feature of the action; but clearly not every instance of *aidōs* and its relatives will be important in quite this way: some occurrences are incidental to the main action of the play, yet none the less provide data which a history of the concept cannot ignore. Treatment of these passages, which shed light upon the meaning and operation of *aidōs* in a more general way, will therefore precede and follow an examination of those in which our concepts are important in the dramatic movement of the plays.

3.1. GENERAL

3.1.1. *Competitive Honour*

The need to maintain personal and collective honour in the face of the challenges and affronts of others is as important a source of motivation in Aeschylus (and his fellow tragedians) as it was in Homer. In the *Oresteia* concern for *timē* is an important ground for the pursuit of vengeance and retribution; in *Eumenides* (95-8) the ghost of Clytemnestra complains of her lack of *timē* among the dead and of the disgrace of her position (she wanders *aischrōs*, 98), and blames this on the failure of the Erinyes, her avengers, to exact retribution. Similarly, in *Choephori* the disgrace suffered by Agamemnon is acutely felt by his children,[3] and is an important element in their determination to seek revenge. As in Homer, however, the code of honour envisaged by the trilogy is such that it may be seen as discreditable to dishonour another person; Agamemnon died *aischrōs* according to Electra at *Choephori* 494, and this is seen as an impairment of his honour (entailing *oneidē*, 495), but Electra also mentions the deceit employed by his murderers, and deceit in itself may be *aischron*;[4] just as the fact that Agamemnon died not in battle, but by deceit (345-54, 479) reflects badly on his honour, so his murderers' unheroic deceit may

---

[3] Ag.'s ignoble death and lack of proper burial deprived him of *timē* (96-7, 430-43, 479, 483-5, 494), and this loss of *timē* affects both Electra (since her father's dishonour implicates her and she was moreover unable to play a daughter's role in his funeral, 444-50) and Orestes (407-9; his concern to recover his patrimony, 301-4, 973-4, is also a concern to recover his *timē*; see Garvie (1986), on 299-304). On the motivating force of *timē* in the trilogy, see Macleod (1982), 138-44.

[4] Cf. Ch. 2 n. 84, on deceit in Thgn.

reflect badly upon them, and the adverb *aischrōs* need not refer exclusively to Agamemnon's condition. The dishonouring of Agamemnon, of course, began before his death with the adultery of his wife with Aegisthus; thus the latter is described as an *aischuntēr*, one who dishonours another (*Choephori* 990), and a similar term, *kataischuntēres*, is used of both Aegisthus and Clytemnestra (*Agamemnon* 1363); in the same way the chorus-leader reproaches Aegisthus for shaming (*aischunōn*) another man's bed at *Agamemnon* 1626. The dishonour suffered by Agamemnon is clearly stated, and this is the immediate reference of the terms employed, but the function of the utterances in which these terms occur is the discredit of the agents of dishonour, not that of its patient. This is particularly clear in the last passage cited, in which Agamemnon's status as a warrior is contrasted with Aegisthus' position as an effeminate stay-at-home; thus it is clear that to deprive a man of *timē* is not always to win it for oneself, and that it may be seen as discreditable to dishonour another.[5]

These passages concerning *timē* and its defence indicate the background against which *aidōs* can occur; in the *Seven against Thebes* Eteocles does not refer to *aidōs* as a motive behind his resolve to face his brother in battle, but he is clearly affected by a desire to avoid disgrace which might be so described (683–5):[6] 'If one is to bear misfortune,[7] let it be without disgrace [*aischunē*]; this alone is an advantage among the dead, but there is no fame in misfortunes which are *aischron*.' Eteocles' concern for his honour, then, leads him to face

---

[5] Adultery was an offence for the male in Athens, but his offence lay not in his lack of chastity or his disloyalty to his own wife (if he had one), but in his dishonouring of a fellow citizen by the seduction of a woman under his protection, and thus Athenian law on this matter, so structured as to penalize and deter the dishonouring of others in this way, reflects the concern, in a society which cares deeply about honour, that systems of honour should remain relatively stable; for the dishonour, see *Dissoi Logoi* 2. 5 (Dover (1974), 209–10); Lacey (1968), 113–16; cf. the treatment of the killing of Aegisthus (he is an *aischuntēr* whom it is lawful to kill, *Cho.* 990), and for the legal background, see MacDowell (1963*a*), 77; (1978), 114, 124–5. In Homer, too, Aeg.'s adultery discredits him (it is 'excessive' according to Zeus at *Od.* 1. 35, and he was directly warned by the gods about his conduct, 1. 37–43). In a different sense Paris' dishonouring of another (he shamed (ἤσχυνε) the table of his host, *Ag.* 399–401) is also discreditable for himself as an offence against Zeus *xenios* (362–6), and this also reflects the beliefs of a society which seeks to prevent inappropriate dishonouring of others.

[6] Thus G. O. Hutchinson (1985: 149), on 653–719 compares 6. 441–3, where *aidōs* does occur; Snell (1928: 83) has the same comparison, but wrongly believes that Et. fears not the disgrace of imputed cowardice, but that of injustice; his concern for military glory, however, resurfaces at 716–17; see Gagarin (1976), 124; Winnington-Ingram (1983), 35–6, 39.

[7] Or: 'if a god is bringing misfortune' (φέρει for φέροι, G. O. Hutchinson's interpretation (1985: ad loc.)).

his brother. This is not his only motive,[8] nor is it Eteocles' personal motives alone which dictate that he should meet Polyneices in battle, since his father's curse also plays a role,[9] but this is not to say that motives such as this, which are given in the text, are simply to be discounted in favour of explanations based on supernatural compulsion;[10] we shall see over and again in Aeschylus that personal motives, among which *aidōs* is prominent, play a full and significant part in the motivation of conduct and in the ascription of responsibility for that conduct, even where supernatural causation is also present.[11]

Eteocles' expression of his concern for his honour as a warrior, however, is not without ambivalence when seen in a wider perspective; he hopes that the *kakon* to which he proceeds may occur without *aischunē*, but this hope can hardly be fulfilled when the *kakon* involves

[8] He is motivated not only by fear of disgrace but by a passionate desire to face his brother (as the chorus see: 686–8, 692–4), and is convinced that Polyneices has violated *dikē*, of which he himself is the true champion (658–76).

[9] 653–9, 695–7. Since Et. never considers the possibility that he might not face his brother, even though the chorus urge him to resist the curse (698), the question of free will versus compulsion, often raised here, does not really arise, for the demands of the curse do not conflict with Et.'s desire. The chorus's comment at 698, however, indicates that they do not see it as impossible for him to refuse to face his brother (see G. O. Hutchinson (1985: 149), on 653–719 and contrast Lloyd-Jones (1959: 86, who says he has 'no choice'). The effect of the *Redepaare* scene, with its mixture of tenses, is to suggest that, despite the curse, Et. could choose to position himself at another gate (although this is variously explained: see Lesky (1961), 8–10; (1966), 83–4; (1983), 58, 60; Dawe (1963), 33–7; Winnington-Ingram (1983), 24; G. O. Hutchinson (1985), 104–5).

[10] Class (1964: 33) recognizes the coincidence of human and divine motives and rightly rules out any question of a *Gewissensentscheidung* in the passage under discussion, but implies that the curse is more important than the personal motives; this is brought out more clearly by Stebler (1971: 35), who also recognizes the combination of motives, but remarks, 'Wo magische Notwendigkeit wirkt, gibt es keine Möglichkeit des Entrinnens.' That tragic action, however, can be motivated in both human and divine terms in an inclusive rather than a mutually exclusive sense is stressed by Winnington-Ingram (1965) (cf. id. (1980), 150–78; (1983), 23–40), Lesky (1966), and Vernant in Vernant and Vidal-Naquet (1981), 28–62.

[11] The word *aischunē* also occurs at *Sept.* 409–10; Melanippus, the adversary of Tydeus, honours the throne of Aischunē and hates proud words, and this is explained by his freedom from *aischra* and his reluctance to be *kakos* (411); Winnington-Ingram (1983: 31) assumes that all these terms refer to his concern for his honour as a warrior, and relates this to Et.'s desire to avoid *aischunē*. The primary reference here, however, is surely to the moral superiority of the defenders over their Argive opponents (excluding Amphiaraus); line 411 might well explain the bravery of Mel., but his worship of Aischunē clearly differentiates him from Tyd., and we have no reason to believe that Tyd. does not also wish to avoid the disgrace of cowardice; the difference, then, must lie in Mel.'s rejection of his opponent's pride, impiety, and excess (cf. G. O. Hutchinson (1985), on 409). Under either interpretation, however, the personification of Aischunē implies the use of *aischunē* not as 'disgrace' but as a synonym of *aidōs*, a usage we have not met before but which must already have been known and which quickly becomes common.

his facing his own brother in battle. His concern for the disgrace accruing from cowardice thus obscures the *aidōs* which he should feel for his brother as a *philos* and at the prospect of breach of *philia*, and his death will be seen not as glorious, but as *asebēs* (impious),[12] a term referring to his neglect of the familial duty which *aidōs* helps enforce.[13] An indication of *aidōs* in drama may thus alert us to the operation or absence of other forms of *aidōs*, and different kinds of *aidōs*, as in Homer, may conflict.

3.1.2. *Supplication*

Of all the plays the *Supplices* is the richest in instances of *aidōs*, a fact arising from the play's central action, the supplication of the Danaids at Argos. We shall consider the effect of *aidōs* on Pelasgus below, but here we may usefully examine the role of *aidōs* in the chorus's supplication more generally. The Danaids adopt the part of suppliants immediately on entering the orchestra, even though they do not take up position at the altar until 207 ff.,[14] and despite the absence of any representative of the Argives; in the opening lines of the play, then, their supplication is directed towards enlisting the support of the gods, especially Zeus, for their cause. Thus at 27–9 they pray that Zeus and the gods should 'accept the band of female suppliants with an *aidoios* breath of the land'. This is clearly a request that their supplication should be accepted, and as such, an appeal to *aidōs*; thus *aidoios* must be active in sense in 28; the 'breath of the land' does not attract *aidōs*, it manifests it, and the gods are to imbue, by means of this 'breath', the inhabitants of Argos with a disposition towards *aidōs*.[15] The active use of the adjective has hitherto been rare,[16] but in this play it frequently coexists beside the passive. The multivalence of the adjective is further in evidence in 191–6, in which Danaus reminds his daughters of the importance of *aidōs* in their supplication: 'Climb upon the altar as quickly as you can, and, holding the white-crowned suppliant

[12] 831, 'they perished in impious intention' (ὤλοντ᾽ ἀσεβεῖ διανοίᾳ). Cf. 677–82, 718, where the chorus refer to the horror of shedding kindred blood.
[13] On the relationship between *aidōs* and *seb-* words in Aesch., see 3.4 below.
[14] See Kopperschmidt (1967), 55–7; Lesky (1983), 63.
[15] Cf. von Erffa (1937), 87; Friis Johansen and Whittle (1980), ad loc.
[16] Cf. *Od.* 17. 578 (Ch. 1 n. 177; note also the adv. in *Od.* 19. 243) and [Homer] *Epigrams* 2. 2, 6. 6. There is a possibility that overtones of both active and passive senses exist at Pind. *Isth.* 2. 37.

branches, the adornments of *aidoios* Zeus, *semnōs* in your left hands, address the strangers [or: your hosts, *xenoi*] with *aidoios*, sorrowful, and needy words, as befits incomers, telling clearly of your bloodless exile.' It is always possible that *aidoios* Zeus in 192 means 'reverend Zeus', but there is no reason to reject an additional active significance;[17] like *aidoios*, *semnos*, derived from *sebomai*, is normally passive, and so the adverb in 193 is most naturally taken in the sense, 'in such a way as to arouse the *sebas* of others'. Friis Johansen and Whittle (ad loc.), however, in translating 'in a reverent manner', clearly feel that an active connotation is also present beside the passive (of which they are also aware), and this is not impossible. Holding the suppliant branches *semnōs*, the Danaids are to utter *aidoia epē*, and again the adjective is ambivalent; as suppliants, the maidens will speak in such a way as to arouse the *aidōs* of others, but in the following lines Danaus speaks not of others' reaction to his daughters, but of their behaviour towards those they will encounter; they are to speak as befits newcomers (195), avoid boldness (197), appear composed in countenance (198–9), be neither forward nor reluctant in speech (200–1), and, above all, to yield to their prospective hosts (202). All this, particularly the references to boldness and the 'quiet eye' (composed countenance),[18] suggests that they are to manifest *aidōs* as a means of attracting it; they are women, and women attract *aidōs* by conducting themselves as their own *aidōs* bids them.

Thus *aidōs* promotes behaviour which attracts the *aidōs* of others, and, in this case, both suppliant and supplicated are expected to show *aidōs* in a reciprocal manner; in connection with this supplication, therefore, it is correct to say that '*aidōs* is common to both parties in the encounter, or is characteristic of the encounter itself'.[19] One should not, however, force these observations into an over-rigid schema; in Homer and elsewhere in tragedy *aidōs* is far more regularly the reaction expected of the supplicated, and in the passages cited the ambivalence of *aidoios* should be seen in the light of (*a*) Aeschylus' pregnant style; (*b*) the nature of the supplication (the Danaids are using an altar dedicated to the city's gods to further their supplication, and a respectful manner is more likely to win acceptance); (*c*) the sex of the suppliants (the supplicated will be better disposed to accede to

[17] Von Erffa (1937: 87) points out that the active sense might be supported by the request to Zeus to 'honour his suppliants' in 815.

[18] Cf. the Danaids' 'quiet eye' with the 'steady-eyed *aidōs*' of the Oceanids at *PV* 133–4 (below, 3.1.3), and on *aidōs* and the eyes, see above, Ch. 2 n. 37 etc.

[19] Gould (1973: 87) using some of the examples cited from *Supp.* as his evidence.

the claims of women who behave properly, and *aidōs* is expected of women in general); and (*d*) Aeschylus' thematic purpose in raising the question, 'how will the Danaids behave?'

One cannot, then, assume that *aidōs* will always exist as a reciprocal element common to both parties to a supplication in any systematic way, even though supplication at an altar may demand *aidōs* of the suppliants and even though *aidōs* can certainly be a feature of the bond which is created between suppliant and supplicated *after* the supplication has been accepted.[20] In personal supplication, however, the suppliant must disclaim or overcome any *aidōs* he might feel, in order that the self-abasement which is essential to supplication in this form can take place;[21] one kind of *aidōs*, then, concern for one's own honour, would actually threaten the performance of such supplication.[22] Central to both kinds of supplication is *timē*: the *timē* of the gods is invoked through contact with an altar or by the ritual gestures of personal supplication; the suppliant is invested with *timē* by the gods, yet disclaims *timē* on his own account; and the *timē* of a protector is committed to the protection of those whose supplication he has accepted. Supplication, in short, creates a powerful and tense situation by focusing on *timē*, by putting a hierarchy of *timē* under stress, and thus *timē* is important in the situation in different ways; it is therefore natural that *aidōs*, which responds to the *timē* of self and others, is also, in different ways, a central feature of supplication, and it is certainly true that Aeschylus' multivalent application of *aidoios* helps bring this out.

3.1.3. *Sex and Sexuality*

Aidōs is also active in the familiar sphere of sexual relationships and encounters between male and female in Aeschylus. That the chorus of

---

[20] *Aidoios* is probably ambivalent again when used of Pelasgus, the Danaids' protector (*proxenos*) at 490-1; in becoming their protector he manifested *aidōs* (cf. 641, where the Danaids praise the *aidōs* accorded them by the Argives) and now deserves their *aidōs* in return.

[21] On the two types of supplication, see Kopperschmidt (1967), 46–53; Burian (1971), I, 4–5; Gould (1973), 75–8; on self-abasement in personal supplication, see Gould (1973), 79, 94–5. (On supplication in tragedy, see, besides Kopperschmidt and Burian, Vickers (1973), 438–9.)

[22] As, indeed, we see at Eur. *Hel.* 947–9; *Pho.* 1622–4. Cf. *IA* 900–2, where such *aidōs* is disclaimed, and see 5.2.2 below.

Oceanids in *Prometheus Vinctus* (133–4)[23] feel the need to explain their presence before the male Prometheus, and thus the abandonment of their usual 'steady-eyed[24] *aidōs*', immediately characterizes them as respectable young women, who have abandoned the modesty required of them only in what they see as exceptional circumstances.[25] Their *aidōs*, which is manifested in their eyes or facial expression, would have kept them in seclusion in their cave, as it keeps respectable Athenian girls in seclusion in their quarters, had it not been dispelled by the noise of Hephaestus' hammer and their subsequent curiosity.[26]

Although differences in the role and status of women have been detected between Homeric society and classical Athens, the relationship of women to male honour, the background against which the Oceanids' remarks on *aidōs* must be seen, remains a constant.[27] A respectable woman's *aidōs* should protect her own honour, but this honour is, in all normal circumstances, bound up with that of a man; we have seen already how Clytemnestra's adultery with Aegisthus was a source of dishonour for Agamemnon, and it is dishonour of this kind which Danaus, the *kurios* (guardian) of his unmarried daughters, seeks to prevent when he warns them to avoid any implication of sexual scandal (*Supplices* 991–1009); Danaus' concern here is for his own honour, as his entreaty that his daughters should not shame him (996) or implicate him in *aischos* (1008) makes clear.

The *aidōs* of Cassandra at *Agamemnon* 1203,[28] the prophetess explains, previously prevented her admission of the sexual nature of

---

[23] The doubts cast on the authenticity of the *Prometheus* by Griffith (1977), have been challenged (e.g. by Conacher (1980), 141–74), but not dispelled. It is therefore advisable to treat the play with caution and to avoid using it as a basis for generalizations about Aesch., but in view of the traditional association and the likelihood that the play, given its echoes of sophistic ideas, is 5th-cent. in date (see Griffith (1977), 253; West (1979), 146–8), it seems sensible to treat the few relevant passages it offers in this chapter. These passages are, in any case, relevant to our study only as indications of the general usage and background of the period, and not of a particularly Aeschylean approach to *aidōs*.

[24] The adjective employed, *themerōpis*, is rare (elsewhere only at Emped. B 122. 2 DK), but Hesych. glosses *themeros* by *bebaios* (steady), *semnos*, and *eustathēs* (balanced).

[25] So Griffith (1983), ad loc.

[26] The connection between *aidōs* and the eyes, and the appropriateness of *aidōs* for young women are further documented in fr. 168. 21–4 Radt (references to 'eyes' (probably) and 'eye' in lines 21–2 respectively).

[27] On the position of women in classical Athens, see Lacey (1968), 151–76; Dover (1974), 95–8, 209; Just (1975, 1989); Pomeroy (1975), 57–119; Gould (1980); and, with particular reference to the social background to tragedy, Vickers (1973), 109–19; Goldhill (1986), 108–37.

[28] Transposed to follow the chorus-leader's question at 1204 by Hermann and subsequent editors.

her relationship with Apollo. Her concern to protect her honour, however, has diminished with her status, and she now has no need for the 'delicacy' which, the chorus-leader aptly comments (1205), more readily attends good fortune than bad. This passage reflects the double prospective/retrospective aspect of *aidōs* which we have noticed already; Cassandra's *aidōs* is occasioned by an event in the past, but inhibits speaking of this event in the future; the immediate reference of the words used ('I had *aidōs* to speak of these things') is to prospective inhibition, but this inhibition itself presupposes a subjective emotional and evaluative reaction to a past event; Cassandra's attitude to her relationship with the god may thus encompass retrospective shame as well as reluctance to disclose a discreditable fact, and, indeed, the two aspects may be inseparable. The form of words chosen need not restrict the reference to fear of future disapproval alone.

Aidōs is also an emotional reaction of a multivalent nature in a difficult lyric passage of *Supplices* (578-9), where the chorus sing of Io's release from the torment of the gadfly and her return to human shape; transformed by the touch of Zeus,[29] she 'sheds her sorrowful *aidōs* of tears'.[30] Friis Johansen and Whittle (ad loc.) insist that the verb translated 'sheds' must mean 'expels' or 'loses', but none of their parallels is strong enough to support this interpretation, which only makes a difficult passage more difficult; it is impossible to imagine that Io, having contained her *aidōs* during her career as a cow, should now lose that *aidōs* on regaining human form, especially since the touch of Zeus signifies the moment of conception of her child. The phrase, then, must connote the expression of *aidōs* in tears. The reference of this *aidōs* is unspecified in the text, but we are aware of Io's circumstances at this point, and so we must assume that these make the occurrence of *aidōs* intelligible. It is significant, for example, that Io expresses her *aidōs* precisely at the point at which she regains human form; *aidōs* is the human emotion *par excellence*;[31] transformed, Io is at least able to react to her situation as a human being, and thus her *aidōs* is part of a release of pent-up emotion. The essential event is Io's breaking down in tears, and the observation that these tears express her *aidōs* belongs to the chorus, who must therefore see her situation as offering grounds for *aidōs*. Either Io's past sufferings (she has

---

[29] See Friis Johansen and Whittle (1980), on 578-9.

[30] δακρύων δ' ἀποστάζει πένθιμον αἰδῶ.

[31] Cf. Friis Johansen and Whittle (1980), on 578-9.

endured humiliating treatment)[32] or her present situation (she is subject to the erotic attentions of Zeus) would adequately motivate her *aidōs*, and, indeed, the passage is such that there is no need to regard these as mutually exclusive; her *aidōs*, which is here most definitely an affect, manifested as it is in a flood of tears, suggests here embarrassment and self-consciousness at her situation *in toto*. The words used to create this picture are few, but they none the less impart an acute and remarkable representation of feminine emotion.

In relating her *aidōs* at speaking of a past sexual episode in her life, Cassandra (*Agamemnon* 1203) was describing an inner emotional state of her own. Such a description, however, is not in question in the superficially similar passage at *Choephori* 917. Orestes is, to be sure, drawing on traditional coyness regarding sexuality when he expresses his reluctance (*aischunomai*) to reproach his mother openly with her adultery with Aegisthus; it is also true that Clytemnestra's offence does represent a stain on her son's honour, but the purpose of his statement is not description of his own emotional state or his motivation, but an insulting expression of his contempt.[33] His use of *aischunomai* places his mother's conduct in the category of the shameful, and thus constitutes an oblique reproach:[34] another example of the complex ways in which emotion-words can be used in utterances whose purpose is not simply the description of occurrent emotion.

---

[32] This possibility (recognized by the scholiast on 578-9) is rejected by Friis Johansen and Whittle (1980), on 579, but their objection, that *aidōs* is not found of retrospective shame before Eur. is invalid; *aidōs* can be caused by past events even in Homer, and we have just looked at an example from the *Ag.* Io's *aidōs* may arise from her past sufferings in the same way as Cassandra's, and need not be regarded as expressing the notion of retrospective shame unambiguously as such. Friis Johansen and Whittle underestimate the retrospective element in locutions which are formally prospective. (Similarly, in discussing *aidōs* in Eur. we shall have to evaluate the prospective element in uses which are formally retrospective.)

[33] See Garvie (1986), ad loc.; Goldhill (1984), 181 and n. 151.

[34] The indirectness of Or.'s words here, given their relation to his *aidōs/aischunē*, constitutes an ironic fulfilment of his observation (at 663-7) that the *aidōs* which is traditionally present when the sexes meet (cf. Gould (1980), 56; Garvie (1986), ad loc.) makes for indirectness in their conversations, whereas men address men with *tharsos* (again boldness as a positive antonym to restrictive *aidōs*) and say what they mean; Or.'s meaning in 917, however, is abundantly clear, despite his indirectness and his *aidōs/aischunē*.

3.2. CRUCIAL PASSAGES

3.2.1. *Pelasgus*

Aidōs, as we have seen, is important in the *Supplices* simply by virtue of that play's nature as a suppliant drama, but it is in the play's central decision scene, in which the king of Argos is led to accept the Danaids' supplication, that *aidōs* plays its most significant part in the action.

From Pelasgus' entry (234) until line 332 the origin of the Danaids, both immediate and ancestral, is the central issue, but the theme of supplication is reintroduced at 333-4 and dominates the action until Pelasgus gives in. The king indicates his readiness to behave properly towards the suppliants (340), but soon recognizes that to do so to their satisfaction will involve conflict with their opponents; the theme of war, which will concern the city of Argos as a whole, is already introduced, and it is a prospect which the king does not relish (342). Against his reluctance to go to war on their behalf the Danaids set an appeal to *aidōs*, urging him to feel *aidōs* for the altar of the city's gods to which they cling and which they have decked with their suppliant emblems.[35] As commonly in such contexts, the injunction 'show *aidōs*' amounts to a plea 'accept our supplication', but in this case the object of this *aidōs* is not the suppliants themselves but the altar at which they supplicate, *qua* focal point of the supplication. The altar may, perhaps, stand metonymously for the suppliants, but it is also an object invested with significance, with honour and power, in its own right, as a symbol of the honour and power of the god who underwrites the ritual. The injunction to show *aidōs* is an injunction to recognize this honour, just as an appeal to *aidōs* for the suppliant himself invites recognition of the honour or *timē* invested in him by Zeus.

Pelasgus immediately indicates that he is moved by this appeal by referring to the shudder he experienced on seeing the altar decked out for supplication (346), and the shudder itself is explained[36] as a response to the power of the wrath of Zeus, the protector of suppliants. The instinctive reaction of Pelasgus' shudder is important, in that it conveys clearly the tension caused by the supplication and the power of the sanctions which support the suppliants' case, and it

---

[35] αἰδοῦ σὺ πρύμναν πόλεος ὧδ᾽ ἐστεμμένην (345).
[36] By the chorus-leader or by P. himself; see Friis Johansen and Whittle (1980), on 347.

may even be a physical manifestation of the *aidōs* which is demanded in such situations. No less important, however, is Pelasgus' appreciation of his dilemma in these lines; to accept the supplication may endanger the city, but to ignore the suppliants' pleas is to invite the anger of Zeus *hikesios*, and there is an obvious parallelism between the two alternatives; both are 'grievous' (342, 347).

The dilemma is then extended over the ensuing epirrhematic section (348–437) and stated as unresolved in the king's speech at 438–54. The Danaids stress their suppliant status (348–53), reiterate their appeal to *aidōs* (359–62), and remind Pelasgus both of the anger of Zeus (381–6, 402–6) and of the consequences of ignoring their supplication (418–37), but Pelasgus continues to emphasize the difficulty of the choice and the balanced antithesis of evil alternatives (376–80, 407–17, 438–54). The essence of his inability to decide lies in his consideration for the city and its people: acceptance of the supplication will bring war 'which the city can do without' (358), and the fact that the Danaids' supplication takes place before a public altar means that the citizens, who will be affected should any pollution (*miasma*, see 366) result from the supplication,[37] must have their say (365–9). Thought of the citizens, then, can furnish reasons for the king's inability personally to accept the supplication (the danger of war), but it also makes him unwilling to take a personal initiative in rejecting it, thus exposing the city to pollution should the Danaids suffer violence from their enemies. At the same time, however, in recognizing the danger of pollution the king recognizes a formidable reason for accepting the supplication, and the chorus immediately seek to exploit his concern for pollution as an argument in their favour (375). The general notion of the 'wrath of Zeus' has crystallized into that of pollution; pollution or war are now the alternatives, and the people will be involved in both.

This balance and parallelism of the alternatives creates the king's dilemma, and in the face of this dilemma he feels himself helpless,[38] seeking to evade the decision entirely.[39] We have seen already that

---

[37] The distinction P. draws between supplication at a civic altar and that at the home (or hearth) of an individual is probably a legitimate one; see Gould (1973), 89; on *miasma* as the result should any harm come to those who supplicate at an altar, see Parker (1983), 182–6, esp. 185.

[38] His helplessness (*amēchania*, see esp. 379–80) is stressed by Snell (1928), 60; Kopperschmidt (1967), 62; Lesky (1983), 64–5.

[39] His hope that the chorus may be persuaded to pursue their claims in accordance with the *nomoi* (laws, customs) of Egypt (387–91) is an indication of his desire to avoid the dilemma as it stands, and probably implies a hope that the suppliants will be

Pelasgus did respond positively to the Danaids' appeal to *aidōs* (his shudder at 346), demonstrating a susceptibility to such *aidōs* and a proclivity towards the proper behaviour thus demanded; on the one hand, then, *aidōs* creates a disposition favourable to acceptance. Immediately, however, the king recognizes the consequences of taking the decision upon himself, and feels unable to decide. That this inability is also a result of *aidōs* is suggested by 397-401: 'The judgement is no easy one; do not choose me judge. I said before, I cannot act without the people, even though I am in charge,[40] lest the people should ever say, if something goes wrong, "By paying honour [*timē*] to incomers you ruined the city."' So Pelasgus fears the censure of the people in the event of disaster,[41] and imagines their reproaches in vivid direct speech. His position is thus analogous to that of Hector in *Iliad* 22 (104-7);[42] Hector recognizes his responsibility for the ruin of his city, Pelasgus does not wish to be responsible for the ruin of his, and both fear what their fellow citizens may say; Hector expresses his concern in terms of *aidōs*, and Pelasgus' concern is identical. His choice, then, is not between giving in to *aidōs* or rejecting it, but between the demands of two different sorts of *aidōs*—*aidōs* for the suppliants, for the ritual, and for its sanctions inhibits rejection of the appeal, and *aidōs* based on the king's responsibility to his people, and his concern for his own *timē* among them, inhibits both acceptance and rejection as involving dire consequences for the city and severe disapproval for himself. We have already seen that *aidōs* may be undesirable when initiative is called for, and that it can lead to indecision or diffidence; here it inhibits both of a pair of alternatives, and leads to complete *amēchania*.

The Danaids now realize that something must be done to secure the

persuaded to leave the altar, freeing him from the anger of Zeus and the danger of pollution; for this tactic, see Gould (1973), 82; cf. Parker (1983), 184 and n. 219. For P.'s desire to avoid a decision, cf. 397, 453-4.

[40] I take οὐδέ περ κρατῶν as concessive rather than conditional (which would be 'not even if I were in charge'); P.'s statements of his personal power at 250-9 are understandable coming from a king who does exercise sole power but later finds that he must consult his subjects, but not from a king who, it is later revealed, is constrained by a democratic constitution. There is no mention of such constraint in the play. P. has the power to decide for himself, but such is the gravity of the matter and its implications for the city that he does not want to; see Burian (1971), 53-7; (1974*a*), 7; Friis Johansen and Whittle (1980), ad loc. (also on 365-9).

[41] Cf. 484-5.

[42] 'An almost certain reminiscence', Friis Johansen and Whittle (1980), on 401; that they are right is demonstrated especially by the close similarity of expression in the imagined reproach (modal part and main verb).

king's support—they threaten to hang themselves on the altar and
Pelasgus gives in. The Danaids preface their threat with the injunction
(455), 'Hear the end [or culmination, *termata*] of *aidoioi logoi*'. The
adjective *aidoios*, ambivalent earlier in the play,[43] also bears the fullest
significance here; the threat is an end of 'reverend words' in that it is
the culmination of the chorus's attempts to elicit Pelasgus' *aidōs*; but it
also constitutes an abandonment of their pleas as helpless suppliants;
it is an end of *aidoioi logoi* both as a departure from the normal, passive
suppliant appeal to *aidōs* and as an abandonment of the *aidōs* actively
urged on the Danaids by their father—they no longer speak 'as befits
incomers' (195). The paradox, however, is that the Danaids' abandonment of *aidoioi logoi* in the latter two senses does serve as a culmination
of *aidoioi logoi* in the former sense, for it is by means of the threat that
they ensure that the king's *aidōs* for the wrath of Zeus, protector of
suppliants, prevails over his *aidōs* for the opinions of the *dēmos*; he still
stresses the terrible consequences of heeding the appeal (461-71, 474-
7), but now realizes that there is no escaping *miasma* if he does not
heed it (472-3), and concludes (478-9, picking up the words of the
chorus in 347, 385, 427): 'Nevertheless, it is necessary [*anankē*] to
aideisthai the wrath of Zeus, protector of suppliants; for this is the
greatest source of fear among mortals.'

Aidōs is thus central to Pelasgus' decision, and his is a decision in the
full sense of the word, for its results from consideration of two
alternatives, and from an estimation of the consequences of those
alternatives, including that of the responsibility which the individual
will bear for his decision.[44] This is not to say that the decision is taken

---

[43] Cf. 3.1.2 above, and esp. *Supp.* 194, where *aidoia epē* (reverent/reverend words)
corresponds to *aidoioi logoi* here.

[44] On the importance of P.'s decision, see Snell (1928), 52-65; Class (1964), 30-3;
Lesky (1966), 78-80. It is certainly true that the decision does not immediately spring
from the recognition of the alternatives and their consequences (Rivier (1968), 18, 34-6;
cf. Lesky (1966), 80), and that the Danaids' threat does tip the scales in their favour
(Lesky, 79), but these points cannot be used to limit P.'s freedom to act or to attribute his
decision to external compulsion; it is precisely because he can decide that he finds it so
difficult to do so, and the necessity of which he speaks in 478 is not some form of external
compulsion (so Rivier (1968), 18, and Stebler (1971), 94; the latter seems to imagine that
the gods somehow force P. to accept the supplication), but the virtual compulsion that is
imposed upon a man of ordinary sensibilities by the recognition that the consequences of
alternative *a* are really much more serious than those of alternative *b*. The threat is not
something new and external to the dilemma P. has already faced, but rather makes the
prospect of *miasma* (473), already prominent as an unpleasant consequence of disregarding the plea (366, 375, 429-33), inevitable; the compulsion is not absolute, but arises from
the king's own appraisal of the situation.

in absolute freedom; Pelasgus seeks to reconcile the conflicting claims made upon him with his own desire to behave properly, and it would therefore be impossible for his choice somehow to exist independently either of the demands made on him by others or of his own subjective response to those demands; this is not how decisions are made in 'real life', either, and even though Pelasgus' doubts and eventual decision are manifestly products of the dilemma with which he is faced, which is in turn both a function of the plot and a reflection of conflicting themes which were doubtless developed over the trilogy as a whole, it is clear that his decision is motivated and effected in a way which invites comparison with 'real life' experience and prompts discussion of Aeschylus' use of psychological realism.[45]

In the motivation which makes such realism possible *aidōs* is central, yet the word occurs explicitly only in contexts of respect for the Danaids' supplication and the god who underwrites it; behind the explicit references, however, *aidōs* plays a wider role, and, indeed, it is part of the function of the explicit references to alert us to this. Pelasgus' shudder in 346, a recognition of the force of the chorus's appeal to *aidōs* in 345, and his statement of the necessity of showing *aidōs* for the anger of Zeus in 478 refer to the recognition of the *timē* which is central to the ritual of supplication (that of the gods, that of the altar, and that of the suppliants). But he also recognizes his obligations towards his people and he is scrupulous about the need to consult them; his *aidōs* here is revealed by his concern for disapproval, but this concern itself implies that Pelasgus values an image of himself as a king who meets his obligations, and so the *aidōs* which inhibits his decision is not merely fear of reproach, but includes reluctance to act in a manner which he himself regards as inappropriate. It is these indications of *aidōs* which make the king's indecision more than simply a device for the creation of a dramatic and suspenseful impasse; the essential inhibitory nature of *aidōs* is exploited to effect the projection of the dilemma created by the external action of the play into the king's character. His *aidōs* recognizes the conflicting claims made upon him, with the result that these seem to cancel each other out, and it foresees that the consequences of his actions are likely to prove unacceptable, with the result that he feels unable to act at all; in short, *aidōs* plays a powerful part in creating an impression of emotional uncertainty and unease in an individual who, although he knows he can act, is unwilling to exercise that ability.[46]

[45] See Lesky (1966), 80.   [46] Cf. Snell (1928), 143.

3.2.2. *Agamemnon*

The so-called carpet scene of the *Agamemnon* has been much discussed, and its importance variously estimated.[47] Modern scholars rightly insist on the visual and dramatic aspect of the scene,[48] or stress its importance as a manifestation of Clytemnestra's mastery of language in the conflict between female and male,[49] but it seems to me that the traditional search for Agamemnon's motivation for giving in, fraught with difficulties though it is, cannot simply be abandoned if we are to make sense of the scene; it is simply that such a search must base itself on the information given in the text rather than on 'reading between the lines'.[50]

Agamemnon is initially reluctant to walk on the fabrics, but eventually agrees to do so, persuaded by his wife. Some reluctance remains, however, and at 948–9 he explains his decision to remove his shoes, an attempt to mitigate his offence and avoid *phthonos*[51] (944–7), in terms of *aidōs*: 'There is much *aidōs* to trample the substance of the house, wasting wealth and silver-bought weavings.'[52] His *aidōs* here refers immediately to the act of wasting the wealth of the house, but it would be wrong to imagine that it is only under this aspect that the act of

[47] Most commentators, even though their views differ widely, stress the importance of the scene in the scheme of the play, but for a dissenting view (of its unimportance) see Dawe (1963), 48 n. 2.

[48] See Taplin (1978: 79–83), whose emphasis on the fabrics as a path of blood leading to the central door of the *skēnē* is shared by Vickers (1973), 366–7, 370.

[49] Taplin (1978), 82; Goldhill (1984), 74–9; (1986), 12–14.

[50] For fruitful approaches along these lines see Easterling (1973); Vickers (1973), 367–70; Winnington-Ingram (1983), 90–3. Meridor (1987) is right to remind us of the importance of Cassandra's visual presence on stage and of her status, like the vestments, as a valuable possession (954–5), but fails to establish that Ag. actually gives in to Clyt.'s persuasion even partly out of a concern that his concubine be accepted.

[51] *Phthonos* is usually translated 'envy' or 'jealousy', but often has connotations closer to 'malice'; as a reaction to human prosperity it can be manifested by both gods and men; see Walcot (1978). Word order suggests that θεῶν in 946 goes with ἁλουργέσιν and not with φθόνος (cf. Denniston and Page (1957), ad loc.; for the opposite view, see Easterling (1973), 11 n. 2), but even construing thus we must assume that it is divine *phthonos* that Ag. principally fears here (hence his observation that 'a god from afar' (note πρόσωθεν in both 947 and 952) looks kindly on those who rule gently (951–2); Ag. attempts to present his behaviour favourably to the gods). See Fraenkel (1950) ad loc.; cf. Meridor (1987), 41 n. 22.

[52] Von Erffa (1937: 94) persists in regarding *aidōs* in such locutions (where the noun is followed by an inf., cf. 17. 336 and *Od.* 3. 24) as equivalent to 'it is *aischron*', but while to say, 'there is *aidōs* to do *x*' (i.e. the prospect arouses the *aidōs* of those faced with it) may come to the same thing as 'it is *aischron* to do *x*', *aidōs* does not *mean* 'disgrace' in this context.

treading on the garments arouses *aidōs*; rather Agamemnon's expression of his *aidōs* sums up the reluctance which he has hitherto expressed and which he has now almost, but not quite, overcome, and its cause or causes are therefore to be sought not only in the immediate context but also in the entire scene from line 905 onwards.

Clytemnestra prefaces her invitation to tread on the purple cloths with the wish that *phthonos* (resentment) should be absent, but if there is one fact which is clear in the audience's mind at this point it is that Clytemnestra is dissimulating; she does not wish her husband well, and she hopes not that her praise will not attract *phthonos*, but that it will; her device of the purple path is a means of attracting *phthonos* to her husband. Agamemnon himself recognizes this in his reply; the path that lies before him is *epiphthonos* (liable to *phthonos*, 921), and it is so because for Agamemnon to tread this path is to go beyond the limits which normally contain him; he feels that such an ostentatious celebration of success places him on a level with an eastern potentate (919-20)[53] and regards the honour which his wife proposes as more fitting for the gods than for a man (922 and 925).[54] Agamemnon's apprehension, then, which he expresses as *aidōs* in 948, is based on his awareness of the inappropriateness for one in his position of what he is being asked to do, and a particular consideration in his mind is the danger of divine, rather than human disapproval.

Clytemnestra, however, manages to overcome these concerns; first of all she attempts to remove his misgivings about the dangerous nature of the act by suggesting that it is not intrinsically wrong, and makes Agamemnon admit that in other circumstances (if he had vowed to the gods to walk on the cloths, 933-4),[55] and for another agent (an eastern potentate like Priam, 935-6), the act might take on a different aspect. The point of this startling exploitation of the sophistic commonplace that the character of an action may vary according to agent and circumstance[56] is the failure of Agamemnon to grasp what is

[53] The eastern potentate, as exemplified in Hdt.'s histories, is the type of the pride in human prosperity which goes before a fall occasioned by jealous gods; see Walcot (1978), 22-37.

[54] Both *timalphein* in 922 and *sebein* in 925 refer to the acknowledgement of *timē*.

[55] On the correct interpretation of these lines, see Fraenkel (1950), ad loc.; cf. Winnington-Ingram (1983), 92.

[56] This is 'non-sceptical' relativism, and is distinguished from sceptical relativism or subjectivism by its implication that the character of an action can be objectively discovered providing the particular circumstances are known; for sophistic applications of both kinds of relativism, see the *Dissoi Logoi* (in general) and cf. Nill (1985), 29-30; on Clyt.'s use of this argument, see Goldhill (1984), 77; (1986), 12-13.

only too apparent to the audience—that the character of the action does in fact *change* with the circumstances; Clytemnestra implants in Agamemnon the suggestion that an action which is not absolutely and in itself inappropriate is positively appropriate in any circumstance, but her argument itself turns on the point that Agamemnon has already recognized the action as inappropriate for one in his position;[57] she deflects this concern by appealing to other circumstances in which the character of the act may differ, and it is this difference which impresses itself on the minds of the audience.

This argument, then, is intended to assuage Agamemnon's anxiety, his *aidōs*. This is also Clytemnestra's purpose in the next part of the dialogue (937–9). She recognizes that Agamemnon's reluctance is a result of *aidōs* and related to the concept of *phthonos*, but interprets both of these concepts in a restricted sense. Since it is not such a bad thing to trample expensive fabrics,[58] Agamemnon is now to put all *aidōs* for human censure out of his mind;[59] he is reminded that, in spite of his protestations of the power of popular disapproval (938), human jealousy is a natural concomitant of success; one who does not attract *phthonos* is one whose position is not to be envied. Clytemnestra, therefore, interprets the *phthonos* towards which Agamemnon's *aidōs* is directed in a narrow sense which stresses his position *vis-à-vis* other human beings, and Agamemnon himself does not take the opportunity to object that his *aidōs* is concerned with more than simply human disapproval.[60] Clytemnestra's argument here is obviously based on the ambiguity of *phthonos* as divine and human resentment,[61] but Agamemnon is not simply defeated by an equivocation. Clytemnestra's arguments on resentment as a sign of success constitute her last attempt to dispel her husband's *aidōs* (from this point on the debate is not concerned with his reluctance to walk on the fabrics, but with her determination to prevail (940–3)), and so, since his *aidōs* is mitigated to the extent that he does walk on the garments, we must presume that this argument is effective. Commentators are right to stress the power of Clytemnestra's rhetoric in this scene,[62] and this feature is certainly vividly represented in the 'battle' language of 940–3, but it

---

[57] In particular, he has rejected eastern luxury only lines before; cf. Easterling (1973), 13; Winnington-Ingram (1983), 92.

[58] Note the inferential particle νυν in 937.

[59] μή νυν τὸν ἀνθρώπειον αἰδεσθῇς ψόγον (937).

[60] See Easterling (1973), 13.

[61] Cf. Winnington-Ingram (1983), 91.

[62] e.g. Goldhill (1984), 77–9; (1986), 13–14.

would be a strange sort of persuasive rhetoric which persuaded by some means other than by the arguments it presents. Agamemnon's *aidōs*, then, is assuaged, but not allayed, by a restriction of his scruple to the human level; and on the human level his desire to attract positive envy as proof of his success outweighs his fear of critical resentment,[63] or, to put it another way, *aidōs* at excess, transgression, or inappropriateness is overcome by the positive desire for honour.[64]

The fact that Agamemnon's *aidōs* is not completely dispelled, however, is of the greatest significance. Its persistence, still with reference to *phthonos* and in the context of his consciousness of himself in relation to the gods (944–52), indicates that it cannot without remainder be equated with simple concern for others' disapproval; it is not equivalent to the calculation, 'Can I get away with it?', but is rather a sense that all is not well, that what Agamemnon is about to do is inappropriate in terms of the values and religious beliefs of his society; he hopes to mitigate his offence by removing his shoes, but the effect of the persisting *aidōs* to which this gesture is a concession is to reveal that he is doing wrong[65] and to contribute to the atmosphere of apprehension and tension which grows from this point until the murder is committed.[66]

The form which Agamemnon's *aidōs* takes also reflects the fact that it would be impossible to claim with regard to Aeschylus, as has been done with Homer, that *aidōs* is nothing more than a reaction to others' disapproval; in the tragedian, in fact, the stress on popular disapproval in contexts in which *aidōs* occurs is much less than in Homer. This does not mean, however, that we should regard *aidōs* in Aeschylus as a concept which has changed or developed considerably from epic usage. In particular, we should not be misled by the religious element in Agamemnon's apprehension into positing a new, religious significance.

As this and other passages suggest, *aidōs* can readily be used of

---

[63] See Winnington-Ingram (1983), 93.

[64] Ag. does want to be honoured, but as a man, not as a god (925); this is the distinction which Clyt.'s rhetoric blurs.

[65] Cf. von Erffa (1937), 94.

[66] The importance of the 'carpet scene' in the creation of apprehension is recognized by Vickers (1973: 367); I would contend that Ag.'s lingering *aidōs* is an important element of this. De Romilly (1958: 73–5) has a brilliant exposition of the crescendo of prophetic fear which builds up from the reactions of the chorus following Ag.'s departure into the palace (975–87) and grows into the paroxysms of the Cassandra scene, but does not notice that Ag.'s own apprehension, his own fear (924) and his *aidōs*, may be regarded as beginning this sequence.

respect for the gods,[67] or the lack of it, but it is not restricted to such applications, and its operation in them is analogous to that in non-religious contexts. *Persae* 809–10 will help illustrate this point. Here the ghost of Darius describes how the Persian troops who invaded Greece under Xerxes 'felt no *aidōs* to plunder the images of the gods or to burn their temples'. These are acts of sacrilege, and no doubt would meet with the disapproval of both gods and men, but the stress in the text is on the lack of scruple which led to the crimes rather than on the sanctions, human and divine, which await them. *Aidōs* should have prevented these crimes simply because their perpetrators should have recognized their 'inappropriateness'; *aidōs* is the reaction which inhibits such inappropriate conduct, whether the force that dictates that it is so is popular opinion, the gods, or one's own moral sensibilities. Similarly, in the 'carpet scene' Agamemnon's *aidōs* is not a specifically religious scruple, but a sense that he is faced with the performance of an action which is inappropriate for him to perform. Inappropriateness may be resented by the gods, particularly since the gods are now felt to lay down the standards by which men should live, but it need not be, and *aidōs*, as Clytemnestra's argument at *Agamemnon* 937 makes clear, is not restricted to the divine sphere.

The inappropriateness to which *aidōs* responds must still, however, be seen against the background of *timē*, since it is *timē*, both of oneself and others, which unifies the concept of *aidōs* throughout the range of its applications. Agamemnon's conduct, and that of the Persian force, is inappropriate in that it fails to take into account the relationship between one's own *timē* and that of others, including the gods; Agamemnon is persuaded that he can assert his superiority in *timē* over other men, but his initial apprehension recognized the gulf in *timē* between men and gods, and his action in spite of this apprehension constitutes an encroachment upon the *timē* of the latter. Similarly, the Persians offend directly against the gods by stealing and burning the objects by which the gods are paid *timē*. But men also possess *timē*, quantitatively but not qualitatively different from that of the gods, and the frequency of religious uses of *aidōs* in Aeschylus only reflects the inclusion of gods and men under the same broad system.[68]

Agamemnon makes two decisions in the play which bears his name;

---

[67] Cf. the examples in *Supp.* (345, 478–9); cf. 3.4 below on *aidōs* and *sebas*.

[68] The continuity of divine and human values, including that of *timē*, is frequently stressed by Adkins; he conveniently refers us to his writings on the subject at (1982*b*), 36–7; see also (1982*c*).

to walk on the purple fabrics is his second, and the first, reported by the chorus, is his decision to sacrifice his daughter.[69] The parallelism which many have detected between the two scenes[70] is reflected in the similarity of his motivation in both places, motivation which is to be understood in terms of *aidōs*. Agamemnon's choice in the first matter is clearly set out: either he can do what would in normal circumstances be inconceivable, and sacrifice his daughter,[71] or he can give up his leadership of the alliance and, as he puts it, desert (206-13). Both alternatives, like those which faced Pelasgus in the *Supplices*, are 'grievous',[72] both will have serious consequences,[73] and both can be seen as actions which *aidōs* should inhibit. On the one side is the possibility of what Agamemnon sees as desertion,[74] an unthinkable option for a warrior and a crime which in Athens was punishable by *atimia* (disfranchisement, loss of citizen *timē*),[75] while on the other there is the murder of a member of his own family, a crime against *philia* which, according to the chorus at 222-3 requires 'shameful-minded delusion'.[76] Agamemnon will have known as well as the chorus do that to kill a member of one's own family is *aischron*, and this will

[69] Decisions again; the chorus describe Ag.'s consideration of two alternatives, and his eventual preference for one over the other, so it can hardly be maintained that he does not have a choice; *anankē* in 218 need not indicate absolute or external compulsion (Dover (1973), 65). For the view that Ag. has no choice, see Page in Denniston and Page (1957), pp. xxiii-xxix; Lloyd-Jones (1962), 187-99, esp. 191-2. Rivier (1968: 9-10) and Stebler (1971: 53) recognize that he does have a choice, but stress his lack of freedom; such, however, is the very nature of difficult choices. Hammond (1965: 47) sensibly points out that 'no choice' in this context can only mean 'no real choice'. We are hardly justified, however, in treating Ag.'s decision as a philosophical issue; he is liable for the sacrifice of Iphigeneia no matter how far his freedom of choice is restricted, and his act calls forth Clyt.'s retribution whatever the nature of his decision; see Gagarin (1976), 197 n. 17 (but note that he also (n. 18) rejects the idea that Ag. is absolutely compelled to act as he does).

[70] See Vickers (1973), 368; Winnington-Ingram (1983), 92-3; even if the carpet scene were only about the destruction of the valuables of the house, as Jones (1962: 85-8) insists, this would be enough to effect the link between the two episodes which he deprecates (85 n. 2); Iphigeneia is the 'adornment of the house' at 208 (Winnington-Ingram, 92).

[71] Cf. Gagarin (1976), 92.

[72] βαρεῖα μὲν ... βαρεῖα δ' ..., 206-8; cf. *Supp.* 342, 347.

[73] 211; cf. *Supp.* 442.

[74] It is Ag. who, as quoted by the chorus, sees the matter in terms of desertion, and so in terms of martial values, and therefore the representation of the choice as between the alternatives of murder and desertion reflects his priorities and his motivation; we cannot be sure that the designation of one alternative as desertion is the only possible interpretation, much less that the possibility of desertion is here rejected by Aesch. himself, as Page in Denniston and Page (1957: p. xxvii) claims.

[75] See MacDowell (1978), 160-1.

[76] αἰσχρόμητις ... παρακοπά, 222-3.

presumably have occasioned *aidōs* at the prospect. This *aidōs*, however, he overcomes, and he does so as a result of his reluctance to behave in a way that is disgraceful for a warrior; 'how can I become a deserter and lose my alliance?' he asks in a rhetorical question 'by which', as Lesky well points out,[77] 'he envisages the disgrace and shame he would incur by deserting his post'. He thus chooses to put his own honour before his loyalty to the family,[78] and as in the carpet scene this concern, in this case itself identifiable with *aidōs*, overcomes his *aidōs* in another direction. Again the abandonment of hesitation, of *aidōs*, suggests the dubious moral character of the subsequent action, and again *aidōs* is central to the vivid presentation of a character's uncertainty in a difficult and tense situation. *Aidōs*, in fact, appears to be central to Aeschylus' representation of the crucial moral choice.

3.2.3. *Orestes*

In the next play of the trilogy *aidōs* again intervenes at the crucial moment, when Orestes is faced with the prospect of killing one whom he should not kill.[79] At 896–8 Clytemnestra bares her breast[80] and appeals to her son's *aidōs* for this emotive feature of the mother–child relationship,[81] so invoking the imperatives of loyalty to one's *philoi* and gratitude to one's parents for the nurture one has received, and constructing a scenario which appeals to traditional norms of honour and obligation and stresses the gravity of their disruption. This appeal destroys Orestes' resolve, and he asks (899), 'Pylades, what am I to do? Am I to feel *aidōs* to kill my mother?' This question, like Agamemnon's intention to kill Iphigeneia, is all the more striking for being unthinkable in any normal context.[82] Unlike Agamemnon, however, Orestes is

[77] (1966), 81.

[78] Cf. Gagarin (1976), 92; also Stebler (1971), 53.

[79] See *Cho.* 930. The meaning of this line for Or. is probably that, although he recognizes that it is wrong in any normal circumstance to kill one's mother, his deed is justified as retaliation for Clyt.'s, which for him is the initial wrong; for the audience, however, the words are a sign that Or.'s vengeance is thematically and morally parallel with that of his mother; see Garvie (1986), ad loc.; cf. Snell (1928), 120; Pearson (1962), 20.

[80] Or the male actor playing the part makes some equivalent gesture (Taplin (1978), 61; Garvie (1986), ad loc.).

[81] Cf. Hecabe at 22. 82–4 (and Ch. 1 n. 133); as in that place, the breast is the direct object of the verb *aideisthai*, both metonymously for the person, and as an object whose exposure puts normal categories of honour and shame under stress.

[82] Cf. Gagarin (1976), 99.

not really involved in deliberation between two alternatives, rather a decision already made is in danger of being unmade in the face of his recognition of the full horror of its consequences.[83] There are two deliberative subjunctives in line 899, and Orestes is thus clearly faced with a choice; he is free to spare his mother,[84] but, reminded by Pylades of the danger of making enemies of the gods,[85] he does not do so. Orestes' hesitation, his susceptibility to *aidōs*, is obviously a considerable theatrical effect, threatening the purpose which has been so consistently expressed in the previous action of the play, and it acts as a foil for the even more dramatic effect of the sudden speech of Pylades, the hitherto silent third actor; but there is more to his hesitation than that. Orestes' response is clearly instinctive and involuntary, and it springs automatically from his awareness of the most deeply held traditional beliefs;[86] his susceptibility to *aidōs*, then, is an indication of the character of his act in terms of these beliefs, and the fact that he overcomes it demonstrates the moral ambivalence of his revenge.[87] Thus, as in the other 'decision scenes' we have looked at, *aidōs* is instrumental in the creation of tension, in the delineation of motive, and in the moral characterization of crucial actions; that this intervention of *aidōs* in scenes of such significance should form a recurring pattern suggests that the dramatist saw its utility—as an inhibitory emotion and a mechanism regulating one's conduct among

[83] Or.'s 'decision' precedes the play's beginning (Rivier (1968), 28-9; Stebler (1971), 31), but his resolve is strengthened at several points, notably in the *kommos*; for the view that Or. fully realizes what his decision involves only at 899, cf. Garvie (1986), ad loc.
[84] Snell (1928: 133-4) is right to emphasize Or.'s choice, but wrong to see it as a struggle in his heart between divine forces (cf. Class (1964), 44); Clyt.'s Erinyes have not yet entered the equation, and Ag.'s Erinyes desire the same end as Apollo; cf. Garvie (1986), p. xxxii. Rivier (1968: 25, 28-9; cf. Stebler (1971), 91) maintains that Or. has no choice, but see Garvie on 899; the very mention of the punishments laid down should Or. disobey Apollo's command (271-96) shows that disobedience is not impossible (Garvie, p. xxxi).
[85] Thus Goldhill (1984: 180; 1986: 84) rightly refers to a 'hierarchisation' of *philia* here; Or. is faced with a choice of 'friendship' or 'enmity' with two individuals, one his mother and one a god; he chooses to make a friend of the latter and an enemy of the former; the opposite choice would have yielded the converse situation. Thus as gods are brought within the same standards of *timē* as mortals, so they are included within the scheme of *philia*.
[86] Or.'s act is thus in conflict with his instinctive appreciation of basic values, and to that extent his *aidōs* must be seen as proceeding from his conscience (Snell (1928), 131, 133; Stebler (1971), 91). Stebler rightly stresses Or.'s *Gewissens-Not*, and categorizes his reaction as a manifestation of the (Jungian (op. cit. 14; cf. Ch. 1 n. 289)) 'moral' (instinctive) conscience, yet maintains that his personal conscience is overcome by divine compulsion; but Apollo does not compel, at least not absolutely (n. 84 above).
[87] Contrast Arrowsmith (1959: 49) for the idea that Or.'s hesitation mitigates his guilt.

one's fellows—in the setting of individual psychology against the background of the values of society.

3.3. THE REJECTION OF *AIDŌS*

We have seen that the rejection of *aidōs* may be a danger sign; we turn now to a number of passages in which the rejection is explicit, and the emphasis somewhat different. Bruno Snell[88] uses fragment 132c Radt (= 225 Mette)[89] as a basis for the delineation of a particular feature of Aeschylean tragedy, which he also regards as a new element in the development of Greek society and the Greek mind. The beginning of each line in the papyrus is lost, and the text becomes more fragmentary towards the end, but the general sense is clear enough for our purposes. Achilles is the speaker (line 2) and he is faced with the strongest possible disapproval from the Greek army following his withdrawal from battle (he is under threat of stoning, 1); he is unrepentant, however, and rejoices in the knowledge that his absence has caused a rout of the Greeks and so demonstrated his pre-eminence (9–11). In line 11, however, the loss of the beginning of the line makes more of a difference; Achilles infers from the effect of his withdrawal either (Snell) that he could destroy everything for the Greek army, or (Schadewaldt *et al.*) that he *is* everything to the Greek army. To utter such thoughts, he goes on, occasions no *aidōs* in him,[90] for none of the other Greek leaders is nobler than he (12–14).[91] Achilles claims, then, that he feels no *aidōs* either at placing himself above all the other Greeks or at contemplating the possibility that he should go so far as to betray his erstwhile comrades; the latter entails a more striking lack of *aidōs*, but the former involves very much the same thing; in either case Achilles feels no *aidōs* at considering his own claims to the exclusion of those of anyone else.

---

[88] (1964), 1–22.

[89] The ascription of this fragment to Aesch. has been challenged (see Page (1941), 136–41; Lloyd-Jones (1957), 590–3), but objections rest largely on literary and dramatic arguments which stop far short of proof. The balance of probability is still that the fr. is by Aesch.; see Lesky (1983), 101 (and even Lloyd-Jones has now changed his mind (1973: 192; 1987: 13), persuaded by the discovery of a uniquely Aeschylean form as the true reading in line 14; see Radt's apparatus, ad loc.).

[90] οὐκ αἰδώς μ' ἔχει, 12.

[91] That Ach. justifies his boast indicates that the *aidōs* he disclaims is not to be imagined merely as a force which inhibits boasting *per se*; it must concern a boast of which the content could conceivably be seen as inappropriate, thus Ach. claims the content of the boast is not inappropriate, in view of his status.

According to Snell,[92] Achilles' denial of *aidōs* means, 'I do not care what you think. I shall stand by what I have done, by my convictions, and shall carry it through against your resistance.' He thus sees the fragment as the first indication of a tendency towards subjective evaluation of one's own account without reference to the universal standards of society, as an indication of the development of a personal moral conscience. He recognizes that it is not in itself new that someone should reject *aidōs* (referring to Archilochus' insouciance over the loss of his shield)[93] and he might also have mentioned any of a number of characters in Homer who are, for whatever reason, insensitive to *aidōs*;[94] these characters, however, do not say, 'I am not ashamed', and therein, for Snell, lies the difference. Certainly in real life people who say 'I am not ashamed', if they are not trying to conceal the effect the criticisms of others *are* having on them,[95] may be seeking to oppose their evaluation of an act or a situation to that of other people,[96] and clearly in the latter instance the possibility of subjective judgement of one's own actions does arise. Here Achilles is clearly setting his own estimation of himself and his prowess against the loyalty to the army as a whole which is demanded by others; this, however, was also his position in the *Iliad*, where his refusal to act as *aidōs* for his comrades' demands is equally apparent.[97] The emphasis in the fragment, it must be admitted, is somewhat different: in the *Iliad* Achilles wishes his own opinion of himself to be validated by the other Achaeans; here he seems to exult in his own knowledge of his worth without reference to the opinions of others; we cannot be sure, however, that his desire for recognition of his prowess was not stressed elsewhere in the play, and should notice that the Homeric Achilles manifests a similar awareness of his own value to the army at *Iliad* 9. 348–55. Snell is certainly right to point out that Achilles is standing up for his own position in the face of the strongest disapproval from

[92] (1964), 8; cf. Stebler (1971: 69), who, like Snell, compares *Ag.* 1373 and, unlike him, *Sept.* 1029–30.

[93] (1964), 8.

[94] The situation of Paris might be thought analogous to that of Ach. in the fr.; Paris is scarcely perturbed that others accuse him of slacking and cowardice (discussion in 1.2.2 above), and it should be noted that he defends his own skills (the gifts of Aphrodite, 3. 64–6) in the face of Hector's criticism. Paris is a bad example—is the Aeschylean Ach.?

[95] 'Sticks and stones. . . .'

[96] 'I am not ashamed', however, need not always mean, '*x* is normally shameful, but I do not consider it so'; it could simply mean 'there is no reason to be ashamed of *x*'; see text below on *Ag.* 614.

[97] Cf. 1.3.2 above, on the embassy of 9.

his fellows, and this last element constitutes a difference between the situation here and that of the *Iliad*, where his anger was, at least until he rejected appropriate compensation, regarded as understandable. We should beware, however, of interpreting his denial of *aidōs* as a simple representation of his conscientious desire to be true to himself. We need, in particular, more information before we can be sure that Achilles' lack of *aidōs* is not reprehensible, an indication of his *anaideia*. We cannot regard as a hero of conscience everyone who asserts his contempt for the restraints placed upon him by his society; a murderer who feels no guilt is certainly opposing his values to those of the group, but this response is normally seen as different in kind from that of the prisoner of conscience. Precise distinctions may be impossible, but there is surely a difference between one who rejects conformity out of sincere belief in a higher imperative and one who ignores the norms of society in order to indulge his own desires, even though the latter may believe that pursuit of one's own desires is right.

Snell's identification of the rise of the personal moral conscience in this passage is therefore dubious, particularly in its over-confident use of such fragmentary evidence. Snell is also wrong to assert that Aeschylus is the first author to use the denial of *aidōs* as a means of presenting loyalty to one's own principles as against conformity to the group,[98] for Solon 32 West, in which the verdict of popular opinion is disputed and opposed to Solon's conviction that he has behaved creditably, is a much clearer example of the phenomenon Snell discusses than the Aeschylean fragment.[99]

Snell also cites other Aeschylean passages as examples of the same phenomenon, and here our access to the context puts us on firmer ground. At *Agamemnon* 613–14 Clytemnestra rounds off her protestation of loyalty to her husband with the claim that her 'boast, full of truth, [is] not *aischros* for a noble woman to utter'. The similarity with the Achillean fragment, however, the lack of inhibition regarding a boast, is only superficial; the loyalty which Clytemnestra feigns is precisely the virtue expected in a wife, and so she is not placing a positive interpretation of her own on conduct criticized by others; her 'not *aischros*' thus means, in fact, 'positively *kalos*', and so this passage has no bearing on Snell's thesis.

There is equally no question of self–other conflict in Clytemnestra's denial of shame at *Agamemnon* 855–8, where, in a preface to a speech expressing her longing for her husband in his absence, she explains

[98] (1964), 9.   [99] See 2.3.3 above.

that she will not be ashamed (οὐκ αἰσχυνοῦμαι) to speak of her 'husband-loving ways'[100] before the chorus; it is implied that such private matters are best kept private, but Clytemnestra explains that time has blunted her inhibition in this area. In both these passages the *aidōs* which she claims to ignore is, on the surface at least, of an insignificant kind, and there is no question of Clytemnestra setting her personal convictions against mere conformity. But the point of the utterances for the meaning of the play is that they are lies; it was almost certainly well established at this period that deceit is *aischron*,[101] and the audience will realize that Clytemnestra's denials of *aidōs*[102] conceal her more significant lack of *aidōs* with regard to her deceit, deceit which itself reveals her lack of *aidōs* with regard to her disloyalty and adultery. In the context of her deceit these remarks dismissing *aidōs* reveal her cavalier attitude towards propriety, towards the chorus, who are aware of the truth, and towards Agamemnon's honour, which her actions are calculated to diminish. It is this, the essence of her *anaideia*, which emerges in a third passage at 1372–6; she will feel no shame (οὐκ ἐπαισχυνθήσομαι) at the open contradiction of her previous lies, since these were justified as a means of executing her vengeance. Here she does attempt to justify conduct which *aidōs* might have prevented with reference to the right of retaliation, and so the passage may legitimately be considered as an instance of the individual's setting her subjective justification of her conduct against conventional criticism; but evident too are Clytemnestra's defiant and bare-faced admission of conduct normally considered discreditable, her lack of *aidōs* at telling lies and admitting that she has done so, and the wider lack of *aidōs* for her husband and the limitations imposed on her as a woman, and these are the more important aspects for the meaning of the play. The effect of all three passages is cumulative—Clytemnestra is

[100] The phrase can also mean 'man-loving ways', and this must remind us of her adultery with Aegisthus (cf. Snell (1928), 122; Stanford (1983), 141; Fraenkel (1950), on 856, denies the double meaning, but there is no good reason to do so).

[101] See Ch. 2 n. 84; cf. *PV* 685 (which is probably later than the passages under discussion); Adkins (1960*a*), 181.

[102] I think it is safe so to describe the two passages cited: in the former her affirmation that her boast is not *aischros* indicates that she would feel no *aidōs* at uttering it (and since her boast is a lie this indicates that she feels no *aidōs* at lying; her boast, *qua* lie, *is aischros* for a noble woman to utter), and in the latter the verb *aischunomai* expresses exactly the same sense as would *aideomai*; indeed, in every case of the occurrence of *aischunomai* in Aesch. (*Ag.* 1373; *Cho.* 917; (*Sept.* 1029, see n. 105 below)), the verb is synonymous with *aideomai*.

entirely without *aidōs*, which, for a woman, is most likely more reprehensible than it is for a man.[103]

The conviction that one is right, then, may actually reveal that one is wrong, at least in terms of traditional values,[104] and there is more (or less) to the passages Snell cites than the depiction of individual principle. Two of the passages, however, fragment 132c Radt and *Agamemnon* 1372–6, do at least suggest familiarity with the argument that one's own idea of right can be opposed to society's idea of wrong, but this is no more than we should expect in Aeschylus' day, since we have observed the same phenomenon in a fragment of poetry written more than a century before the performance of the *Oresteia*.[105]

3.4. *AIDŌS* AND *SEBAS*

We have now covered most of the instances of *aidōs* etc. in Aeschylus, but comment on some passages has been postponed, in order that we may observe the relationship between two complexes of terms, *aidōs*-words and *sebas*-words. We have already seen that *sebas* etc. can operate in similar spheres to those in which *aidōs* etc. are found; in Aeschylus *sebas* is, in certain areas, by far the commoner term, and has taken over many of the functions of *aidōs*, but the take-over is not complete, and the considerable degree of overlap not only allows us to discover what the terms have in common, but also helps pin down essential aspects of *aidōs*.

The most obvious point of contact is to be found in *Persae* (694–703), where the chorus explain their inhibition towards the ghost of

---

[103] Cf. Fraenkel (1950), on 1373 (which he relates to 856); on the revelation of Clyt.'s general *anaideia* through her lies, cf. Goldhill (1984), 89; (1986), 14.

[104] As Snell, in fact, recognizes (1964: 10–11).

[105] *Sept.* 1029–30, where Antigone argues, much as she does in Soph.'s play, that she is not ashamed to disobey the order that Polyneices should go unburied, is a clearer example of the phenomenon Snell is describing, but he presumably omits it from his discussion because of the doubts about the authenticity of the end of the play (on which see G. O. Hutchinson (1985), on 1005–78; Lesky (1983), 61–2; for an argument for authenticity see Lloyd-Jones (1959); further lit. in all three). He includes, however, *PV* 266, to which similar reservations apply; Prometheus proudly claims that he offended (ἥμαρτον) willingly and so reveals that he regards his transgression against the will of Zeus as justified, indeed laudable. (For *hamartia* as offence or transgression, see Bremer (1969), 32 (on this passage), 30–64 (generally).) The phenomenon which Snell identifies is clearly present in 5th-cent. lit. (*PV* at least, if not the end of *Sept.*, is likely to be 5th-cent.), but it is not a specifically Aeschylean development.

Darius: they feel *sebas* to look directly at him,[106] *sebas* to speak in his presence, and attribute this to their 'ancient dread' of their former king. Darius then paraphrases their reserve as *aidōs* (699), before they go on to reiterate it in terms of fear,[107] which the king describes as *deos* (703). The connection with fear recalls the association of *aidōs* and that emotion in contexts of respect for those of special status in Homer, and it is clear that the chorus's response is one of veneration for one whom they regard as pre-eminent in *timē*. The chorus's reluctance to look the ghost in the face (694) indicates that this characteristic shame-reaction, which is often found in contexts that we might describe in terms of modesty, embarrassment, etc., also occurs in contexts of respect, and presumably the similarity of the manifestations of inhibition across the range of these uses is one reason why Greek applies a unitary term where English sees difference.

Thus *sebas* and *aidōs* overlap as responses to those of greater power and *timē*. The link with *timē* in the use of *sebas* as recognition of another's power is most apparent at *Agamemnon* 258-60, where the chorus-leader describes himself as 'revering' [*sebizōn*] Clytemnestra's power [*kratos*]', and explains that he does so 'because it is right to pay *timē* to [*tiein*] a ruler's wife'. Like *aidōs*, then, *sebas* is a response to *timē*, and can obviously be used of mortal superiors.[108] But *sebas* does not simply respond to power as such: at *Agamemnon* 779-80 Dikē feels no *sebas* for (pays no honour to) 'the power of wealth, falsely stamped with praise'; the new regime of Clytemnestra and Aegisthus, although not lacking in power, is said, at *Choephori* 55-7, to have lost the *sebas* which once belonged to the royal house, and so to have forfeited the respect of the people; and at *Agamemnon* 1612 the chorus-leader refuses to *sebein* Aegisthus, even though the latter has already assumed the place of ruler, because of his hubristic exultation at Agamemnon's death. *Sebas*, therefore, is not simply fear of the powerful, but encompasses admiration of authority which one regards as legitimate; it responds to the value of the powerful person, not simply to the fact of his power.[109] The power of the gods, at least in the eyes of ordinary

[106] The verb *sebomai* here occurs with an inf. in an inhibitory sense analogous to that of *aideomai*.

[107] On the verb *diomai* here, see Broadhead (1960), on 700-2; however the form is explained, 'I fear' is clearly the sense, and the connection with fear is, in any case, guaranteed by *deos* in 703; this is the only certain instance of *deos* in Aesch.; see Italie's *Index*, s.v.; cf. de Romilly (1958), 59, 111 n. 1.

[108] Cf. *Ag.* 785-7, 833, 925, 1612.

[109] Thus at *PV* 937 Prometheus' association of *sebas* with flattery recognizes that it encompasses an active expression of admiration for its object.

mortals, is analytically legitimate, and both *aideomai* and *sebein* etc. are found of reverence for the gods.[110] This, however, does not make even *sebas*, which is much more common in such contexts than *aidōs*, an exclusively religious concept;[111] it is only possible to regard *aidōs* and *sebas* as 'religious awe', directed fundamentally towards the sacred and the numinous, if we assume that they respond to the same qualities when used of humans, and this is plainly not the case. The link, in both cases, between the divine and human spheres is *timē*.[112]

The link between *aidōs*, *sebas*, and *timē* can, in fact, be observed in Aeschylean usage, since both *aideomai* and the verbs based on *sebas* occur frequently in contexts of the acknowledgement of honour, value, or importance. In *Eumenides*, for example, Orestes claims that Zeus became his saviour πατρῷον αἰδεσθεὶς μόρον (760),[113] which Verrall translates, 'in pity of my father's fate',[114] and which Gagarin[115] paraphrases as 'in a sense of respect and shame at his father's death', but the point is that Zeus has *preferred*, that is, considered more important, the death of Agamemnon to that of Clytemnestra. Thus Athena declares (at 739–40): 'I shall not prefer [attach more *timē* to, προτιμήσω] the death of a woman who killed a man, the overseer of the house.' Similarly at 640 the chorus-leader, in recapitulation of Apollo's argument in 625–39, observes, 'according to you, Zeus attaches more *timē* to [προτιμᾷ] the death of the father'. The similarity in sense between *aideomai* and (*pro*)*timan*, and the association of these

---

[110] *Aideomai*: see *Ag.* 362–4, where the chorus's *aidōs* for Zeus *xenios* is not general reverence for a deity, but awe at the manifestation of his power in punishing Paris (cf. von Erffa (1937), 93–4); cf. also *Supp.* 478–9. *Sebas* also recognizes the power of the divine to punish (*Supp.* 755–6; *Cho.* 912), and is by now the more common term used to designate man's attitude to god: *Sept.* 529–30; *Supp.* 222–3, 921–2, 1024–5; *Cho.* 960; *Eum.* 12–13, 897.

[111] On the other hand, regular association of *sebas* with recognition of the *timē* of the gods means that the adj. *eusebēs* (stock translation 'pious') and *asebēs/dussebēs* (impious) tend to occur most often in religious contexts (e.g. *Ag.* 338, 372; *Cho.* 122; *Eum.* 910, and generally in 5th-cent. and later lit.; see Burkert (1985), 272–5), but they also describe proper behaviour in human relationships in which the gods have an interest (*Supp.* 340, 419, supplication; *Cho.* 704, *xenia*), and can, particularly since the gods now have such an interest in human conduct, refer to general right and wrong doing (*Supp.* 941; *Eum.* 532); see Adkins (1960*a*), 132–8. Perhaps the particular association of these terms with the gods arises from the fact that 'lack of *sebas*', in general contexts where no object is named, naturally suggests disregard of divine rather than human authority; but where a human object is specified *eusebeia/dussebeia* can acknowledge/disregard his authority (see Ch. 4 n. 13 on Soph. *Ant.*).

[112] Cf. 3.2.2 above, on *Pers.* 809–10.

[113] 'Out of *aidōs* for my father's death.'

[114] (1908), ad loc.

[115] (1976), 78.

with *sebas*, is confirmed at 545-9 by the use together of *aidomenos* and προτίων ('attaching more *timē* to', here governing 'the *sebas* of parents', a locution equivalent to 'feeling *aidōs* for parents'). *Eumenides* 760, then, means 'putting my father's fate first', that is, giving it its due importance, responding, as if it were a person, to its *timē*.[116] *Sebō* is used in a similar sense at *Eumenides* 715 and 749,[117] and both *aideomai* and *sebō* etc. can, when governing a direct object, be translated as 'acknowledge the *timē* of', 'honour'.

As a result of this fundamental association with *timē*, *aidōs* and *sebas* are very close, and can be used almost interchangeably, both when conveying the acknowledgement of the *timē* of mortals and gods in general and in those particular relationships to which *timē* is essential. Thus in supplication both *aidōs* and *sebas* can indicate the response (*a*) to the altar in which is invested the *timē* of the gods,[118] (*b*) to the suppliants themselves,[119] and (*c*) to the god who guarantees the ritual.[120] A similar institution to supplication is that of the oath, and in *Eumenides* the verb *aideisthai* is used three times (483-4, 680, 710)[121] of the attitude towards its maintenance of those who have sworn an oath, with the oath itself (or a periphrasis, 483) as the direct object of this *aidōs*. In this case *aidōs* responds to the oath, as it does to the altar in supplication, as a 'thing' invested with *timē*, something in which the power of ritual and the gods inheres. Supplication and the oath resemble each other in that both institutions invoke the sanction of divine punishment,[122] make use of the sanctity of ritually pure places,[123] and place structures of honour under stress. The suppliant abandons

---

[116] Aesch. is rich in the use of such quasi-personal objects with *aideisthai*; cf. *Supp.* 345, 478; *Ag.* 937; *Eum.* 483-4, 680, 710; fr. 135 Radt.

[117] Cf. *Ag.* 274, 779-80; *Cho.* 637.

[118] *Aidōs*: *Supp.* 345 (cf. 3.2.1 above); *sebas*: *Supp.* 222-3. At *Cho.* 106-8 *aidōs* is thought of as responding to the power of an altar in a more general way, when the chorus-leader explains that she feels *aidōs* for Agamemnon's tomb as she would for an altar. The tomb embodies the *timē* of the deceased, now a revered object of ancestor worship, while the altar partakes of that of the gods.

[119] *Aidōs*: *Supp.* 641; *sebas*: *Supp.* 815, *Eum.* 151.

[120] *Aidōs*: *Supp.* 478-9; *sebas*: *Supp.* 671.

[121] Cf. Soph. *OT* 647. Here, however, the oath is not one sworn by oneself, but by someone else, and the *aidōs* it receives as an entity endowed with *timē* is analogous to that which one might accord the gods, its guarantors.

[122] Albeit slightly differently in each case: the suppliant is protected by the gods from harm, while the swearer of an oath invokes destruction on himself in the event of his perjury; but divine anger is the result of transgression in either case, and this anger proceeds directly from the *timē* of the gods, which is injured in cases of offence.

[123] This applies, of course, to supplication before an altar or hearth, not to personal supplication.

his own claim to honour, and relies on that of Zeus, while the swearer of an oath commits his honour on the question of its veracity and its fulfilment; not only does perjury involve disregard of the honour of the gods, it reveals both the perjuror's lack of concern for the honour of those before whom the oath was sworn and a reprehensible lack of concern for his own honour—for the exposure, that is, of his falsehood which the public nature of the institution makes inevitable.[124] *Aidōs* for the oath, then, is a recognition of its power, of the various ways in which *timē* is invested in the institution, just as *aidōs* for the swearer of the oath[125] is a recognition of the fact that he has created a powerful situation by invoking the honour of the gods and placing his own honour at risk; to believe him is to recognize his *timē*, to refuse is to slight it.[126] Burkert[127] and Parker[128] stress the way in which these institutions invoke the divine sanction and the concept of the sacred to protect important human relationships; the emphasis in their works is rightly on the ritual and sacred aspects of the institutions, and their relationship to systems of *timē* is not explored, but while the elements of the ritually pure and the numinous in such situations are un-questionably important, it is equally important to recognize that it is not primarily to these that *aidōs* and *sebas* respond. The sacred nature of an altar or an oath is no doubt inseparable from its status as an element in a system of *timē*, but it is under the latter rather than the former aspect that they attract *aidōs* and *sebas*.[129]

---

[124] Thus, to commit perjury is to ignore *aidōs* (Hes. fr. 204. 82 MW) and to manifest one's *anaideia* (Ar. *Knights* 298, in the contest of *anaideia* between the Sausage Seller and Paphlagon, 275 ff.; cf. 1239).

[125] Soph. *OT* 652-3; Creon, according to the chorus-leader, is 'big in oath', and so deserves *aidōs*.

[126] On honour and oaths, see Pitt-Rivers (1966), 32-4. More general discussions of the oath as an institution may be found in Hirzel (1902), and Plescia (1970).

[127] (1985), 250-4 (on the oath).

[128] (1983), 180-8 (on supplication and the oath).

[129] As we saw, an altar can be regarded as an object invested with *timē*, and its posses-sion of *timē* is inseparable from its sanctity; similarly, a wide range of precious objects, especially but not exclusively those connected with ritual and the divine, can be regarded as possessing *timē*, e.g. by virtue of their associations with gift-giving and the status of the giver. When such objects are involved in ritual and sacrifice, as in the examples collected by Gernet (1981: 73-111; article also in Gordon (1981)), their *timē* may itself explain their choice as sacred objects or their status as sacred objects may enhance their *timē* (Gernet refers to the *timē* of the valued object at pp. 103-4 of his study). But Gernet is too insistent on the religious and magical aspects of the early Greek concept of value, even to the extent of translating *timē* as 'religious quality' (104), and might have done better to explore further the concept of *timē* itself; for *timē* *is* value, both of persons and of objects, and there need be nothing religious or magical in the way in which objects enjoy

Aidōs and *sebas* also naturally overlap in those other spheres of human relationships, notably *xenia* and *philia*, to which *aidōs* was central in Homer; here, too, both respond to the special status of the other as a party to a given relationship. Thus in *Supplices* (707-9) it is one of the 'ordinances of Dikē' that parents should receive the *sebas* of their children[130] and in *Eumenides* (269-72) lack of *sebas* for the gods, a guest,[131] or one's parents is said to be punished. Likewise Eteocles and Polyneices face and kill each other 'with *asebēs* intention',[132] and their lack of *sebas* might also be seen in terms of lack of familial *aidōs*.

So far we have used *aidōs* and *sebas* as shorthand for the complexes of terms related to those concepts, but the inaccuracy of this in reflecting Aeschylean usage is revealed by a number of passages in which *sebas* is not a reaction to another person or some object which arouses awe,[133] but that quality which occasions or is the object of such a reaction.[134] Thus in fragment 135 Radt *sebas* refers to a homosexual relationship for which one party failed to show *aidōs*; *sebas* thus stands for a *philia* relationship and attracts *aidōs* accordingly.[135] Similarly, *sebas* may be the object of the verb *sebein* (*Eumenides* 92); *aidōs* is never the object of the verb *aideisthai* and is only rarely used of the quality which attracts the *aidōs* of others.[136] In other applications of the substantive *sebas*, however, the active sense, 'respect', is clearly what is

timē, even though religious and magical objects will obviously have a special claim to that quality. Throughout the classical period, all everyday items of commerce will have had their own *timē*, since *timē* is ordinary Greek for 'value' or 'price' (see LSJ, s.v. ii). In this context we might remember the carpet scene of the *Ag.* and Ag.'s *aidōs*; the fabrics on which Ag. walked were expensive, precious, and associated with the gods (on the most likely reading of 946, they actually belong to the gods, but they are, in any case, the sort of object which might be destroyed in a propitiatory ritual (933)), and he felt *aidōs* at destroying the wealth of his house (948-9); one aspect of Ag.'s *aidōs*, then, responds to the *timē* of the precious objects spread before him, and *aidōs* thus bears its usual relationship to *timē*. (On the value of the fabrics in the carpet scene, cf. Gernet (1981), 82-3.)

[130] Cf. *Eum.* 545.
[131] Cf. *aidōs* for guests at *Eum.* 546-8.
[132] *Sept.* 831 (cf. n. 12 above).
[133] As it was in Homer; see 1.6.3 above.
[134] Thus *sebas* is often the possession of the gods (*PV* 1091; *Supp.* 396; *Cho.* 644) or can be predicated of a god (*Ag.* 515). For *sebas* as that which one *sebei*, cf. fr. 99. 5 Radt; *Cho.* 157-8, 243.
[135] The fr. belongs to the *Myrmidons* (like fr. 132c Radt in 3.3 above) and the relationship is that of Achilles and Patroclus; one reproaches the other for his ingratitude, but it is unclear to which of the two the complaint should be attributed and in what context the words were uttered (see Radt, ad loc.). For similar complaints of ingratitude in a homosexual context, cf. 2.3.4 above.
[136] Cf. Ch. 1 n. 44 (two instances in Homer); also 2.2 above on *h. Hom. Cer.* 214; no examples in Aesch.

required, while in others it is either unnecessary or impossible to
choose between the two senses.[137] Yet it remains a difference between
aidōs and *sebas* that the ambivalence of the substantive *sebas* between
the subjective and objective, the active and passive spheres, is much
more regular than that of *aidōs*.

The verb *aideomai* also enjoys a wider range of usage than do the
sebas verbs; in general, in Aeschylus and the other tragedians the two
verb systems overlap only where both take a personal or a quasi-
personal object, in situations, that is, where both may be rendered
'respect'; in Homer *sebomai* etc. could be followed by an infinitive, and
thus express an inhibitory sense similar to that of *aideomai*, but in
Aeschylus this happens only at *Persae* 694-6, and there the chorus's
inhibitory *sebas* is based on their *sebas* (respect) for their former king.
The personal objects of *sebas* verbs, moreover, normally denote the
direct recipients of one's respect, and the verbs do not, as can *aideomai*,
focus on a generalized group of 'other people'. But the most important
difference between the two groups of terms is more fundamental:
aidōs, like *sebas*, acknowledges the *timē* of others, but *sebas*, unlike *aidōs*,
has no central reference to oneself, to one's own *timē*. Consider the
difference in sense of two derivative adjectives—*asebēs*, 'without *sebas*',
connotes disregard of others' (especially the gods') authority *tout court*,
but *anaidēs*, while suggesting lack of respect for the status of others,
also entails indifference with regard to one's own status and reputation; to be *anaidēs* is to lack respect for oneself as well as for others.[138]
The two groups of terms are obviously very close, and from Homer
onwards there exists the possibility of contamination from one to the
other, but even considering the central reference of both to *timē*, the
essence of *aidōs* emerges more clearly by contrast as well as by
comparison with *sebas*.[139]

---

[137] See *Eum.* 545, 885, *Supp.* 83-5, 755, and, in particular, *Cho.* 55-7, where *sebas* must
be both the quality in the royal house which arouses the respect of the people and that
respect itself, which now 'stands aside' (see Garvie (1986), ad loc.). The development of
sebas from 'awe' to 'that which occasions awe' can also be traced in *h. Hom. Cer.* 10-11
(Ch. 2 n. 36). In many passages there is probably no clear distinction between the two
senses.

[138] See Arist. *Rhet.* 1383[b]15-17; *anaischuntia* (= *anaideia*) is a kind of contempt for and
indifference towards misfortunes which can lead to ill-repute; the *anaideis* are commonly
indifferent to the opinions others have of them (e.g. Archilochus, according to Critias
(Ch. 2 n. 64), the Sausage Seller and Paphlagon in Ar. *Knights*, etc.).

[139] *Sebas* etc. occur in the other major tragedians, as in Aesch., with greater frequency
than do *aidōs* etc., but the pattern of usage established in this chapter holds good for
Soph. and Eur. too, and there will be no need to treat *sebas* systematically in subsequent
chapters, although we shall continue to note important cases of overlap. One might point

The greater frequency of *sebas* etc. as compared to *aidōs* in Aeschylus is particularly reflected in the *Eumenides*, where *sebas*, with some help from *aidōs*, is central to the establishment of the Areopagus as the centrepiece of a system of justice. Both the Erinyes and Athena stress the role of deterrence,[140] and fear of punishment is seen as essential if human beings are to have any respect for justice.[141] Fear, *sebas*, and *aidōs*[142] go together, but this does not imply that respect for justice rests on mere fear of punishment.[143] *Timē* is, as we have seen, crucial to both concepts; the gods who enforce justice and Justice herself have *timē*, and the Erinyes, who enjoy *timē* as a result of the fear they inspire as ministers of justice, are determined both that deterrence should not be abandoned and that they should not lose their prestige.[144] Athena assures them that this will not happen, restates the utility of fear, and indicates that the new homicide court will itself be an object of reverence; legitimately constituted and impartial, however, the new system will be superior to the old.[145] As the final step in the resolution of conflict the *timē* of the Erinyes is to be recognized in a civil cult.[146]

The new civic system of justice laid down by Athena in the *Eumenides* thus takes over the function, and so the *timē*, of the divine

---

out, however, that the use of *sebas* as a response to the status of another mortal appears to be felt as specifically 'tragic' or poetic; in Hdt., for example, it is *aidōs* which denotes the response to a mortal superior (3. 72. 3, 77. 1, although it can take a divine object, 9. 7a. 2), while *sebein* etc. respond exclusively to the prodigious, the supernatural, and the divine (1. 66. 1, 86. 2, 138. 2; 2. 141. 6, 172. 4; 5. 7; 7. 115. 3); cf. the religious reference of *sebein* in its only occurrence in Thuc. (2. 53. 4; also *asebein* etc. at 4. 98. 7; 6. 27. 2, 53. 1). So in prose (e.g. Thuc. 3. 14. 1, respect for humans and the divine) and in Aristophanes (*Wealth* 981, 988, 1077) it is generally *aischunomai* (the prosaic equivalent of the more poetic *aideomai*), not *sebō*, which denotes respect for other mortals.

[140] 490–565, 690–706.

[141] 517–25 (who would accord Justice *sebas* without fear?), 538–49 (punishment awaits those who do not show *aidōs* for the altar of Justice, and such *aidōs* itself promotes due regard for the *sebas* of parents and *aidōs* for guests); cf. Athena at 699.

[142] On 'good fear' and its association with *aidōs* and *sebas* in the resolution of the trilogy, see de Romilly (1958), 111–14; Macleod (1982), 135–6. Both de Romilly (114) and Macleod (135, 138) relate the good fear of the *Eum.*, which is the healthy counterpart of the terror that affects the characters earlier in the trilogy, to the sequence of distortion or corruption in *Ag./Cho.* and resolution in *Eum.* which has been noticed by so many writers (Peradotto (1964), on nature imagery; Zeitlin (1965), (1966), on sacrificial imagery; Haldane (1965), on musical imagery; Gantz (1977), on nature imagery).

[143] Cf. Macleod (1982), 136.

[144] See 778–93 (= 808–23), 837–47 (= 870–80).

[145] 700–6.

[146] 804–7, 834–6, 852–69, 890–1. The Erinyes, too, will pay *timē* to the city in return (917, 992–5, 1029).

Erinyes;[147] like them, it attracts respect by virtue of its ability to punish, but such respect does not, either in the case of the Erinyes or in that of the Areopagus, simply respond to naked power; rather it is a recognition of legitimate authority, of an authority which adopts a moderate position between coercion and licence[148] and which helps maintain the values that the community holds most dear.[149] Both *aidōs* and *sebas*, therefore, are promoted by fear of punishment,[150] but are not synonymous with such a fear; rather punishment implies power, and power which one recognizes as legitimate embodies the *timē* that attracts *aidōs* and *sebas*. The theory of the judicial system which is expounded in the *Eumenides*, then, rests fundamentally on *timē*; *aidōs* and *sebas* for the homicide court are perhaps derived from the *aidōs* and *sebas* one might accord the gods as superior beings, but it is crucial that these responses, which are regarded as fundamental to civilized life, are now to be shown towards the institutions of the state. Aeschylus thus transforms *aidōs* and *sebas* from responses to persons (or gods envisaged as persons) who enjoy some claim to *timē* vis-à-vis oneself to an acknowledgement of the *timē* of an impersonal entity, a civic institution, and the transcendence of the personal and the partial demonstrated by the institution of the homicide court is mirrored in the move from personal to impersonal *aidōs* and *sebas*. The utility of *aidōs* in Aeschylus' political theory is thus rather different from that accorded the concept in other theories which we shall consider, which tend to take *aidōs* in a much more traditional way as a social entity, active in interpersonal relationships within the community rather than in the relationship between the individual and the state.

[147] The embodiment of the *timē* of the Erinyes in the Areopagite court, like their defeat in the trial by Orestes and Apollo, leaves them *atimos* (n. 144 above) until they are given new *timē* by Athena; the resolution of the sequence of conflict succeeds because the loss of *timē* to one's opponent (Or.'s recovery of his patrimony, 754–60, also signifies the recovery of his *timē*) which usually accompanies defeat in competition is made good. On *timē* in *Eum.* and in the trilogy as a whole, see Macleod (1982), 138–42.

[148] The wish of the Erinyes that life should be neither free from control nor subject to despotic coercion is answered, in almost the same words, by Athena at 696–7; the principle which the citizens are to *sebein* (697) is that of submission to a degree of authority which they themselves recognize as appropriate.

[149] At 545–9 the deterrence which the Erinyes maintain is seen as promoting two of the most canonical of Greek values, respect for parents and for *xenoi*, and at 701 and 706 the new homicide court is to be the salvation and protection of the community.

[150] Von Erffa (1937: 104) would distinguish *aidōs* and *sebas* with reference to the association of the latter, but not the former, with fear of punishment; but punishment follows absence of both (cf. 517–25 with 538–49). Neither, however, is equivalent to fear of punishment.

[151] Cf. de Romilly (1957: 112–13), who contrasts the role of *aidōs* and *aischunē* as fear of disgrace in Pl.'s *Laws* with Aesch.'s concentration on respect for legitimate authority.

4

Sophocles

The extant plays of Sophocles belong to an age in which the idea that there are two sides to every story became a commonplace, and problems based in sophistic relativism—that people may differ over the meanings of words, may have subjective ideas of what is right and what is true, and find it difficult, sometimes impossible to communicate—loom large in his work. Sophocles understands partiality, aware that people often hold views or attitudes that are contradictory and that they interpret events and situations to suit themselves;[1] accordingly, it is common in his work for one kind of *aidōs* to be set against another, and his characters often have only a partial grasp of what *aidōs* is, and of what course of action it dictates; conflicts of values, sometimes irreducible, underlie much of the tragic force of Sophocles' plays, and it is in such cases that his use and treatment of *aidōs* are most important and intriguing.

Von Erffa[2] contends that we have no opportunity in Sophocles, as we had in Aeschylus' *Supplices*, to observe the operation of *aidōs* over the course of an entire play; with this I cannot concur. The first part of this chapter will consider the more incidental of Sophocles' uses of our terms, although even here we should note the importance of *aidōs* as an element of the supplication-theme in the *Oedipus at Colonus*. The second part, however, considers three plays, *Ajax*, *Electra*, and *Philoctetes*, in which the role of *aidōs* is such that it must be treated as a theme of great significance for our understanding of each play as a whole.

4.1. GENERAL

4.1.1. Oedipus Tyrannus

Our terms occur with relative frequency in the *Tyrannus*, but the relevant passages are largely heterogeneous, and are not central to the meaning of the play; few therefore require discussion, although some are

---

[1] Cf. in general Blundell (1989), ch. 8.
[2] (1937), 107.

used in corroboration of other points elsewhere.[3] We cannot, however, ignore the role of *aidōs* in the concluding scenes of the play, for it is here that the complex of values with which we are concerned is most prominent in the motivation of the main character.

Having been revealed as an incestuous parricide Oedipus is regarded as a bearer of contagion and an object of revulsion; in lines 1424-8 Creon appeals, presumably to a group of attendants, as follows: 'But if you no longer have shame before the children of mortals, at least feel shame before the flame of lord Helios, which nourishes all,[4] at thus revealing such defilement, defilement which neither earth nor sacred rain nor light will accept.' The disgrace and pollution with reference to which the attendants are expected to feel *aidōs* (or *aischunē*) are not their own, yet it is they who are responsible for the fact that the sight of Oedipus affronts both human beings and the Sun,[5] and so they are felt to share any reproach or revulsion which the exposure of his pollution may arouse.[6] If *aidōs* is to be the reaction of those whose duty it is to keep Oedipus out of sight, then we might expect that he himself would be all the more liable to that emotion, but in fact no word of *aidōs* ever crosses his lips.

It is, however, clear that Oedipus' situation constitutes grounds for reproach. Creon prefaces the remarks quoted above with a denial that he has come to mock or reproach (*oneidiōn*, 1423) his misfortunes, while Oedipus himself at 1486-1502 (see especially 1494, *oneidē*, and 1500, *oneidieisthe*) recognizes that his daughters will be taunted with the deeds of their father for the rest of their lives. He also, at 1407-8, laments the fact that he has committed 'all the acts which are *aischista* among men', and he goes on to say that, since he has done that which

---

[3] See, e.g., Ch. 3 nn. 121, 125, on 647, 652-3, and 5.3 below, on 1079 as an instance of retrospective shame.

[4] Note the equivalence of the verbs *kataischunesthai* and *aideisthai* in ἀλλ' εἰ τὰ θνητῶν μὴ καταισχύνεσθ' ἔτι γένεθλα, τὴν γοῦν ... φλόγα αἰδεῖσθ'. ... Although in this passage the former occurs with a human object and the latter with a divine, the roles could easily have been reversed; in both cases the object of the verb is the focus of an inhibition based on the evaluation that a particular state of affairs is *aischron*.

[5] On the Sun as the god who sees all and so most resents pollution, see Parker (1983), 293, 310, 316-17.

[6] Because people shun and express revulsion for that which is polluted, the consequences of pollution and disgrace converge; see Parker (1983), 94, 205, 313-18. While it is true that pollution is an objective form of guiltiness which adheres whether others perceive it or no, it is notable that both the common association of pollution with the all-seeing eye of the Sun and this convergence of pollution and disgrace place this objective stain within the sphere of the outward and the visible in which *aidōs* etc. often operate.

it is not *kalon* either to speak of or to do, he should be concealed or put to death, in order that he might never be seen again (1409–12). Oedipus is thus quite aware of his disgrace, and in wishing to be removed from sight he is exhibiting both a classic shame reaction and the kind of *aidōs* which Creon urges on the attendants at 1424–8. Much more importantly, however, his self-blinding is also related to his desire for concealment, and therefore to his shame. Conceptually, unseeing and unseen are very close, and by depriving himself of sight Oedipus expresses the same impulse which later drives him to seek concealment. At 830–3, referring to his fear of the deeds prophesied by the oracle, he wishes that he should never *see* the day of their fulfilment, and that he should vanish from the sight of men, become invisible, rather than see that he has incurred such defilement; his conviction, then, that he would be unable to bear the sight of such pollution is linked to a desire to disappear from the sight of others, should he be revealed as polluted. This passage finds an echo in 1384–5, after the blind Oedipus has reappeared on stage; having justified his self-blinding in terms of his inability to look others in the face (his parents in Hades, his children, the city of Thebes, 1371–83), he concludes: 'Having revealed such defilement [*kēlis*, cf. 833] as my own, was I about to look these people straight in the eye [literally 'with straight eyes', ὀρθοῖς ὄμμασιν)?'

Oedipus' self-blinding is thus a consequence of his inability to face others,[7] an extension, as is made quite clear in 1385, of the impulse which leads one, when subject to *aidōs*, to avert one's gaze; this is indication enough that he is experiencing a classic *aidōs*- or shame-reaction; but the association of the desires not to see and not to be seen both before and after the self-blinding indicates that these two impulses, both manifestations of *aidōs*, are inseparable strands in Oedipus' reaction. In a sense, it is in this situation, where Oedipus, the revealer, stands revealed as a sight which affronts gods and men, and where he can bear neither to see nor to be seen,[8] that all the language

[7] For which cf. Class (1964), 74.

[8] Oedipus also, however, wishes to be shown to the people of Thebes, according to the *exangelos* at 1287–9; Soph., of course, has to get him back on stage somehow, but perhaps he also makes a virtue of necessity in adding a detail which may be taken as a sign of the complexity of O.'s reaction, of his desire to punish himself by exposing himself to the very revulsion he fears. Would this quasi-masochistic response prove bewildering to the original audience? No doubt a modern psychoanalytic account of such behaviour would be conceptually beyond the average 5th-cent. Athenian, but I doubt that he would have been unable to cope with a natural coexistence of the impulse to conceal oneself and the impulse to punish oneself. The combination of these impulses is, in any case, apparent elsewhere in the *exodos* (see main text above).

of seeing and showing which so permeates the play finds its culmination; and both Oedipus' behaviour at this point and the language in which it is described make it inevitable that the audience will categorize his response as *aidōs*, a concept which, as we have seen, is closely related to ideas of seeing and visibility, and particularly associated with the eyes.

It is not, however, simply the prospect of others' reproach which troubles Oedipus: his words in the final scene often take the form of the strongest self-reproach (for example, 1337–46), and he is clearly horrified at what he has done (1357–61, 1398–1408); he also wishes to be punished (1409–15), and even expresses remorse over his wrongful accusation of Creon (1419–21). His pain, which is so vividly presented, lies less in fear of disgrace than in his knowledge of what he has done, in his μνήμη κακῶν ('memory of evils', 1318); he is 'wretched both in his fate and in his knowledge of it', says the chorus-leader at 1347. If Oedipus' reaction, then, is one of *aidōs*, it is clearly based on a subjective awareness of the horror of what he has done; this being so, his reaction is also compatible with the emotion which we, in ordinary usage, call guilt.[9]

That Oedipus' response may be seen in terms of guilt, however, is no mere consequence of the imprecision of ordinary English usage; even the abstract conceptual distinctions between shame and guilt advanced by specialists could not exclusively categorize his response in terms of one or the other. We noted that Oedipus was unable to face his parents, and we saw in Homer that the parental or paternal model constituted the very focus of one's *aidōs*. In the psychoanalytic definitions we looked at earlier,[10] punitive parents and their interdictions were said to be the focus of guilt-feelings, loving parents (and their example) of shame-feelings; shame occurred when one failed to live up to an ideal image of oneself as a whole person, guilt when one transgressed a boundary by a specific act. But it is idle to speculate

[9] On O.'s guilt-feelings, see Class (1964), 84–8; Stebler (1971), 82, 95–8; I would not dispute the general import of their observations, but it seems to me that both place too much emphasis on O.'s repeated references to his *kaka*. Stebler (97) claims that *kaka* in the *exodus* is 'doppelsinnig ... als Unglück und Leid, Schlechtes und Böses'. There is, however, no instance of the word in which the primary sense is not 'misfortunes' rather than 'misdeeds' (see esp. 1330). O., as Class (87) points out, bears no *Schuld* in the objective sense, he is not 'morally responsible' for what he has done, yet he experiences a *Schuldgefühl* which is entirely natural ('Oidipus wäre kein Mensch, wenn die Stimme des Gewissens bei ihm ausbliebe', Class, ibid.); neither this point, however, nor any general appreciation of O.'s sense of guilt depends on the interpretation of his *kaka* as 'misdeeds'.   [10] See Introd. 0.3 above.

whether Oedipus is unable to face his parents because he has failed to live up to their ideals or because he envisages them as sources of punishment; it is quite clear that Oedipus' crimes are both transgressions of the most profoundly felt traditional imperatives and a failure to conform to ideals set by others, that he feels himself defiled, and that he abhors his specific actions, and so neither the distinction between guilt and shame as the concomitants of transgression and failure respectively, nor the related distinction between focus on what one does rather than what one is, can be much help to us. Where one's personal awareness of the character of one's own actions is concerned there will often be little effective difference between anxiety described as shame and that described as guilt, and it would be entirely arbitrary to state categorically that Oedipus is suffering from the one rather than the other. That he does experience *aidōs*, however, I regard as certain, even in the absence of the word itself, and this is a valuable indication that *aidōs* cannot be identified wholly with some concept of 'shame' which is to be entirely and sharply distinguished from 'guilt'.

4.1.2. Antigone

There is only one reference to *aidōs*[11] in the *Antigone*, but it is one which illustrates very well the temperament of the heroine and the breakdown of communication which has occurred between Antigone and Creon. At line 508 stichomythia between the two begins, the issue being the degree of support which Antigone's defiance enjoys among the chorus and the people of Thebes. Creon maintains that Antigone is alone in her belief, expressed in 502–7, that her deed is glorious, that it is pleasing to the old men of the chorus, and that he is simply taking advantage of the prerogative of the absolute ruler to do and say what

[11] There are, however, several minor uses of related terms; the concept of *aischrokerdeia* ('base gain') is mentioned by Teiresias at 1056, and Creon uses the adjective *aischros* with a similar reference to the pursuit of wealth or advantage by dishonest means at 299, 313, and 1047 (cf. Haemon at 747). One might also see self-regarding *aidōs* as lying behind the concern of both Ant. and Cr. with their status and reputations; Ant.'s statement at 5 that there is nothing *aischron* or *atimon* (dishonourable) which is not part of the ills of her family is but one indication of the concern for personal and familial honour which is one of her chief motives (cf. Gellie (1972), 30–1), while for Cr. it is a particular matter of honour that he should not be worsted by a woman (484–5, 525, 677–80) or by his son, a mere boy (726–7), himself the slave of a woman (746, 756); cf. Heracles' resentment that he should be brought low by a woman, and himself be reduced to the status of a woman (*Trach.* 1062–3, 1071–5).

he will; at 509 Antigone replies with a reiteration of her conviction that the chorus side with her, but Creon prefers to ignore this, and insists that their opposition to her conduct is an acknowledged fact (510): 'Do you feel no *aidōs* [οὐκ ἐπαιδῇ], if you think differently from these men?' To this, however, Antigone makes an unexpected answer (511): 'It is nothing *aischron* to honour one's kin [τοὺς ὁμοσπλάγχνους σέβειν].' Creon's question insinuates that Antigone is out of step with popular opinion, and that she should feel *aidōs* on that account;[12] he reproaches her, in effect, with failure to conform, failure to react as did Ismene, who affirmed the inability of women to oppose men (61-2) or to act against the wishes of the citizens (βίᾳ πολίτων, 78-9). The *aidōs* to which Creon thus refers would, were Antigone susceptible to it, be based simply on the knowledge that others disapproved of one's conduct, regardless of one's own evaluation, and this would be a recognizable and traditional form. Antigone explains her lack of *aidōs*, however, with reference to quite different standards. In effect, the question she answers is not, 'Do you not feel shame, if you think differently from these men?' but, 'Do you not feel shame at what you have done?' For her, any *aidōs* she might feel would depend on her own interpretation of her actions, not on that of other people; in itself, her statement in line 511 is quite in keeping with traditional values (all things being equal, most people would have agreed that it is not *aischron* to honour one's kin),[13] but it remains quite clear that for

---

[12] He thus 'makes the fact of Antigone's deviation a reproach against her' (Jones (1962), 199).

[13] The idea of 'honouring (*sebein*) one's kin' raises the possibility, *sebein* and *aideisthai* being so close in such contexts, that Ant. feels *aidōs*, of the kind appropriate within the family, for her brother. Clearly, it would be possible for her attitude to Polyneices to be so designated, but Soph. achieves a significant effect by describing it in terms of *sebas*, since throughout the play he exploits to the full the various senses and applications of *sebein*, *eusebeia*, etc. (on which see Adkins (1960*a*), 132-8). *Sebas* is not originally or exclusively a religious term, but it and its relatives are commonly used of the response to the divine, and it is this application of the words, together with that centred on loyalty within the family, that Soph. assigns to Ant. (511, 922-4, 943; see, e.g., Stebler (1971), 108). Haemon supports her form of *eusebeia* at 745, and Cr. recognizes its religious nature (777-80), but with contempt. For him, *sebein* is to be a patriot, to obey those in authority, and, ultimately, to bow to *his* power (166, 301, 514, 516, 730, 744). The chorus also pronounce on the nature of *eusebeia*: at 872-5 they recognize that the *eusebeia* of both Ant. and Cr. is entitled to be so called, and point out the failure of the former to recognize the totality of the concept (cf. 365-75). In the end, however, it is Ant.'s *eusebeia* that is seen as more important, and Cr.'s failure to grasp this that is condemned: 'in divine matters one should do nothing *asebes*' (μηδὲν ἀσεπτεῖν, 1349-50; on the two choral comments, cf. Kirkwood (1958), 126). Cr. and Ant., then, differ in their conceptions of *aidōs* and *eusebeia*, as on the meanings of many common words (cf. Goheen (1951), 17; Kirkwood (1958), 125; Knox (1964), 90).

Antigone it is her own judgement of what is or is not *aischron* that matters,[14] that it is her own personal conscience rather than convention which determines for her the character of her actions.[15] It is not, of course, novel that one should possess standards of one's own to which one is committed, but the contrast which the poet has contrived between adherence to personal standards and conformity is a striking one, appropriate to an age which is coming to a clear realization of the difference between the two.

4.1.3. Oedipus Coloneus

The *Oedipus Coloneus* is a suppliant drama, and since the process of supplication provides the play with its dramatic impetus, we do find (as we might expect, given the close association of *aidōs* with that process) much that is relevant to our study. The standard motifs of suppliant drama, however, are employed in complex and unusual ways,[16] and the role of *aidōs* is accordingly not as straightforward as one might expect. In particular, *aidōs* of a humane, other-regarding kind is requested and mentioned in the context of supplication, but this kind of *aidōs* is shown to conflict with other standards of honour which themselves make use of *aidōs*.

Oedipus himself does not refer to *aidōs* in any of his appeals to the stranger, to the chorus, or to Theseus; already in this respect he is an atypical suppliant. It is left to Antigone, when her father is in danger of being expelled from the country,[17] to employ a more typical suppliant appeal (237-53) for pity and for *aidōs*; the chorus are apostrophized as *aidophrones*[18] and their *aidōs* for Oedipus is requested at 247; Antigone pleads for pity for herself (242), and the wretched state of both

[14] See von Erffa (1937), 108-9; Stebler (1971), 69. Adkins (1960a: 184) misses the point, which is precisely that Cr. does *not* ask Ant. 'whether she is not ashamed of having tried to bury Polyneices in defiance of his orders'.

[15] On Ant.'s 'conscience', see Stebler (1971), 107-11. As Stebler points out (107, cf. Gellie (1972), 29, 32), Ant. has a number of motives, but one of them is certainly her independent recognition of an absolute moral imperative.

[16] See Kopperschmidt (1967), 89-91; Burian (1971), 207-62; (1974b).

[17] O. has already been persuaded to leave the sacred precinct and to relinquish contact with it; his supplication is thereafter 'figurative', and it might therefore be easier for the chorus to have him expelled from Attica (which they wish to do on learning of his identity (229-36)).

[18] *Aidophrōn* ('of reverent mind', i.e. liable to manifest *aidōs*) first occurs at Eur. *Alc.* 659, and was presumably coined in order to convey the sense 'showing *aidōs*' which can only ambiguously be expressed by *aidoios*.

suppliants is stressed (241, 244-5, 246, 248). The chorus do feel pity
(255), but their doubts about Oedipus have not been dispelled, and
accordingly the latter now makes his famous speech of self-vindica-
tion.[19] The combination of these two, very different, appeals results in
the chorus's abandonment of their intention to expel Oedipus and
their decision to await the arrival of their king (294-5).

The expectation that the suppliants would have to repeat their
appeal before Theseus, however, is disappointed.[20] The king enters at
551, recognizes Oedipus, and expresses his pity (556), basing his
sympathy on a recognition of common humanity (567-9); since
'showing *aidōs*' is a regular description of the act of accepting supplication, Theseus' conduct could presumably be so construed, but, equally,
his concern for another human being might also be described as *aidōs*;
aidōs would thus be relevant as an act-description and as a motive.
More readily recognizable forms of *aidōs*, however, also have their
parts to play in his acceptance; at 636 he says that he will allow
Oedipus to remain out of *sebas* (*sebistheis*) for his status as suppliant
and divine protégé and for the tie of *xenia* which exists between them,
and *aidōs* and *sebas* are virtually interchangeable in such contexts.[21]
Grounds for *aidōs* are also in evidence in 902-3, where Theseus,
despatching his attendants to free Antigone and Ismene, speaks of the

[19] As Adkins points out (1960a: 105), O.'s language in expressing his moral innocence
(that he suffered rather than did, 266-7, cf. 538-9) is novel, and akin to the kind of
argument found in the tetralogies of Antiphon (see esp. *Tetr.* 3. d. 3-6), but this does not
mean, as Burian assumes (1971: 222 n. 26; 1974b: 414), that the passages present 'a
distinction between objective guilt (pollution) and moral responsibility' which is also
novel. This distinction is already present in Athenian homicide law, which was very far
from new when *OC* was written (see Gagarin (1981), 1 and *passim*), and which
distinguished between intentional, unintentional, and justified homicide, regardless of
pollution (see MacDowell (1963a), 47, 58-81). This long-established legal distinction
between degrees of responsibility on the one hand and objective pollution on the other is
thus, not surprisingly, present in *OC*; O.'s pollution is still relevant, even though he
maintains his essential innocence (see, e.g. 1132-4); pollution still adheres even though
he is 'pure in law' (νόμῳ καθαρός, 548; he is so, it seems, because he acted in self-defence
and in ignorance, 270-2, 547-8), and this pollution is presumably indelible by virtue of
the intrinsic horror of his crimes (cf. Parker (1983), 124). The 'distinction between
subjective and objective guilt', then, is not something that was discovered in the years
between *OT* and *OC*, as Lesky (1983: 177) seems to imply. On the subject of 258-91, we
should note the presence of the argument from the reputation of the supplicated at 258-
62, 282-3; essentially, this is an appeal to *aidōs*, but of a more self-regarding kind than is
the target of the simple appeal for *aidōs qua* suppliant. Perhaps, too, the whole argument
on O.'s moral innocence is a variation of another common suppliant appeal, the
argument that the suppliant's position is just, *dikaion* (cf. Aesch. *Supp.* 343, 384, 395, 406,
419, 430).
[20] Cf. Burian (1971), 231; (1974b), 414.   [21] See 3.4 above.

danger of ridicule should he fail to protect those whom he has taken into his care; the honour of the supplicated is committed by his acceptance, and concern for one's reputation as a strong protector is very often an important motive in ensuring that the supplicated continues actively to protect the suppliant.[22] The centrality of *aidōs* in the context of supplication is thus highlighted once more; concern for the suppliant as a human being prepared to undergo the indignity of acknowledging his misfortune and begging for assistance constitutes one possible manifestation of *aidōs*, but this is combined, here as elsewhere, with recognition of the suppliant's special status, imparted by the gods, while, as is typical in situations in which *aidōs* responds to the status of another, concern for one's own status is also elicited. The richness and diversity of the manifestations of *aidōs* in such contexts indicate both the effectiveness of the ritual in placing systems of honour under stress and the inclusivity of *aidōs* as a response, in various ways, to the honour of self and others.

In sharp contrast to the *aidōs* of the admirable Theseus, the suppliants' protector or *sōtēr*, is the *anaideia* of Creon, their enemy (*echthros*).[23] Creon is twice charged with *anaideia*, first at 863, where the basis for the charge lies in his attempt to lay hands on Oedipus, in disregard of any claims the latter may have to *timē*, and at 960-1 where the accusation of *anaideia* is coupled with one of *hubris* (both being connected with disregard of another's *timē*): 'Oh shameless temper, whom do you imagine this *hubris* affects, me, an old man, or yourself?'[24] Although the speaker of these lines is hardly unbiased, their wording does suggest that, in certain circumstances, the attempt to dishonour (*kathubrizein*) another can rebound to the discredit of the person making the affront.[25]

After Creon has been seen off, the pattern of the suppliant drama is complete,[26] but it is at this point that a second suppliant, Oedipus' son

[22] Cf. 5.2.2 below.

[23] The terminology is that of Kopperschmidt (1967), employed by Burian (1971) and (1974*b*). Burian also points out that Cr. himself takes on the role of the enemy herald in this play (1971: 235; 1974*b*: 418).

[24] ὦ λῆμ' ἀναιδές, τοῦ καθυβρίζειν δοκεῖς, | πότερον ἐμοῦ γέροντος, ἢ σαυτοῦ, τόδε;

[25] Cf. Ch. 3 n. 5 etc. Cr.'s *anaideia* is revealed in one further passage, at 978-80, where O. asks whether he is not ashamed (οὐκ ἐπαισχύνῃ) to compel him (O.) to speak of his incest with Cr.'s own sister; out of family loyalty and a sense of family shame he should refrain from mentioning his sister's disgrace, and the fact that he does so reveals his lack of concern for propriety (cf. von Erffa (1937), 118; since this sentence is a question, we need a question mark (Dawe (Teubner)), rather than a colon (Pearson, Lloyd-Jones and Wilson (OCT)) after τάχ').

[26] Burian (1971), 242; (1974*b*), 421.

Polyneices appears. Oedipus is at first determined not to see him, but eventually gives in on two grounds, having noted Theseus' remark on the sanctity of Polyneices' place of supplication and on the possibility of divine displeasure (1179-80), and out of deference to his daughter's plea (1189-91), in which Antigone, as in the drama which bears her name, subjects retributive justice to a higher standard, the *themis* (right, 1191) of the familial relationship; she is prepared to concede that Polyneices himself has breached this standard, but claims that even if his conduct had been completely lacking in *sebas* (if he had done *ta dussebestata*, 1190) retaliation would not be *themis*.

Mention of the family, *themis*, and *sebas* already suggests that Antigone is appealing to the *aidōs* which is appropriate within the family, and this is confirmed when we see that Polyneices himself, after he has left the altar of Poseidon, expresses an appeal to similar standards in terms of *aidōs*.[27] In the face of his previous ill-treatment of his father he reminds him that (1267-9) 'Aidōs shares the throne of Zeus in all matters—let her stand by your side too, father.' Here *aidōs*, opposed as it is to resentment for a wrong done which would encourage retaliation rather than compassion, takes on positive connotations of forgiveness, and is invested with considerable importance, sharing the throne of Zeus in all matters. *Aidōs* is, of course, appropriate here as the response normally demanded by suppliants, but, with its positive connotation of forgiveness, it is said to apply in all situations, not just in supplication; in the Greek context, however, perhaps any request for forgiveness is seen as akin to placing oneself in a position of humility analogous to that of the suppliant. Given this association with forgiveness, one might compare Polyneices' appeal with the institution of *aidesis* (pardon) in Athenian homicide law, by which an exiled homicide could be allowed to return, if granted the pardon of the relatives of the deceased.[28] The problem with Poly-

---

[27] It is obviously in Pol.'s interests to set a high value on *aidōs*, but the fact that he is not disinterested need not lead us to suppose that he is insincere or that he is being presented unsympathetically (see Whitman (1951), 211; Burian (1971), 247-8; (1974*b*), 472-5; Winnington-Ingram (1980), 276; Blundell (1989), 242 n. 51; against Kirkwood (1958), 152; Vickers (1973), 473); his sympathy for his father and sister is quite spontaneous and he is candid in admitting his own faults (1254-66)—there is no sign that he is dissimulating.

[28] The noun *aidesis* is the technical term at Arist. *Ath. Pol.* 57. 3 and Demosth. 21. 43, but the verb used of the act of *aidesis* is *aideisthai* at Demosth. 23. 72 and 77, 37. 59, 38. 22. The institution and the procedure for its implementation are mentioned in Dracon's homicide law (IG I². 115 (I³. 104); ML 86.) See the discussions in MacDowell (1963*a*), 118-25; Stroud (1968), 49-51; Gagarin (1981), 48-52, 137-40; and, above all, Heitsch (1984). Probably *aidesis* could only be granted in cases of unintentional

neices' appeal for forgiveness, however, is precisely that there is something to forgive—he *has* wronged his father, and so the *aidōs*-standard
conflicts with another, the need to retaliate in order to preserve one's
timē, to pursue retaliatory *dikē*, and the confrontation of these two
traditional sets of values produces the dilemma which exists in all
those tragedies in which retaliation within the family is pursued or
contemplated.

Oedipus himself makes this opposition of *aidōs* and *dikē* quite
explicit at 1375–82:

Such curses I previously launched against you, and I now call on them to come
to me as allies, so that you two should think fit to honour [*sebein*] your father
and not deprive him of *timē* on the grounds that it was of a blind father that two
such as you were born. These daughters did not act thus. So my curses are
superior to your 'supplication' and your 'claim to the throne', if indeed Dikē,
declared long ago, exists, who sits beside Zeus by his ancient laws.

In a pointed rejoinder Oedipus opposes *dikē* to Polyneices' *aidōs* as
Zeus' companion. He does not depreciate *aidōs*, but rather insists that
his sons were first to neglect it; they failed to *sebein* a parent, to show a
father the *aidōs* he deserves.[29] To disregard such *aidōs* was to deprive
Oedipus of *timē*, and as a result he is not now prepared to acknowledge
the *timē* of Polyneices the suppliant. In referring to *dikē* Oedipus
obviously appeals to a principle which the audience will have understood as a traditional and a powerful one, and they will also have
identified 'honouring one's parents' in 1377 as one of the canons of
traditional values, yet it is by no means certain that Oedipus' harshness
is presented unambiguously for their approval.[30] His wrath, for

homicide; see Heitsch, 12–18, against Gagarin, 50–1, 137–40. *Aidesis* as absolution in
cases of homicide may be derived from the element of compassion which exists in *aidōs*
in its common association with pity, especially in contexts of supplication (Heitsch, 9);
we remember, though, that in Homer supplication was often accompanied by the offer of
ransom (and that compensation was offered to the relatives of a victim of homicide,
9.632–6), and it seems probable that an approach by the relatives of an exile to the
relatives of the victim with a view to obtaining *aidesis* was, at least in Dracon's time, and
possibly also later, accompanied by an offer of compensation (Heitsch, 9–12). Perhaps
the description of this procedure as *aidesis* has its origins in a period in which actual
supplication of the relatives of the victim by the perpetrator or his relatives did take
place (a situation probably envisaged by 9.632–6; for a parallel from Bedouin society, see
Abou-Zeid (1965), 254–5; cf. Ch. 1 n. 217); even if supplication and the payment of
compensation did not occur in the classical period, there must have been some personal
contact between the two parties, and this will have placed the petitioners in a position of
inferiority *vis-à-vis* the recipients of the request, a position analogous to that of a
suppliant. For *aidōs* in a sense similar to that of *aidesis*, cf. Ch. 5 n. 88.

[29] *Aideisthai* could easily replace *sebein* in this context.   [30] Cf. Burian (1971), 254.

example, conflicts with the idealism not only of Polyneices, who is biased, but also of Antigone, who is concerned for her father and her brother alike, and his rejection of supplication, 'the only such formal suppliant appeal rejected in all of Greek tragedy',[31] contrasts sharply with the humanity of Theseus.

Before the play ends, however, there is yet another twist in its deployment of the motifs of suppliant drama. At 1399–1413 Polyneices declares his intention of facing his brother and begs Antigone to see to his funeral should his father's curse be fulfilled; now it is Antigone who becomes, figuratively, the suppliant ('I beg you', ἱκετεύω σε, 1414), but once again her appeal to family loyalty is ignored. Polyneices claims it would be impossible to lead his army back 'having once trembled' (1418–19), and that it would be as *aischron* for him to flee, as it would be for him, the elder, to be ridiculed by his brother (1422–3). Polyneices is thus subject to a familiar form of *aidōs*, but of a different nature from that which he urged on his father at 1267–9, i.e. not the respect for the claims of another human being which would lead one to abandon retribution, but that which envisages one's own humiliation and which demands retribution as vindication of one's own honour. Some hold that the contrast between these two attitudes reveals Polyneices' essential hypocrisy and selfishness,[32] yet his reaction is a traditional and understandable one, and one does not have to be a hypocrite to be blind to the fact that one expects from others behaviour different from that which one is ready to manifest oneself. The fact remains, however, that he appeals to familial and other-regarding *aidōs* when attempting to dissuade his father from pursuit of *dikē* and consideration of his own injured *timē*, yet disregards it when his own desire for revenge and his concern for his own honour intervene; his partiality thus overcomes his idealism, and there is an obvious, Sophoclean irony in the way in which this comes about, not the least part of which is the eventual similarity which emerges between father and son.[33]

In Polyneices, then, two attitudes to *aidōs* are opposed; for himself he requests forgiveness and recognition of his status as a *philos*, but when the opportunity arises for him to exhibit this form of *aidōs* himself, he responds instead to straightforward concern for his own honour. Polyneices' partiality, his failure to accept the universalization

---

[31] Burian (1971), 250.
[32] Kirkwood (1958), 152–3.
[33] See Winnington-Ingram (1980), 276–7.

of his own arguments, indicates how the principles of retaliatory justice, of helping one's friends and harming one's enemies—principles which define one's obligations to others with primary reference to one's own honour (narrowly conceived)—tend to overcome any recognition of another's status which might inhibit retaliation when an affront has been suffered. The same priority is revealed in Oedipus himself (although he is consistent in the application of his ideals of strict reciprocity in a way that Polyneices is not),[34] and as Winnington-Ingram has brilliantly shown,[35] it is as a symbol that this is simply the way of the world that Oedipus is elevated to the status of a hero. And yet, Oedipus' heroization gives us no straightforward resolution of the conflicts of the play; the pursuit of retaliation within the family is never unproblematic, and the self-regarding concern for one's own honour is only one, albeit very powerful, aspect of the traditional code, which by no means obliterates those elements that embody the possible grounds for inhibition of self-assertion; and if Oedipus' elevation indicates the universal force of retaliatory *dikē*, there remain the humane, if idealistic, examples of Antigone and Theseus.

4.2. *AJAX, ELECTRA, PHILOCTETES*

These three plays are those in which the role of *aidōs* demands detailed analysis, not because they are necessarily rich in instances of the term itself—*Ajax* and *Electra* have their fair share, but in *Philoctetes* the term *aidōs* does not actually occur—but because the instances of *aidōs* and other relevant terms, even if relatively scarce, indicate the central importance of the schemes of values to which they refer. In *Ajax* and *Philoctetes*, in particular, the significance of the values centred on *aidōs* is not only thematic (their proper evaluation being necessary for any interpretation of the play), but also sociological, the subtlety of Sophocles' technique bringing out the complex nature of the emotions and values with which we are concerned.

---

[34] Cf. Blundell (1989), 258, 262.
[35] (1980), 277-9, 325-9; cf. (with different emphasis) Blundell (1989), 253-9.

4.2.1. Ajax

Much has been written about the Homeric character of *Ajax*,[36] about
similarities between Ajax and the Homeric Achilles,[37] and those
between the Sophoclean and the Homeric Ajax;[38] and it is certainly
true that the values exhibited in martial contexts in the *Iliad* form the
moral background to the play, and that the play does contain 'the one
conspicuous and extensive reproduction by Sophocles of a specific
Homeric passage'[39] (*Ajax* 430–595, recalling *Iliad* 6. 390–502). Yet
Sophocles' Ajax is much more extreme in his pursuit of *timē* than
anyone in Homer,[40] and, as has been demonstrated,[41] Homeric motifs
are employed for contrast as well as for comparison; there is also the
figure of Odysseus, whose conduct must be judged on the basis of
different, though still related standards.

One of the essential attitudes which the play explores is expressed
by Athena in the prologue (79), when, in reply to Odysseus' request
not to call Ajax, his enemy, out of his tent, she asks, 'Is not mockery of
one's enemies the most pleasant kind of mockery?' This supposition
that pleasure is to be found in the disgrace of one's enemies is, as we
shall see, shared by all but one of the characters of the play; it assumes
a strict polarity of friends and enemies, and notions of the importance
of 'what people say' which are quite traditional. That Ajax himself
shares these attitudes is shown by his first appearance on stage; he is
pleased with his 'success' and wishes to boast of it (96); in one sense,
this is a traditional or Homeric attitude, for Ajax believes he has
defeated his enemies and expects that his strength and prowess in
doing so will be recognized; yet the *echthroi* he believes he has
attacked are his fellow warriors, those who should be his *philoi*,[42] and
the Homeric ideal in disputes between *philoi* is compromise. For Ajax,
however, it is his own *timē* that is paramount (98), and he clearly does
not believe that it could be diminished by breaches of the social

---

[36] See esp. Kirkwood (1965); Winnington-Ingram (1980), 15–19.

[37] Winnington-Ingram (1980), 17; Garner (1990), 59; cf. Whitman (1951), 64.

[38] Kirkwood (1965), 59–62; Winnington-Ingram (1980), 16 (on Aj.'s 'preoccupation
with *aidōs*' in the); Garner (1990), 54–63.

[39] Kirkwood (1965), 56; cf. Easterling (1984); Garner (1990), 51–2.

[40] Winnington-Ingram (1980), 16–19.

[41] Kirkwood (1965), 57–9, 62, 65, 67; Winnington-Ingram (1980), 16; Easterling
(1984), 6–8; Garner (1990), 52.

[42] Cf. Goldhill (1986), 85 (and 85–106 on conflict over 'friends and enemies' in Soph.
in general, as exemplified in *Ajax* and *Antigone*).

aspects of the heroic code.[43] The crucial ideas introduced in the prologue, then, are the closely related ones of the disgrace of competitive failure and the mockery of enemies which accompanies, exacerbates, and in one sense even constitutes the disgrace; but other standards, also part of the Homeric code of honour, remain in the background.[44]

With the entry of the chorus we see that Ajax's *philoi* identify with and are troubled by his disgrace; the reports they have heard signify *duskleia* (ill-repute, 141–3) and if they are true they will entail disgrace (*aischunē*) not just for Ajax, but also for his *philoi* (174). They are reluctant to believe those who would rejoice in their leader's misfortunes (150–7), and regard those who do so as guilty of *hubris* (151–3). Now, *hubris* is a pejorative term, and so the chorus clearly see the exultation of others in Ajax's ills as discreditable, but it is also clear that they are using the word in a polemical sense. In using *hubris* of the desire of Ajax's enemies to glory in his disgrace they are applying the term in a fundamental sense, that of the attempt to dishonour another person,[45] but it is far from certain that mockery of one's enemies would objectively be regarded as *hubris*; although there are some indications in earlier literature that such mockery or exultation is not to be pursued,[46] it is generally accepted that one's enemies *will* mock, and certainly Ajax himself had plans to humiliate his enemy, Odysseus,

[43] On his concern for his *timē* and *atimia*, see Knox (1964), 29; Winnington-Ingram (1980), 27; on his disregard for his social context, Winnington-Ingram (1980), 24; Goldhill (1986), 86.

[44] To mention this is not to 'make an issue' of it, something which Heath (1987: 173) sternly forbids. Heath is probably right to argue that in the play's opening and subsequent scenes the audience are induced to sympathize with Aj., and it is true that the plot to kill his fellow Greeks does not receive explicit condemnation until Menelaus calls it *hubris* at 1061 (cf. 1088). But the audience can sympathize with Aj. without regarding his conduct as blameless (as Heath is well aware), and Heath goes wrong in attempting to mitigate his offence by appealing to 'Homeric values'; it is true that 'Achilles' first impulse in 1 is to kill the man who has insulted him (and Athene, when she intervenes to prevent this, does not suggest that it would be *wrong*: only that restraint will in this case promise a more effective restitution)' (ibid.), but, as we saw, Nestor approaches the matter rather differently, insisting on the *timē* of both parties and urging compromise (see 1.3.3 above, in general). And why does Athena intervene? Is she simply concerned that Ach. should maximize his advantage, or does she use this as her argument to induce him to behave in the way which is generally desirable, i.e. to refrain from upsetting the social order?

[45] On *hubris* in *Ajax* and its connection with dishonour, see Fisher (1979), 33–6.

[46] See the maxim of Pittacus (5 DK) and Democ. B 107a, 293 DK. The stress on common humanity in the Democ. frr. is particularly relevant in the context of Od.'s behaviour in this play. Elsewhere such scruple seems to be restricted to mockery of the dead (*Od.* 22. 411–12; Aesch. *Ag.* 1612). Cf. Blundell (1989), 56.

when he thought he had him in his power (105-17). It therefore seems likely that mockery of the disgrace of enemies is more likely to be termed *hubris* when it is the mockery of *them* against *us*, and thus in this play the possibility that *hubris* may be partial, a term one applies to the behaviour of one's opponents, is a real one.[47] The relevance of this to our enquiry lies in the fact that to describe the dishonouring of Ajax by his enemies as *hubris* is to regard it as illegitimate dishonouring, and thus as a breach of the *aidōs* which should respond to the *timē* of others; and yet the chorus, while they deprecate the absence of this *aidōs*, clearly have no realistic expectation that it will be forthcoming, something which can only be the case because they regard its absence in one's enemies as natural; the ultimate irony, however, will be that such *aidōs* will be forthcoming, from one quarter at least.

Thus the question of the *aidōs* which responds to the *timē* of others is implicitly raised by the remarks of the chorus on *hubris*; but it is also clear that the situation in which they and their leader find themselves is such as to excite the *aidōs* which defends one's own *timē*. The question of *aidōs* on Ajax's part is first raised at 344-5, but this *aidōs* (the chorus-leader hopes that Ajax, once he has been exposed to the gaze of his fellows, will compose himself, presumably ashamed to be seen raging or grieving) is mentioned merely as a foil, to suggest the idea of *aidōs* in the minds of the audience, for when Ajax does appear he gives every impression of being troubled by another kind of *aidōs*. He contrasts his present *atimia* with his past greatness (364-5, 418-27) and imagines the mockery of his enemies (367, 382); he also believes that he has been treated with *hubris* (367, presumably referring to his delusion), without reflecting that this *hubris* only served to deflect him from the murder of his fellows. It is entirely, then, with the prospect of humiliation that he is concerned, and the moral character of his actions is no consideration with him at all.[48]

---

[47] On the natural tendency of people to regard as discreditable in others what one might do oneself in identical circumstances, see Adkins (1960a), 61.

[48] Cf. Class (1964), 72; Stebler (1971); Winnington-Ingram (1980), 27. Class, however, also writes of Aj.'s 'klar[es], voll[es] Bewußtsein, daß er etwas vollbracht hat, wofür er ganz verantwortlich ist und das sich nicht rückgängig machen läßt', and continues, 'Von der νόσος [disease] der Aias ... läßt sich eine Linie ziehen zur νόσος des euripideischen Orestes, der unter dem schlechten Gewissen leidet, nämlich dem Bewußtsein, Furchtbares getan zu haben.' Aj. does realize what he has done, and that his action will have its consequences, but he attributes its initiation not to himself as a responsible agent, but to Athena (367, 401-2); and the fact that he is not troubled by the rightness or wrongness of what he has done, but only by the ignominy in which it involves him, is part of his extreme concern with his honour, part of his character, and is in no way attributable to the play's (presumed) early date; the difference between Aj. and Eur.'s Orestes need not be seen in terms of development towards a greater understanding of 'conscience'.

In the iambic scene that follows, Ajax at first goes over much of the same ground again (430–80), before being drawn into that dialogue with Tecmessa which is so clearly based on the farewell of Hector and Andromache in *Iliad* 6. In the first speech Ajax's *aidōs* is still very prominent; he contrasts his own *atimia* (440), consisting in the original slight (the judgement of the arms, 441–4), the disgrace of the slaughter of the animals (453), and the mockery of the Atreidae (445–56), with the *eukleia* of his father (434–6). So much for the past; in contemplating the future (457–80), his thoughts return to his father, who is the very focus of his *aidōs*;[49] he is determined to show his father that he is not unworthy of his birth or his inherited nature (470–2), and he manifests a typical *aidōs*-reaction in his inability to contemplate facing his father without some proof of his success at Troy (462–6).[50] All this leads him to thoughts of death, for it would be *aischron* to live a life which is less than admirable (473–6); the *eugenes* (well-born) must either live *kalōs* or die *kalōs* (479–80).[51]

The chorus-leader comments that Ajax's speech was entirely like him, but that he should still give in to the advice of his *philoi* (481–4), and then it is the turn of Tecmessa to speak. As Kirkwood says, 'She presents a concept of values and duty significantly opposed to that of Ajax,'[52] but she does so not because the suppositions on which she bases her argument are entirely different from those on which Ajax bases his, but because she exploits aspects of the complex of values to

[49] Cf. Heath (1987), 180–1. Aj.'s concentration on his father here reveals the strength of his attachment to the heroic ideal; in the it is the father's hope that his son will be a better warrior than he is himself (Hector at 6. 479, recalled by Aj. at *Aj.* 550–1) and the father shares in the son's glory (6. 446, 8. 285); the converse is also true, and both Glaucus in the (6. 209) and Telemachus in the *Od.* (24. 508) are reminded by their fathers of the need to preserve family honour. Cf. the stress placed on Neoptolemus' *phusis* as son of Achilles in *Phil.* (4.2.3 below; Blundell (1988)). (On the question of focus on the parental model as a criterion for the development of guilt or conscience, see Introd. 0.3 and 0.4 above.)

[50] Note 'what eye shall I show to my father?' (462); Aj. also imagines that his father will be unable to bring himself to look upon him (463)—such will be the disparity in *kleos* between the two (465) that Telamon will also experience *aidōs*. As a sign of *aidōs* the inability to look others in the face may simply be an indication of embarrassment, or it may be a sign that one shares the negative judgement of one's own conduct or situation which one expects in others, and thus, as Class puts it (1964: 74–5), a *Gewissensregung*.

[51] Devotion to their own standards of *eugeneia* is a characteristic of the heroes; see Knox (1964), 28; cf. Diller (1956). The standards to which a *eugenēs* must aspire may be, to a large extent, laid down by others, but devotion to these standards must also presuppose a personal self-image.

[52] (1958), 105.

which he subscribes which, in this particular case, conflict with the
conclusions he draws.[53]

Tecmessa begins with the need to accept changes of fortune (485–
6), as she herself has done (487–90); she was once free, but is now a
slave, Ajax's concubine, and as such she appeals to him on the basis of
their sexual relationship, of her own feelings for him, and of the power
of Zeus, guardian of the hearth and home (490–3). Her appeal,
however, is couched in terms which he should be liable to understand,[54] for it is to his concern for his *timē* that she appeals, and thus to
his sense of *aidōs* at diminution of that *timē*, and this is an emotion to
which he has already shown himself to be susceptible. Ajax is affected
by the thought of his failure in competition, his failure to demonstrate
his strength and prowess; Tecmessa attempts to demonstrate to him
that an equivalent failure will result from neglect of his co-operative
obligations to his dependants. Thus she points out that his enemies
will mock if she becomes the property of another (494–5), that, if he
dies, she and Ajax's child will become slaves (496–9), and that the
taunt of their masters will be (501–5): '"See the bedmate of Ajax, who
was the strongest of the army, see what drudgery she has exchanged
for her admirable position." That is what they will say; in my case,
destiny will drive me on, but for you and your family these words will
be disgraceful [*aischra*].' The *aidōs* to which she appeals may promote
co-operation, but should Ajax decide to accept this argument he would
be doing so out of self-regarding concern for his own honour;
Tecmessa has widened the focus which Ajax had brought to bear on
heroic values, and again we see how closely linked are its co-operative
and competitive aspects.[55]

Line 505 is transitional;[56] from the implicit notion of *aidōs* at the
prospect of the taunts of others Tecmessa now turns to the *aidōs* which
one owes one's *philoi*, particularly one's parents (506–9), and to pity,
which she first invokes in the name of their son (510–13). There is a
change of emphasis here, but not a particularly great one, for the
other-regarding *aidōs* to which she now (explicitly) appeals is merely
the other side of the coin in relation to the self-regarding *aidōs* she
sought to arouse in the earlier part of her speech, since *aidōs* for one's
parents may be based both on respect for their special status *vis-à-vis*

---

[53] See Winnington-Ingram (1980), 18–19, 29–31; Easterling (1984), 2–4; Heath (1987),
181.

[54] Cf. Easterling (1984), 2–4; Blundell (1989), 76–7.

[55] Cf. 1.2.3, 1.2.4, 1.3 above.

[56] Cf. Heath (1987), 182.

oneself and on the idea that such respect is a duty which it is discreditable to neglect; even when reminding Ajax of the *aidōs* he owes his
parents, then, Tecmessa may excite his concern for his own reputation.
Similarly, although in appealing to pity for Eurysaces Tecmessa
appeals to an emotion which is normally regarded as altruistic,[57] she
also stresses both the boy's ignoble status as an orphan and Ajax's
responsibility for it (510–13), and it is surely discreditable in itself that
a hero's son should be in such a pitiful condition. Tecmessa's appeals
to self- and other-regarding impulses are thus virtually inseparable.
Likewise, when she comes to speak of the pitiful nature of her own
condition (514–19), it is not to pity itself that she appeals, but to *charis*,
the obligation to show gratitude (520–4), which she represents as a
duty of the *eugenēs* (523–4), and while to return a kindness is to benefit
another person, the impulse to do so may be based on the knowledge
that reciprocity is an imperative which it is discreditable to ignore; and
in suggesting that Ajax will not be regarded as *eugenēs* if he fails to
return the *charis* of their relationship Tecmessa is clearly attempting to
arouse his *aidōs* at the prospect of conduct which would undermine his
status.

The definition of *eugeneia*, the idea with which both Ajax and
Tecmessa end their speeches, is one aspect of the conflict of values
between the two,[58] and related to this is their difference over what the
eugenēs should find disgraceful, over *aidōs* and its proper object. As
Reinhardt says, 'Ajax' thoughts of his father, his home, his son, respect
and shame [*aidōs*] are to him reasons for committing suicide; but
precisely the same ideas appear to Tecmessa as reasons for *not*
committing suicide. . . .'[59] They do, therefore, place quite different
interpretations on the same material, and in the sequel Ajax is not
persuaded, but it is not quite true to say that they 'speak different
languages';[60] Tecmessa's whole speech takes its argument from that of

---

[57] Cf. Kirkwood (1958), 106.

[58] Winnington-Ingram (1980: 29) refers to Tec.'s use of *eugenēs* as 'a "persuasive" redefinition' of Aj.'s, but the idea that the man of good birth should return favours is
certainly not foreign to the traditionalist outlook of, e.g., the Theognid corpus (cf. 2.3.4
above). Winnington-Ingram may be right, however, to suggest (30) that more obviously
self-regarding concerns may override such sentiments, and that the claims of a concubine
to *charis* may not be particularly strong. The fact remains, however, that Tec. bases her
argument on aspects of the heroic code.

[59] (1979), 21–2.

[60] Segal (1981), 134; cf. Reinhardt (1979: 21), who claims that neither listens to the
other, that Aj. hears nothing of what Tec. says, and that 'neither speech refers to the
other, they do not touch or lead to any argument for or against. . . .'

Ajax, and it is expressed in terms which are likely to strike a chord in him; and strike a chord it does, for although Ajax does not reply directly to Tecmessa, in his speech to his son (550–77) he does answer her on precisely those points on which she attempted to arouse his *aidōs*: he declares that the boy will not suffer *hubris* or *lōbē* (560–1) because Teucer and his fellow Salaminians will protect him (562–6), and he is confident that his son will be able to perform the function of providing for his parents (567–70).[61] It is not, then, that he denies that the eventualities set out by Tecmessa would harm his posthumous honour, simply that he does not believe that they will come about.[62] Only for Tecmessa's appeal to *charis* has he no answer (although he does express his pity for her and the child at 652–3),[63] and this suggests that he is not susceptible to her claim that to fail to show *charis* would be to impair his *eugeneia*.

Ajax concludes his general reflections in the *Trugrede* with remarks on the mutability of friendship and enmity (678–83), and it is the theme of friends and enemies, introduced in the prologue, which is to dominate the remainder of the play. As in the prologue, the central idea is that one's own disgrace and sorrow is one's enemies' joy; Teucer echoes the sentiments of Athena at 79 when he says that

[61] See Easterling (1984), 5; Heath (1987), 181–3, esp. n. 34.

[62] Thus he does not quite *reject* Tec.'s reminders of his obligations, as Goldhill (1986: 86) claims; he recognizes the obligations, but claims that they will be met. We need not suppose, however, that Aj. can foresee, however dimly, the events of the rest of the play (as does Taplin (1979), 126), and should note that, in so far as his perspective makes no allowances for the crucial intervention of Odysseus, he is wrong to be so confident (Winnington-Ingram (1980), 31); Od.'s intervention is an ironic substantiation of the principle, which Aj. only pretends to accept, that *echthroi* can become *philoi* (679–80).

[63] Since this statement comes in the deception speech, we have no way of knowing for sure whether this pity is real or feigned; Aj. is brusquely dismissive of pity in 580, but some will say that he has changed his mind. Certainly, it *could* be genuine without affecting the feignedness of other aspects of the speech, but for my money the pejorative ἐθηλύνθην ('I have been made feminine') in 651 suggests that his pity is part of the deception. Aj. also speaks of 'yielding to the gods and honouring [*sebein*] the Atreidae' in 666–7, which might suggest that he is accepting the kind of *aidōs* for one's superiors which Menelaus urges in 1071–86; but Winnington-Ingram (1980: 49) and Heath (1987: 187) are surely right to point out that the application of *sebein* to a human object and 'yielding' to a divine inverts, ironically, the relationship we should expect to find where *both* these objects are mentioned (contrast Taplin (1979: 128), who points out, correctly, but inappositely, that *sebas* is not exclusively a response to the divine); Aj., therefore, does not yield, does not honour the Atreidae (contrast Sicherl (1977), 82). It follows that I do not believe that he accepts any recognizable kind of *sōphrosunē*, in spite of his reference to that concept in 677 (cf. Reinhardt (1979), 24; Winnington-Ingram (1980), 50–6; Segal (1981), 119, 150; Heath (1987), 188; contrast Whitman (1951), 77; Sicherl (1977), 82–8; Taplin (1979)). On 'yielding' in Soph. in general, see Diller (1956), 75–8.

'everyone' longs to mock the mighty dead when they have fallen (988–
9); Tecmessa describes her woe as Odysseus' joy at 954–5; at 955–60
the chorus lament the mockery and *hubris* of Odysseus and the
Atreidae which they regard as inevitable; and when the chorus-leader
sees Menelaus approaching he immediately assumes that mockery is
his intention (1042–3).[64] There are clearly two strands of thought in
such passages, that it is discreditable to mock a dead enemy and that it
is natural to do so; both find support in epic. (Odysseus forbids
exultation over his dead foes at *Odyssey* 22. 411–12,[65] but exultation
over enemies dead or dying is common in the *Iliad*. This is perhaps a
grey area; but dishonouring of an enemy can go too far, and become
unambiguously inappropriate, as in the case of Achilles' maltreatment
of Hector.)

When Menelaus does appear we learn that he indeed intends to
dishonour Ajax (by depriving him of burial, 1062–5), and that his
motivation in doing so is one of retaliation for the dishonour which
Ajax attempted to inflict on him and his fellows (1057–9). Menelaus
also has important remarks to make on the nature of Ajax's error; his
attempt on the lives of his comrades and superiors was an act of *hubris*
which a god turned against the sheep and cattle (1061).[66] At 1071–86
Menelaus sets Ajax's *hubris* in a wider, civic context: a city cannot exist
without obedience, and the fear (*deos*, 1074) which promotes it, nor
can an army be ruled with discipline (*sōphrosunē*, 1075) without fear

[64] The chorus and Teucer are obviously disturbed by the prospect of the mockery of
others, and presumably they believe that it can do some damage, both to Aj.'s honour
and their own, as members of his contingent. Such concern for their collective honour
will presumably be related to *aidōs*. Interestingly enough, this concern is not shared by
Tec., who takes the attitude that the mockery of the Atreidae can be ignored, and finds
comfort in the fact that they will feel the lack of Aj. in battle (961–5); she accepts that
they will mock, but maintains that their mockery will not harm its target (966–70), and
that Od.'s *hubris* will thus be in vain (971). This is roughly the attitude of Apollo at 24. 54
(it is 'dumb earth' that Achilles mutilates, not Hector), but while this attitude is possible
it clearly requires a certain amount of detachment from ideals of *timē* (such as may be
found in women and gods?) which other characters are unable to share. (Cf., e.g., Priam's
concern for the state of Hector's body at 24. 406–9, and Hermes' reassurance at 411–23.)
[65] Cf. n. 46 above.
[66] The indiscriminate slaughter of helpless beasts and the complete disregard of the
rights of all those whom he intended to kill, whether they had offended against him or
not, is presumably a more objective kind of *hubris* than that of which Aj.'s party first
complained, but Heath (1987: 173; cf. 200) is right to point out that Aj.'s action is only
described in this way at this late stage, and that the description affects neither our
sympathy for Aj. nor our antipathy towards Men. Heath's insistence on the antipathy one
normally feels towards the 'adversary' in tragedy, regardless of any abstract value in his
arguments, is valuable: see 58–9, 87, 96–7, etc.

(*phobos*) and *aidōs* (1076), but even the physically strong must be aware that they can fall from pre-eminence. He who has *deos* and *aischunē* (synonymous with *aidōs*) has safety (*sōtēria*, 1079–80), but where *hubris* and doing whatever one likes prevail, that city is doomed (1081–3).

In its stress on the utility of the traditionally related ideas of fear and *aidōs* in the state this speech is particularly reminiscent of similar arguments in the *Eumenides*,[67] and probably makes use of ideas which are both traditional and part of contemporary discussion of the nature of civil life and the need for justice in the community.[68] In general, Menelaus' remarks seem to be justified as an analysis of Ajax's conduct; there is certainly nothing 'distasteful' in his general observations,[69] and Pearson[70] is probably right to see them as 'an orthodox exposition of the civic virtues'—the chorus-leader calls them 'wise maxims' at 1091. Menelaus, therefore, like Tecmessa, draws attention to aspects of *aidōs* which Ajax's preoccupation with his own *timē* ignored.[71] Seen in their wider context, however, Menelaus' maxims emerge in a different light, for he uses Ajax's *hubris* and lack of *aidōs* as justification for his own retaliation (1067–70, 1085–90); he thus manifests a concern similar to that which motivated his enemy,[72]

---

[67] See 3.4 above, *ad fin.* Both *Eum.* and *Aj.* passages discuss the utility of fear in the state, but the Aeschylean passages are more explicit about the need for positive respect for the institutions of punishment, whereas Men.'s remarks about 'falling (from a favoured position)' in 1077–8 reveal that he is thinking primarily of *aidōs* as related to disgrace and of fear as related to punishment, rather than of positive respect for one's superiors (although that idea is certainly present). We saw (n. 63 above) that Aj. ironically rejected the respect for his superiors which Men. demands here.

[68] The idea that it is fear, of both punishment and disgrace, which makes one amenable to state or military authority seems to reflect the 5th-cent. preoccupation with the origin of the institutions of civilization and the question, 'Why should one be moral?'. Men.'s argument has certain affinities with the position of Protagoras, as far as it can be reconstructed (see 6.2 below). Rose (1976: 53) identifies *sōtēria* (as in 1080) as a sophistic catchword, the aim of the pre-social struggle for survival which is analogous to the state of man before the acquisition of *aidōs* and *dikē* in Plato's *Prot.* myth (322ab); here, however, as in the *Philoctetes* (see Rose, 79, on *Phil.* 1396), *sōtēria* is the product of *aischunē* and *deos* (so at *Prot.* 322b6 in trying and failing to found cities men were seeking *to sōzesthai* (= *sōtēria*); this, however, they only achieve with the acquisition of 'political skill' through *dikē* and *aidōs*).

[69] *Pace* Whitman (1951), 78.   [70] (1962), 194.

[71] Tec., of course, does, as we saw, get through to Aj. to a certain extent, in that he does make provision for his dependants. But she is also careful to emphasize the implications of the fate of his dependants for his own honour; Aj. himself does not reflect that he also owes them *aidōs* as a response to *their* special status, and it is reasonable to suppose that it is on the basis of the implications for his own honour that he considers the question, even though Tec. does ask him positively to respond to the special status of his parents.

[72] Cf. 1134 and Kirkwood (1958), 107.

creating a parallelism which emerges quite explicitly at 1087-8: 'These things alternate. Previously he was a flagrant *hubristes*, but now it is my turn to think big.' In spite of his commendable remarks, then, Menelaus sees *hubris* not as a bad thing which one should not commit at all, but as a legitimate weapon against one's enemies. He thus condemns himself out of his own mouth and maintains the partiality of *hubris* which we have already noted;[73] he is prepared to ignore *aidōs* just as he says Ajax did. The chorus-leader's comment (1091-2), therefore, is fully justified: 'Menelaus, do not put forward wise maxims and then yourself insult the dead.'[74]

The *hubris* that is the attempt to dishonour one's enemies dominates the subsequent exchanges between Teucer and the Atreidae; accusations of *hubris* (1151, 1258) and lack of *sōphrosunē* (1259) fly, Menelaus and Teucer both maintain that it would be beneath their dignity (*aischron*) to continue the argument (1159-60, 1161-2), and Agamemnon and Teucer attempt to bring disgrace on each other by mutual accusations of barbarian origins (1259-63, 1291-8), the latter adding, for good measure, some unsavoury details from the history of the Pelopidae. It is Teucer, however, who finally comes back to the issue at hand, suggesting that the true occasion for shame ($\alpha i\sigma\chi\acute{v}\nu o\iota\mu\iota$, 1305) is not his own birth, but Agamemnon's conduct in denying burial to Ajax ($\acute{\epsilon}\pi\alpha\iota\sigma\chi\acute{v}\nu\eta$, 1307); the polarity of friends and enemies and the reciprocity of *hubris* are maintained by the attempts to excite the other's shame over facts which were entirely beyond his control, but eventually Teucer raises the question of shame over one's own actions, and with it the assumption that it is discreditable to insult the

---

[73] i.e. although Men.'s description of Aj.'s *hubris* may be such as to find support among the impartial, he confesses himself prepared to commit *hubris*. (I think Fisher (1979: 34) is wrong to claim that Men.'s 'thinking big' is not to be identified with *hubris*; whatever may be the normal relationship between 'thinking big' and *hubris*, Men.'s remarks on reciprocity strongly suggest that he is now accepting the requital of *hubris* with *hubris*; his attitude of 'thinking big' is ot to be sharply divorced from his attempt to dishonour Aj. by denying burial.) With the prohibition of burial, however, the *hubris* of Aj.'s enemies also takes on a more objective character (it is no longer just a term which Aj.'s party apply to their opponents' conduct), since denial of burial is almost certainly to be seen as going too far in the attempt to dishonour (it is an infringement of divine law in *Ant.*, and in this play it is opposed by the morally scrupulous Od.). (Cerri (1979: 17-50) argues that it was Soph.'s own belief that denial of burial was always wrong, even though it was part of the punishment for treason at Athens.) Given the possibility that the denial of burial is to be seen as objectively wrong, it is worth remarking that the partiality of choral comments decreases somewhat from the point at which it is threatened; see the leader's criticisms of Teucer's abuse of Men. at 1118-19, implying that, in misfortunes, dignity and moderation should be shown by all (and cf. 1264-5).

[74] Lit. 'become a *hubristēs*', echoing Men.'s own word at 1088.

dead. These two modes of conduct, the opportunist desire to capitalize on one's enemy's weaknesses and the concern for impartial standards of behaviour, stand in sharp opposition to each other at the point at which Odysseus re-enters the play.

Odysseus returns at 1316, and the chorus-leader hopes that he can break up the quarrel (1316–17); on the one hand, the spectators have been encouraged to believe that he, too, will exult in Ajax's misfortunes (953–4, 955–60, 971), yet they have also seen the prologue, and are perhaps not entirely disposed to accept the assumptions about Odysseus' future conduct made by Tecmessa and the chorus. However this may be, it is the promise of the prologue rather than the expectations of Ajax's party that is fulfilled; Odysseus immediately places himself outside the scheme of partiality and retaliation (1320–4), forcing Agamemnon to admit that he has not only received, but also dealt insults (αἰσχίστους λόγους, 1320; *aischra*, 1324). In his speech at 1332–45 he states his opposition to the prohibition of burial, gives his reasons, and restates Ajax's *timē*.

Unlike the Atreidae, Odysseus distances his personal bias from his estimation of Ajax's worth; his enmity, he says (1336–41), will not lead him to deny that Ajax was best (*aristos*) at Troy, after Achilles, to deny him, that is, the *timē* he deserves. He bases his impulses on 'justice', *dikē*: to leave Ajax unburied is to give in to the temptations of force and to trample on *dikē* (1332–5); Ajax's *aretē* is such that it is not just that he be dishonoured by Agamemnon (1342, cf. 1363); to dishonour Ajax is not to destroy him, but to destroy the laws of the gods (1343–4); and it is not *dikaion* to harm the *esthlos* in death, even out of hatred (1344–5). Odysseus thus clearly subscribes to the belief, reiterated throughout the play, that it is wrong to exult in others' misfortunes, especially that it is wrong to insult the dead, and thus his idea of *dikē* happens to coincide with that of Teucer at 1125,[75] but his appeal to these standards has greater validity by virtue of its impartiality.

But what precisely are Odysseus' principles in opposing the dishonouring of Ajax? He responds to his enemy's *aretē* and is reluctant to deprive him of *timē*. This belief, that others should be accorded the *timē* they deserve, is a Homeric one,[76] and to accord others the *timē* they deserve in Homer was to show *aidōs*; and so it is here, for in answer to Agamemnon's question (1356), 'Are you so moved to *aidōs* for this enemy's corpse?' Odysseus replies (1357), 'Yes, for his *aretē*

---

[75] Cf. Winnington-Ingram (1980), 66.
[76] Cf. above, 1.3.3, and 1.3 in general.

weighs more heavily with me than my enmity.'[77] So Odysseus experiences a positive feeling of respect for Ajax's *aretē*; but this is also allied to a more general feeling that it is not right to deprive others of such respect, and this feeling is expressed with reference to *dikē—dikē* 'is presented in terms of *timē*'.[78] This concern of the impartial observer that another should have his due *timē* was not explicitly related to *dikē* in Homer, but we saw that Nestor's intervention in the dispute between Achilles and Agememnon did express that concern, and that he was thus appealing to an implicit notion of 'justice' based on the title to honour.[79] It is this implicit notion of 'justice in honour' that Odysseus makes explicit here; it is not a sharply defined, legalistic concept of justice,[80] but one based to a large extent on traditional ideas of limit and appropriateness.[81] These ideas are also prominent in the passage, in as much as the standard of *to kalon*, that which is praiseworthy and appropriate, is referred to the concept of limit in one's hatred (1347) and in one's pursuit of one's own advantage (1349).[82] Again, as it is *aidōs* that responds to another's *timē*, so it is *aidōs* that responds to the standard of appropriateness, to what is *kalon*.

So Odysseus is following certain traditional beliefs;[83] but the most striking aspect of his response to the situation is that it is un-expected and shared by none of the other characters.[84] In particular, Agamemnon gives in not because he believes or even understands what Odysseus says (he continues to think in terms of friendship and enmity (1356, 1360) and of his own reputation (1362)), but out of deference to their friendship (1370-1), while Teucer, in refusing to allow Odysseus to participate in Ajax's burial (in spite of Odysseus'

[77] As Jebb points out (1896: ad loc.), the sense of this line, the contrast between *aretē* and enmity, is guaranteed by the context, although editors differ as to how the text should be emended. My translation paraphrases the OCT of Lloyd-Jones and Wilson (reading πλέον for πολύ), although one is tempted to go further and substitute something like Pearson's κινεῖ for MSS νικᾷ.

[78] Winnington-Ingram (1980), 66.

[79] See Ch. 1 n. 154; cf. 2.1 above on *aidōs* and *dikē* in Hes.

[80] Cf. Pearson (1962), 195.

[81] The laws of the gods are also relevant (1343-4), but the two points are separate; Od. believes both that it is not *dikaion* to deprive Aj. of *timē* and that it is not *dikaion* to transgress the laws of the gods; divine law does not subsume the concern for the honour of another human being.

[82] In the latter place the idea is of *kerdos* (profit), which is not *kalon*; cf. 2.1 and 2.3.4 above on *kerdos* in Hes. and Thgn., and n. 11 above.

[83] Cf. Heath (1987), 203-4.

[84] On its unexpectedness, see 1382. Of course, Teucer and the chorus would not dispute what Od. says, but their concern for Aj. and his body is partial where his is not.

desire to do so),[85] reaffirms the polarity of friends and enemies at the play's close (1393–1401). Odysseus, then, is isolated, and his ideas of *to kalon* and *dikē* depend on his own sensitivity, his own interpretation of right and wrong, his own personal conscience.[86] They also, as we have seen, depend on his *aidōs*, and so it should be clear that this *aidōs* is not simply an impulse to conform, a fear of being out of step with convention, for it is based on principles which are subjective and activated instinctively. Odysseus could clearly 'get away with' maltreating Ajax's body, and so popular disapproval is not a consideration with him; and yet his *aidōs* is of a traditional type, based on standards which are quite traditional. Behind his response to the body of Ajax and its burial, therefore, lies a realization, which may or may not be 'new', that to behave in accordance with traditional ideas depends on the sensitivity of the individual rather than simply on fear of punishment or disgrace.[87]

In Ajax, then, we are faced with a recurrent contrast between individualistic values (preoccupation with one's own honour, including the related impulses to dishonour one's enemies and to retaliate for dishonour suffered) and values which, while still traditional, none the less emphasize more social, humane, and other-regarding aspects of

[85] Od. is thus denied the opportunity to act as did Achilles in 24, where he helped prepare his enemy's body for burial (571–90; cf. 6. 418–19, where Ach. personally sees to the burial of Eëtion, for whom he felt *sebas*).

[86] This is, in effect, denied by Stebler (1971), 71; she recognizes that Od. acts out of concern for *dikē*, but writes: 'Im Blickpunkt steht noch nicht das eigene Selbst, das eine Verletzung der göttlichen νόμος [law] nicht mit sich vereinbaren kann, aus tiefst-innerer, wesensmässiger Gefolgschaft, sondern die δίκη [*dikē*], die νόμοι [laws], die zu wahren sind, damit der Mensch weiter in ungetrübter Beziehung zu den Göttern stehen kann. . . .' The idea of 'das eigene Selbst . . .' she finds in *Ant.* (pp. 106–16 of her work), but I see no difference between Od.'s conviction that one should not break divine law and Ant.'s (nor is Od.'s *dikē* simply a matter of divine law). Both *dikē* and the laws of the gods in *Aj.* are interpreted in line with Od.'s own moral principles, and so, just like Ant., he is opposing his own moral conscience to the will of others.

[87] On the relevance of this to Democ. B 264 DK etc., see 6.3.2 below. Od. does, it need hardly be said, motivate his conduct in several different ways: there is the aspect which most concerns us, his sense of what is *dikaion* and *kalon*; then there is his belief that divine law forbids the exposure of a corpse; and there is his (in this play) characteristic humanity, his ability to see his own fate in that of another, expressed both at the beginning (121–6) and the end (1365–7) of the play (cf. Theseus at *OC* 567–9 and, fundamentally, Achilles and Priam in 24). In both these places he points out that his pity for Aj. as a human being is based on consideration of his own interests as well as those of his enemy (cf. Democ. B 107a, 293 DK, n. 46 above), and Jones (1962: 184–8) is at pains to explain this element of self-reference to 'the reader educated in a morality of altruism' (186). I do not think, however, that his sentiments will place any strain on those familiar with the phrase (often repeated in explanation of Christian altruism), 'There but for the grace of God go I' (cf. Stanford (1983), 27; Blundell (1989), 99).

the complex of honour. The effect is that of the placing of the individualistic values, the more obvious aspects of the code of honour, in their wider context, of the delineation of the limits of self-assertion at the point at which self-assertion itself becomes a violation of the code. It is salutary to note that Sophocles does not in any way have to innovate to create this effect; he simply sets the parts of the traditional complex in the context of the whole.

4.2.2. Electra

The same pattern is detectable in the *Electra*. This is also a play of retaliation and reciprocity, as emerges with greatest relevance to our theme in the *agōn* between Electra and Clytemnestra which stands at its heart. It soon emerges, however, that the *agōn* itself is representative of a recurrent process of retaliation and mutual recrimination.[88] The background to this is one of *atimia*,[89] and concern for *timē*, both Agamemnon's and her own, is Electra's chief motivating force.[90] It is out of this background that there arises the process which we shall see at work in the *agōn*. Electra's retaliation for her own and her father's *atimia* consists in her persistence in grief, disobedience to the authority of Aegisthus and Clytemnestra, and maintenance of her miserable condition;[91] this annoys her enemies, but honours her father (355–6); to desist would be cowardice (351).[92] Electra thus lives and acts as she does in order to annoy her enemies; not surprisingly, therefore, she believes them to be motivated by a similar concern—indeed, she regards the conduct of Clytemnestra and Aegisthus as specifically designed to undermine her status; their sexual union, for example, she regards as 'the ultimate *hubris*' (271–4)[93]

[88] Cf. Linforth (1963), 116; Winnington-Ingram (1980), 222–3; Blundell (1989), 163–4.
[89] Cf. Knox (1964), 28–30; Winnington-Ingram (1980), 240–1.
[90] See 100–20, 266–74 (cf. Chrysothemis at 419–21), 442–6 (cf. the chorus at 486–7); El. believes that she will win fame by restoring her father's honour (975–83), while at 1153, believing Orestes dead and contemplating the ruin of her cause, she imagines the mockery of her enemies. Her own *atimia* is recognized by Or. at 1181 and 1427.
[91] Cf. Whitman (1951), 165; also Linforth (1963), 114–15; Blundell (1989), 157, 159.
[92] In thus seeing the course of action recommended by Chrysothemis (moderation and compliance towards authority, the 'normal' woman's reaction) as cowardice El. seems to be undertaking a role more in line with male values than with female.
[93] Cf. her designation of the sexual relationship at 586 as 'the most *aischron* acts of all'; *aischista* here may refer to the disgrace of Clyt.'s adultery or simply to the distaste El. feels for the acts themselves, but she clearly resents these acts, and feels that their 'ugliness' diminishes her own and her father's honour. On her preoccupation with her mother's adultery, see Jones (1962), 149–53; Blundell (1989), 153.

and complains of her mother's reproaches and *hubris* in the face of her troubles (278–93; especially 293, *exubrizei*).[94] Of her mother's part in the process of recrimination, then, she is clearly aware.

The process is enacted before our eyes in the *agōn*, and there are constant signs that this is but one further episode in a continuing and long-standing series.[95] The pattern is one of mutual recrimination and abuse, as Clytemnestra acknowledges in 523–4, justifying her own abuse of Electra as retaliation for the abuse she has received; clearly, therefore, we are concerned with honour and shame here, since abuse is designed to enhance the honour of the agent and impair that of its recipient. We have seen that Electra believes that the conduct of her mother and her paramour is expressly designed to humiliate her; similarly, on the other side of the equation, Clytemnestra, in her first words in the *agōn* (516–18), expresses her annoyance that Electra's unrestrained and unmaidenly behaviour,[96] brings disgrace on her family (αἰσχύνειν φίλους, 518); there can be no doubt that shaming those who, in any normal circumstances, would be her *philoi* is precisely Electra's intention—it is the obverse of her honouring of her father. Each, then, regards the other as attempting to implicate her in dishonour, and thus each sees the other as behaving without *aidōs*. This theme is kept before us as the *agōn* progresses. It is also clear that the recurrent pattern of mutual recrimination involving Electra and Clytemnestra only mirrors the sequence of crime and vengeance in the house of Atreus. The pattern of insult and retaliation exhibited in the *agōn* and adumbrated elsewhere in the play, therefore, must influence our attitude towards the issues raised by the larger pattern of crime and revenge within the family.[97]

Clytemnestra then proceeds to a justification of the murder of Agamemnon with reference to the sacrifice of Iphigeneia, and Electra duly responds with a statement of her interpretation of the same

[94] Similarly, she sees Clyt. as reacting with *hubris* to Or.'s death at 790 and 794.

[95] See 520–4: Clyt. complains that El. is always denouncing her and complaining of her *hubris*, but claims that she only abuses El. in retaliation. Clyt.'s awareness of the charges El. makes against her corresponds to El.'s awareness at 278–93. Cf. 552–3, El.: 'You cannot say I started it this time'; 556–7, Clyt.: 'If this were the way you always spoke to me . . .'; 596–7, where El. accurately observes that Clyt.'s constant complaint is one of a daughter's abuse of her mother (as at 523–4); and 605–7 (with 612–15), El. challenges Clyt. to make her usual charges against her, and she does so.

[96] Cf. Kells (1973), on 517–18.

[97] I am conscious that the following does little more than develop a suggestion made by Kirkwood (1958: 140–1); the approach of Winnington-Ingram (1980), is also in close harmony with mine.

events (525–609). Thus they debate the justice (*dikē*) of Clytemnestra's deed, but there is no real attempt to persuade,[98] and it is clear enough that this passage is but another round in the recurring pattern.[99] There is no need to get involved in the rights and wrongs of this exchange; the position is exactly what one familiar with the *Oresteia* would expect; the rights of retaliation are stressed, but so too is the impropriety of retaliation against one's *philoi*.

Clytemnestra's argument is simple: she killed Agamemnon justly because he sacrificed her daughter. Electra's is less simple (558–60): 'You say you killed father; what argument could be more *aischron* than that, whether you killed him justly or not?' Electra appears to dismiss the argument from justice, but returns to it in 561–76, arguing that her mother's action was not *dikaion*. So the concession made in 558–60 is merely rhetorical; Electra is at pains to designate her mother's conduct *aischron*, of course because she believes it was, but also because to implicate her in disgrace is part of her strategy.

Adkins, however, sees more in the passage:[100] 'To say an action is *aischron* is to play the ace of trumps: to justify performing it, one cannot press the claim that it is *dikaion*, for that is of less importance, but must maintain that it is in fact not *aischron* after all.' We can dismiss the curious assumption that, in any real context, a word may be an 'ace of trumps',[101] for it is not central to Adkins's argument, which is, presumably, that if one accepts that one's action is *aischron* one cannot go on to justify it on other grounds, even those of *dikē*. But this is also a rather artificial argument; if one does believe that one's conduct was *dikaion*, the judgement that it is also *aischron* rarely comes from oneself. And yet there does exist a number of passages in which people do admit that they have acted or may act in a way commonly regarded as *aischron*, but justify this in terms of the necessity of achieving some more important objective. Such, for example, is Sophocles, fragment 352 Radt: 'It is not *kalon* to tell lies, but for one for whom the truth brings terrible destruction, it is pardonable to say even what is not *kalon*.'[102] Any of those passages, moreover—and there are many—in which someone is advised or decides to abandon *aidōs*, the emotion which categorizes a course of action as *aischron*, would also show that

[98] Kirkwood (1958), 140.
[99] Whitman (1951), 158; Linforth (1963), 97; Winnington-Ingram (1980), 219–22.
[100] (1960*a*), 156.
[101] See Dover (1983), 41.
[102] Adkins denies that 'not *kalon*' is the equivalent of *aischron* in Homer (1960*a*: 43–4), which is in itself unlikely, but there is no equivalent denial with regard to later literature.

recognition of a given action as *aischron* does not mean that its performance cannot be justified. Perhaps the most apposite parallel is that of Aeschylus' Orestes,[103] whose *aidōs* at *Choephori* 899 shows his awareness that it is normally *aischron* to kill one's mother, but who proceeds to do so on the basis of *dikē* and the divine command, a basis on which he defends his conduct in *Eumenides*. Characters can, then, justify conduct which is *aischron* in other terms.

The passage quoted, however, is not Adkins's last word on the subject. Some pages further on[104] he goes on to claim that Electra's words in 558–60 constitute Sophocles' 'solution . . . to the problem set by the crime within the family'; that is to say, Sophocles attempts to subject the competing claims of *dikē* in the feud to a higher standard, under which it is always wrong to pursue retaliation against a member of one's own family. The problem with this is that Adkins appears to envisage an innovation on Sophocles' part, a contribution to a problem not yet solved; but this is a completely false picture of the facts. It is in no way new to represent the crime within the family as *aischron*—Clytemnestra's deed is *aischron* even in the *Odyssey* (11. 432–4),[105] being both a fundamental breach of the obligations of *philia* and against all the imperatives of loyalty to one's husband inherent in women's *aretē*. Electra thus has traditional values on her side, and Sophocles himself may even have agreed with her interpretation, although we could never be sure about this. But Sophocles is most emphatically not giving us an innovative solution to the problem set by the crime within the family; rather he represents it in its most fundamental aspect; injustice, wrong, or insult against oneself or a member of one's family calls forth retribution (*dikē*), and the requirement to pursue *dikē* is a powerful one, but to pursue it within one's family must inevitably involve an action which is *aischron*.[106]

Electra, then, is able to state the problem which bedevils the history of her family, and accuses her mother of an unpardonable breach of familial *aidōs*. Her arguments are thus part of the pervasive theme of shame and dishonour which is intrinsic to the process of recrimination

---

[103] See 3.2.3 above.

[104] (1960a), 185.

[105] Cf. 1.4.1 above; also Blundell (1989), 166–7.

[106] Cf. Blundell (1989), 167. For the *aischron/dikaion* antithesis in the same context, cf. Eur. *El.* 1050–1, *Or.* 194; implicit in Aesch. *Cho.*, it seems to become a *topos* in the other plays. In the Euripidean passages, there is certainly strong emphasis on the horror of retaliation within the family, but this can only be emphasis on one of the traditional aspects of the situation, not an innovation on Eur.'s part.

in which the two women are involved. Just as, however, attempts to implicate the other in dishonour are common to both women, so Electra's remarks about the primacy of the *aischron*-standard over the requirement to pursue *dikē* take their place in the equilibrium and parallelism which exists in the arguments of both parties; in short, Electra is ignorant of the application of her own words to herself. This becomes particularly apparent at 577–83 where she recognizes that Clytemnestra's case rests on the legitimacy of the *lex talionis*, and suggests that a rigid application of these principles would lead to her own death; she would be first to die, Electra claims, if she were to meet with *dikē* (583). She thus recognizes, but depreciates, Clytemnestra's claim to *dikē*, yet she herself acts on the same principle and will, as we who have seen Orestes know, bring the hypothesis of 583 to its fulfilment.[107]

So much for the similarity between Electra and Clytemnestra in point of *dikē*; in the final section of the speech, as Electra's temper rises, it is the possibility of the shamefulness of her own conduct which comes to the fore. At 595 she abandons her argument on the nature of her mother's conduct—she will never convince Clytemnestra,[108] because the latter's only concern is the absue she endures at her daughter's hand.[109] Electra thus recognizes that her mother's complaint is based on her own failure to show proper *aidōs*, to respond appropriately to another's *timē*; at the same time, as we have seen, her

---

[107] Cf. Segal (1966), 536, 540; Kells (1973), on 582–3; Winnington-Ingram (1980), 221; Blundell (1989), 168. Heath (1987: 136–7) argues that El.'s remarks on the *lex talionis*, prompted by 'the rhetoric of the situation' (Dale (1954), p. xxvii), make a point against Clyt. which is not to be invested with any wider significance; I am not so sure that the audience's familiarity with rhetoric would have blinded them to the application of El.'s words to herself (see further Blundell (1989), 21–3 and n. 72), but more importantly, Heath seems unaware that this passage is only one of many which reveal that El.'s motives are of the same moral character as Clyt.'s. Heath also tries to stigmatize the interpretation of these lines which I favour by saying that it 'belong[s] with a reading of the play that is irretrievably faulty'; but to agree with Kells (and others) on lines 582–3 does not entail agreement with his views on the impropriety of Or.'s question to Apollo in the prologue (32–7); quite clearly, the point Kells takes from these lines cannot be made so obliquely, and his interpretation errs in its attempt to uncover negative characterization of Or. and El. at every point. Or. is fairly colourless, but El. is presented sympathetically, and we are on her side; the moral dubiety of her position does not detract from this sympathy—it enhances it. Not only in the theatre, but also in life, we can sympathize with those who commit even the most terrible crimes, if we can understand the circumstances, the pain, and the suffering that drove them to do so.
[108] So Clyt. recognizes that her arguments will never persuade El. (547, 551; cf. Winnington-Ingram (1980), 246).
[109] Precisely Clyt.'s complaint at 523–4.

own complaint is that her mother and Aegisthus positively undermine her own *timē*. The similarity in complaints, however, becomes a similarity in character when, as the exchange develops into the invective which we are to regard as the normal pattern of communication between the two, Electra concludes (605–9): 'So denounce me before all as worthless [*kakē*], garrulous, full of *anaideia*—whatever you like; if I am [by nature, *pephuka*] familiar with these things, I hardly put your nature to shame [σχεδόν τι τὴν σὴν οὐ καταισχύνω φύσιν].' Electra *is* vulnerable to the charge of *anaideia*, of deficiency in the *aidōs* she owes her mother, and it is important that she acknowledges, albeit ironically, the legitimacy of this charge. Even more significant is the possibility of a similarity in *phusis* (nature) between the two women. In saying that she does not *kataischunein* her mother's *phusis*, Electra is both offering a perversion of the traditional ideal, normally appropriate to men rather than to women,[110] that one should live up to the reputation of one's parent, and affecting irony, because it is clear that she is trying to shame her mother by imputing to her the negative qualities of 605–7; but the real irony is that the similarity in *phusis* between the two is genuine.[111]

Clytemnestra immediately takes up the challenge, accusing her daughter of *hubris* (613)[112] and *anaideia* (αἰσχύνης ἄτερ, without *aischunē* = *aidōs*, 615). Electra has just claimed that she is indifferent to any charge of *anaideia* her mother might make, and to any damage such a charge might do her reputation; her reaction to Clytemnestra's words in 612–15 is therefore surprising (616–21):[113] 'Know well that I am ashamed of these things [τῶνδέ μ᾽ αἰσχύνην ἔχειν],[114] even if I do not seem so to you. I know that my conduct is excessive and unfitting; but your enmity and your actions compel me by force to act in this way; shameful deeds [*aischra*] are taught by shameful deeds [*aischra*].' It might be possible to regard the sentence 'I know ... unfitting,' as referring only to Electra's failure to act in accordance with her status, and thus to relatively minor breaches of decorum, such as being seen

---

[110] Cf. 1.2.1 at n. 85.

[111] Cf. Kirkwood (1958), 140; Segal (1966), 499; Winnington-Ingram (1980), 246; Blundell (1989), 169, 172.

[112] The offence which, she recognizes (5232–4), El. most often attributes to her (cf. 271, 790, 794).

[113] Cf. Linforth (1963), 118. On the depth of El.'s self-awareness here, see Whitman (1951), 165; Lesky (1983), 167; on self-awareness in Soph. in general, see Diller (1956). Stebler (1971: 87) sees El.'s *aischunē* here as a 'bestimmte Form des Gewissens'.

[114] This use of *aischunē* with an objective genitive may be considered as a periphrasis for a retrospective use of *aischunomai*; see further below, 5.3.2.

out of doors, were it not for the fact that she says τῶνδε μ' αἰσχύνην
ἔχειν ('I am ashamed of *these things*'), for 'these things' must refer to
Clytemnestra's accusations of *hubris* and lack of *aischunē* (= *aidōs*),
specifically lack of *aischunē* for her mother. Electra therefore does
experience an instinctive feeling that her lack of respect for her
mother is reprehensible; but she goes on to justify her unseasonable
and unseemly conduct with regard to the need to retaliate (as, in effect,
did Clytemnestra at 523-4)—shameful deeds are taught by shameful
deeds; is this not the justification of conduct which is *aischron* in terms
of *dikē*? Such justification is thus (*pace* Adkins) clearly possible; the
significance is that while Electra exploits this line of argument herself,
she refuses to allow Clytemnestra to do the same.[115]

In 605-9, moreover, Electra suggested that if she was full of *anaideia*,
this was due to the *phusis* she inherited from her mother; in 616-21
she accepts the charge of *anaideia*, but explains it in terms of the
education she has received at her mother's hands; in terms of both
sides of the great fifth-century antithesis between heredity and
education, *phusis* (nature) and *nomos* (convention, law), Electra's
character, from which springs her conduct, including her eventual
participation in matricide, is the counterpart of her mother's.

In the *agōn*, then, the theme of *aidōs*, both the familial variety and
that appropriate in women, keeps before our eyes a parallelism
between Electra and Clytemnestra and a balance of contradictions in
Electra's own arguments which play no small role in the articulation of
the moral dialectic of the play. The effect created by the *agōn*, however,
is also apparent at earlier stages in the action. The *kommos* which
doubles as the *parodos* of the play comes to an end with five lines in
which *aidōs* appears in a traditional guise (245-50): 'For if he that died
lies wretched, mere earth, nothing, and they do not pay the penalty
with their lives, all mortals will lose their *aidōs* and *eusebeia*.' The theme
of the departure of *aidōs* from a corrupt world is a common one,[116]
while the notion that punishment of the guilty will reinforce traditional values recalls the arguments of the Erinyes in *Eumenides*.[117] In

---

[115] Clyt.'s response to this is to dismiss, as did El. at 558-60, the argument from retaliation and to concentrate on the disgraceful aspect, the lack of *aidōs* of the other's
conduct; El. has just shown signs of *aidōs*, but Clyt. hears only one more reference to her
'shameful deeds'. Again, in spite of the moral partiality of her argument, our sympathies,
especially in this moment of weakness, are with El.

[116] Cf. Hes. *WD* 197-200 (2.1 above); Thgn. 289-92, 647-8 (2.3.4 above); Eur. *Me.*
439-40 (Ch. 5 n. 30 and 5.5 below).

[117] 490-516; cf. 3.4 above at n. 140.

this passage both *aidōs* and *eusebeia* may be the impulses which prevent one committing murder, especially within the family (and *eusebeia* may have a specifically religious connotation), but there may also be a subsidiary notion that both these qualities are required in those who avenge the murder of their kin, and so it seems likely that Electra believes that her retaliation is demanded by *aidōs* and *eusebeia* and that she will manifest these qualities in carrying it out.

In her next utterance, however, in the ensuing spoken scene, the theme of *aidōs* resurfaces in a rather different light; already in 254-60 she expresses sentiments which are very close to those of 616-21, admitting that her own conduct is discreditable but justifying it in terms of the need to retaliate: 'I am ashamed [*aischunomai*], ladies, if you imagine that my grief is excessive, but, since force compels me to act in this way, excuse me. For how could any noble woman not act thus, seeing paternal ills, as I do day and night, growing rather than declining?'[118] Although Electra's *aischunē* here is less significant than in the later passage (merely embarrassment regarding conduct unfitting in a woman of her status, whereas in 616 it also implies disquiet with regard to her lack of *aidōs* for her mother), it is important that she recognizes something of the ambivalence of her conduct; her *aischunē* indicates that she is not behaving as a noblewoman should in normal circumstances, yet she justifies her conduct in terms of loyalty to her own nobility (*eugeneia*).[119] The 'compulsion' which makes her act in this way is compelling only in terms of her own values and outlook, and it is part of her tragedy that she is compelled to act in ways which she perceives, with more or less clarity, to be discreditable.

So Electra's statement that she is acting to safeguard *aidōs* is immediately qualified by a statement that this very conduct causes her to act in ways which *aidōs* (or *aischunē*) should preclude. There was also mention of *eusebeia* in 250, and just as her statement of the need for *aidōs* is immediately balanced by the opening lines of her speech at 254-60, so her remark about *eusebeia* is qualified by the words with which she concludes the same speech at 307-9; unless her father's murderers pay the penalty, she claimed, *eusebeia* would depart from the earth; she thus sets herself up as champion of *eusebeia*, a position she maintains throughout the play;[120] it is therefore surprising that she

[118] With the words of force and compulsion in 256 cf. 620.
[119] Cf. n. 51 above.
[120] See 589-90, 968-9, and cf. the chorus at 1058-97; El. claims *eusebeia* for herself no less than does Ant. (n. 13 above); cf. Lesky (1983), 163-4.

ends the speech, in which she justifies her retaliation with reference to the insults she suffers at her mother's hands, with the words: 'In such circumstances, my friends, it is not possible to *sōphronein* or to *eusebein*; rather in the midst of evils there is every necessity to practise evils.' The pursuit of *eusebeia*, then, necessitates its negation.[121] For Electra herself the sense, both of these lines and of 254–60, is that propriety (for the reference of *sōphronein* and *eusebein* in 307–8, as of *aischunomai* in 254, is to behaviour appropriate for an unmarried noblewoman) must be sacrificed to higher imperatives, but the effect of these two passages, which open and close her speech, is to highlight the problematic nature of her conduct; indeed, the very parallelism between Electra and her mother, which is articulated in the *agōn* by means of the theme of shame, is foreshadowed—'in the midst of evils there is every necessity to practise evils.' Both justify conduct which is *aischron* in terms of *dikē*.[122]

In three plays, then, *Oedipus Coloneus*, *Ajax*, and *Electra*, the contrast between limited, personal, and self-assertive aspects of the conglomerate of traditional, honour-based values and wider aspects, which to a large extent limit the self-assertion of individuals, constitutes a major theme. In these plays the two fundamental, traditional, and related senses of *aidōs* as concern for one's own honour (concern with what most immediately concerns one's own honour) and positive respect for the honour of others (which raises the issue of the ways in which one's own honour relates to that of others and to generalized standards of appropriateness) are repeatedly set at variance in a way which underlines the moral partiality of several characters and which contributes in no small degree to the articulation of the ethical background against which the action takes place.

[121] Cf. Winnington-Ingram (1980), 225. The sentiment contrasts with that of the Aeschylean Electra, who wanted to be 'more *sōphrōn*' and 'more *eusebēs*' than her mother (*Cho.* 140–1). Sheppard (1918*a*: 137) suggests that the *sōphrosunē* and *eusebeia* of El. may have become a *topos*, and (1918*b*: 84–5) develops the idea that Soph.'s treatment of these themes reveals the essential contradiction in El.'s conduct which constitutes a large part of her tragedy. On *Cho.* 140–1 and *El.* 307–9, cf. Segal (1966), 500; Lesky (1983), 163.

[122] 308–9 clearly bear comparison with 621; cf. Winnington-Ingram (1980), 223–4; Blundell (1989), 171.

4.2.3. Philoctetes

There is no instance of the word *aidōs* in the *Philoctetes*, yet the play none
the less provides us with a perceptive and convincing representation of
the emotion in circumstances in which the ethical suppositions on
which it rests are put to the test. The question of *aidōs* is raised by the
issue of deceit, the basic assumption being that it is *aischron* to tell lies.[123]
Odysseus first alludes to the deception of Philoctetes in lines 50-3, in
which he prepares Neoptolemus for the hearing of something *kainon*
(new, unusual, 52), in the execution of which the youth must prove
himself *gennaios* (noble, 51); much of the remainder of the play will be
concerned with the question of whether one who is truly *gennaios* can
bring himself to carry out such a plan. The plan is then unveiled (54-69);
Neoptolemus is to claim that he left Troy in anger at being denied the
arms of his father—an extreme 'heroic' response, calculated to impress
upon Philoctetes that Neoptolemus is *gennaios* in the sense that his
character is true to that of his father.[124] In lines 64-7, on the other hand,
the contrasting, unheroic nature of Odysseus is revealed; Neoptolemus
may say anything he likes against him in the course of his tale; nothing,
no matter how bad, will cause him pain. This Odysseus, then, does not
care what people say about him—he is *anaidēs*.[125]

The subject of *anaideia* is raised explicitly in the conclusion to
Odysseus' speech (79-85): he knows that lies are foreign to Neoptolemus' nature, his *phusis*,[126] and admits that the execution of the plan

---

[123] Cf. frr. 79 and 352 Radt. Segal (1966: 475) suggests that the remarks of Orestes in
the prologue of Soph.'s *El.* (57-63) on the use of deceit as a means of overcoming Clyt.
and Aeg. are to be read with the discreditable nature of deceit in mind. This may be true;
certainly the action of his father's murderers is frequently described as deceitful (114,
125, 197, 279, etc.; cf. Segal (1966), 511; (1981), 254), and thus we may have another
parallelism between El.'s side and Clyt.'s. Or.'s rhetorical question ('What does it pain me
... ?', 59-60), however, need not be taken as a sign of his hesitation—the words could be
delivered so as to suggest that Or. feels *no* misgivings. Nor are his words to be seen as
referring directly to deceit; as Garner (1987: 15) points out, their immediate reference is
to be the ill omen of fabricating one's own death, an omen Or. is prepared to risk. Yet he
expresses himself in a way that draws attention to the moral dubiety of his enterprise: 'In
my opinion, nothing that is said with profit [*kerdos*] is bad' (61); this obvious overstep-
ping of the mark must alert the audience to the possibility of *aischrokerdeia* (see n. 11
above); cf. Blundell (1989), 173 and n. 84.

[124] Even Achilles, however, does not express his heroic resentment by actually leaving
Troy, although he contemplates doing so (9. 356-63).

[125] Cf. the Merchant at 607-8.

[126] Achilles' hatred of duplicity appears at 9. 312-13; cf. Knox (1964), 121; Kamerbeek
(1980), 21.

will require *anaideia*[127] on Neoptolemus' part, but holds out the promise of success (victory, *nikē*), and suggests that *anaideia* in the present will not rule out a future reputation for justice and *eusebeia* (thus suggesting that concern for such a reputation must for the moment be suspended). More than this, however, is the implication that success in itself can secure a reputation for justice and *eusebeia*, even if the means to that success involve *anaideia*.[128] Thus, as with his use of *gennaios* in 51, he retains the prescriptive sense of these words (he does not deny that a reputation for justice or *eusebeia* is a good thing to have), but distorts the descriptive (implying that one can act in ways normally considered *adikon* or *dussebes* and yet still be called *dikaios* and *eusebēs*).

This argument makes it clear that it is Neoptolemus' *aidōs* that Odysseus is trying to forestall. He assumes, therefore, and not unreasonably given the traditional connection between *aidōs* and 'what people say', that he will be able to do so if he allays the youth's fears that his reputation may suffer. Yet he himself makes pointed reference to Neoptolemus' *phusis* (79–80), and this suggests something more than mere concern for reputation; if it is against one's *phusis* to act in a certain way, will the intellectual appreciation that one can act in that way without damage to one's reputation be enough to enable one to perform the action without qualms? This question is already fore-shadowed by the reference to Neoptolemus' *phusis*, but it is one of which Odysseus is unaware; for him the end justifies the means, and any doubts about the moral character of a course of action can be dispelled by the knowledge that it can be carried out with no ill effects.[129]

---

[127] 83–4, νῦν δ' εἰς ἀναιδὲς ἡμέρας μέρος βραχὺ | δός μοι σεαυτόν. It is likely that εἰς ἀναιδές is to be taken in isolation, rather than that ἀναιδές also qualifies μέρος (von Erffa (1937), 117; Webster (1970); Kamerbeek (1980); against Jebb (1898), ad loc.). Jebb, however, is right to point out that if ἀναιδές = ἀναίδεια we should expect the article, and it is beside the point to argue, as does Kamerbeek, that the abstract noun proper (ἀναίδεια) could occur without the article, since the argument is not about the usage of abstract nouns, but about that of substantival adjectives. The other possibility considered by Kamerbeek, which is von Erffa's interpretation, is to translate 'for a shameless deed'; here one might expect τι, but perhaps the ellipse of τι is less surprising than that of the article. The use of the adjective, however interpreted, is certainly unusual, but if the passage is corrupt, no convincing emendation has been forthcoming; I suspect that εἰς ἀναιδές is an attempt to convey the sense of εἰς τὸ ἀναιδές, which must have proved metrically recalcitrant at this point. Webster can adduce no real parallel for his suggestion that the phrase is adverbial.

[128] See M. C. Nussbaum (1976–7), 37 with 51 n. 29.

[129] On Od.'s 'consequentialist' reasoning, see M. C. Nussbaum (1976–7), 29–39.

The opposition between Neoptolemus' concern for the character of one's actions and Odysseus' stress on results is maintained in the ensuing dialogue; Neoptolemus replies by paraphrasing the *aidōs* which the plan arouses in him (he is pained to hear Odysseus' proposals and abhors the idea of carrying them out, 86–7) and by referring to the incompatibility of such conduct with his *phusis* (88–9).[130] His reaction, then, is instinctive, as we might expect from one whose *phusis* it is to reject deceit. Yet he is unwilling also to reject his mission outright; he has been sent as Odysseus' assistant by the army, and he is reluctant to be called a traitor (93–4). This concern is not ultimately decisive in ensuring Neoptolemus' co-operation, but it does suggest his inability to follow the dictates of his *phusis* at this early stage; it is also, recognizably, rooted in *aidōs*. One kind of concern for his honour and reputation, therefore, different even from that envisaged by Odysseus, makes him susceptible to Odysseus' arguments; but he is not yet ready to give in—he would rather behave honourably and fail (καλῶς δρῶν ἐξαμαρτεῖν, 94–5) than succeed basely (νικᾶν κακῶς, 95).

Neoptolemus thus uses the adverbs *kalōs* and *kakōs* in a co-operative moral sense, and values means and intentions over ends and results. His moral scruples here, moreover, are clearly rooted in his sense of honour; but honour is never a uniquely co-operative concept, and in the stichomythia which follows Neoptolemus is forced to choose between co-operative and competitive aspects of his concern for honour. At first he remains true to his principles (100), and protests that lying is *aischron* (108); Odysseus denies that this is so if lying brings success (security, 109; cf. 111, *kerdos*),[131] but for Neoptolemus this is simply a sign of his elder companion's *anaideia*.[132] Odysseus' sophistic arguments, then, do not convince the youth, yet in 112 Neoptolemus asks after the nature of the *kerdos* to which reference was made in 111, and, on learning that he cannot become the sacker of Troy without Philoctetes' arrows, he agrees at 120 to the deception, 'dismissing all *aischunē*' (= *aidōs*). Odysseus does hold out other

[130] His awareness of his own *phusis* will prove important; see Diller (1956), 71.

[131] Security, *sōtēria*, is an important idea in the play; Rose (1976: 53) regards this as an indication of Soph.'s adaptation of sophistic theories of the origin of culture.

[132] 110, 'How can one bring oneself to say such things with a steady eye?' (πῶς οὖν βλέπων τις ταῦτα τολμήσει λακεῖν;) N. thus alludes to the common manifestation of *aidōs* in the eyes and to the fact that *aidōs* should make it difficult to look those who disapprove of one's conduct in the eye. Cf. n. 50 above; also Class (1964), 74; Stebler (1971), 103. N.'s use of τολμήσει also hints at *anaideia*, which is commonly felt to require boldness or daring.

inducements, to the effect that Neoptolemus' reputation will not suffer through deceit (119), but it is the possibility that he may lose the glory of being the sacker of Troy that convinces the latter. The position of neither has changed—Odysseus still promotes end over means and Neoptolemus still holds that lies are *aischron*; it is simply that he is willing to abandon his *aischunē* in order to win fame as a warrior, and believes that to do so will be as easy as Odysseus says it is. He is plainly portrayed as naïve, and his swift abandonment of his untested principles may have struck some in the original audience as the inevitable compromising of youthful idealism in a harsh world; yet there are indications enough of the reprehensible nature of Odysseus' plan, of which any audience cannot but be aware, and it will be clear that, in ignoring a feeling of *aidōs* or *aischunē*, Neoptolemus is doing something which rarely comes off well in tragedy. His change of heart may not appear inevitable, but such an eventuality must at least be present as likely or possible in the minds of the audience as they watch the play unfold,[133] and this must colour one's impression of the young man's subsequent words and deeds.

Neoptolemus' decision to abandon his *aischunē* is very soon put to the test by his association with Philoctetes. First, the plan requires that Neoptolemus win the confidence of his prey, and accordingly a form of *philia*, though based on deceit, is created between the two. Even this false friendship, however, brings him into contact with one whose ethical suppositions seem close to his own, as he expressed them in the prologue.[134] Then there is the possibility of pity, which is raised, in all sincerity, it seems,[135] by the chorus at 169–90. Neoptolemus is also placed in a position of stress by Philoctetes' supplication, which takes place at 468–506, after the former has made as if to depart at 461. Although the irony of this passage is that Philoctetes entreats Neoptolemus to do exactly what the execution of the plan requires (to

[133] Likely: Seale (1972), 98; possible: Linforth (1956), 105; Erbse (1966), 182.

[134] See Rose (1976: 64–80) on the development of ties of friendship between the two men which eventually become genuine; Rose relates this to sophistic 'social contract' theories. On real points of contact between the two even before N. confesses his deceit, see Rose (1976: 67) on 411–60, where there does seem to be a genuine agreement on the merits of the heroes at Troy; cf. Kirkwood (1958), 146; Alt (1961), 151. Erbse (1966: 189–90) rules this kind of interpretation illegitimate, since N. has given no sign that he is not merely carrying out the plan of deceit, but the point is that the audience have seen the prologue, they know where N.'s deepest sympathies lie, they are on the alert for a change of heart, and it will often be unclear to them, as the play progresses, to what extent N.'s words and deeds betoken mere deceit or genuine identification with Phil.; see Seale (1972), 98.

[135] See Linforth (1956), 106; Seale (1972), 99; Rose (1976), 66 and n. 42.

take him on board ship), part of the effect of the appeal is also to reveal that the arguments used by Odysseus in the prologue may be employed to quite different ends and that there are alternatives to his definitions of important terms.

At 485 Philoctetes falls at Neoptolemus' knees, and thus probably effects the ritual contact of 'full' supplication; in doing so he creates a situation of tension in which *aidōs* is felt to be appropriate and which places structures of honour under stress; we have seen that Neoptolemus is susceptible to *aidōs* and concerned about honour, and it can hardly be that the supplication has no effect on him, especially when he is faced with the appeal to pity (501) of a lame and helpless individual grovelling at his feet. Most importantly, though, Philoctetes also employs the regular suppliant appeal to the concern of the supplicated for his own reputation.[136] Like Odysseus, then, he uses the argument from reputation, and, to complete the parallel, employs many of the same terms (473–9):[137]

The conveyance [of Philoctetes back to the Greek mainland] is a source of much annoyance, I know [ἔξοιδα, 474; cf. 79], but endure [τλῆθι, 475; cf. τόλμα, 82]; truly, for the noble [*gennaioi*] the shameful [*aischron*] is inimical and the good [*chrēston*] glorious. If you fail to perform this action, an ugly reproach [an *oneidos* that is not *kalon*] awaits you, but if you do perform it, great will be your fame, if I return alive to Oeta.

To Odysseus' perverse use of *gennaios* in 51 Philoctetes now opposes a general formulation with which few would disagree, and offers Neoptolemus good repute if he helps him and bad if he does not. Philoctetes' argument from reputation, however, is based on co-operative standards, and so the chief point in these lines is that they remind Neoptolemus of the co-operative side of the code of honour to which he himself subscribes; thus we can imagine that the maxim that the *gennaios* hates the *aischron* painfully recalls to Neoptolemus his abandonment of his commitment to his own standards of nobility in favour of a course of action which he recognized instinctively as *aischron*.

Rose[138] claims that Philoctetes' idea of *gennaios*, 'boldness',[139] and *eukleia* is 'worlds away' from 'traditional heroic virtues', implying that

---

[136] Cf. *OC* 258–62, 282–3 (cf. n. 19 above), 902–3 (n. 22 and text above).

[137] Cf. Kirkwood (1958), 243 n. 23.

[138] (1976), 68; cf. Blundell (1989), 199–200.

[139] Referring to τλῆθι (475) and τόλμησον (481), which, however, denote 'endurance' rather than 'boldness' here.

he is adapting these terms to a non-traditional application. This, however, is incorrect; we saw in the Theognidea[140] how any number of co-operative moral virtues could be seen as requirements in those designated by essentially aristocratic terms like *gennaios*, and we should not forget that for an audience watching a play in 409 BC it is not only the harshest elements of the morality of the *Iliad* that are 'traditional'. Equally, there are instances enough in the *Odyssey* of good reputation being acquired by helping others,[141] and this is of particular relevance in the case of those who help guests and suppliants, while the idea that the *gennaios* should pursue the good (*chrēston*) and reject the shameful (*aischron*) is fundamental.[142] Both Neoptolemus and the audience, then, will recognize that Philoctetes' use of these terms in a co-operative context is normal and traditional, and Neoptolemus will be reminded of his own abandoned commitment to the quieter side of the code of honour.

Given the impression of Neoptolemus' character conveyed in the prologue, one is bound to consider the effect that Philoctetes' words may be having on their addressee; dramatic irony here produces a formidable emotional effect, as our recognition of the essential decency of both characters leads to unease at Philoctetes' uncomfortable reminders of the standards which Neoptolemus has abandoned and to sympathy for Philoctetes, the victim of deception. Our unease at Neoptolemus' abandonment of his untested and unreflective principles is increased and exacerbated as the shortcomings and difficulties of his acquiescence in deceit are highlighted, and we are on the look-out, I feel sure, for equivalent signs of discomfort on his part. This being so, it is significant that we are given frequent reminders of the values espoused by Neoptolemus in the prologue, particularly of his commitment to honour and desire to avoid disgrace. At 524–5, for example, Neoptolemus is made to feign one particular kind of *aidōs*—as part of the deceit, the chorus (507–18) and their leader (522–3) have affirmed their pity for Philoctetes and their willingness to convey him homeward, and Neoptolemus affects embarrassment that he should show less initiative in helping a *xenos* than his inferiors: 'It would be

---

[140] 2.3.4 above. Note also that at Thuc. 3. 82. 7 and 83. 1, the *locus classicus* on the kind of cynical misapplication of moral terminology practised by Od., *gennaiotēs* is used of the civilized, gentlemanly qualities which are opposed to the ruthless self-seeking of those involved in faction.

[141] See 1.3.5 above, *ad fin.*, with Ch. 1 n. 194.

[142] Cf. Adkins (1960*a*), 189 (on the prologue of this play); M. C. Nussbaum (1976–7), 44–5.

unfitting [*aischra*] for me to appear deficient in comparison with you as far as appropriate action is concerned.' There is a note of aristocratic politeness about this, and Neoptolemus may be simulating the gentlemanly qualities which Philoctetes expects in the *gennaios*; certainly, his use of *aischra* in the context of failure to help another echoes the latter's words at 475–9.[143] The point is, however, that since the words are a simulation, we have no way of knowing whether they conceal any real *aidōs* on Neoptolemus' part, whether he does in fact share the values of Philoctetes; at the same time, they keep the theme of nobility and honour, and the thought of Neoptolemus' scruples in the prologue, before us, and maintain the emotional tension.

The prospect of *aidōs* on Neoptolemus' part is further raised when, after Philoctetes has fallen into an exhausted sleep following the attack of his illness, Neoptolemus rejects the chorus's promptings (827–38) that he should take the bow and leave the man. This is impossible, he replies, for the prophecy demanded both (841), and thus to imagine that possession of the bow alone constituted success would be an empty boast—'it brings an *aischron oneidos* to boast falsely of success in an unfinished task' (842). As Winnington-Ingram notes,[144] in this sentence Neoptolemus combines the twin considerations between which he had to decide in the prologue—that it is disgraceful to fail and that it is disgraceful to lie. It is, however, the competitive aspect which is the stronger here, and the disgrace which is explicitly referred to is that of leaving an enterprise unfinished, the context in which *aischron* makes its first appearances in Greek literature.[145] Is Neoptolemus, however, solely concerned with success? On the one hand, he does not simply carry out Odysseus' original plan, the aim of which seemed to be the acquisition of the bow and arrows (77–8, 113–15); on the other, it is unlikely that the statement that the prophecy mentioned both Philoctetes and his weapons is a mere excuse: even Odysseus (at 101) said that Philoctetes must be captured, and the Merchant, too, seems in no doubt but that both the bow and the man are required (591–7). We should assume, then, that Neoptolemus does believe what he says about the prophecy.[146] At the same time, he also

---

[143] Cf. Rose (1976), 69 (who, however, claims that N. imitates Phil.'s 'untraditionally humane ethics').

[144] (1980), 288.

[145] Cf. 1.1.3 above.

[146] On the progressive and partial revelation of the prophecy, see D. B. Robinson (1969), 45–51; Seale (1972), 96; Easterling (1978), 31–4; Winnington-Ingram (1980), 292. All are agreed that, while the final version, given by N. at 1324–36 and endorsed by

echoes both Philoctetes' words at 476-7 and his own of the prologue, and it can hardly be that thoughts of the moral character of deceit and the contradiction this poses to his desire for a good reputation are not to be imagined as occurring to him when he uses these terms. This is not the first time he has prevaricated (cf. 639-40), and it seems that his expression of a conventional kind of *aidōs* (his words in 842 are virtually a *gnōmē*) conceals a growing uncertainty about his behaviour.[147]

Sophocles has thus used terms from the *aidōs*-complex to keep the question of *aidōs* on Neoptolemus' part before us, and, if we entertained suspicions that use of these terms masked growing discomfort with his mission, we are proved right when Neoptolemus finally expresses the pain which the deception is causing him, and describes it as vexing him *palai* ('long since', 906, 913).[148] The expression of this discomfort is finally caused by means of the pressure built up by Philoctetes' assumption of nobility in Neoptolemus;[149] at 874-6 he congratulates Neoptolemus on the 'ease' ($\dot{\epsilon}\nu$ $\epsilon\dot{\nu}\chi\epsilon\rho\epsilon\hat{\iota}$) with which he bore the sight and sound of his sufferings, and attributes this to his *phusis*, which is $\epsilon\dot{\nu}\gamma\epsilon\nu\dot{\eta}s$ ... $\kappa\dot{a}\xi$ $\epsilon\dot{\nu}\gamma\epsilon\nu\hat{\omega}\nu$ ('noble and of noble stock'), but Neoptolemus' position is far from easy; he can go on no longer, and gives voice to his difficulty[150] at 897. Philoctetes then asks if the 'difficulty' (or 'annoyance', *duschereia*)[151] of the disease has persuaded him not to take him on board ship (900-1), but in fact the *duschereia* of the disease has persuaded him in quite another direction, and produced in him a different sort of 'difficulty': 'All is *duschereia*, when one abandons one's own *phusis* and does what is not fitting' (902-3). Philoctetes' own pain, then, has induced an analogous pain in Neoptolemus,[152] the pain of conscience.[153] His feeling is clearly

---

Heracles at 1418-40, may be authoritative, it cannot be read back into all stages of the drama; it is pointless to treat the characters' knowledge of the oracle historically and to ask, in connection with the present passage or 1324-36, how N. knows and why he does not say what he knows sooner. Cf. also Lesky (1983), 175-6 (with further references).

[147] Cf. D. B. Robinson (1969), 48.
[148] Cf. 966; also, on the significance of *palai* in these lines, Winnington-Ingram (1980), 284; Lesky (1983), 172.
[149] Cf. Linforth (1956), 131.
[150] Difficulty or *aporia* is the dominant note of this scene; cf. 895, 908, 969, 974; see Alt (1961), 159, 163; Stebler (1971), 104-5; Lesky (1983), 172.
[151] Cf. 473, also in the context of the disease.
[152] See Rose (1976), 73; cf. Segal (1981), 336.
[153] Cf. Stebler (1971), 104, on N.'s *Gewissensnot*. For words indicating pain, see 806, 906, 913, 1011. Some commentators attempt to deny all reference to psychology and inner life in the play; Erbse (1966: 178) says there is 'no psychological development in

instinctive,[154] it arises in spite of the efforts he must have made already to ignore it, but it is also reflective, based on an appreciation of his own *phusis* and on a prolonged confrontation of a dilemma.[155] That this feeling may be described as *aidōs* is suggested by the mention of appropriateness (τὰ μὴ προσεικότα) in 903, and confirmed by 906: 'I shall appear *aischros*; this has long been a source of pain to me.' Fear of appearing 'base'[156] and concern for 'how things look' quite clearly indicate *aidōs*—here based on the fact that Neoptolemus has 'hidden what he should not and spoken the most *aischron* of words' (908-9). It is thus clear that this *aidōs* has a retrospective aspect: it is based on action in the past. It is also, however, articulated with the familiar reference to the future disapproval of others (φανοῦμαι, 906); but this does not mean that Neoptolemus is afraid of opprobrium and no more. Despite his concern for the outward aspect of his conduct, he has no very clear idea of whose disapproval he might incur, unless that of Philoctetes. There is also the question of his *phusis*. To do what is not fitting is to abandon one's *phusis* (903-4); Neoptolemus thus believes that he has acted contrary to his essential nature, and it is this which causes him pain. He does not simply acknowledge that other people find deceit disgraceful; he states, *tout court*, that deceit is wrong (ἃ μὴ δεῖ, 909), and it is part of his very being to believe that this is so.[157] Stebler[158] claims that Neoptolemus' *phusis* cannot be seen as 'seine eigentliche Ich-Natur' (or, as we might say, cannot form the basis of his

the modern sense' in N.'s case, without defining 'development', or enlightening us as to what the 'modern sense' is and how N.'s characterization differs from it. Similarly, Vidal-Naquet, in Vernant and Vidal-Naquet (1981: 178), is contemptuous of those who find 'psychology' in *Phil.*, preferring to see N.'s development in terms of the civic institution of the *ephebeia* which he believes is embodied in the play; but this is to deny the obvious import of the text in favour of an abstract substratum of symbolism.

[154] Cf. Alt (1961), 160.

[155] On the way in which N's commitment to his principles develops from emotional unease to informed moral decision (a process which she relates to Arist.'s views on excellence of character and *proairesis*), see Blundell (1988), esp. 139-42.

[156] Applied to a person *aischros* usually bears a physical sense (ugly); for this transferred use, cf. 1284.

[157] N.'s moral standards and his *aidōs* thus seem to be part of his *phusis*, but this hardly allows us to attribute to Soph. the view that *aidōs* can exist by nature, because first, the poet is not writing a systematic discourse on *nomos* and *phusis* and secondly, it is not necessary to suppose that, because a certain kind of *aidōs* is part of one's *phusis* as a young adult, it is innate. The play itself might support the view that both innate capacity and education (that which N. receives at the hands of Phil.) are necessary for the development of a sound character (see Rose (1976), 85-9); this is the Protagorean/Democritean position (see 6.2 and 6.3.2 below), and Soph. may have been aware of ideas such as that of Democ. B 33 DK, to the effect that education can create a new *phusis*.

[158] (1971), 104.

own idea of his self), because it also encompasses imperatives based on loyalty to aristocratic virtue, represented by the accumulation of terms such as *gennaios* and *eugenes*, and to his father (cf. 904–5, also 89); but Neoptolemus *is* of noble birth, and his background must be an essential part of himself—in living up to aristocratic standards he is also being true to himself.[159] His concern to live up to the image of his father is also important, given that the paternal model is a frequent focus of *aidōs*;[160] but reference to this model does not indicate observance of external standards, since a human being's most deeply internalized moral standards are likely to be based on precisely this source of reference. Again, there is the difficulty of deciding whether fear of falling short of parental standards can be regarded exclusively as a guilt- or as a shame-reaction;[161] in this case, too, it would be possible to describe Neoptolemus' *aidōs* in terms of both, but wrong to claim that either must exclude the other.

The psychology of Neoptolemus' *aidōs*, then, is realistically presented, and the combination of the concern for outward appearances with the reference to personal standards is entirely natural. Thus far, however, he has only given expression to his dilemma; he has abandoned the deceit, but not yet his commitment to the mission itself; he retains the bow which Philoctetes entrusted to him at 776. Philoctetes, however, maintains the pressure on Neoptolemus' sense of *aidōs*; his vehement denunciation of the deceit contains a reproachful reference to Neoptolemus' lack of *aischunē* (= *aidōs*) for a suppliant (929–30),[162] and at 934–5 he observes that his reproaches have been effective—Neoptolemus no longer speaks to him but turns his head away, not because he is deaf to his appeals for the return of the bow, but because he is ashamed.[163] Similarly, at 967–8 Philoctetes once more reminds Neoptolemus of the discreditable nature of deceit, urging him not to set up an *oneidos* for himself in the eyes of men.[164]

---

[159] On N.'s aristocratic *phusis*, see Diller (1956), 71; Lesky (1983), 175 (191–2 on *phusis* in Soph. in general); Blundell (1988); the aristocratic aspect of the references to *phusis* should not be exaggerated, however, to the extent of claiming that, in N., Soph. dramatizes the 'Pindaric' notion of inherited virtue. N.'s essential 'nobility' and his *phusis* must meet with proper education to become effective (see Rose (1976), 87; Blundell (1988), 145) and, as Winnington-Ingram (1980: 310) suggests, terms originally denoting aristocratic virtues may long since have become 'simply those of traditional morality'.

[160] Cf. n. 49 above.

[161] Cf. Introd. 0.3 and 0.4, 4.1.1 (with n. 10), and n. 49 above.

[162] οὐδ᾽ ἐπαισχύνῃ μ᾽ ὁρῶν | τὸν προστρόπαιον, τὸν ἱκέτην, ὦ σχέτλιε; We have seen enough to know that this rhetorical question should be answered in the affirmative. (Cf. Phil. at 1382, where he feels N.'s commitment to helping him is waning.)

[163] See Class (1964), 73; cf. line 110 (n. 132 above).   [164] Cf. Phil.'s words at 477.

Neoptolemus' *aidōs* is not solely concerned with the opinions of others, but these words must none the less increase his difficulty; his direct response to the mention of an *oneidos* is an expression of despair (969–70).

The arrival of Odysseus precludes any decision for the moment, and Neoptolemus remains silent during the exchange between the two old enemies. Even in his silence, however, he apparently gives signs of his discomfort, and Philoctetes regards his pain as provoked by both remorse and pity (1011–12).[165] Neoptolemus, he recognizes, has committed a *hamartia*, an error.[166] Neoptolemus himself had referred to *hamartia* in the prologue when he said that he would rather fail nobly than succeed basely (94–5, καλῶς | δρῶν ἐξαμαρτεῖν μᾶλλον ἢ νικᾶν κακῶς). There the sense of the *hamart*-word was entirely non-moral,[167] but Philoctetes has raised the possibility of moral *hamartia*, and it is with this that we are concerned when Neoptolemus and Odysseus return to the stage at 1222.[168] Neoptolemus says (1224) that he intends to undo his previous *hamartia*, and at 1228 defines this as consisting in his 'disgraceful (*aischrai*) deceptions';[169] at 1234 he explains his desire to give back the bow, and bases this on the recognition that he acquired it *aischrōs* and without *dikē*, and, again, this must refer to deceit.[170] In reply to Odysseus' threats and specious arguments (1241–8) Neoptolemus simply restates his desire to remedy his shameful (*aischra*) *hamartia*.[171]

[165] N. has, then, recovered his principles of the prologue, and Od. recognizes this by acknowledging that his nobility, his *gennaiotēs*, could lead him to jeopardize their mission (1068). This recognition of N.'s qualities by Od. is not new (cf. 79–80), but his use of *gennaios* in 1068 contrasts with that in 51, and reveals that he is aware of the ordinary significance of the word. This use of *gennaios* agrees with that of Phil. at 475–6 (cf. 1402), and there can be no doubt that we are supposed to regard this as the proper application of the word. Rose (1976: 90), however, while recognizing that Od.'s redefinition at 51 is specious and that 1068 represents a popularly acceptable sense, refuses to allow that Phil.'s use at 475–6 is also recognizably conventional. On *gennaios*, see also Alt (1961), 147; Avery (1965), 289; M. C. Nussbaum (1976–7), 32, 36, 44.

[166] On the three senses of *hamartanō* ('miss', 'err', 'offend') in 5th-cent. Gk., see Bremer (1969), 31–64; cf. Ch. 3 n. 105.   [167] See Bremer (1969), 32 n. 32.

[168] Cf. Bremer (1969), 34.   [169] Cf. Phil. at 1136.

[170] Taplin (1971: 36) refers to this scene as a 'reversal and refutation of the prologue'; cf. Goldhill (1987), 72, on the senses of *hamartia*. Poe (1974: 29–31) points out that N.'s concern in attempting to undo his *hamartia* is most emphatically based on his own ideas of what is right, and not on any concern for the will of the gods, and both he (41) and M. C. Nussbaum (1976–7: 47) note that N. is evincing an unusual concern for the rights, as opposed to the interests, of another; this concern is especially manifested in his ultimate decision to abandon Troy and his own and Phil.'s destiny in the name of friendship.

[171] On *hamartia aischra* in this passage Adkins (1960*a*: 183) writes: 'Under traditional

Neoptolemus thus recognizes that he has done wrong in committing his *hamartia*, and takes full responsibility upon himself.[172] Again, since he feels that his conduct has been *aischron*, his reaction to it is presumably one of *aidōs*, but in this scene his *aidōs* is entirely directed at his past actions, and there is not the slightest hint that he is concerned at the prospect of future damage to his reputation. It is clear, then, that in this passage (1224 ff.) we are confronted with an individual who acts according to the promptings of his own conscience, who can characterize his own actions negatively in retrospect without reference to others' opinions, and who, like Odysseus in the *Ajax* and Antigone in the play which bears her name, is prepared to defy the group in order to carry his convictions through (1250-1).[173] His terminology, however, is still that of the *aidōs*-group, and it is therefore of the greatest significance that these terms can be used in the context of an individual's retrospective evaluation of his own conduct, in the context of the moral conscience. Sophocles, it appears, has recognized that when one experiences *aidōs*, one is not simply reacting to the prospect of others' disapproval, but may be responding on the basis of standards which have become part of one's character. Any feeling of *aidōs*, of course, even when it is explicitly related to

values, a *hamartia aischra* is a mistake that has led to a failure.' 'Mistake' seems to render *harmartia*, but, as Bremer (1969: 31–64) demonstrates, *hamartia* is not exclusively non-moral in the 5th cent.; 'that has led to a failure' seems to paraphrase *aischra*, but at no period is there an intrinsic reference to failure *per se* in the adj., except in so far as to do something *aischron* is to fail to match some standard of propriety; but the standard could be any one of a large number of traditional imperatives, and need not simply be the requirement to succeed *simpliciter*. Correspondingly, Adkins's subsequent remarks on this passage are invalid. He goes on: 'To be able to use such a phrase . . . in a situation where a success has been gained, indicates a firmly rooted change in values. . . . The new usage is sufficiently rooted to be understood without explanation, but only a minor assault might be needed to overset it.' Since he finds it 'significant' (1960*a*: 183) that this phrase occurs in a late play of Soph., Adkins presumably regards the 'change in values' as a phenomenon of the later 5th cent. Yet in Hes. success is not to be pursued at all costs, and in the Theognid corpus (2.3.4 above) theft (the pursuit of *kerdos* by improper means) is *aischron* (and note that in Thgn. 607-10 it is profit made from deceit which is *aischron*). One might even claim that the 'firmly rooted change' goes back to the beginning of Gk. lit., for although the evidence for the usage of *aischron* in Homer is scant, the suitors of the *Od.* could, despite their manifest success, be implicated in *aischos* by virtue of their dishonouring of another (see 1.1.3 etc. above).

[172] Stebler (1971: 106) notes the absence of any attempt to excuse himself.

[173] Cf. Rose (1976), 76: this passage 'does mark a particularly self-conscious internalization of the heroic "shame" ethic; terms which normally derive their validity from the approval or disapproval of the group are here held up as a basis for defying the group's opinion.' Rose also relates this to sophistic thought, and hints at Democritus, without mentioning the passages which would best illustrate the phenomenon, viz. Democ. B 84, 244, 264 DK.

'other people' will indicate the activation of an internal source of references based on the standards of society,[174] but the importance of this passage and, to an only slightly lesser extent, of Neoptolemus' earlier manifestations of *aidōs* at 895–975, lies in their presentation of the working of an internalized standard, one which the individual has made his own, as such. We have met passages in which a subjective evaluation of one's own conduct is used as an explanation for the absence of any pang of *aidōs*,[175] but it is only in the *Philoctetes* and the *Ajax* that we have so far encountered a clear and unambiguous representation of *aidōs* as a subjective awareness that a given course of action is against the agent's own principles, regardless of the correspondence or otherwise of those principles with the opinions of others.[176] Thus, while it has always been possible that *aidōs* should rest on standards which one has made one's own, the realization that it can proceed from the moral conscience of the individual may be a phenomenon of the later fifth century.[177]

There is a certain paradox in all this: Neoptolemus' *aidōs* is based on interpretations of key terms like *aischron* and *gennaios* which must roughly correspond to orthodox fifth-century senses, yet in responding to conventional standards he is forced to use his own subjective judgement and to defy the rest of his society—out of obedience to his sense of honour he is prepared to give up the honour that comes from

---

[174] Cf., e.g., 1.7 above.

[175] Cf. 2.3.3 and 3.3 above.

[176] On N.'s conscience, Stebler (1971: 106) writes: 'Neoptolemos' kurze Angaben von 1234 . . . und 1246 zeigen weiter, daß er mit der Vorstellung seines Gewissens-Inhalts den inneren κανών [standard] des spontanen Rechts-Empfindens umgreift, noch nicht aber sein Ich als zentrale Instanz (noch nicht: "Ich habe getan, was mir nicht entspricht.")—In Antigone werden wir auch dieser Stufe von Ich- und Gewissens-Bewußtsein begegnen.' This is quite arbitrary; N. *says*, 'Ich habe getan, was mir nicht entspricht' at 902–3. Stebler claims, however (151 n. 255), that in spite of the stress on *phusis* and 'that which is unfitting' in those lines, the presence of other motives (concern for noble birth, status, shame, etc.) renders the meaning quite different from *Ant.* 523 (the famous statement about Ant.'s loving *phusis*). But N.'s *phusis* drives him just as much as Ant.'s does her, and the latter is also subject to motives other than loyalty to her *phusis*. Nor do I see how a phenomenon present in *Ant.* should be seen as 'not yet' present in *Phil.* Stebler (151 n. 256) also seems to regard Ant.'s positive commitment to do what is right as more important than N.'s retrospective, 'bad' conscience, but this, again, appears to me a quite arbitrary preference.

[177] We shall meet it again in the frr. of Democritus; see 6.3.2 below. Blundell (1988: 142–3; 1989: 211–12, 219) also notes resemblances between N.'s consistency in abiding by his convictions, even to the point of sacrificing valued external goods, and Plato's Socrates; the parallel is certainly relevant, but Soc.'s commitment comes less obviously from *aidōs* than does N.'s (see below, 6.4.2, *ad fin.*).

success and its recognition by one's peers;[178] the subjective aspect of
his *aidōs* is thrown into relief by the fact that it entails a corresponding
neglect of any *aidōs* with regard to the criticism of others, and thus the
roots of Neoptolemus' *aidōs* in his conscience are highlighted in a way
which would be difficult in one whose ethical assumptions were shared
by the rest of his society. Philoctetes, however, does subscribe to the
same standards as Neoptolemus eventually does, and the bond created
between them, in effect, creates a society outside that represented by
Odysseus, and it is to the values of this 'group' that Neoptolemus
responds[179]—but only because these are the values he has made his
own. A deeper paradox, however, confronts the audience of the play:
the relationship between Neoptolemus and Philoctetes and the
commendable conduct of the former surely demonstrate the bank-
ruptcy of the argument that the end justifies the means, yet in this case
the end must be achieved, and it is the will of the gods that it should be
so. There is thus no comfortable solution in which the spectator may
bask, but rather each member of the audience, each reader of the play
is compelled closely to examine his own values in the face of this
fundamental paradox.[180]

The relative paucity of instances of *aidōs* in Sophocles belies the great
importance of the concept; the poet's use of different kinds of *aidōs*
and his creation of tension between them form an important part of
his dramatic technique, and the influence of contemporary thought is
clearly shown in the partiality with which his characters often
approach the terms with which we are concerned. Of crucial importance for our study are the psychological realism, the sheer emotional

---

[178] Cf. Blundell (1989: 219), who points out (220; cf. O'Brien (1967), 33–5) that N.'s
sense of honour, in obedience to which he is prepared to forgo considerable extrinsic
benefits to himself, leads him to manifest a particularly altruistic respect not even for the
interests of a friend, but for his wishes and his rights (cf. n. 170 above).

[179] Cf. Rose (1976), 64–80.

[180] For a summary of views on the play's 'two endings', see Easterling (1978: 33–9),
who herself tends towards the view that the *deux ex machina* produces a positive resolution to the problems set by the play—Phil. goes to Troy, but without giving in to the
Atreidae. Others see the departure of N. and Phil. as the 'real' ending, with the epiphany
of Heracles as a mere addition to square Soph.'s account with the standard version
(Linforth (1956), 150–5; D. B. Robinson (1969), 51–6), while the study by Poe (1974), is
designed to demonstrate the pessimism of the play's close, as revealing the absence of
divine justice and the 'futility of mankind' (51); Winnington-Ingram (1980: 301) notes the
absence of agreement, and Goldhill (1987: 72–3) suggests that final agreement is impossible. Unable to support one suggested interpretation over all others, I wonder whether
this is exactly the response which the play demands.

verisimilitude, of all the extant plays, and in particular, the portrayal of the individual moral conscience at odds with the rest of society in *Antigone*, *Ajax*, and *Philoctetes*.

In term of usage we find that *aidōs* is now less frequent than *aischunē*; *aischunomai* etc. occur ten times, *aideomai* etc. six times, and both are increasingly used not of apprehension for the future, but of concern over an action on the present. Neither is used with an infinitive, but both occur with present participles,[181] and two instances with a conditional clause reinforce this connection with present action.[182] This clearly represents a certain shift in usage, and it is certainly significant that these verbs are now used more frequently of an action that is already begun than to inhibit one which is merely contemplated. Perhaps this concern with present actions does facilitate a move towards a subjective interpretation of the character of one's own conduct, but no very sweeping conclusion should be drawn as regards changes in values or society; it is obvious, for example, that *aidōs* with regard to one's present conduct may still be related to others' future disapproval (as in *Antigone* 510).

---

[181] *aischunomai* etc.: *Aj.* 1307; *Ant.* 540; *OT* 635; *Phil.* 929, 1383; *aideomai*: *Aj.* 506–7.

[182] *El.* 254: *aischunomai*; *Ant.* 510: *epaideomai*. In the remaining instances the two verbs take a direct object.

5

Euripides

Euripides offers the student of *aidōs* a range of occurrences which can only be paralleled by the Homeric poems. This is not simply a consequence of the fact that he survives in greater bulk than do the other tragedians, for even within individual plays *aidōs* and its relatives often occur with considerable frequency. The relative domesticity of setting in many of his plays means that Euripides is often as useful a source of sociological data on *aidōs* as is Homer, but in general the data which emerge regarding the contexts in which *aidōs* is at home rarely make a significant difference to the conclusions we have been able to glean from Homer and others. In the following, then, I have attempted to concentrate on that which is new, significant, or of great thematic importance in the interpretation of individual plays. Thus while I begin by discussing, in turn, self- and other-regarding uses of *aidōs* (and the ways in which these are inextricably linked) and conclude with a survey of passages which extol the value of *aidōs*, the most important sections of this chapter focus on new, retrospective usages of the verbs *aideomai* and *aischunomai* and their relationship to concepts of conscience (5.3), and on the place of *aidōs* in attitudes towards sex and sexuality (5.4), in which connection many interesting questions are raised by the *Hippolytus* in particular.

5.1. PERSONAL HONOUR AND STATUS

5.1.1. Aidōs *in Battle*

Concern for one's personal honour is a basic and pervasive motivating force in Euripidean drama, and is naturally prominent in the martial context. The competitive values of the Homeric poems remain in the forefront; victory is *kalon*, defeat *aischron*,[1] and *aidōs* may still cause one

---

[1] *Supp.* 529–30; cf. the Iliadic exhortation to avoid *aischunē* (disgrace) at *Hcld.* 839–40. The reference to the *polis* here indicates that the community which gives rise to sentiments of collective honour is different from that in Homer, but otherwise the ideas

to be reluctant to flee.[2] Such values are so often the springs of action that they must be regarded as current and uncontroversial. This is not to say, however, that Euripides always presents them uncritically. In *Phoenissae*, for example, Eteocles is subject to exactly the same concern for his honour as are his namesake in Aeschylus and his brother in Sophocles. He sees it as 'unmanliness' to lose the greater share and get the smaller, and is ashamed (*aischunomai*) that his brother should come and get what he wants by force;[3] it would be a reproach on the honour of Thebes if he were to give up his right to rule to his brother in fear of Argive arms (509–14). Eteocles represents himself as concerned both for his own reputation and for that of his city, but his justification is couched in terms which reveal only selfishness; to say that it is *anandria* to give up the greater for the smaller share is to confuse greed with manliness, while his concern for the honour of Thebes barely conceals his reluctance to give up his own privileges. What are understandable motives in Aeschylus and Sophocles are base and mean in Euripides, and Eteocles' selfishness is further highlighted by contrast with the fairness of his brother and through the criticism of his mother.[4]

An instructive contrast with the behaviour of Eteocles in *Phoenissae* is provided by Menoeceus, another character who acts to preserve his

---

are thoroughly Homeric; von Erffa, however (1937: 142), holds that, 'Der Zuruf αἰδώς ist positiv, die Mahnung οὐκ ἀρήξετ' αἰσχύνην negativ' (cf. his discussion of *Hcld.* 813, ibid.); but *aidōs* is inhibitory, and so 'negative' in Homer (see Ch. 1 n. 5). On the disgrace of cowardice in battle, cf. *Hcld.* 700–1, 828–9; also *Tro.* 1190–1. Results may not always be everything, however; at least the defeated can console themselves that defeat after noble resistance is not *aischron* (*Tro.* 401–2). With the ability of the speaker here to deny that a situation popularly considered *aischron* is so, cf. *Supp.* 767–8 (see Szlezak (1986), 57); Theseus' rejection of ordinary opinion in favour of common humanity here is often considered 'new' or 'enlightened' (G. G. A. Murray (1913), 97; Adkins (1960a), 184), but if there is any novelty it can lie only in the expression of the lines, not in their content; the humanity of Thes. in taking part in the burial of fellow human beings not bound by a tie of *philia* is shared by Achilles in the (6. 418–19, 24. 571–90); cf. Odysseus in Soph. *Aj.* (4.2.1 above, with Ch. 4 n. 85) and Thes.'s lack of concern for pollution in *Her.* (Collard (1975), on *Supp.* ad loc.; Vickers (1973), 154–5; 5.3 below).

[2] *Hel.* 805.

[3] This (*Pho.* 510–12) is the first time we have met *aischunomai* with a noun clause; von Erffa (1937: 158) suggests that the verb has its 'root meaning' ('I consider it *aischron*'), but clearly the belief which is constitutive of the emotion of *aidōs* and which is present in any instance of *aideomai* might also be expressed as 'I consider it *aischron*', and, in fact, *aideomai* occurs with a comparable noun clause at *Hcld.* 43–4.

[4] At 531–2 Jocasta asks Et. why he worships Philotimia (Ambition, love of *timē*), the 'worst of divinities', while at 506 Et. himself claims that he holds Tyrannis the greatest of gods. To these two deities Joc. opposes Isotēs (Equality) at 536 and 542; cf. Soph.'s later opposition of Aidōs and Dikē in *OC* (4.1.3 above).

reputation and avoid the charge of cowardice. Menoeceus who, according to Teiresias (913–14), must be sacrificed to secure the safety of Thebes, initially feigns acceptance of his father's plan to save his life, but soon reveals his resolve to commit suicide. Important in his decision is his belief that to flee would be cowardly (994), but his concern for his reputation is combined with a strong sense of responsibility to others; there is no excuse, he says (995–6) for his betrayal of the land that bore him, combining the idea of the opinion of others with a quasi-familial loyalty to his country.[5] Self-regarding and other-regarding motives are further entwined at 999–1005: it would be *aischron* if he were to flee when others are prepared to die in battle; it is the act of a coward to leave, and wherever he might go, he would be revealed as *kakos*. He thus considers how his conduct might compare with that of others and takes account of the external aspect of his actions; but he also considers his responsibility to others (it would also be cowardice to betray his father, his brother, and his city, 1003–4), and it is on this co-operative note that he ends his speech: if everyone contributed to the common good to the best of his ability, cities would have fewer ills and might prosper in the future (1015–18). The indissoluble combination of self- and other-regarding impulses in Menoeceus' motivation is a feature of the traditional notions, first, that it is reprehensible, and so bad for oneself, to fail in one's duty to others and, secondly, that an acknowledged concern for one's honour and one's image is proper and commendable, but there may also be some input from contemporary debate on the compatibility of other-regarding behaviour with self-interest.[6] In Menoeceus there is a perfect coincidence of the two, and he undertakes the ultimate subjection of self to community out of concern for his own reputation.[7] That other-regarding behaviour is often motivated in this way is a particular Euripidean theme; another recurrent technique is the demonstration that a given action or attitude is harmful or reprehensible in one situation or individual, helpful or commendable in another. This, too, may be related to contemporary thought, to that form of relativism which recognizes that the character of a particular action (or

[5] On the reinforcement of patriotism through identification with loyalty to the family, cf. Blundell (1989), 44 (citing Lys. 13. 91 etc.).
[6] On the debate, see Nill (1985).
[7] Cf. Macaria's speech justifying her self-sacrifice at *Hcld.* 500–34, in which concern for the status of herself and her family is combined with fear of mockery, the obligation to show gratitude, and other, practical considerations relating to the quality of life Macaria and her family could expect if she did not offer herself for sacrifice.

whatever) is not fixed but dependent on circumstances;[8] in the contrast between Eteocles and Menoeceus we see that concern for one's reputation is not always good or bad, but sometimes one, sometimes the other.

5.1.2. *Non-Martial Contexts*

It is not only in contexts of war and battle, however, that we find characters expressing concern for their reputations and status. Concern for *timē* is a basic motivation,[9] disgrace is to be feared or avenged,[10] the disgrace of one member of the family affects the others,[11] and the mockery of one's enemies is felt to be unbearable.[12] In the *Alcestis* we see the interplay of self-regarding notions of manliness, extended beyond the martial sphere, with both concern for popular opinion and respect for one's obligations; Admetus accuses his father of cowardice in refusing to die in his stead (642, 717, 721, 723); therefore, he says (725), Pheres will die in disgrace when he does die; this does not bother the old man, however (726), and Admetus laments (727) the prevalence in the old of *anaideia*, reprehensible indifference to one's image in the eyes of others. Pheres, however, picks up the idea of *anaideia* and extends its reference (728): he may be *anaidēs*, but Alcestis was not; she, presumably, had a proper respect for public opinion, but also possessed *aidōs* for her husband as a woman should. Pheres' reply thus combines the two senses of *aidōs* as 'shame'

[8] 'Non-sceptical' relativism; see Nill (1985), 29; cf. *Dissoi Logoi* 2. 2–8 (whether an action is *kalon* or *aischron* depends on where, how, and by whom it is performed).

[9] e.g. in the case of Megara in *Her.*, who describes her concern for the honour of the family to which she belongs (see 284–94) as imitation of her husband, perhaps even 'imitation of a man' (294).

[10] Particularly in the *El.*, where the heroine is preoccupied with the overwhelming dishonour inflicted upon her by Aegisthus; for her the very suggestion that, on his return, Orestes would do anything other than take revenge is *aischron* (274). Cf. the attitude towards loss of status manifested by Polyxena and Hecabe in *Hec.* 551–2, 822 (also by Hec. at 968–73, where she feigns *aidōs* at her loss of status—hence she cannot look Polymestor in the eye—as part of her plan to obtain revenge). In *Hel.*, too, both Menelaus and Helen are sensitive about the former's current sorry state (see Men.'s *aischunē* and *aidōs* at 414–17, his desire not to shame his *kleos* at 845–6, Hel.'s horror that she has been reduced to begging for food at a foreigner's door at 790–1).

[11] Gnomically expressed at *Her.* 292–3; cf. *El.* 47–9, 1154; *Hel.* 134–6, 200–2, 686–7. Related is the idea that children should live up to the reputation of their parents: *El.* 336–8; *Ion* 735–7; *Or.* 1169–71; *Ba.* 265; *IA* 505.

[12] *Me.* 383, 404–6; *Her.* 284–6; *IT* 502; *Or.* 1159–60; *Ba.* 842; *IA* 371–2. In fr. 460 N² it is seen as inevitable that one's enemies will mock one's misfortunes.

and 'respect' which answer to the two senses of the verb *aideomai* with a direct object in Homer.

Obviously, though, these two senses are closely linked; to acknowledge the status of another is to know one's own place, and to know one's own place is to see oneself as part of a wider group, a group which is liable to disapprove of both excessive self-assertion and dereliction of obligations towards others; since, therefore, society may disapprove of a failure to show *aidōs* towards one who deserves it, *aidōs* for others of special status may easily encompass *aidōs* at 'what people say'. This is very much the case in this *agōn* between Admetus and Pheres: Admetus' major accusation is that it was cowardly of his father to refuse to die, but it is also part of his case that he failed to return an obligation of *charis*— Admetus did not dishonour Pheres, but was *aidophrōn* towards him (658–9),[13] yet, he implies (660–1), his *aidōs* was not returned. Pheres' own accusations against his son are exactly parallel; Admetus reproaches others with cowardice, yet he has been outdone in bravery by a woman and is a coward himself (696–8, 701–2), while his determination to avoid death even at the cost of his wife's life has convicted him of *anaideia* (694–6).[14] The aim of both parties in this *agōn*, as is typical, is to implicate the other in disgrace, and it is noteworthy that this can be done as much by allegations of lack of respect for others as by the charge of failure or weakness; to respect others is a function of one's concern for one's own reputation in the inclusive codes of honour which persist from Homer to the fifth century.[15] As we saw, Pheres virtually admits his son's

[13] On *aidophrōn*, cf. Ch. 4 n. 18. The connection with *timē* in the present passage is instructive; to be *aidophrōn* is not to *atimazein* the object of one's *aidōs*.

[14] Admetus' *anaideia* in striving to fight off death is multivalent; he disregards the opinions and the rights of everyone else in pursuing his own advantage, he disregards the accepted limits of human conduct, and he shows little *aidōs* for a wife whom he expects to show *aidōs* for him. Lombard (1985: 11 n. 34) points out that, in 694–6, Ad.'s *anaideia* properly consists in his attempt to avoid death, not in his 'murder' of his wife (against von Erffa (1937), 133); but his attempt to avoid death did culminate in his allowing his wife to die, so it seems pedantic to deny that his *anaideia* also covers lack of respect for a *philē*. Lombard also claims (9) that in this passage 'at last we have a negative form of *aidōs* censuring the absence of the inner restraint demanded by Democritus [B 264 DK etc.]'. Ad., he claims, is convicted of '*anaideia* on the existential level'. I cannot, however, see why Lombard should imagine that *aidōs* of this type is rare or why he should refer this passage specifically to Democ.; Pheres refers to his son's concern for himself to the exclusion of all others, and such disregard for the claims of others is a recognizably traditional form of *anaideia*. This *anaideia* does involve 'an absence of inner restraint', but not remarkably so— *aidōs* is an inner restraint even 'in the context of social conventions' which Lombard would contrast strongly with 'the existential level'.

[15] Cf. *Hcld*. 567–71: Demophon says it would be *aischron* for him to disregard Macaria's request that her sacrifice should be attended only by women, on the grounds both of her bravery and of *to dikaion* (justice); it would be *aischron* for Dem. to deny her the honour she

accusation of *anaideia*; similarly Admetus, in a quieter moment, reveals that he is sensitive to the charges made by his father, when, in the Homeric manner, he imagines 'what someone will say' (954-7); in a vivid representation of the acute *aidōs* to which he is subject, he feels himself under the gaze of an enemy who points to his disgrace in allowing, in a cowardly and unmanly fashion, his wife to die in his place. This is not to say that Admetus is not also sensitive to the charge of having failed his wife,[16] simply that in this passage his self-pity brings his concern for his own reputation for manliness to the forefront.

Contemporary Athenian attitudes towards social status and the hierarchy of honour which goes with it seem to lie behind several passages in the *Ion* and the *Electra*. In the former, Ion is concerned about his reputation in two ways: first, he is apprehensive lest he incur the resentment of the Athenians in taking up a position of importance in the city despite being, as he believes, the incomer son of an incomer king. He knows that the autochthonous Athenians resent incomers (589-90), and he fears that he will incur their disapproval no matter how he acts: if he keeps quiet out of fear of reproach, they will call him a nobody (593-4), and if he is at once active in the state, his inferiors will hate him and the upper classes, who remain aloof from politics, will call him a fool for courting popular disapproval (595-601). Ion's *aidōs* (for such his concern obviously is) stems from his desire to act in accordance with his status as it stands in relation to that of others;[17] and is so acute that he cannot see any way of avoiding the reproaches he fears.[18] It is not, however, misplaced, given that the chorus of Athenian women express their city's hatred of foreigners at 719-22 and 1074-5.[19] The other aspect of Ion's deserves, and, since her sacrifice frees him from a dilemma (either he must acquire a reputation for abandoning those under his protection, 461-3, or he must enter a battle he knows he cannot win), it would be *aischron* for him to fail to show gratitude. (On *to dikaion* in the context of the requirement to show gratitude, see Pearson (1962), 136-60.)

[16] He mentions the debt of gratitude he owes her at 950-3 and (in refusing the woman brought by Heracles) at 1057-61, where he is concerned lest the citizens (or his *dēmotai*, 'demesmen') reproach him for having betrayed his benefactress. On one's *dēmotai* as one's severest critics, cf. Ar. *Knights* 319-20, with Neil (1901), ad loc.

[17] Cf. 636-7, where he says it is 'unbearable' to have to give way to one's inferiors in the street (a mark of *aidōs* and acknowledgement of *timē*; cf. giving up one's seat to another at Tyrt. 12. 41-2 West; Ar. *Clouds* 993).

[18] The intensity of Ion's *aidōs* is presumably a function of his youth; cf. Telemachus in the *Od.* and Achilles in *IA* (5.4.3 below); on the importance for the young of honour and 'what people say', see Arist. *Rhet.* 1389ᵃ10-12, 28-9.

[19] 1074-5 is explained by Wilamowitz (1926: ad loc.) as the chorus's reaction to the participation of a non-Athenian in the Eleusinian procession; they assume that the god (Iacchus) shares their hostility. For a view of the negative aspects of the theme of autochthony in the play, see Saxonhouse (1986).

aidōs is his fear that he may turn out to be of low or servile birth;[20] illegitimacy would be *aischron* for him (1526), and it would be better never to discover his mother than to find that she was a slave (1382). He thus takes a view of slavery which is very different from that of Creousa's old retainer at 854-6, who believes that only the name of slave brings *aischunē* and that a slave who is *esthlos* is no more *kakos* than a free man; even if this disregard of the social rather than the moral aspect of these terms would not find complete acceptance, the slave's remarks do suggest that the equation of birth with moral worth is now under attack.[21]

Questions of this kind are raised most explicitly in the *Electra*. The eponymous heroine is deeply disturbed by her loss of status, dwelling on it with much exaggeration at 300-13 and ending (312-13) with an expression of her shame[22] that she whose hand was once sought by Castor, now a god, should now be married to a peasant.[23] This marriage, however, allows the poet to explore the legitimacy of the equation of birth with virtue, for it emerges that the Farmer is no less conscious of his status than Electra, and, just as she does, he experiences *aischunē* at the divergence in their rank. He is proud of the fact that he comes from noble stock,[24] but the wealth and nobility of his line have declined, and so he is now inhibited with regard to those of greater status. He feels that he would *aischunein* Electra if he were to sleep with her (43-4), and he is ashamed (*aischunomai*) to lay hands on her, a child of a rich father, and dishonour (*hubrizein*) her, since he is unworthy (45-6). The Farmer's *aischunē*, then, takes account of his own status and that of others, and is dependent on a stratification of honour and status in which inferiors are expected to know their place;

[20] Cf. the shame (at Oedipus' low birth) attributed by O. to Jocasta at Soph. *OT* 1078-9.

[21] Obviously such remarks are more likely to come from slaves than non-slaves (cf. *IA* 858), and slaves can be protective of their honour even in Homer (Eumaeus at *Od.* 14. 38), but there is a number of similar passages in Eur. (cf., with Adkins (1960*a*), 177 and 207, *Hel.* 730-1; frr. 511, 831 N²), and the disjunction between rank and moral worth is exploited in *El.*

[22] Page's emendation, *aischunomai* for *anainomai*, quoted with approval by Denniston (1939: ad loc.), and accepted by Diggle (OCT).

[23] Cf. 404-5, where she berates her husband for inviting guests 'greater than himself' to his humble abode, and 658, where she explains her conviction that Clyt. will come to her on hearing of her childbirth in terms of the presumed desire of her mother to bemoan the wretched circumstances of the birth. For various views on El.'s preoccupation with her status and its significance, see Arnott (1981), 185; Gellie (1981), 3; Michelini (1987), 187-94.

[24] 'I shall not be shown up in that respect,' he says at 36.

but the idea that concern for one's own honour must encompass awareness of the status of others is not new or confined to the lower classes, since it is apparent even in the aristocratic society of the Homeric poems. In this play, however, there is a contrast between the classes, for while the Farmer's awareness of his low status leads him to show regard for others,[25] Electra's causes her to think only of herself. Electra and Orestes are thoroughly appreciative of the Farmer's recognition of his place, and express their approbation in terms of his *eusebeia* (253-4) and his *sōphrosunē* (261).[26] Paradoxically, however, they also express it by means of words which refer in their origin to noble birth: he is *gennaios* at 253 and 262, and it is recognition of this 'nobility' which leads to Orestes' disquisition on the proper application of terms such as *euandria*, *gennaios*, *kakos*, *agathos*, and *eugenēs* at 367-90.[27] The wider paradox behind this speculation is that, while it is the Farmer's acceptance of class distinctions which leads him to act as he does, his conduct leads to conclusions that undermine those very distinctions.[28] It is the Farmer's *aidōs* or *aischunē*, as the force which makes it impossible for him to consider dishonouring another person, that lies behind this behaviour, earns him these terms of praise, and, ultimately, contrasts his character favourably with the two representatives of the house of Atreus, whose *aidōs*, such as it is, is entirely self-regarding.[29]

5.2. FRIENDS, SUPPLIANTS, AND GUESTS

Aidōs remains active in the three areas of other-regarding behaviour with which it was particularly associated in Homer, and promotes very much the same values. Perhaps the most interesting aspect of these themes, however, is the indissoluble link between other-regarding and self-regarding behaviour. This is not, of course, a new thing; in Homer, too, it was discreditable to neglect one's obligations, and focus on the

---

[25] The Farmer's concern for the honour of others is apparent at 47-9 in his sympathy for Orestes on the basis of his sister's loss of status, and is assumed at 364-5, where Or. believes that he is motivated by an unwillingness to destroy his (Or.'s) reputation.

[26] Sheppard (1918a) shows how the motifs of *eusebeia* and *sōphrosunē*, applied to El. in *Cho.* and Soph. *El.* (cf. Ch. 4, n. 121), have been transferred in this play to the Farmer.

[27] See Adkins (1960a), 177; cf. Denniston (1939), ad loc.

[28] There may, however, be a further twist, in that anyone who wishes to may see the Farmer's moral 'nobility' as a product of his atavistic social 'nobility'. One senses a certain playfulness in Eur.'s exploitation of this theme.

[29] Cf. Goldhill (1986), 162-5.

status of others was the obverse of focus on one's own status; but whereas in Homer, when *aidōs* occurred in the context of other-regarding behaviour, it often did so as a description of the other-regarding response itself, with the implications for the honour of the agent implicit in the background, in Euripides we more frequently find that respect for *philoi*, suppliants, and guests is expressed in ways which suggest that *aidōs* for one's own honour is the main concern. Perhaps this is greater 'realism', or perhaps, with the influence of contemporary rhetoric on Euripides' speeches, characters tend to motivate their own actions and to motivate others to action with as many plausible arguments as possible, rarely failing to add *utile* to *honestum*.

5.2.1. Philia

Aidōs does still occur as positive respect for a *philos*,[30] and positive respect for one's *philoi* is still required, but other terms now tend to do the work done by *aideomai* in Homer. *Philia*, for example, looms large in the *Alcestis*; Alcestis herself is pre-eminently loyal to her husband,[31] while the mutual responsibility expected in both partners is repeatedly mentioned.[32] It is expressed, however, not by *aideomai*, but by *sebomai*, *sebein*, *presbeuō*, etc., in terms which convey the sense 'I honour you'

[30] e.g. Creousa's *aidōs* for her *eunai* (marriage) with Xouthus, *Ion* 977; cf. frr. 109 (parents), 593 N² (the 'fetters of *aidōs*' that bind Theseus and Peirithous (= Critias B 20 DK)). See also *Me.* 439–40 (the chorus draw the moral from Jason's breach of *philia*—the *charis* of oaths is no more and *aidōs* has left Greece (a *topos*—cf. Ch. 4 n. 116; *IA* 1089–94)); cf. 469–72 (in appearing before a *philē* he has wronged, Jas. manifests *anaideia*, though this is properly his effrontery in facing his victim). *Anaideia* may, however, cover lack of respect for a *philos* at *Alc.* 728 and 954–7 (in 5.1.2 above). At *Hipp.* 1258–60 Thes.'s *aidōs* for the gods and for H. prevents his taking pleasure in the latter's destruction; his *aidōs* for the gods presumably implies their disapproval of exultation in the misfortunes of a *philos*, while his *aidōs* for his son, which is explained with reference to the paternal relationship, must be positive regard for H. *qua philos*. At *Hcld.* 6–9 Iolaus explains his participation in the labours of Heracles as motivated by *aidōs* and by respect for their kinship (αἰδοῖ καὶ τὸ συγγφενὲς σέβων); both of these motives, *aidōs* and *sebas*, may denote positive respect for one's kin, but *aidōs* could equally refer to Iolaus' recognition that it would be discreditable for him to neglect a *philos* (cf. Szlezak (1986), 58–9 n. 81). *Aidōs* as the proper response to one's *philoi* is implied by *IA* 378–80, where to abuse one's brother with an unflinching gaze is *anaides* (although Ag. thinks that one can abuse one's brother appropriately (with *sōphrosunē*) by averting one's gaze somewhat (!); on the association of *aidōs* with *sōphrosunē* and the avoidance of excess, cf. North (1966), 78 n. 116).

[31] And thus a model of feminine *aretē*: 152, 323–5, 1000–1.

[32] Cf. Pearson (1962), 148–51.

more directly than does *aideomai*. The reciprocity of this respect is evident at 279 and 282, in which Admetus' protestation of regard for Alcestis (*sebomai*)³³ is answered by an equivalent on her part (*presbeuo*).³⁴ It remains, however, *aischron* to betray a tie of *philia*,³⁵ and *aidōs* or periphrases for *aidōs* may describe reluctance to do so.³⁶ Sometimes the stress is on the desire to do the right thing, sometimes on the unpleasant consequence (disgrace) of failure to do the right thing, but the situation is rarely so clear-cut that one can state unambiguously that a given character is concerned only with duty or only with his own reputation. In refusing to accept the woman Heracles has brought him, for example, Admetus (1057-60) is worried lest people say he betrayed his benefactress, but equally he represents himself as afraid of the censure of his dead wife, surely a less pressing sanction and one which can more readily be understood as a projection of his commitment to the obligation of loyalty. Of this obligation he is, in any case, aware, pointing out that Alcestis deserves his respect and that he must show great consideration for her (1060-1).

The interdependence of concern for one's *philoi* and for one's own reputation also emerges clearly in the case of Orestes and Pylades in the *Iphigeneia among the Taurians*. Only one of the two, it appears, can be saved, but neither is willing to abandon the other. Both agree that to do so would be *aischron* (606, 674), and, for Pylades in particular, this judgement encompasses a considerable regard for public opinion: he would incur a charge of cowardice and baseness, and when he returned

³³ With Alc.'s reverence for the relationship itself (φιλίαν σεβόμεσθα), cf. *Or.* 1079 and *Hcld.* 6.

³⁴ Cf. προτιμῶσα (paying *timē* to) at 155, with Dale (1954), ad loc.; also 433-4, where Ad. deems his wife worthy of *timē* in that she alone was willing to die for him; Alc. honoured Ad. and he will honour her in return.

³⁵ *Me.* 166-7, 501 (*aischros* used non-physically of a person; cf. Soph. *Phil.* 906), 695, 1328; *Hipp.* 1290-1 (cf. 1331-4, Artemis' failure to protect H. implicates her in *aischunē*); *Supp.* 296; *El.* 1051; *Or.* 194, 499; *IT* 605-7, 674; *IA* 1187; *Hyps.* fr. 60 Bond, 41-2. At *Hec.* 251-3 Hec. asks Od. whether he is not ashamed (does not consider it *kakon* or (perhaps) feel himself *kakos*; the verb *kakunomai* is a coinage analogous to *aischunomai*; cf. *Hipp.* 686) to demand Hec.'s daughter for sacrifice after she, Hec., had once saved his life; at 310-11, however, Od. points out that Achilles, whose ghost demands the sacrifice, is also a *philos* whom it would be *aischron* to abandon in death. Od. is right about the relative importance of the two ties of *philia*, his own towards Hec. and that of the Greeks towards Ach., but surely he uses these arguments to immoral ends? (Human sacrifice is unambiguously condemned as early as 23. 176, and so Od. is out of step with 'basic Greek values'.) I should support Pearson (1962: 144-6) rather than Adkins (1966: 196-9) here.

³⁶ *Aidōs*: *Or.* 460-7 (retrospectively; Or. feels *aidōs* at facing Tyndareus because his matricide is a betrayal of the nurture and *timē* he received at his grandparents' hands as a boy); periphrasis: *Hcld.* 26-30; *IT* 676-86.

home people would think that he had betrayed his friend and saved himself, or even that he had killed Orestes himself (676–82). The opinions of 'the many' (678), then, do weigh heavily with Pylades, and his fear of unpleasant consequences is the main motive to which he gives voice. He is afraid of such charges, he says, considering them *aischron* (683), and so he is determined to be sacrificed along with Orestes, because he is his friend and because he is afraid of reproach (684–6). Only in the reference to his status as Orestes' *philos* in the last line of his speech is there any indication of a positive feeling of obligation or loyalty, yet it would be entirely illegitimate to disregard this phrase and consider Pylades as entirely motivated by prudential concerns.

The passage does indicate the tendency of the Greek to express his sense of obligation in terms of external sanctions, but should not be taken as evidence that concern for such sanctions replaces any sense of obligation. Pylades' very fears show that he is acutely concerned for his reputation for loyalty as such (by subsuming disloyalty to the head of cowardice he relates it to the area of male values about which a young nobleman in his position might be most concerned);[37] he fears the charge of disloyalty because, for him, disloyalty is unthinkable. Orestes immediately agrees with this outlook (the disgrace Pylades envisages will be his if he destroys his friend by implicating him in his own ruin, 689–91), but earlier, at 605–8, in explaining precisely the same concern, he gave voice to sentiments which sound much more altruistic: betrayal of one's friends' interests is *aischiston*; Pylades is his *philos*, and he is as concerned for his life as he is for his own. It is not that this altruism degenerates into egoism as the scene progress; rather the scene demonstrates that both positive respect for those who deserve it and the recognition that failure to show such respect will bring disapproval are regarded as appropriate, indeed laudable expressions of one's sense of honour. Pylades is not committed to loyalty only in so far as disloyalty can be taken for cowardice; it is more a case of competitive and co-operative, self-regarding and other-regarding aspects of the code of honour being so inextricably linked as to render any hard and fast disjunction between them unhelpful.[38] The

[37] At *Me.* 465–6 Medea regards Jason's desertion of her as cowardice, presumably because her intention is to represent his conduct in as disgraceful a light as possible.

[38] Roisman (1984: 173) claims that, in *IT*, 'only the chorus . . . fulfills the requirements of loyalty', apparently because the motivation of Pyl. and Or. is tinged with self-interest; in their cases, however, apparently self-regarding concerns lead each to wish to subordinate his own material interests entirely to those of the other; the attitude that it is

'realism'[39] of the Greeks means that the individual's *aidōs* is typically concerned both with the disgraceful character of the act and with the harm to one's reputation which is its consequence, while the *aidōs* one feels in recognition of others' claim to honour readily overlaps with *aidōs* based on the implications for one's own honour.

5.2.2. *Supplication*

Aidōs, as we have seen, is active in several ways in the institution of supplication. Firstly, for supplication to occur at all, the suppliant must place himself in a position of inferiority *vis-à-vis* the supplicated, thus abandoning any claim to parity or superiority in honour and overcoming any *aidōs* which this might entail. In some cases characters are reluctant to do this, and *aidōs* inhibits or prevents the supplication. Adrastus, for example, prefaces his appeal to Theseus (*Supplices* 164–5) with a reference to his *aidōs*[40] at undergoing ritual humiliation, yet recognizes that undergo it he must.[41] Once supplication is begun, *aidōs* on the part of the supplicated may follow, most straightforwardly in the form of the *aidōs* which is virtually a technical term for acceptance of supplication, and which recognizes either the honour of the suppliants *qua* protégés of the gods or that of the gods themselves. Thus in the *Heraclidae* the chorus inform the enemy herald[42] that it is seemly to *aideisthai* the gods' suppliants and not to force them to leave their place of refuge (101–3). Ideally, then, the suppliant deserves *aidōs*

in one's ultimate best interests to sacrifice oneself for another's sake may differ from the recognition that it is one's (categorical or unpleasant) duty to do so, but one ends up chasing one's own tail if one attempts to categorize it absolutely as either altruistic or self-regarding.

[39] Dover's description (1974: 225).

[40] The phrase used, ἐν αἰσχύναις ἔχω (164), seems to paraphrase *aischunomai* (see Collard (1975), ad loc.; cf. δι' αἰσχύνης ἔχω at *IT* 683).

[41] Like Adr., Clyt. (*IA* 900–2) recognizes the possibility of *aidōs* at performing supplication, but ignores it as inefficacious in the present circumstances; for her to *epaideisthai* when her daughter's life is at stake would be inappropriate pride or pretentiousness (*semnunesthai*, 901). When supplication is necessary, then, *aidōs* is unhelpful. Other characters, however, stand by their *aidōs*: Menelaus refuses to supplicate Theonoë (947–9) because to do so would be cowardice and a disfigurement (*aischunein*) of the glory he won at Troy; Men. cuts a rather ridiculous figure, but the *aidōs* which rules out supplication is also found in a more serious context at *Pho.* 1622–4, where Oedipus refuses to appear *kakos* or to betray his *kleos* by supplicating Creon.

[42] Who enters unusually early, before the suppliants have met their prospective protector (Burian (1971), 96).

qua suppliant.[43] Related to this positive respect for the suppliant (indeed, not normally distinct from it), is the recognition of the force exerted by the ritual itself; the ritual contact of supplication creates a situation in which a decision must be made; if the suppliant cannot be persuaded to abandon his appeal, either force must be used or the supplication must be accepted. This tension can create its own sort of *aidōs*, as in the case of Creon in *Medea*. At 324 Medea begins a suppliant appeal, but Creon dismisses her pleas (325), confirming, in answer to her question (326), that he will not respect (*aideisthai*) her entreaties (*litai*). Medea has taken on a position of inferiority *vis-à-vis* Creon, begging him in a wheedling tone to be allowed to remain in Corinth, but so far her supplication has probably been figurative, without ritual contact.[44] By 339, however, she has made contact, and begs to be allowed to remain one more day (340-7). Now Creon gives in, although he knows that he is making a mistake (348-51): 'My character is not at all as a monarch's should be; rather have I already done much damage because of my *aidōs* [*aidoumenos*]. Now, too, although I see that I am making a mistake, still you shall get what you want.' Ritual contact, then, does make a difference, since it brings Creon to the point at which he must carry out his threat (335) to use force against Medea. This, however, he cannot bring himself to do, because he is prone to *aidōs*.[45] His reference to the *aidōs* which has been detrimental to his interests in the past indicates that he sees his present conduct in the same terms, and perhaps this is so simply because acceptance of a suppliant appeal is commonly described as 'showing *aidōs*'. Yet the tension created by ritual contact does seem to have been decisive, and it seems likely that the stark recognition of the two alternatives, compliance or the use of force to break the suppliant's hold, has also produced in Creon *aidōs* as an instinctive reluctance to undertake a course of action that he regards as unacceptable. This inhibitory *aidōs* is very close to, but none the less distinct from that which responds spontaneously to the *timē* of the suppliant and the gods, and may arise in those, like Creon, who are initially inclined to reject supplication but unable to contemplate the

---

[43] For *aideisthai* in an appeal meaning 'accept my supplication', cf. *Hec.* 806. Similarly, at *Or.* 682 Menelaus' statement ('I feel *aidōs* for your head') seems simply to indicate his recognition of the force of Or.'s supplication.

[44] See Gould (1973), 85.

[45] His use of the part. *aidoumenos* may simply be a reference to repeated acts of *aidōs* in the past, but since there is a contrast with a 'tyrannical spirit', it probably also refers to a disposition to behave as *aidōs* demands.

use of force when ritual contact makes either that or acceptance unavoidable.

Some characters are convinced outright by the moral and religious requirement to accept supplication.[46] But others take, or must be persuaded to take, other considerations into account. Even in these cases, however, *aidōs* is often central to both appeal and acceptance. In the *Heraclidae* there is, in view of the violence threatened by the enemy herald,[47] really only one decision Demophon can make, yet even though he decides quickly and with scarcely any hesitation, his decision does not arise from any one simple consideration. Iolaus' appeal for protection employs three main arguments which supplement the basic argument that it is right to honour those who are under the protection of the gods.[48] First, by indulging in extensive praise of the Athenian spirit, he demonstrates that the Athenians have a reputation to maintain. There is a suggestion that Athens is concerned for justice and the rights of suppliants as such (193-6), but much more is it Iolaus' intention to suggest that failure to protect will be taken as a sign of weakness (191-2, 197-8); thus when he observes that the Athenians will fight on the suppliants' behalf, because 'good' men (*esthloi*) take more account of *aischunē* than of their own lives, there may be a suggestion that to betray a reputation for piety, justice, and altruism is disgraceful, but more obvious is the suggestion that for the Athenians to fail to fight would be an *aischunē* which would impair their *aretē* as warriors.

Iolaus' remaining arguments are closely linked: Theseus and Heracles were related, and so Demophon is related to the suppliants (207-13), and is thus under an additional obligation to protect them (205-6). But there was more to the *philia* of Theseus and Heracles than simple kinship, for Heracles freed Theseus from Hades (214-19), and Iolaus, using the third of his arguments, now claims that *charis* back (220).[49] Having made these points, he sums up (223-31), mentioning the pitiful situation of the suppliants and the divine sanction (221-2, 224-5), but also drawing his arguments from reputation, kinship, and *charis* together; Demophon is to honour the suppliants, to show himself their kinsman and *philos* (227-30); to do

---

[46] e.g. *Supp.* opens with the commitment of Aethra to the suppliants' cause, a commitment based on pity and respect for the divine sanction (34-6).

[47] See 65, 67-8, 105-6, 159-60; Burian (1971), 97-8.

[48] On these *Bitt-Topoi*, see Kopperschmidt (1967), 150.

[49] For the argument from *charis* and *philia*, cf. *Or.* 453, 646-64 (*charis*), 665-9, 674 (*philia*).

otherwise, to allow kinfolk to be dragged from their suppliant position, would be *aischron*, not just as a sign of weakness, but also as a failure to honour one's kin and to return a favour. Iolaus is thus appealing to Demophon's *aidōs* on three different grounds, none of which answers to the simple argument that suppliants deserve *aidōs qua* suppliants. In his reply Demophon shows that he is affected by these arguments; he takes the divine sanction fully into account (238–9), but he is also influenced by the arguments from kinship and gratitude, which he takes together (240–1), and, thirdly, by the argument from *to aischron*, which he mentions at greatest length and to which he grants most consideration (242–6), observing that both his own reputation for bravery and his city's as an independent state are at stake.[50] In acting in a way which might itself be described as 'showing *aidōs*', then, Demophon reveals his susceptibility to *aidōs* on other grounds, and *aidōs* appears as a deeply pervasive element in the context of supplication; the suppliant, it emerges, has a variety of appeals at his disposal which might draw their power from their relationship with this central aspect of the situation.[51]

In *Heraclidae* Demophon clearly has self-interested reasons for according protection, but there is no suggestion whatever that his motivation is anything less than admirable. The interaction of self-interest with the ritual of supplication, however, is not always so straightforward: suppliants may misuse the ritual gestures, which in theory demand absolute and unconditional acceptance, for illegitimate ends, while the supplicated may emerge in a poor light in accepting a supplication for purely selfish reasons.[52] Particularly relevant for our

[50] Cf. 256 and his remarks to the Argive herald at 284–7; on the theme of the city's reputation, cf. Iolaus at 69–72 and the worries of the chorus-leader at 461–3.

[51] We have seen that *aidōs* can be inappropriate in those who are about to make an appeal. The suppliants themselves, however, may manifest other kinds of *aidōs*; *aidōs* may, for example, promote the kind of proper behaviour most likely to win sympathy (as in Aesch. *Supp.*, see 3.1.2 above), or it may form part of the successful suppliant's gratitude towards his protector (Ch. 3 n. 20; cf. *Hcld.* 315—the suppliants *sebein* their protector). A suppliant may, moreover, experience a natural form of *aidōs* at the prospect of being overcome by his enemies; the taking of the suppliant by force may be *aischron* for the suppliant himself (*Hcld.* 450), as well as for his protector. Furthermore, since respect for a suppliant is a fundamental form of *aidōs*, it follows that the enemies of suppliants are *anaideis* (e.g. Lycus: *Her.* 165–9, 299–301, 554–7; Eurystheus: *Hcld.* 458–60), and maltreatment of the suppliant may, as in *Hcld.*, be *aischron* for suppliant, saviour, and enemy (see *Hcld.* 255 with Demophon's reply, 256, and note how the same action may be *aischron* for both agent and patient).

[52] See Dalfen (1984) on this topic. Medea and the Nurse in *Hipp.* are characters who exploit ritual for their own ends (Dalfen, 67–72; cf. Hermione at *Andr.* 859; she who had persecuted the suppliant Andr. now turns suppliant for her own protection; cf. also Ion's

purposes here is the role of the personal honour of the supplicated. This features regularly in both appeal and response (particularly in Euripides, but not exclusively so), and need not, as we saw in *Heraclidae*, imply either an unpleasant use of threats by the suppliant or vanity in the supplicated.[53] A combination of the desire to do the right thing and a proper awareness that one's own honour may be at stake thus seems quite normal in this, as in other contexts.

This is certainly the case in the supplication scene in *Helen*, where both Helen and Menelaus, seeking Theonoë's help in order to escape from Egypt, appeal both to her sense of justice and piety and to the reputation for these qualities she shares with her dead father; the standards to which, they argue, Theonoë must aspire are not abstract but rather embodied in the ideas of her own status and reputation and of the paternal model.[54] In Helen's speech, in particular, virtue and the reputation for virtue are inseparable, and in urging Theonoë to maintain her reputation and live up to her father's standards she is essentially urging her to be true to herself. Theonoë's reply, in turn, shows that she has taken these arguments to heart (998–1004): 'I am by nature such as to *eusebein* and I want to, I love myself[55] and I would not defile the *kleos* of my father, nor would I render my brother a favour by means of which I should be revealed as ill-famed. There is a great temple of Dikē in my nature; and since I inherited this

complaints on the misuse of supplication at *Ion* 1312–19); others accept ritual because it suits them, or ignore legitimate uses of ritual in pursuit of their own interests. (See Dalfen, 72–5. Hec.'s supplication of Ag., *Hec.* 787–856 (Dalfen, 74) is a good example of self-interested acceptance; Ag., having heard all that Hec. is going to say about the justice of her case, moves away (812), an action which Hec. interprets as rejection (813); he changes his mind, however, in response to her appeal to his sexual relationship with Cassandra (824–40), revealing his sensitivity about this in 855–6. Cf. Kovacs (1987), 102–3, and contrast Adkins (1966), 202.) It emerges from Eur.'s handling of this theme that the absoluteness of the ritual of supplication is problematic; it can be harmful to accept a supplication, and thus some people consider only their own interests when confronted with the ritual, but to consider only what is harmful or beneficial to oneself leads to disregard of legitimate claims; the absolute requirements of the ritual are sometimes a bad thing, but not always.

[53] For a further uncontroversial instance, see *Andr.* 575–6. At *Hec.* 806, however, Hec.'s phrase ταῦτ' οὖν ἐν αἰσχρῷ θέμενος αἰδέσθητί με ('regard these things as *aischron* and show me *aidōs*') refers to her previous description of the crimes (against hospitality) of Polymestor, not (*pace* Adkins (1966), 201) to the possibility of Polymestor's conduct, or Ag.'s failure to punish him, being *aischron* for Ag.

[54] See 900–2, 919–23, 940–3 (Hel.); 954–8, 966–8, 973–4 (Men.). Men.'s speech essentially repeats the points made by his wife, but in cruder form, relying more on threats, both of loss of reputation and of violence (975–87). His stress on Theonoë's reputation is in harmony with his own reluctance to undertake formal supplication (see n. 41 above).

[55] φιλῶ τ' ἐμαυτήν, 'I treat myself as *philē*'.

from Nereus I shall try to save Menelaus.' Von Erffa[56] is right to compare *Iliad* 6. 442-4[57] with this passage, for Theonoë resembles the Homeric Hector in her active desire to act in accordance with principles which have become, as we might say, 'second nature', and, although Theonoë identifies her motives in a more analytical fashion than Hector does, the responses of the two characters do not, in fact, differ widely.

Theonoë, then, refers unambiguously both to personal standards of behaviour (in 998 and in the reference to the temple of Dikē, 1002)[58] and to her reputation (999-1001); she responds to Helen's appeal to self-image and parental model, and to Menelaus' to simple reputation, but also presents her commitment to the relevant principles under a more abstract aspect. It is clear that her concern for her own reputation and that of her father, together with her commitment to the paternal or ancestral model, indicates *aidōs*, for these are traditional applications of the term, and I should argue that the element of conscience in her response is also capable of description in terms of *aidōs*; without using the term itself, Theonoë refers to those elements of subjective evaluation of the character of one's own actions, and concern for the outward aspect of those actions, which we have seen to be part of the *aidōs*-reaction from the beginning.

Theonoë's self-love is also interesting; this is clearly to be regarded as positive,[59] but it is not certain whether it belongs in sense with the

[56] (1937), 149.

[57] Cf. 1.2.3, 1.7 above.

[58] On the temple of *dikē*, cf. (with Kannicht (1969), on 1002-4) [Demosth.] 25. 35, where the best of men are said to possess altars of dikē, *eunomia*, and *aidōs* in their hearts, analogous to the literal altars to these powers set up in public places. For F. Eckstein (*LIMC* i. 1, 351), this demonstrates a 4th-cent. Athenian familiarity with public altars of *aidōs* (attested for Athens by Hesych., s.v. Αἰδοῦς βωμός; Eustath. on 22. 451; cf. Paus. 1. 17. 1), but there are good reasons for considering speech 25 spurious and late (see Gigante (1956), 286-92; Guthrie, iii. 75). Concepts such as *aidōs* are readily personified (in Eur., see *Ion* 336-7, *Her.* 557), but even where granted cult status, personification of *aidōs* remains on a more figurative level than that of (e.g.) Nemesis (see von Erffa (1937), 57; Wilamowitz (1959), i. 347 n. 1). On the significance of the *Hel.* passage as an acknowledgement of the location of the standard of justice in the conscience of the individual, see Stebler (1971), 74; cf. Pippin (1960), 159.

[59] In contrast to the same concept at *Me.* 85-6 and fr. 452 N², where self-love is seen as selfishness (see A. Harder (1985), 102, on the latter). We might compare *Hipp.* 1080-1 where Theseus accuses Hippolytus of 'revering himself' (σαυτὸν . . . σέβειν) rather than his father; too much respect for oneself is thus discreditable (cf. the pejorative sense of the adj. *semnos*). These passages refute the contention of Michelini (1987: 188) that the Greeks had no words for the concepts of 'selfishness' or 'egotism'. Kovacs (1987: 24, 125 n. 4) uses a similar argument against those who find negative traits in the character of H.; the Greeks had no word for 'smug'. Well, perhaps not, but the absence of an exact

reaction based on internalized principles, as expressed in 998, or with the response to the possibility of loss of reputation in 999–1001.[60] On the face of it, it seems equally possible that the enlightened *philautia* to which Theonoë refers should refer either to the self-respect which renders one true to one's own principles or to the impulse towards self-protection against the criticisms of others. Since, however, both concerns are expressed in the immediate context, there can be no possibility of relating this *philautia* exclusively to one or the other, and, indeed, since the two aspects of her response are clearly inseparable, it is perfectly possible that it covers both. Given that Theonoë's *philautia* probably does carry positive connotations of 'self-respect', von Erffa[61] may be right to relate it to the reflexive uses of *aideisthai* in Democritus B 264 DK etc., but while 'loving oneself' and 'feeling *aidōs* before oneself' may belong together, the two expressions can no more be synonymous than can *philein* and *aideisthai*.[62] However that may be, the passage remains a clear demonstration of the compatibility in the Greek moral outlook of self-regarding and other-regarding motives, of moral principle with concern for reputation, and, if Theonoë's self-love encompasses her commitment to her own principles, it will take its place in the dispositional background from which her *aidōs* at ignoring the arguments of the suppliants springs.

The argument from reputation in *Helen*, then, produces an exemplary response, and again concern for one's honour appears as proper and admirable. This is not the case, however, in the *Iphigeneia at Aulis*. In this play Clytemnestra supplicates Achilles in order to elicit his support for Iphigeneia against Agamemnon and the rest of the army. Achilles has the young nobleman's typical susceptibility to *aidōs*,[63] and it is this quality which Clytemnestra hopes to exploit in framing her appeal.[64] This she begins at 903, having first assured Achilles that she feels no *aidōs* at undertaking supplication (902).[65] Encouraged by the sense of grievance that Achilles has already (897–9) expressed with regard to the misuse of his name by Agamemnon, she argues that the

equivalent for that particular adj. does not prove Kovacs's point; Thes. is certainly capable, in the lines cited above, of recognizing the element of narcissism in H.'s desire to witness himself weeping (1078–9), and this belongs with the tendency towards *semnotēs* criticized by H.'s servant (93–6; cf. Thes. at 1064).

[60] See Kannicht (1969), on 998–1001.
[61] (1937), 149.
[62] On 'good' *philautia* and Democ. B 264 DK etc., see Ch. 6 nn. 79, 239.
[63] Cf. von Erffa (1937), 154; 5.4.3 below.
[64] Clyt. recognizes Ach.'s *aidōs* (821) and praises it (as *sōphrosunē*) at 824.
[65] Cf. n. 41 above.

bogus marriage between Achilles and Iphigeneia creates a kind of *philia* between them which means that it would be discreditable (an *oneidos*) for him to abandon her (906–8). She also, however, refers to Achilles' *onoma* (his name) as that which has brought about her destruction, and says that he must now act to restore that name (910). Her intention, then, is to suggest that the mere use of Achilles' name implicates him in the affair, both as a quasi-bridegroom and as a contributory cause of Iphigeneia's misfortune, and so he must act to help her, in order both to avoid a breach of *philia* and to dispel the impression that his name has been the instrument of another's death. These attempts to represent Achilles as under an obligation, however, are unquestionably tenuous, and, accordingly, she devotes most of her appeal to the attempt to arouse Achilles' pity (903, 911–16).

Achilles is not oblivious to the appeal for pity (932–4, 942–3), but he says much more about his good name and its misuse by Agamemnon, convinced by Clytemnestra's point that his *onoma* is partly to blame for Iphigeneia's plight (938–9, 941, 947) and deeply resentful that he has been used.[66] At many points, however, he does show an appreciation of the issues involved: he will obey the Atreidae if they 'think well', but not if they do not (928–9), implying that the plan to sacrifice Iphigeneia is (at the least) ill-advised; and he would consider himself defiled should he be the unwilling agent of Iphigeneia's ruin (940–3), suggesting that he does feel a certain revulsion for the plan. At 959–69, however, he gives himself away: he has no desire for marriage with the girl, but resents the *hubris* Agamemnon has perpetrated against him (959–61); Agamemnon should have asked for permission to use his *onoma* (962), in which case he would gladly have participated in the deception of Clytemnestra and the sacrifice of Iphigeneia (963–7); as it is, his permission was not sought and he feels that he has been treated as a nobody by his commanders. There are elements in Achilles' speech, such as his discursive *prooimion* (919–31) and his aside that 'myriad girls' seek him as their husband (959–60), which, though they might seem to us to indicate pomposity and narcissism, we might play down in deference to the rhetorical character of Euripidean rhesis and the millennia of cultural change which separate Euripides' world from ours, but surely in 959–69 Achilles reveals that he is totally absorbed in himself and his fame to the exclusion even of those external moral

[66] From 954 it appears that he believes that the honour of his homeland is at stake if he does not resist such treatment at the hands of Agamemnon.

considerations which he appears to recognize elsewhere in his speech?[67]

Achilles' response to the supplication, then, goes beyond Clytemnestra's use of the argument from reputation in its exclusively self-regarding nature, and serves to indicate how the acceptance of supplication on the basis of the argument from *to aischron* can contribute to negative characterization. The proclivity of this Achilles to resent any and every insult to his *timē* is clearly based on the Homeric model; it is rooted in the dispositional *aidōs* of the young warrior which Achilles manifests on first encountering Clytemnestra, but is perhaps best related to the Homeric *nemesis* at another's breach of *aidōs* in failing to recognize one's own *timē*. The shabbiness of the heroic response in Achilles, moreover, is reflected in the treatment of *aidōs* elsewhere in the play; Agamemnon, for example, has such an acute concern for his image that, when informed that his wife and children have arrived, he describes his *aidōs* at the prospect both of weeping and of not weeping (451-3)—apparently he is the sort of person who feels uncomfortable at not weeping when he thinks he should.[68] This impression of shallow pomposity is confirmed by the remarks which precede this observation; at 446-9 Agamemnon envies the low-born their ability to say what they like and to weep when they feel like it, whereas people like himself must protect themselves with their own self-importance (*onkos*, 'pomposity', 450) and are slaves to popular opinion. In this character, then, the nobleman's traditional concern for his reputation, his *aidōs* (which Agamemnon identifies as a virtue of the nobly born at 380, 446-53)[69] is held up as something faintly ridiculous; and just as Agamemnon equates *aidōs* with *onkos*, so other characters, notably Clytemnestra, express the idea that, in certain circumstances, a too profound regard for one's own status may not be *aidōs*, but mere *semnotēs* or *habrotēs*.[70] The play thus explores the inappropriateness of *aidōs* in certain circumstances, a traditional idea, but also one which suits Euripides' interest in the shifting validity of traditional values.

---

[67] Cf. Blaiklock (1952), 117-21.

[68] Cf. the braggart Menelaus at *Hel.* 947-53; he feels it unmanly to weep, yet has heard that it is *kalon* to do so in time of trouble. On rejection of weeping as unmanly, cf. Soph. *Aj.* 319-20; *Trach.* 1071-2; see also *Or.* 1047-8, where Or. experiences *aidōs* at displaying his feelings towards El. The position of Od.'s *aidōs* at weeping in *Od.* 8. 86 is complicated by the fact that Homeric heroes can shed tears with no hint of *aidōs* (Ch. 1 n. 191).

[69] Cf. 2.2, 2.3.4 above.

[70] Cf. 858, 900-1 (n. 41 above), 997, 1343-4.

The question of the character of the self-regarding response to supplication arises with greatest difficulty in the *Supplices*, where the play's main departure from the canonical pattern of suppliant drama, the presentation of two parallel sets of appeals and replies,[71] creates a disjunction between the possibility of spontaneous acceptance of the suppliants *qua* suppliants and acceptance on other grounds.

The climate initially seems favourable to the suppliants when, at 34–41, Aethra expresses her pity, reveals her respect for the institution of supplication, and announces that she has summoned her son in order that he might resolve the situation. Adrastus' appeal to Theseus (163–92), however, fails, because the latter is more interested in the imprudence (161), injustice (224, 228, 233), and impiety (231) of the expedition against Thebes than in Adrastus' attempt to arouse his pity.

Adrastus' speech is remarkable for the absence of most of the typical suppliant appeals; even the gods' protection of suppliants goes unmentioned. The *topoi*, however, do find a place in Aethra's subsequent appeal on the suppliants' behalf (301–31). She makes three main points: first (301–2), Theseus must be careful not to ignore the role played by the gods in supplication; next, she refers to the dangerous precedent which will be set should the Thebans be allowed to maltreat the dead with impunity (306–13). She has observed in passing, however, that Theseus stands to win *timē* by helping the Argives (306), and this leads her to her third and longest argument, an appeal based on the reputation of the supplicated (314–27). Although she concludes this section with an implication that it is discreditable in itself not to help those in need (326–7), most of this part of her appeal turns on the argument that others will regard Theseus as a coward if he avoids conflict with the Thebans; people will say he shirked a fight out of fear and *anandria* (314–16), and they will belittle his previous exploits if he is found to be a coward in this case (316–19); she even goes so far as to suggest that she would disown him were he to act in the manner she describes (320). This is clearly a more audacious form of appeal than could be employed by any suppliant, but in essence, if not in degree, this appeal to the self-regarding *aidōs* of the warrior is of the same kind as that employed by Iolaus in *Heraclidae*.

Aethra thus adduces three grounds for acceptance (the gods, Panhellenic custom, and popular disapproval), but it is only the last of these that is acknowledged by Theseus in his reply (337–46); both Aethra's hint that he must live up to his reputation as an Attic

---

[71] See Kopperschmidt (1967), 133–5; Burian (1971), 137–8.

286 *Euripides*

Heracles-figure (316-17, cf. 339-42) and her reference to her own disapproval (320, cf. 343-5) are taken up. This point, however, is often ignored; Kopperschmidt,[72] for example, thinks that the reference to the gods in 301 is the main point of Aethra's argument and sees Theseus' negative and positive responses as manifestations of a regard first for *Polis-Recht*, then for *Götterrecht*. He recognizes that Theseus gives in out of *aidōs* but does not explain what this *aidōs* is.[73] Zuntz[74] emphasizes Aethra's appeal to *nomos* and describes her argument as a successful attempt to subject the claims of pity to the test of reason, but wholly ignores the character of Theseus' response, in which divine and Panhellenic law do not rate a mention.

On the other hand, there are those who positively emphasize the appeal to Theseus' fear of the charge of cowardice and its obvious acceptance, and assume that these indicate irony in the presentation of his character.[75] Burian attempts to find a middle way: 'The question of Theseus' reputation', he writes, 'is ... inseparable from the ethical and political considerations inherent in ... the appeal.'[76] This is true, to the extent that *Aethra* believes that her son will incur disapproval by failing to do what she regards as pious and proper, but she does not say that it is on these grounds that he will be reproached, but for cowardice, and it is to this argument that he responds. Again, Burian is right to point out that the force of Aethra's religious and legal (or moral) arguments remains despite Theseus' lack of response to them, and that Theseus actually uses the same arguments against the Theban herald (531-41, 558-9); it is also true that Theseus' earlier dismissal of Adrastus' appeal failed to take account of this, the central aspect of the mothers' supplication. The argument from Panhellenic custom is valid, and it can hardly be wrong of Theseus to act in support of this custom; yet Euripides is perfectly well aware that people may often do the right thing for the wrong reasons.

In evaluating the tone of Theseus' reply one must certainly bear in mind that it is in no way inherently discreditable for a character like Theseus to be concerned for his reputation;[77] that in revealing his

[72] (1967), 135-6.
[73] (1967), 138.
[74] (1963), 7-8, 10; cf. Grube (1961), 233; Conacher (1967), 102; Vickers (1973), 459; Lesky (1983), 266.
[75] Greenwood (1953), 108-9; Fitton (1961), 431-2.
[76] (1971), 159; his discussion in (1985), 135-7, 214-15 n. 12, essentially repeats his earlier position.
[77] Cf. Burian (1971), 164; Walcot (1976), 98-9; Heath (1987), 15 n. 18.

commitment to his reputation he is remaining true to himself; and that the reputation which he seeks to maintain is based on noble exploits as chastiser of the *kakoi*,[78] an aspect of their national hero which is likely to have struck the Athenians as one with which they had been familiar since childhood.[79] It may be, then, that Theseus' entirely self-regarding reply simply demonstrates the compatibility of the demands of morality and religion with those of self-interest in this particular case. Yet the fact that Theseus at this point mentions only one of the many possible motives for accepting the supplication leaves this reader uneasy, especially since the recovery of the bodies which his intervention ensures leads both to the rehabilitation of those whose injustice and impiety he himself had criticized, and, ultimately, to a renewal of the conflict through the *epigonoi*.[80] If the Athenian audience were encouraged by Theseus' concern for his personal honour to regard his acceptance of the suppliants as commendable, they may have had reasons for changing their minds by the end of the play, when the complex of values based on honour emerges in a less positive light; perhaps Theseus' motivation modulates between the two parts of the play, unproblematic at first sight but somewhat ambivalent in retrospect.

The prominence of *aidōs* in the context of supplication is readily apparent, as is the variety of ways in which it can become involved; both suppliant and supplicated may manifest *aidōs* in their different ways, and in the response of the supplicated in particular *aidōs* may take a number of different forms—now as a response to the moral and religious arguments, now as a recognition of the various ways in which one's own honour is at stake; here as a reaction rooted in one's most deeply held moral principles, there as a fear of others' reproach; sometimes positive, occasionally negative. All this, moreover, must be seen in terms of the shifts of character undergone by the institution itself, the absolute response which it demands being appropriate or otherwise depending on the context. The multifaceted nature of *aidōs* in the context of supplication, in short, may serve as a paradigm for the diversity of character and application in Euripides' use of the concept.

---

[78] Burian (1985), 136.

[79] Cf. in general Shaw (1982).

[80] For the 'ironical' interpretation of the second part of the play (including the notorious and, to my mind, clearly problematic Funeral Speech), see Fitton (1961), 438–41, followed by Burian (1971), 191–5; (1985), 137–8, 145–55, 218–19 n. 38; against, see Collard (1972), 39, 43–9; Lesky (1983), 269, 272; Shaw (1982), 12 n. 22, sits on the fence.

5.2.3. *Guest-Friendship*

Like supplication, guest-friendship is an institution by means of which outsiders are brought within the group and thus within the range of privileges to which *philoi* are normally entitled; accordingly, as we saw in Homer, strangers and guests are felt particularly to deserve *aidōs*, and *aidōs* also enters into the relationship, as it might among *philoi* or in the context of supplication, as an emotional response to the prospect of transgression,[81] as an awareness that the principles of *xenia* are generally upheld by society,[82] and as a fear that a host's failure to accord hospitality can be criticized as a failure to meet the obligations which his privileges and status entail.

In *Alcestis*, *aidōs* governs the concern for appropriateness and good manners of both parties to the relationship; Heracles expresses his unwillingness to intrude on his host's grief in terms of *aidōs* (542),[83] and Admetus, for his part, stresses the impropriety of troubling a guest with one's own grief (549–50). Both parties, as we have seen, must be committed to the enjoyment of hospitality;[84] Heracles finds the imbalance in mood between the two parties uncomfortable and Admetus attempts to play it down, each considering both the awkwardness of the situation and the position of the other party.

That Admetus is motivated by *aidōs* in insisting that Heracles remain emerges more clearly from his reply to the criticisms of the chorus-leader (553–60); his grief would not have lessened had he turned Heracles away, but he would have lost a *xenos* whose *aretē* reflects well on himself and whose hospitality he hopes to enjoy in the future, and the *kleos* of his house would suffer. Superficially, Admetus' concern is entirely for his own reputation and advantage, but there is every reason to believe that this merely rationalizes his reluctance to ignore the requirements of *xenia*. He cannot simply be calculating the

---

[81] e.g. *Ba.* 441–2, where Pentheus' servant experiences *aidōs* at maltreating a *xenos*. Such *aidōs* is lacking in the Polyphemus of *Cycl.* (416, 592).

[82] See *Hec.* 1247–8, where Ag. describes the killing of a guest as universally *aischron* among the Greeks.

[83] 'It is *aischron* for guests to be entertained in a house which is in mourning.' If this indicates a desire not to trouble one who already has troubles of his own, such a concern for the privacy of others might be seen as the converse of the desire not to involve others in one's own problems which is expressed at *Her.* 1162, 1200; *Or.* 280–2; *IA* 981–2. Cf. *IA* 327–31: since one's business is one's own and no one else's, it takes *anaischuntia* to interfere in another's affairs.

[84] Cf. Ch. 1 n. 193.

consequences for his own reputation, since Heracles showed no sign that he would be offended if not accorded hospitality, but rather gave evidence of his sympathy for Admetus' position and even declared that he would be grateful if allowed to depart (544). Admetus, of course, could not be sure what Heracles might say in the future, or of what those with malicious intent might make of his predicament, yet it remains true that the mismatch between Admetus' response and Heracles' motives is a strong argument for the proposition that he simply cannot bring himself to deny hospitality.

This emerges more clearly as the episode draws to a close; for Admetus the main thing is that Heracles should not, in any circumstances, be allowed to leave, even if this means deceiving a *philos*, for, as he points out in conclusion, his house does not know how to reject or dishonour a guest (563–7). Admetus, then, is determined to do what is generally thought commendable and what he imagines to be in his own best interests, but is not simply trying to maximize his own advantage.

The nobility of Admetus' attitude receives favourable comment both in the subsequent choral song, where his *philoxenia* is explained in terms of his *aidōs* and seen as a product of his noble birth (597–601), and in the scene following the *agōn* between Admetus and Pheres, where the possibility, raised by Pheres, that Admetus may have been guilty of *anaideia* (694), is contrasted with his *aidōs* as a host; the Servant explains his master's reluctance to send Heracles away as *aidōs* (823) and Heracles recognizes that he has been the recipient of this *aidōs* (857).[85] Admetus' behaviour is thus seen both as rejection of conduct felt to be inappropriate and as positive regard for the honour of another person, and, since Heracles recognizes that he has been the recipient of Admetus' *aidōs*, he is determined to reciprocate; it becomes a matter of honour for him to honour Admetus in return, to show himself worthy of Admetus' nobility (855–60). It is therefore apparent that in a reciprocal relationship of this kind concern for one's own honour and regard for that of the recipient of one's actions go hand in hand. The obligations here are expressed entirely in concrete, personal terms, as concern for one's own honour, recognition of the other's honour, and awareness of popular opinion as a force in the background, but this does not rule

---

[85] These two occurrences of *aideisthai* demonstrate the operation of *aidōs* both as prospective inhibition (823) and as positive recognition of another's honour (857). For Ad.'s concern for Her.'s honour, cf. 567, 1037.

out the kind of absolute commitment to particular standards of behaviour manifested by Admetus.

The *aidōs* accorded strangers and guests emerges in an especially
altruistic light in a passage of the *Iphigeneia among the Taurians* (947–
54), in which Orestes tells his sister how, when he first went to Athens
for purification, no *xenos* would accept him on account of his pollution.[86] He goes on, however, to explain how 'those who had *aidōs*'
(949) did eventually accord him hospitality, but although they admitted him to their houses, they would not allow him into their
company. These people clearly had no need to fear that their fellows,
who refused to have anything to do with the matricide, would disapprove if they, too, were to reject him, and since they endanger themselves by allowing a polluted person under their roof,[87] their *aidōs* must
spring from their own ideas of what is right and from their sympathy
for the unfortunate.[88]

[86] This is the reaction Or. fears at *El.* 1195.

[87] Here one might compare 'those who claimed some share of *aretē*' at Thuc. 2. 51. 5;
these are people who, out of *aischunē* (= *aidōs*) risked infection in order to care for sick
philoi, and who thus demonstrated that the strength of their *aischunē* outweighed their
concern for their own safety. (Thus it is unlikely that this *aischunē* is a simple fear of
reproach.) On the passage in Thuc., see Creed (1973), 220; Gomme's n. (1956: ad loc.) is
slightly misrepresented by MacDowell (1963 *b*: 129)—Gomme has for *aretē* 'primarily
courage and a sense of duty', not just 'primarily courage'. This use of *aretē* is, of course, by
no means novel, since obligations towards one's *philoi* have always been associated with
that quality, but it is important, as Creed notes, that this co-operative manifestation of
aretē can entail greater regard for the immediate interests of others than for one's own.
(It is, of course, always possible to argue that self-sacrifice is in one's own *ultimate* best
interests.) Creed's remarks on this particular passage go unnoticed in Adkins's reply
(1975); rather he implies (218) that the actions performed by the *agathos* for his *philoi*
cannot be altruistic. This, however, needs to be argued, and with due regard for the role
of self-reference, as opposed to self-interest, in other-regarding behaviour.

[88] The other-regarding aspect of *aidōs* can, as we have seen, coexist with more self-
regarding concerns, and may, as in the passage just discussed, come quite obviously to
the fore. Most of the relevant passages deal with specific ties or obligations, whether of
philia, *xenia*, or supplication; but there are a few passages in which *aidōs* arises spontaneously as a response to another person not covered by any pre-existing obligation.
Such is *Tro.* 717–18: Talthybius speaks of his uncertainty as to how he might best break
the news to Andromache of the decision to kill Astyanax; she interprets his apprehension as *aidōs* (but wishes to hear the worst), and this *aidōs* must involve the desire to
spare another's feelings. It is to this kind of *aidōs* that Tal. himself refers in 786–9, where
he remarks that to be the bearer of such tidings is a task better suited to one more pitiless
and more prone to *anaideia* than he. In these passages, as in that from *IT* in the text
above, *aidōs* seems to take on positive connotations of pity (Tal.'s *aidōs* in *Tro.* is very like
his pity in *Hec.* 518–20), a concept with which it is traditionally associated; cf. *aidōs* in
legal contexts as 'consideration/clemency' (Ant. 1. 26–7, 4. a. 1; Pl. *Laws* 867e, 877a; cf.
also perhaps *Hcld.* 1027), and *aidesis* in Athenian homicide law (Ch. 4 n. 28). *Aidōs* arises
in a similar context at *Hec.* 515, where Hec. asks Tal. whether the Greeks sacrificed Pol.
aidoumenoi or treated her as an enemy even in death; the use of the part. may bear a

5.3. HONOUR, REPUTATION, RETROSPECTIVE SHAME, AND GUILT

The idea of concern for one's image in the eyes of others has bulked large in the foregoing discussion of self- and other-regarding *aidōs*, although we have seen evidence enough that this idea may coexist with positive commitment to standards which the individual has made his or her own. In the following pages we trace these two aspects of the *aidōs*-reaction with particular reference to new uses of the verbs *aischunomai* and *aideomai* and to Euripides' allusions to the concept of conscience.

5.3.1. Aidōs, *Guilt, and Pollution*

In the *Heracles* concern for 'what people say' and 'how things look', specifically expressed as *aidōs*, is prominent in Heracles' reaction on awakening to the enormity of his crime, but Heracles' *aidōs* merits particular discussion because of the questions it raises about the relationship between *aidōs*, guilt, and pollution. Heracles learns that he has murdered his family at 1135-9, and in his first continuous speech thereafter immediately expresses his desire to kill himself.[89] He is concerned about his reputation, but not with that alone, for in expressing his desire to escape *duskleia*, he employs a metaphor from the ritual of purification by fire (1151-2),[90] thus combining the ideas of ill-repute in the eyes of others with the objectively adhering stain of pollution; and he also conceives an image of himself as juror in his own case (1150), picturing his death as just punishment for his crime (1148-50). His fear of disgrace, then, is combined, naturally with grief, but also with a desire to punish himself which implies subjective recognition of his objective guilt;[91] and there is the first of several combinations of the ideas of disgrace and pollution.

Heracles does allude to the disgrace which he foresees even before

reference to sexual propriety and Pol.'s status as a virgin (cf. 568-70), but even so it must also encompass respect for a person who is bound to the Greeks by no specific obligation.

[89] Thus he manifests a wish for death as a means of escaping disgrace which is close, but not identical to the choice of death rather than future dishonour; for parallels, cf. Dover (1974), 237; Lesky (1983), 279.

[90] See Parker (1983), 227.   [91] Cf. Adkins (1966), 214.

Theseus arrives, but it is certainly true, as Parker points out,[92] that his distress increases noticeably with the latter's arrival. This is not, however, just because Theseus is a witness to his plight, but also because he is Heracles' kinsman and *philos* (1154); he is distressed at being seen by Theseus, but also at affecting a *xenos* with his pollution (1155–6).[93] As a result of these concerns, Heracles veils his head (1159–62), explaining his action both in terms of the *aischunē/aidōs* caused by his crimes and with reference to his desire not to infect an innocent person. The veiling of one's head is a typical *aidōs*-reaction, a consequence of the fear of being seen and part of the general complex of associations between *aidōs* and the eyes,[94] but, since pollution can be transmitted by sight, it is also an obvious means of avoiding affecting others. In spite of the fact, however, that *aischunē* and the wish not to affect another are given as distinct reasons for the veiling of his head, they must rather be seen as two aspects of the one feeling of inhibition; Heracles' *aidōs/aischunē* should not be sharply distinguished from his concern for another person, since precisely this concern not to involve outsiders in one's troubles is more than once in Euripides expressed by means of the verb *aischunomai*.[95] In this sense, then, Heracles' *aidōs* and his awareness of his pollution and its effects on others are inextricably linked, as indeed such concerns will tend to be, since, as Parker shows,[96] the immediate danger of pollution for the polluted party lies not in the stain itself but in the reaction of others to it, and the attitude of the polluted person to the horror, revulsion, or reproach of others will take the same form as it would were these reactions aroused for any other reason.[97] Heracles' inhibition before Theseus thus encompasses inner and outer aspects, a sense not only of the stain which adheres to him and of the enormity of his actions, but also of the

[92] (1983), 318. This observation, however, should not be taken to differentiate Heracles' response sharply from guilt, for private suffering of guilt may just as easily be exacerbated by the presence of another who knows of one's misdeed.

[93] See Bond (1981), ad loc., on the transmission of pollution through sight (with parallels).

[94] For a simple restatement of the proverbial association of *aidōs* with the eyes, see fr. 457 N² (*Cresphontes*; see A. Harder's commentary (1985), 118–20).

[95] *Or.* 281–2 and *IA* 981–2; cf. *Alc.* 542 and n. 83 above. Szlezak (1986: 54) notes the presence of this type of *aidōs* in Eur., but seems to imply that its prominence in his work distinguishes Eur. from other authors; positive respect for the rights and status of others, however, is a regular application of *aidōs*. Cf. also Arist. *EN* 1171ᵇ5–6: 'Everyone is reluctant to be a cause of pain to his *philoi*.'

[96] (1983), 316–17 (also 94, 205); cf. Ch. 4 n. 6.

[97] Conversely, the language of pollution may be used to express extreme moral revulsion (Parker (1983), 313–14).

impact of these on other people; and a sense of the impact of pollution on others may encompass concern both for the other person and for oneself.

The association of *aidōs* and pollution is more or less present in several other Euripidean passages in which the head is veiled in shame. In the *Hippolytus* (243–6) Phaedra asks the Nurse to cover her head;[98] she feels *aidōs* at what she has said and has already made her *aischunē* (here a synonym for *aidōs*) plain by the lowering of her eyes. Phaedra is clearly motivated more by shame at her own conduct and shyness at being seen by others than by any thought of pollution, but the ultimate object of her *aidōs*, her illicit love for Hippolytus, is the kind of sexual transgression which might, at least figuratively, be described in terms of that concept.[99] The title of Euripides' first *Hippolytus* (*Kaluptomenos*, 'Veiled') suggests that the eponymous character veiled his head at some point, which in turn suggests that the identification of the shameful and the impure featured in his reaction to Phaedra's love in both plays;[100] and commenting on *Heracles* 1159 Wilamowitz compares *Orestes* 459–61, a close parallel in that both Heracles and Orestes are polluted, both feel shame at what they have done,[101] and both are reluctant to be seen by one who is bound to them by a tie of *philia*.[102]

Emphasis on contagion decreases after Theseus convinces Heracles, in his speech at 1214–28 and in the stichomythia at 1229–54, that he will not be deterred from helping a friend by considerations of

[98] On this passage, see also below, 5.3.2 and 5.4.4.

[99] She herself refers to her love as a *miasma* at 317, and H. reacts to the Nurse's report of her passion as if her very words brought contagion (653–5; cf. Thes. towards H. at 946–7; Parker (1983), 313).

[100] The veiling of H.'s head may have been accompanied by the exclamation (fr. 436 N²): 'O Lady Aidōs, would that you associated with all mortals and took the shameless-ness [τἀναίσχυντον, their *anaischuntia*] from their minds.' So, e.g., von Erffa (1937), 160; Vickers (1973), 145; Michelini (1987), 287–8. Webster (1967: 68) suggests another location for the fr., but does not contest the significance of the play's title. Craik (1987), however, argues that the title cannot refer to H.'s veiling of his head (but rather refers to the presentation of his covered corpse at the play's close), on the grounds that no one ever veils his head as a reaction to the shameful conduct of *other* people; but this objection is invalid, since at Aeschines 1. 26 we are told how 'right-minded men' covered their heads in shame (on behalf of the city) at the sight of the disgraceful condition of Timarchus' naked body. Since one can be affected by another's disgrace, one can veil one's head in response to it.

[101] Cf. *Her.* 1160 with *Or.* 461.

[102] On *philia* in this passage, cf. n. 36 above. The breach of *philia* is the major reason for Or.'s *aidōs*, but he is none the less a polluted person, and Tyndareus treats him as such at 479–81.

pollution,[103] but Heracles is still afraid of reproach in the future, and part of his fear, at least, must be based on the awareness that others less well disposed to him than Theseus will shun him as polluted.[104] Accordingly, at 1286–90 he imagines the reproaches of those whom he will encounter should he leave Thebes, and his shame persists to the end of the play, where, at 1423–4, he refers to the disgrace in which he has ruined the house and the fact that he will henceforth be a wretched burden on Theseus.

By that stage, however, he has given up his intention to commit suicide, and just as *aidōs* contributed to his resolve to die, so it has a role to play in its undoing. Heracles, in fact, is won over by the argument that failed to convince Sophocles' Ajax, that there is more occasion for *aidōs* in choosing to kill oneself than in facing the tribulations of life, even a life beset by disgrace.[105] But traces of the old *aidōs* persist: at 1378–85, he wonders whether he will be able to carry his murderous weapons in the future. So strongly does he feel that the weapons will be a reminder of his crimes that he sees them, metaphorically, as witnesses who will reproach him in future (1379–81). Again, however, his concern for his past glory as a warrior and fear of future disgrace at the hands of his enemies lead him to persevere, to continue to be the Heracles he was, and so he will retain his weapons (1382–5).

Aidōs is clearly of great importance in the play, and it works on Heracles in different ways, both suggesting the idea of suicide and encouraging him to stay alive. It also has two distinct aspects, one particularly concerned with the judgement of others, another based on

---

[103] See esp. 1231–4; Thes. removes Her.'s fears of polluting the Sun, of polluting a *philos*, and of incurring reproach, at least from Thes. himself (cf. Chalk (1962), 13). On the complex question of the novelty or otherwise of Thes.'s ability to ignore the danger of pollution, see Parker (1983), 309–11; cf. Vickers (1973), 153–5. Michelini (1987), 258–60, is in no doubt that Thes. is being modern and enlightened.

[104] Even if he is purified, as Thes. (1323–5) promises he will be, he will still risk revulsion as one who has committed crimes which are felt to involve pollution, and presumably this revulsion will take little account of formal purification.

[105] On the contrast, cf. Lesky (1983), 280. The thought that suicide is the coward's way out, however, is not overtly prompted by Her.'s interlocutor, but arises within himself (1347–51); cf. Michelini (1987), 260. On the cowardice of suicide and the positive value of endurance, see Chalk (1962), 13; cf. Michelini (1987), 265, 267 n. 158. Adkins (1966: 218) is right to say, in modification of Chalk's argument, that Her. is still motivated by fear of disgrace, and that this, a demand of traditional *aretē*, is not a new *aretē*. Yet Her. has changed his mind as to the nature of disgrace, and has, in effect, decided to live a life which might be seen as disgraceful in traditional terms. Thus, while he does base his decision to live on an aspect of traditional *aretē*, he also rejects one traditional response, and if he does not make endurance a 'new' *aretē*, he does subsume it under *aretē*.

his own recognition of what he has done.[106] We have seen, for example, that Heracles wishes to remove himself from Theseus' sight and that he retains a concern for what other people will say of him in the future (1155–62, 1286–90), while his decision to endure is grounded in his reluctance to be called a coward or to fall prey to his enemies (1347–8, 1382–5). At the same time, however, his resolve to live also draws its strength from a renewed confidence in his own worth which enables him to face the prospect of future opprobrium, and we saw that his very first utterance on discovery of the murders contained not only a reference to his *duskleia*, but also a desire that he should receive his just punishment (1146–52). At the core of his response, then, lies a self-image, first diminished and then restored, which forms the inner basis on which all Heracles' other-directed responses are predicated. One passage not so far discussed shows how these 'inner' and 'outer' aspects are combined, and united under the head of *aidōs*. At 1199–1201 Amphitryon explains to Theseus why Heracles hides his head:

$$\text{αἰδόμενος τὸ σὸν ὄμμα}$$
$$\text{καὶ φιλίαν ὁμόφυλον}$$
$$\text{αἷμά τε παιδοφόνον.}^{107}$$

The zeugma of different applications of *aideisthai* unites inhibitory and retrospective senses;[108] according to Amphitryon, Heracles feels inhibition at being seen by Theseus, respect for Theseus as his *philos*, and shame at what he has done. Of these three senses, the last implies a new use of *aideisthai* with a non-personal object indicating retrospective shame (a point to which we shall return presently). There should be no doubt that Amphitryon is correct in attributing these motives to Heracles, since all he does, in effect, is to rephrase the concerns expressed by Heracles himself at 1153–62 when he first saw Theseus approaching.

---

[106] See Zürcher (1947), 93–4, 96; Stebler (1971), 98.

[107] 'Feeling *aidōs* for your eye, for your kindred *philia*, and for the blood of murdered children.' Wilamowitz (1895: ad loc.) refers φιλίαν ὁμόφυλον to the chorus, but Thes., son of Poseidon, is a kinsman of Her., son of Zeus (cf. 1154 and Bond (1981), on 1200), and referred to Thes. the line picks up Her.'s reluctance to harm the innocent (1161–2), a reluctance which is probably to be seen as *aidōs* (cf. text above with n. 95).

[108] Cf. Bond (1981), ad loc.

5.3.2. *Retrospective Shame*

The most interesting aspect of this passage is Heracles' retrospective
shame, which raises the possibility of a subjective, negative, and
retrospective evaluation of one's actions which would not be far away
from the phenomenon which we call guilt. That this possibility is
realized is, in fact, irrefutable, because in giving the three objects of
Heracles' *aidōs* Amphitryon is clearly not simply saying the same thing
three times over; if Heracles' *aidōs* before Theseus' gaze is to differ
from his *aidōs* at the blood of his children, the difference must lie in the
reference of the former to inhibition before others and of the latter to
the character of one's own actions and one's responsibility for them. It
is significant, however, that it is Amphitryon who makes the
distinction; when Heracles speaks on the subject, he mentions only
aidōs, aischunē, duskleia, and so on; we can distinguish different aspects
of his *aidōs*, but for him these are all part of one total emotional
response. Accordingly, when he speaks of his shame, inhibitory and
retrospective aspects are inseparable. A good example is his own
explanation of his veiling his head at 1160—αἰσχύνομαι γὰρ τοῖς
δεδραμένοις κακοῖς.[109] It is clear that he regrets what he has done and
that his horror of it instils in him a profound sense of shame; he knows
that what he has done is reprehensible and feels responsible for it, yet
this knowledge still produces inhibition and the desire to avoid the
(possibly critical) gaze of others. The dative, τοῖς δεδραμένοις κακοῖς,
moreover, is not the object of his shame but the reason for it (it is a
causal dative),[110] and the possibility thus arises that *aischunomai* refers
as much to prospective inhibition as to the recognition that he has
done something disgraceful. In the same way, Heracles' feeling that his
weapons will be a constant source of reproach to him as they hang by
his side (1379–81) is simply a projection of his shame at what he has
done and of the fear that he will find it hard to live with the memory of
his crime; but the fact that he projects these feelings on to an external
source of reference at all shows how the idea of guilt or remorse and
the awareness that the object of his guilt may also be the object of

---

[109] 'I am ashamed because of the wrongs I have done.'

[110] On the causal dative with *aischunomai*, see, e.g., Goodwin's *Greek Grammar*²
(London, 1894) § 1181. (G.'s citation, 'Ar. *N.* 1355', should be emended to 'Ar. *N.* 992, *Eq.*
1355'.) Bond's description 'instrumental dative' (1981: ad loc.) seems to require a quasi-
passive sense of the verb, though the distinction between causal and instrumental dat.
will not be very precise.

others' disapproval can be combined within him, as indeed they are commonly combined in the Greek context.[111] Let it be clear, however, that neither of these aspects cancels the other.[112]

It is important not to go to extremes in our eagerness to discover what is new about the usage of *aidōs* in the tragedians; we saw in Homer that *aidōs* could entail awareness of the wrongness of the action inhibited, and that prospective locutions could encompass retrospective evaluation of the character of one's actions.[113] The element of 'conscience' is present in many prospective uses, and is not a concomitant of the retrospective sense alone, but obviously the ability to use *aideisthai* and *aischunesthai* retrospectively allows expression of concern for the character of one's actions without explicit reference to future disapproval, and this is clearly what we have in Heracles' shame at shedding the blood of his children at *Heracles* 1199-1201.

Passages like *Heracles* 1160, however, in which *aischunomai* is used with a causal dative, need to be treated with some caution: it is not enough simply to translate, 'I am ashamed of ...', and to assume retrospective conscience. In *Heraclidae* (541-2), for example, Demophon tells Macaria, 'I am not ashamed as a result of your words, but I am pained by your misfortune', and here the question of retrospective shame does not arise, because the *aischunē* which Demophon denies is not occasioned by his conduct at all. In saying that Macaria's words do not occasion any *aischunē* in him he means that there is nothing about her declaration of her readiness to die which makes him concerned for his own honour.[114] There is a third use of

---

[111] Also comparable in this respect is Her.'s statement that he has ruined the house in *aischunai* (1423). This entails self-reproach and the recognition that he has done wrong, but he will also be aware that others tend to criticize those whose actions have, on their own admission, been disgraceful.

[112] Cf. Bond (1981), on 1287: 'Such mockery or scorn was a natural concomitant of the guilt which the fifth-century Greek felt.' If this implies that guilt and fear of mockery can coexist as manifestations of the one general emotional state, one should approve it. Bond goes on, however, 'The Stoic-Christian notion of the *mens sibi conscia recti* which disregarded public opinion was still far away.' True; recognition of the reprehensible nature of one's own actions is very often accompanied by fear of mockery in the Greek context, but there are examples enough of those who disregard public opinion in standing by their own idea of what is right—Solon, 2.3.3 above; Antigone, 4.1.2; Odysseus, 4.2.1; and see below, 6.3.2, on Democritus. [113] See 1.7 above.

[114] Perhaps he implies that he does not imagine that he will incur reproach for allowing a suppliant to die, or that he is not concerned at being outdone in heroism by a woman. For the idea that it is discreditable for women to take the initiative over men, cf. *El.* 932-3, and for the idea that it is *aischron* for men physically to be worsted by women, cf. *Ba.* 798-9 (Ar. *Lys.* 271-2, 450-1, 485; Hdt. 1. 207. 5, 8. 93. 2; cf. the disgrace of comparison with women at Hdt. 2. 102. 4, 106. 2, 7. 11. 1, 9. 107. 1).

298 *Euripides*

the causal dative at *Orestes* 460-1, where Orestes explains his reluctance to face Tyndareus,

$$οὖ μάλιστ᾽ αἰδώς μ᾽ ἔχει$$
$$ἐς ὄμματ᾽ ἐλθεῖν τοῖσιν ἐξειργασμένοις.^{115}$$

Here the causal sense of the dative is apparent, since the *aidōs* phrase is also followed by an infinitive in the regular, prospective manner. Orestes is clearly troubled by the enormity of what he has done,[116] and his past conduct occasions his present response, but he is also afraid of adverse judgement at the hands of Tyndareus, and goes on to give specific grounds for his fear of disapproval from that quarter in particular. It is not that Orestes is only concerned about the prospect of Tyndareus' disapproval, for, in order for him to fear that disapproval, he must realize in what way he has invited it, and so as well as his awareness of the horror of matricide, Orestes also manifests a recognition that he has failed to meet the obligation to show gratitude to one's *philoi* (462-7).[117]

The situation in passages like this, then, is not far removed from that in *Iliad* 22 (104-7), where Hector is aware that he has caused the destruction of the host, something which he knows is 'wrong', but combines his knowledge with a prospective fear of disapproval.[118] A similar situation is envisaged at *Troades* 1025-8, where Hecabe, expressing her revulsion for Helen, observes bitterly that, in view of what she has done,[119] she should manifest *sōphrosunē* rather than her present *anaideia* by dressing in rags, trembling with fear, and shaving her head. Here the *anaideia* referred to is specifically a failure to show proper inhibition towards others on account of past transgressions, and there is thus both a retrospective aspect (Helen should recognize her faults for what they are) and a prospective, inhibitory aspect, in that she is expected to modify her conduct in the face of others' disapproval.[120] Helen reacts almost as Hecabe would like at *Orestes* 97-105, where she explains, with reference to *aischunē* (98), her inability

---

[115] 'I am especially seized by *aidōs* at the prospect of appearing before him on account of what I have done.'

[116] As Willink points out (1986: ad loc.), 461 recalls the famous line 396.

[117] Cf. nn. 36, 102 above.

[118] Cf. 1.2.3, 1.7 above; also 2.3.3 on Solon 32 West, which is comparable.

[119] ἐπὶ τοῖς πρόσθεν ἡμαρτημένοις, 1028.

[120] On the opposition of *to sōphron* and *anaideia* in this passage in the context of women's modesty, cf. North (1966), 69.

personally to make an offering at Clytemnestra's tomb.[121] Here von Erffa is right to note that the reason for Helen's *aischunē* lies in the past,[122] but it is misleading of him to regard this as an instance of retrospective shame, since 98, δεῖξαι ... αἰσχύνομαι ('I am ashamed to show myself'), is a straightforward instance of the prospective use of the verb with an infinitive. It would be more correct to say that Helen's prospective *aischunē* is based on the knowledge that she has done something for which she is liable to be criticized. It emerges from the context, however, that criticism alone is her concern (102); she is afraid of the reproaches of those who lost their sons at Troy.[123]

We saw at the end of the last section that the *Heracles* passage (1199–1201) furnished an instance of *aideomai* with a non-personal accusative object, facilitating the sentiment 'I am ashamed of *x*', which could not be expressed by traditional uses of the verb. This use, is, then, a new development, but a locution of which Euripides seems particularly fond. It first occurs in the martial context in *Heraclidae* (813–16), and here, as in the *Heracles* passage, we have a zeugma of different senses of the verb.[124] The Messenger describes Eurystheus'

---

[121] Electra refers to Hel.'s reluctance, which she had expressed by means of *aischunomai*, as *aidōs* (101), thus demonstrating the essential synonymy of *aischunomai* and *aideomai*, *aischunē* and *aidōs*. For the unselfconscious switch from one to the other, cf. *IA* 1341–2; Soph. *Aj.* 1076–9; Thuc. 1. 84. 3; Ant. 1. 26–7. (The fact that, in this last, both *aidōs* and *aischunē* connote 'mercy' or 'consideration' tends to refute Wilamowitz's contention ((1927) on Ar. *Lys.* 1015) that whereas *anaidēs* can mean 'ruthless', *anaischuntos* could not).

[122] (1937), 158.

[123] The association of *aidōs* with fear of unpleasant consequences is traditional, but this can be combined to varying degrees with a recognition that others' reproaches are justified. There is not much of this in Hel.'s *aidōs* here, and in this respect she contrasts with El., whose inability to look upon her mother's tomb (and thus to make the offering on Hel.'s behalf, 105) is probably an indication of a kind of *aidōs* which is based exclusively on her recognition of the enormity of what she and Or. have done (so Lombard (1985), 7–8). Hel. counters with another kind of *aidōs* which contrasts as trivial with El.'s, claiming that it is *aischron* that she should neglect her duty to her dead sister by allowing slaves to bear her offering (106).

[124] Eur. is fond of the zeugma of different senses of *aideisthai*; cf. also *Hipp.* 1258–9. There is a zeugma of a kind which appears superficially similar to that in the present passage at *Rhes.* 926–7 (since the *Rhes.* does not otherwise demand our attention, the question of its authenticity does not concern us). The Muse laments how she bore her son, the dead Rhesus, only to cast him away, 'out of *aidōs* for her relatives and her maidenhood' (συγγόνους αἰδουμένη | καὶ παρθενείαν). As in the *Hcld.* passage, the verb governs a personal and a non-personal object, but in *Rhes.* the non-personal object is not the conduct of which the agent is or should be ashamed, but a term indicating the status/ role which is the focus of the agent's respect, disregard of which would be a source of disgrace; cf. *Od.* 16. 75 = 19. 527: εὐνήν τ' αἰδομένη πόσιος δήμοιό τε φῆμιν ('out of *aidōs* for her husband's bed and for popular opinion').

cowardice in the face of a challenge from his opponents: 'Neither out
of *aidōs* for those who could hear him nor for his own cowardice,
general though he was,[125] did he dare to take the field, but he proved
himself most worthless.' Here 'out of *aidōs* for those who could hear
him' expresses exactly the Homeric reaction of concern for the
opinions of witnesses,[126] but the use of the participle with a non-
personal object is far from Homeric; the speaker clearly means not 'he
did not respect his cowardice', but 'he was not ashamed of his
cowardice', and the phrase 'general though he was' adds to the
criticism by giving grounds for *aidōs* based on Eurystheus' status and
responsibilities. Eurystheus, then, did not care what others thought of
him and failed to reflect on the inappropriateness of his conduct for
one of his status. Now, any occurrence of *aidōs* or any fear of loss of
reputation presupposes a claim to honour, a subjective appreciation of
one's own worth, but the novelty of this passage lies in its explicit
reference, by means of the new use of the verb, to the internal source
of reference as such.[127] The thought behind the passage is wholly
traditional—cowardice is *aischron*—but it is recognized that when one
rejects a course of action as *aischron* one is not simply responding to
the prospect of others' disapproval.

Clearly, the usage of *aideomai* has widened since Homer, first of all
with the occurrence of the verb with participial and conditional
clauses, relating it more closely to present action, and now with the
taking of a non-personal object; the past or present action itself may
now become the explicit focus of *aidōs*, whereas in Homer the explicit
focus could only be an action in the future (*aideomai* with infinitive), or
a person or group of persons (the accusative uses). The development
of *aideomai* from inhibitory to retrospective uses is noted by Barrett,[128]
but, regrettably, his explanation of the phenomenon, in terms of
contamination from *aischunomai* to *aideomai*, will not survive examination of the evidence.[129] In Homer the usage of both verbs is parallel,

125 οὔτε τοὺς κλύοντας αἰδεσθεὶς λόγων | οὔτ' αὐτὸς αὑτοῦ δειλίαν στρατηγὸς ὤν, . . .
126 *Pace* von Erffa (1937), 142 ('the positive force of *aidōs* is lost'); cf. n. 1 above.
127 Cf. Lombard (1985), 10 n. 14. Von Erffa (1937: 142) may thus be right to refer this
passage to Democ. B 264 DK etc.
128 (1964), on *Hipp.* 244.
129 I say 'regrettably', because Barrett's explanation has won widespread acceptance;
see Kannicht (1969), on *Helen* 415-17; Solmsen (1973), 423; A. Harder (1985), 149 (on
Cres. fr. 457 N²). Barrett has the support of Ammonius (§ 17 Nickau), quoting Aristoxenus
(fr. 42 a Wehrli; cf. frr. 42 b-c), at least in so far as they distinguish between *aidōs* as
respect and *aischunē* as retrospective shame; but this does no more justice to the
evidence than does Barrett himself. Barrett's distinction is also found in the Stoic

and in the one passage in which *aischunomai* governs an object it does so in exactly the same way as *aideomai*,[130] and while *aischunomai* is much more common with the participial construction in Sophocles than *aideomai*, this reflects only the obsolescence of the latter,[131] not a particular association of the former with shame over one's own conduct. There is, in fact, only one passage, which may or may not be earlier than that under discussion, in which *aischunomai* may legitimately be translated 'I am ashamed of *x*', and that is in Sophocles' *Oedipus Tyrannus* (1079), where Oedipus offers in explanation of Jocasta's conduct the opinion that 'she is ashamed of my low birth' (τὴν δυσγένειαν τὴν ἐμὴν αἰσχύνεται). Even if the *Tyrannus* were unquestionably earlier than *Heraclidae*,[132] one previous instance of *aischunomai* with a non-personal accusative would hardly be enough to prove that the sense 'I am ashamed of *x*' is original to *aischunomai* and only later transferred to *aideomai*. It is much more likely that both verbs, as synonyms, develop this meaning in parallel fashion.[133]

These new uses, it must be stressed, do not necessarily or unambiguously express concepts of guilt or conscience. The usage clearly does suggest a move away from consideration of the visibility of

definitions of *aidōs* and *aischunē* as types of fear quoted by Nemesius (*SVF* iii. 416, p. 101, ll. 29–39)—*aischunē* is a 'sinking feeling' caused by one's own actions, *aidōs* is fear of illrepute; but here it is also noted that 'the ancients' often use *aidōs* and *aischunē* interchangeably. Note, too, that other Stoic classifications of fears (*SVF* iii. 407, 409) mention *aischunē* alone and define it in exactly the terms used in fr. 416 to define *aidōs*. These later distinctions between *aidōs* and *aischunē* are probably the results of comparison of older, poetic uses of *aidōs* with the dominant contemporary and unpoetic sense of *aischunē*.

[130] *Od.* 21. 323; cf. *Od.* 16. 75, 19. 527 for *aideomai* in the same sense.

[131] The obsolescence of *aideomai* is noted by Barrett (1964), on *Hipp.* 244. See 4.2.3 above, on Sophoclean usage; and cf. that of Thuc (*aidōs* once (1. 84. 3), *aischunē* and *to aischron* more frequent) and Ar. (*aidōs* twice (*Clouds* 995; *Wasps* 447), in contexts which suggest its poetic and old-fashioned nature (in *Clouds*, the Just Argument, the representative of the old ways, personifies *aidōs*, while the *Wasps* passage alludes to the proverb '*aidōs* in the eyes')).

[132] The argument of Knox (1979: 112–24) strongly suggests that *OT* is to be dated, if not to 425 BC, at least to between 430 and 425. This view is rejected, but not, I think, refuted by Müller (1984), who argues for a date in the 430s. This would make *OT* slightly earlier than *Hcld.* (dated to 430 by Zuntz (1955), 81–8), but not sufficiently so for Barrett's thesis to be sustained on these foundations alone.

[133] The fact that we do find a retrospective use in Soph. at least suggests that the retrospective sense of the verbs, though frequent in Eur., does not represent a Euripidean innovation in Attic usage. The retrospective sense of *aischunomai*, furthermore, is presupposed by the use of *aischunē* with an objective gen. at Soph. *El.* 616. Since retrospective uses are also frequent in post-Euripidean prose, perhaps the sudden proliferation of instances of *aideomai* and *aischunomai* with a non-personal obj. in Eur. is to be set down to his use of a prosaic locution avoided by the other tragedians.

actions, or their openness to criticism, towards evaluation in subjective and personal terms, but equally clearly some retrospective uses will involve no element of conscience whatever. In the line from the *Tyrannus*, for example, the *aischunē* which Oedipus attributes to Jocasta does focus on an event in the past (which is envisaged, however, as having led to a present state of affairs), but the event in question is not, at least as Oedipus conceives it at the time, one for which Jocasta could possibly regard herself as responsible. One can, in Greek as in English, be ashamed of an action committed by someone else or of something that one has suffered rather than done,[134] and both shame at one's sufferings and mere embarrassment, as well as shame based on one's own misdeeds, may be expressed retrospectively. Even when the verb does refer to the agent's own actions, the emotional response which is described may retain much of its traditional character. In the passages from *Heracles* and *Heraclidae*, for example, the zeugma of senses unites both inhibitory and retrospective aspects, and this may be the case even where there is no such zeugma. For instance at *Ion* 367, Ion urges Creousa not to question Apollo about the child he fathered because the god αἰσχύνεται τὸ πρᾶγμα ('is ashamed of what he has done'); this does attribute an awareness of the discreditable nature of the act, but Ion is equally concerned that the god will be reluctant to have his misdeed exposed (μὴ 'ξέλεγχέ νιν, 'do not show him up', he urges).[135] Similarly, in the *Hippolytus* (244) Phaedra's αἰδούμεθα γὰρ τὰ λελεγμένα μοι ('I am ashamed of what I have said') may indicate recognition of the discreditable nature of the passion which lies behind her ravings, but it is also clear that Phaedra's words when mad now occasion embarrass-

---

[134] This is the case at *Ion* 341 and *IA* 848; the past actions, expressed in the acc., of which the subj. of the verb (*aischunomai* and *aideomai* respectively) is ashamed were performed by someone else (although the former passage is complicated by the fact that the *adikia* suffered by Creousa's friend is rape, for which the victim, it seems, could be blamed (below, 5.4.2)). Cf. the instance of *aidōs* with an objective gen., answering to a use of the verb with non-personal acc., at *Hel.* 417—Menelaus is ashamed, or embarrassed, at his *tuchē*, at what has happened to him; as a result, he was ashamed (ἠσχυνόμην, from *aischunomai*, 415) to approach people in order to find out where he was. Under the influence of Barrett, Kannicht (1969: on 415–17) claims that the verb *aischunomai* and the noun *aidōs* in this passage have exchanged roles, the one being used in a sense which belonged 'originally' to the other.

[135] Cf. the *aidōs* of Apollo with regard to his past prophecies (another case of noun + obj. gen. = verb + acc.) at *IT* 713 (this leads him to drive Orestes, whose presence in Greece would be a constant reminder of the disreputable oracle and a possible source of reproach, as far away as possible). With this passage, cf. *Ion* 1557–8 and *Hel.* 884–6, where Apollo and Aphrodite respectively fear disapproval arising from the presence of a mortal whom they have treated shabbily.

ment before those who were witness to her madness, and this aspect of her emotional reaction is expressed both in her desire for concealment (243) and in the reference to her eye turning to *aischunē* (246)—an indication that she has adopted an expression which is typical of inhibitory *aidōs*. This is not to say that *aideomai* etc. in these passages express concern only with appearances rather than with the character of one's actions, simply that *aidōs* typically involves a reference to the outward aspect of one's actions which does not disappear with the new retrospective uses; by the same token, the element of subjective evaluation of the character of one's own conduct was often present even in locutions which referred explicitly to the judgement of others. A retrospective use of *aideomai* or *aischunomai*, then, may well encompass an element of retrospective, 'guilty' conscience, but this element will rarely constitute the totality of the response; *aidōs* is a term of wider extension than any of the modern concepts which may be invoked in explanation of it.

5.3.3. *Conscience*

The coexistence of the sense that one is under the scrutiny of others with an element of retrospective conscience is apparent even in the play in which Euripides' interest in conscience emerges in its clearest light. We have seen already how, in the play that bears his name, Orestes' awareness that he has done wrong leads to unwillingness to face the reproaches of Tyndareus. His conscience, however, emerges unambiguously as such in the famous line 396, in which he explains his affliction in terms of 'awareness, the fact that I am conscious of having done terrible things'. This line is universally seen as the first reference to the phenomenon of conscience as such in tragedy,[136] and it clearly belongs with other passages in late fifth-century literature in which the phenomenon is articulated by means of the verb *suneidenai*.[137] In this

---

[136] See Zucker (1928), 7-8; Seel (1953), 298-9; Class (1964), 102-7; Stebler (1971), 118-19.

[137] 'To share knowledge', 'to be aware, conscious of something', often, in the passages most relevant to our enquiry, with a reflexive pronoun. On *suneidenai* elsewhere in Eur., see Zucker (1928), 8 n. 12; Class (1964), 102-7; Stebler (1971), 120; on 'conscience' in Eur. in general: Class, 91-107; Stebler, 47-9, 83-4, 88-9, 91-2, 98-102, 117-19; on *sunesis* in this passage: Class, 106; Willink (1986), ad loc.; on *suneidēsis* etc. in other authors, cf. 6.1 below. Rodgers (1969) sensibly points out that both Or.'s *sunesis* and *suneidēsis* in general refer basically to 'awareness'; a simple assumption that any instance of *suneidenai* etc. is an example of 'conscience' is thus unwarranted. I remain convinced, however,

case the emphasis is on Orestes' intellectual apprehension of his crime,[138] and thus there is no mention of *aidōs*, which, while it may sometimes perform the function of categorizing one's actions as *aischron* and no more, usually suggests affective or dispositional consequences of that awareness. Euripides therefore separates the element of retrospective conscience from its effects and manifestations here, and identifies the cognitive element in the emotional reaction. Elsewhere, however, it is clear that *aidōs* is one of many aspects of Orestes' response to his crime. He hides his body, says Electra at line 43,[139] feels *aidōs* at the approach of Tyndareus at 459–69, and expresses a fear that he will cause the latter pain at 544–5.[140] The wider action of the drama clearly shows that Orestes' awareness of what he has done does lead to *aidōs*, and *aidōs* and conscience are not to be regarded as mutually exclusive in this context any more than in the others we have considered.

The language of conscience is also apparent in the Nurse's description of Hermione's behaviour in *Andromache* (804–15); Hermione is supposed to be troubled by her 'awareness' (*sunnoia*, 805) that she has done wrong in attempting to have Andromache and her child put to death—she 'repents' (experiences 'after-pain', 814) and recognizes that she has acted in a way that was not *kalon* (814–15). The Nurse thus reveals a familiarity with the experience of remorse,[141] yet she also makes it clear that Hermione fears punishment at the hands

that such locutions can describe the phenomenon of conscience, and Rodgers's demand that conscience proper must always spring from moral values which are personal to oneself seems unreasonable. She herself (242–3) recognizes that retrospective conscience in English is often felt to encompass awareness of one's culpability in terms of external sanctions; I should point out that such awareness, even if it does lead to fear of punishment, does not necessarily exclude recognition that one has failed to live up to one's own standards. (Cf. the sound common sense of Dover (1974), 220–6.)

[138] An apprehension which has, however, emotional and psychological consequences; see Class (1964), 106–7; Willink (1986), ad loc.; cf. Wilamowitz (1959), ii. 387 n. 1.

[139] Cf. Class (1964), 104.

[140] This concern for the feelings of another person might well be the same as the *aischunē* that Or. expresses with regard to El. at 280; cf. n. 95 above. Or. also (557) claims that he feels *aidōs* at referring to Clyt. as his mother. He has been representing himself to Tynd. as troubled by what he has done (e.g. 546), and so this *aidōs* may be based on his gross breach of *philia*, but it is more likely, since he has progressed to the subject of Clyt.'s adultery, that his *aidōs* is to be seen as reluctance to associate himself with a mother whose conduct he despises (as at Aesch. *Cho.* 917); 559–60 support this view, and, in that case, Or.'s *aidōs* here is part of his defensive rhetoric and not of his psychological reaction to matricide.

[141] See von Erffa (1937), 160; Grube (1961), 208; Class (1964), 99–102; Stebler (1971), 83.

of Neoptolemus and the dishonour which punishment would bring (808–9).[142] The Nurse, then, believes that these motives are combined in Hermione, as indeed they might be. But Hermione has already revealed herself as an ignoble character; her distress as reported by the Nurse emerges only when she is faced with the prospect of punishment, and, most importantly, when she reappears on stage, although her distress is acute, she is concerned with her conduct towards Andromache only in so far as it makes her own position vulnerable (833–5, 919–20).[143] This does not, however, mean that apparent references to conscience in Euripides are illusory—merely that the Nurse attempts to place the best construction on her mistress's behaviour by suggesting that she is troubled by genuine recognition of her own moral error rather than panic at the thought of punishment.[144]

The retrospective uses of *aideomai* and *aischunomai* may thus be seen against the background of the familiarity of the Euripidean corpus with phenomena which may be grouped loosely under the heading of conscience. The emotional fullness of tragedy, however, and the complexity of the concept of *aidōs* are such that the responses expressed in the locutions with which we are concerned rarely fall into the simple moral/non-moral, internal/external, shame/guilt dichotomies so beloved of modern commentators; and if the range of aspects which may be united by one application of the verb *aideomai* indicates a comparative lack of differentiation in Greek moral vocabulary, this has the happy consequence for tragedy of allowing the depiction of emotional states with depth and complexity.

5.4. SEXUALITY AND THE SEXES

5.4.1. *General*

Euripides' female characters, and those of the other tragedians, clearly cannot be regarded as specimens of contemporary Athenian

---

[142] Cf. Stebler (1971), 84.

[143] *Pace* Class (1964), 101; Heath (1987: 93) also takes a different view.

[144] Cf. 918, where Herm. claims that Men. gave way to Peleus out of *aidōs*; this he manifestly did not, and thus Herm.'s attribution of such sensitivity to her father is simply an attempt to disarm Or.'s surprise that Men. should be defeated by a weak old man (cf. Dalfen (1985), 73). In both these passages partiality leads a character to place a favourable, but false construction on another's motives.

womanhood, and it must be assumed that they often act and speak in ways which would have been quite inappropriate for any Athenian woman.[145] Yet there are, especially in Euripides, very many details which manifestly do not stem from the heroic world, and, while it may be difficult to posit abstract, categorical distinctions between dramatic and real life, it is a relatively uncontroversial assumption that there is constant allusion in Euripidean tragedy, often in fairly trivial ways, but sometimes as an important dramatic theme, to the situation of women in contemporary Athens. Often such details merely serve to demonstrate the ordinary role of *aidōs* etc. in women's behaviour, but occasionally, as in the *Hippolytus*, Euripides is able to use the association of *aidōs* with sexuality and sexual morality to explore the role and value of the concept as a motivating force in a profound and disturbing manner.

Women's *aidōs* is most regularly concerned with the requirements of loyalty to husband or father and freedom from any imputation of sexual impropriety, the best way to avoid any such imputation lying in the limitation of the woman's opportunity for contact with the opposite sex.[146] *Aidōs* and *sōphrosunē* maintain the standards both of loyalty and of propriety,[147] and failure to observe them is *aischron*.[148]

[145] e.g. such phenomena as the appropriation by females of competitive male values in times of stress, found in all three tragedians, must have been alien to the experience of most Athenian women. The female characters of tragedy, however, need not replicate the ordinary behaviour of Athenian women in order for their portrayal to provide important information on the role of women in Athenian society and on Athenian (male) conceptions of their nature; cf. Just (1989), 10–11.

[146] See *Hcld.* 41–4, where it is the male protector of a group of young women who experiences *aidōs* at their appearance in public and among men (cf. *Pho.* 93–4: if Antigone appears in public, blame will attach both to her and to her *paidagōgos*). That men and women should not meet face to face is called a *nomos* (offered as an explanation of Hecabe's *aidōs*) at *Hec.* 974–5. These lines may be interpolated (Diggle, after Dindorf and Hartung), but their irrelevance in the context might well indicate Hec.'s search for one further excuse for her inability to look Polymestor in the face.

[147] *Aidōs*: *Pho.* 1276 (such *aidōs*, with its attendant symptoms and behaviour patterns—blushing, veiling the head—is denied by Antigone at 1485–92); *sōphrosunē*: *Hcld.* 474–7; *Andr.* 235, 365, 594, 595–601; *Hel.* 932; *Pho.* 1692. We saw above that at *Tro.* 1027 *sōphrosunē* could be opposed to *anaideia* as the proper attitude in a woman aware of her infamy, and clearly *sōphrosunē* and *aidōs* are very close in this context (cf. North (1966), 69, 71, 74).

[148] *Hec.* 443; *Tro.* 773, 1041, 1114; *Or.* 118–19, 1154, 1361–2—all with reference to Helen (cf. von Erffa (1937), 133); cf. *Hel.* 66–7, 686–7; *Or.* 99. On the disgrace for a woman of appearing in the company of men, cf. *Andr.* 876–7; *El.* 343–4; women's sexual indiscretions are *aischron* also at *Ba.* 487–8, 1062. At *Andr.* 220, 238, and 244 it is women's insatiable appetite for sex that is disgraceful, and so not to be spoken of. For this, the orthodox view of women's sexual appetite, cf. frr. 401, 410, 493, 662 N², 882a (Snell, suppl. to N²).

Under these conditions, then, it is not surprising that all respectable women are expected to manifest a certain decorum with regard to sexual matters[149] and that unmarried women often show an acute sensitivity bordering on fear.[150] We may examine some of these ideas in two plays, *Ion* and *Iphigeneia at Aulis*, in which they are important in the ethical background, before considering the *Hippolytus*, in which the *aidōs* appropriate to contexts of sex and sexuality is prominent in the motivation of both major characters in subtle and suggestive ways.

5.4.2. Ion

Since it is a basic premiss of the plot of *Ion* that a woman has been raped, it is to be expected that women's *aidōs* has an important role. Upon meeting Ion, Creousa initially conceals the fact that it is she herself who has been raped, yet her *aidōs* is still apparent, as she attempts to bring herself to relate the sufferings of her 'friend';[151] Ion does not find her *aidōs* at all out of the ordinary, taking it, we must presume, as an ordinary expression of a woman's reticence about sex. The real reason for her *aidōs*, however, must be her shame at having been raped, a reaction which Ion himself regards as quite natural in a woman. Having heard Creousa's tale that her 'friend' was raped by Apollo, Ion is shocked, and attempts to exonerate the god by claiming that Creousa's friend must be seeking to conceal a crime committed by a mortal—'That cannot be; it is a man's offence (*adikia*) of which she is ashamed' (341). This instance of retrospective shame is envisaged as applying not to something one has done, but to something one has suffered,[152] and although a man who commits rape does wrong or breaks the law (*adikein*), it is assumed that the woman will be ashamed

[149] See esp. the passages from *Andr.* in n. 148 above.
[150] See *IT* 372–6, where Iphigeneia describes how, out of *aidōs* occasioned by her forthcoming 'marriage', she could not bring herself to embrace her infant brother before leaving her father's house. Here *aidōs* appears as an undifferentiated (and powerful) inhibition-feeling caused by the prospect of the transition from virginity to womanhood. Cf. n. 201 below.
[151] The reason for Cr.'s inhibition is given in 288, where she explains why she reacted with such vehemence to Ion's mention of the Long Cliffs—she is 'aware of something disgraceful in the caves'. At 336 she is about to divulge the story which is to form the basis of her consultation of the oracle, but *aidōs* holds her back, and this draws from Ion a remark on the traditional force of *aidōs* (personified as a *theos*, cf. *Her.* 557) in inhibiting action. Cr.'s *aidōs* resurfaces whenever she has to talk about her disgrace: see 859–61, 934; cf. 1471.
[152] Cf. n. 134 above.

of the experience; this is not, however, something which should surprise the modern reader. Nor is it the case that rape is shameful only for the victim, for at 367 *aischunomai* is used, retrospectively once more, of the god's shame at his own wrongdoing.[153] Yet Creousa's shame is not simply a manifestation of a regrettable but understandable tendency in the victim to experience feelings of self-disgust and unworthiness as a result of an episode for which no reasonable person would hold her responsible; for it appears from 392–400 that a woman might expect to be criticized, even denigrated, for having been a victim of rape. Creousa urges Ion not to reveal anything of what she has told him to her husband, lest she incur *aischunē*, disgrace, for stirring up what should remain hidden (395–6), and ends with a *gnōmē*: women's lot is an unhappy one, and good women incur hatred through simple association with the bad (398–400). Creousa is no doubt concerned lest Xouthus should ever discover the truth of her own disgrace, but she is able to motivate her anxiety in terms of male attitudes which she expects Ion to understand, and these seem to include not only criticism of a woman who talks about sex at all, but also a readiness to consider a woman who had been raped as 'bad' (*kakē*), someone to be shunned by her 'respectable' sisters. In this respect the Athenian attitude seems to differ, if not from our own, at least from that which we should like to be our own, and, seen in this context, the intensity of Creousa's *aidōs* at her past experiences[154] becomes entirely understandable.[155]

[153] It is, I suppose, possible that Ion considers rape shameful when perpetrated by a god (as being beneath his dignity), though not by a man; but more likely he thinks rape shocking in itself (at least he knows that it is an *adikia*), even if what is disgraceful for a mortal is *a fortiori* disgraceful for a god. Ion does not tell us precisely why he thinks the god is ashamed of his rape of Cr., although it is clear that he believes the god to be afraid of exposure (365, 367). Even if we imagine that to be the god's only concern, this in itself reveals that rape is something for which the perpetrator would be criticized (cf. Athena at 1557–8). At 895 Cr. sings of the *anaideia* which the god manifested when he forced himself on her, thus referring to his lack of respect for another's person, for the honour of her *kurios*, and for public standards of proper behaviour.

[154] As Conacher points out (1967: 282), Cr.'s *aidōs* is the chief obstacle to a speedy resolution of the complications of the play.

[155] Clearly, a woman who had been raped and who had thus been the vehicle of the dishonour of her *kurios* might be blamed by him and by others. It is not at all clear, however, whether social disapproval in such cases was matched by legal disabilities. A woman who had been *seduced* was subject to punishments; see A. R. W. Harrison (1968), 35–6; MacDowell (1978), 125; Garner (1987), 84–5. Harrison (36) suggests that a woman who had been raped might be 'liable to just the same treatment as she who had been a willing co-operator in the adultery'; but does 'liable' mean 'in law' or just 'in practice'? Garner (84–5) takes it in the former sense, but this interpretation, even if it is what Harrison meant, is doubtful. Certainly a man exercising his right to kill an adulterer caught *in flagrante* with a woman under his tutelage might not have known for certain

5.4.3. Iphigeneia at Aulis

This play is richest of all in examples of polite *aidōs* towards the
opposite sex. We meet it first of all in the young women of the chorus,
when they sing (at 185-91) of how they overcame their inhibitions
(which caused their cheeks to blush with 'the *aischunē* of youthful
freshness', 187-8).[156] The chorus return to the theme of *aidōs* in the
first stasimon, in which it is specifically related to proper conduct in
the sphere of sexual relations.[157] The antistrophe deals with the *aretē* of
women, which, in its limited application to the shunning of secret
loves, is contrasted with that of men, which takes countless forms and
can make a city great (568-72). Education makes a great contribution
to *aretē* (561-2), and *aidōs* (*to aideisthai*, 563), the force which discerns
the proper course of action, the course which will bring good
reputation, is seen as a product of education (563-7).[158]

Aspects of the education which fosters *aidōs* are apparent elsewhere
in the play.[159] Agamemnon, for example, is seen enforcing the
imperatives of women's education when he reminds both his daughter
(678-9) and his wife of the need to avoid contact with the world of
men (735). It is in the confrontation between Clytemnestra and

that she was being seduced rather than raped (Harrison, 34); and if he killed an offender
who turned out to have raped rather than seduced, given that rape was a less serious
offence for which the *kurios'* right of self-help did not exist (Lys. I. 32), he would, in order
to avoid conviction, have to maintain in court that the woman had in fact been seduced
rather than raped; thus in this, and presumably in other ways (e.g. a woman's allegation
of rape might not be believed), a woman who had been raped might be taken for an
adulteress and treated accordingly. But none of this in any way proves that a woman who
had been raped, and who was acknowledged as having been so, was liable in law to the
same penalties as one who had been seduced. The Athenians were certainly capable of
distinguishing between the disloyalty of a seduced wife and the absence of disloyalty in
one who had been raped; the speaker of Lys. I. 32-3 holds that the penalty for seduction
is more severe than that for rape precisely because the seducer has made the woman
disloyal and has cast the paternity of her children into doubt; and in *Hipp.* Phaedra feels
it is better to die with her husband believing that she has been raped than to risk the
charge that she had attempted to consummate an adulterous passion.

[156] For the symptoms, cf. *Pho.* 1485-90, and, on the overall sense, [Aesch.] *PV* 132-5
(3.1.3 above) also motivating the entrance of a chorus of maidens.
[157] Szlezak (1986: 55), however, unaccountably assumes that *to aideisthai* in 563 refers
to respect for the rights of others, above all the weak. The context clearly shows, though,
that the job of *to aideisthai* is to promote the conduct demanded by *aretē*, namely, in the
case of women, to shun illicit sexual relationships. On the themes of marriage, sex, and
the role of women in the choral odes of *IA*, see Foley (1985), 78-84.
[158] For a more detailed interpretation of this passage, see 5.5 below.
[159] Cf. Foley (1985), 80.

Achilles, however, that the consequences of the belief that women should not be seen in public are exploited to greatest effect.

Clytemnestra's abrupt words of greeting at 819–20 reveal that the rules against women appearing in the company of men, enforced by women's *aidōs*, may also involve *aidōs* on the male side, for Achilles is shocked, and immediately invokes *aidōs* at finding himself in the company of a woman of such distinguished appearance (821–2).[160] Achilles' youthful *aidōs* is obviously acute, activated as it is by the mere sight of an unaccompanied woman; Clytemnestra, however, approves his *aidōs*, and recognizes it as the proper response, an indication of his reverence for *sōphrosunē* (824).[161] Achilles' *aidōs* persists, however, and, thanking Clytemnestra for her brevity in disclosing her identity, he makes to leave, since it is *aischron* in his view to converse with women (829–30). His embarrassment, accordingly, intensifies when Clytemnestra goes on to offer him her hand as a preliminary to the marriage ceremony, and he reiterates his *aidōs* (833–4) in terms of his fear of what Agamemnon might do were he to touch what he should not.[162]

Clytemnestra, however, continues to talk about marriage, and construes Achilles' incredulity as another kind of *aidōs*, a natural bashfulness at meeting one's prospective in-laws and being reminded of marriage (839–40). She assumes, then, that young men and not just young women (as at *Iphigeneia among the Taurians* 372–6) may experience shyness with regard to marriage. Yet one feels that, even though Achilles does show considerable coyness *vis-à-vis* the opposite sex, the shyness with regard to marriage in general with which Clytemnestra credits him would, if it were ever experienced by any real

---

[160] His exclamation, 'O Lady Aidōs, . . .' is also that of Hippolytus in fr. 436 N² (n. 100 above).

[161] Ach.'s reverence (*sebein*) for *sōphrosunē* presumably implies the latter quality on his part, although there is probably also an implication that *sōphrosunē* is required in both parties when the sexes meet. Cf. North (1966), 78, on this passage.

[162] αἰδοίμεθ' ἂν | Ἀγαμέμνον', εἰ ψαύοιμεν ὧν μή μοι θέμις. Ach. does not say that, out of respect for or shame before Ag., he will refrain from touching his wife, but that he would feel *aidōs* before him if he were to touch his wife, and this can only mean that he would be embarrassed to appear before Ag. if the latter were aware of what had transpired between Clyt. and Ach. *Aideisthai* here does encompass a recognition that the other person possesses *timē* for which he will be concerned (and Ach. does firmly believe that it is wrong, μὴ θέμις, to lay hands on another man's wife), but the use of the potential optative seems also to express the thought in prudential terms, relating to the embarrassment of exposure. Ach. does, however, show genuine respect for another's honour at 1028–32 (following the supplication scene), where he is scrupulous to ensure that Clyt. moves through the camp unseen; to be detected would shame (*aischunein*) her house and her father, who does not deserve to be dishonoured. This is the heart of the prohibition on women being seen abroad; men's honour is vulnerable through women.

bridegroom, be a rather milder thing than the *aidōs* of the bride, given the seclusion in which the latter will have been brought up.

With Achilles' persistence in denying all knowledge of marriage, however, it dawns on Clytemnestra that she has been deceived, a realization which turns the tables by occasioning *aidōs* in her to balance that of Achilles. 'I feel *aidōs* about this' (αἰδοῦμαι τάδε), she says at 848, and while this is clearly another instance of *aideomai* with a non-personal object referring to an event in the past (her acting as matchmaker in a marriage which did not exist, 847–8), once more the reference of the phrase as a whole is to present inhibition or embarrassment. Clytemnestra has not herself done anything disgraceful, rather she has been placed in an embarrassing situation by someone else (as Achilles recognizes, 849); her phrase then means something like 'I am embarrassed at this', and, despite Achilles' words of consolation, her embarrassment persists, manifested in her downcast eyes as she makes to quit the scene (851–2).

Lombard notes the effect of parallelism and contrast in the way in which both Achilles and Clytemnestra, at the beginning and the end of their short dialogue respectively, feel impelled by *aidōs* to leave the scene,[163] but I see no evidence for his further assertion that the poet is employing 'a technique of juxtaposition and contrast' that is intended 'to highlight the difference between traditional notions, motivated by external sanctions, and more advanced concepts, grounded in inner ethical attitudes'.[164] Rather the contrast is between two ordinary and traditional forms of *aidōs*. Achilles' shyness at being in the company of a woman is both an inner ethical attitude, in that it operates in him instinctively and is part of his upbringing and social role, and a response to the external standards of convention; he feels that it is wrong to associate with another man's woman and fears disapproval for doing so. There is, on the other hand, scarcely any sign of an inner ethical attitude on Clytemnestra's part; no doubt she disapproves of the deception that has been perpetrated against her, but this attitude is not equivalent to her *aidōs*, which relates to the fact that she has been treated in a way which she sees as undermining her status (847, 852). Her embarrassment, then, has nothing to do with 'a subjective feeling of inner shame for having actually told a lie';[165] her words ψευδὴς γενομένη ('having been proved false', 852) do not refer as such to a belief that lies are *aischron*, but to the fact that she has been shown to have been talking about a non-existent marriage, which troubles

---

[163] Lombard (1985), 6–7.   [164] (1985), 6.   [165] Lombard (1985), 7.

her because she is standing face to face with one who knows she has been talking virtual nonsense and who realizes that she, a woman of her status, has been the victim of a hoax. Accordingly, her reaction is not 'inner shame', but straightforward embarrassment, which may be a profoundly 'inner' experience, but is none the less produced by no 'inner ethical attitude'.[166]

The education in *aidōs*, therefore, is clearly apparent in Achilles, and the chorus's reference to their own youthful *aischunē* (188) thus heralds the importance of this as a theme. Similar qualities are apparent in the characterization of Iphigeneia herself. She is one of those Euripidean maidens, like Macaria in *Heraclidae* and Antigone in *Phoenissae*, who are presented initially as inexperienced and full of the modest *aidōs* which is particularly appropriate in those of their sex and age, but who eventually reject the maiden's role out of devotion to some higher cause.[167] We first hear of her *aidōs* at second hand, when, at 992–7, Clytemnestra asks Achilles: 'Do you wish her to embrace your knees as a suppliant? That would be unmaidenly; but if you wish, she will come, keeping her eye free in *aidōs*. But if I may obtain from you the same favour in her absence, let her remain at home; for she has a maiden's pride. Still, one must *aideisthai* as far as is possible.' This is a difficult passage, but the general sense is clear; if Iphigeneia were to come, she would conduct herself with *aidōs*. This must mean that she would not entirely abandon her *aidōs* by abandoning her claim to honour in the unmaidenly action of supplication; somehow she would enjoy the best of both worlds by supplicating without total self-abasement, retaining her *aidōs* for her own status in the look of her eye. When manifested in the eyes *aidōs* indicates that the gaze is averted downwards, and although 'free' (*eleutheron*, 994) does not immediately suggest 'downcast' this must be the sense here.[168] Iphigeneia's free status would be reflected in her downcast eyes.

On the whole, however, it would be better if she stayed at home,[169]

---

[166] Lombard's contention (1985), then, that Eur. consistently applies a technique of contrast between conventional and advanced uses of *aidōs* remains, on the evidence he cites, not proven. Of the three passages he cites (the present, *Alc.* 600 ff. (n. 14 above), and *Or.* 97–105 (n. 123 above)), only in the last is there any real contrast between superficial or conventional *aidōs* and something deeper, and Electra's *aidōs* at approaching her mother's tomb (if that is what it is) is in no way novel. The theme of *aidōs* in *Hipp.*, however, may admit of an approach similar to Lombard's; see 5.4.4 below.

[167] Cf. Snell (1928), 151–2; Grube (1961), 428.

[168] Cf. von Erffa (1937), 153.

[169] Iph. does supplicate her father at 1245–8, using the infant Orestes as a lever and appealing to *aidōs* and pity, but Ach. is an outsider where Ag. is not, and so to supplicate him would require Iph.'s overcoming her *aidōs* to a greater degree.

since her modest regard for her virginity is acute. This seems to be the force of 996: σεμνὰ γὰρ σεμνύνεται, 'for she has a maiden's pride'—literally 'she reveres (*semnunesthai*) reverend things (*semna*)'.[170] In the next line,[171] Clytemnestra qualifies her observation of her daughter's *semnotēs*, which probably has negative overtones of 'haughtiness',[172] by reformulating it as *aidōs*, a more positive designation and something which one should seek to maintain as far as possible, but which, it is implied, must sometimes be abandoned. The idea that *aidōs* can be taken too far and thus be equated with negative qualities such as *semnotēs* or *habrotēs* is a prominent one in this play,[173] which receives its clearest expression when Iphigeneia comes to voice her own *aidōs* at 1341–4. At 1338 the girl sees a crowd of men approaching, and on learning that her 'bridegroom', Achilles, is among them, experiences *aidōs* so acutely that she wishes to hide herself (1340). Her mother, however, recurs to the pragmatic, even cynical view of *aidōs* she has expressed before, and in response to Iphigeneia's embarrassment, which she expresses by simple *variatio* in terms of both *aischunē* and *aidōs* (1341–2),[174] points out that there is no room for *habrotēs* (delicacy)[175] or *semnotēs* (stuffiness) in the present situation (1343–4). Clytemnestra's paraphrases for *aidōs*, then, do not simply recast her daughter's words, but rather place a negative construction on her conduct. She draws, obviously, on the traditional ambivalence of *aidōs*, but this ambivalence may take on new life under the influence of the rhetorical capacity to place good and bad constructions on the same behaviour (I say *aidōs*, you say *semnotēs*, I say 'thrifty', you say 'mean', and so on), and possibly also against the background of contemporary interest in the proper definition of words (is *aidōs* always *aidōs*, even when it is unhelpful?). All this, in turn, fits well in a play in which conventional standards of behaviour are questioned, playfully exploited, and even ridiculed, as Iphigeneia abandons the maiden's role,

---

[170] Cf. von Erffa (1937), 153.

[171] 997, ὅμως δ' ὅσον γε δυνατὸν αἰδεῖσθαι χρεών. The γε seems to be limitative, belonging to Denniston's (1954: 140) category (ii), cases in which an extension of application is excluded ('as far as possible (but no further)'). Cf. von Erffa (1937), 153.

[172] For the pejorative connotations of *semnunomai* and *semnotēs*, cf. 901 and 1344 (respectively).

[173] Cf. n. 70 above.

[174] Iph.'s *aidōs* at the unhappy outcome of her marriage plans in 1342 has overtones of the embarrassment at being made to look a fool manifested by Clyt. at 847–8.

[175] For *habrotēs* as a pejorative equivalent of *aidōs*, cf. Aesch. *Ag.* 1203–5. Cf. *IA* 858, where Clyt.'s retainer, a plain speaker, informs us that he does not *habrunesthai* on account of his servile status.

Clytemnestra shows her concern to be less for honour than for the
ends which she wishes to achieve, and the 'heroic' values of Agamemnon and Achilles are satirized. In our next play, produced more
than twenty years before, we meet again the notion that a concept
which changes its prescriptive force (whether it is 'good' or 'bad')
according to context, might better be distinguished by separate names.

5.4.4. Hippolytus

It is in the *Hippolytus* that *aidōs*, as a considerable element in the
motivation of both the central characters, plays its most celebrated
Euripidean role. The concept does work in different ways in the play,
but its overall prominence is surely to be attributed to the poet's
focusing on the power of Aphrodite; the aspect of *aidōs* which renders
it most relevant to the main theme of the play, then, is that of its
association with sexuality and the social roles of men and women.

Hippolytus indicates the place of *aidōs* in his own character almost
immediately after his entrance; with his companions he sings a hymn
to Artemis, then proceeds to dedicate a garland to the goddess (73–
81):

I bring you, mistress, this woven garland I have fashioned from an unspoilt
meadow, where no shepherd thinks it right to pasture his herds, nor has iron
yet come, but unspoilt is the meadow, and the bee passes through it in
springtime, and Aidōs gardens with river waters, for those for whom nothing is
taught but whose lot is constant *sōphrosunē* in all respects, for them to pluck,
but for the base [*kakoi*] it is not right.[176]

The meadow is plainly symbolic, and characterizes Hippolytus at once
as chaste and pure, and it is with these qualities that the personified
Aidōs and the innate *sōphrosunē* of 79–81 belong. Hippolytus thus
regards *aidōs* and *sōphrosunē* as particularly his own,[177] and he
subsumes them under his worship of Artemis, which he regularly sees
in terms of another of his characteristics, *eusebeia* (εὐσεβοῦς ἄπο,
83).[178] The association of *aidōs* and *sōphrosunē* is common; applied to a
young male, their combination is as old as the *Odyssey*, in which the

---

[176] Translation after Barrett (1964).
[177] On his *sōphrosunē*, see 667, 949 (Theseus, ironically), 995, 1007, 1013, 1034–5, 1365,
1402; cf. North (1966), 70; Berns (1973), *passim*; Gill (1990), 80–5.
[178] See 656, 996, 1061, 1309, 1364, 1368, 1419, 1454.

youthful modesty and shyness of Telemachus could be described as both *aidōs* and *saophrosunē*.[179] Indeed, precisely these qualities are frequently regarded as typical of the young,[180] the closest parallel to Hippolytus in the Euripidean corpus being the youthful Achilles of the *Iphigeneia at Aulis*, whose *aidōs* and *sōphrosunē* are especially active in the sphere of coyness and propriety *vis-à-vis* the opposite sex.[181] Thus the association of *aidōs* and *sōphrosunē* in a young male, and even in the context of that person's shyness with regard to sex, is not unusual. And yet the overall effect of this passage is precisely to characterize Hippolytus as unusual.

The regular association of *aidōs* and *sōphrosunē* in modest young men, first of all, normally indicates their general shyness, the modesty of their bearing, their proneness to blush, and so on; associated with virginity and heterosexual chastity, however, both terms more readily suggest the behaviour of women than that of men: it is only in the context of women's behaviour, for example, that one would be tempted to translate *sōphrosunē* as 'chastity'.[182] But this is perhaps not decisive; the *sōphrosunē* commended in youths, for example, might also connote their chastity towards homosexual advances. More cogent evidence for the unusualness of Hippolytus' *aidōs* and the character in which it belongs is offered by the wider implications of both the image of the meadow and the worship of Artemis.

The poetic beauty of Hippolytus' picture of the meadow is often remarked upon;[183] less frequently noted, however, is the specific debt of the passage to lyric poetry,[184] yet the associations brought to the text by the lyric echoes are crucial to its proper understanding. Bremer[185]

---

[179] *Od.* 3. 24, 4. 158–60; cf. 1.3.4 above.

[180] See Ar. *Clouds* 960, 992–5, 1006, and esp. Pl. *Charm.*, a dialogue about *sōphrosunē* in which the youthful Charmides exemplifies that concept in his modesty and bashfulness; see *Charm.* 158c2–7, where Socrates asks Charm. whether he possesses a sufficient share of *sōphrosunē*, Charm. blushes, and Soc. interprets his blush as *to aischuntēlon* (*i.q.* *aidōs*), appropriate in one of his age; and note also Charm.'s definition of *sōphrosunē* as *aidōs*, 160e2–5. On the appropriateness of *sōphrosunē* for women and young males, cf. Cornford (1912), 252–3, with refs.

[181] See 5.4.3 above.

[182] On *aidōs* and *sōphrosunē* of women's modesty, see n. 147 above, and 5.4.1 in general.

[183] See Barrett (1964), ad loc. Kovacs (1987: 35) notes the poetic density of the passage but has no reference to lyric, and regards the passage as designed simply to endear H. to the audience.

[184] Nothing, e.g., in Garner's supposedly comprehensive survey of 'the allusions' in *Hipp.* (1990: 127–8).

[185] (1975), drawing on the work of Motte (1973). I differ from Bremer slightly in placing more emphasis on the Ibycus fragment, which I also interpret slightly differently.

shows that the meadow is normally an erotic image in lyric, and cites in particular two fragments which share several features with the present passage.[186] One of these, Ibycus 286 *PMG*, is particularly close in its language, and if Euripides is not relying on his audience to catch echoes of this poem specifically, he is at the very least making use of associations which the Ibycus fragment shares with other erotic poems, and which thus serve to give the present passage its paradoxical character. In common with our passage, Ibycus' poem has the river waters, an unspoilt (*akēratos*, as in *Hippolytus*) garden (cf. Aidōs the gardener), and the detail of springtime; significantly, too, the garden is said to belong to the maidens (*parthenoi*, 3). The inviolate garden, then, is, as in the *Hippolytus*, associated with virginity. But the virginity of the garden and its maidens is strongly contrasted with the erotic passion of the poet's persona; his love never 'goes to bed' and he is subject to violent storms which proceed from Cypris, the goddess Aphrodite. Thus it is strongly suggested that the erotic attentions of the narrator are to be directed towards the inhabitants of the garden, whether the *parthenoi* themselves or those associated with them. So the inviolate garden is under threat from Cypris; and the suggestion is there that Cypris will conquer, for the fruits of the garden, quinces and vines, are ripening in due season and will soon be ready for plucking. The lyric associations of the present passage, therefore, suggest the coming of Love to those who had previously been inviolate, and this accordingly creates a discord in relation to Hippolytus' determination to remain chaste.[187] This discord is powerfully emphasized by the location of Aidōs the gardener in the erotic meadow, and the incongruity thus created serves to underline the tensions inherent in Hippolytus' rejection of sex and his worship of Artemis.

Hippolytus' quasi-feminine concern for sexual purity[188] emerges in greater relief when we consider his devotion to Artemis in general. Here too the meadow is relevant; the meadow of Artemis is mentioned again under a different aspect in the *Iphigeneia at Aulis* as the location of Iphigeneia's sacrifice (1463), a sacrifice which was first represented as a marriage and becomes a symbolic marriage of

---

[186] Sappho 2 LP and Ibycus 286 *PMG*, with the Cologne Epode of Archilochus (fr. 196a West²) as corroboration. Cf. Anacreon 417. 5 *PMG*, where the meadows in which the Thracian 'filly' romps represent the sexual innocence which the singer threatens to end.

[187] See line 87: 'May I finish my life as I began.'

[188] See Segal (1970), 293; Devereux (1985), 19–32; cf. 1006: H. has a 'virgin soul' (παρθένον ψυχὴν ἔχων).

death;[189] Iphigeneia's passage from life to death thus takes place in a setting which, as we have seen, has associations with the passage from virginity to sexual maturity,[190] and the prominence of Artemis in this context must recall the association of that goddess with women, the stages of their lives, and their deaths.[191] In particular, Artemis is associated with the change of status from maiden to wife.[192] Certainly, she is also associated with male transitions,[193] but not, as far as I can discover, with the passage of the male from virginity to sexual activity as such.

Where Artemis is of particular relevance to male rites of passage, as far as the status of Hippolytus is concerned, is in connection with the progress of the ephebe to the status of warrior,[194] a topic which has recently received some attention in the context of Attic tragedy.[195] Hippolytus' worship of Artemis, his hunting, and his chastity all fit the typology of the ephebe as identified by Vidal-Naquet.[196] What is problematic about Hippolytus is that his chastity is never to be abandoned,[197] that he intends never to make the transition from ephebe to hoplite, youth to manhood.[198] More than this, however, his specific rejection of sex conflates the status of the young male with that of the young woman. 'Marriage is for the girl what war is for the boy,' writes Vernant;[199] the initiation of the male may prepare the way for his

[189] See Foley (1985), 65–105.

[190] Cf. Foley (1985), 70.

[191] See *RE* ii. s.v. Artemis, coll. 1346–8 (marriage, childbirth, woman's goddess), 1351–3 (maiden goddess); Lloyd-Jones (1983); Burkert (1985), 150–2.

[192] Artemis received sacrifice from girls about to be married at Athens and elsewhere (*RE* ii. coll. 1346–7; Burkert (1983), 62–3 with n. 20 (cf. (1985), 151, 221); Lloyd-Jones (1983), 94; cf. *IA* 433, 718, 1111–13)).

[193] e.g. as Orthia at Sparta (see *RE* ii. col. 1346, with other evidence for the goddess's association with young males as well as females, particularly with ephebes; also Burkert (1983), 65; Lloyd-Jones (1983), 91, 97, with 98–101 on male as well as female initiations; Burkert (1985), 152; Burnett (1986), 177 and nn. 66–7).

[194] See the discussions cited in n. 193 above.

[195] See Vidal-Naquet in Vernant and Vidal-Naquet (1981), 175–99, for an attempt to related Soph. *Phil.* to the institution of the *ephebeia*; also Goldhill (1987), 73–5, on the *ephebeia* and tragedy. Vidal-Naquet's essays on the *ephebeia* in general (*inter alia*) have recently appeared in English (1986); two of these also in Gordon (1981).

[196] On the association of chastity with hunting, Artemis, and the rites of passage of young men, see Lloyd-Jones (1983), 99–100; cf. Burkert (1983), 60–1.

[197] The chastity which Lloyd-Jones (1983: 99–100) associates with athletic training and the practices of pre-agricultural hunters is strictly temporary (cf. Burnett (1986), 174). Even if chastity were demanded of all youths below the age of majority, it certainly was not demanded in the male after he had attained adulthood (cf. Cornford (1912), 257–8).

[198] See Zeitlin (1985), 56; Burnett (1986), 177; Goldhill (1986), 120–1; Luschnig (1988), 55.

[199] (1980), 23.

marriage (although marriage normally came at a considerably later stage), but it is for the girl that the post-transitional stage is typically seen as marriage—it is the girl who must obtain release from Artemis in order to be married,[200] and it is the girl who is characteristically reluctant to enter the stage of sexual activity.[201] The displacement occasioned by the poetic image of the meadow is thus matched by that in the ritual background, and this serves to indicate that Hippolytus, whatever his moral deserts and however sympathetic or unsympathetic he may be,[202] is an anomalous and problematic figure; his

[200] Plut. *Arist.* 20. 6 (see Braund (1980), 184 and n. 7) says brides and bridegrooms both sacrificed to Art. Eukleia; normally, however, the sacrifices by young males to Art. are connected with the *ephebeia*. Apparently, no Athenian girl could be married who had not been consecrated to Art. at Brauron or Mounichia (Schol. Ar. *Lys.* 645; Harpocr., s.v. ἀρκτεῦσαι = Craterus, *FGH* 342 F 9; see Burkert (1985), 263; Vidal-Naquet (1986), 145-6). Lucian, *de Syr. Dea* 60, says bridegrooms as well as brides offered a lock of hair to Hippolytus (*sic*), but the offering of the males may have taken place on entry into the *ephebeia* (see *RE* viii. s.v. Hippolytos, col. 1866; on the hair-offerings of young men on coming of age, see Burkert (1985), 70, 373-4 n. 29; Garland (1990), 179, 326-7.

[201] Cf. Iphigeneia's *aidōs* as she set off ostensibly to be married at *IT* 372-6 (n. 150 above). For a contrast between the pleasantness of maidenhood and the uncertainties of marriage, see Soph. fr. 583 Radt, and Deianeira at *Trach.* 144-50 (this passage is also instructive in its use of vegetation imagery in the context of the virgin's growth to maturity). On the girl's fear of marriage and the common association of marriage with death in tragedy, see Foley (1985), 86-9 and *passim*; Seaford (1987). Foley (87; cf. Garland (1990), 222-4) relates the 'marriage of death' complex to the myth of Persephone (or *Korē*, the Maiden), and sees Hippolytus as a *korē* figure, noting the relevance of the *aition* which concludes the play; H.'s resistance to Aphrodite thus becomes a consolation to *girls* making the transition from maidenhood to marriage. (Foley is anticipated here by Reckford (1972), 414-16; cf. Dimock (1977), 241; see also Zeitlin (1985), 66-7; Segal (1986), 58-60.) The girls will dedicate locks of hair to H. before marriage (1425-6); this perhaps connects with H.'s garland and his meadow, since *akēratos* can mean 'unshorn' of hair (*Ion* 1266), and since vegetation and hair are commonly associated (see Barrett (1964) on 210: Phaedra's wish to lie in a 'hairy meadow' which is clearly that of H.); if H.'s garland is a figurative hair-offering (as Braund (1980: 185) suggests) it is an offering for a transition which never takes place; the norm is re-established at the end of the play in the *aition*. On the 'incompleteness' of H.'s initiation, see Burnett (1986), 177.

[202] Several recent accounts stress H.'s essential moral innocence: Heath (1987: 84-5) claims he is 'blameless' (cf. Vickers (1973), 293; also 146-7: H.'s chastity and devotion to Art. are 'perfectly normal'). The most thorough exculpation of H. in the recent literature is that of Kovacs (1987); the issue, however, is not as black and white as Kovacs *et al.* would have us believe. In some sense H. may be blameless; there is no crime or moral offence, in the senses in which we understand these words, for which he is punished; but in terms of the anthropomorphic religion of the play he can hardly be blameless in his contempt for Aphrodite. (If polytheism makes his worship of Art. natural—Vickers (1973), 146, following Lloyd-Jones (1965), 166—it also makes his rejection of Aphr. dangerous.) So much for the level of literal anthropomorphism; Kovacs also rules out any symbolic interpretation of Aphr. which would stress the unusualness of H. in rejecting the power of sex (24-9); but he is wrong to claim that there is no indication of eccentricity in the text, and wrong, too, to claim that, if H.'s rejection of Aphr. were to be seen

appropriation of *aidōs* and *sōphrosunē* to his particular life-style serves the same end.[203]

Hippolytus' speech in dedication of his garland, so indicative of the peculiarity of his character, is explicitly recalled later in the play, in the *agōn* between Hippolytus and his father, in which this peculiarity is one of the most crucial issues. For Theseus, Hippolytus' virtue was just a sham—it is he, who regarded everyone but himself as *kakos* (81), who is *kakistos* (945), and his claims that he, an exception among human beings, enjoys intercourse with the gods (948-9, recalling Hippolytus at 84-6, cf. Aphrodite at 17), that he is *sōphrōn* and untainted by evil (*akēratos*, 949, cf. 73, 76) are hypocritical boasts. Theseus, then, knows all about Hippolytus' claims to be *perissos* ('exceptional', but also 'odd'), and is made to refer back to the very passage in which his son's oddness is originally and most strikingly presented; the meadow passage is clearly a major contribution to the understanding of

metaphorically as a problematic suppression of the sexual urge, the passion Phaedra feels towards him would have to be a necessary consequence of his 'repression' (126-7 n. 13). This is to conflate vehicle and tenor of the metaphor; on the literal level Ph.'s passion is part of Aphr.'s revenge; on the symbolic level all that is required is a general sense that total rejection of sex is dangerous. Aphr. cannot be wholly symbolic, but neither is she merely a tremendously powerful being whom H. happens to have offended. Kovacs also begs the question when he assumes (24-9) that to regard H. as unusual is to 'patronize' (25) or even to 'hate' him (26), and thus to take moral satisfaction in his death; lack of sympathy for H. at the beginning of the play does not entail satisfaction at his death— there is a significant shift of sympathy towards H. at the end of the play (cf. Vickers (1973), 294). The anomalies in H.'s worship of Art. need not arouse disapproval, but they do characterize him as a problem figure; the negative element in his characterization comes from his exclusivism—he regards everyone whose *sōphrosunē* is not innate as 'base' (81); in spite of our knowledge of the falsity of Ph.'s accusation, we therefore have mixed feelings when he is later suspected of being 'base' himself (942, 945, 959, 1031, 1071, 1075, 1191), until our sympathy is finally won over by his undeserved suffering.

[203] A closer link between H.'s *aidōs* and his worship of Artemis might be suggested by the appearance of the letters *ΑΙΔΟΣ* (AIDOS) designating the figure of Art. on an Attic red-figure amphora (depicting the rape of Leto by Tityus) by Phintias (Louvre G 42; *ARV*² 23, i; Boardman (1975), fig. 41. 1; for the inscriptions, see Hoppin (1919), ii. 368). That this constitutes an association between the goddess and *aidōs* is the position of Kretschmer (1894: 197), Norwood (1954: 76 n. 2), and Schefold (1978: 68). Certainly analogous titles/epithets exist—the cult of Art. Eukleia is discussed, with reference to the *Hipp.*, by Braund (1980), and Schefold (1978: 290 n. 152) points to a possible description of Art. as Aretē on a black-figure neck amphora by the Antimenes Painter (Basle iii, 3; the figure so designated, however, is not certainly Art.). But the view of von Erffa (1937: 58) and F. Eckstein (in *LIMC* i. 1, 352-3) that the letters are an abbreviation of the gen. *Artemidos* is not to be dismissed, notwithstanding Kretschmer's assurance (1894: 197) that *ΑΙΔΟΣ* not [*ΑΡΤΕ*]*ΜΙΔΟΣ* is the correct reading (note that the vase also names Leto in the gen.). An association of Art. and *aidōs* makes sense, and a cult would not be impossible, but we should be wary of assuming either from such doubtful evidence.

Hippolytus' role in the play. Accordingly, when it comes the turn of Hippolytus to defend himself against the charge of rape, he, too, is made to recall the characterization of the prologue, with all its problematic aspects; the references to *aidōs* (998), *sōphrosunē* (995, cf. 1007), and *eusebeia* (996) are all intended to indicate the impossibility of Phaedra's accusations given Hippolytus' unique life-style. Here *aidōs* is used to underline Hippolytus' exclusivity; he has *philoi*, but they are people of high ethical standards (in implicit contrast to others unnamed), people who would not attempt to do wrong and whose *aidōs* would prevent them sending wicked messages or treating disgracefully those who have dealings with them. What Theseus can only see as an irrelevant defence of Hippolytus' hunting companions is, of course, a reference to the conduct of Phaedra, as Hippolytus construes it,[204] but the real point of the reference to *aidōs* and its associated qualities is to remind us of their prominence in Hippolytus' crucial first speech, and to underline the fact that the characterization conveyed by that speech is, in fact, the chief obstacle to the resolution of the problems of the present scene. Theseus is incensed by his son's sanctimoniousness, a reaction which we, the audience, can understand, even though our knowledge of the truth and of the suffering of Hippolytus in his inability to break his oath ensures both that we recognize the profundity of Hippolytus' moral principles and that we sympathize with him as a victim of injustice.

In a very real sense, the character and the virtues of Hippolytus, as outlined in his speech of dedication, contribute to his ruin. Just as Theseus can only see Hippolytus' reference to his companions' *aidōs* in 998 as an appeal to a profession of virtue which he himself has already rejected as false, so he is unlikely to understand the reference in 996 to Hippolytus' *eusebeia* for the gods in anything but the most general sense; but the point of that line lies in its allusion to Hippolytus' eventual decision, after initial reluctance in 612, to keep his oath not to reveal the subject of his conversation with the Nurse. It is this compunction which he calls *to eusebes* in 656. In the present passage the irony is that it is precisely the virtue to which he alludes that prevents Theseus' understanding the allusion.[205]

[204] See Barrett (1964) on 997–9.
[205] We remember that the keeping of an oath is frequently regarded as a demand of *aidōs*; see 3.4 above. Hippolytus, however, refers only to his *eusebeia*, and while it may simply be that the two terms are virtually interchangeable in this context (since *aidōs* for the oath entails *aidōs* for the gods who are its guarantors, and because *eusebeia* might just imply the kind of proper behaviour which is promoted by *aidōs*), he does use the term in

Hippolytus, of course, remains true to his principles to the end of the play, even in the face of the deepest opprobrium. His *eusebeia* for his oath is clearly a powerful force. He also conspicuously maintains his particular brand of *sōphrosunē*, with which *aidōs* is very closely connected, and so remains true to his concept of his *phusis* as he articulates it at 79–81. As in the case of the Sophoclean Neoptolemus, then, Hippolytus' principles, from which his *aidōs* arises, constitute part of his nature and do not merely depend on other people. He can recognize, however, that *sōphrosunē* can be misused or inefficacious (1035), and it is clear that in an important sense his virtues are his downfall; this is not to say that such virtues are wrong or to be abandoned, merely that they can be harmful to their possessor; we shall see that this point is also relevant in Phaedra's case.

At 997–1001 Hippolytus implies that Phaedra was without *aidōs*; this is far from true, but there is none the less a difference in the attitudes of the two principals to the concept. Hippolytus is quite sure about *aidōs* and links it to his inborn nature, while his very unconventionality indicates that he has little time for the *aidōs* of ordinary people which simply promotes conformity to traditional standards; ultimately he chooses to keep his oath rather than to attempt to clear his name. Phaedra, on the other hand, does care what people say about her and does show concern for conventional standards; she does have her own standards of right and wrong, but finds it difficult to live up to them; and in her case *aidōs*, I feel sure, emerges in an ambivalent light.

Phaedra's *aidōs* develops as the play progresses, but its basis is to be found in the fundamental demands of women's *aretē*—she struggles to be faithful to her husband and to reject adultery, just as the chorus of the *Iphigeneia at Aulis* (568–70) recommend.[206] Phaedra recognizes that her passion itself is *aischron* and that it would be *aischron* for her to give in to it;[207] the situation, therefore, is such that

a specific rather than a general way. For him the *aidōs* which is normally felt as a result of the public nature of the oath is less important than reverence for its divine guarantors, a reverence which is an essential part of Hippolytus' being.

[206] On her attempt to overcome *erōs* with *aidōs*, cf. Zürcher (1947), 85–7.
[207] See 331, 408, 411, 499, 503–6; at 408 and 420 the idea that she would dishonour Thes. is also present. On the dishonour suffered by the husband of an adulteress, cf. *Tro.* 1041 and fr. 662 N². The Nurse only confirms the traditional disgracefulness of adultery when she argues that τὰ μὴ καλά are often ignored in practice (462–6) and that *aischra* are better for Ph. than *kala* (500). Later, when he believes that Ph. had been raped by H., Thes. sees the crime as *aischron* for himself (944–5, 1165, 1171–2; at 1040 he claims that it involves him in *atimia*). The presumed rape is also disgraceful for H., its agent—he is 'shown up as *kakistos*' for disgracing his father's bed (944–5), and Thes. expresses his revulsion for him by regarding him as polluted (946).

we cannot help but see *aidōs* as one of the dominant elements in her
motivation.

In order to understand Phaedra's *aidōs* we must understand its role in
her great speech (373–430). Her remarks on *aidōs* here come in the
notoriously problematic lines 375–87, of which there are almost as many
interpretations as there are interpreters; of these some are frankly out-
landish,[208] some merely vague,[209] while others, despite their merits, fail
fully to satisfy the requirements of this particular passage;[210] one recent
critic even claims that the lines do not admit of any precise interpretation and so should not be forced into one.[211] Much work has been
done on the passage, however, since the appearance of Barrett's commentary, and the best of these contributions have, at the very least, clar-
ified the issues.[212] The attempt to understand Phaedra's speech as a
meaningful contribution to the play must still, surely, be made.

Any interpretation of the passage which goes against the movement
of thought in the speech as a whole cannot be correct, and, fortunately,
the significance of the speech as a whole is not difficult to establish.[213]
Phaedra has pondered the ways in which the lives of men have come
to ruin (375–6): their failure lies not in their appreciation of what must
be done (not in their *gnōmē* or intelligence, 377, 380), but in their
failure to put this into practice (381).[214] But this is not going to happen

[208] e.g. Conacher (1967: 35, 54–5) believes 'that the "bad *aidōs*" here regarded as a
pleasure refers to the distracting enjoyment of "taboo" subjects which, when not treated
with reverence, lead to shame'. This ingeniously employs two Eng. terms regularly
associated with *aidōs*, but answers to no sense of the Gk. word that I can identify.

[209] e.g. the commentaries of Barthold (1880) and Wecklein (1885) speak merely of
Ph.'s 'weakness'.

[210] See the judgement of Lesky (1983), 237. Here I would include Dodds (1925);
Winnington-Ingram (1960); Barrett (1964) on 385–6; Solmsen (1973).

[211] Michelini (1987), 300.

[212] The recent interpretations which any student of the passage must consider
(without ignoring those mentioned in n. 210) are: Willink (1968), 11–26; Segal (1970);
Claus (1972); Manuwald (1979); Kovacs (1980). I have benefited from all of these, though
I cannot fully agree with any one. My attempt to use what seems to me of value in each,
however, is not intended merely to reach a well-meaning compromise between views
which often diverge widely.   [213] See the account of Manuwald (1979), 143–7.

[214] This disjunction between knowledge and action makes it certain that Ph. is talking
about the phenomenon of *akrasia* (weakness of the will) which is regarded as impossible
by Plato's Socrates in the *Prot.* (see Irwin (1983)). The intellectual terms *gnōmē* (377), τὸ
εὖ φρονεῖν (good sense, 378), and the verbs in 380 cannot be taken in undifferentiatedly
dispositional senses (combining knowledge, volition, and emotion), *pace* Barrett (1964)
on 377–81, Willink (1968), 11; the use of these terms cannot be divorced from Ph.'s
description of 'the way of her *gnōmē*' in 391–402, and it is clear that *gnōmē* refers to the
intellectual aspect of moral decision-making (note 'I examined', ἐσκόπουν, 392; 'I made
plans', προυνοησάμην, 399; 'I decided', ἔδοξέ μοι, 401; 'the best of plans', κράτιστον
βουλευμάτων, 402). In any case, as Irwin points out (1983: 190–1), if both our intellectual

to Phaedra (388–90)—the judgements of her *gnōmē*, which she outlines in 391–402 (prolonging into her enunciation of her attitude towards adultery, 403–30), will be put into practice. Thus Phaedra is not explaining to the chorus the reasons for her own failure in conceiving an illegitimate passion for her stepson, but rather insisting that she intends to behave entirely properly now that she has conceived such a passion.[215] The ultimate point, however, is that Phaedra's attempts to put her *gnōmē* into practice come to grief; she has failed to keep silent about her love (393–7), failed to overcome it by means of *sōphrosunē* (398–9), and, although she is now resolved to die without further ado (400–2), in this, too, she will fail, instead allowing the Nurse to attempt a 'cure'. Thus her optimism about her ability to carry out the judgements of her *gnōmē* is misplaced—she is, after all, one of those people who know and understand the good, but do not work it out.[216]

Phaedra's reference to *aidōs* comes in her explanation of *why* people do not put their knowledge into practice (380–7):

We know and understand the good, but do not work it out,[217] some out of idleness, others because they prefer some other pleasure in place of what is *kalon*;[218] there are many pleasures in life, long conversations and leisure, a

awareness and our motivational states were correct, our failure to act (οὐκ ἐκπονοῦμεν, 381) would be inexplicable (unless by the intervention of some external agency, a possibility not raised by Ph.). That there should be an allusion to the historical Socrates himself is very likely (see below, this section *ad fin.*), but for our immediate purposes the question is immaterial. The relevance of the Socratic thesis is upheld by Barthold (1880), on 380; Snell (1948); (1964), 59–67; Dodds (1951), 186–7; Manuwald (1979), 147–8; Irwin (1983); contrast Barrett (1964) on 377–81; Claus (1972), 235–7. Moline (1975) goes to unnecessary lengths to disprove the thesis of Snell (1964) (cf. id. (1948)), that Ph.'s words represent the opinions of the poet in a polemic forming part of a protracted philosophical dialogue between Eur. and Soc.; Snell clearly takes little account of the facts that Eur. is a dramatist and *Hipp.* a play. Yet the poet does present the occurrence of *akrasia*, and, unless he dramatizes what he believes to be impossible, he is opposed to the Socratic view. On *akrasia* in Eur., see Walsh (1963), 16–22; cf. Fortenbaugh (1970), 233–41.

[215] As Claus (1972), 225, 230, 233; Manuwald (1979), 143, and Kovacs (1980), 291, rightly insist.

[216] This (obvious) point is stressed by Manuwald (1979: 145), but ignored or under-estimated by Claus (1972), and Kovacs (1980). Lines 388–90 are also relevant here; Ph. *does* ruin her resolve with a *pharmakon* (drug, remedy); indeed, these remarks, rather odd in their initial context, only achieve their full significance in their ironic reversal.

[217] Reading τὰ χρήστ'... οὐκ ἐκπονοῦμεν δ', as approved by Barrett (1964: 433), rather than ἃ χρήστ'... οὐκ ἐκπονοῦμεν, approved by Willink (1968: 13–14); there is little to choose between the two in sense, and for our purposes the distinction is immaterial.

[218] We must, I think, translate ἡδονὴν... ἄλλην τιν' as 'some other pleasure' (Willink (1968), 14; Claus (1972), 228; Kovacs (1980), 293–4), rather than as 'something else,

pleasant evil—and *aidōs*. There are two [kinds ?], the one [or 'one' ?] not bad, the other [or 'another' ?] a burden on the house; if what is appropriate were clear,[219] there would not be two things with the same letters.

Phaedra's concluding remarks have long been seen as a recognition of the traditional ambivalence of *aidōs*, in the same spirit as the famous lines of Hesiod's *Works and Days*.[220] The ambivalence of *aidōs* is certainly mentioned in Euripides,[221] but this passage is essentially different,[222] and the traditional ambivalence of *aidōs* is no evidence for its interpretation. Nor is it universally accepted that *aidōs* is ambivalent in this passage; three scholars have recently made a strong case for referring *dissai* (translated 'two [kinds ?]' above) not to *aidōs*, but to

namely pleasure' (Barrett (1964), on 381–5; Manuwald (1979), 137); the 'other pleasure' will be τὸ καλόν not ἀργία (see Kovacs, loc. cit.; ἄλλος ἀντί equivalent to ἄλλος ἤ). There is no problem with this; pleasure may accompany the performance of what is fine, noble, or merely 'looks good', and awareness of one's good reputation or personal rectitude may be pleasant. I, however, unlike Luschnig (1988: 59), cannot follow Claus (1972: 231) in his insistence that τὸ καλόν means 'good name' and no more; in itself the use is completely general, and cannot be limited to one specific significance. When we consider, however, what the *kalon* might be in Ph.'s own case, the answer can only lie in her statement (401–2) that suicide (as a means of escaping erotic passion) is the best of counsels; this is the end she intends to achieve by allying her *gnōmē* to the necessary tenacity, and this end involves her both avoiding that which she regards as morally wrong and securing her reputation. See text below.

219   It would do no real harm to take the *kairos* in 386 as temporal: indeed, the idea that *x* is now appropriate, now inappropriate might fit well, depending on our interpretation of the rest of the passage (*pace* Kovacs (1980), 297 n. 19); taking *kairos* as 'right time' the sense would be, 'If the occasion were clear we should know when to practise *x* and when not', i.e. when it is 'good' and when it is 'bad'. I see nothing 'roundabout' in this; but Barrett (1964: ad loc.) is certainly right to point out that the temporal sense is only one among many in 5th.-cent. literature.

220   See 2.1 above, and, for the argument that Eur. had *WD* 317–19 in mind when composing Ph.'s speech, Cook (1901), 341; cf. Segal (1970), 299.

221   Not just in the *Erechtheus* fr. (365 N²) which is often mentioned in this context, but also in *Ion* 336–7; *IA* 900–2, 992–7, 1341–4; these passages refer to the typical inefficacy of *aidōs* where outspokenness is required (cf. Soph. fr. 928 Radt and fr. trag. adesp. 528 N²).

222   If one kind of *aidōs* is opposed to *to kalon* here, then the reference is not simply to the need to overcome one's apprehension that a given action may be *aischron* in order to achieve an end which one sees as expedient or necessary (cf. Kovacs (1980), 296). In his note on 385–6 Barrett (1964) essentially explains the traditional ambivalence of *aidōs* rather than the more complicated remarks of Ph. (On the inadequacy of his interpretation, cf. Willink (1968), 15; Claus (1972), 228–9; Kovacs (1980), 288.) We need some explanation as to how *aidōs* can inhibit *to kalon* in Ph.'s case, and the traditional ambivalence of *aidōs* does not provide this. *Aidōs* can, however, inhibit *to kalon*; see Solmsen (1973), and cf. *Supp.* 297–300: out of a fear of criticism lest she, a woman, be regarded as presumptuous, Aethra is reluctant to speak, even though she has something *kalon* to communicate. In such passages, what is *kalon* in one respect is readily construed as *aischron* in another.

pleasures (*hēdonai*, 383).[223] In favour of this we should note that there is no explicit change of subject between 383 ('there are many pleasures in life') and 385 ('there are two [kinds ?]'); and that *aidōs* has no plural to construe with *dissai*. If *dissai* referred to *aidōs*, we should expect a demonstrative pronoun to mark the change of subject and a singular *dissē*.[224]

There are, however, also arguments against—why should the *kairos* not be clear, and why should there be two things with the same letters, if the sense is merely that there are good and bad pleasures, since presumably each pleasure, good or bad, is adequately distinguished from the others by the possession of its own name?[225] The complaint about two things having the same name, the argument goes, makes more sense applied to a specific than a generic concept; it is rather as if one were to say, 'Some animals are tame, others are wild; if the *kairos* were clear, there would not be two things with the same letters.' But this objection is hardly cogent; first, it assumes that *dissai* (twofold) must divide pleasures into one set of unambiguously good and one of unambiguously bad, which need not be the case; and secondly, members of the genus 'pleasure' do share a common name, and the complaint may simply be that this common name does not isolate the good from the bad.

One might, however, argue that *dissai* may mean simply 'two' rather than 'two kinds', and if it does, there is surely no problem in the fact that a plural of *aidōs* is not found; if the scholiast on 385 can coin a plural in order to understand this passage, so presumably could the original audience, even assuming that it is not pure accident that the plural of *aidōs* is not attested elsewhere. Finally, if the reference of *dissai* is to two kinds of pleasure, what is the reference of ἡ μὲν ... ἡ δ'? We can only understand *hēdonē* with these demonstrative articles, and if the locution means 'the one ... the other ...', as most often, then it seems as if we are dealing not with two kinds of pleasure, but with two pleasures, which is absurd.[226]

Neither the argument for two kinds of pleasure nor that for two kinds of *aidōs* is clearly decisive in itself; the plural *dissai* does seem to suggest that this word should be referred back to εἰσὶ δ' ἡδοναὶ πολλαὶ

[223] Willink (1968), 15–16, followed by Claus (1972), 228, and, with further argumentation, by Kovacs (1980), 294–5.
[224] Willink (1968), 15; Kovacs (1980), 295.
[225] So Manuwald (1979), 139; cf. Michelini (1987), 299 n. 97.
[226] Cf. Manuwald (1979: 138), who points out that we should expect αἱ μὲν ... αἱ δ' in connection with two kinds of pleasure.

βίου ('there are many pleasures of life') in 383, but with the proper stress on the emphatic *aidōs* in 385 and on the subsequent διοσαὶ δ' εἰσίν, the lines could just as well refer to *aidōs*. We are compelled, then, to assess the probability of the two interpretations. If we take ἡ μὲν . . . ἡ δ' as 'the one . . . the other . . .' it becomes easy to take *dissai* as meaning 'two'; this would construe well with the neuter *duo* in 387, and rule out a reference to pleasure. Crucially, however, ἡ μὲν . . . ἡ δ' need not be so construed, but may be used to give representative (rather than exhaustive) examples of a class, in the sense 'this one . . . that one . . .', or 'one . . . , *an*other . . .'.[227] The pleasure which is 'not bad' and that which is 'a burden on the house' would then be representative of the two kinds of pleasure (and 'two things' in 387 is sufficiently vague to accommodate two classes rather than two particulars). The point which, in my estimation, just tips the scales in favour of relating *dissai* to *hēdonai* is the use of the plural without explicit change of subject; had Euripides wanted to refer to the duality of *aidōs* he could easily have composed the line in such a way as to make this perfectly clear; that he did not do so argues fairly strongly for taking *dissai* with the plural subject of the previous sentence; and there is no problem in Phaedra's complaint that if the *kairos* were clear, there would not be two things with the same letters, since this may be less a complaint that it is difficult to distinguish between different things all having the generic title, pleasure, than an observation that if that title were accorded simply on the basis of what is appropriate, what is 'good for us', then bad or harmful pleasures would not be called pleasures at all. At the very least, therefore, we should recognize that there is no convincing argument which proves that the two kinds of *aidōs* of traditional interpretation are present in the text, and that, on balance, two kinds of pleasure seem more likely; absolute certainty one way or another, however, is not attainable.

The significance of *aidōs* in the speech, however, still remains to be explained. Claus and Kovacs both assume that the statement that pleasures are of two kinds means simply that some pleasures are (always) good, some (always) bad, and that *aidōs* is included in the list in 384–5 as one of the unambiguously good pleasures.[228] But to say that pleasures are of two kinds need not split the category into two

---

[227] See Gildersleeve (1980), 216; cf. Xen. *Cyr.* 8. 2. 5.

[228] Claus (1972), 231; Kovacs (1980), 297; contrast Luschnig (1988), 41–2. *Aidōs* must, in any case, be a pleasure, and von Erffa (1937: 166) and Barrett (1964: on 377–81) are wrong to try to deny the obvious significance of the text. Cf. Willink (1968), 15; Segal (1970), 285–6 n. 4.

unambiguous sub-classes; Hesiod's two kinds of *eris* (strife)[229] do not refer to two distinct and consistently opposed classes, but to one concept which is now helpful, now harmful. There may be some circumstances in which *eris* is always bad, and there may be circumstances in which pleasure (or a given pleasure) is always bad, but even a distinction between good and bad pleasures need not rule out the possibility of a single pleasure being good in some circumstances, bad in others. The phenomenon which such locutions isolate is not the possibility of subdividing terms into sub-classes, but that of contextual ('non-sceptical') relativism.[230]

Against the position of Claus and Kovacs that *aidōs* is a good pleasure which one never chooses in preference to *to kalon* must be set the general impression created by Phaedra's argument; we hear nothing about the two kinds of pleasure until after we have heard that people choose some pleasure other than *to kalon*; the many pleasures of life are then exemplified in long conversations, leisure, and *aidōs*—a strange list, as many commentators have noted, and the implication is there, particularly given the occurrence of τερπνὸν κακόν ('a pleasant bane') in 384, that these pleasures are such as one might, in certain circumstances, choose in preference to *to kalon*. If Phaedra's subsequent remarks on the two kinds of pleasure are intended to add, in the way of an afterthought, that some pleasures, perhaps including *aidōs*, are or can be harmless, they do not altogether dispel the negative effect created by the preceding lines. It remains open whether *aidōs* may not, after all, be a pleasure which is sometimes harmful and which interferes with the pursuit of *to kalon*.

The immediate reference of *aidōs* in the list of pleasures is not, I think, far to seek. All three pleasures named are to be seen against the background of the seclusion in which respectable (Athenian) women lived. This is clear for 'long conversations and leisure', and should be no less so in the case of *aidōs*, for it is *aidōs*, as the disposition which renders her sensitive to her own honour, to that of her *kurios*, and to the expectations of society, that motivates a woman's observance of the norms which keep her in seclusion.

Such seclusion, however, while safeguarding the honour of the *kurios*, the legitimacy of his children, and the integrity of his

---

[229] *WD* 11–41.
[230] Cf. Willink (1968), 16 (though I cannot endorse the more detailed aspects of his argument); Luschnig (1988: 42) points out that the pleasures which Ph. actually mentions are all capable of ambivalence according to circumstance.

328 *Euripides*

household, has its negative side—the woman's isolation with none but her own kind for company might constitute an environment in which destructive erotic passions could develop.[231] The ambivalence of the named pleasures derives from the fact that they are capable of contributing to that pleasure which is uppermost in Phaedra's mind—that of illicit sex, indulgence in which truly is 'a burden on the *oikos*'.[232] Yet in the case of *aidōs* this is deeply paradoxical, for if *aidōs* is potentially harmful in so far as it contributes to an unhealthy environment in which dangerous erotic passions can develop, it is also much more regularly and traditionally the salutary virtue which maintains a woman's commitment to honour and *to kalon*. This means, I think, that the emphatic inclusion of *aidōs* in the list of pleasures will have posed a problem in the minds of the original audience and prompted them to further reflection. Of course, the point could simply be that since seclusion of women can actually foster destructive *erōs*, anything that contributes to seclusion is, or can be, bad; but this leaves unanswered the crucial question of the sense in which the *aidōs* which actually promotes rather than shuns improper sex may be a pleasure. In what sort of person and in what circumstances might *aidōs* be pleasant, yet harmful? To answer this question we have to think further, and to do this, I believe, we must investigate the role of *aidōs* and the possibility of its ambivalence in the motivation of Phaedra herself.

In this connection we should remember the overall significance of Phaedra's speech; she is determined to put her correct judgement of her situation into practice, but she has failed to do so in the past, and will fail once more in the future; her remarks thus have a forward and a backward reference, and although intended as an explanation of others' failure, they tell us more about Phaedra than she knows herself. The strongest case for the ambivalence of *aidōs* as an element in Phaedra's motivation will emerge if *aidōs* can, without special pleading, be shown to fit in this scheme of failure of purpose. Although, then, it has been claimed that Phaedra's remarks on *aidōs* have no relevance to

[231] On the pleasures named by Ph. as the background in which her passion might have developed, see Winnington-Ingram (1960), 174–7. An indication of male suspicions as to what goes on in an atmosphere of long conversations and leisure is provided by Semonides fr. 7. 90–1 West: the good ('bee') woman does not 'take pleasure in sitting among women, where the topic of conversation is sex [ὅκου λέγουσιν ἀφροδισίους λόγους]'.

[232] On the threat to the *oikos* posed by female adultery, see Lys. 1. 33; cf. Seaford (1990), 160. For making me see that the 'burden on the house' is, ultimately, *erōs* I am very grateful to Mrs E. M. Craik, who kindly showed me successive drafts of her article, "Αἰδώς in Euripides' *Hippolytos*: Review and Reinterpretation" (forthcoming, *JHS* 1993).

her own situation[233] or that they are not to be referred to previous occurrences of *aidōs* in the play,[234] possible connections must at least be explored before being discounted.

There have been three occurrences of *aidōs*-terms so far in the play; Phaedra's remarks on the failure of human beings to carry out their resolve obviously have no relevance to Hippolytus, yet, at 73–81, he obviously does take pleasure in the chastity of which his *aidōs* is a part, and, since his particular life-style and his personal virtues contribute to his downfall (and since the dangers inherent in Hippolytus' brand of *aidōs*, *sōphrosunē*, and *eusebeia* have already been highlighted), any member of the audience alerted by Phaedra's remarks to the significance of the theme of *aidōs* might well reflect that here is an instance of the harmfulnes or inefficacy of that emotion;[235] but while Hippolytus may rejoice in his *aidōs* to the detriment of his own best interests, prudentially conceived, he cannot be said to chose *aidōs* over *to kalon*.

Phaedra's own *aidōs* is first mentioned at 244–6; the very fact of her coming to her senses, together with the realization that she has suffered an attack of temporary insanity, causes her pain,[236] and allied to her pain is a feeling of embarrassment at her uninhibited ravings; she is ashamed of what she has said and her eye has turned to *aischunē*.[237] This *aidōs* contributes to the observation that death is better than either being in one's right mind or being mad, and so cannot conflict with *to kalon*; nor is it a pleasure—quite the reverse. The very fact that it is painful, however, is surely to be related to the general theme of the harmfulness or inefficacy of *aidōs*;[238] the *aidōs* of the great speech is a pleasure, such, we assume, as might be preferred to *to kalon*; the *aidōs* of 244–6, on the other hand, is the mirror-image, a painful kind of *aidōs* which belongs with Phaedra's painful resistance to her passion, with her attempt to achieve *to kalon*.

---

[233] Solmsen (1973), 420–1.

[234] Kovacs (1980), 289.

[235] Since the theme of the harm caused by H.'s resistance to sex is not absent from the play (n. 202 above), his *aidōs* may also be harmful as the force which lies behind such resistance.

[236] Cf. Class (1964), 97–8.

[237] See the discussion of this passage above, 5.3.2, *ad fin.*

[238] Dodds (1925) saw *aidōs* in this passage as the 'not bad' *aidōs* of 385; this is not entirely wrong, since here *aidōs* is allied to Ph.'s desire to do the right thing; but even on the traditional interpretation of two kinds of *aidōs*, it is not enough simply to identify these wholly with the two previous instances of Ph.'s *aidōs* (even the 'good' *aidōs* is painful; cf. in general Winnington-Ingram (1960), 193–4); and if the notion of ambivalence remains even after the banishment of the 'two kinds of *aidōs*', this will be of a more subtle kind than Dodds's interpretation suggested.

These two passages are clearly relevant to the terms of Phaedra's great speech; at the very least they serve to indicate, as Winnington-Ingram says, that *aidōs* 'is playing a dubious part in the action'.[239] The *aidōs* of 244-6, in particular, seems tailor-made to contrast with a form of *aidōs* which is pleasant rather than painful, but morally harmful rather than helpful; it remains, then, to discover whether there is any room in the play for the pleasant *aidōs* which inhibits *to kalon*. And indeed there is; for when Phaedra mentions *aidōs* a second time the context satisfies all the requirements of 380-7; Phaedra fails to do what she knows to be right (*chrēston* or *kalon*), but rather prefers to respond to *aidōs*, an *aidōs* which emerges distinctly as a pleasure.

At 325-6 the Nurse, seeking to discover the reason for her mistress's desire for death, undertakes supplication by clasping Phaedra's hand and her knees, refusing to let go. Immediately the supplication begins, the idea of revealing her secret seems to become more attractive to Phaedra (329-35):

PHAEDRA. You will destroy me. Yet the matter does bring me *timē*.
NURSE. And then you conceal it, although the object of my appeal is worthy?
PHAEDRA. Yes, for I am contriving good things from shameful [*aischra*].
NURSE. Then will you not appear more honourable [*timiōtera*] if you speak?
PHAEDRA. I beg you, go away and let go of my hand.
NURSE. No, I won't, since you do not give me the gift I deserve.
PHAEDRA. I shall give it; for I feel *aidōs* for the *sebas* of your gesture.

Explicitly, then, Phaedra gives in out of *aidōs* for the Nurse's supplication,[240] yet at 329 the idea that her struggle brings her credit also crosses her mind, and it is after the Nurse's suggestion that she will enjoy greater *timē* by divulging her secret that she gives in. There are thus two strands to her yielding, and both motives are important; it is certainly true that her concern for her *timē* reveals a desire to share her knowledge of her struggle against her passion,[241] but the Nurse's supplication also creates the context in which she can give in to this desire,[242] and breaks a deadlock which might not otherwise have been broken; had Phaedra not given in she would have been obliged to

---

[239] (1960), 193.

[240] On *aidōs* and *sebas* here, cf. 3.4 above.

[241] Cf. Dodds (1925), 103; Barrett (1964) on 333-5; Winnington-Ingram (1960), 179, 193; Knox (1979), 209. This is denied by Kovacs (1987: 131 n. 46), who ignores 329 and, in particular, the effect of μέντοι (yet), which clearly indicates Ph.'s awareness of a reason for giving in.

[242] Cf. Dodds (1925), 103; Gould (1973),86-7; Taplin (1978), 69-70.

attempt to break the Nurse's hold by force, something she is unlikely to do in her weakened condition and which would entail an improper disregard for the suppliant gesture and all that it implies, even as that gesture is misused by the Nurse. Phaedra does want to give in, but she does so in a situation in which the pressure upon her is intense.

It is therefore this passage which suggests the fullness of the ambivalence of *aidōs*. Phaedra's concealment of her love for Hippolytus is motivated by the awareness that her passion is discreditable, a motive which perhaps issues in her *aidōs* on regaining her senses at 239–49, yet she also believes that she is being virtuous in her resistance and is attracted by the thought of the *timē* that her resistance might bring. The two motives are obviously incompatible, since, in order to enjoy *timē* for her resistance, Phaedra must reveal its object—a disgraceful passion, a *miasma* (317) which might attract the revulsion of others.

Phaedra does prefer *aidōs* to *to kalon* in this passage, then, and, significantly, her yielding to the Nurse's supplication entails the failure of her resolve to keep silent about her love (393–4), a stage of her resistance ('the way of her *gnōmē*', 391) which probably both antedates and accompanies her attempt to overcome her malady by means of *sōphrosunē* (398–9). The *aidōs* Phaedra accorded the Nurse's supplication is thus highly relevant to the central theme of the great speech, and it brings the *aidōs* which is mentioned in 385 into relation with the stages of her resolve, indicating quite clearly how *aidōs* can be preferred to *to kalon*, not just by those from whom Phaedra dissociates herself, but in her own case. Thus whatever Phaedra herself might mean by *aidōs* in 385, her remarks on the concept are to be related to her own conduct, just as her determination to follow the dictates of *gnōmē* is to be related to her failure to do so in the past, which also implies the possibility of failure in the future.

The sense in which *aidōs* is to be regarded as a bad pleasure emerges when we note that the *aidōs* for the supplication which is the external motivation for the revelation of Phaedra's secret occurs in the same context as other terms with which *aidōs* is intimately concerned (*timē*, 329; *aischra*, 331; *timiōtera*, 332). Phaedra is contriving *esthla* (good) out of *aischra*, and thus, as 244–6 suggest, *aidōs* at the disgraceful nature of her passion must be relevant. *Aidōs*, therefore, is playing a familiar role, as the feminine virtue which promotes loyalty to the *kurios*, and as the disposition which is protective of one's honour. Together with this, however, there belongs her positive desire for her *timē* to be recognized (329, exploited by the Nurse in 332), and this positive desire for honour is inseparable from the dispositional *aidōs* which underlies Phaedra's resistance. It is, then, part of the *aidōs* with which Phaedra rejects adultery that she takes a certain pleasure in her virtue; her *aidōs* for the Nurse's supplication in 335 serves as a verbal indication of the wider presence of *aidōs* in the scene.

Phaedra, moreover, has every opportunity to reflect on the inappropriateness of her positive desire for honour and of the misplaced *aidōs* for the Nurse which is its concomitant, since her disclosure of her passion is immediately met by the horror of the Nurse (352, 353-61); significantly enough, Phaedra's own initial reaction is to pretend that she has not, in fact, given away her secret. Thus at the point at which she delivers her remarks on *aidōs* Phaedra feels that she would have done better to die without revealing her love, indeed, her speech as a whole is designed to reassure the chorus that she can still do the right thing in spite of the enormity of her passion and in spite of her having given in to the Nurse. Her 'pleasures' in 383-5 all have their relevance to her situation,[243] but *aidōs* is the emphatic member of the group, precisely because *aidōs* is the only one of the three pleasures which we have been able to witness so far in the play as an obstacle to *to kalon*, and because Phaedra is herself, although perhaps only dimly, aware of the complications which have arisen in her attitude towards *aidōs*, *timē*, and *to kalon*.[244] Lines 385-7 perhaps correct any impression that all pleasures, including *aidōs*, are all bad, but they do not have the effect of showing that *aidōs* is all good.[245]

The pleasures, as we have seen, are those of the respectable, secluded married woman, and *aidōs*, the emphatic pleasure, is a woman's virtue *par excellence*, its chief object the maintenance of loyalty to father or husband, its field of operation the sphere of honour and disgrace, of *timē*, *to kalon*, and *to aischron*. *Aidōs* is thus inseparable from

---

[243] See n. 231 above.

[244] The emphasis on *aidōs*, moreover, makes it certain that it is the ambiguity of this concept that will engage the audience's attention; even if the reference of *dissai* in 385 is to pleasures, it is not the ambiguity of pleasure (which has already been mentioned in a conventional manner in 384; cf. the ambivalence of *erōs* as pleasure and pain 347-8), but the presence of *aidōs* in the list of pleasures which demands explanation.

[245] *Aidōs* thus has different aspects and varies in character according to circumstance. On this idea in Eur., see Dalfen (1984), who also (70-2) notes the respect paid by both Ph. and H. to religious sanctions which the Nurse misuses for her own ends, and considers it in the light of the idea that context determines the usefulness or otherwise of such conventions. Cf. n. 52 above, and *Ion* 1312-19, with the comments of Segal (1970), 284.

Phaedra's (and any woman's) moral outlook as a whole, and is the disposition which underlies her concern for her *timē*. The inefficacy of Phaedra's *aidōs* resides in one aspect of the whole, in an element of Phaedra's attitude to the honourable and the disgraceful which even she recognizes as inappropriate. We have seen her *aidōs* promote *to kalon* (244-6), when it led to the decision to die (248-9), and this *aidōs* was related to her recognition of the disgraceful character of the passion itself; in 335, however, *aidōs* is concerned, on the surface, with external ritual and, on a deeper level, with reputation, rather than with the moral character of one's conduct. The *aidōs* which opposes *to kalon*, therefore, is that which is concerned with the outward aspect of one's behaviour in the eyes of others, as opposed to that which classifies a given course of action as inconsonant with one's own notions of what is *kalon* and what is *aischron*. These, of course, are traditionally combined in *aidōs*, and must, even in Phaedra's case, be very close, but Segal is certainly correct in identifying 'internal' and 'external' strands in her reaction.[246] Had her private shame at her illicit passion dominated her reaction she would have perished without disclosing it, but as it is, that aspect of her *aidōs* which relates to 'other people' leads first to disclosure, then to the destruction of Hippolytus.

The two aspects of her *aidōs* are, as Segal has shown, most prominent in the great speech itself; she is *not* merely concerned with her outward reputation;[247] rather she knows that both the act of adultery and the passion or sickness which lies behind it are ignoble (*duskleēs*, 405). She feels revulsion for adulteresses (405-14), and rejects a mere reputation for chastity without the substance (413-14), wondering how women who conceal their adultery can be so lacking in *aidōs* as to look their husbands[248] in the face without fear either of the darkness which is their accomplice or that the timbers of the house might cry out.[249] At the same time, however, she expresses herself in

---

[246] (1970), 281-8, followed by Vickers (1973), 288-95, and, to some extent, by Michelini (1987), 300-4. Cf. Gill (1990), 89-90 with nn. 55-9.

[247] As Claus (1972), 230-1, claims; contrast Manuwald (1979), 142; Kovacs (1987), 48-9, 131 n. 53; Michelini (1987), 301-2.

[248] Or perhaps 'bedfellows', since this is the basic sense of ξυνευνετῶν; Willink (1968: 24) suggests the women are envisaged as shameless before both their husbands and their secret lovers.

[249] Ph. thus implies that a knowledge of her own misdeed would be insupportable, would occasion in her persistent *aidōs* (cf. Barrett (1964), on 413-14); she also, however, exhibits a tendency, which is a traditional component of *aidōs*, to project the subjective awareness of the character of one's own conduct on to external critics; thus the darkness and the house itself become witnesses to the crime who might bring about its exposure (cf. *Her.* 1378-85 in 5.3.2 above and Kovacs (1987), 131 n. 53). There is no evidence at

ways which create the impression that she is more concerned with
seeming than with being good; she hopes (403-4) both that her *kala*
will not escape notice and that she should not have many witnesses
when doing *aischra*, an awkward *gnōmē* which is out of place in her
explanation of her resolve to be rid of her passion in death. She
recognizes, to be sure, that adultery (or the passion behind it)[250] is
aischron, but appears to countenance behaving disgracefully provided
she can get away with it. This is not to be taken as the whole truth
about her moral standards, but, in context, her remarks constitute
another hint that she might not be able to achieve *to kalon* by putting
her *gnōmē* into practice.

Further remarks suggest that her rejection of shameful behaviour
encompasses prudential fear of detection—she hopes never to be
caught shaming her husband or her children (420-1), and wishes never
to be *seen* among the *kakoi* (430).[251] It must be stressed that the
elements of subjective judgement of the character of an action and
concern for how things look are traditionally combined in *aidōs*,[252] but
Phaedra has made the disjunction between the reputation for virtue
and the thing itself (413-14), and has even given the impression that
she might be content with the former (403-4). She also, in her remarks
on the importance of a parent's good name for the status of one's children, refers to the concern which will lead to her denunciation of
Hippolytus.

It has, however, been denied that this last can be seen as in any way

this point in the text for the view (Barrett, loc. cit., Willink (1968), 23; Claus (1972), 230)
that Ph. envies those women who can behave in the shameless way that she herself
rejects (cf. Gill (1990), 103 n. 59). In view of Ph.'s subsequent behaviour the assumption
of such envy in retrospect would not be wholly unwarranted, but I cannot see how we
could be expected to detect such a hidden emotion at the time.

[250] Ph.'s subsequent remarks suggest that by αἰσχρὰ δρώσῃ ('committing *aischra*') she
means 'being in love', and thus 403-4 may mean only that she wishes her secret, now that
it is out, to go no further than the Nurse and the chorus, but her expression must raise
the possibility that she might attempt to commit adultery in secret; cf. (roughly) Willink
(1968), 20; I do not believe, though, that these lines reveal that Ph. is deterred from transgression by fear of discovery alone; rather the inapposite expression suggests an inappropriate element in Ph.'s *aidōs*.

[251] These remarks become somewhat ambivalent in Ph.'s case, but such locutions are
not normally to be taken as evidence that Greek morality is based exclusively or mainly
on fear of external sanctions; in considering such expressions in tragedy, Garner (1987:
17) assumes that a desire never to be regarded as such and such, which may encompass
outright rejection of the action itself, indicates fear of detection alone, a readiness to
perform the action provided one remains undetected.

[252] Cf. the combination of the two elements in the choral comment at 770-5.

a failure or a case of Phaedra's preference for *aidōs* over *to kalon*.[253] Her action, it is held, is legitimate 'heroic' retaliation, satisfying the requirement to harm one's enemies. This approach, however, is unsatisfactory for several reasons. First of all, Hippolytus is at bottom Phaedra's *philos*, and even if personal enmity breaks out among *philoi*, retaliation in this context is rarely unproblematic; secondly, Phaedra's accusations are unjust, they are lies, and the attitude to lies in tragedy is generally unfavourable;[254] thirdly, even if our sympathy for Phaedra is never wholly or even significantly alienated, we are encouraged to sympathize more strongly with Hippolytus as the play draws to a close— we regret (to put it no more strongly) that Phaedra felt compelled to take the action she does. In addition, the concern for the reputation of her children, the desire for revenge, and the reluctance to face Theseus with her shameful passion known (717–21), all of which lead her to denounce her stepson, prove misplaced; despite his initial hesitation (612), Hippolytus has no intention of breaking his oath (656–8), and the truth can be revealed only because of the action Phaedra took to avoid exposure; what she wishes to prevent happening happens precisely because of the actions she takes to prevent it, and while this last point does not prove that the outward aspect of her *aidōs* is anything like 'morally bad', it does at least show that it is unhelpful.

Phaedra is ultimately left trying to preserve the outward appearance of virtue because the option which she regards as *to kalon* is no longer open to her. She allows the Nurse to approach Hippolytus, and thus can no longer keep her secret within a small circle of the well disposed. This failure to follow the course suggested by *gnōmē* is not, let it be clear, obviously or immediately occasioned by an occurrence of *aidōs*, but the *aidōs* passage of the great speech is still relevant in that, once again, Phaedra falters by preferring some other pleasure (that afforded by the prospect of successful adultery) to *to kalon*, and the course which appears pleasant to her does so precisely because of ambivalences in her moral outlook, her concern for her *timē*, her *aidōs*. The Nurse engages her in a 'long conversation', and tempts her first of all with the prospect of concealed adultery (462–81), and then with an ambiguous *pharmakon* (508–24). The Nurse's proposals of an illicit and covert affair are, she knows herself, *aischra* (500) and not *kala* (466), a

[253] See esp. Kovacs (1980), 300–2; (1987), 60 with 135–6 n. 85; Heath (1987), 85.

[254] In Eur., see *Andr.* 451–2 (Menelaus' pursuit of his aims by saying one thing and doing another is *aischrokerdeia*); *IA* 1144–5 (lying involves *anaischuntia* (= *anaideia*)); *Hyps.* fr. 60 Bond, 58–9 (Amphiaraus' *aischunē* before his patron Apollo, the god of true prophecy, prevents his telling a lie).

judgement which she shares with Phaedra (499, 503, 505), yet Phaedra herself finds the Nurse's words attractive; they are *kaloi* (487) and 'pleasant to the ears' (488), even if they would not make one *eukleēs* (489).[255] Most significantly of all, the attractiveness of the Nurse's words threatens to weaken Phaedra's resolve even before the Nurse mentions the *pharmakon* (503–6): 'Do not, I beg you, proceed with these words, for although you speak well your words are *aischra*; my soul is well and truly made ready by passion, and if you express the disgraceful course in attractive terms I shall be brought to the destruction from which I now flee.'[256] Phaedra thus sees the danger in her desire to do as the Nurse suggests; there is a disjunction between the pleasant and *to kalon* and she is attracted to the former. This is not all, however, for Phaedra also makes it clear that the pleasant course, which she regards as *aischron*, and which she opposes to the morally *kalon*, is none the less, in its own way, *kalon*—the Nurse's words are 'too *kaloi*' (487), they are *aischra* spoken well (*kalōs*, 505). There is, then, a further disjunction between that which is *kalon* in word and that which is *kalon* in deed, the outer attractiveness of that which is pleasant and sounds attractive and the inner fineness of the proper course of action. The fact, therefore, that Phaedra exhibits a failure to align her affective motivation with her rational choice of the good sets up a disjunction which Euripides is able to relate to the ambivalence of *aidōs* by presenting it in terms of a conflict between competing conceptions of what is *kalon*; for *aidōs* is in essence that disposition which governs one's attitude to *kalon* and *aischron*.

It is also significant that the Nurse, as she did in the supplication scene, pursues her aims by working on her mistress's concern for her reputation. Sensible people, says the Nurse, turn a blind eye to the sexual indiscretions of wives or sons; the typical practice of the clever is λανθάνειν τὰ μὴ καλά ('to let what is not *kalon* escape notice', 466), a phrase which recalls verbally Phaedra's desire that her *kala* should not escape notice (403), but whose content recalls her desire not to have many witnesses when committing *aischra* (404).[257] These lines precede

---

[255] In 488–9 note esp. the echo of the opposition between *to kalon* and *hedonē* in 382–3.

[256] The play on senses of the antonyms εὖ/καλῶς–αἰσχρά here is obvious, and the contrast between that which merely looks good and the truly noble thus implied relates to the topic of the aspects of *aidōs* under discussion. (Cf. 487–9; also 490–1: for the Nurse, accused of 'too attractive words' and of saying what is merely pleasant to the ears rather than the *kala* which make one *eukleēs*, Phaedra's words about the moral *kalon* are merely 'of fine appearance', λόγων εὐσχημόνων, her scruple mere *semnotēs*.)

[257] Cf. Vickers (1973), 289; Gill (1990), 102 n. 48.

those in which Phaedra admits the attractiveness of the Nurse's proposals (487–8) and confesses the danger of her giving in (503–6); because she is 'made ready by *erōs* (erotic passion)' she is susceptible to the Nurse's argument, but she is also susceptible because there is a side of her which is open to the argument that what the eye does not see, the mind does not grieve over, and when she wavers once more and allows the Nurse to pursue the plan of the *pharmakon*, we are quite sure that she is not simply deceived by the Nurse's ambiguities. The inappropriate element in her concern for her reputation, which is part and parcel of her *aidōs*, has contributed to her abandoning the plan which she saw as best, to her abandoning *to kalon*. After the Nurse has approached Hippolytus, *to kalon* is no longer possible, and Phaedra, as a *pis aller*, attempts to salvage enough of her reputation to secure the position of her children; concern for *eukleia* (or *aidōs*, of one sort) must now inevitably take preference over *to kalon*.

There can be no doubt that Phaedra herself regards the Nurse's approach to Hippolytus and its effects as constituting a failure; the Nurse has ruined her (596), and she is ashamed and disgusted with herself (*kakunomai*, 686); she can no longer die *eukleēs* (687–8). She never says that her denunciation is a way of preserving her reputation in full, merely that it will preserve that of her children and avoid inflicting the disgrace of an adulteress on her Cretan home (715–19). She explains that she cannot face Theseus charged with shameful deeds (720–1), but this means only that she will avoid any reproach Theseus might level against her passion or against her having urged the Nurse to approach Hippolytus, not that her reputation after her denunciation will stand as high as it would have, had she died without allowing the Nurse to pursue the plan of the *pharmakon*. A woman who has been raped may be thought more virtuous than one who has conceived an adulterous passion for her stepson, and Theseus, reserving all his vitriol for Hippolytus, clearly does not blame Phaedra in any way; but he also feels himself dishonoured,[258] and for this to be the case, Phaedra's honour must also be impaired, even if this attracts no censure from those who are well disposed towards her. As we saw in connection with the *Ion*, even a woman who has contributed nothing towards her dishonour may be regarded with suspicion.[259]

---

[258] See n. 207 above.

[259] To make these observations is not to 'patronize' Ph. or to hold that she 'should' have gone on living knowing that H. might denounce her at any moment, as Kovacs (1987: 134–5 n. 84) thinks; see Vickers (1973), 290.

Phaedra's remarks in her great speech on *aidōs*, *to kalon*, and pleasure thus fall into place in the context of her role in the play as a whole; we do have two contrasting passages in which *aidōs* receives contrary predicates (*kalon*-promoting but painful versus *kalon*-inhibiting but pleasant), but these occurrences do not in themselves constitute the totality of the ambivalence of *aidōs* to which Phaedra refers in 380–7; rather they are indicative of the ways in which her *aidōs*, which is the root of her moral values and the source of her sense of the *kalon* and the *aischron*, can issue in conflicting impulses and fail to bring success either in moral terms or in terms of self-interest. In the character of Phaedra Euripides is exploring problems of human motivation on a level with the greatest of Greek thinkers; he identifies the elements involved in moral struggle—the moral judgement that a given course is *kalon*, the educated, emotional disposition to pursue *to kalon*, and the factors of pleasure and pain which accompany moral action and moral choice in different ways and to varying degrees. We might think first of Plato and the tripartite soul, with its three goals of truth, honour, and pleasure,[260] but reflection reveals that the approach of the *Hippolytus* has more in common with Aristotle[261]—when we first see Phaedra, and when we first hear of her *aidōs*, she is, in Aristotelian terms, an encratic; the effortless virtue which pursues the judgement of *to kalon* with pleasure and without a hint of struggle is beyond her, but she does have a judgement of the noble by which she is determined to abide, even though she is tempted by the pleasant course, even though it causes her some pain to resist. Ultimately, however, Phaedra slides into *akrasia*; painful self-control gives way to temptation, and a noble best judgement is overcome by pleasure (a fact, incidentally, which lends support to Aristotle's view that women tend to *akrasia* because their deliberative faculty is *akuron*, 'without authority').[262] The analysis of action against one's principles afforded by

[260] See 6.4.3 below.

[261] For the hierarchy, *sōphrosunē*, *enkrateia*, *akrasia*, and *akolasia*, see first of all *EN* 7, and cf. 6.5.3 below (at nn. 228–30). On the relationship of these states to pleasure and pain, see Charles (1984), 168–77, with discussion by Cairns (1989). Arist., of course, bases his account of *akrasia* on a dialectical examination of the opinions of the many and the wise, and one might be inclined to argue that Eur.'s dramatization of *akrasia* in Ph. simply manifests the opinion of the many that *akrasia* can occur (so, roughly, Barrett (1964), 229). For me, however, there is much more to the characterization than that; Eur., at the very least, also considers the opinions of the many and the wise (the allusion to Soc.), and is thus offering a reflective dramatization of *akrasia*.

[262] *Pol.* 1260ᵃ13; see Fortenbaugh (1977: 138), who goes on (139) to illustrate Arist.'s view, 'a common view of women', with ref. to Eur.'s Medea; cf. id. (1970), 240–1, where the relevance of Ph. in *Hipp.* is also, cautiously, admitted.

Phaedra's conduct in the *Hippolytus*, then, is no banal dramatization of the viewpoint of the ordinary man,[263] but is rather conducted in terms which are those of future philosophical discussion.

If Phaedra's *aidōs* is ambivalent, then the seeds of her destruction are to be found in the very qualities which constitute her virtue. The same, as we saw, can be said of Hippolytus; he, too, we remember, is motivated by *aidōs*, and while his *aidōs* does not manifest the tension between 'inner' and 'outer' aspects prominent in Phaedra's responses, it remains ambivalent in one sense, in that, although a positive trait of character, it is not a force which promotes the interests of its possessor. For the youth Hippolytus, as for the woman Phaedra, moreover, *aidōs* is close to, even interchangeable with the virtue of *sōphrosunē*; but *sōphrosunē*, as Hippolytus is aware (1035), can be misused to the detriment of its possessor. If, then, Phaedra's conduct and her articulation of her principles in the great speech suggest opposition to Socrates on the possibility of *akrasia*, the ultimate fate of both Phaedra and Hippolytus questions the (related) Socratic thesis that our virtues must promote our own interests.[264] This, and the hints of an Aristotelian approach to *akrasia*, given that Aristotle's own account is closely based on the questions posed by Socrates, suggest that there is more than mere allusion to the views of the historical Socrates in the drama; what is important for our purposes, however, is the fact that Euripides articulates the issues through his emphasis on the ambivalence of the concept of *aidōs*. Like his philosophical contemporaries and successors,[265] Euripides' representations imply not merely an analysis of the conceptual reference of *aidōs*, but an account of its role and its importance in the motivation of the moral agent; the motivational force of *aidōs* is not straightforward—it may belong with absolute and unassailable commitment to internalized moral principles, or with the painful struggle to maintain one's principles in the face of temptation, or with the tendency to base one's moral conduct on the external rewards and sanctions of honour and disgrace, and thus with a liability to succumb to the pleasures of doing

[263] Such is the suggestion of Barrett's rather perfunctory observation (1964: 229) that 'the notion of acting against one's moral convictions is fairly common in Eur.', and his remarks about 'straightforward statements of a straightforward position'.

[264] At Pl. *Charm.* 160e–161b Socrates induces Charmides to abandon his definition of *sōphrosunē* as *aidōs* on the grounds that a virtue such as *sōphrosunē* cannot share the well-known ambivalence of *aidōs*, i.e. cannot be 'bad' for its possessor. Cf. Ch. 6 n. 86. For another view of the relevance of *Charm.* to *Hipp.*, see Gill (1990), 95–7.

[265] See Ch. 6. On *Hipp.* and the question of 'doing wrong in secret' (see 6.3 below), cf. Gill (1990), 92–3.

wrong in secret; and whatever its role in one's character, *aidōs* does not guarantee success. These are major topics of fifth- and fourth-century ethics; they are also, transformed into modern terms, some of the questions which most exercise the modern commentator.

5.5. THE IMPORTANCE OF *AIDŌS*

It seems fitting to end this chapter on an author who gives *aidōs* such a major role by collecting those passages in which its importance is the main point; for, in spite of the frequent complexity, even ambivalence, of *aidōs* in Euripides, the traditional utility and positive value of the concept are repeatedly extolled.[266] A traditional way of expressing this utility, one which seems to have become a poetic commonplace, is the presentation of the decline in contemporary morality in terms of the departure of *aidōs* from a decadent world. We noted the occurrence of this *topos* in *Medea* (439–40),[267] and the same idea recurs in one of the plays in which *aidōs* is most prominent, at *Iphigeneia at Aulis* 1089–97, where the chorus draw the moral from Agamemnon's desire to sacrifice his daughter: 'Where can the face of *aidōs* or of *aretē* have any strength, when impiety [lack of *sebas*, τὸ ἄσεπτον] is powerful and *aretē* is abandoned by mortals, *Anomia* conquers law, and mortals do not strive to avoid the *phthonos* of the gods.' The context is again, as in the *Medea* passage, one of neglect of *philia*, but in a way which involves a perversion of ritual, and so the references to the gods are relevant not just in the general sense that the gods are felt to support loyalty among *philoi*. *Aidōs* is associated with *aretē*, and although both belong together in the maintenance of one's obligations towards *philoi*, they are also given a more general reference here as factors which ensure respect for law and custom; it requires *aretē*, then, to meet traditional standards both in one's relations with one's *philoi* and in general, and *aidōs*, as a dispositional trait to manifest the emotion in its occurrent sense, is the force which renders one susceptible to the requirements of those standards. There is nothing untraditional here; mention of the gods reinforces the conventional tone and suggests that the sentiments expressed would not be considered novel.

Aretē is also associated with *aidōs* in an earlier ode of the same play. At 558–72 the chorus sing:[268]

---

[266] Cf. Szlezak (1986), 58–9, on the importance of *aidōs* in Eur.
[267] Cf. n. 30 above.   [268] Cf. 5.4.3 and n. 158 above.

Varied are the natures of mortals, varied their ways; but the truly good [*esthlon*] is always clear, and an educated upbringing makes a great contribution to *aretē*. For *to aideisthai* is wisdom [*sophia*], and has the excellent grace of discerning with the help of intelligence [*gnōmē*] what should be done [or 'one's duty', *to deon*],[269] where reputation brings ageless fame to life. It is a great thing to hunt *aretē*; women do so in the sphere of hidden love, whereas in men good behaviour in its myriad forms promotes a city's growth.

These meditations on traditional women's *aretē* are remarkable for their almost philosophical precision in identifying, with such economy of expression, the role of *aidōs* in excellence. Allowance is made for innate capacity (558-9),[270] but the varied natures of human beings do not entail the relativity of the good, which is objective and, as the aim and focus of *aretē*, apprehended, to a large extent, as a result of education. The association of *aidōs*, moreover, with education is accepted as needing so little explanation that it can be assumed that to point out the utility of *aidōs* is to demonstrate the contribution of education to *aretē*. *Aidōs* is identified as *sophia* (wisdom), which perhaps only reflects the traditional association of the concept with terms denoting good sense, or perhaps simply indicates that *aidōs* is in the best interests of its possessor, but possibly there is also the suggestion that *aidōs* is the product of learning and experience. Mention of *sophia* presupposes the cognitive side of *aidōs*, but the continuation, that *aidōs* discerns the proper course of action with the help of *gnōmē*, implies that although *aidōs* does have this cognitive side, that is not all there is to the concept. *Aidōs* also bears its traditional relationship to reputation and fame, but while these are the results of proper action there is no suggestion that one does 'what is necessary' (*to deon*) merely in order to gain these rewards. All in all, the passage reveals subtle understanding of the nature of *aidōs*, and hints at more extensive debate on the subject in contemporary thought. As we shall see in the next chapter, the questions of the relationship between education and innate capacity, and of the nature of our motivation to be moral, loom large whenever *aidōs* appears in sophistic contexts.

The association of *aidōs* with education, however, is not new. It is

---

[269] In 563-6 I take τὸ αἰδεῖσθαι as the subject of ἔχει. Von Erffa (1937: 161-2), followed by Szlezak (1986: 55-6), takes ἐσορᾶν τὸ δέον as the subject, and seems to imagine that ἐξαλλάσσουσαν (surpassing) must have a comparative sense. Thus he sees a contrast between instinct (*aidōs*) and intelligence (*gnōmē*); but (*a*) *aidōs* has already been described as *sophia*, (*b*) τε . . . τε does not indicate any sort of contrast (quite the reverse), and (*c*) ἐξαλλάσσουσαν need not be comparative.

[270] Cf. 'Protagoras' at Pl. *Prot.* 327bc.

apparent, for example, in Theognidean passages such as 409-10,[271] where there is also an association with *aretē*, and even in *Iliad* 6 (441-6),[272] where Hector sets his *aidōs* in the context of his having learned to be *esthlos*. But in Euripides the idea is recurrent, and this probably does reflect contemporary preoccupations. In the conclusion to Adrastus' Funeral Speech (*Supplices* 909-17), for example, *aidōs* is seen as a product of a good upbringing and every man who has practised noble behaviour is said to experience *aischunē* at the thought of becoming *kakos* (911-13). This much is conventional, and does not take us far from the implicit position of Hector in *Iliad* 6. In the next sentence, however, we move firmly into sophistic territory, as *euandria*, a synonym for *aretē* in its narrow, competitive, martial sense,[273] is said to be teachable in the same way that a child learns to speak a language without formal tuition (913-15).[274] Other passages stress the importance of acquiring a sense of *aidōs* by pursuing *kala* and avoiding *aischra* in childhood and youth, so that *aidōs* at the prospect of acting inappropriately is an automatic adult response,[275] and its absence in the adult a sign of inadequate moral education or 'sense'.[276] All these passages, then, firmly suggest that the fully developed capacity of *aidōs* with its cognitive ability to distinguish between right and wrong, *kalon* and *aischron*, is not something which is innate but is developed in the process of socialization and education,[277] and this, by no means an unsophisticated position, indicates that even in passages dealing with conventional forms of behaviour Euripides is applying a familiarity with important currents of thought on the nature of *aidōs* itself. Clearly, too, these Euripidean passages reveal that *aidōs* is a major element in that *aretē* which is acquired by education and habituation.

[271] Cf. 2.3.4 above.   [272] Cf. 1.2.3 above.

[273] *Euandria*, however, denotes excellence in a wider sense at *El.* 367-70, a passage which also suggests that environment and upbringing, rather than heredity, are the more important factors in the development of character.

[274] This point is made, with reference to a wider sort of *aretē*, by 'Protagoras' at Pl. *Prot.* 327e, and I should be inclined to see Protagoras as the main influence behind all these passages on *aidōs* and education. On *aidōs* and education in the fragments of Prot. and in the Platonic dialogue which bears his name, see 6.2 below.

[275] See fr. 1027 N²; *Hec.* 599-602 (deleted by Sakorraphos, but clearly representing ideas similar to those found in other, undisputed passages). The former deprecates the acquisition of bad habits, since these become ingrained (*emphuton*) features of the adult character—a thoroughly Aristotelian sentiment, which also, in its recognition that acquired traits can become part of one's *phusis*, corresponds to the observation of Democ. B 33 DK.

[276] *Hcld.* 458-60; *Her.* 299-301 (*aidōs* absent in the stupid but found in the *sophoi*).

[277] Thus Hippolytus, who rejects education yet values *aidōs* (*Hipp.* 78-80), is an isolated figure.

6

The Sophists, Plato, and Aristotle

The role of *aidōs* in the doctrines of the sophists is a topic to which the preceding chapters have already alluded; the present chapter, therefore, begins by following up some of these indications of the trends in fifth-century thought that are most important for our study. Consideration of *aidōs* in Sophocles and Euripides, in particular, has identified a growing recognition of the interaction of that concept with the internalized self-regulatory mechanism that we call conscience, as well as insight into the role of *aidōs* as an important factor in the development of character. Accordingly, we look first at the evidence for the popular conception of 'conscience' in later fifth-century Athens, before turning to the evidence for the doctrines of some of the major contemporary thinkers themselves, with particular reference to one particular controversy (that concerned with the problem of 'doing wrong in secret') which sheds considerable light on ancient views of the nature of *aidōs*, and, indeed, brings the view expressed in our ancient sources into relationship with the modern discussions of the nature of shame and guilt with which we began our study. This focus on the essence of *aidōs*, on its relation to internal or external sanctions, on its nature as a feature of the ethical and psychological outlook embedded in the texts under discussion, and on its relevance or otherwise to the concept of 'conscience', is then extended into the discussion of its place in the ethics and moral psychology of Plato and Aristotle. Essentially, our discussion now comes full circle, as we consider ancient views which reveal important perspectives on the issues raised in the Introduction.

6.1. CONSCIENCE AND THE ORDINARY ATHENIAN

We saw that conscience and its expression as such (that is, in terms of the individual's own assessment of the character of his or her actions, as opposed to modes of expression—references to Erinyes, and the like—which might or might not be regarded as alternative ways of

construing the same phenomena) form a topic in which Euripides
seems to take a particular interest, and it is normally assumed that this
interest, together with his uses of *sunesis*, *suneidenai*, and so on, reflects
not the everyday usage of contemporary Athenians, but a new recognition of the phenomenon of (retrospective) conscience which has not
yet permeated to the popular level. Accordingly, when (for example)
the verb *suneidenai* is found reflexively in another fifth-century author,
this is felt to indicate the influence of the same 'enlightened' opinions.
One rarely meets the observation that the phenomena and locutions
which we place under the heading of conscience may have been
perfectly normal features of everyday speech and experience;[1] yet
there does exist a number of passages in which the popular context of
the utterance suggests that such an observation is warranted. This, of
course, is not to imply that the absence in earlier literature of locutions
which present the phenomenon of conscience as such is simply fortui-
tous; Homeric language, as we saw, does not and presumably cannot
express quite the concepts of retrospective shame and conscience
whose presence we noted in Euripides; yet the passages considered
below do suggest that the development of Greek moral and psychological vocabulary had facilitated an unselfconscious familiarity with
ideas of remorse and personal conscience on a widespread and popular
basis. This familiarity may be attributable to gradual development, or
perhaps insights won in the earlier part of the fifth century had
become part of the popular consciousness, just as (for example) a
popular and distorted form of Freudianism is now a familiar part of the
intellectual baggage of huge numbers of non-specialists.

6.1.1. *Antiphon 'the Orator'*

The relevant passages of the speeches of Antiphon are somewhat
ambivalent evidence for the existence of a popular concept of conscience. Antiphon himself was clearly no ordinary Athenian, but an
aloof intellectual and a contributor to contemporary philosophical
debate,[2] and the exploitation of the idea of conscience in his speeches

---

[1] See, however, Wilamowitz (1959), ii. 386, on the popular character of the concept of
suneidēsis.

[2] On the identity of Antiphon 'the Orator' and 'the Sophist', see, above all, Morrison
(1961) and cf. his remarks in Sprague (1972), 109–11; cf. also Avery (1982) and contrast
the reiteration of the separatist position by Pendrick (1987). That there is, at least, no
possibility of a positive distinction between the sophist and the orator is accepted by

is not matched by any of his oratorical successors.[3] Yet the homicide speeches were designed to be heard in popular courts, while the exercises contained in the tetralogies must be intended to represent the kind of argument which might sway a jury, and it is therefore extremely unlikely that the speeches contain ideas that would have seemed novel or unfamiliar to the ordinary Athenian. The references to the concept of conscience in the speeches, then, must be considered to represent views current among at least a good proportion of those liable to constitute a jury.

Reflections on guilt and conscience, however, are not introduced arbitrarily or gratuitously into the speeches. All have their point, and in terms of purpose and application may be divided into two categories, those which warn the jurors of the possibility that their consciences will trouble them should they reach an unjust verdict, and those in which the main point is the clear conscience of the speaker himself. Those in the first category are mostly based on the idea of the jury's duty, which in a case of homicide is a religious one (a requirement of *eusebeia*)[4] analogous to that of the prosecution in avenging the deceased.[5]

Summing up his second speech for the defence, the speaker of 2. d. 11–12 appeals to the jury for *eusebeia* and *aidōs*, and concludes by

Guthrie, iii. 293–4, Kerferd (1981*a*), 50; Rankin (1983), 64–5. Such reservations as these scholars express towards Morrison's thesis are largely 'political', i.e. they retain some doubt that the so-called 'democratic' sentiments in the 'Sophist' can be reconciled with the 'conservatism' of the Rhamnusian orator. These arguments are taken to extremes by Luria (1963), who claims that the author of Antiphon B 44 B DK col. 2 (on the unnaturalness of class and racial distinctions) 'cannot' be the right-wing orator, that the speeches of the orator reveal conservative attitudes which must have been held by their author, and that Thuc., who praises the oligarch, 'could not' have agreed with the views of the author of the anarchistic papyrus fragments. But (*a*) we know nothing of the ideology of the oligarch (and it is dangerous to assume that 5th-cent. right-wingers believed exactly as their counterparts today); (*b*) the conservative attitudes of the speeches would surely have been retained by their author on publication precisely because such attitudes are more likely to win over a jury—their appearance shows merely that their author thought them efficacious; (*c*) the papyrus frr. are not necessarily anarchistic, and it is far from certain that Thuc. would have disagreed with their content, even supposing that his praise of the oligarch in Book 8 is contingent on agreement with detailed aspects of his doctrines; see Moulton (1972), 365–6; cf. Avery (1982), 147–51. I treat 'the Orator' here and 'the Sophist' below (6.3.1), not because I believe they are different people, but because the data gleaned from the speeches and from the frr. in DK need, for the purposes of our study, to be set against different backgrounds.

[3] Note how many of Dover's passages on conscience (1974: 220–2) come from Antiphon.
[4] See 2. d. 11, 2. d. 12, 3. b. 11, 3. b. 12, 4. b. 7, 5. 88, 5. 96, 6. 51.
[5] See 6.7.

reminding the jurors that a hasty verdict will afford them ample opportunity for repentance:

By undertaking such an unjust prosecution they, who are seeking to have me put to death *anosiōs* [impiously], say that they are pure, but that I, who am urging you to *eusebein*, am acting impiously [*anosia*]. But, pure of all the charges as I am, on my own behalf I urge you to respect [*aideisthai*] the *eusebeia* of those who have committed no crime,[6] and on behalf of the deceased I remind you of his vengeance and advise you not to let the guilty party escape by condemning the innocent. Once I am dead no one will continue to seek the culprit. Out of respect [*sebesthai*] for these considerations, then, acquit me piously [*hosiōs*] and justly, and do not recognize your error with the pangs of remorse. For in such matters remorse [*metanoia*] has no remedy.

It certainly seems that the speaker is warning the jurors that their own subsequent recognition that they have reached an unjust verdict will cause them pain, but the picture is complicated by the obvious stress on the religious aspect. Given the concern for pollution and purity in the rest of the passage, as evidenced in the warning that if the speaker is condemned the real murderer, a source of pollution, will remain free,[7] it is possible that the *metanoia* of the jurors may be occasioned by their recognition that they have brought pollution on themselves and their city.[8] If, then, the jury's *metanoia* is to be caused by the sense that they are being pursued by some avenging spirit, we are not dealing with remorse as such, although such a superstitious fear would not, I think, be totally removed from the experience which many a God-fearing Christian might describe as remorse or repentance. At the same time, however, in both 2. d. 12 ('respect the *eusebeia* of those who do not *adikein*') and 3. b. 12 ('respecting the *eusebeia* of these actions and *to dikaion*') the verb *aideisthai* is used of the jurors' positive respect for justice and 'piety' or 'righteousness',[9] and it is clearly possible that

[6] For *eusebeia* as the object of *aideisthai*, cf. the closely similar 3. b. 12. The overlap of *aideomai* and *sebomai* in this, a prose passage, is striking, and gives a somewhat poetic and archaic flavour. Cf. the use of *epaideomai* and *sebomai* as synonyms in Antiphon B 44 B DK col. 2, 1–6.

[7] See Parker (1983), 105, 110.

[8] In other passages, both the condemnation of an innocent man (3. d. 9, 4. b. 8, 4. d. 10) and failure to condemn the true killer (2. b. 9–11, 3. b. 11–12, 4. a. 3, 4. b. 2) may bring the wrath of the victim down upon the jury.

[9] These non-personal objects are the recipients of *aidōs* in exactly the same way as persons—they are qualities which are in themselves worthy of honour and which are indicative of the right to honour of their possessor. That *aidōs* is to be the response which recognizes such qualities as 'justice' and 'piety' indicates the ease with which Greek can base a sense of justice or fairness in traditional notions of the entitlement to honour.

any repentance they might experience after the trial might also be occasioned by a sense that they have failed to accord justice and *eusebeia* their due. Unless we believe, moreover, that fifth-century Athenians were literally pursued by the avenging spirits of the dead or subject to the pollution of shed blood, we are bound to see the phenomena which they describe with reference to such concepts as indications of basic human emotions, and it is likely that such apprehensions conceal an anxiety that we might describe in terms of conscience. This much, however, does not take us beyond the world of Aeschylus,[10] and clearly expressions of conscience in these terms do not refer unambiguously to the concept as such.

Similar warnings nevertheless occur in the speech *On the Murder of Herodes* (5. 89, 91-2), and although reservations based on the theological aspect of homicide do still obtain, they do so to a far less significant extent in this, a genuine court speech, than in the tetralogies.[11] In the last sentence of §88 the jury are informed that it is a *hamartia* and an *asebeia* to convict an innocent man of murder; the next sentence (§89) explains that it is more serious for a jury wrongfully to convict than for a prosecutor wrongfully to accuse; and §89 closes with a warning that the consequences of a wrong verdict (whatever they may be) are inescapable. In §91 Euxitheus proceeds to make a distinction within the category of *hamartia*, saying that to acquit unjustly is 'more *hosion*' than to convict unjustly; the former is a mistake (*hamartēma*), the latter an impiety (*asebēma*). In the latter case a mistake cannot be remedied and recognition of one's mistake and repentance are more harmful.[12]

There are certainly religious elements in this passage, but the threat of pollution is not explicitly brought out.[13] Parker,[14] however, is sure that the warning that the jurors cannot escape the responsibility for any *hamartia*[15] envisages only 'pollution or spirits' as the consequences of error. Yet there is emphasis on the jurors' recognition of their own *hamartia*, which in itself is said to be a source of *blabos* (harm), and it is

[10] e.g. in his description of the fear of divine punishment at *Ag.* 179-81. This, again, is not unlike the kind of 'bad conscience' of which a fundamentalist Christian might warn.
[11] Cf. Parker (1983), 126: '... there is a noticeable contrast between the *Tetralogies*, where the argument from pollution occurs with obsessive regularity, and its merely intermittent presence in the forensic speeches'; also 127, 'Arguments from the *Tetralogies* recur, but in the most muted of tones.'
[12] Cf. §92: a conscious decision which turns out to have been wrong admits of no excuse. [13] Cf. Parker (1983), 127.
[14] Ibid. [15] 5. 89, repeated, almost verbatim, at 6.6.

impossible categorically to decide whether the harm arises from the fact that recognition leads to fear of consequences or from the individual's own self-reproach.[16] In fact, since the purpose of the argument is to create uncertainty and hesitation, the openness of the matter is such as to prove effective, allowing the individual members of the jury to construe the 'harm' either in superstitious terms or in terms of personal conscience.

That Antiphon is thinking of conscience in this passage might be suggested by the sequel (§93), in which the vocabulary of conscience is exploited to suggest the innocence of the defendant:

> Know well that I would not have come to this city, if I had such a thing on my conscience [or 'were aware of such a thing in myself']. But as it is, I place my trust in justice [*to dikaion*], whose value as a partner in litigation is unrivalled, if one is conscious that one has done nothing *anosion* or committed no impiety against the gods. For in such a case, if the body gives up, the soul preserves it, since it is willing to undergo hardship on account of its having nothing on its conscience. But if one has a guilty conscience ['for one who is aware of something in himself'], then that in itself militates against one; for even if the body is still strong, the soul abandons it, considering the punishment in which it is involved to be punishment for its impieties. I, however, stand before you with no such thing on my conscience.

The repetition of reflexive use of the verb *suneidenai* in this passage is most striking, and this degree of emphasis must be intended to make the point that one's own awareness of one's innocence is of the utmost importance. As Dover points out,[17] the representation of conscience in this passage strongly resembles similar descriptions in the fragments of Democritus, to which, as we shall see, *aidōs* is relevant.[18] Antiphon may, however, stop short of a wholly Democritean explanation of conscience; the weakness of the *psuchē* of the man with a bad conscience occurs because he feels that what is happening to him is a punishment for his *asebēmata*, and a fear of supernatural punishment may enter the picture at this point, although the guilty party may simply realize that his indictment on a charge is a prelude to the punishment he deserves.[19] (Note that the psychic disturbance is a consequence not of the thought of punishment, but of the knowledge of

---

[16] Cf. Dover (1974), 221.

[17] (1974), 222.

[18] 6.3.2 below.

[19] For the idea that awareness of culpability leads to weakness of the *psuchē*, cf. Creon at Soph. *Ant.* 491–4.

culpability, which causes the *psuchē* to give up when the offender is put on trial.)[20] Even if certain reservations must be entertained, however, the passage certainly reveals an obvious familiarity not only with the phenomenon of the guilty conscience, but also with the influence of a clear conscience on the maintenance of moral fortitude.[21]

The passage is, however, not a gratuitous digression; rather it exemplifies the exploitation (as an argument from probability) of the jurors' response to the speaker's demeanour, as he invites them to conclude from his confidence that he is innocent. The converse of this argument, open to his opponents, would be that his confident exterior, in the face of compelling proof of his guilt, is a sure sign of *anaideia*.[22]

The speech *On the Chorister* opens with a similar argument from conscience;[23] the greatest of benefits for one facing danger is a clear

[20] Parker (1983: 254) leaves it open whether that which is a punishment for acts of impiety is the agent's physical weakness or his trial; the former might indicate some supernatural intervention, while the latter merely suggests that the guilty party realizes that he is about to receive his just deserts. It seems to me rather more likely that 'this' (ταύτην) is the trial, since the point at issue is the demeanour in court of the innocent and the guilty. It is certainly not quite right to say, with Rodgers (1969: 249), that the guilty man's mental unease is caused by his fear of punishment; rather he sees what has already happened to him as punishment; the point seems to be that the guilty man recognizes that his crimes have caught up with him, and so he cannot deny the charge with confidence.

[21] The passage thus refutes Snell (1930b: 27), who claims that, in the pre-Christian era, where a moral evaluation enters into the idea of conscience, it is always in the context of the 'bad' conscience. Rodgers's discussion of this passage (1969: 248–9) is not totally wrong, but she claims that the element of psychological insight is not in any way conveyed by the reflexive uses of *suneidenai*. This requires the claim that the instances of the relevant locutions refer only to the speaker's knowledge that he has not, in fact, done that of which he is accused; but Euxitheus is not just saying that, as far as he is aware, he did not murder Herodes, and so the illocutionary force of his uses of *suneidenai* etc. is inextricably bound up with his antithesis of the confidence of the innocent and the fear and psychic disturbance of the guilty.

[22] For such accusations of *anaideia* in Antiphon, see 3. c. 1, 3. c. 5, 4. c. 6; in these *anaideia* is coupled with *tolma*, daring; cf. 1. 28, 4. c. 4, 5. 15, 5. 57, 6. 51 with *tolma* alone. Charges of *anaideia/anaischuntia*, together with accusations that one's opponent has acted *aischrōs*, constitute the major applications of our complex of terms in the orators.

[23] Garner (1987: 17–18) regards this passage (6. 1) as the 'one fifth-century passage which especially seems to assert the importance of something like conscience or an internal standard independent of outside circumstances'. This ignores the passages just cited from the Herodes speech, not to mention numerous others elsewhere in 5th-cent. literature. A clear conscience, Garner goes on, 'is not a good in itself. It is merely the best in a bad situation.' Obviously one would rather not be accused or condemned for something that one has not done, but the fact that a clear conscience can be seen as a consolation in such circumstances suggests that it is something on which a high value is placed, with no implication that it is not valued in itself. Garner, moreover, ignores the speaker's claim that one cannot be considered *kakos* or be implicated in disgrace when one knows that one's downfall is not caused by one's own wrongdoing.

conscience, so that, even if the worst should happen, it does so without
the implication of baseness (*kakotēs*) and without disgrace (*aischunē*),
by chance rather than by wrongdoing (6. 1). Again, the true deter-
minant of the character of the situation is the conscience of the
individual, and it is claimed that no matter what others may think, no
matter how one's situation may appear, no *aischunē* can accrue to one
who has done no wrong. This is not the traditional view, and contrary
opinions are found in Antiphon himself,[24] but such explicit statements
of the autonomy of one's own judgement of one's actions have been
increasingly common in the literature since Solon. Here the awareness
that one has done no wrong is said to free the speaker from fear and
inhibition, even from the effects of the taunts of others; a little later he
makes the converse point, that the awareness that one has done wrong
causes one to submit oneself to justice, even in the absence of compulsion; someone who kills a person under his control (a person who thus
has no one to avenge him by prosecuting his killer) nevertheless voluntarily seeks purification, out of respect for convention and the divine
sanction (τὸ νομιζόμενον καὶ τὸ θεῖον δεδιώς, 6. 4). The verb used is
one of fearing, and its reference to the divine sphere clearly does
indicate fear of external sanctions, but 'fear' of current usage or custom
suggests not merely fear, but *aidōs*;[25] nor does it seem that this *aidōs* is
directed primarily at others' reproaches, but rather, taking the form of
respect for prevalent modes of behaviour, it indicates an assumption
that the individual agrees with conventional standards and is keen to
behave in accordance with them. This readiness, moreover, to submit
to the prescriptions of law or custom is described in terms of
conscience—'anyone who was aware that he had done such a deed'
would abide by the law relating to such matters. The context here is
entirely that of the pollution of shed blood, but it is maintained that a
conscientious desire to do what is right can coexist with fear of supernatural agency;[26] obviously the speaker hopes that such idealistic
sentiments will help in his own case, but they could hardly be expected
to do so were they not acceptable and familiar to his audience.

[24] e.g. at 5. 18 Euxitheus, who also protests his clear conscience, argues that his
wrongful imprisonment has brought an *oneidos* on his family.

[25] Cf. Thuc. 1. 49. 4 (*deos* of fear of reproach), 2. 11. 4–5 (salutary fear, *deos*, in a context
which suggests *aidōs*), 2. 37. 3 (*deos* covering both fear and fear of disgrace; cf. von Erffa
(1937), 190), 6. 24. 4 (fear of disgrace, *deos*, answering to the *aischunē* which Nicias
deprecates at 6. 13. 1).

[26] Cf. Parker (1983), 254, on the 'explicit awareness of the mechanism of religious
scruple'.

The speeches of Antiphon, then, place great emphasis on the subjective evaluation of right and wrong, and see it as uncontroversial that people should be concerned to do what is right even in the absence of external sanctions.[27] We note, moreover, that there is no disjunction between behaviour motivated by *aidōs* and that described in terms of conscience or religious scruple, but rather an easy and natural coexistence of interrelated forces in which one element reinforces the others.

These passages, with their indications of the concept of conscience and their respect for individual principle, obviously do not deal with these topics in any purely theoretical way, and no doubt the varieties of conscience outlined fail to satisfy those who demand that conscience proper must relate exclusively to the inherent character of actions without reference to their consequences or to the currency of opinion for or against them. No doubt, too, the search for a philosophical concept of conscience that is more rigorous and less subject to internal contradiction than that of ordinary speech is justified; but this is no reason to deny that a popular concept of conscience is present in passages such as those under consideration. There is no justification for criticizing the popular ideas of the Greeks for their failure to anticipate the theories of later thinkers; if we rather compare like with like, we shall recognize that in this particular area the popular concepts of the Greeks are echoed very closely by our own. The supernatural elements and the references to external sanctions which complicate the picture may differ in specific details from those which might obtain in the modern world, but not, I think, in essence, and if we must be wary of regarding apparently promising passages in classical literature as references to a moral conscience uncontaminated by fear of consequences, the same wariness will often be in place in approaching ordinary uses of conscience in our own language.

6.1.2. *Aristophanes*

Further evidence for the popular nature of the concept of conscience at Athens is provided by several passages in Aristophanes in which adumbrations of conscience are introduced with a familiarity which suggests that they would have been in no way novel or baffling in the

---

[27] Cf. 6. 23: free men tell the truth under cross-examination 'for their own sakes and for that of *to dikaion*'. Cf. 5. 41, 49–50; Dover (1974), 221–2.

eyes of the audience. In *Knights* (1354-7), for example, we have an example of that combination of retrospective and inhibitory aspects in a feeling of *aischunē* which we found to be so common in Euripides. Demos bows his head[28] and changes his stance (1354), and explains this behaviour as *aischunē* caused by his previous errors (*hamartiai*, 1355). Consciousness of past error leads to present inhibition in the presence of others, but the suggestion of remorse is clearly present, since the Sausage Seller seeks to assuage Demos' concern by insisting that he was not responsible for actions performed under the persuasive influence of demagogues such as Cleon/Paphlagon (1356-7). The notion of self-reproach is also present in *Wasps* (743-9), where the chorus imagine Philocleon's recognition of his past mistakes and consider it possible that he is reproaching himself, although they themselves seem to acquit him of responsibility in that they claim that his errors were committed when he was 'mad' (744) and hope that he will now 'come to his senses' (748). Similar ideas recur at 999-1002,[29] where Philocleon exclaims: 'How shall I cope with this on my conscience, to have acquitted a defendant?[30] What will become of me? O most honoured gods, forgive me; I didn't know what I was doing—it's completely out of character.' The joke, of course, is that Philocleon regards conviction as his duty, imposed by the gods, and therefore sees acquittal as a breach of that duty and an offence which will involve divine punishment, and the point of the joke must lie in its allusion to the use of similar language in real contexts. Indeed, the value of the passage lies precisely in its evocation of an everyday reaction. As such, the reaction lacks philosophical precision; Philocleon implies that he cannot bear the thought of having on his conscience an action which is against his personal principles; yet he also believes that these principles are upheld by the gods, and that the gods will punish him for their breach. He feels responsible for what he has done, yet at the

---

[28] Cf. *Frogs* 1474, where it is implied that consciousness of a wrong one has committed should lead to an inability to look the wronged party in the face. The proverbial association of *aidōs* with the eyes is prominent in Ar.: it is expressed as such at *Wasps* 447; *aidōs/ aischunē* causes one to avert one's gaze at *Thes.* 902 and *Wealth* 367-8; and at *Ach.* 289-91 and *Knights* 1239 an unflinching gaze is characteristic of *anaideia*.

[29] Cf. Seel (1953), 301.

[30] πῶς οὖν ἐμαυτῷ τοῦτ' ἐγὼ ξυνείσομαι . . . ; This sentence further highlights the falsity of Rodgers's claim (cf. n. 21 above) that reflexive uses of *suneidenai* denote simple awareness and do not in themselves refer to the phenomenon of conscience; it would be ludicrous to take Philocleon's words as, 'How shall I be aware of this in myself?' Since this is the case, and since the sentence clearly refers to the idea that knowledge of action in contravention of one's principles creates a feeling of discomfort, then we must conclude that it is the verb *suneidenai* itself which carries the reference to conscience.

same time denies responsibility (he says he acted *akōn*) and seeks to mitigate his culpability by pleading previous good character. Allowing for the element of comic distortion, however, we can recognize in Philocleon's panic all the confusion of motive and inconsistency that we might expect in such a popular context; in particular, the compatibility of the sense of responsibility with the awareness or the claim that one was not essentially at fault is common, and indicates only that an emotional response is not entirely determined by an intellectual grasp of the situation,[31] while the reference to divine disapproval does not in any way imply that the standard breached is one which has been imposed on one from outside and to which one has no personal attachment.[32]

The inhibition which is caused by consciousness of wrongdoing is the subject of a joke again in *Knights* (182–5). The Sausage Seller, surprisingly, declares that he feels himself unworthy of high office (182), and Demosthenes wonders if this indicates that he has something *kalon* on his conscience.[33] Take away the comic inversion, and we have an unselfconscious recognition that awareness of a discreditable fact about oneself can lead to a feeling of unworthiness to exercise power over others. The fact, too, that the comic *kalon* clearly implies an original *aischron*, demonstrates that such inhibition, which has clear affinities with *aidōs/aischunē*, may be the result of an

[31] Cf. the reaction of the god Plutus in *Wealth* after he has been released from his blindness; he is ashamed of his condition and of his association with worthless men (774–5), and realizes that this behaviour was 'wrong' (778), yet he knows quite well that he acted *akōn*, without knowledge of what he was doing (775, 777). His *aischunē* in 774 illustrates his inhibition before other people, and he is determined to demonstrate to all that he acted *akōn* (780–1), but his concern for his reputation is not simply based on dislike of criticism, regardless of its object, but on a moral sense which is appalled at mistakes committed in ignorance and which finds it unacceptable that others should consider him to be morally worthless.

[32] Rodgers (1969), in particular, goes too far in assuming that recognition that an action is liable to external sanctions positively rules out a sense that it is incompatible with one's own standards (see 246–7, on the *Wasps* passage). This is not to say that there are never occasions when an apparent reference to conscience contains little of the element of personal commitment; Cephalus at Pl. *Rep.* 330e–331a probably represents the unreflective view of many when he represents concern over one's past misdeeds as arising only because of the fear of approaching death (see Rodgers (1969), 248). Cephalus' naïve pronouncements need not, however, be understood as indicating that ordinary decent people like himself abstained from wrongdoing out of fear of post-mortem punishment alone, even if the reference to such punishment is the best prudential justification they can think of for being moral.

[33] ξυνειδέναι τί μοι δοκεῖς σαυτῷ καλόν, 184; cf. Seel (1953), 300–1. Rodgers (1969: 246) completely fails to notice that the inversion presupposes a more normal *aischron* for *kalon*.

awareness (of something *aischron* in one's past), which is here expressed in terms of a reflexive use of *suneidenai*, but which could equally be conveyed by a retrospective use of *aideomai* or *aischunomai*.

Such passages as these illustrate the place of 'conscience' in the moral outlook of the Athenian layman, and at the very least it must be taken as established that a faculty capable of subjective evaluation of the character of one's own actions coexists alongside fear of external sanctions from such quarters as the gods, the legal system, and popular disapproval. The element of individual conscience, moreover, may presuppose an emotional attachment to moral principles and a corresponding emotional disturbance at any breach of those standards, and the importance of this is that it demonstrates that, in at least one strand of ordinary Greek opinion and usage, it is taken as obvious that people are not deterred from wrongdoing or disturbed at their transgressions merely because they calculate that transgression may lead to punishment.[34] Where *aidōs*, *aischunē*, and related terms occur in the context of conscience, moreover, it is not the case that they are sharply distinguished from that phenomenon as that element in the overall reaction which responds solely to the external sanction of popular disapproval.

6.2. PROTAGORAS AND MORAL EDUCATION

We have seen in a number of places in tragedy the influence of an approach to political theory which stresses the coercive role of both statutory punishment and social control in promoting obedience to the values of the state. Aeschylus, for example, stresses the deterrent effect of punishment (civil, but with elements of the divine) in the *Eumenides*,[35] and Sophocles' Menelaus recalls these arguments in his discourse on the role of fear and *aidōs/aischunē* in maintaining civil and military discipline in the *Ajax*.[36] *Aidōs* and the terms related to it are relevant in such contexts because of their intimate relationship with

[34] One final and straightforward example may illustrate the point: at 5. 75. 1 Hdt. gives as the Corinthians' reason for withdrawing from an expedition against the Athenians the simple realization that the course upon which they had embarked was unjust—σφίσι αὐτοῖσι δόντες λόγον ὡς οὐ ποιοῖεν τὰ δίκαια. The Corinthians thus ignore the possibility that other participants on the enterprise might criticize their action as cowardice (or failure to complete what one has begun, etc.), and the outward aspect of their actions is no consideration with them.

[35] See 3.4 above.   [36] See Ch. 4 nn. 67 and 68.

conventional values and social disapproval; their frequent appearance
in association with fear of punishment, however, might suggest that
aidōs is envisaged solely as a response to external sanctions. In this
present section we shall look at one particular exposition of the social
nature of *aidōs* and its role in the maintenance of civil discipline, before
considering, in the next section, certain ramifications of this sort of
approach which appear to have occupied Greek thinkers themselves.

Given the paucity of direct evidence, any attempt to reconstruct the
broad outline of Protagoras' ethics will inevitably be driven to consider
the accounts given of his views by Plato, both in the eponymous
dialogue and in the *Theaetetus*, and this raises obvious questions about
the reliability of Plato's testimony. Of the arguments put forward in
these two dialogues, however, only those of the so-called Great Speech
of the *Protagoras* (320c–328c) concern us in detail, and there must be a
strong presumption that, if views which may be reliably attributed to
Protagoras are to be found anywhere, it is here, where he is represented as freely offering his own opinions without interruption, that
we shall find them.[37] It is, of course, impossible to be completely
confident that the speech does give the views of the historical
Protagoras, but we can at least be sure that it does not attribute
doctrines to him which could not have been espoused during his
lifetime, since the speech is firmly in the mainstream of older sophistic
thought (that tradition which has left traces in Sophocles and
Euripides, as well as in the pseudo-Aeschylean *Prometheus*), and since
the strengths and weaknesses of the doctrines there expressed are
reflected in the discussions of younger contemporaries such as
Antiphon and Democritus. Given that the speech does treat major
topics which also engaged other fifth-century figures, and is therefore
not a wholly Platonic invention, there is no reason to deny its essential
authenticity as an indication of the general trend of Protagorean
thought, for, even if Plato does, deliberately or otherwise, misrepresent
details of Protagoras' doctrines, it is difficult to imagine that he would
have gone to the trouble of composing a dialogue called *Protagoras*

[37] On the legitimacy of seeking the views of the historical Prot. in the Great Speech,
see Heinimann (1945), 115 (and the older lit. cited in his n. 14); Gagarin (1969), 134;
Guthrie, iii. 186; Nill (1985), 5–6, 15–20. Nill's extended comparison of the treatment of
Prot. and Gorgias in the dialogues which bear their names is enough, it seems to me, to
refute Maguire (1977), who argues that the ambiguity between 'political *aretē*' as (*a*)
administrative skill and (*b*) the moral capacity to live in a city (on which see also Adkins
(1973)) represents Pl.'s manipulation of Prot.'s non-moral approach into his own view of
moral virtue. That the speech has a Protagorean core is also accepted by Farrar (1988:
78–81).

which fathered the opinions of some *other* fifth-century figure on the eponymous character; why introduce Protagoras at all if the dialogue does not at least take Protagorean doctrine as its starting point?

The myth (320c–322d), which Protagoras relates in order to prove his contention that political *aretē* can be taught, gives a two-stage account of human progress, the first stage being bestial and uncivilized, the second bringing civilization and 'political skill' through the intervention of Zeus and his gift of *aidōs* and *dikē*. These, then, are the forces which allow human beings to live together successfully,[38] and both obviously inhibit their impulses to harm each other, presumably in the Hesiodic sense that they limit self-assertion in the face of others' claims to honour and to property. In the post-mythical section of the speech *aidōs* and *dikē* are directly replaced by *sōphrosunē* and *dikaiosunē*,[39] but although the more fashionable terms do perhaps bring certain associations of their own, there remains a basic equivalence between the two pairs; *aidōs* and *dikē*, *sōphrosunē* and *dikaiosunē* all connote recognition of one's place as one among many and acceptance of the obligations entailed by the legitimate claims of others. *Aidōs* thus appears under a traditional aspect, as a valued disposition or trait of character encompassing a sense of the ways in which one's own honour and status are bound up with those of others; the passage draws on the poetic tradition, in which *aidōs* is the social virtue *par excellence* and an ally, if not an element, of *aretē*; and the reformulation of *aidōs* in terms of *sōphrosunē*, a member of the select group which, in Plato's early and middle dialogues, establishes itself as a classification of the cardinal virtues, suggests a readiness to regard dispositional *aidōs* as itself an *aretē* or part of *aretē*. That *aidōs* is an *aretē*, however, is as we shall see, a view that is rejected by both Plato and Aristotle.

In the myth *aidōs* and *dikē* are imparted by divine gift, but in the subsequent *logos* the acquisition of *sōphrosunē* and *dikaiosunē* is, though allowance is made for innate capacity, seen largely in terms of education, and since *aidōs* is subsumed and presupposed by *sōphrosunē*, we must assume that, regardless of the divine apparatus of the myth, *aidōs*, too, is the product of education.[40] In support of the proposition

---

[38] Cf. those passages in which the withdrawal of *aidōs* is seen as a sign of the breakdown of moral order (Hes. *WD* 200–1; Thgn. 289–92, 635–6, 647–8; Soph. *El.* 245–50; Eur. *Me.* 439–40; *IA* 1089–97).

[39] At 323a and thereafter; *aidōs* occurs again at 329c in a reference by Soc. to the myth; its combination here with *dikaiosunē* rather than *dikē* shows that the latter two terms are regarded as equivalent, and *aidōs* itself is quickly rephrased as *sōphrosunē*

[40] This is sometimes disputed (see Maguire (1977), 111 n. 24, and the earlier

that *aretē* can be taught much reference is made to the practice of punishment (323d–324c, 325a, 325d, 326d), since this is held to indicate society's opinion that the faults of its members are remediable; but the corrective and deterrent effects of punishment come into play only when the subject has failed to absorb the precepts imparted in the process of education, a process which Protagoras presents as the instruction of each member of society from the earliest age in the standards and values of the community. At several points Protagoras' account of this process strongly suggests the inculcation, rather than the exploitation, of a sense of *aidōs*.[41] At 325cd, for example, we learn that a child's nurse, mother, *paidagogos*, and father all strive to improve their charge, pointing out 'this is *dikaion*, that *adikon*, this is *kalon*, that *aischron*, this is *hosion* and that *anosion*, and do this, don't do that', and thus the child learns to subscribe to the same values as its teachers.[42] The pairs of adjectives in this list correspond to

authorities cited by Kerferd (1953), 42 n. 5) on the grounds that, since all those who were unable to possess *aidōs* and *dikē* were to be put to death early in the history of mankind (322d), all now alive must possess these qualities by nature. There are several arguments against this (see Kerferd (1953), 43; (1981*a*), 134), but the point which clinches the matter comes in the analogy of the pipe-players at 327cd; as all pipers are pipers *simpliciter* in comparison with non-pipers, even though within the category itself there may be a wide range of talent and ability, so all citizens, although they vary widely in *aretē* and justice, are just in comparison with those who do not enjoy a civilized life in a political community. Even the most unjust citizen, we are told, would appear an expert in justice compared with those who had no contact with the institutions of civilization. If, then, men possess a minimal capacity for justice, they do so because of their membership of a civilized community, not because they are men; the process is reciprocal—*aidōs* and *dikē* are required in order for cities to exist, and membership of a citizen body makes it inevitable that one will possess some degree of *aidōs* and *dikē* (cf. Kerferd (1953), 45; Farrar (1988), 90). The Prot. of the dialogue, like the historical Prot. (B 3 DK), does believe that education exploits varying degrees of innate capacity; it is natural ability that enables one musician to excel over his fellows (327bc), and this implies that men may differ in the degree of their *dikaiosunē* according to their nature (Guthrie, iii. 67–8). Clearly, however, innate capacity cannot produce justice on its own. Prot. does not tell us what this innate capacity is, but it is unlikely that it should be *aidōs* or *dikē*, since these occupy a position analogous to *dikaiosunē* (cf. Kerferd (1953), 43). If *aidōs* and *dikē* do not exist by nature, the ability to acquire them presumably does (cf. Heinimann (1945), 115–16; Guthrie, iii. 67–8; Adkins (1973), 7; Nill (1985), 14; people must be able to acquire these qualities otherwise they simply would not acquire them), but this is not a point upon which Prot. lays any emphasis; the important point is that the natural ability to acquire these qualities must be developed in a social context or else it will remain ineffective. On the coalition of innate capacity and education, cf. Democ. B 33, 182–3 DK.

[41] Cf. Kerferd (1953), 44; (1981*a*), 135; also Guthrie, iii. 67; Gagarin (1969), 144.

[42] Cf. Simmons (1972), 530. This is no place for a detailed discussion of child development, but it is my view that Prot.'s thumbnail sketch of the ordinary course of early childhood education at Athens does not rule out, and indeed positively suggests, the acquisition of internalized moral standards.

the three parts of *aretē* at 324e–325a, namely *dikaiosunē*, *sōphrosunē*, and
τὸ ὅσιον εἶναι (= *hosiotēs*, 329c5), and, in so far as the child does not know
instinctively what is *dikaion* or *adikon*, it seems that the efforts of the
teachers at this stage are designed to instil precisely these parts of *aretē*,
which are those that enable the child to recognize what is *dikaion*, what
adikon, etc. Protagoras himself avoids the word *aidōs* outside the myth,
but the learning of what is *aischron* and *kalon*, while it corresponds only
to *sōphrosunē* of the three parts of *aretē*, strongly suggests the learning of
aidōs.[43]

Protagoras thus sees the social virtues, including *aidōs*, which
promote conformity to the standards of society as imparted in the
process of socialization, a theory which, as we have seen, appears to
have been influential and current in the later fifth century.[44] He
believes, moreover, both that it is necessary for the existence of the
social and political community that citizens should acquire these
qualities, and that it is in the interests of the individual, since their
possession benefits citizens mutually (327b).[45] It is also clear from his
stress on education and emulation that he assumes that citizens
internalize the values imparted in the process of education,[46] and so,

[43] This general impression is confirmed by the subsequent stages of education, in which
several points suggest the application of *aidōs*. The learning of *eukosmia* (discipline, deport-
ment) with the *didaskalos* (325de) and the practising of *sōphrosunē* with the *kitharistēs* (326a)
suggest the development of the youthful sense of *aidōs*, and physical training is linked to the
requirement to avoid cowardice (326bc), a requirement also enforced by *aidōs*. At several
points, too, there is stress on learning by example (from the poets, 325e–326a, and from the
laws, 326c), suggesting the acquisition of positive goals and a spirit of emulation which will
imply *aidōs* as a correlative when a goal is not reached.

[44] Cf. the links between *aidōs* and education in Eur. (5.5 above). Similar ideas appear
to lie behind Archidamus' account of the role of *aidōs* and *sōphrosunē* in Spartan education at Thuc. 1. 84. 3; cf. Xen. *Const. of the Lacedaemonians*, 2. 2, 3. 4–5. Hussey (1985: 123–
4) relates the Thuc. passage specifically to Democritus; this is not implausible, but
Protagoras and even Antiphon might also be candidates, or such ideas may have been of
fairly widespread currency in 5th-cent. intellectual circles. (Clearly, too, sophistic discussions of the interaction of *aidōs* and education draw on the traditional association of the
two in, e.g., the Theognid corpus.)

[45] i.e. my justice benefits you, and yours me; this is another argument for the advanta-
geousness of moral virtue beyond that embodied in the myth, where the acquisition of
those qualities which allow men to live together successfully is assumed to be desirable, it
being better for human beings to live in civilized communities. This suggests a minimal
social contract theory, although there is no explicit mention of agreement in the myth
(see Kahn (1981), esp. 98 with n. 10; cf. Guthrie, iii. 137, Döring (1981), esp. 110–11, Nill
(1985), 26, and contrast Sinclair (1967), 58, Kerferd (1981*a*), 147–8; cf. Simmons (1972),
524–6, who takes the myth literally); a contract theory would certainly fit with the
opinions attributed to Prot. at *Tht.* 167c ('what each city considers just is just for itself').

[46] At 326d the laws of the city which continue the process of education after the individual has finished with formal schooling are compared to the lines drawn on the slate to
help those who are *not yet* good at writing; if this analogy holds in detail it implies the

despite all his stress on the coercive and corrective force of the state, its laws, and its customs, he cannot be said to believe that morality is maintained by external sanctions alone. Yet the stress on external sanctions is there in the text, and it would be possible for a contemporary, drawing on traditional aspects of *aidōs* and *dikē*, to construe these simply as respect for what the city holds appropriate and just, on the sole basis of the sanctions (of opprobrium and punishment) against transgression which the community, as the authority which lays down moral and legal standards, has at its disposal;[47] *aidōs* could still be a disposition acquired in the process of socialization, but it would be a disposition to respond to external rather than internal sanctions.[48]

Protagoras does, moreover, place considerable emphasis on advantage; he believes that the laws and customs of a city are a conventional arrangement designed to secure the advantage of the citizen-body as a whole, and thus his discussion will, in the contemporary context, invite the objection that individual and communal advantage may not coincide.[49] To this he has an answer—that it is in the interest of the individual that the city should exist and that each citizen benefits from the justice of the others. But he does admit that citizens vary in the degree of their observance of justice (and presumably in their susceptibility to *aidōs*), and while he might plausibly argue that the preservation of the state requires the minimal degree of justice that he says all its members possess, a minimal degree of justice allows for a considerable degree of injustice stopping short of actually endangering

prospect that, eventually, adults can acquire the ability to behave properly without need of further correction.

[47] Cf. the remarks of Pericles at Thuc. 2. 37. 3. Like Prot., Per. stresses respect for law and custom, but ascribes conformity above all to fear, which seems to encompass fear of the 'agreed disgrace (*aischunē*)' entailed by transgression of unwritten laws. (The 'unwritten laws' probably refer to Athenian belief in general; anything the Athenians considered *aischron* might be proscribed by an 'unwritten law'; cf. Ostwald (1973), 88–9. I cannot, however, understand why Ostwald (100) implies that 'unwritten laws' such as these could not have originated in custom.) This has similarities with Prot.'s stress on deterrence and his deployment of *aidōs*, but seems to envisage external sanctions alone as enforcing conformity.

[48] Such an approach, I should stress, would have to take a view of *aidōs* and *dikē* which is almost certainly not that of Prot.; see Farrar (1988: 91–8, 102), who stresses the internalization of social virtues in Prot.'s theory, contrasting his view with forms of contract theory (such as that put forward by Glaucon in *Rep.* 2) which construe political behaviour in terms of response to external sanctions. But neither in the dialogue nor in any of his meagre fragments does Prot. explicitly argue for internalization, and there are ancient thinkers (such as Antiphon) and modern commentators for whom it would not appear analytically true that *aidōs* and *dikē* involve internalized standards (cf. Farrar (1988), 116).

[49] In line with the views of justice taken by Thrasymachus in *Rep.* I and Callicles in *Gorg.*

the state. For our purposes, then, the main weaknesses of his theory as it stands lie in the failure explicitly to argue for the citizen's commitment to his acquired standards of behaviour and in the fact that it would allow the maximization of individual self-interest by means of a combination of minimal justice, motivated by fear of external sanctions alone, with unjust pursuit of one's advantage.[50]

6.3. DOING WRONG IN SECRET: OR SHAME-CULTURE VERSUS GUILT-CULTURE

If the Protagorean theory of the acquisition of moral standards and the origin of the *polis* finds echoes in tragedy and elsewhere, so too do the attacks made by other fifth-century figures on that sort of position. The counter-attack focuses on the social nature of the Protagorean theory and on its association of justice and self-control with advantage; it sees Protagorean *aidōs* and *dikē*, *sōphrosunē* and *dikaiosunē* as forces which promote mere conformity, and raises the possibility that an admixture of justice and injustice might best promote individual advantage.

6.3.1. *Antiphon*

It seems that one major avenue of attack on the view which based justice and self-control in the mutual advantage of all members of the community lay in raising the question of doing wrong in secret.[51] Echoes of debate on this subject survive in contemporary literature,[52]

---

[50] For a detailed discussion of these points, see Nill (1985), 8–10, 38–51; cf. Adkins (1960*a*), 237–8.

[51] This problem is an important theme in the study by Nill (1985) of the views of Prot., Ant., and Democ. on the compatibility of morality and self-interest; see esp. his remarks on p. 57.

[52] See Soph. *Trach.* 596–7 and Eur. *Hipp.* 403–4, in which the view is taken that disgraceful action can be undertaken provided it remains undetected. In neither play, however, does this view go uncontested (see 5.4.4 above, on the juxtaposition of the concerns for internal and external sanctions in *Hipp.*). Cf. Thuc. 1. 37. 2, where the Corinthians claim that the Corcyreans avoided alliances in order that they should be able to proceed with their *adikēmata* without having to experience *aischunē* at the opinions of the witnesses of their misdeeds; on this view shame requires a real audience to be effective, and people tend to transgress where no audience exists. The problem of doing wrong in secret comes most explicitly to the fore in the celebrated fragment of the satyr-play *Sisyphus*, attributed in antiquity both to Critias (B 25 DK) and to Eur. (see Dihle (1977)). This fr. is notable for the setting of its observations in the context of an account

but for our purposes the most relevant statement of this view is to be found in the papyrus fragments of Antiphon. In fr. B 44 A DK, Antiphon criticizes a view which defines justice as 'not to transgress the *nomima* [norms both moral and legal] of the city in which one happens to be a citizen' (col. 1. 6–11).[53] Criticized from the point of view of advantage, however, this view entails no deterrent force in circumstances in which external sanctions are unlikely to be brought to bear, and one might maximize one's advantage by obeying the laws in front of witnesses and obeying 'the things of nature' when no witnesses are present (col. 1. 12–23).[54] This is because transgression against law and custom, the products of agreement, entails no necessary disadvantage, provided one escapes the notice of those who are party to the agreement,[55] whereas attempted transgression of natural

of human progress similar to that offered by the *Prot.* myth. It is assumed that the conventional nature of law and custom indicates that people are deterred from wrong-doing only by external sanctions, and, since these are ineffective where the subject believes his transgression will remain undetected, some sanction which might deter even secret wrongdoing is required, in this case that of divine punishment. The other way to enjoy wrongdoing with impunity, of course, is to be strong enough to get away with it: see Thrasymachus at *Rep.* 344ac on ordinary wrongdoers and tyrants; cf. Xen. *Mem.* 4. 4. 21 (also Mackenzie (1981), 126).

[53] That Ant. does not himself uphold this view of justice, is demonstrated by his subsequent argument that the requirement of justice may be ignored when it is advantageous to do so. See Saunders (1977–8), 219. Kerferd (1956–7: 27–9) shows that Ant. is not putting forward his own positive views in this fragment, although he is clearly criticizing a thesis from the standpoint of his own views. Cf. Furley (1981), 91; Nill (1985: 53, 104 n. 12) misunderstands Kerferd when he takes him to mean that even Ant.'s criticisms are not his own. (Admittedly, it is difficult to establish just how much Kerferd is willing to attribute to Ant.) It is a priori likely that Ant. should be criticizing the view of a major contemporary, and this in itself would make Protagoras a candidate, even if this possibility were not strengthened by the fact that the definition of justice corresponds exactly with the position attributed to Prot. at Pl. *Tht.* 167c; the statement that 'the things of the laws are *epitheta*' (adventitious, arbitrary, col. 1. 23–5) and the familiarity with social contract theory (coll. 1. 27–2. 3) are also compatible with the position implied by the *Prot.* myth. For the view that Ant. has Prot. in mind, see Nill (1985), 51, 54, and *passim*; cf. Bignone (1938), 74–5; Sinclair (1967), 70–1.

[54] This is presented as a consequence of the definition of justice when submitted to the criterion of individual advantage, not as an injunction to break the law in secret; see Moulton (1974), 136 n. 21; Barnes (1982), 513–14; Nill (1985), 54; contrast Guthrie, iii. 108; Adkins (1970), 116; Saunders (1977–8), 219.

[55] Cf. the argument of Glaucon at Pl. *Rep.* 358e–360d; a social contract to abide by *nomos* and to refrain from injustice arises as a compromise because, although everyone wants to do wrong, no one wishes to suffer it (with this view of the post-legal stage of human development contrast the positive conception of Prot. in the *Prot.* myth); but no one would refuse Gyges' ring, which would allow one to do wrong without fear of consequences. On this view, as for Ant., the mutual and social benefits of *nomos* are not enough; justice must be shown to be beneficial for the individual in itself if it is to be accepted as in the agent's own interests.

law brings disadvantage regardless of whether the act is public or private (coll. 1. 23–2. 23).[56]

In his criticism Antiphon singles out two consequences of public law-breaking, *aischunē* (disgrace) and *zēmia* (punishment, col. 2. 7–8),[57] and it is probable that he uses these terms in order to encompass the entire range of the term *nomos*, both codified 'law' and uncodified 'custom', since, although *aischunē* would follow conviction for a crime proscribed by law, it also naturally follows breach of convention.[58] Antiphon thus affects to see the virtues which promote social cohesion, which Protagoras described as *aidōs* and *dikē*, in terms of concern for external sanctions alone, and so he anticipates those who describe classical Greece as a 'shame-culture'. Whether or not the view of justice he criticizes is that of Protagoras, it is clear that he is reacting against accounts which recognize the conventional nature of social institutions but none the less proclaim their utility, and he does succeed in uncovering weaknesses in such theories. He exposes the gap between the interests of the community and personal advantage, and shows that a view which stresses the embodiment of justice in statutory law and the role of other people in social control might be seen as promoting conformity without commitment; and, in so far as *aidōs*, *aischunē*, and the rest commonly refer to 'witnesses' (and the earliest accounts of the nature and development of political communities do stress their coercive and disciplinary role), his argument both exploits traditional aspects of the Greek moral outlook and

[56] The opposition between *nomos* and *phusis* is constant in the papyrus frr., and nature, or that which is advantageous by/to nature, is clearly to be preferred; the question, however, of precisely how Ant. construes *phusis* and its requirements is a vexed one, which cannot be discussed here; see Kerferd (1956–7), 32; (1981*a*), 115–17; Havelock (1957), 257–8, 274 ff.; Moulton (1972), 333–43; Furley (1981), 89–90; Nill (1985), 54–61, 105–7 nn. 27–34.

[57] Similarly, Thras. at Pl. *Rep.* 344b sees punishment and disgrace as the consequences awaiting those ordinary wrongdoers who fail to escape notice.

[58] Cf. Heinimann (1945), 139 (who notes the parallel with Thuc. 2. 37. 3, n. 47 above). Guthrie (iii. 138) and Moulton (1972: 333) think that Ant. is more interested in written law, but he also considers unwritten *nomos* at B 44 A DK col. 5. 4–8 (the *nomos*-abiding behaviour of those who treat well parents who have treated them badly is against nature) and at 44 B coll. 1. 35–2. 15, where *aidōs* and *sebas* for the well-born are said to rest on a distinction which has no basis in *phusis*. Both these passages suggest that *aidōs* (such as might, in the former, lead one to respect a parent who had shown one no kindness) is based in conventional standards and may be disadvantageous. The former is enough to refute the contention of Saunders (1977–8: 227–30) that Ant., much like Hippias at Xen. *Mem.* 4. 4. 24, saw traditional *gnōmai* or 'unwritten laws' as a category of *nomoi* which were natural, social, and automatic in effect; 'honour your father' (Cleobulus 2; cf. Solon 8, Chilon 8, Thales 6, 7, 8, Periander 12 in DK's 'Seven Sages') is just such a maxim, and Ant. rejects it as contrary, at least in some circumstances, to nature.

focuses on the particular character of much contemporary discussion. Yet it also ignores the unreflective popular belief that people just do have a commitment to their standards of proper behaviour (presumably on the grounds that such beliefs merely disguise our essential egoism), and it also has nothing to say on the subject of moral education, a topic stressed by Protagoras and one which is traditionally relevant to the question of the nature and depth of one's moral and social principles, especially *aidōs*. Antiphon thus overlooks the area in which an opponent might find a basis for a counter-argument to the effect that, even where no external sanction appears likely, real human beings may none the less be unwilling or unable to do wrong in secret. Such a counter-argument, of course, would not necessarily prove morality advantageous for the agent—even if one accepts the objection that some people simply find wrongdoing distasteful, one might argue that it would be in their best interests to divest themselves of this distaste; but it would at least reveal the falsity of the 'doing wrong in secret' argument as an empirical claim about the nature of social values.[59]

6.3.2. *Democritus*

Democritus,[60] like Antiphon, is aware that fear of punishment and fear of disgrace are not sufficient to deter all wrongdoing, but rather lead

[59] Ant., of course, does not necessarily advocate doing wrong in secret, and he seems to have argued that uninhibited pursuit of one's desires would for most people entail more disadvantage than advantage; see Bignone (1938), 82–3; Untersteiner (1954), 247; Guthrie, iii. 289–91; Adkins (1970), 115–16; Nill (1985), 69–73; Farrar (1988), 118. If, however, he did argue for conformity to traditional values as a means of promoting one's advantage, as many of the citational frr. assigned to his *On Concord* (B 44a–71 DK) suggest, he must still allow that doing wrong in secret would be advantageous where one could be sure to escape notice. That the argument on doing wrong in secret may be vulnerable even on its own prudential terms is suggested by Soph. *Trach.*: at 596–7, Deianeira observes that disgraceful acts performed in secret do not bring disgrace, but at 721–2, resolving to die rather than live with her reputation in ruins, she recognizes that her confidence that she could avoid disgrace was ill-founded. No one, unless in possession of Gyges' ring, can be sure that their acts will remain secret, and this may be used as an argument for caution; this much is noted by Adeimantus at *Rep.* 365cd, but, as he says, the rewards may make the attempt worthwhile.

[60] On the question of the authenticity of the ethical frr., see the surveys of Guthrie, ii. 489–91; Nill (1985), 110–11 n. 4. In so far as those frr. considered here treat topics current in Democ.'s lifetime, their inclusion is justified. The 'Democrates' frr. are often considered especially doubtful, but in many cases they corroborate ideas found in the rest of the corpus, and thus should, at least in these cases, be considered legitimate evidence; cf. Kahn (1985), 2–4; Farrar (1988), 193–5.

some simply to attempt to conceal their vices;[61] unlike Antiphon, however, but like Protagoras, he stresses the role of education, and he has a conception of the individual conscience which plays an important role in his attempt to demonstrate that, at least for those who have had the benefit of an adequate moral education, wrongdoing has intrinsic as well as extrinsic disadvantages for the wrongdoer. Central to his argument on these subjects, moreover, is the most sophisticated analysis of the essential operation of *aidōs* offered by any classical thinker.

That Democritus does recognize the inability of external sanctions to deter in every case is shown most clearly by fragment B 181 DK, where he observes that one who is merely compelled to avoid injustice by law (*nomos*) is likely to do wrong in secret; encouragement and verbal persuasion are more likely to promote *aretē*, and one who is brought to his duty (*to deon*) by persuasion is unlikely to do anything untoward either in secret or openly; which is why one who behaves properly with knowledge and understanding becomes both brave and sensible. Persuasion, then, gives reasons, in order that the individual may do what he must (*to deon*) with a proper understanding of the reasons for doing so,[62] and *nomos*, probably strictly conceived as statutory law, is insufficient to promote proper behaviour in the absence of such an understanding.[63] Democritus thus stresses personal insight and appreciates the limitations of external sanctions; compare B 41, 'Do not abstain from wrongdoing because of fear, but because of *to deon* [what must be done].'[64]

---

[61] On the relationship between the views of Democ. and Ant., see Moulton (1974); Nill (1985), chs. 3 and 4. That Democ. is seeking to refute the view that only external sanctions can deter wrongdoing is also the position of Konstan (1988: 17-18).

[62] The fr. does not actually say that these reasons must be self-interested (*pace* the implication of Nill (1985), 76), although it does not rule out such an interpretation.

[63] Democ. does, however, appreciate the considerable benefits of *nomos* elsewhere: B 245, 248, 252, 255 DK; cf. Havelock (1957), 135-9; Adkins (1970), 111; Lloyd-Jones (1971), 131-2; Moulton (1974), 131, 137; Nill (1985), 75-6; Farrar (1988), 253-6.

[64] It is impossible to be absolutely categorical as to whether *to deon* indicates that Democ. had a view of the intrinsic value of moral actions or merely refers to what must be done to achieve some further end (in B 42 'what must be done', ἃ δεῖ, is probably colloquial and prudential—'it is a great thing to know what to do in time of misfortune'); we do, however, have the evidence of the frr. and ancient testimony that he did conceive of contentment or well-being as the end (variously designated: see A 1, 167-9; B 3-4, 170-1, 174, 189, 191, 215-16, 257, 286 DK), and so 'what is necessary' *could* be merely that which promotes this end. (Cf. B 83, 'The cause of wrongdoing is ignorance of what is better'; but must this mean 'better for oneself'?) That this is so is the view of Nill (1985), 113 n. 37, and Farrar (1988), 237, but see also Voros (1974). The 'necessity' of moral action, it seems to me, might more plausibly be referred to the appreciation that a given

This insight is presumably to be seen as acquired in a process of education, broadly conceived, and this is a notion which also receives some emphasis in the fragments:[65] it takes learning (*mathēsis*) and toil to produce *kala*, *aischra* come automatically (B 182), and a traditional education of the young tends to produce *aidōs*, which implies *aretē* (B 179). The relationship in the adult between *aidōs* and the insight which prevents wrongdoing is suggested by fragment B 264:

One should not *aideisthai* [experience *aidōs* before] other people to any greater extent than one does before oneself, nor should one do wrong if no one is going to know any more than if everyone is. One should *aideisthai* oneself above all,[66] and let this be established as a *nomos* in one's soul, so as to do nothing inappropriate.

B 84 and 244 express the same idea using *aischunesthai* rather than *aideisthai*:

The one who does *aischra* should *aischunesthai* himself first of all.

Even if you are alone, do not say or do anything base; learn to *aischunesthai* yourself much more than other people.

This, then, is Democritus' answer to the problem of doing wrong in secret; the individual has his own standard of right and wrong, and values his own opinion more than that of other people. Both *aideisthai* in B 264 and *aischunesthai* in B 244, as is shown by the contrast between 'self' and 'others' as object and the stress on *preventing* wrong-doing, are prospective uses of the 'I feel shame before' type, and thus the primary reference of these fragments is not to self-respect or retrospective shame, but to inhibition of a contemplated action, inhibition which focuses not on others as the prospective witnesses, but on oneself. This, however, presupposes that one can be a source of reproach to oneself much as can other people, and so suggests a familiarity with subjective senses of guilt or remorse. The sense of *aischunesthai* in B 84 is less easily established. There it is 'the one doing *aischra*' (τὸν αἰσχρὰ ἔρδοντα) who is to experience *aischunē*, and while

action is required by the 'law in the soul' of those who have a disposition to experience self-directed *aidōs* (B 264). *To deon* in Democ.'s theory would then occupy the place that is taken by *to kalon* in Arist.'s (see n. 254 below)—doing 'what is necessary' could still be a means to *euthumia*, but the agent who characterized an act as 'necessary' would not have its utility as a means to a further end as his motive at the time of action.

[65] See B 33, 183, 208 on the contribution of *phusis* and education to character, and 242 on the greater importance of education.

[66] ἑωυτὸν μάλιστα αἰδεῖσθαι.

this could mean that one who has begun a disgraceful action should abandon it out of prospective *aischunē* before himself, or that habitual offenders ought to experience an *aischunē* which would prevent offence, it might also mean that one who does *aischra* should experience a self-directed sense of retrospective shame, perhaps as a necessary prelude to reform, perhaps in contrast to shame before the reproaches of others. The other two fragments, however, firmly establish Democritus' awareness of *aidōs* as a prospective check which can inhibit action not because it is liable to attract the censure of others but because it fails to correspond with one's own ideals. If *aischunesthai* in B 84 is retrospective, this will only suggest that a failure to avoid wrongdoing out of prospective *aidōs/aischunē* for oneself may entail retrospective shame over one's own conduct.[67]

Democritus' concept of *aidōs* cannot be unrelated to his ideas of conscience and guilt, but these are not quite as closely linked to his views on *aidōs* as we might have hoped. The effects and manifestations of a guilty conscience are described in B 174, where they are referred to his central concept of *euthumia* (contentment, well-being, etc.). The *euthumos*, since he behaves in accordance with justice and *nomos*, is confident and free of care, whereas those who disregard *dikē* and do not do 'what must be' are discontented and, when they remember their misdeeds, are fearful and reproach themselves.[68] It is possible that this fear is not entirely object-specific, that it is simply the converse of the confidence and placidity of the good man, and the self-reproach may indicate genuine regret unprompted by the thought of unfortunate consequences; but it is on the face of it more likely that the fear should at least encompass fear of unpleasant consequences and that self-reproach should include a prudential sense that it would have been better not to transgress.[69] B 262, however, is more hopeful, in that it is claimed that the injustice of one who, out of desire for profit or pleasure, contravenes the law by acquitting the guilty must remain with him as an *enkardion*, something which lies in his heart. Here it is the injustice itself which is to be 'on his conscience', and it appears to be accepted that the awareness of wrongdoing can in itself

[67] In that *aideisthai heauton* presumably does imply self-reproach and may suggest retrospective shame as a correlative, it is clearly compatible with guilt, but in the two frr. in which the sense of the locution is clearest, it cannot, since it is prospective, actually denote guilt (*pace* Lloyd-Jones (1987), 21).

[68] Cf. B 215; Konstan (1988), 17.

[69] So Nill (1985), 89; Procopé (1989: 319–20), however, may be right to argue that Democ. need have no specific object of fear in mind.

be painful.[70] Equally, in B 43 repentance in one who has performed disgraceful deeds is said to be salutary, and this presumably also recognizes the importance of a subjective awareness of the character of one's own actions.[71]

Democritus' explicit pronouncements on conscience and remorse may go little further than those found in the forensic speeches of Antiphon, but they do at least allow for the presence of negative evaluation of one's own actions alongside fear of their consequences; we saw, too, that as far as prospective conscience or awareness of right and wrong is concerned, he recommends abstaining from wrongdoing not out of fear of consequences, but out of concern to do the right thing (B 41). He seems, moreover, to have believed that wrongdoing inevitably involves loss of the contentment that is his ideal,[72] and thus considered the intrinsic disadvantages of wrongdoing more important than the extrinsic. His concept of *aidōs* may be related to his stress on the intrinsic consequences of wrongdoing, in the sense that, in practice, the *aidōs* of the person with a proper insight into 'what must be done' may forestall the self-reproach of one who realized that he had diminished his own *euthumia*, yet the proposition entailed by the verb *aideomai* is not 'this is bad for me', but 'this is *aischron*', and so *aideisthai heauton* cannot refer to a merely prudential calculation of consequences.[73]

[70] The word *enkardion* recalls *enthumion* at Ant. 2. c. 10, 3. a. 2, 3. d. 9 (see Stebler (1971), 63–6; Parker (1983), 252–4; Procopé (1989), 318), but the *enthumion* has a supernatural aspect which *enkardion* is not likely to share, given that Democ. deprecates fear of post-mortem punishment in B 297 (which contains, according to Snell (1930b: 23), the earliest occurrence of the noun *suneidēsis*). *Enkardion*, however, presumably shares a similar origin with *enthumion* (or is a coinage based on *enthumion*), which shows that Democ. is willing to borrow words employed in describing fear of the supernatural in order to adumbrate a sense of conscience which has no reference to supernatural forces.

[71] Cf. von Erffa (1937), 199; also Farrar (1988), 236, on B 297, 43, etc.

[72] See B 45: the perpetrator of *adikia* is worse off than its victim. This is presumably to be related to B 191, in which the psychic disharmony of those who are subject to the kind of desires which might make them unjust, in contrast to the *euthumia* of those who moderate their desires, is outlined at greatest length; see Nill (1985), 84–91, on Democ's attempt to link disadvantage with wrongdoing. B 191 is also the most promising fr. in terms of the establishment of a link between Democ.'s ethics and physics (Guthrie, ii. 497); see Vlastos (1975b) (originally published 1945/6), with the criticism of Taylor (1967); cf. Barnes (1982), 533–5; Nill (1985), 110 n. 3. For a recent and extensive argument for the continuity of Democritean ethics and physics, see Farrar (1988), 197–230, esp. 221–30 on B 191 and Taylor's criticisms of Vlastos.

[73] Plato, of course, often insists that *aischron* and *kakon* are equivalent in the sense of 'disadvantageous for the agent' (e.g. *Gorg.* 474d–475e). But that this would not appear analytically true to the ordinary Greek is shown by the disjunction made by Polus in *Gorg.* (474c) and Cleinias in *Laws* (661e–662a). Both these accept that the base may act in a disreputable and disgusting manner (*aischrōs*), but not necessarily in a way that is disadvantageous or displeasing to themselves.

Democritus, moreover, also stresses the role of an education which, in the early stages at least, takes a traditional form, and it is this which develops the sense of *aidōs*. Since it is unlikely that he envisaged a universal course of instruction inculcating *ab initio* his own ideas of contentment and well-being, he presumably believed that traditional moral education creates a disposition to proper behaviour based not on the calculation of advantage but on the unreflective sense that certain things are wrong (or not nice); recognition that this behaviour is in one's own interests will arise in adults who have already made these acquired standards their own and who subscribe to them because they regard them as intrinsically right. If Democritus is determined to show us that traditional moral virtue is compatible with self-interest, his persistence in referring to wrongdoing in traditional terms (as injustice, *hamartia*, that which is 'untoward' or 'unfitting', etc.), his stress on *to deon*, and, above all, his recognition of the role of *aidōs* suggest that he did not entirely *reduce* morality to self-interest, but rather believed that moral standards to which one is committed as such might also be regarded as promoting one's own ultimate good.[74]

Whatever the place of Democritus' self-directed *aidōs* in his scheme of contentment and psychic harmony, however, it is for their psychological insight that his observations are valuable.[75] Even if he does believe that a proper understanding of the good for individuals will reveal that the *aidōs* which inhibits wrongdoing also helps maximize

[74] Even if instances of *to deon* etc. are to be denied all reference to 'duty', the absence of a categorical imperative in Democ. does not entail the absence of a concept of conscience. Even those who are not deontologists may regard themselves as possessing a sense that certain behaviour is to be rejected as such, and the possession of such a sense is not incompatible with the desire to justify one's moral responses in non-deontological terms. The Greeks, needless to say, never achieve a Kantian perspective on the objectivity and impartiality of obligation, but they do, as is obvious in such works as Soph. *Phil.* (4.2.3 above) and in passages like Thuc. 2. 51. 5 (Ch. 5 n. 87), possess an ordinary concept of duty which can entail observance even of obligations which frustrate one's own material interests; if pressed to justify such principles, however, their tendency, at the popular and the philosophical level, is to appeal to a higher degree of social or personal advantage.

[75] In particular, we should distinguish the value of Democ.'s arguments against doing wrong in secret as empirical psychology from the matter of his success in proving injustice bad for the agent. It is always possible to argue that justice or morality is in one's own ultimate interest, but difficult to prove that injustice or immorality entails inevitable disadvantage, and while Democ. does show that people who have been adequately socialized may not be tempted by the prospect of doing wrong in secret, he has no compelling argument to offer those who happen still to be deterred by external sanctions alone, since any claim that even the thoroughly wicked suffer psychic disturbance as a consequence of their wrongdoing is unlikely to win acceptance. (For a reconstruction of Democ.'s efforts in this area, see Nill (1985), 86–91; cf. also Irwin (1977), 32.)

one's advantage, he is clearly also committed to the view that human beings can possess an affective attachment to standards of behaviour which may operate without exclusive reference to external sanctions. His view of *aidōs*, therefore, is not in any way undermined by his concept of the intrinsic disadvantages of wrongdoing (indeed, many might agree that the operation of the ordinary prospective conscience is thoroughly compatible with an awareness that one would 'feel bad' were one to ignore its promptings);[76] rather they belong together in minimizing the role of popular opinion, a traditionally powerful force,[77] and grounding moral behaviour in the disposition and the insight of the individual.

The expression *heauton aideisthai* has both novel and traditional aspects. Most obviously, *aideisthai* is not normally a reflexive verb,[78] and when it governs a personal object it normally manifests a relationship with the opinions or the status of other people.[79] Any feeling of *aidōs*, however, will have its subjective and self-directed aspects, since even in cases in which it expresses inhibition before the criticisms of others, it is still up to the individual to supply the standard against which he or she wishes to be measured; any such feeling entails an appreciation or a fantasy that a particular description of one's actions fails to match a valued internalized ideal. This is true even where *aidōs* connotes simple embarrassment, but is all the more relevant to Democritus' thesis where it inhibits an action which the agent

[76] One might, of course, reject an action simply in order to avoid the unpleasant consequences of fear of detection, but this motive is distinct from the recognition that one will suffer from remorse based on the moral character of the act itself, in which case the recognition of the intrinsic disadvantages of wrongdoing is inseparable from the judgement that the action is wrong.

[77] Cf. B 48, where the *agathos* is said to pay no heed to the criticisms of the base; in other frr. there is an equally untraditional stress on the intentions and the will behind one's actions, as opposed to their outward aspect (B 62, 68, 89).

[78] There are, however, other instances of *aischunesthai* used reflexively: Pl. *Tim.* 49cd, *Ep.* 7. 328c; Demosth. *Ep.* 3. 37 (note both 'self' and 'others' as objects; cf. 48. 2, where *aischunomai* is used absolutely rather than reflexively, but is coupled with 'considering oneself a worthless person'). Pl. *H. Maj.* 298b, 304cd seem also to allude to reflexive *aischunē*. These may all be later than the Democritean frr., but it would be rash to claim that they all ultimately derive from Democritean coinage. For other, later formulations, see Procopé (1989), 323 n. 109. Democ.'s reflexive uses of *aideisthai* and *aischunesthai* may have had some basis in popular usage, but this does not detract from the significance of his remarks as a riposte to the 'external sanctions' approach.

[79] Thus von Erffa (1937: 198) looks in vain for parallels, finding only two linguistic similarities, examples of verbs not normally used reflexively being so used (Soph. *OC* 960–1; Eur. *Hel.* 999), which are no real parallels at all. The line from the *Helen*, however, is relevant in content, in that it deals with a positive form of *philautia*. On the relationship of this and Democ. B 264 etc. to Aristotelian *philautia*, see n. 239 below.

instinctively rejects as inappropriate, where even explicit reference to 'other people' need not rule out commitment to a standard which one has made one's own. As we have seen, indeed, references to or representations of the operation of the internalized standard as such have become increasingly common in literary works in which *aidōs* occurs or is otherwise adumbrated. The experience of *heauton aideisthai* thus antedates Democritus' formulation of the expression, and in spite of the untraditional flavour of much of what he has to say on the importance of one's own judgement as against that of other people, the validity of his view of *aidōs* rests on its exploitation of the possibilities of the concept, even in traditional guise.[80] Democritus' contrast of self- and other-directed *aidōs* recognizes that in ordinary language *aidōs* is normally other-directed, but in exhorting his audience to experience self-directed *aidōs* he is clearly not urging them to do the impossible, and the significance of this for our purposes lies in the explicit and unambiguous recognition by a native speaker of classical Greek that *aidōs* may belong with a response to internal rather than external sanctions.

6.4. PLATO

Although the works of Plato are comparatively rich in instances of our terms and in manifestations of the wider complex of values to which they belong, it would at this stage be superfluous to pursue all the ramifications of *aidōs*-related values in the relatively minor contexts in which they occur; Democritus' response to the issues raised by his contemporaries and predecessors has narrowed the focus of our enquiry in such a way that the subsequent study of Plato (and

[80] Thus the real parallels for *heauton aideisthai* are to be found in tragedy, particularly in Soph. *Aj.* and *Phil.* (4.2.1, 4.2.3 above; cf. 5.3 and 5.4.4 *passim* on Eur.). That ideas similar to those of Democ. appear in the *Aj.* (see Ch. 4 nn. 46, 87), might seem to rule out a direct relationship between the theory of that philosopher and Soph., since the production of *Aj.* is conventionally dated to the 440s, and the birth of Democ. to *c.*460, but the alternative birthdate of *c.*470 might just allow direct influence. (On Democ.'s dates and life see A 1 and 2 DK.) More probably, however, the presence of these ideas in a play of the 440s indicates the extent to which such things were 'in the air' in the second half of the 5th cent. (One should not, however, rule out the possibility that Prot. was a direct influence on Soph. and that Democ. borrowed from him. Even if this was not so, the similarity between the two Abderites remains; in particular, Democ.'s view of *aidōs* may, to some extent, be regarded as bringing out what was implicit in Prot.'s view, as represented in the Great Speech, of the acquisition of *aidōs* through education. Cf. Kahn (1985), 28 n. 59.)

Aristotle) must concentrate on their approach to these same issues in order to discover whether they replicate, contradict, or go beyond the conclusions of Democritus. We no longer need the sorts of data on the nature of *aidōs* collected in previous chapters, because the issue is no longer whether *aidōs* can be a response to internal sanctions rooted in a form of conscience, but whether Plato and Aristotle realized that it could. Accordingly, the subsequent sections focus on the views of the nature of *aidōs* which emerge from the works of the two philosophers, with particular reference to its role in their psychology, its connection with their conceptions of moral excellence, their views regarding its reference to external or internal sanctions, and the possible role of *aidōs* in any conception of conscience they may possess.

6.4.1. *Conventional Approaches*

The notion of honour is prominent in the Platonic dialogues as a subject discussed in its own right,[81] but it is also a pervasive element in the moral background against which the discussions take place, and conventional aspects of honour are frequently taken for granted or adapted to the practice of dialectic.[82] Similarly, even in contexts in which there is explicit discussion of the concept, views of *aidōs* rarely go beyond the conventional. In the *Euthyphro* (12ac), for example, Socrates, demonstrating the difference between genus and species, opposes his view that *aidōs* (*qua* fear of a reputation for depravity) is a

---

[81] For a study, see Venske (1938).

[82] e.g. ignorance, pretending to know what one does not, and failure to pursue the truth are commonly regarded as *aischron* (etc.) or as occasion for *aidōs* (*Ap.* 29b, 29de, *Euthyph.* 15d, *La.* 201ab (*aidōs* to be disregarded in order that the ignorant may learn), *Theag.* 130c, *Tht.* 196d, etc.), and the dialectical search for knowledge is seen as an important enterprise requiring bravery (*La.* 194a, *Charm.* 160de, *Euthyd.* 294d, *Tht.* 203e, 205a; cf. *Phil.* 21d, *Soph.* 241c), in which one should feel *aidōs* at slacking or at endangering the integrity of the argument (e.g. *Prot.* 341ab, 348c, *Gorg.* 458d, *Phil.* 28a (*asebeia*), *Tht.* 151d, 183e, 190e, *Pol.* 268d). Reputation, too, may be vulnerable in the competitive atmosphere of the *elenchos*, which typically involves exposure of inconsistency and can be humiliating (e.g. *Lys.* 211bc, *Am.* 135a, *Charm.* 169c, *Euthyd.* 295b, 297a, 303d (ironically), *Gorg.* 457c–458a, *Phil.* 19a, 23a, etc.). Socrates and Plato, however, more than once express or imply disapproval of the more competitive aspects of dialectic—e.g. Hippias is satirized for his *philotimia* in *H. Maj.* (cf. *Prot.* 337d); at *Prot.* 338bc Soc. implies that his colleagues are too concerned with prestige, while at *H. Min.* 372c he claims that he is not ashamed to learn by being proved wrong (cf. *Soph.* 230ce: the *elenchos* may lead to *aischunē*, but one whose ignorance remains unexposed is *aischros*). The competitive spirit is condemned as inappropriate in philosophical argument at *Rep.* 451a and *Laws* 638b.

species of fear to that of a fragment from post-Homeric epic (*Cypria* fr. 24 Davies; compare Epicharmus 221 Kaibel) which contains the *gnōmē*, 'Where there is fear [*deos*], there too is *aidōs*.'[83] Here, the treatment of *aidōs*, such as it is, is popular and unreflective, even frivolous, and tells us little about Plato's real views.[84]

The association of *aidōs* and fear recurs in the *Republic* (465ab); the poetic terms *aidōs* and *deos* are employed (probably with an allusion to *Iliad* 15. 657–8), but the former is not seen in terms of the latter, rather *aidōs* as positive respect for one's father (which Socrates claims will obtain in all relationships between younger and older members of the guardian class, given that one will not know one's natural father) is distinguished from *deos* as fear of punishment at the hands of those who would be prepared to come to the aid of an older man assaulted by a younger. Here *aidōs* is used in a traditional sense, but is distinguished from straightforward fear of external sanctions; *aidōs* for one's father may encompass regard for his opinions, but here it is clearly also envisaged as inhibitory reverence in the context of a special tie of *philia*, and thus a special claim to honour. Similarly, in the seventh Letter (337a)[85] *aidōs* and *phobos* appear as the factors which would induce those defeated in civil strife to abide by the new settlement; they would experience fear because the victors had demonstrated their superior strength, and *aidōs* because they had shown themselves superior to their own desires for revenge and ready

---

[83] ἵνα γὰρ δέος ἔνθα καὶ αἰδώς. The meaning of the original is presumably that fear of one who is superior in power and prestige necessarily leads to inhibition before that person, but even so, and even in spite of the regular epic association of *aidōs* and *deos*, it seems to be going too far to say that *all* fear of the more powerful implies *aidōs*. The text in the first half of the line of the fr. in which the *gnōmē* occurs is uncertain (see Burnet's (OCT) and Davies's *app. crit.*), but the reference of *aidōs* is to inhibition before Zeus, no matter which reading or emendation is preferred. Since this is so, Soc. is clearly equivocating when he moves from the *aidōs* (= respect) of the fr., which implies a personal object, to the *aidōs* which takes a non-personal object (αἰδούμενός τι πρᾶγμα καὶ αἰσχυνόμενος) in his expression of his own view. The shift in meaning of the verb *aideisthai* in this context, in fact, requires elucidation (in *Euthyph.* 12b6 does the *aidōs* whose occurrence is ruled out connote respect for sickness and poverty (which would certainly be absurd) or shame at these states of affairs (which would be quite possible)? Is the use of the verb with a non-personal object in 12b10 prospective or retrospective?), but it would be to treat the passage out of all proportion to its importance to go into detail here.

[84] The shift from personal to impersonal object might be taken as indicating that the latter usage is the more familiar by this period, but 'I respect' uses do continue, with *aischunomai* in place of *aideomai* (e.g. Demosth. 27. 65, 54. 22 (*bis*); Aeschines, 1. 24, 180). On Soc.'s (deliberate ?) misunderstanding of the *Cypria* fr., cf. Wilamowitz (1959), i. 348 n. 1.

[85] On the authenticity of the Letters, esp. *Ep.* 7, see the survey of Guthrie, v. 399–401.

themselves to abide by the law. Used with a personal object, then, *aidōs* connotes positive respect for those who deserve it rather than fear of the stronger.[86]

The traditional association of *aidōs* with *sōphrosunē* comes to the fore in the *Charmides*. The role of *aidōs* in the *sōphrosunē* for which Critias so extravagantly praises Charmides (157d) is suggested by the latter's own behaviour; for when Socrates asks him whether he agrees that he possess a sufficient degree of *sōphrosunē*, he blushes, and Socrates comments on the appropriateness of his *aidōs*[87] in one of his years (158c). The affective basis of Charmides' *sōphrosunē* in *aidōs* is then further suggested by his *aporia* as to whether he should agree or disagree and by his modest reluctance to praise himself (158cd), and may also be traced in his first definition of *sōphrosunē* as behaving in an orderly and quiet manner (159b). It comes as no surprise, therefore, that Charmides, in his second definition, brings *aidōs* into explicit relation with *sōphrosunē* (160e); his identification of the two, however, is rejected with reference to the traditional ambivalence of *aidōs* (*Odyssey* 17. 347), an ambivalence which, Charmides agrees, cannot be shared by a virtue like *sōphrosunē* (161a).[88] It may be that there is a foreshadowing in this of an Aristotelian distinction between *pathos* and *hexis*, affect and settled state,[89] but this is hardly a prominent aspect of a passage in which the treatment of *aidōs*, such as it is, is extremely superficial.

Aidōs also appears in thoroughly traditional guise in the *Laws*,

---

[86] Cf. Chilon 12 (DK, 'Seven Sages'); Arist. *Pol.* 1314^{b}18–20.

[87] Here expressed as *to aischuntēlon*, *aischuntēlos* being an adjective used to qualify a subject as disposed to feel *aischunē/aidōs*. The (rare) active sense of *aidoios* which conveyed this sense in earlier literature has by now disappeared.

[88] For the point that a virtue cannot be bad for its possessor, cf. *La.* 193d, *Prot.* 349e–350b. Cf. *Prot.* 333bc, where Prot. agrees with Soc. that *sōphrosunē* cannot be used to unjust ends, while recognizing that many people say it can. There is, then, popular support for the view that Soc. rejects, that *sōphrosunē* can be used to produce morally bad as well as morally good results. This question, however, whether a virtue can be misused, should be distinct from that of whether it may be incommodious for its possessor, yet Soc. rejects Charm.'s definition of *sōphrosunē* as *aidōs* by confronting his recognition that *aidōs* may be disadvantageous with his intuition that *sōphrosunē* cannot be misused, that a bad man cannot be *sōphrōn* (*Charm.* 161a); there is no attempt to argue for the assumption that '*x* is bad for me' = 'the possession of *x* makes me a bad person', or to supply the missing link which would prove that it is always good for a person to be a good person. The general point is that the ordinary Athenian might equally say of *aidōs* everything that Soc. says of *sōphrosunē*, and vice versa. (Note that the pseudo-Platonic definition of *aidōs* (*Def.* 412c8–10) builds 'rightness' and 'seasonability' into the concept in the same way as Pl./Soc. seek to make the goodness/utility of virtues such as *sōphrosunē* analytic.)

[89] So Crombie (1962), 212–13.

where the association with fear is once more a dominant aspect. The discussion of the propaideutic use of alcohol and the symposium in the first and second books centres on *aidōs*, and at 646e-647a *aischunē*, quickly reformulated as *aidōs*, is introduced as a kind of fear distinct from the fear of harm (*phobos*), the difference between the two kinds being illustrated in the paradigm case of martial bravery—fear of the enemy is to be banished, but fear of the opinions of one's fellows encouraged, and the soldier must be both fearless and fearful (647b).[90] The lessons of this discussion are then applied to the symposium, in which one may learn to overcome one's *anaischuntia*, a reprehensible form of confidence (647ab), by means of exposure to the shameful; wine removes one's inhibitions (649b),[91] and thus allows examination of one's character (649d-650b), but if this is done in a controlled environment, the inappropriate conduct of those with a tendency towards *anaischuntia* may be checked by means of censure, and a sense of *aidōs*[92] which is less easily dispelled fostered in its place (649bd; cf. 648bc for the application of reward and punishment, and 671ce on the importance of rules and of control of the symposium by strict 'generals', disobedience to whom is to entail disgrace, *aischunē*).[93] *Aidōs/aischunē* are here persistently related to fear of the external

[90] This point, and the general argument behind it that an education in replacing fear with confidence must be accompanied by an education in self-control, are related to that made in *Pol.* 310de on the need to combine, in the individual and in the state, the qualities of *sōphrosunē* and *andreia*; here *aidōs* is, as in *Charm.*, related to *sōphrosunē* but ambivalent—interbreeding of those whose souls are too full of *aidōs* and untempered by self-assertiveness would produce, over generations, totally supine offspring. On the opposition of *andreia* and *sōphrosunē* here and its implications for the doctrine of the unity of the virtues, see Görgemanns (1960), 125-6 (128-9 on *Laws*); North (1966), 170-1, 184-5; O'Brien (1967), 178-9; Guthrie, v. 191-2; Klosko (1986), 193-4. For the opposition of *sōphrosunē* and *mania* (which is the result (310d) of extreme *andreia* untempered by *sōphrosunē*), cf. *Rep.* 573b. The view of the *Pol.* of *aidōs* as a character trait which may be educated to produce virtue and avoid *mania* is discussed and applied to Eur. by Szlezak (1986).

[91] Cf. 666bc: older men, who are embarrassed at singing (665de, 667b), can lose their inhibitions under the influence of wine; for the sentiment that excessive indulgence in wine dispels *aidōs*, cf. Thgn. 482. Pl.'s stress on the utility of the symposium in *Laws* doubtless owes much to the parainetic elements of sympotic poetry apparent in the elegies of Thgn.; on the influence of archaic poetry on the *Laws*, and the extent to which the *Laws* itself resembles earlier literary/educational works, see Görgemanns (1960), 19-20, 61-2, 66, 69-71, 104, etc.; cf. Solmsen (1962), on Hesiodic motifs in Pl.

[92] Wine is thus a means of instilling *aidōs* in the soul, 672d.

[93] At 671d the *aidōs* and *aischunē* which prevent over-indulgence in the symposium are described as 'divine fear', θεῖος φόβος. This phrase, however, carries no implication that these are specifically religious qualities; the adjective is used in a simple commendatory sense which would be familiar to the Athenian's two Dorian interlocutors. Similarly, the four cardinal virtues are 'divine goods' at 631c, as is *timē* at 727a.

sanction of disgrace, but the creation of a sense of *aidōs* which can withstand the influence of alcohol also suggests the acquisition of an instinctive disposition towards self-control; this may be no more than implicit in the text, but the dispositional sense of *aidōs* (a sense which agrees with the identification of *aidōs* as a malleable trait of character in the *Politicus*) is certainly there.

Aidōs is again associated with *phobos* at 699c, where, as the fear of the censure of one's *philoi* which (as at 647b) promotes bravery in battle, it is said to be partly responsible for Athenian success at Marathon.[94] The importance of this kind of fear in the state is then stressed in an exposition of the benefits of limited authoritarianism and the dangers of too much freedom (699d–701e) illustrated by an account of Athenian decline which exploits the traditional motif of the departure of *aidōs*.[95] Disregard of traditional forms in music, the core of the aristocratic education, created a tendency for performers to play to

[94] Here again Pl. is being traditional; cf. Demaratus' explanation of Spartan resistance to Persian power in terms of their fear of *nomos* at Hdt. 7. 104. 4–5 (cf. Guthrie, v. 332 and n. 1); both Pl. and Hdt. have the contrast between fear of a tyrant and the Greek peoples' fear of legal and social sanctions, and the operation of Hdt.'s *nomos* in securing discipline in battle strongly suggests *aidōs*. Pl.'s text at this point, however, is doubtful. The paradosis, reproduced by Burnet (OCT), England (1921), and des Places (Budé) gives: 'All these were the considerations that created in them a sense of mutual *philia*—I mean the fear (*phobos*) they experienced at that time and that fear which was born of their former *nomoi*, the one they acquired in servitude to their old laws; this is the one we have often called *aidōs* above, and which, we said, those who would become *agathoi* must serve; the coward, however, is free of such fear and unaffected by it; [but] if *deos* had not seized him [the coward] at that time, he would never have come together to fight back, nor would he have defended the temples . . . as he did in fact do, but we would have been scattered in little pieces, all dispersed in different directions.' This is puzzling because the presumption must be that *deos* substitutes for *aidōs*, with which it has a long association in poetry (see England (1921), ad loc., adducing 15. 657, *Cypria* fr. 24 Davies, and Soph. *Aj.* 1073–83); but if the coward is free of *aidōs* and never experiences it, how could his experience of *aidōs* (= *deos*) in 490 BC have proved salutary? An alternative would be to regard *deos* as fear of danger (= *phobos*), but since the whole point of the passage is to defend the salutary fear which has its basis in respect for *nomos*, this would be both irrelevant and inapposite (for the decline which Pl. goes on to describe can scarcely be ascribed to a reduced tendency to be afraid of danger). The fault presumably lies in ὃν εἰ τότε μὴ δέος ἔλαβεν (699c6), which makes the coward (ὁ δειλός) the subject of all that follows (especially difficult with συνελθών, 'coming together'), and a conjecture such as Ritter's ὃ . . . δῆμος δέος ἔλαβεν, identifying *deos* with *aidōs*, and expressing its salutary influence on the Athenian people, would solve the problem (though I feel that *deos* should remain the subject of the verb).

[95] *Aidōs* occurs in a similarly archaizing context at 713e as one of the pleasant consequences for men of their being ruled by *daimones* in the age of Cronus. Similar, too, is *Rep.* 560de, where the moral decay of 'democratic man' is seen in terms of the driving out of *aidōs* and its replacement with *anaideia*. (For the reversal of the normal significance of moral terms in this passage, cf. Thuc. 3. 82. 4–8.) Cf. also the reversal of values under tyranny at 562e, which involves the son's failing to *aischunesthai* his parents.

the gallery and brought about a 'theatrocracy' in which the ordinary man's pride in his own opinion led to the abandonment of the fear which held the state together and thus to *anaischuntia*, self-confident disregard of the opinions of one's betters (700a–701b). As a result, people became unwilling to serve the authorities, began to disobey the admonitions of parents and elders, and ultimately sought to avoid obeying the law; regard for oaths, pledges, and even for the gods themselves vanished (701bc). This familiar catalogue of woes suggests the departure of *aidōs* at several points, most obviously in the rise of 'boldness' and *anaischuntia* (701ab), but also in the lack of respect for parents and elders and in the disregard of oaths; the complaint is one of increased self-assertion in place of respect for authority, but also of lack of concern for the opinions of others, and thus we are dealing with a concept of *aidōs* that is comprehensive in its scope, covering both respect for one's fellows and one's superiors and consciousness of one's own status as affected by the opinions of fellows and superiors. Thinking oneself superior to the laws, however, is another manifestation of this lack of inhibition, and so it appears that Plato also envisaged *aidōs* as covering respect for the institutions of the state in the same quasi-personal way as did Aeschylus.[96] The whole passage, then, belongs with the earliest expressions of the role of *aidōs* in the state which stress the external sanctions of punishment and popular opinion and advocate deference to human and institutional authority.[97]

In all this there is no explicit suggestion that *aidōs* involves anything more than fear of disgrace or inhibition before more powerful or august forces, and much that suggests that it does not. Much of the *Laws*, indeed, seems designed to foster concepts of honour which focus on the outward aspect of actions and encourage conformity rather than commitment;[98] even sincere heterodoxy, for example, is to

[96] Cf. 3.4 above.
[97] Cf. 3.4 above, *ad fin.*, Ch. 4 nn. 67–8, and 6.2 *ad init.* Pl.'s remarks elsewhere on the utility of *aidōs* etc. in the community tend simply to replicate the position of the *Prot.* myth that such qualities are necessary if communities are to survive; cf. *Ep.* 6. 323b (*aidōs* and *dikē*, perhaps wholly derived from the *Prot.* myth), *Gorg.* 507d–508a (*sōphrosunē* and *dikaiosunē*), *Rep.* 351ce (*dikaiosunē*).
[98] For the use of public honour (praise) and disgrace (blame) in making proper behaviour pleasant and improper painful, see 631e–632c, 634a, 663c, 671e, 711c, 721d, 730b–731a, 742b, 755a, 762a, 762c, 773e, 774c, 784d, 808e, 841e, 879e, 881bc, 921d–922a, 926d, 944de (the coward to be treated as a woman), 952bc; see Venske (1938), 30–3; Gould (1955), 75; Görgemanns (1960), 121–2, 169–71; Stalley (1983), 124, 138. Cf. also the importance of openness and public knowledge as a means of ensuring that each gets his proper *timē* at 738e. Pl. occasionally stresses the disgrace of discovery rather than the impropriety of the act, and at 841ac, 841e, 845bc it is the discovery *rather than* the act

be punished.[99] On the other hand, it is important that, if possible, the citizens should be rather than merely seem good,[100] and it is acknowledged that some people at least are not deterred from wrongdoing by external sanctions alone.[101] These last observations, however, might also be compatible with a view that gave *aidōs* no role beyond that of fear of disgrace. Yet the great stress on education and habituation in the work[102] suggests that individuals would actually internalize their values of the honourable and the shameful, and the claim that the members of a true *politeia* must be willing subjects (832c), just as the Athenians were once, on account of their *aidōs*, voluntary slaves of their laws (700a), also indicates that members of the community may share its values. There are also, in Plato's incidental uses of the term, indications enough that *aidōs* involves rather more than his explicit pronouncements on the subject might suggest. At 813cd, for example, the *aidōs* of the official in charge of children, which is responsible for his positive desire to choose the right men and women as his assistants, clearly has no reference to 'what people say', but rather is

that is disgraceful (cf. Guthrie, v. 355). Yet the very fact that, in the exceptional cases of sexual morality in 841, Pl. sees the efficacy of making discovery disgraceful, rather than the act itself, seems to indicate an acknowledgement that to be disposed to believe that a given act is *aischron* is not merely to fear detection, since otherwise there would be no point in distinguishing the disgracefulness of discovery from that of the act itself.

[99] As noted by Stalley (1983: 150), citing 799b and 908e–909a. These passages help refute the interpretation of 863e–864b as upholding the integrity of one who acts in good faith; see O'Brien (1957); Görgemanns (1960), 137–40; Saunders (1968), 428–34; Stalley (1983), 157–9.

[100] Cf. Görgemanns (1960), 169. One might use 729bc as an example: taking as his starting point a Theognidean *gnōmē* (cf. Thgn. 409–10, 1161–2) that *aidōs* is the best legacy one can bequeath to one's children, the Athenian maintains that *aidōs* (= respect) is best instilled not simply by urging the young to respect (*aischunesthai*) everyone, but by example; the elders should respect and practise self-restraint before the youth, ensuring that they never do or say anything *aischron* in their presence. (Note how the sense of *aischunesthai* in this passage covers both 'respect' and 'shame before'.) Needless to say, this does not necessarily imply that one may do or say *aischra* provided young persons are absent.

[101] e.g. at 632c the custodians of the legal system are to possess either knowledge (*phronēsis*) or true opinion about what is right, and at 727a–728c the argument on the importance of 'honouring the soul' (= a good form of *philautia*) presupposes a positive commitment to moral improvement (cf. 731d–732b on bad *philautia*, honouring oneself more than the truth, which can cause one to avoid taking the measures which would make one truly good). Cf. 875cd: there is no human being who is so rational as to be able to do without laws entirely, but traces of the reason which enables one to do right without the guidance of law are found in small doses (d3).

[102] Esp. in Bks. 1–2, 643a–674c, and 7, 788a–824a. On education in *Laws*, see Gould (1955), 77–87, 110–18; Barker (1960), 35–6, 430–4; Morrow (1960), 297–398; Görgemanns (1960), ch. 1; North (1966), 187–92; Stalley (1983), 42–4, 123–36; Klosko (1986), 202–6.

linked to his sense of the importance of the task entrusted to him (813d1).[103] There is room, then, in the *Laws'* conception of *aidōs* for positive commitment to one's values, but, not surprisingly perhaps in a work of such traditional stamp, this is not a point that receives great emphasis in the work itself.

6.4.2. *Whose Opinions?*

The association of *aidōs* with 'other people' is also prominent in the *Symposium*. Phaedrus includes in his praise of homosexual love the observation that *aischunē* over *aischra* and *philotimia* over *kala*, which are essential to the success of cities and individuals alike, are most intense between homosexual lovers; there is no one's opinion the lover values more than the beloved's, and so if he is found to have (literally 'if he becomes obvious having') done something *aischron* or to have suffered something *aischron* through unmanliness, he is more pained at being seen by his beloved than by anyone else; likewise the beloved before his lover. Thus an entire city or army of lovers would be a powerful force, such would be its determination to avoid disgrace and pursue honour (178d–179a).[104] The importance of honour, of the *kalon* and *aischron*, in homosexual relationships is then developed as the dialogue progresses, as first Pausanias (180c–185c) stresses the need for propriety in love, outlining the standards of *aischron* and *kalon* which do and should obtain, and finally Diotima (through Socrates, 204d–212a) gives pursuit of *to kalon* a metaphysical basis that is, however, built on the foundations of the individual's desire for *kleos* and his recognition of *to kalon* in another.

In all this there is an increasing discrimination between mere concern for others' opinions and concern for those of the truly noble, and both the pursuit of honour, which Phaedrus saw as a by-product of homosexual love, and *erōs* itself ultimately become dependent on

[103] Cf. 837c: the *aidōs* and *sebas* of the chaste lover for *sōphrosunē*, courage, magnificence and good sense motivate the purity of his conduct towards his beloved; but physical gratification he rejects as *hubris*. Here, then, *aidōs* involves positive respect for standards of decency and leads one to avoid outrage and excess.

[104] This passage is discussed by M. C. Nussbaum (1980: 395–6), who sees in it notions of 'self-respect' and 'personal separateness'; her account might have benefited, however, from a wider consideration of the thoroughly traditional, not to say unreflective, nature of Phaedrus' remarks on *aischunē*. Much sounder in this respect is Venske (1938: 23–4), who notes the stress on the visual aspect in such words as *katadēlos* (manifest) and *ophthēnai* (being seen).

objective standards of *to kalon*. Accordingly, the implication of Phaedrus that lovers should care for each other's opinions without qualification rather than *qua* good men is modified, as both Socrates and (disingenuously) Alcibiades imply that only the opinions of the wise really matter (194c, 218d). This is a distinction we meet elsewhere in Plato, notably in the *Crito*, where Socrates attempts to dissuade Crito from his concern for the opinions of the many by advocating *aischunē* only for the opinions of the expert who really knows (46c–48a).[105] Similarly, at *Laws* 886a, the distinction between the Athenian's fear that his atheist opponents will ignore Cleinias' naïve 'proofs' of the existence of the gods and the *aidōs* which, he says, he would never experience before *them* suggests that *aidōs* is being reserved for positive respect for the opinions of those who really matter. Yet even though such passages admit a degree of subjectivity in one's judgement of what is *aischron*, *aidōs* and *aischunē* remain linked to the opinions of others, and there is no overt suggestion that they might cover commitment to one's own standards regardless of others' opinions.[106]

There are, however, just a few passages which do express such commitment in terms of *aidōs*. Clearest and least ambivalent of these is *Gorgias* 522d. The best form of self-defence, Socrates tells Callicles, is to be innocent of *adikia* towards gods or men in both word and deed. He goes on: 'If someone were to show me up as unable to defend myself and others in this way, I should be ashamed to be so exposed, whether before many or few or in private by one man alone. . . .' Socrates does not believe that he is unable to avoid injustice, but if someone were to prove that he were, he would experience *aischunē*.

---

[105] Cf. *Ap.* 28be, where Soc. rejects the suggestion that he should be ashamed of having engaged in practices which have now landed him in court on a capital charge, insisting instead on his determination to be *dikaios* and *agathos*; he does not, however, directly oppose this to the concern for one's standing in the eyes of others (implied by the imaginary interlocutor's use of *aischunomai*), but rather to fear of death (cf. 32a). His desire to avoid injustice at all costs subsumes a desire to avoid *to aischron* (28b and d), and he compares himself to an Achilles who, by his account, wished to avoid being a figure of ridicule (28d); this might well suggest a subjective sense of *aidōs/aischunē*, but *aischunomai* is used only of the response which he deprecates.

[106] In the *Crito* passage, and in others such as *La.* 184d–185e, concern for the opinion of the many is contrasted unfavourably with regard for true virtue, which resides in the soul (*La.* 185e: thus only the opinions of those who understand and can foster this inner good are worthy of account; cf. *Crito* 47b–48a), but there is no suggestion here that *aidōs/aischunē* might protect the inner good of a healthy soul in the same way as it forestalls loss of reputation, except in so far as it responds to the prospect of the expert's criticism. For reputation as an external good, cf. *Rep.* 358b–367e *passim*, *Euthyd.* 279a–281e, *Meno* 78cd (Venske (1938), 27–30).

He does talk about *elenchos* (exposure), but there can be no doubt that his shame subsequent to such exposure would be occasioned by his failure to live up to his own standards; the 'one man alone' of the hypothesis would merely be the catalyst—Socrates would be ashamed of his failure regardless of its public or private status. Nevertheless, the normal asociation of *aischunē* with an audience is presupposed, and Plato does not actually go so far as explicitly to acknowledge the possibility of self-directed shame in the absence of any external catalyst.

There are also, interestingly, reflexive uses of *aischunesthai* in Plato which recall Democritus' 'aidōs before oneself'.[107] In the *Timaeus* (49cd) it is said that one should be ashamed of oneself to insist that an entity which is in a state of constant change can be called one thing rather than another, while in the *Hippias Major* Socrates twice alludes to a form of self-directed shame by mentioning, with cryptic irony, his concern for the reproaches of the one person (namely himself) who would criticize his lack of *aischunē* were he to acquiesce in the inadequate definitions acceptable to Hippias (298b, 304cd). Similarly, the seventh Letter (328c) tells how Plato set off for Sicily out of concern for his self-image in his own eyes, lest he appear to himself a man of words and not of deeds.[108] These passages certainly do make use of a form of *aischunē* which is related to the standards one sets oneself, and they are enough to indicate Plato's awareness that *aidōs/ aischunē* are not entirely dependent on the opinions of others, but none has the explicit emphasis of the Democritean fragments on the importance of self-directed *aidōs*, and none really goes the full distance in presenting *aidōs* as a prospective form of conscience which inhibits wrongdoing; nor do they occur in the context of an argument which would demonstrate the falsity of the claim that human beings will necessarily do wrong in secret where external sanctions are inapplicable.

Plato, then, even on the basis of the evidence we have examined so far is aware of the possibility of a commitment to personal ideals rather than mere conformity on the basis of external sanctions and, even if in his explicit discussions of *aidōs/aischunē*, he places much more stress on traditional, other-directed senses, his own usage is sufficiently wide

---

[107] Cf. n. 78 above.

[108] αἰσχυνόμενος μὲν ἐμαυτὸν τὸ μέγιστον, μὴ δόξαιμί ποτε ἐμαυτῷ, etc. The close analogy between this concern for one's own view of oneself and fear of others' disapproval is quite striking.

to allow us to gather from it something of the more complex nature of the concept. *Aidōs*, however, plays little overtly significant role in the search for the kind of internalized conception of morality that is, for example, embodied in the integrity and personality of Socrates, even though the passages collected above which concern Socrates' self-directed shame and his commitment to personal standards of *kalon* and *aischron* are certainly all of a piece with his determination to be consistent in maintaining his principles.[109]

6.4.3. *The Tripartite Soul*

Plato's major contribution to the search for an internalized conception of morality comes, of course, in the *Republic*, where he undertakes to prove that justice is intrinsically good for the individual, taking as his starting point the sophistic view, which we have already met in Antiphon, that human beings are deterred from transgression by external sanctions alone.[110] Plato, however, is concerned less to attack this view as empirical psychology than to demonstrate the intrinsic benefits of justice and the intrinsic harm caused by wrongdoing, and therefore his account goes beyond, and indeed does not lay much emphasis on, the simple argument that some people in some cases will not do wrong even though they know they can get away with it. Yet the crucial element in his attempt to prove that no one who has a proper understanding of his or her own good will have reason to do wrong even in secret, namely the doctrine of the tripartite soul,[111] may

[109] Soc., of course, has his *daimonion*, on the surface a promising candidate for consideration as a form of instinctive conscience, but 'hardly anyone' apart from Soc. has ever possessed such a thing (*Rep.* 496c), and so the *daimonion* is not to be taken as an *Umschreibung* of any ordinary form of conscience, unless we believe that Pl. saw conscience as a very rare phenomenon indeed. In general, Soc.'s sense of commitment and his stress on consistency seem to me to spring much more obviously from his faith in the *elenchos*, in which inconsistency is the greatest failing, and in the possibility of scientific knowledge of what is right as a result of the *elenchos*, rather than from an acknowledgement of the emotional and dispositional basis of the sort of conscience with which *aidōs* is concerned, even though his intellectual commitment to consistency may presuppose *aidōs* at the prospect of failure.

[110] Suggested by Thrasymachus at 344bc, developed by Glaucon at 358e–361d, and Adeimantus at 362e–367e.

[111] For general discussion of tripartition, see Crombie (1962), 341–59; Graeser (1969); T. M. Robinson (1970); Cooper (1984); Klosko (1986), 64–80; on the question of the development of the doctrine in dialogues later than *Rep.*, see Rees (1957); Görgemanns (1960), 122–3, 137, 142; Saunders (1962), 38–41; Graeser (1969), 100–5; Fortenbaugh (1975), 23–5; (1979), 150; Mackenzie (1981), 172–4; Stalley (1983), 46–8.

also be seen as a contribution to the study of human motivation which establishes precisely this point.

Our study of tripartition, however, must be limited to consideration of the degree to which the doctrine bears on *aidōs*, and thus we are not concerned with such questions as the establishment of distinct 'parts' by means of the principle of conflict,[112] or the relationship of the parts of the soul to those of the state.[113] These may be the aspects of the doctrine which most invite criticism, and which contribute most to its weaknesses, but they do not affect the question of the essential psychological verisimilitude of much of Plato's observation, and it is under this aspect, as an account of human motivation, that the doctrine concerns us.

The role of *aidōs* in the tripartite soul, however, is not immediately apparent, since Plato does not locate the emotion specifically in any one of the psychic 'parts'.[114] Fortenbaugh makes a case for the situation of *aidōs/aischunē* in the *logistikon* in certain passages of the *Republic*, citing 571c9, 606c3–9.[115] But these passages hardly constitute convincing evidence; in the former, the bestial part of the soul, which gives rise to unnatural desires in wish-fulfilment dreams while the rational part (*to logistikon*) sleeps, is without *aischunē* or *phronēsis*; Fortenbaugh must hold that both these reside in the sleeping *logistikon*, but the text does not go so far as to say this. Similarly, in the other passage, which concerns the impropriety of finding amusement in the representation of vulgar characters in comedy, laughter is said to be directed at jokes one would be ashamed to make oneself, and to gratify impulses that one has restrained in oneself by means of reason.[116] Shame and reason thus clearly oppose baser desires in both these passages, but the relationship between the·two is never made explicit. The nature of the relationship, however, may be supplied from another passage which deals more directly with the functions of the

[112] On the difficulties involved in the principle of conflict (436b–441c), e.g. that it may allow an indefinite proliferation of psychic parts, see Crombie (1962), 345–56; R. Robinson (1971); Stalley (1975); Irwin (1977), 326 n. 18; Annas (1981), 137–42. The deficiencies of the argument by which Pl. introduces tripartition, however, need not concern us; it is sufficient that the parts of the soul should each include some aspects of human motivation which can plausibly be seen as belonging together (cf. Crombie, loc. cit.).

[113] See Cornford (1912), Williams (1973).

[114] I use the term 'part' with the reservation that, in *Rep.*, at least, the notion of partition is perhaps not to be too rigidly interpreted; see Stocks (1915), 216–18; Graeser (1969), 15–16; Guthrie, iv. 425. But cf. n. 131 below.

[115] Fortenbaugh (1975), 32, with n. 1; cf. 37–8 n. 3, 46.

[116] Cf. 605e–606b, on the analogous experience in tragedy.

parts of the soul. At 441a it is said that the third part of the soul, the spirited part (*thumos* or *thumoeides*) sides with reason against desire, unless it has been corrupted; if *aischunē* were associated with the *thumos*, the passages cited by Fortenbaugh could be taken as referring to this alliance of reason and spirit; and that they are so to be taken is suggested by 606ab, where the cause of our approval in the dramatic character of conduct which we should consider *aischron* in ourselves is given as the inadequate education of 'that part of us which is naturally best'; but since the inadequacy of this education lies not only in intellectual training (*logos*), but also in affective habituation (*ethos*), the clear implication is that these lower desires are opposed both by reason and by the emotions that are allied with reason, *aischunē* being a representative of the latter.[117]

The evidence, moreover, that *aidōs*/*aischunē* is associated with the *thumoeides* is incontrovertible. In the *Republic* the *thumoeides* is actually introduced by means of an example which strongly suggests *aidōs*-related standards, for the anger of Leontius at his desire to look at corpses (439e–440a) takes the form of a self-reproach which clearly has the unworthiness of the desire as its object, and which thus presupposes a judgement of one's own conduct similar to that entailed by retrospective shame. The relevance of *thumos* to a complex in which *aidōs* belongs is further suggested by its manifestation as the anger of one who has been wronged (440cd); Greek definitions of anger tend, rightly or wrongly, to stress the reference of that emotion to one's own honour and status,[118] and anger is typically seen as resentment of an affront, an emotion which was, in Homer, described as *nemesis* and which has *aidōs* as its natural correlate; such resentment turns on one's sense that the offender has failed to acknowledge a legitimate claim to honour, either one's own or that of another. This connection of the *thumos* with honour, moreover, later emerges as fundamental, when, at 548c, it is seen as the part which gives rise to *philotimia* (ambition, love of honour) and *philonikia* (competitiveness, love of victory).[119] The *thumos*, then, is intimately related to the ideal of oneself presupposed by the concept of *timē*, and covers the desire for *timē*, the anger of one who has fallen below his own ideal of himself, and the resentment of one whose self-image has failed to find validation in the eyes of others.

[117] Cf. *Phdr.* 256a, where the two better parts of the soul resist 'with *aidōs* and reason'.
[118] e.g. [Pl.] *Def.* 415e11; Arist. *Rhet.* 1378ᵃ30–2 (*et seq.* on the conditions of anger), *Top.* 127ᵇ30–1, 151ᵃ15–16, 156ᵃ32–3; cf. *DA* 403ᵃ30–1.
[119] Cf. 581ab, and the attachment to honour of timarchic man at 549a, 549d–550b.

The recent accounts of *thumos* which stress its relationship with ideal self-image are thus entirely justified in doing so.[120]

The role of *aidōs* in all this emerges in the *Phaedrus* myth of the soul's chariot. The myth of the chariot is applied to the soul of the lover at 253cff., the charioteer and his two horses being the three 'forms' (*eidē*) of the soul. The nobler horse is a lover of *timē* with *sōphrosunē* and *aidōs*, obedient to the command of the charioteer (253de, 254c), and in the conflict which ensues, when the lover is confronted by the corporeal beauty of the beloved, this good horse supports the desire of the charioteer for true beauty and checks itself under the force of *aidōs* (254a2),[121] while the bad horse strains for sexual gratification (253e–254a); with the victory of the two better parts, the whole soul follows the beloved with *aidōs* (254e9; contrast the *anaideia* of the bad horse at 254d7). The scheme is transparently that of the tripartite soul, the *aidōs* of the noble horse springing from the love of honour which is the characteristic of the *thumoeides*;[122] and this is only what we should expect, given the relationship between

---

[120] Notably Gosling (1973), 41–51; cf. Annas (1981), 127–8; Cooper (1984), 14–15; Klosko (1986), 68, 125; cf. also Price (1990), 262–4, on Pl.'s *thumos* and Freud's superego and ego-ideal. Gosling's account is illuminating, but is flawed by its insistence that the ideal associated with *thumos* is always and only one of manliness; but while it is *thumos* that contributes most to the Auxiliaries' *andreia* (375a–376c, 429a–430b, 440d, 442bc), *andreia* having an analytic connection with manliness, and while Pl., like other Greeks, does tend to associate *timē* with martial values, it is clear—from the *Phdr.*, from the case of Leontius, and from the relation of *thumos* as anger to one's sense that one is in the right rather than in the wrong (440cd)—that ideals other than those of manliness are involved; in principle, *thumos* can be attached to any ideal, as in the oligarchic man, in whom it is attached to the ideal of wealth (553d). Gosling recognizes that other ideals may be involved (50), but claims that Pl. subsumes these under manliness (49, 258–9, a claim which allows him to criticize Pl. for concentrating on manliness to the exclusion of other ideals, 255–9). It is true that Pl. does want to say that the ability to preserve one's convictions about what is and is not to be done is *andreia* (430ab, 442bc), but while it may require 'manliness' or courage to retain one's convictions, this does not mean that those convictions necessarily involve ideals of manliness. We, too, talk about having the courage of our convictions without meaning that our only conviction is to be courageous. Penner (1971: 112) is sarcastic about the 'many eloquent words' spent on *thumos* as a conception of self, and claims that grief (an appetite, according to Pl. at 606a) involves a notion of selfhood no different from that involved in indignation; but whereas grief requires the thought that it is *I* who am bereaved, indignation requires the further thought that to be treated in a particular way is incompatible with my status or that of some individual or group with whom I identify.

[121] Cf. *aischunē*, 254c4, and the *aidōs* of the beloved at 256a6. For *aischunē* as the proper response to the idea of homosexual intercourse, cf. 251a1.

[122] Cf. O'Brien (1967: 168–9), who notes the similarity between the action of the *thumos* in the case of Leontius and the *aidōs* of the good horse, in that both cases represent 'an inner struggle against a debasing appetite'. Cf. also Guthrie, iv. 422; Cooper (1984), 15.

thumos and honour in the *Republic*. Thus there is no question that Plato is unclear about the role of *aidōs/aischunē* in his psychology; it belongs clearly with the functions which are situated, in a collocation that is coherent and plausible, in the *thumos*.[123]

The importance of Plato's location of *aidōs* in the *thumos* lies in the nature of the *thumos* itself, in particular in its relationship with reason. Plato's explicit comments here go no further than the remarks that *thumos* naturally sides with reason against passion, but is not its inevitably ally, since it may be corrupted by bad upbringing.[124] What this might mean is suggested by the argument of 440ad, where *thumos* is said to follow the calculation which opposes desire (440b1-2), to abide by what reason has chosen (b5), and to be capable of being recalled and soothed by reason (d2-3). From this it might appear that *thumos* has no cognitive content of its own, that the opinions on which it depends are supplied by reason.[125] Yet *thumos* can receive, obey, and retain these opinions (441e-442c), and in general Plato's personificatory language suggests that it has opinions of its own (spirit can attempt to rule and issue orders of its own, 442ab, 443de, 550b, 587a).[126] That there is, however, no

---

[123] Arist. *Top.* 126ᵃ6-12, pointing out that genus and species must 'come to be in the same thing', says that fear cannot be the genus of *aischunē*, since *aischunē* belongs in the *logistikon* while fear belongs in the *thumoeides*. Although *Topics* does, in general, employ Academic opinion in its examples (Düring (1968), 202), this particular passage does not correspond with Academic doctrine, according to which *aischunē* is a species of fear (cf. [Pl.] *Def.* 416a9 and the passages cited above from *Euthyph.* and *Laws*; on the Academic origin of *Def.*, see Ingenkamp (1967), 106-14), and it conflicts with those passages which suggest that the place of *aischunē* in tripartition is in the *thumoeides*. Perhaps the reference to the place of *aischunē* in tripartition is only *exempli gratia*, as an illustration of a logical point, which could be used to refute an opponent who argued that *aischunē* was a species of fear, but also held that *aischunē* belongs in the *logistikon* and fear in the *thumoeides*. (Contrast Fortenbaugh (1975: 32; 1979: 153 n. 48), who takes this passage as evidence for Academic doctrine, precisely because his purpose is to criticize the inadequacy of *Rep.*'s tripartition in dealing with emotions such as *aischunē*; but Pl. should not be saddled with the difficulties of this odd passage, which answers to nothing in his own account. Stark (1972: 132) regards the passage as evidence for an early stage in Arist.'s own thought; but Arist. is not necessarily committed to the validity of the opinions used as examples in *Top.*, even though many do conform with his views in the later treatises (Düring (1968), 209)).

[124] 440b, 441a; cf. *Phdr.* 253de, 254c, 256a. *Rep.* 440b, distinguishing spirit from appetite, does go too far in suggesting that *thumos* never opposes reason, but this is quickly modified in 441a. Contrast Penner (1971: 111), who claims that, since *thumos* always sides with reason, Pl. had no argument which would distinguish the two. True, the principle of conflict is not explicitly applied to distinguish reason from *thumos*, but it could be applied to the example of Odysseus' restraint of his anger in a way exactly analogous to its application to Leontius' anger at his desires.

[125] That this is the case is suggested by Klosko (1986: 68).

[126] Cf. Moline (1978), 10-13.

contradiction here is demonstrated by the argument for the distinction between reason and *thumos*. *Thumos* has seemed to depend entirely on reason; to show that this is not so, reference is made to its presence in children and animals (441ab); this, again, seems to push spirit to the extreme of mere temper. But the next point shows that this is not the case; Odysseus' restraint of his *thumos* in resisting his impulse to effect immediate punishment of his unfaithful maidservants[127] is held to demonstrate the difference between 'the element which reasons about better and worse' and 'the element of irrational *thumos*'. But this *thumos* is clearly irrational only in so far as it does not calculate about better and worse; it is not completely devoid of intellectual content, since it relies on Odysseus' belief that the disloyalty of the maidservants diminishes his honour, and this is not a belief that is supplied by the *logistikon*.[128]

The situation, then, is this: reason supplies judgements about the better and the worse, spirit about the honourable and dishonourable, and a judgement that *x* is dishonourable may or may not be congruent with the judgement of reason as to what is best.[129] The role of reason is therefore limited; it does not supply the belief-content of a spirited emotion, but is capable of setting the opinion involved in the emotion against a long-term concept of the agent's good.[130] Nor does reason necessarily supply the ideal upon which spirit rests; spirit has its own

[127] *Od.* 20. 17, quoted at 441b6.

[128] Perhaps, then, the *thumos* of children and animals is seen as having a minimal belief-content (that they have been 'offended'); or the behaviour of children and animals may simply display the affective symptoms and tendencies which, in adult human beings, develop into the concept of one's own worth that is central to spirit; or perhaps these tendencies are simply analogous to the manifestations of spirit. Cf. Gosling (1973), 47-8; Annas (1981), 126-7; Cooper (1984), 15-16.

[129] Reason has its own desire (for truth, 581b), and when reason dominates in the soul, 'better and worse' will be determined with reference to the true good; but reason may still determine advantage or disadvantage when other elements of the soul dominate, in which case better and worse will depend on standards of the overall good supplied by the dominant element (e.g. 553d). The former case describes, in the terminology of Kraut (1973), 'normative', the latter 'predominant' rule of reason; cf. Klosko (1982); (1986), 71-5; Annas (1981), 133-6. The main passages which establish the notion of normative rule, when one element dominates and the whole soul pursues that element's goal, are also those which demonstrate that those character-types that are not dominated by reason none the less possess reason; see 553d, 580d-581c, 586d-587a, 588b-591b. All citizens thus possess tripartite souls, but all are typified by one source of motivation (cf. Stocks (1915), 213-14; Annas (1981), 149-50), and, if those who are typified by a source of motivation other than reason are to be members of a just community, they must rely on the reason of their superiors (590d-591a).

[130] Cf. Irwin (1977), 194-5; Cooper (1984), 16-17 with nn. 18-19.

desire, for honour (581ab),[131] and while in the best case *thumos* may regard as honourable that which reason identifies as conducive to the true good, in the case of the type dominated by *thumos*, reason will be compelled to regard as conducive to overall good that which contributes to the honour pursued by *thumos*.[132]

Therefore, says Plato, the *thumos* of the young must be educated to side with reason[133] and this education, in the process of habituation which begins from earliest childhood, precedes the training of reason itself.[134] A properly educated *thumos*, then, results from a thorough musical and literary education, the outcome of which is a character in which aesthetic discrimination between beautiful and ugly, *kalon* and *aischron*, is matched by a closely related moral discrimination (400c–403e). This character is ready to be harmonized with the aims of reason because the curriculum has been constructed on the basis of reason's apprehension of the true nature of moral and aesthetic beauty, but presumably Plato believes that the commitment to ideals of the honourable is fostered by education and habituation even where

[131] The personificatory language which attributes opinion and desire to the *thumoeides* thus succeeds in isolating the thumoeidic emotions as a group without totally divorcing them from either the appetitive or the intellectual capacities of the whole person. There is thus no need to hope (with White (1979), 129) that Pl.'s attribution of cognition to the lower parts is merely a *façon de parler*, or to despair (with Klosko (1986), 73) that Pl. allows the *thumos* its own opinions; since emotions and desires, as functions of rational beings, are intentional, they presuppose an element of cognition, and any discussion of emotion which saw the element of evaluation or the belief-component as extrinsic to the emotion itself would be unsatisfactory. On the strengths of Pl.'s 'personification' of the parts, see Annas (1981), 142–6; cf. Stocks (1915), 217; Moline (1978), 22–6; Price (1990), 260, 267–70. One might think, therefore, that Pl. has satisfied R. Robinson's (1971: 46–7) demand for an account in which the 'psychic parts' are merely collective names for the functions and events which they group together; but Pl.'s use of the principle of conflict in introducing tripartition seems designed to establish that the parts are, in some sense, separate 'entities' (Crombie (1962), 348; Penner (1971), 104–5; Stalley (1975), 116). It is this argument that is responsible for the initial impression that the two lower parts have no share of cognition whatever (see Annas (1981), 139; cf. White (1979), 241; Cooper (1984), 9).

[132] For the dominance of the *thumoeides*, see 550b. Even in this case reason could presumably conflict with *thumos*, if a given thumoeidic response were to conflict with a rational plan to maximize one's honour.

[133] 441a3, 441e–442a, 589b.

[134] At 441e–442a the education of the *thumos* is equated with the traditionally based education in *mousikē* which is outlined in Books 2–3; the education which will satisfy reason's desire to apprehend the truth is described in Book 7 (see 522ab on the inadequacy of the education which sufficed for the *thumos* in training the reason to the required degree). On the role of education in training the *thumos*, see O'Brien (1967), 142–3, 149–53; Gosling (1973), 76–9; Irwin (1977), 194–5, 201–3; Burnyeat (1980), 79–80; Klosko (1986), 120–6.

the ideals imparted are not the correct ones.[135] The importance of this education of the *thumos*, the *thumos* which comes to embody the ideal image of the self as a bearer of honour, is precisely that it has this aesthetic aspect, which suggests that the habituated subject rejects that which he has been habituated to regard as *aischron* in the sphere of acts with much the same instinctive revulsion as he would reject dissonant music.[136] The habituated *thumos*, then, presupposes the operation of *aidōs* as an instinctive revulsion *vis-à-vis* certain conduct rather than as mere fear of disapproval, and this sense of moral revulsion is, in fact, exactly what we find in the anger of Leontius.

The account of the *thumos* thus demonstrates considerable insight into the nature of the emotions involved. Its development through education and its role as a corrective and supportive force on the side of reason demonstrate Plato's recognition that a capacity of moral significance may be created by the acquisition of internalized ideals in the process of socialization. The insufficiency of the *thumos*, however, also conveys another salient fact about emotions—that in spite of their cognitive-evaluative content and even where they are attached to rational goals they are in themselves less than fully rational; that while emotional responses may be judged on rational criteria and criticized for irrationality, they need not immediately replicate a rational appraisal of the situation. One example of this is given by Plato, in Odysseus' hasty anger which would conflict with his rational plan for vengeance;[137] another might be that of Telemachus' *aidōs* in *Odyssey* 3, which persists even though its grounds are removed.[138] Plato's identification of the *thumoeides*, then, has much to tell us on the nature of *aidōs* that is illuminating; we learn with what kinds of response *aidōs* belongs, how it is acquired, and that it and the ideals from which it springs are indispensable to the proper moral development of the individual.

Disparagement of the *thumoeides* is therefore unwarranted.[139] Obvi-

[135] This is suggested by the remark at 441a3 that the *thumoeides* may be corrupted by bad upbringing.

[136] On the 'aesthetic' nature of the ordinary moral conscience in *Rep.*, see Crombie (1962), 285–8; cf. Irwin (1977), 202–3.

[137] Irwin (1977: 194) and Burnyeat (1980: 84) compare Arist. *EN* 1149ᵃ25–ᵇ2.

[138] Cf. 1.3.4 above.

[139] For the view that the *thumoeides* is awkwardly introduced into the scheme of tripartition or is determined by the political analogy alone, see Cornford (1912), 259–64; T. M. Robinson (1970), 44–6; Penner (1971), 96, 111–13; the significance of the *thumoeides* as a contribution to moral psychology is upheld by Cross and Woozley (1966), 120–3; O'Brien (1967), 165; Gosling (1973), 41–51; Irwin (1977), 193–5 with 328 n. 19; Annas (1981), 126–8; Mackenzie (1981), 168–9; Cooper (1984), 16–17.

ously, however, there are deficiencies. Plato is interested in those emotions which most contribute to the acquisition of moral standards, and it is a strength of his account of the *thumoeides* that he recognizes the extent to which such standards may be rooted in the habituated dispositions among which *aidōs* belongs. But his ethical interest means that he is not concerned to isolate emotion as a psychological category, and he offers no account of emotion in general. The *thumos* is certainly not coextensive with the category of emotion.[140]

Plato also seems to want to say both that the strong attachment to honour entailed by the *thumoeides* promotes fear of disgrace rather than commitment to internalized ideals and that the converse is true. In the anger of Leontius and in the good horse of the *Phaedrus* there is no suggestion of mere concern for others' opinions; rather the emotion involved expresses exactly the sort of distaste one would expect to result from a habituated disposition to regard some things as *kalon*, some as *aischron*.[141] Plato, moreover, often stresses that the education which develops the *thumos* and attaches it to the right ends creates a strong and deep-seated commitment to certain standards.[142] Elsewhere, however, to be concerned for honour seems largely to be concerned for the outward aspect of one's actions.[143] At 548b, for example, it is said that citizens of the first degenerate society, which is dominated by *thumos* and love of honour, will tend to do wrong in secret, because they have been educated by force rather than persuasion. This education which encourages fear of external sanctions rather than positive commitment is apparently due to the dominance of *philotimia* and the thumoeidic type in this society, which in turn is related to a failure to base education on the precepts of true reason and to an overvaluation of physical at the expense of literary/musical

---

[140] The doctrine of tripartition is rehearsed at 602c–605c, and applied in the sequel (605c–609b) to the emotions (admiration, grief, pity, etc.) which are excited by poetry and drama; because poetic representation aims at pleasure, all these emotions are sited in the appetitive part, and the *aischunē* which would prevent our behaving in the manner represented (605de, 606ac), should, it is implied, prevent our vicarious experience and enjoyment of the emotions being portrayed. Cf. Crombie (1962), 351; Fortenbaugh (1975), 37; Annas (1981), 131.

[141] Cf. 560a on the *aidōs* which temporarily restores equilibrium in the democratic youth.

[142] 396de, 402a, 413e, 429c, 430ab, 442bc.

[143] Cf. 604a: the good man who loses his son will, out of *aischunē*, restrain his grief before witnesses, but will not be ashamed to grieve in private. Here, however, the standard may be not 'to grieve is *aischron*' but 'to display one's grief in public is *aischron*', and so the passage need not imply that all cases of shame involve concern for the opinions of witnesses and no more.

education. It is not explained why education in this society should rest on force rather than persuasion, but probably the disciplinarian tendencies of Spartan society made it plausible to assume that such an education would be typically timocratic.[144] An education, then, which employs punitive and unjustified sanctions alone in inculcating values is liable, in Plato's view, to produce individuals who are concerned mainly for external sanctions. The other two points about the deficiencies of timocratic education seem to go hand in hand; the education system does not embody the aims of reason, and so *mousikē*, which does so much to create the harmonious character that is receptive to reason, is undervalued. Instead, emphasis is placed on athletic training, which presumably encourages the desire to win and excel over others.

Since, therefore, the timocratic state and the timocratic character are intended to illustrate what will become of *thumos* if it is allowed to dominate, it appears that Plato regards competitiveness and concern for appearances as attributes of the unfettered love of honour, a view doubtless strongly coloured by his understanding of honour-based values in his own and other contemporary societies.[145] Yet he himself has already shown that this is not the only possible model; properly developed, an ideal self-image can encompass co-operative as well as competitive aspects, and can operate with reference to internalized standards rather than simply to the opinions of other people. The model of the honour-based society, then, is an extreme one, created under conditions that are arbitrarily imposed, and the role of honour in that society is not the only one envisaged by Plato's account. If he believes that it is only in the perfect society that ideals of the

---

[144] Arist. (*(Pol.* 1270ᵇ34–5) notes that the enforced austerity of Spartan life gives rise to attempts to enjoy sensual pleasures in secret. This is clearly a case of external force rather than persuasion, since the austere life of the ordinary Spartiate is contrasted with the relative luxury of their rulers, the ephors.

[145] Pl. has, of course, manufactured the premisses of this argument in order to yield the kind of society he wishes to condemn; on the face of it, it seems in no way necessary that a society which is not structured in accordance with philosophical knowledge of the true good, but which rather sets great store by honour, should educate its members by force rather than persuasion, and neglect *mousikē* in favour of *gumnastikē*; why should those in charge of education not attempt to persuade their charges of the truth of their (erroneous) opinions as to how one should live? At 590e–591a Soc. appears to concede that the aim of law and education in existing states is to develop in their members a regulating faculty which may operate independently of outside control. Obviously, though, the degenerate societies of Book 8 do not and could not represent real societies; Pl. is therefore not committed to the view that a society which educates entirely by force rather than persuasion or whose values are enforced by external sanctions alone actually exists.

honourable may be internalized, it is here that he goes wrong,[146] but it must be stressed that the contrast between the tendency to be governed by external sanctions in the timocratic society and the commitment to standards one has made one's own in the ideal state is one between two different concepts of honour, not between honour and something else. There is thus no essential contradiction in his view of honour; the perfect society develops the love of honour correctly, deviant societies do so incorrectly.

Plato clearly does believe that affective attachments to ideals acquired from childhood onwards are insufficient to promote reliable adherence to proper standards of behaviour,[147] and without following him in his belief that reliably just behaviour may only be expected in a state ruled by those who have knowledge of the transcendental Good, we can agree—someone who merely has a sense that certain behaviour is 'not nice' may come to countenance that behaviour if it is somehow presented as attractive, and some sort of reflective moral outlook which sees reasons for one's moral likes and dislikes is clearly to be preferred.[148]

Paradoxically, however, it is the citizen who has an unreflective, 'aesthetic' commitment to certain standards of behaviour, rather than the philosopher-ruler, who appears most likely to be motivated by conscience in Plato's state; the philosopher eventually goes beyond the commitment to do *x* because it is right, and comes to see that to do *x* is more beneficial, for himself and for the whole community; because Plato identifies moral insight with the knowledge of the Good, the higher and more developed features of the moral conscience never come explicitly to the fore.[149] But though to expatiate on the developed moral conscience may be the mark of a deontological perspective, one need not be a deontologist to possess a conscience. Presumably the Platonically good man is one who used, as a younger man, to reject certain actions as intrinsically wrong, but who now,

[146] The *aidōs* of the democratic youth at 560a, mentioned above, seems to be a vestige of the quasi-aesthetic discriminatory faculty that is developed, in the Guardians and Auxiliaries, by *mousikē*, and thus indicates Pl.'s intuition that such a sense may also exist in a non-ideal society. (Since this *aidōs* seems to come from the oligarchic element in the youth's character, it perhaps arises from a mistaken exaltation of the ideal of wealth, but this does not negate the point that it represents residual attachment to an ideal rather than fear of disgrace.)
[147] Cf. also *Phdr.* 256c: those who are attached to honour rather than to transcendental beauty will tend to lapse in the control of their desires.
[148] Cf. Crombie (1962), 288.
[149] Cf. Gosling (1973), 266–70.

since he has true knowledge of the Good, knows that the good action benefits the soul and instantiates the Good, and thus that he has no reason to perform bad rather than good actions. Yet Plato's account leaves the way open for cases in which a person with knowledge of the Good and concern for the best part of himself has to strive to remain true to his vision, in much the same way as did Socrates in his determination to be just, and clearly this would, in certain circumstances, require behaviour which we should regard as typically expressive of the reflective moral conscience. So such a thing is possible on Plato's account. It is, however, on the less developed, instinctive conscience that he lays real emphasis; and here at least it is clear that most, if not all in a well-run state need properly trained dispositions,[150] and that an ordinary, unreflective moral conscience is a real possibility for most, if not all people.

To sum up: the basis for an affective form of conscience may be discerned in the functions of the *thumoeides*; it is here that *aidōs* is situated, and thus *aidōs* relates to the positive ideals that *thumos* involves. Therefore, even though neither the *Republic* nor the *Phaedrus* offers a specific or systematic account of the nature of *aidōs*, it is clear that its location in the *thumos* places Plato firmly on the side of those who recognize that *aidōs* involves more than fear of external sanctions. Plato's most deeply considered views on *aidōs* and the affects and dispositions among which it belongs thus offer little support for the position that ancient Greek society was a shame-culture, whether that term signifies a society whose moral and social standards are enforced by external sanctions alone or one in which the conditions for a form of conscience which assesses the intrinsic character of one's actions are not realized.

---

[150] Both the Guardians (cf. O'Brien (1967), 163; Crombie (1962), 98) and the Auxiliaries will undergo the affective training of Books 2 and 3; one would think that the harmony of the classes that is justice in the state entails that the emotional commitment to proper standards should extend even to the lowest class, but Pl. never explicitly discusses their education. This question, however, is distinct from the considerably more vexed one of whether all citizens in the just state would be just in the Platonic sense, or, if not, in what way they might be considered just at all; on this, see Kraut (1973); Vlastos (1973), 111–39; Williams (1973), 198–9, 203; Irwin (1977), 329–30 n. 26, 331 n. 29, 333 n. 33; Klosko (1982).

6.5. ARISTOTLE

6.5.1. *Aristotle on the Emotions*

Study of *aidōs* in Aristotle begins from the point at which our remarks on Plato left off, namely from the role and concept of the emotions in his philosophy. Here we are on somewhat firmer ground than with Plato, since Aristotle tells us both that he believes *aidōs* to be a *pathos*, an affect,[151] and, more or less, what he conceives such affects to be. *Pathos* is a term which Aristotle uses in several senses, senses which span the width of his interests from logic to biology, but the basic unity of the term is to be found in its reference to that which is non-abiding or non-essential, and in the associated connotation of passivity, of being affected. A *pathos* may be either an attribute (an affection) or an event/experience (an affect), but there remains a link between these two senses, in that, *qua* non-essential attribute, a *pathos* is typically that which is capable of change, of being otherwise, while, *qua* experience, a *pathos* is the process of change, of alteration (*alloiōsis*) itself.[152] Aristotle's view of the *pathē*, then, must be seen in the context of his general account of change (*kinēsis* or *metabolē*).[153]

---

[151] *EN* 1128ᵇ10-15, *EE* 1220ᵇ12-20; cf. *Rhet.* 1383ᵇ11-16 on *aischunē*.

[152] See *Metaph.* 1022ᵇ15-19, where the sense of *pathos* as quality is closely related to that of *pathos* as a process of alteration, in that the latter is defined as the actualization of the alteration which is possible in respect of the former (cf. 1020ᵇ8-12). It is clear from *DA* 403ᵃ25-7, *Rhet.* 1378ᵃ20-3 that the emotional *pathē* with which we are particularly concerned conform to this scheme (anger is a *kinēsis*, *DA* 403ᵃ26, *pathē* involve *metabolē* in their subjects, *Rhet.* 1378ᵃ20-1). *Alloiōsis* in general is defined as change in respect of quality (*Cat.* 15ᵇ11-12, *Phys.* 226ᵇ26-7), but no alteration is possible in respect of essential qualities (*Phys.* 226ᵃ27-9; see *Phys.* 5. 1-2 in general); the process of alteration that is a *pathos* is thus alteration in respect of a non-essential quality, and the qualities which are *pathē* are those that can be or have been affected by *pathos qua* alteration. At *Cat.* 9ᵃ28-10ᵃ10 Arist. introduces two kinds of 'affective quality', (*a*) qualities of things which produce *pathē* in other things, and (*b*) qualities of things which are produced by *pathē* in the things themselves, and the latter category seems to form a subset of that of *pathē* as non-essential qualities. In this passage a *pathos* (process of alteration) is said to give rise to an affective quality only if the relevant *pathos* is persistent or natural and produces a permanent or persistent condition in the patient; otherwise the patient is simply affected. By way of illustration a distinction is made between the man who reddens through shame (*to aischunthēnai*, 9ᵇ30-1) or pales through fear and the man who is ruddy or pale; shame and fear are both *pathē*, and so *alloiōseis*, but they produce no change from one quality to another; this need not mean, however, that they are not changes in respect of quality at all, but only that some changes in respect of quality are fleeting, interrupting the possession of an existing quality rather than causing change from one persisting quality to another.

[153] Clearly, however, we cannot go into Arist.'s views on change in any detail here; see, first, *Phys.* 3. 1-3; further, *Phys.* 3-8 in general and *Metaph.* 9; there is an excellent exegesis of Arist.'s analysis of change in Lear (1988), ch. 3.

Since it is with the *pathē* as processes of alteration that we are concerned, and with the operation of these processes in human beings, our focus narrows on to what Aristotle calls the *pathē* of the soul. But a further narrowing of focus is required, for the *pathē* of the soul cover everything that 'happens' to or in the soul (or rather, to the organism in so far as it is ensouled), and thus include changes such as those of perception. In the ethical works, however, *pathē* are typically what we should regard as emotions, and elsewhere, too, emotions constitute an important and relatively self-contained subset of *pathē* of the soul, and are consistently employed as typical examples of the class.[154] A case in point is *De Anima* I. 1, which considers the question of whether there is any *pathos* of the soul that is not also a *pathos* of the whole organism; the examples given of *pathē* are *thumos*, mildness, fear, pity, confidence (*tharsos*), joy, liking, and hating (403[a]17-18). These, like 'all' the *pathē* of the soul ([a]16, a less tentative formulation than 'most' in [a]6), are said to be 'with body' ([a]16-17), to be accompanied by a *pathos* in the body ([a]18-19).[155] But the bodily change is not all there is to the *pathos*; *pathē*

---

[154] Even where *pathos* is used in its narrowest of senses, however, the class signified by the term is wider than that of emotion, for it includes appetite (*epithumia*, *EN* 1105[b]21, *EE* 1220[b]13). Perhaps Arist. is to be commended for noticing similarities between appetite and emotions, e.g. in their intentionality or in their association with pleasure and pain, pursuit and avoidance, but his refusal or failure to isolate the emotions as such is still noteworthy. This is a point one could expect to see emphasized much more clearly in Fortenbaugh's account (1975), especially since he takes Pl. to task for failing to isolate the emotions as a class (e.g. p. 37). Arist. never gives a detailed account of how or whether that which holds good of the (typically emotional) examples he selects also holds good of non-emotional *pathē*, precisely because, in my view, he is more impressed by his perception of similarity across the entire range of the term *pathos* than by criteria which would establish the emotions as a distinct class, and thus demand an account of how the class of emotional *pathē* relates to that of *pathē* as a whole. On the nature of *pathē* as they affect Arist.'s ethical theory and the relationship with appetite and desire, cf. Engberg-Pedersen (1983), 129–42; Hutchinson (1986), 75–8.

[155] 'Most' implies reservations about the case of theoretical intellect, which may be a function of the soul that is separable from body (cf. 429[a]24–430[a]25). In this passage the *pathē* in question clearly cover everything that 'happens' in or to the soul; thus, though the examples given are exclusively emotional, what is said will hold good also of 'affections' such as sensory perception; cf. Hardie (1980), 74–5. The connection between, say, anger and sensory perception lies in the fact that both are caused by external stimuli and involve change in the recipient, a change which, in both cases, is caused by the transmission from outside of a 'form', an *eidos* or a *logos* (the *logos* of a thing is of its *eidos* and the *eidos* is a *logos* in the thing; we remember that *pathē* are *logoi enuloi* (enmattered forms/accounts), and that the dialectician's account of anger as the evaluation of a state of affairs gives the *eidos* or *logos*); on perception as the sense-faculty's adoption of the form of the sensible object, see *DA* 424[a]17–24, 425[a]23–4; note also *Phys.* 202[a]9–11, 257[b]10: *all* change occurs because form is introduced. Arist. presumably believes that perceiving the form of an external object is analogous to perceiving an external state of affairs in terms of a certain *logos*, a *logos* which is then instantiated in the perceiver.

are 'enmattered *logoi* (forms, essential accounts, etc.)' (^{a}25), and any definition of a *pathos* must take a form such as, 'Being angry is a sort of movement [or change; *kinēsis*] of a body of a particular kind or of a part or capacity of a body because of x and for the sake of y' (^{a}26-7). A proper definition, then, of an emotion such as anger must specify both the bodily change and the efficient and final causes. In the case of an emotion, though presumably not in that of absolutely every *pathos*, these last appear to be or to involve beliefs, since the notion of a correct definition is illustrated (403^{a}28-^{b}2) by means of the definitions of anger given by the natural scientist and the dialectician: the former calls it 'the boiling of the blood and hot stuff around the heart', and the latter 'the desire for retaliation', the one giving the matter and the other the form (*eidos*) and rationale (*logos*). It is to be noted that a simple combination of these two accounts does not yield a definition of the form Aristotle desiderates, but they do provide the material for such a definition; 'desire for retaliation' presupposes not only the goal of retaliation, but also the belief that an affront has occurred, and thus a combination of this with the biologist's account would yield the definition, 'Being angry is a boiling of the blood and hot stuff around the heart caused by the belief that one has been insulted and encompassing the desire for retaliation.' Aristotle's view is thus that an emotion like anger requires a belief as its efficient cause,[156] and this means not that the belief causes the emotion, which is the boiling of the blood and nothing else, but that the belief is in an important way part of the emotion (the relevant beliefs constitute the *logos*, and the emotion is an 'enmattered *logos*'). An account of an emotion which did not specify its belief-content would therefore be deficient; equally, however, a proper account must accommodate the fact that emotions involve bodily change, indeed cannot, it seems, occur without bodily change (403^{b}2-3).[157]

[156] Cf. *Top.* 151^{a}16-17 (the pain of anger is caused by the belief that one has been insulted; cf. 156^{a}31-3), *Rhet.* 1378^{a}30-2; Fortenbaugh (1975), 11-15; (1979), 144-6; Sherman (1989), 169-71. Thinking, imagination, and sense-perception, themselves enmattered and thus involving bodily change, appear as causes of bodily feelings also at *MA* 701^{b}16-22, 703^{b}18-20, *DA* 432^{b}26-433^{a}1 (cf. Furley (1977), 56-9; M. C. Nussbaum (1978), 146-58, 382).

[157] It is impossible that, in the account of anger in *DA*, 'desire for retaliation' is to be regarded as wholly reducible to 'the boiling of the blood and hot stuff around the heart', any more than, for Arist., form is reducible to matter (Sorabji (1979), 55; Guthrie, vi. 281). Clearly, the purely physical explanation of what goes on in anger does not suffice, and the psychological explanation provides a necessary 'something else'. This 'something else', however, is presumably also 'with body', since there is no *pathos* of the soul (excluding those involved in the problematic activity of pure intellect) that is not with body. Thus

This procedure for the definition of an emotion is followed by Aristotle in his other works. The definition of *pathē* in the *Rhetoric* ($1378^{a}19\text{-}26$) adumbrates the physical aspect by mentioning pleasure and pain,[158] but also makes it clear that an adequate account, particularly in rhetorical theory, where it is a matter of arousing emotions and changing people's minds, must also include the objects of the emotion (e.g. the kind of people against whom one might feel anger) and its grounds.[159] An emotion such as anger, then, cannot be aroused without the implanting of certain beliefs; once these have been implanted, a physical change presumably takes place, and the desire for retaliation which is specified as part of anger (at $1378^{a}30$ in the immediate context) may be enlisted in support of the speaker's case. The subsequent definitions of particular emotions follow this pattern, giving both summary indications of the physical changes (in terms of 'pain', 'disturbance', etc.) and the belief which is the emotion's cause (together with any desire for a goal that may be relevant).[160] Typical is the definition of *aischunē* ($1383^{b}12$ ff.): *aischunē* is given as 'a kind of pain or disturbance concerning those evils (ills, misfortunes) which seem to lead to ill-repute, whether they be present, past, or future' ($^{b}12\text{-}14$), its opposite, *anaischuntia*, being 'a kind of contempt or indifference with regard to the same things' ($^{b}14\text{-}15$); and the definition is followed up by an account of the conditions of *aischunē*: first in terms of the acts or states of affairs which are its impersonal

the belief that causes the bodily change and the desire that is involved in (say) anger will also be enmattered and must depend on physical processes, but they will not be reducible to those physical terms which characterize the bodily change that is typically associated with the emotion itself (see n. 156 above). For a wider discussion of the issues raised by Arist.'s application of the distinction between form and matter to the relationship between body and soul, see the articles by Kahn, Barnes, and Sorabji (all repr. (1979) in *Articles on Aristotle*, iv); Hardie (1980), 74-93; Guthrie, vi. 279-85, 307-8; Charles (1984), 213-43; Irwin (1988), 279-302.

[158] For pleasure and pain as part of the definition of *pathē* in so far as they bear on ethics and politics, cf. *EN* $1105^{b}21\text{-}3$, *EE* $1220^{b}12\text{-}14$. The *EE* passage qualifies the pleasure or pain as 'perceptual'; this relates to the status of *pathē* as *alloiōseis*, for, according to *Phys.* 7. 3, *alloiōseis* occur in the part of the soul that perceives (*to aisthētikon meros*) and involve being affected (*paschein*) by sensible objects ($245^{b}3\text{-}5$, $248^{a}6\text{-}9$), and bodily pleasure and pain are themselves *alloiōseis* of the perceptual part which depend on perception or sensation ($247^{a}7\text{-}18$); cf. Dirlmeier (1963), 243, and Woods (1982), 110-11, on *EE* $1220^{b}14$.

[159] Cf. Fortenbaugh (1979), 141-2; Sherman (1989), 169-70.

[160] e.g. $1378^{a}30\text{-}2$ (anger), $1382^{a}21\text{-}2$ (fear), $1385^{b}13\text{-}16$ (pity), etc.; cf. *Top.* $127^{b}30\text{-}2$ (a recognition that both pain and the belief that one has been insulted are offered as definitions of anger). On Arist.'s application of his psychophysical view of emotion in *EN*, see Hardie (1980), 76.

objects (ἃ αἰσχύνονται, generally misdeeds, faults, or shortcomings, 1383ᵇ18–1384ᵃ21),[161] and secondly in terms of the nature and qualities of the audience that forms the focus of the 'mental picture (*phantasia*) of ill-repute' that *aischunē* is said to be (1384ᵃ22–1385ᵃ13; generally those whose opinion one values or fears for whatever reason). *Aischunē*, then, is not merely a form of pain or disturbance; to exist at all it requires beliefs about acts or states of affairs pertaining to oneself and about the character and response of any audience.[162]

Aristotle is therefore quite clear that emotions involve cognition, and that some belief is generally constitutive of the emotion. Yet it also seems that an emotion is properly defined in terms of bodily change as well, and this not merely in the sense that some physical (biochemical, electrical, or whatever) process underlies the belief, but that the *pathos* properly so called encompasses a characteristic bodily change. Aristotle's account of those *pathē* that we should regard as emotions thus gives priority to occurrence, indeed only an occurrent emotion would qualify as a *pathos*.[163] This indicates another way in which Aristotle's class of *pathē* cannot without further ado be assimilated to the class of emotion, and has important consequences for his conception of *aidōs*.

6.5.2. *Emotional Dispositions*

If we think about it, we recognize dispositional and occurrent senses of emotion-words; even if we believe that the focal meaning of emotion-words ultimately presupposes occurrence, we none the less acknowledge that the words can be used in a variety of ways which imply no bodily change or physical symptoms. One typical non-occurrent use of an emotion-word involves the reference to dispositions towards the occurrent emotion with no implication that the latter is actually being experienced (for example, 'John is afraid of the dark'), but we also noted the existence of second-order dispositions (for example, 'John is a timid person'), which involve the possession of established traits of

---

[161] For each of these, the person subject to the emotion will believe that the given act or state of affairs pertains to him and that that act or state of affairs is *aischron*, either in his own eyes or in those of others whose opinion he values (1383ᵇ16–18).

[162] The orator will thus apply his knowledge of the nature and conditions of *aischunē* by constructing scenarios by means of which he can arouse the *aischunē* of his audience or portray *aischunē* or its absence in those whose conduct he wishes to characterize.

[163] Cf. *EN* 1106ᵃ4–6. Hence the interest shown in classifying the physical symptoms of emotions, including *aidōs* etc., in both genuine and spurious works (*Cat.* 9ᵇ30–2, *Prob.* 957ᵃ9–17, 960ᵃ36–ᵇ7, *Physiog.* 812ᵃ30–3, fr. 761 Gigon).

character implying marked tendencies towards a given emotion.[164]
The significance of this classification for our purposes, as we have
noted, is that *aidōs* is found in all three senses, the same concept
denoting both the occurrent affect and the two forms of disposition.

The conceptual distinction between disposition and occurrence is,
of course, far from foreign to Aristotle. He has a developed terminology which makes similar distinctions: a *pathos* is an affect, and is
always occurrent, but behind *pathē* lie capacities (*dunameis*), and
settled states (*hexeis*), both of which may involve some kind of non-
occurrent disposition towards the various emotions.[165]

Aristotle's threefold classification of *pathē*, *dunameis*, and *hexeis*,
however, clearly does not simply overlap with that in terms of
occurrent affects, first-order, and second-order dispositions; Aristotle,
in fact, never explicitly acknowledges the existence of the first-order
disposition, never shows himself aware that one can, for example, be
afraid without feeling afraid in the sense of experiencing the characteristic bodily change. There should, however, be a place in Aristotle's
scheme for the second-order disposition, but it is not immediately
clear whether he would regard such a disposition as a *dunamis* or as a
hexis, or as in some cases one and in some the other.

6.5.3. Hexeis

The criteria which determine what it is to be a *hexis* are more readily
apparent and more obviously self-consistent than those for *dunameis*,
so we shall consider these first.[166] A *hexis* is a kind of disposition
(*diathesis*),[167] one which is long-lasting and hard to change,[168] and one
which is, as Hutchinson puts it, 'evaluatively significant',[169] that is, one
who possesses a *hexis* (of character) is either well or badly off, well or
badly disposed, with regard to a particular *pathos*.[170] Thus far, the class

[164] See Introd. 0.2 above.
[165] On *dunameis* and *hexeis* as qualities (*poiotētes*), distinct from *pathē*, which are not
qualities, but may imply affective qualities, see *Cat.* 8ᵇ25–10ᵃ10, with the discussion of
Ackrill (1963), 104–7. According to *EN* 1105ᵇ19–28, *pathē*, *dunameis*, and *hexeis* are 'the
three things that come to be in the soul' (cf. *EE* 1220ᵇ7–20, *MM* 1186ᵃ9–19); for a
detailed account of the relationship between *pathē*, *dunameis*, and *hexeis* in Arist.'s theory
of virtue, see D. S. Hutchinson (1986).
[166] There is a detailed exegesis of what it is to be a *hexis* in D. S. Hutchinson (1986:
ch. 2).   [167] *Cat.* 9ᵃ10–13.
[168] *Cat.* 8ᵇ27–9ᵃ10.   [169] D. S. Hutchinson (1986).
[170] *Met.* 1022ᵇ10–12, *EN* 1105ᵇ25–6, *MM* 1186ᵃ16–17; cf. the different form of expression (which, however, comes ultimately to the same thing) in *EE* 1220ᵇ9–10, 18–19.

of *hexis* seems a likely candidate for overlap with that of second-order dispositions, and we do find that dispositions which, in our scheme, are of the second order appear to be, in Aristotle's terminology, *hexeis*.[171] There is, however, one crucial way in which Aristotle's *hexeis* involve more than our second-order dispositions. The two classes might seem to overlap closely if we consider a *hexis* simply as a matter of being well or ill disposed with regard to a particular emotion, because, for us, second-order dispositions (timidity, irascibility, the disposition to manifest pity or sympathy, etc.), since they indicate marked tendencies with regard to the relevant emotions, imply that their possessor displays these qualities to a greater degree than is usual, and thus where the quality is a valued one we will see the individual as well disposed, and where it is a negative one we will see him or her as badly disposed. There are clearly many degrees of being well or badly disposed, and we might imagine that there are degrees of good and bad in *hexeis* too; Aristotle often, for example, refers to health as a *hexis* (not, obviously, a *hexis* of character, and so not one of the *hexeis* with which we are concerned),[172] and clearly there can be degrees of good or ill health, involving several intermediary stages between excellent or perfect health and utterly poor health; we might thus expect some *hexeis* to be excellences (*aretai*), some to be deficiencies (*kakiai*), and some to be neither, or intermediate between the two. This, however, is precisely what Aristotle does not admit; all *hexeis* are either perfections, and so *aretai*, or departures from perfection, and so *kakiai*; there is no third possibility, no intermediate stage between the two.[173] Thus, when we read the ethical treatises and recognize that the excellences of character constitute a sub-class of *hexeis* of character, we need to guard against the assumption that *hexeis* of character can cover evaluatively significant dispositions which are neither *aretai* nor *kakiai*; if something is neither an *aretē* nor a *kakia*, then it is not a *hexis*.[174]

[171] e.g. irascibility (*orgilotēs*) a defect of character in all three ethical treatises, and so necessarily a *hexis* (*EN* 1108ᵃ7-8, 1125ᵇ29, 1126ᵃ13-18, *EE* 1220ᵇ38, 1221ᵃ15-16, 1231ᵇ5-26, *MM* 1186ᵃ17-18, 1191ᵇ23-38). The *MM* contains Aristotelian doctrine on any account, whether it is a later abridgement of one or other of the ethical treatises, a student's notes on *EE* (Kenny (1978), 220), or an early work by Arist. himself (Dirlmeier (1964), *passim*; cf. the hypothesis of Cooper (1973), that the *MM* is someone's notes on an updated version of an early work).

[172] e.g. *Metaph.* 1022ᵇ12, *EN* 1129ᵃ15.

[173] *Phys.* 246ᵃ11-17; for *aretē* as perfection (*teleiōsis*, ᵃ13), cf. *Metaph.* 1021ᵇ14-23, with D. S. Hutchinson (1986), 20-35, esp. 20-1.

[174] It might be thought that Arist.'s frequent distinction between simple performance of the thing's function and excellent performance of its function (which is therefore the function of its excellence, e.g. *EN* 1098ᵃ8-12, 1106ᵃ15-24, 1139ᵃ15-17, *EE* 1218ᵇ37-

Thus *hexeis* are not simply settled states of character in the same way as our second-order dispositions, for we would not accept that these latter are in themselves necessarily excellences (or virtues) or deficiencies (vices). Since Aristotle's ethical *hexeis* are either excellences or defects of character, they imply all that goes with his concept of excellence, and thus involve more than the simple disposition to experience emotion E to a degree significant enough to require comment; rather they involve coping with emotions rightly or wrongly, in accordance with the doctrines of the mean and of practical reason. Thus, while some *hexeis* resemble second-order dispositions (e.g. irascibility, a defect), most do not; in our terms, the second-order disposition with regard to fear is timidity, the trait of character which explains one's tendency to experience fear more than usual, but the corresponding *hexis* in Aristotle's scheme is not timidity but cowardice, and one can be timid without being a coward.[175] Cowardice,

1219^{a}8, 1219^{a}19–28) leaves room for a degree of indifference between goodness and badness (e.g. the description of excellence as the best *hexis* at *EN* 1139^{a}15-17 and *EE* 1218^{b}38–1219^{a}1, 32-3 appears to leave room for degrees of goodness in *hexeis* between best and worst; cf. *EE* 1219^{a}6-8), but if excellence is perfection then anything less than excellence is clearly a defect. A more serious case for the existence of intermediates between excellence and defect, however, can be made with reference to the qualities of *enkrateia* (continence, self-control) and *akrasia* (incontinence, weakness of will) which are intermediate between *sōphrosunē* (an excellence) and *akolasia* (licentiousness, a *kakia*) (see *EN* 1150^{b}29–1151^{a}28; cf. *MM* 1202^{b}38–1203^{a}29, 1203^{b}12–1204^{a}18); of these, the former is a good *hexis* (1151^{a}27, ^{b}28), but not an *aretē* (1145^{a}18; cf. 1128^{b}33-4), and the latter a bad (1151^{a}28, ^{b}29), a *kakia* only in a qualified sense (1151^{a}5-11). On the other hand, the guarded expression which introduces the *EN*'s discussion (where *kakia* and *askrasia* are distinguished as 'things to do with character that are to be avoided', *aretē* and *enkrateia* distinguished as their contraries, 1145^{a}16-18) is replaced in the *MM* by a formulation which calls *enkrateia* and *akrasia aretē* and *kakia* respectively (1200^{a}37–^{b}2), albeit *aretē* and *kakia* of an unusual and anomalous kind; similarly *enkrateia* is an *aretē* at *EE* 1223^{b}11-12; these are perhaps mere slips or loose expressions, but there may also be a notion that *enkrateia* can be an *aretē* in a reduced or qualified sense. Thus we have a good *hexis* (perhaps even an *aretē* of a sort) stopping short of perfection (although any *hexis* short of perfection is supposed to be a *kakia*) and a bad which none the less is better than absolute *kakia*. There is definitely a problem here; but Arist. could presumably resolve it by arguing that, relative to the excellence of *sōphrosunē*, both *enkrateia* and *akrasia* are *kakiai*, but that some *kakiai* are relatively good (even, relative to other *kakiai*, close or analogous to *aretai*) while others, though bad, are not as bad as the very worst; this comes to much the same as arguing that *aretē* and *kakia* can be used in both absolute and qualified senses, and thus accommodates the tendency to speak of *enkrateia* as an *aretē*. Nevertheless, there are signs that Arist. has not entirely worked out how these intermediate qualities conform to his accounts of what it is to be a *hexis*.

[175] Arist. would deny that a timid person could be courageous (since such a person feels more fear than is right); timidity would thus preclude excellence, and would presumably be a defect, but, clearly, timidity and cowardice, even in Aristotelian terms, are not the same defect.

one of a trio of *hexeis* which involve right and wrong ways of being disposed to fear, is further removed from the simple disposition to experience fear that is timidity, and, although both may be defects of character, cowardice signifies, in a way which timidity does not, a failure to organize one's responses to fear-inducing situations in accordance with one's appreciation of the nature of the good life. Second-order dispositions, therefore, are not to be identified wholesale with Aristotelian *hexeis*, but presuppose a rather different, less teleological way of classifying traits of character. We have seen that there exists, quite regularly, a second-order disposition *vis-à-vis aidōs*, a disposition which is itself normally called *aidōs*; but it will not do to assume that, simply because such a disposition exists, it must be an Aristotelian *hexis*; *aidōs* will have to satisfy other criteria if it is to be a *hexis*.

6.5.4. Dunameis

If the *pathē* which are emotions are kinds of change, then, like all forms of change, they require a *dunamis*, the potentiality which is actualized in the change. This is the basic sense of *dunamis* for Aristotle, and this basic sense persists in all the various applications of the term; though *dunamis* can be used in a number of special senses, all *dunameis* are capacities for the actualization of activities or experiences. These capacities, however, can exist at different levels and take on different forms; that which is a capacity in one respect may be an actualization (of a capacity) in another,[176] and thus there exist different levels of *dunamis*, from simple to developed potential.[177] Aristotle, therefore, shows himself aware that the capacities of a human being take different forms and come to be in different ways—some are innate potentialities, some are acquired by practice or habit, and some are learned.[178]

The *De Anima* has an important discussion of the degrees of potentiality and actuality;[179] the actualization of a simple potentiality can itself be a capacity for activity, and one can think of this situation in terms either of two levels of actualization or of two levels of potentiality: knowledge, for example, is an actualization of the capacity

---

[176] *Phys.* 201ᵃ19-22.
[177] On the relativity of potentiality and actuality, see (from different perspectives) Irwin (1988), 230-1, 236, and Lear (1988), 103-6, 118-19.
[178] *Metaph.* 1047ᵇ31-5.
[179] See *DA* 412ᵃ10-11, 22-8, 417ᵃ21-9.

to acquire knowledge,[180] and a capacity for the activity of using knowledge;[181] it is a first-level actualization (the actualization of a first-level capacity) and a second-level capacity (a capacity for the second-level actualization). One important upshot of this is that a *hexis* (for such is knowledge)[182] can be a *dunamis*,[183] and this is important because, in the ethical treatises where *hexeis, dunameis,* and *pathē* are 'the three things which come to be in the soul', *hexeis* are distinguished from *dunameis*.[184] This, therefore, does not mean that *dunameis* involve potentiality while *hexeis* do not, but must mean that, in the ethical works, *dunamis* refers to a particular kind of capacity. The term presumably does not denote the kind of capacity which one learns as one does a skill or an organized body of knowledge (for this would hardly be a *dunamis* in respect of emotional *pathē*), so the remaining possibilities are that it refers to (*a*) nothing more than the potentiality to experience a given emotion which all normal human beings presumably have at birth by virtue of their being the kind of creature they are, (*b*) some form of innate capacity to manifest a particular emotion to a particular degree, or (*c*) a developed and acquired capacity which proceeds from either or both of the other two and which would answer quite closely to a second-order disposition *vis-à-vis* a particular emotion.

The *Eudemian Ethics* offers some indication that the *dunamis* which is relative to *aidōs* will correspond to our second-order disposition of *aidōs* as a trait of character (1220[b]6–20):

We must say, then, in accordance with what in the soul characters become of a given kind.[185] They do so in accordance with the *dunameis* [capacities] for feelings [*pathēmata*], according to which people are described as *pathētikoi*, and in accordance with the *hexeis*, according to which people are said to be in a certain condition with respect to those feelings,[186] by virtue of their experi-

---

[180] 412[a]23–7 (knowledge, like the soul, is a first actuality).

[181] 417[a]27–8, [a]30–[b]2, [b]5–7.

[182] As is evident from 417[b]16—acquiring knowledge is change towards acquisition of a *hexis* and of one's nature.

[183] This emerges also from *EN* 1103[a]26–34, which, arguing that the virtues do not arise by nature (since in the case of what is by nature we do not acquire the capacity by performing the activity), indicates that in the case of the *aretai* (which are, of course, *hexeis*) we do acquire a capacity through repeated performance of the appropriate actions.

[184] See *EN* 1106[a]6–12, *EE* 1220[b]7–10, 16–20, *MM* 1186[a]14–17.

[185] Translating ποῖ᾽ ἄττα (MSS) rather than ποιότης τὰ (Spengel).

[186] The words 'in a certain condition' translate the supplement πως ἔχειν proposed by D. S. Hutchinson (1986: 126), comparing *EN* 1105[b]25–6 (ἔχειν was already suggested by Spengel, but, if that was intended to construe with the subsequent πως, we should have a

encing them in a certain way or being unaffected [*apatheis*]. There follows the division, found in the finished discussions [?], of the *pathēmata*, the *dunameis*, and the *hexeis*.[187] By *pathē* I mean such things as *thumos*, fear, *aidōs*, and appetite, in general all those things which are in themselves usually attended by perceptual pleasure or pain. With respect to these there is no quality, one just experiences them, but there is quality in respect of *dunameis*. I mean by *dunameis*[188] the things according to which those who actualize [i.e. those who possess the *dunameis* and manifest the affects] are described in terms of the *pathē*,[189] as, for example, irascible, insensitive, lustful, *aischuntēlos*, or *anaischuntos*. *Hexeis* are what are responsible for the occurrence of these *pathē* in accordance with reason or otherwise, such as bravery, *sōphrosunē*, cowardice, licentiousness.

This passage strongly suggests that *dunameis* in respect of *pathē* are developed tendencies towards the particular emotions; 'being *aischuntēlos*' is the *dunamis* relative to *aidōs*, and to be *aischuntēlos* is to be particularly prone to manifest *aidōs*. Here, to possess a *dunamis* and so to be *pathētikos* is apparently to be liable or prone to experience the particular emotion, rather than simply to be capable of experiencing it. In the other two ethical treatises, however, *dunameis* in respect of *pathē* are defined in terms of ability to manifest an emotion, rather than tendency to manifest it to a significant degree;[190] both agree with the *Eudemian Ethics* that by virtue of one's possession of a *dunamis* one is called *pathētikos*, but to be *pathētikos* is explained in terms of possession of a capacity, rather than with reference to the fact that those who are *pathētikoi* are qualified by epithets derived from the names of the *pathē*. In the Nicomachean context, furthermore, the capacity to manifest a particular *pathos* is regarded as innate.[191] The term *dunamis*

rather odd word order). This solution seems to me preferable to Russell's deletion of τῷ, adopted by Walzer and Mingay (OCT). Dirlmeier (1963: 242) believes the text can stand, but τῷ πάσχειν πως ἢ ἀπαθεῖς εἶναι most likely forms one instrumental phrase, and thus without the supplement the MSS text does not divulge *what* people are said to be in respect of these *pathē*.

[187] On the meaning of this sentence, see Dirlmeier (1962), 35–43; but the view of D. S. Hutchinson (1986: 126), that it is a marginal comment and should be deleted, is attractive.

[188] Omitting τὰς, with Susemihl.

[189] There is no need to transpose οἱ to precede κατὰ τὰ πάθη (Ross and Walzer *apud* Woods (1982), 205); the statement that οἱ ἐνεργοῦντες are called after the *pathē* makes good sense, given that a list of adjectives derived from the names of the *pathē* follows.

[190] *EN* 1105^b23–5 and *MM* 1186^a14–16, where the *EE*'s expression, '*dunameis* are the things in respect of which we are described as *pathētikoi*', is expanded by, 'e.g. according to which we are described as capable of feeling anger, pain, or pity'. Note that at *EN* 1106^a7–8 these *dunameis* are explicitly equated with 'simple ability to be affected' (τῷ δύνασθαι πάσχειν ἁπλῶς).

[191] *EN* 1106^a9–10.

thus appears to span two senses in which one might be said to be capable of manifesting an affect: that of simple potentiality, according to which a person is capable of manifesting an emotion or acquiring a character trait, and that of developed capacity, according to which one who is not actually experiencing an emotion may be characterized in terms of that emotion as being prone to manifesting it.

It might seem that Aristotle is employing the former sense in the Nicomachean passage and the latter in the Eudemian, with no implication that the two are the same;[192] the Eudemian passage, after all, says nothing about *dunameis* for *pathē* being natural or innate, and employs terms which signify character traits (*orgilos, aischuntēlos, anaischuntos*, etc.) where the *Nicomachean Ethics* and the *Magna Moralia* explain 'being *pathētikos*' in terms of simple ability. Nevertheless, all the evidence suggests that the Eudemian and Nicomachean accounts agree that the *dunameis* that have to do with *pathē* are innate. The former, unlike the latter, has, following its treatment of the individual excellences of character and prior to its discussion of justice, a reference to 'natural excellence' (introduced in the context of the explanation of why some means, including *aidōs*, are not *aretai*). *Aidōs*, like the other non-virtuous means, is a *pathos* (1234ª27), and because such *pathē* are 'natural' (*phusika*), they contribute to the natural excellences (ª27–8), *aidōs* contributing to the natural excellence of *sōphrosunē* (ª32).[193]

Now, 'natural' does not necessarily mean 'innate', for what is natural may be that which grows naturally as well as that which is present from the beginning, yet there is a discussion of natural virtue also in Book 6 of the Nicomachean treatise (one of the 'common books' shared by the Nicomachean and the Eudemian versions), and here the natural virtues are explicitly said to be present in us from birth.[194] There is a reference forward in *Eudemian Ethics* 3 to a subsequent discussion of natural and full excellence, and there must be a certain presumption that that reference is to the passage of the common book.[195]

[192] So Woods (1982: 109) and, apparently, D. S. Hutchinson (1986: 115–16), both assuming that, *qua* traits of character, the *EE*'s *dunameis* are acquired.

[193] That *aidōs* contributes to the natural virtue of *sōphrosunē* also correlates with the relative positions of *aidōs* (a *pathos*), 'being *aischuntēlos*' (a *dunamis*), and *sōphrosunē* (a *hexis*) at 1220ᵇ12–20. The natural virtue of *sōphrosunē*, of course, is distinct from *sōphrosunē* itself (as being without *phronēsis*), but if *aidōs* contributes to *sōphrosunē qua* natural virtue, it will also contribute to full *sōphrosunē*.

[194] See *EN* 1144ᵇ1–17, esp. 4–6 'right from birth'.

[195] Kenny (1978: 50–9) considers these forward references in the early books of *EE/EN* which are fulfilled in the common books, and concludes that they strongly suggest a Eudemian origin for the latter.

If it is the position of the *Eudemian Ethics* that the natural virtues are in fact innate, then anything which contributes to a natural virtue will also be innate, and the *Eudemian Ethics* will thus be advocating the view that emotions such as *aidōs* are biologically given; this is a view held by some modern psychologists,[196] but one which cannot be accommodated in a conception of emotions as socio-cultural constructs which, while they do include the biologically given, also depend on evaluative categories which must be acquired during socialization. Since the latter appears to me to be the correct view of emotion, it follows that I regard any statement that *aidōs* is innate as untenable.

A statement that *aidōs* the *pathos* is innate, however, while it does require that, in some sense, a *dunamis* for *aidōs* should also be innate, does not actually require that the *dunamis* by virtue of which one is called *aischuntēlos* be innate—it may be an acquired capacity to experience an innate effect to a greater degree than is normal.[197] Yet, if the common book, *Nicomachean Ethics* 6, or that part of it which deals with natural excellences, does belong with *Eudemian Ethics* 3, then there is no reason to deny that such *dunameis* are regarded as innate, for in that place even *hexeis* such as justice, *sōphrosunē*, and bravery are regarded as, in some sense, present from birth.[198] There must, in any case, be a strong presumption that, in all three ethical treatises, the *dunameis* which merit consideration as qualities of character are those which furnish the natural capacity to acquire excellence of character which all three recognize.

There is thus no reason to deny that both the *Eudemian* and the *Nicomachean Ethics* regard the *dunameis* which are related to *pathē* as innate. Thus far, then, the two treatises may be seen as consistent. If, however, they are wholly consistent, and nothing which is said of a *dunamis* in one is to be regarded as denied or modified by the other,

---

[196] Such claims usually rest on the observation of characteristically emotional behaviour patterns and responses (e.g. facial expressions) in the very young; see, e.g., Izard (1977), 408, who claims that infants are capable of shame from the age of 4–5 months; but while these responses may be incorporated in the developed syndromes which constitute emotions, they are not the emotions themselves. See, e.g., Averill (1980), 39, 58, 63.

[197] Note, however, that the statement of *EE* 1234^{a}26–8, that all the questionable means are *pathē* and that, since they are natural, they conduce to natural excellence, implies that *anaischuntia* (a *dunamis* at 1220^{b}18, and one extreme in the triad in which *aidōs* is a mean) is also natural. (It remains puzzling how a *pathos* can be a mean, and how such a *pathos* can have a contrary which is a *dunamis*; see text below.)

[198] *EN* 1144^{b}4–6, 8–9 (*hexeis*).

then we are faced with some problems. The Nicomachean treatise says, explicitly, that the relevant *dunameis* are the qualities by virtue of which we are *capable* of experiencing the emotions, and that these are innate, while the Eudemian says that it is by virtue of our possession of these *dunameis* that we are qualified as irascible, *aischuntēlos*, or *anaischuntos*. If these statements are to be reconciled at their face value, then it seems that Aristotle asumes that the capacity to manifest the emotions that human beings are born with (or perhaps rather the affective tendencies according to which an infant may be described as, say, placid or bad-tempered) are the same as the developed or acquired capacities towards the emotions which are present in the characters of adults. But while we might agree that the capacity to manifest an emotion may be innate, or that all human beings are initially capable of manifesting the emotions (although perhaps to different degrees), we surely do not believe that we call a person irascible because that person is naturally capable of feeling anger, or shameless because he or she is by nature incapable of feeling shame. Rather these adjectives indicate that the person is liable or not liable to the particular emotion in a degree that exceeds or falls short of the norm. If, therefore, the *dunamis* of the Nicomachean treatise, which renders us capable of experiencing a particular emotion, is the same as that of the Eudemian, by virtue of which we are called irascible etc., then Aristotle does not distinguish either between the capacity to feel anger possessed by the irascible and the mild-mannered alike, and the capacity to feel anger more than is normal that is characteristic of the irascible person, or between the innate bashfulness, which might plausibly be attributed to a shy individual, and the developed capacity to discern and categorize certain things as *aischron*, which may draw on and develop the innate tendency, but cannot be identified with it. One's initial bashfulness may contribute to one's acquisition of a sense of shame, but it does not entirely duplicate it.

I do not think Aristotle should be saddled with these difficulties. That he should be unable to distinguish between bare potentiality, innate capacity, and acquired capacity is wholly implausible given the discussion of degrees of potentiality in the *De Anima* and the recognition of innate, habituated, and learned capacities in the *Metaphysics*.[199] The possibilities, then, are three: (*a*) all three ethical

[199] *DA* 412ª10-11, 22-8, 417ª21-9, *Metaph.* 1047ᵇ31-5 (cited above, nn. 178-81). We note, too, that the approach of the *EN* to innate and acquired potential, and to degrees of potentiality, is wholly compatible with the distinctions made in the *DA* and *Metaph.*;

treatises are consistent, and regard significant character traits such as shamelessness as innate; the expression of the Nicomachean version and of the *Magna Moralia*, which appears to refer to capacity rather than tendency in fact refers to the latter. This, however, is unlikely, since the difference between the explanations '*dunameis* are those things by virtue of which we are called, for example, irascible . . .', and '*dunameis* are those things by virtue of which we are described as capable of experiencing the emotions' is quite marked, and offers little indication that these expressions are interchangeable. That *dunameis* are expressly equated with simple ability to undergo a *pathos* (*EN* 1106ᵃ7–8) seems to rule this interpretation out.

A second possibility (*b*) is that all three are consistent, but what they regard as innate are mere impulses or affective tendencies (*hormai*, to use the expression of the *Magna Moralia*).²⁰⁰ In this case the *dunameis* of the *Eudemian Ethics*, including *anaischuntia* and 'being *aischuntēlos*', will refer not to these qualities as developed states of character but only to the germ of their presence in children, and the discussion of natural excellences in *Eudemian Ethics* 3 and *Nicomachean Ethics* 6 (*Eudemian Ethics* 5) will be a discussion of qualities which approximate to the true excellences in an attenuated or analogous sense; the 'natural excellences' will involve little more than the qualities by virtue of which, according to *Nicomachean Ethics* 2. 1, we are by nature able to acquire the virtues—they themselves will be natural *dunameis*.²⁰¹ This approach is more hopeful, since the discussion of natural excellence in the common book clearly can be harmonized either with the view of the *Eudemian Ethics* that traits such as *anaischuntia* are *dunameis* (*dunameis* being innate) or with the view of the *Nicomachean Ethics* that our innate capacities to acquire the virtues consist of much more limited tendencies.²⁰² If we follow the latter course, regarding the sense in which we can be said to possess justice, *sōphrosunē*, and the rest from birth as attenuated or figurative (adducing the *Magna Moralia* as evidence for the view that these are to be considered as mere *hormai*),

---

see *EN* 1103ᵃ18–ᵇ25 on acquiring a *hexis* (a form of potentiality *vis-à-vis* the *energeia* of using one's *hexis*) by habituation (a process which must rely on an anterior potentiality, such as the potentiality for acquiring the excellences, *EN* 1103ᵃ24–5).

²⁰⁰ *MM* 1197ᵃ39.

²⁰¹ Corroboration for this view of the natural excellences may be found in *HA* 588ᵃ17–ᵇ3 (see 588ᵃ30–1, *phusikē dunamis*); it is, in any case, the obvious view of the *MM*.

²⁰² See Dirlmeier (1964: 349–50), who interprets the accounts of natural excellence in both *EE* 3 and *EN* 6 in the light of *MM*, and so sees all three as consistent on the point that the natural component of excellence consists of mere *hormai*.

then we may be disposed to treat the Eudemian *dunameis*, such as *anaischuntia*, in the same way, as referring only to qualities such as the innate impudence which hardens into shamelessness in the mature individual. The stumbling-block for this intepretation, however, is the statement of the *Eudemian Ethics* that it is by virtue of *dunameis* that we are *called orgiloi, anaischuntoi, aischuntēloi*, for the fact is that, although people may in some sense be called 'irascible' or 'bad-tempered' by virtue of qualities present from infancy, this is certainly not true of qualities such as *anaischuntia*—we are typically called *anaischuntoi* because we have failed to acquire a proper disposition in respect of the evaluative categories of the *kalon* and the *aischron*, because we have no respect for propriety or for other people. If, therefore, the Eudemian *dunamis* of *anaischuntia* is simply a sort of natural impudence, then it is only in a qualified sense that people who possess it are described as *anaischuntoi*, whereas the text refers quite plainly to that quality in respect of which people are actually called *anaischuntoi*.

The third possibly (*c*) is that both the Eudemian and the Nicomachean accounts regard *pathētikai dunameis* as the innate basis from which excellence of character may develop, but only the former sees these as considerable traits such as irascibility and shamelessness, while the latter regards them as more basic tendencies. This interpretation is strengthened if we consider that the account of the natural excellences in *Nicomachean Ethics* 6, according to which we possess our characters, in one sense, from birth, is Eudemian, and that this is modified by the more cautious approach of the remainder of the Nicomachean version, according to which that which is innate is the natural capacity to develop traits of character (an approach which is reflected in the view of the *Magna Moralia* that natural excellences are mere *hormai*). While I am inclined to believe that this last hypothesis is true, it is not, however, necessary that it should be so in order for it to be true that the *dunameis* of the *Eudemian Ethics* are not those of the *Nicomachean Ethics* or *Magna Moralia*. The Nicomachean account is, in any case, scrupulous in stressing that *dunameis* are simple capacities for the *pathē*, and never says that we are qualified by epithets drawn paronymously from the *pathē* by virtue of our possession of these *dunameis*. Nor does the Nicomachean version even come close to exhibiting a view that substantial traits of character are innate, except on an interpretation of the passage from the common book which fits better with the *Eudemian Ethics* than with the rest of the *Nicomachean*. The discussion of *pathē, dunameis*, and *hexeis* in the *Eudemian Ethics*, on the other hand, is much closer to the account of quality in the *Categories*, normally considered an early work: only the Eudemian version introduces the discussion with explicit reference to quality (*poiotēs*),[203] and if we are right that the *dunameis* of the *Eudemian Ethics* are, like those of the *Nicomachean*, innate, then the view of the former that the *dunamis*, irascibility, is innate will tally wholly with that of the *Categories* that the 'affective quality' of irascibility is innate;[204] the *Nichomachean Ethics*, on the other hand, is quite clear that we become irascible (*orgiloi*) by habituation, by dealing repeatedly with anger in a certain way (1103^{b}17–21).[205] These links with the *Categories*,[206] to my mind, suggest that the *Eudemian Ethics* is relatively early, and that the discussion of natural excellence in the common book *Nicomachean Ethics* 6 belongs with a correspondingly early view that considerable

---

[203] 1220^{b}5–7, 14–15.

[204] For the discussion of the relevant qualities in *Cat.*, see 8^{b}25–10^{a}10. 'Bad temper' (*orgē*, the quality which makes us *orgiloi*), an affective quality, is said to be present from birth at 9^{b}35–10^{a}2. We notice, too, that the only form of *dunamis* considered by *Cat.* is the 'natural *dunamis*' (9^{a}14–27). The class of affective qualities as a whole is odd and heterogeneous, and it is no surprise that it occurs nowhere else; it is particularly perplexing how a quality such as bad temper can be present from birth and yet be caused by 'a certain *pathos*' (9^{b}35–6). There is a degree of interchangeability between affective qualities and *diatheseis* (hotness a *diathesis*, 8^{b}36, an affective quality, 9^{b}3), and between *diatheseis* and *dunameis* (health, 8^{b}37 and 9^{a}15, 21–3 respectively), and it is difficult to escape the conclusion that affective qualities are better seen in terms of one or other of these categories. (It is entirely proper that some *diatheseis* should be *dunameis*, since a *diathesis* can be 'an arrangement of a thing that has parts . . . in respect of . . . *dunamis* . . .', *Metaph.* 1022^{b}1–2. The statement that boxers and runners are not so called because they are disposed in some way, but because they possess a natural capacity to do something easily (9^{a}19–21), need not mean that their *dunamis* is not also a *diathesis*, but only that in these cases the attribution of the qualification '*puktikos*' or '*dromikos*' is made on the basis that the relevant quality is better regarded as a *dunamis* than a *diathesis*. The overlap between affective quality and *diathesis*, on the other hand, suggests the redundancy of the former.)

[205] This last point is perhaps not conclusive proof that the doctrine of the *EN* differs from that of the *EE*, for at 1103^{b}13–25 Arist. is talking about the acquisition of excellences or defects of character (i.e. *hexeis*) by means of performance of the appropriate activities, and *orgilotēs* is a genuine defect of character, part of a genuine trio of mean and defects, and therefore necessarily acquired by habituation, in the *EE* too (1220^{b}38, 1221^{a}15–16, 1231^{b}5–26). The *orgilotēs* that is a *dunamis* at 1220^{b}17 may thus be different from that which is an acquired defect of character, and this might suggest that the *EE* works with a distinction between innate character traits that are *dunameis* (irascibility in one sense) and acquired traits that can be *hexeis* (irascibility in another sense). Yet it still seems significant that in the *EN* irascibility is always a *hexis*, never a *dunamis*.

[206] It may just also be significant that the *EE*, despite its enumeration of *pathē*, *dunameis*, and *hexeis* at 1220^{b}7–20, also makes frequent mention, in the immediate context, of *diatheseis* (e.g. 1220^{a}19, 22–3, 26, 29), a form of quality in *Cat.* 8^{b}27–9^{a}13; but even *EN*, although it insists that only *pathē*, *dunameis*, and *hexeis* exist in the soul, uses the term *diathesis* as variation for *hexis* (a kind of *diathesis*; e.g. 1107^{b}16, 1108^{a}24, ^{b}11).

traits of character, such as the second-order disposition with regard to *aidōs*, are innate—a view which is modified in the *Nicomachean Ethics* and the *Magna Moralia*.[207]

On this view, the *Eudemian Ethics* alone succeeds in identifying something like the second-order disposition for *aidōs*, calling it the *dunamis* of being *aischuntēlos*, but makes the mistake of regarding this quality as innate. It follows that when the Nicomachean treatise modifies this view of innate character traits, it forfeits the ability to place the second-order disposition for *aidōs* in the category of *dunamis*, for the *dunamis* with regard to *aidōs* will now be the simple capacity to experience *aidōs*, which will answer to, at most, an affective tendency rather than a developed disposition. This, I think, is the most plausible view, but absolute certainty is not attainable. Of the other possibilities, only (*b*), that in all three treatises both natural excellences and *dunameis* for *pathē* are minimal capacities, is at all likely, and in this case not even the designation of 'being *aischuntēlos*' as a *dunamis* in the *Eudemian Ethics* will come close to isolating that disposition for *aidōs* which is a developed trait of character.

In the last two sections we have examined the criteria which *aidōs* must meet if its dispositional aspects are to be considered under the headings of either *hexis* or *dunamis*. That *aidōs* may be a *hexis* is not explicitly ruled out by the definition of the latter concept, but the alternative conceptions of what it is to be a *dunamis* seem unable to capture the essence of *aidōs* as a developed trait of character—on the one hand, according to the Eudemian conception, the tendency to experience an emotion to an extent which makes that tendency a significant trait of character is innate, contrary to the common (and correct) view of the fifth and fourth centuries that neither emotions such as *aidōs*, which involve complex evaluative categories, nor dispositions for those emotions can be innate; on the other hand, the view of *dunameis* as minimal capacities for emotions, encompassing certain affective tendencies, but not duplicating the developed traits of the mature individual, will not be a candidate for the genus of *aidōs* as a settled and mature disposition.

Hexeis and *dunameis*, however, certainly are the categories of quality into which, in the ethical works, any non-occurrent quality in respect

---

[207] The view that the common books are Eudemian in origin is persuasively argued by Kenny (1978), but his opinion that the *EN* is the earlier seems to me unlikely. For the view that the *EE* is earlier, see Rowe (1971).

of an emotion must, apparently, be fitted; we know that, in ordinary Greek, *aidōs* is used in non-occurrent and dispositional senses, but it remains to be seen how (or whether) Aristotle will accommodate both these and the occurrent senses of *aidōs* in his scheme.

6.5.5. *The Place of* Aidōs *in Aristotle's Scheme*

We have seen that in at least one place Aristotle does recognize the existence of a capacity or tendency to experience *aidōs*; he does not tell us the name of the *dunamis* that is a capacity to experience *aidōs*, but since, by virtue of possessing it, one is called *aischuntēlos*, he presumably would not object if we called it *to aischuntēlon*. *To aischuntēlon*, however, is merely a synonym for *aidōs* or *aischunē* in the dispositional rather than the occurrent sense. Yet Aristotle does not seem explicitly to acknowledge that the term used to convey the occurrent sense may also be used in a dispositional sense. *Aidōs/aischunē*, like anger, fear, etc. is always a *pathos*, never (explicitly) a *dunamis* or a *hexis*.[208] This, however, creates difficulties over the inclusion of *aidōs* in a triadic scheme of mean, excess, and deficiency. *Aidōs* is included in such a scheme in both versions of the *Ethics* (and the *Magna Moralia*), opposed to *anaischuntia* on the one hand and *kataplēxis* (shyness)[209] on the other.[210] For in these triads *aidōs*, as the mean, presupposes the idea of seasonability,[211] and seasonability

---

[208] See n. 151 above. The inclusion of *aidōs* in the Eudemian table of means, excesses, and deficiencies is often thought to indicate that Arist. there regards *aidōs* as an *aretē* (Stark (1972), 125; Woods (1982), 110), since the table is introduced at 1220ᵇ35-6 with reference to the need to record 'what sort of mean *aretē* is and with what sort of mean it is concerned'. But the list of means that follows is offered as a basis for further discussion (ᵇ36-7), and the further discussion uses the table to distinguish between those means that are virtues and those that are not. The list, therefore, is a table of means, not of virtues, and, when it is the turn of *aidōs* to be discussed (1233ᵇ26-9, 1234ᵃ26-33), it is explicitly described as a mean that is not a virtue, though it is said to conduce to the natural virtue of *sōphrosunē*. On the means that are denied the status of *aretai* in the three ethical treatises, see Fortenbaugh (1968) (also Dirlmeier (1963), 350-1; (1964), 299-302). *Aidōs* is described as an *aretē* at *EN* 1116ᵃ28-9, but it is clear that this can only refer to *aretē* in a loose or qualified sense, since the motivation involved is inferior to that of the brave man who acts for the sake of *to kalon*.

[209] *Kataplēxis* implies 'dumb-struck', and denotes an excessive sense of *aidōs* that inhibits even actions that must be performed or that a normal person would perform with equanimity. It thus corresponds to the negative aspect of *aidōs* identified in many of the passages in which the concept is regarded as ambivalent.

[210] *EN* 1108ᵃ30-5, *EE* 1221ᵃ1, 1233ᵇ26-9; cf. *MM* 1193ᵃ1-10.

[211] Cf. [Pl.] *Def.* 412c8-10.

cannot be an attribute of the affect in its purely occurrent sense. One might think that the passages in which *aidōs* appears as a non-virtuous mean indicate Aristotle's awareness that, in one sense at least, it is not a *pathos*. In the *Nicomachean Ethics*, for example, *aidōs* is explicitly said not to be an *aretē*, yet the person who possesses *aidōs* (the *aidēmōn*) is praised (1108ᵃ31-2). Only paragraphs before, however, we are told that no one is praised for their *pathē* (1105ᵇ31-1106ᵃ2),²¹² and this suggests that, even if *aidōs* is not an *aretē*, it cannot (simply) be a *pathos*. The same argument, moreover, would rule out the possibility of *aidōs* being a *dunamis*, since (1106ᵃ7-9) we are not praised or blamed for our *dunameis*, either. Indeed, this particular passage (1105ᵇ28-1106ᵃ13) strongly suggests that praise and blame are appropriate only to states, *hexeis*, of which the virtues are a species; yet *aidōs* is consistently, and in the immediate context, denied the status of *aretē*, and also that of *hexis*.²¹³ It is now apparent that Aristotle has some difficulty in fitting *aidōs* into his scheme.

On the basis of the foregoing, and indeed a priori, one would expect that a mean cannot be a *pathos*, but must imply some dispositional quality. There are, however, also signs that Aristotle may have entertained a contradictory opinion that a *pathos* could be a mean, for in the wider contexts of those passages in which *aidōs* is identified as a mean it is also specifically said to be a *pathos*.²¹⁴ It thus seems unlikely that he is making use of a distinction between *aidōs* as a *pathos* and

---

²¹² Cf. *EE* 1220ᵇ14-15: there is no quality in respect of *pathē* (one is just affected), but there is in respect of *dunameis*.

²¹³ The contexts in which *aidōs* is said not to be an *aretē* are also those in which it is identified as a praiseworthy mean; this might be thought to leave room for the possibility that *aidōs* is a *hexis* though not an *aretē* (*aretē* being a species of *hexis*), but this, too, is explicitly ruled out at *EN* 1128ᵇ11 and 15 (discussed in text below). We remember, too, that, strictly speaking, a *hexis* is either an *aretē* or a *kakia* (*Phys.* 246ᵃ11-17, n. 173 above); but, as we saw (n. 174), Arist. does recognize *hexeis* which are neither *aretai* nor *kakiai* in an unqualified sense.

²¹⁴ See *EE* 1234ᵃ23-33, where *aidōs*, a praiseworthy mean, but not an *aretē*, is also described as a *pathos*; cf. 1220ᵇ13, where, immediately before the table of means in which *aidōs* is included, *aidōs* is given as an example of a *pathos*. Thus in *EN* when *aidōs* is said to be one of the means 'in *pathē* and in the things concerned with *pathē*' (1108ᵃ30-1), there need be no indication that *aidōs* is not itself a *pathos*, or more like a *pathos* than anything else (in fact, this formulation mirrors that of the *EE*, where *aidōs* is a *pathetikē mesotēs*, 1233ᵇ18). *Aidōs* is a questionable mean in all three ethical treatises, never an *aretē*, and never called anything but a *pathos*. Thus, whatever their disagreements in other areas, especially on the status of the other questionable means, *EN*, *EE*, and *MM* are in close agreement on the status of *aidōs*. Contrast Stark (1972: 131) and Dirlmeier (1956: 395-6; 1963: 350-1), who, as a result of their desire to chart Arist.'s 'development', seem to me to exaggerate and to manufacture differences between the two treatises in this respect.

aidōs as something else, a non-virtuous mean (a mean that would fail to meet the requirements of *pathē*, *dunameis*, or *hexeis*, which are 'the three things that come to be in the soul');[215] rather he seems not to have faced up to the contradiction between his insistence that *aidōs* is a *pathos* and his denial that a *pathos* can be praiseworthy, and so a suitable candidate to be a mean. *Aidōs*, it seems, can be both a *pathos* and a praiseworthy mean, even though the formal requirements of the elements of this classication conflict.[216]

Those contexts in which *aidōs* is identified as a mean, however, indicate quite clearly that we are dealing with dispositional terms, not with bare affects; *aidōs* is opposed to *anaischuntia*,[217] the *dunamis* in respect of which, as we have seen,[218] one is *anaischuntos*, and the possession of the mean *aidōs* qualifies its possessor as *aidēmōn*,[219] a dispositional term in the same way as is *anaischuntos* and one that is parallel to *aischuntēlos*, which is used to indicate possession of a *dunamis* in the *Eudemian Ethics* (1220^b17). The mean in these cases, then, involves being *aidēmōn*, and thus requires a quality of some sort; Aristotle might have coined the term *aidēmosunē*, but instead he uses the term which has traditionally served to denote the disposition of the *aidēmōn*, namely *aidōs*. In these passages, therefore, *aidōs* cannot, strictly speaking, be a *pathos*. It is, of course, not in itself problematic

---

[215] *EN* 1105^b19-20, *MM* 1186^a10-11.

[216] Dirlmeier (1956: 395-6) believes that Arist.'s statement in *EN* 4. 9, 1128^b11-15 that *aidōs* is not a *hexis* indicates a rejection of the opinion of *EN* 2. 7, 1108^a31-5 that it is a mean; but the passage in Book 4 provides the discussion of *aidōs* that we expect from the introduction of the concept as a questionable mean in Book 2, and there is, in fact, no explicit contradiction of the previous position. It is equally possible, and in my opinion more likely, that Arist. retains his belief that *aidōs* is a mean while, in a way that is certainly puzzling, denying it the status of a *hexis*. A similar (and understandable) assumption that all means are 'dispositions' haunts Fortenbaugh's article (1968) on 'the questionable mean-dispositions' (*sic*); if Arist. actually says that one of the questionable means is not a *hexis*, how does *aidōs* as a 'mean-disposition' fit into his terminology? (Arist., of course, does have a wider term denoting 'disposition', namely *diathesis* (a less stable and long-lasting quality than a *hexis*, *Cat.* 8^b27-8), but it is never suggested that *aidōs* is a *diathesis*). Fortenbaugh, moreover, believes that Arist. is right to see *aidōs* as a questionable mean, on the grounds that it is clearly related to the occurrent emotion of *aischunē* (1968: 224); but (*a*) there is nothing in the slightest way 'questionable' about the fact that a mean-disposition should be related to an occurrent affect; and (*b*) this can only work if *aischunē* and *aidōs* are distinguished, the one as the affect and the other as the disposition, whereas the two are normally synonymous, and Arist. treats them as two aspects of a whole at 1128^b10-35, saying quite explicitly that *aidōs* (not *aischunē*) is more like a *pathos* than a *hexis* (1128^b11).

[217] *EN* 1108^a35, *EE* 1221^a1, 1233^b27, *MM* 1193^a1-10.

[218] *EE* 1220^b16-18.

[219] *EN* 1108^a32, *EE* 1233^b29, *MM* 1193^a7.

that a term used to denote an occurrent affect should also be used of the disposition towards that affect; such, indeed, is the normal position in the case of *aidōs*. But since Aristotle insists that *aidōs* is an occurrent affect, we should expect him to acknowledge, at some point, that he is using the term in a different, if clearly related sense.

Aidōs should at least be elevated from the level of *pathos* to that of *dunamis* in the sense in which 'being *aischuntēlos*' is a *dunamis* in the *Eudemian Ethics*. But if, as such a *dunamis*, *aidōs* can, even in the Eudemian context, be a praiseworthy mean, including the idea of rightness, and if such a *dunamis* could, as is clearly the case, be a persistent trait of character, then it is difficult to see why it should not be accorded the status of *hexis*. In the Nicomachean treatise traits of character such as 'being *aischuntēlos*' are not recognized as *dunameis*, and so it appears even more compelling that, since *aidōs* as the mean quality by virtue of which one is called *aidēmōn* can be neither *pathos* nor *dunamis*, it should be a *hexis*.[220] Are there, then, good grounds for denying *aidōs* the status of *hexis*?

We have seen that Aristotle frequently denies that *aidōs* is an *aretē*, but his most emphatic denial comes at *Nicomachean Ethics* 1128ᵇ10–35:

It is wrong to speak of *aidōs* as an *aretē*; it is more like a *pathos* than a *hexis*. It is defined, at any rate, as a sort of fear of ill-repute, and its effects are similar to those of fear of danger; for those who are ashamed [*hoi aischunomenoi*] go red, and those who fear death turn pale. Both, then, appear to be in a way somatic, which seems to be a feature of a *pathos* rather than of a *hexis*. The *pathos*, moreover, is not suitable for every age-group, but for youth. For we think that people of that age should be *aidēmōn*, because, since they live by their emotions, they often err, but are prevented by *aidōs*. And we praise young men who are *aidēmōn*, but no one would say appreciatively of an older man that he is *aischuntēlos*; for we think that he should do nothing that is attended by *aischunē*. For *aischunē* is not a mark of a decent man, since it occurs at base actions—such things are not to be done. Whether some actions are really *aischra* and others only in belief does not matter; neither sort should be done, so that one should not feel *aischunē*. It is the mark of a base person to be such as to do something *aischron*—to be so disposed as to be ashamed [*aischunesthai*] were one to do some such thing, and to consider oneself decent on this account, would be absurd; for *aidōs* occurs at voluntary actions, but the decent man will never willingly commit base acts. *Aidōs* would be a decent thing on a hypothesis: if he were to do it, he would be ashamed [*aischunesthai*]; but this does not apply to

[220] *EN* 1105ᵇ28–1106ᵃ13 suggests, even if it does not assert, that *only hexeis* are praised or blamed, which, rigidly applied, would entail that *aidōs*, a praiseworthy mean, is a *hexis*.

the *aretai*. For if *anaischuntia* and not feeling *aidōs* at the prospect of doing what is *aischron* are base, this does not mean that to feel *aischunē* when one does such things is decent. Self-control [*enkrateia*] is not an *aretē* either, but a sort of mixture. This will be shown later.

It is frequently suggested that this passage trades on an illegitimate identification of *aidōs* and *aischunē*, characterizing the former in terms proper to the latter.[221] The situation, however, is not so straightforward, for Aristotle neither identifies *aidōs* and *aischunē* nor treats them as two distinct concepts; rather he uses the two terms, for the purposes of this passage, to refer to distinguishable aspects of a single emotional concept. In ordinary Greek *aidōs* and *aischunē* are synonyms, except when the latter refers to a disgraceful state of affairs rather than the individual's reaction to that state, but *aidōs* is the older and more poetic term, and it draws its claim to be considered as a virtue from its use in highly poetic contexts where something of the importance originally accorded the concept is preserved. *Aischunē*, on the other hand, is the regular prosaic word of Aristotle's own day, the one which would generally be used to do the work of *aidōs* both as affect and as a trait of character, although as a trait of character *aischunē* does not bear the exalted connotations of *aidōs*. Aristotle's moves from *aidōs* to *aischunē*, then, are not in any way underhand—ordinary language, in fact, goes further than he does in this passage, in so far as it treats the two as synonyms.

In the present passage *aischunē* is used in an exclusively retrospective sense. That *aischunē* (and *aidōs*) can, by this time, have such a sense obviously helps Aristotle's case, since he is able to use retrospective shame as a sign of imperfection of character—if someone is ashamed of what he has done, then he has done something *aischron*, something that the good man should never do. But the passage does not simply slide from prospective *aidōs*, the rejected candidate for consideration as a virtue, to retrospective *aischunē*, a sign of moral imperfection; rather Aristotle feels that each implies the other, and therefore feels justified in treating them as aspects of the whole.[222] For it is clear that Aristotle has not simply failed to consider prospective *aidōs* as a quality of real moral worth. The young, for example, live by *pathos* and so make mistakes, presumably because their emotional

221 e.g. Guthrie, vi. 368; Irwin (1985*a*), 330.
222 Cf. *Rhet.* 1383^b^12–1384^a^23, where the list of actions and situations of which people are ashamed (*ἃ αἰσχύνονται*) covers both that which one would be ashamed to do and that which one would be ashamed to have done.

response to situations is not guided by the moral insight of the man of practical wisdom;[223] but another aspect of their living by *pathos* is their propensity to *aidōs*, which can prevent their doing wrong (1128[b]16–18). Thus the *aidōs* that is disparaged as appropriate for youth but not for adults is prospective; it may actually inhibit the action that is *aischron*, but it is not therefore, according to Aristotle, an unqualified good. We must assume, then, that the mature adult, if he is 'decent', is no more prone to prospective *aidōs* than to retrospective.

The reason why this should be so emerges at the passage's conclusion: *anaischuntia*, to be entirely without *aischunē* is base, as is failing to experience *aidōs* at the prospect of doing *ta aischra* (31–2),[224] but this does not make *aischunē* when one does *aischra* any more decent (32–3). Here the second member of the sentence is not quite what we expect to follow the first, and there is a move from prospective to retrospective shame; for we expect the sequence, 'If it is base not to feel *aidōs* at the prospect of wrongdoing, this does not entail that such *aidōs* is positively virtuous,' rather than, 'If it is base not to feel *aidōs* . . ., this does not entail that feeling *aischunē* when one does wrong is positively virtuous.' The sentence as it stands appears to allow the possibility that prospective *aidōs* may be decent, since this possibility is not excluded by the observation that retrospective *aischunē* is not decent. Aristotle does, however, wish to exclude this possibility, and he does think that his remarks on retrospective *aischunē* are successful in doing so; he thinks, that is, that susceptibility to prospective *aidōs* entails a susceptibility to retrospective *aischunē*. This is why *aidōs* is decent only 'on a hypothesis' (*ex hupotheseōs*); *aidōs* would be decent if the susceptibility to retrospective *aischunē* which it implies were purely hypothetical ('if he were to do it, he would be ashamed'), if, that is, the disposition to experience *aidōs* excluded actual occurrence of retrospective shame.[225]

As it is, however, *aidōs* does (as Aristotle believes) entail the potentiality for retrospective shame, as we see if we continue to work

---

[223] Cf. the remarks on youth in *Rhet.* 1389[a]3–[b]12, esp. [a]28–9 on the young as prone to *aidōs/aischunē* (*aischuntēloi*); on the importance of *aidōs* in the young, cf. *Pol.* 1331[a]39–[b]1, 1335[a]2–4. On the imperfect, emotional nature of the young, cf. Fortenbaugh (1975), 49–53.

[224] τὸ μὴ αἰδεῖσθαι τὰ αἰσχρὰ πράττειν is clearly prospective.

[225] Clearly, the 'hypothesis' is not simply that *aidōs* would be decent if those who performed *aischra* experienced *aischunē* thereafter, for this has already been excluded by 1128[b]20–8; the hypothesis must be that *aidōs* would be decent provided both the wrongdoing and the retrospective shame which the *aidēmōn* or *aischuntēlos* would experience at such wrongdoing were purely hypothetical.

backwards in the stages of his argument. *Aidōs* occurs at voluntary actions (1128^{b}28), but the decent person will never voluntarily do anything base (28–9). This means, I think, not merely that *aidōs* implies that one has performed or will necessarily perform base actions, but rather that to be so disposed as to experience the *aidōs* which inhibits an action which it is in one's power to perform or not to perform (assuming *aidōs* to be prospective here as elsewhere in the passage) implies that one is also disposed to experience retrospective *aischunē* over base actions which it was in one's power not to perform. This is substantiated by the preceding sentences: (*a*) to be such as to do something *aischron* is the mark of a base person (^{b}25–6); (*b*) to be in such a condition as to experience *aischunē* were one to do something *aischron* offers no warrant for considering oneself decent (^{b}26–8), because to be so disposed as to experience retrospective *aischunē* is to be so disposed as to do wrong (this need not exclude the possibility that one who experiences *aischunē* after doing wrong is better than one who is disposed to do wrong with no feeling of *aischunē*). The crucial step in the argument, however, remains unstated; this is (*c*): to be so disposed as to experience *aischunē* were one to do something *aischron* is entailed by possession of a disposition to experience *aidōs*. This step, however, is easily supplied, since the whole argument is, after all, designed to prove that *aidōs* is not an *aretē*; Aristotle must, therefore, see the disposition to experience retrospective *aischunē* as part of *aidōs* (this much, indeed, is indicated by the fact that the sentence at ^{b}28–9, which follows proposition (*b*) above, begins, 'For *aidōs* . . .').

The objection, then, that Aristotle can only deny *aidōs*, a prospective character trait which inhibits disgraceful action, the status of a virtue by wholly identifying it with the retrospective shame which occurs in those who do perform *aischra* is unfounded. If, instead, we recognize that *aidōs* and *aischunē* refer to different aspects of the same concept, and therefore that they are not used interchangeably, we shall see not only that Aristotle's argument is clear and precise, but that it is convincing. For it is, in fact, true that retrospective shame is (by now) part of the concept of *aidōs*, and we should agree with Aristotle that one who is so disposed as to experience distress with regard to conduct which is *aischron* is disposed to experience that distress whether the conduct is past, present, or future.[226] Both we and the ordinary Greek find it quite acceptable that possession of a sense of

---

[226] Note how the *Rhet.* (1383^{b}15) includes focus on present, past, or future events in its definition of *aischunē*.

shame or *aidōs* should encompass both prospective and retrospective
aspects and yet remain a positive trait of character (a virtue), because
we accept that decent human beings do sometimes go wrong and
because we regard repudiation of past wrongdoing in a positive light.
Aristotle's ideal, however, is perfect virtue, the possession of traits of
character which preclude wrongdoing, and he is therefore right to
oppose any suggestion that *aidōs* could be, in his terms, an *aretē*. Aristotelian *aretē* involves dispositions to choose the *kalon* for its own sake,
whereas the disposition to experience *aidōs* and *aischunē*, Aristotle
points out, implies that, on some occasions at least, one will have
chosen the *aischron* rather than the *kalon*. If this aspect of the disposition with regard to *aidōs/aischunē* cannot be actualized in the good
man, then *aidōs* cannot be an *aretē*, for the good man must not only
have but use the *hexeis* which are his *aretai*.[227] Aristotle is therefore
correct, indeed brilliantly so, in recognizing that the totality of the concept of *aidōs* cannot be accommodated under his conception of *aretē*.

If, however, the passage is a conspicuous success in proving that
aidōs should not be considered an *aretē*, it also contains one conspicuous defect, and that is its failure to recognize that *aidōs*, the name
of an affect, is also the name of a developed trait of character. We have
seen that it is Aristotle's view that *aidōs* somehow involves a
potentiality for retrospective *aischunē* (an occurrent affect); this might
suggest that the relationship between *aidōs* and *aischunē* is that of
potential to actual, *hexis* (or *dunamis*) to *energeia* (or *to paschein*). Yet
the passage begins with a statement that *aidōs* is more like a *pathos*
than a *hexis*, and all instances of *aidōs* or *aideisthai* in the text can be
taken as referring to the prospective, occurrent affect. The passage,
then, does not recognize *aidōs* the disposition; but it does make use of
the concept of a disposition towards *aidōs*, for it is by virtue of this
disposition that 'are in such a condition as to *aischunesthai*'.[228]
Aristotle thus implicitly recognizes a disposition with regard to *aidōs*,
which, he says, implies a disposition to retrospective *aischunē*. This
disposition remains nameless (although by virtue of its possession we
are called *aidēmōn* or *aischuntēlos*), but there is absolutely no reason
why it should not be given its regular title, namely *aidōs*. Thus Aristotle

[227] This, I think, is the implication of the phrase, 'but this does not apply to the *aretai*'
(1128ᵇ30-1), referring to the statement that *aidōs* would only be decent on the hypothesis that actual experience of retrospective shame be excluded.
[228] τὸ οὕτως ἔχειν ὥστ'... αἰσχύνεσθαι, 1128ᵇ26-7; cf. τὸ εἶναι τοιοῦτον, another
dispositional expression, in 25.

should recognize that there is a sense in which *aidōs* is a disposition for the occurrent emotions of *aidōs* and *aischunē*

The passage closes with an additional remark which, properly interpreted, sheds further light on Aristotle's attitude towards *aidōs* and his reasons for refusing to accord it the status of *aretē*. The sentence, '*Enkrateia* is not an *aretē* either, but a sort of mixture' (1128ᵇ33-4) is probably not introduced as an *explanation* as to why *aidōs* is not an *aretē* (Aristotle is not actually saying that if *enkrateia* is not an *aretē*, then neither is *aidōs*, *aidōs* being a species of *enkrateia*), but the presence of the remark in itself suggests that there is some link in Aristotle's mind between the two concepts.

Enkrateia is a less praiseworthy condition than *aretē* in that the *enkratēs* is tempted by the course that his better judgement identifies as wrong, but manages to control himself, whereas the virtuous person, typically the *sōphrōn*, has succeeded in aligning his attitudes to the *kalon*, the good, and the pleasant in such a way that the virtuous course appears to him under all three aspects.[229] This might have something to do with prospective *aidōs*, in that Aristotle might believe that inhibition of an action through prospective *aidōs* is a form of self-control in which the agent actually contemplates and is momentarily attracted by the wrong action, but, if this is Aristotle's opinion, it never permeates to the explicit level; nor is it necessary for the existence of an analogy between *aidōs* and *enkrateia* that *aidōs* be a form of self-control, although it is plausible, and certainly traditional, that *aidōs* should, in certain circumstances, be felt to require such self-control.

Thus, while it may be possible that Aristotle regards *aidōs* as less than an *aretē* because it can involve a degree of moral struggle inappropriate in the truly good, the most obvious link between *aidōs* and *enkrateia* is

---

[229] See *EN* 1150ᵃ9-1152ᵃ36, *MM* 1202ᵇ29-1203ᵃ29, 1203ᵇ12-1204ᵃ18, esp. *EN* 1151ᵇ32-1152ᵃ3, *MM* 1203ᵇ12-23 on the difference between *sōphrosunē* and *enkrateia*. For modern discussion, see North (1966), 202-3; Burnyeat (1980), 86-8; Charles (1984), 169-77. At *EE* 1223ᵇ11-12 *enkrateia*, in flat contradiction of *EN* 1128ᵇ33-4, is said to be an *aretē*; but this is also in flat contradiction of *EE* 1227ᵇ15-16, in which *enkrateia* and *aretē* are different, and so cannot be taken as the considered doctrine of the *EE*, esp. if the common book *EN* 7/*EE* 6 is regarded as Eudemian (there is a forward reference in 1227ᵇ16-17 that at least suggests that the *EE*'s discussion of the relationship between *enkrateia* and *aretē* took the same line as that in the common book). Most probably the statement of 1223ᵇ11-12 (and its counterpart at 1223ᵃ36-7 that *akrasia* is a vice, a form of *mochthēria*) stand to be qualified by the greater precision of the later account. Thus even in *EN* 7, where *enkrateia* is distinguished from the virtue *sōphrosunē* and *akrasia* from the vice *akolasia*, the former is a good *hexis* (1151ᵃ27, ᵇ28) and the latter a bad (1151ᵃ28, ᵇ29), a vice in a qualified sense (1151ᵃ11). (On the question of the sense in which these states can be *hexeis* and yet not *aretai* or *kakiai*, see n. 174 above.)

to be sought elsewhere, in the simple fact that *enkrateia* is one step removed from the best possible state, a good thing in one way, but not the best *hexis* that is *aretē*. *Enkrateia* is worse than *sōphrosunē*, but better than *akrasia* (incontinence), where the wrong action actually is performed,[230] which in turn is better than *akolasia* (licentiousness), where there is no correct moral judgement at all (quite the opposite).[231] This is relevant to *aidōs*, since *aidōs*, too, often appears as a motive of those who stand at one step removed from absolute virtue. This is quite clearly the case, for example, in the accounts of bravery in all three treatises: true bravery entails following the course dictated by *logos*, and *logos* bids one choose what is *kalon*;[232] and doing the right thing for the sake of *to kalon* is contrasted with endurance of danger as a result of other motives, the first of which, because it prompts conduct which is most like true bravery, is *aidōs*, the motive of those who possess civic bravery.[233] Here the point is not that *aidōs* involves control of bad desires, which would make it exactly like *enkrateia*, but that it does not presuppose a rational grasp of *to kalon*; the man of civic bravery is brave out of emotional rather than rational motives,[234] and, though he is concerned for honour and reputation, he is not motivated by the intrinsic nature of the noble action. Thus *aidōs*, even in its prospective form as an inhibitory emotion, takes the second place as a motive inferior to that of the truly virtuous, who perform the noble action because they see its intrinsic nobility, because they know it is good for them, and because they want to.

In these passages on bravery there is a strong suggestion that *aidōs* is concerned with external honour and reputation alone.[235] Honour is

---

[230] Those who experience retrospective shame, then, will be akratic rather than enkratic.

[231] In Cairns (1989) I defend this, the traditional interpretation of the hierarchy, against that of Charles (1984: 169–77), who claims that one type of *akolastos* may actually retain a virtuous best judgement.

[232] *EN* 1115ᵇ11–13, *EE* 1229ᵃ1–2, *MM* 1191ᵃ22–5.

[233] *EN* 1116ᵃ17–29 (with an excursus, 1116ᵃ29–ᵇ3, on that inferior subspecies of civic bravery which is enforced not by *aidōs*, but by fear), *EE* 1229ᵃ13, 1230ᵃ16–21, *MM* 1191ᵃ5–13 (where *aischunē* replaces *aidōs*).

[234] See *MM* 1191ᵃ4: the brave man should not be brave as a result of a *pathos* (the immediate reference is to *pathē* such as sexual passion (cf. *EE* 1229ᵃ20–9, *EN* 1117ᵃ5–9), but the point presumably holds of the *pathos aidōs*, even though brave conduct prompted by *aidōs* is said to be a result of respect for the law, *EE* 1229ᵃ29–30). Bravery, however, is not completely unemotional or unimpulsive, but the impulse must arise from reason on the basis that the brave action is *kalon*, *MM* 1191ᵃ21–3 (cf. *EN* 1116ᵇ30–1).

[235] See *EN* 1116ᵃ18–19: men of civic bravery endure danger on account of the legal penalties (*epitimia*), the reproaches (*oneidē*), and the honours (*timai*); 1116ᵃ28–9: they act out of *aidōs* (here an *aretē* in the same loose way as is *enkrateia* at *EE* 1223ᵇ11–12) and

not an ignoble motive for Aristotle[236] (he even posits particular states
of character which relate to one's attitude to honour),[237] but it is not
the supreme motive for moral action. Thus we find in the passages on
bravery that conduct motivated by *aidōs* is contrasted with that
motivated by the appreciation that the brave action is *kalon* and its
opposite *aischron*,[238] and action 'for the sake of the noble (*to kalon*)' is
the regular and proper choice of the truly good man.[239] It might seem,
therefore, that Aristotle also holds it against *aidōs* that it is concerned
only with reputation and external sanctions, not with the intrinsic
moral character of one's acts. *Aidōs* would then encompass the

out of the pursuit of *something kalon* (namely *timē*) and the avoidance of *something aischron*
(namely *oneidos*). Cf. *EE* 1230ᵇ23-4 (fear of ill-repute not a proper motive for true
bravery), *MM* 1191ª18-21 (only the person who acts believing the action is *kalon*, and
acts whether or not there is an audience is brave; this last condition is presumably
intended to contrast with the case of civic bravery).

[236] Cf. Hardie (1980), 106-7. It is an important external good (*MM* 1184ᵇ4, *Rhet.*
1360ᵇ28, one that the good man can expect to enjoy, *EN* 1123ᵇ35 etc.), but not a candidate for consideration as the good for man: see *EN* 1095ᵇ22-30 (cf. *Rhet.* 1371ª8-10).

[237] See *EN* 4. 3-4, *EE* 3. 5 (and cf. 3. 7, 1233ᵇ34-8, on *semnotēs*), *MM* 1192ª21-36. Cf.,
on *megalopsuchia* (magnanimity), Gauthier (1951), Rees (1971), and Hardie (1978).

[238] *EN* 1115ᵇ21-4, 1116ª11-12, ᵇ3, 31, 1117ª16-17, ᵇ9, *EE* 1229ª1-4, 1230ª26-32.

[239] See *EN* 1115ᵇ12-13: acting for the sake of *to kalon* is the end or goal of *aretē*. Cf.
1120ª11-15, 23-4, 1122ᵇ6-7, *EE* 1230ª27-9, *MM* 1191ª20-1, etc. Thus the good man,
who is most truly a self-lover, since he cares for what is best in himself (and therefore
realizes his full potential as a human being), is he who acts for the sake of *to kalon* (*EN*
1168ᵇ25-31, 1169ª8-13, 25-ᵇ1, *MM* 1212ᵇ3-23); cf. *EE* 1248ᵇ34-7: the *kaloskagathos*
(completely good man, see 1249ª16-17) chooses *to kalon* for its own sake, as opposed to
those who choose virtuous action for the sake of external goods (1249ª14-16). Choosing
an action because it is *kalon* is thus clearly distinct from choosing an action which 'looks
good' because it reflects well upon oneself in the eyes of others (*to kalon* is praiseworthy,
but one still chooses it for itself, not as a means to praise, *EE* 1248ᵇ19-20, *Rhet.* 1366ª33-
4); see Monan (1968), 102; Burnyeat (1980), 78; also, in general, on *to kalon* as the
intrinsic and irreducible end of virtuous action, Adkins (1960ª), 316-17, 318-19; Monan
(1968), 101-3; Allan (1971); Cooper (1975), 76-88 *passim*; Owens (1981); Engberg-
Pedersen (1983), 37-62; Irwin (1985ᵇ), 120-38; (1988), 440-1, 630-1 nn. 3-4; Sherman
(1989), 113-14. On Aristotelian *philautia* (self-love), see Fraisse (1974), 232-7; Gigon
(1975); Hardie (1980), 323-35; Engberg-Pedersen (1983), 37-42. The good *philautos* is
clearly the good man, and thus Stark's attempt (1972: 119-21, 168) to relate Aristotelian
philautia to Democ.'s *aideisthai heauton* is misleading to the extent that the Democritean
individual is allowed both a retrospective and a prospective conscience; he experiences
an emotional inhibition *vis-à-vis* contemplated or inchoate action and a sense of regret
over past action that Arist. would deny his truly good man. Choosing the *kalon* for its
own sake and loving oneself in this way, then, do not seem to involve the elements of
struggle and self-restraint suggested by the Democritean frr.; nor is Democ.'s self-
directed *aidōs* to be conceived solely as 'self-respect' (*pace* Farrar (1988), 238). This is not
to say, however, that there is no connection between Arist. and Democ. here; in
particular, the care for the true self of the good *philautos*, governed as it is by concern for
to kalon, will, as I argue below, retain much of the dispositional and evaluative aspects of
aidōs.

judgement that a given action is *aischron qua* disgraceful in the eyes of others, while the man of true virtue would reject those actions that are *aischron* and pursue those that are *kalon* in his own eyes, without reference to the opinions of others.

There certainly seems to be something of this. In the Nicomachean passage quoted above, in which *aidōs* is denied the status of *aretē*, Aristotle makes use of a definition of *aidōs* as 'fear of ill-repute' (1128^{b}11–12), and many other passages in the corpus demonstrate the traditional association of *aidōs* with the judgements of other people.[240] In other places, however, it appears possible that *aidōs* should refer to internalized standards. Even the *Rhetoric*, for example, does not rule out such a reference, since, even though *aischunē* is there characterized as a response to 'the ills that seem to lead to ill-repute', the reference to ill-repute merely categorizes the *kaka* which are the object of *aischunē* as belonging to a certain class,[241] and the possibility remains that one could experience shame with reference to such a *kakon* even where the audience that is the focus of the emotion was absent, or present only in fantasy. If *aischunē* is a *phantasia* of ill-repute, this need not mean that it amounts to nothing more than fear of criticism, even if no one fears ill-repute apart from the thought of the judgements of others and even if *aischunē* is more intense when witnesses are present. The mental picture of ill-repute is specifically said to be of ill-repute in itself, not of its consequences (1384^{a}24–5), thus *aischunē* is not a simple calculation of possible effects. The emphasis, admittedly, is on the prospect of exposure and embarrassment, not primarily on the character of the action or situation itself, but still the action or situation must be characterized, by oneself, as embarrassing or

---

[240] e.g. the *EE* (1233^{b}26–9) views the triad consisting of *aidōs, anaischuntia*, and *kataplēxis* exclusively in terms of the attitude towards reputation. Cf. *EN* 1115^{a}12–14: to fear ill-repute is to be *aidēmōn*; *Pol.* 1331^{a}39–^{b}1: the presence of witnesses promotes *aidōs* in the young. In the *Rhet.* (1383^{b}13–15) *aischunē* is a pain or disturbance concerning those ills that appear to lead to ill-repute (cf. 1384^{a}23–4, *aischunē* a *phantasia* with regard to ill-repute); thus, since no one cares for reputation without caring for those who form opinions about one (1384^{a}25–6), Arist. gives us a list of those before whom *aischunē* is felt (1384^{a}26–^{b}26), chiefly those whose opinion we respect, those who witness our short-comings, and those who are liable to criticize. Similarly, the section on those who are liable to feel *aischunē* (1384^{b}27–1385^{a}15) concentrates on their attitudes towards witnesses and others whose judgements they fear. Cf. 1382^{b}8–9: as a rule people do wrong when they can, implying that most people are deterred from wrongdoing by external sanctions alone (cf. *EN* 1180^{a}4–5).

[241] In the same way *kala* are characterized as praiseworthy (*EE* 1248^{b}19–20, *Rhet.* 1366^{a}33–4), with no suggestion that a desire to do something *kalon* is merely a desire for praise.

disgraceful, and in many cases in which one categorizes one's own conduct as disgraceful and fears the criticism of others, the standards on the basis of which others criticize will also be one's own.[242]

In addition, Aristotle twice makes a distinction between 'conventional' and 'real' *aischra*. In the *Rhetoric* ($1381^{b}19$-21, 29–32) we are said to be ashamed (*aischunesthai*) of real *aischra* before our friends, but not of those that are only *aischra* 'in terms of opinion', and the point must be that in the former case, but not in the latter, we share the judgement that the situation is *aischron*, and so our *aischunē* encompasses an awareness of our own misdeed or fault, with a possible further implication that some *aischra* are objectively so and others only so by convention.[243] The same distinction is found in the passage of the *Nicomachean Ethics* that is crucial to Aristotle's appreciation of *aidōs*—'if there are some *aischra* that are so in truth and others by convention [or opinion, *doxa*], no matter; neither should be done, so that one should not experience *aischunē*' ($1128^{b}23$-5). Again, this makes it clear that *aidōs* or *aischunē* can relate to 'real' *aischra*; therefore it is not the case that either is a mere fear of others' criticism of faults which one does not oneself regard as reprehensible. Hence Aristotle must believe that *aidōs* can encompass a subjective awareness of the true character of one's own actions, and, if he disparages it, this cannot be because he feels that it is solely concerned with external appearances.[244]

In one passage of the *Nicomachean Ethics*, however, *aidōs* is not disparaged at all, but positively valued in a way that appears to contrast somewhat with the remarks which conclude the fourth book. The work as a whole closes with a discussion of moral education in the

---

[242] The character of the action or situation, moreover, is considered in the section which gives typical objects of *aischunē* (that which tells us ἃ αἰσχύνονται, *Rhet.* $1383^{b}19$-$1384^{a}23$). This section is introduced by the statement that 'Since *aischunē* is as defined, it follows that one experiences *aischunē* over such *kaka* as seem either to oneself or to those who matter to be *aischra*' ($1383^{b}17$-19). Both Cope (1877), ad loc., and W. R. Roberts (in the Oxford translation (Oxford, 1924; Princeton, 1984)) construe ἢ αὐτῷ ἢ ὧν φροντίζει with *aischron*, 'disgraceful either for oneself or for those one cares for'; I take the words, however, with δοκεῖ, and would point out that φροντίζω is used twice in the immediate sequel in the sense 'take seriously', indicating regard for others' opinions ($1384^{a}25$, 33). This is also a more natural sense in the context, and one that is very common in Arist. (see Bonitz, s.v.).

[243] See Cope (1877), ad locc.

[244] We should notice, too, that it is only *EE* which defines the triad of which *aidōs* is a member solely in terms of others' opinions; *EN* ($1108^{a}31$-4) is wholly unspecific as to what it is to experience *aidōs* properly, excessively, or deficiently, while *MM* ($1193^{a}1$-10) refers generally to the (prospective) force which ensures that what we say and do meets the correct standard of appropriateness.

community, of which the following forms part of the introduction (1178^{b}4-20):

> Now if arguments were self-sufficient to make people decent, then, as Theognis says, they would justly win many great rewards, and it would be right to provide these; but as it is, they seem to have the power to encourage and stimulate the civilized among the youth, and to make a noble nature that is truly fond of *to kalon* such as to be possessed by *aretē*, but they are unable to turn the many towards *kalokagathia* [fine-and-goodness]. For they do not, by their very nature, obey *aidōs*, but fear, and they refrain from base actions not because of *to aischron* but because of the penalties; since they live by their emotions they pursue their proper pleasures and the means to them, and avoid the opposing pains, but have not even an idea of what is *kalon* and truly pleasant, since they have not tasted it. What argument could change such people? For it is impossible, or not easy, to remove by argument what has long been adopted as part of one's character. Perhaps we should be content if, having everything we think we need to become decent, we achieve some share of *aretē*.

Here *aidōs* is associated with the possession of a character that truly loves *to kalon*, with avoiding the base because it is *aischron*, and contrasted with fear of external sanctions. Those who possess *aidōs* here are contrasted with those who live by *pathos*, whereas in the previous passage at 1128^b those who possessed *aidōs* were those who lived by their emotions. Here, then, *aidōs* manages to raise its head somewhat above the level of other *pathē*.[245] The real contrast between the two passages, however, is in their tone, not in their substance; in both *aidōs* is appropriate for those at a level lower than that of true virtue, and in

---

[245] This need not, however, imply that *aidōs* itself is not now to be regarded as a *pathos*; the distinctive feature of *aidōs* in this passage is not that it is non-emotional, but that it is an emotion which can carry a reference to the intrinsic character of one's actions, to the *aischron* as such, rather than to the consequences for oneself in terms of pleasure and pain. Note that *aidōs* can still retain the reference of all *pathē* to pleasure and pain, in so far as it belongs with the tendency to regard *to kalon* as truly pleasant (1179^{b}15), and so presumably involves a tendency to find the *aischron* painful. The sequel strongly suggests that *aidōs* is to be seen in terms of the habituated disposition to find pleasure and pain in the right things (e.g. 1179^{b}24-6, ^{b}29-1180^{a}1), a process which clearly involves education of the *pathē*, but which can be opposed to 'living by *pathos*' in as much as it involves control of the *pathē* as opposed to their indulgence whenever they arise. All this suggests that the emotional dislike of *to aischron* that is *aidōs* is acquired by habituation (contrast *EE* 1234^{a}27-8, where *aidōs* is 'natural'). There is, however, a slight suggestion, at 1179^{b}11, that the *aidōs* of the 'civilized' youth may be inherited, for its absence in the many is said to be a matter of their nature (πεφύκασιν); but (*a*) this nature may be that of the developed specimen, formed by the conditions in which the many inevitably live; or (*b*) that which is natural to the many may be an inability to acquire *aidōs*, of which the positive counterpart is not innate *aidōs* but an innate capacity for *aidōs*.

both *aidōs* may encompass a genuine desire to avoid what is truly *aischron*; the difference is that in the earlier passage Aristotle gave the impression that to possess a sense of *aidōs* is nothing very impressive, whereas in the later he indicates the true value of the concept.[246]

There is thus no conflict in doctrine between the two passages; *aidōs* is an indispensable ally in the process of moral development, something which can give one a genuine desire to do what is *kalon* and avoid what is *aischron*, not because of what others might say or do, but because it encompasses a distaste for the *aischron* as such. It appears, therefore, that *aidōs* might actually enable one to act, in some sense, 'for the sake of the noble', avoiding *to aischron*, without reference to the prescriptions of the laws, the honours, and the opinions of other people which made *aidōs* a second best in the discussions of bravery. Yet *aidōs* is still one stage removed from true *aretē*, appropriate, as before, in the young; but where the previous passage saw *aidōs* as a sign of immaturity in respect of the goal of *aretē*, the present sees the same phenomenon, quite reasonably, as a sign of the capacity for progress.

Obviously Aristotle has decided to draw a dividing line between choosing *to kalon* and avoiding *to aischron* out of *aidōs* and doing so for their own sake as a virtuous person would; but where precisely should the line be drawn? Presumably at the point at which, in Aristotle's terms, the merely well-brought-up person becomes the virtuous person, after the acquisition of that intellectual quality, *phronēsis*, that is essential for true virtue. And, indeed, we saw in the discussions of bravery in the ethical treatises that the truly brave man's choice of *to kalon* was the choice dictated by *logos*, by reason.[247] This might suggest that discernment of *to kalon* in the virtuous person differs sharply from that in the pre-virtuous, the person who has been habituated so as to make the proper choices, the one who understands 'the that', but not yet 'the because'.[248] The person of full virtue, we might say, chooses the noble action rationally, because he sees its point, whereas the properly habituated person, responding on the basis of *aidōs*, reacts instinctively and emotionally. If this suggested, however, that *to kalon* is perceived and chosen by the intellect alone, it would be wrong. The noble action of the truly virtuous need not be the product of deliberation or calculation, but may be instinctive and automatic without being any

---

[246] See the excellent discussion of the two passages in Burnyeat (1980: 79–80).
[247] See n. 234 above.
[248] *EN* 1095^b6–7, 1098^a33–^b4. Cf. Burnyeat (1980), 71–3; Sherman (1989), 194.

the less rationally chosen (a result of *proairesis*).[249] And several recent writers stress (what is, in fact, clear in Book 6 of the *Nicomachean Ethics*) that moral virtue or excellence of character and the intellectual capacity of *phronēsis* that is required for full virtue are only logically separable;[250] moral virtue in itself presupposes cognition and evaluation, and it is the powers of discrimination acquired in the process of habituation leading to moral virtue that ultimately give rise to *phronēsis* also; *phronēsis* completes, and therefore requires, habituation. Even in the fully virtuous person, then, choosing *to kalon* is not a matter of purely intellectual judgement, but requires the affective states and capacities that have been developed since childhood.

And here Aristotle's attempts to grapple with the concept of *aidōs* run into difficulty. He is absolutely justified, in his own terms, in denying *aidōs* the status of *aretē*: *aidōs* can connote moral imperfection, both as prospective inhibition of an action one is tempted to perform and even more so as retrospective shame; it is traditionally associated with honour and one's position in the eyes of others; and it regularly suggests an emotional response that may not be wholly responsive to reason.[251] Equally traditionally, however, *aidōs* is fundamentally related to the terms *aischron* and *kalon*;[252] and if the judgement of the person of practical wisdom that such and such is *aischron* may also encompass affective aspects, then there should presumably be a place for *aidōs* in that person's response.

If *to kalon* is the intrinsic and irreducible end of virtuous action, it must be supplied in the individual by that process of habituation which gives rise to *aretē*;[253] in that process, during which the individual is

---

[249] See esp. 1117ª9-22: moral character can produce instinctively the *kalon* action, and this is still a case of action with *proairesis*, provided the action is performed by a truly virtuous person; cf. Fortenbaugh (1975), 70-5. Thus not every case of moral action that is with *proairesis* has to be deliberated; cf. Cooper (1975), 6-10; also Sorabji (1980), 204-5; Charles (1984), 187.

[250] See esp. *EN* 1144ª14-1145ª12; also the full discussions of the issues in Monan (1968), 78-83 etc.; Burnyeat (1980); Sorabji (1980), esp. 210-18; Engberg-Pedersen (1983), chs. 6-8; Dahl (1984), 35-99 *passim*; Charles (1984), 177-87; Sherman (1989).

[251] Burnyeat (1980: 79, 84 (cf. n. 137 above)) aptly compares Pl.'s *thumoeides* and the way in which its judgements may not coincide with those of reason; similarly, Arist. acknowledges the possibility of *akrasia* of spirit at *EN* 1149ª25-b2. A straightforward example would be that of Telemachus in *Od.* 3: he is told that he has no need to feel *aidōs*, yet his *aidōs* persists (3. 14, 24).

[252] This needs no demonstration, but we might note in passing how *Rhet.* 1366b34-5 acknowledges the intimate connection between *kala* and *timē*, and how 1367ª6-14 sees *aidōs* and *aischunē* as promoting *kala* by avoiding *aischra*.

[253] On habituation, see *EN* 1103ª14-b25, 1179b20-1180ª32, *EE* 1220ª39-b3. This last passage sums up neatly what is clear from the first, that habituation is a matter of being

brought to regard *to kalon* as pleasant and *to aischron* as unpleasant, *aidōs* will be indispensable, both as the force which makes one sensitive to the opinions of those, such as parents and teachers, who constitute the media through which one learns to subscribe to the standards of one's society, and as the basis for one's acquired sense of the intrinsically *aischron* or *kalon*.[254] The person who has achieved full excellence, then, must have done so with the help of *aidōs*, and it is difficult to imagine that that person can have left *aidōs* entirely behind. Aristotle, moreover, knows very well that emotions have an important evaluative component, and the evaluative judgement that is constitutive of the emotion of *aidōs* has traditionally had as its content the belief that such-and-such is *aischron*. Admittedly, the correct but unjustified judgement that such-and-such is *aischron* is exactly what Aristotle wishes to distinguish from the judgement of the *phronimos* by means of his distinction between 'the that' and 'the because'; but one who knows 'the because' does not abandon his previous appreciation of 'the that', and so the *phronimos* has no need entirely to leave behind his sense of *aidōs*. An appreciation of *to kalon* and *to aischron* in

repeatedly affected in a certain way; the acquisition of *aretē* thus requires frequent experience of the particular *pathos* in a particular way, and so frequent experience of *aidōs* will be necessary for any developed aversion to *to aischron*.

[254] *To kalon* is Arist.'s word for the intrinsic attractiveness of the correct action as it appears to the good man; given that excellence of character is acquired by habituation, the content of any individual's sense of *to kalon* will initially have been supplied by the values of society, as these are imparted through the medium of parents and others. We remember, too, that the *kalon* is typically characterized as praiseworthy; this suggests, I think, that *to kalon* for the good man is specified as that sort of conduct for which he has been praised since childhood and which he now sees as intrinsically attractive. But if *to kalon* appears as such to the truly good, then it appears as 'beautiful' to one who is achieving his full potential by fulfilling man's function to the highest degree; the objectivity of *to kalon* will therefore presumably lie in the fact that what is ethically 'beautiful' will, under another aspect, be what the *phronimos* would do in order to achieve his full potential and manifest his excellence. We can thus expect objective criteria for the *kalon*, but Arist. leaves us to piece together some idea of what they might be. Engberg-Pedersen (1983: 37–52) and Irwin (1985*b*: 120–38; 1988: 440–1, 630–1 nn. 3–4) define it in terms of the 'common good', but while to promote the common good may be, to a paramount degree, *kalon* (e.g. *EN* 1169ª18–22; cf. *Rhet.* 1366ª36–1367ª6, 18–19) and while one can make a case for the view that all *kala* ultimately promote the common good (using, e.g., *EN* 1169ª11–15), the arguments of Engberg-Pedersen and Irwin stop short of proof that the common good must be included in a definition of *to kalon* or that the content of *to kalon* must be specified with reference to the common good. When the *phronimos* responds to the *kalon qua kalon* he presumably responds in the quasi-aesthetic manner which Irwin (1985*b*: 120–4) rules out, i.e. out of appreciation of its intrinsic beauty. This is not to say, however, that he cannot give a reasoned account of why he finds it beautiful, or justify the performance of a *kalon* action in terms of fulfilment of human nature and achievement of *eudaimonia*. Cf. (roughly) Allan (1971), 69–70.

themselves and without reference to external sanctions suggests not a capacity that is totally distinct from *aidōs*, but a variety of *aidōs* which responds to *to aischron* without reference to external standards.

One can appreciate Aristotle's difficulty with *aidōs*, however; any *aidōs* that might form part of the excellence of the wholly virtuous person would of necessity be that which responds to *to aischron* as such; this would be a recognizably traditional aspect of the concept, and we might think that Aristotle could easily construct an Aristotelian virtue of *aidōs* on that basis. But such *aidōs* (excluding retrospective *aidōs*, *aidōs* inhibiting acts one is strongly tempted to perform, *aidōs* at exposure before the eyes of the worthless, *aidōs* as simple embarrassment, etc.) would not capture the whole of the concept, and the reconstituted virtue thus arrived at would surely be too revisionary for Aristotle's taste. In trying to cope with the range and diversity of the concept he therefore tends to err in the other direction, by attempting to reduce *aidōs* to the occurrent level and failing explicitly to acknowledge the role it might, as a trait of character, legitimately play in the choice of *to kalon* for its own sake.

To return to 1128ᵇ10–35: Aristotle's attempt to deny *aidōs* the status of *hexis* is unsuccessful; even on his own account *aidōs* emerges, *malgré lui*, as a state of character, as an appropriate object of praise; in particular, his observations that *aidōs* involves 'being in such a condition as to *aischunesthai* were one to do something *aischron*' (1128ᵇ26–7) in itself requires a *hexis* which is related to *aidōs* and *aischunē*, and Aristotle should accommodate ordinary Greek usage in designating this *hexis* as *aidōs*.[255] We have seen, however, that Aristotle cannot accept the common opinion that *aidōs* is an *aretē* without either revising *aidōs* to a considerable extent or relaxing his criteria as to what it is to be an *aretē*.[256] On the face of it, this is problematic, since, if

---

[255] There is no reason to speculate that Arist. might regard *aidōs* as a *diathesis* rather than a *hexis*, for *hexeis* are simply those *diatheseis* that are deeply ingrained and hard to lose, and according to which the bearer is well or ill disposed (*Cat.* 8ᵇ27–8, 9ᵃ8–13, *Metaph.* 1022ᵇ10–12; cf. Hutchinson (1986), 8–20). Alex. Aphr. (*Ethical Problems* 21, p. 142. 14 Bruns = Sharples (1990), 55–6) agrees that Arist. should concede that *aidōs* is that particular sort of *diathesis* which is a *hexis*.

[256] In theory, an Aristotelian virtue of *aidōs* could be reconstituted from that recognized by common opinion. The notorious ambivalence of *aidōs* would be no objection, since Arist. himself is prepared to revise *aidōs* to the extent of having it include the idea of seasonability (and so also praiseworthiness); nor would the fact that *aidōs* can be an occurrent emotion debar it, since legitimate excellences of character, such as bravery and *praotēs* (mildness or good temper, *EN* 1125ᵇ26–1126ᵇ10, *EE* 1231ᵇ5–26, *MM* 1191ᵇ23–38), also govern one's disposition with regard to occurrent emotions (on means with regard to emotions, see Kosman (1980)), and Arist. might therefore posit a virtuous

aidōs is to be a *hexis*, then it should be either an *aretē* or a *kakia*,[257] and Aristotle, one might think, would not agree that it is either. Yet the problem is only superficial; *aidōs*, once recognized, as it should be, as a *hexis*, could be a good *hexis* like *enkrateia*,[258] a sort of mixture[259] of excellence and defect which can even, on occasion, be seen as a qualified *aretē*.[260] *Aidōs* would then be a defect relative to the perfection of true *aretē*, but a relatively good *hexis* to have when compared with other, worse imperfections.

Aristotle's only real error, then, in his treatment of *aidōs* is to ignore its dispositional aspect by denying it the status of *hexis*; this, however, is understandable, given that he rightly sees that *aidōs* cannot, as it stands, constitute an Aristotelian *aretē*, and given his sense that any *hexis* which is not an *aretē* must be a *kakia*. He is right, I think, to resist the temptation to create a revisionary *aretē* out of *aidōs*, and clearly prefers to treat the concept as a necessary condition and preliminary for complete *aretē*, a crucial element in the acquisition of an attraction to *to kalon* for its own sake. The only explicit statement of a role for *aidōs* in *aretē*, however, comes in the *Eudemian Ethics* (1234ᵃ32), where it is said to contribute to the natural excellence of *sōphrosunē*, and this is clearly too limited a conception of the contribution of *aidōs* to *aretē*. It is limited because the *sōphrosunē* in question is only that which is anterior to the full virtue governed by *phronēsis*, and because, in any case, even true *sōphrosunē*, for Aristotle, is active in a much more limited sphere (that of sensual pleasure) than that of *aidōs*, which, as the *Magna Moralia* recognizes,[261] is quite generally concerned with the *aischron* and *kalon* across the range of words and deeds. A full account of the place of *aidōs* in Aristotle's theory of virtue, therefore, must take account of its contribution to excellence of character as a whole, recognizing its importance as a source of the affective and evaluative dispositions which can be developed into that complete form of excellence of character which is informed by *phronēsis*. Seen in this light, *aidōs* emerges as indispensable in the inductive process which

mean representing the appropriate attitude towards the emotion of *aidōs* (*aidēmosunē*?). One might object that such a mean would be without *proairesis*, a criterion that excludes *pathē* (and *dunameis*?) from consideration as virtues (*EN* 1106ᵃ2–4) and *aidōs* from consideration as a virtue (along with other means) at *EE* 1234ᵃ24–33; but if the proper disposition towards anger (*praotēs*) can be with *proairesis*, so presumably could the proper disposition towards *aidōs*, even if occurrent *aidōs*, like occurrent anger, is itself without *proairesis*.

[257] See *Phys.* 246ᵃ11–17 (nn. 173, 213 above).
[258] See *EN* 1151ᵃ27, ᵇ28 (nn. 174, 229 above).
[259] *EN* 1128ᵇ34. [260] Cf. n. 174 above. [261] *MM* 1193ᵃ1–10.

develops in tandem the desiderative and the rational aspects of complete *aretē*, and if Aristotle fails to make the part of *aidōs* in all this as clear as he might have, this is to be taken as a mere lacuna, rather than a substantive defect in his account.

Several of Aristotle's explicit pronouncements on *aidōs* are disappointingly negative or unsatisfactorily limited, but what emerges from his treatment of *aidōs* as a whole is an impression of a great intellect grappling with a popular concept whose complexity resists easy absorption into an Aristotelian framework; that the concept is eventually accommodated and accorded something like its true importance without too much violence to the common beliefs is a tribute to Aristotle's determination to do justice to the facts of (Greek) ethical experience, while the very difficulties he faces in dealing with such an intractable concept provide further testimony as to its many-faceted nature and a salutary warning against facile generalization.

Aristotle may leave us to reconstruct his essential position on the true contribution of *aidōs* to excellence of character, but what emerges from such a reconstruction is a mature and suggestive appreciation that *aidōs*, even if conceived as a mere preliminary to complete *aretē*, cannot simply be regarded as a fear of the unpleasant consequences of ill-repute and is thus not incompatible with a form of conscience based on internalized moral standards; *aidōs* can encompass rejection of the *aischron* as such, and it is therefore clear that Aristotle regards it as quite uncontroversial that at least those of his fellow countrymen whose natural aptitudes had received the proper habituation should be concerned for the intrinsic character of their actions rather than simply for their consequences. And once we restore *aidōs* to its proper place as a factor whose dispositional and evaluative elements are incorporated in the moral insight of the good man, we should be prepared to acknowledge its role in that concern for the best part of oneself that is Aristotelian *philautia*. To be true to himself, the *philautos* seeks the *kalon* and rejects the *aischron* as inconsonant with his self-image as a bearer of certain standards which he has accepted and made his own and to which he subscribes for their own sake.[262] It is possible, then, to see in this picture of proper *philautia* a development

---

[262] On *philautia*, acceptance of one's true self, and commitment to *to kalon*, see Irwin (1988), 376–7, 379–81; cf. Lear (1988), 186–91, on endorsing one's character as the fulfilment of one's human nature.

within an Aristotelian framework of that concern for the self as one among many which is characteristic of *aidōs* from Homer onwards.

To attain the goal of complete excellence may be a rare or impossible achievement, but it is an ideal which Aristotle is able to construct on the basis of the categories of evaluation which he found in ordinary moral discourse, and it is an ideal in whose construction he is remarkably successful in combining a system based on a natural teleology of man with an account which saves most of the phenomena of common belief. We should thus see in his overall approach to *aidōs*, and to what may be made of *aidōs* in the good man, a recognition of the central thesis of this work, that *aidōs* is not solely dependent on the judgements of others, that it can spring from a form of conscience based on internalized moral standards, and that it can express a concern for the intrinsic character of one's actions. In this matter, Aristotle is in agreement with Democritus and with Plato; of the three, Democritus seems the most optimistic that such a concern may be possible for a wide cross-section of society, but since the conclusions of all three must, at least to some extent, be drawn from their understanding and observation of the motivation of their fellow Greeks, their ethical theories, though different, converge in offering evidence to contradict the generalizations of the shame-culture theorists.

Epilogue

Full rehearsal of the issues raised and conclusions drawn in the Introduction and subsequent chapters of this work would be inappropriate here; I hope, rather, that the reader will see the individual chapters as fulfilment of the general approach set out in the Introduction, and thus feel no need for an exhaustive summary and conclusion. Nevertheless, some valedictory remarks are clearly in order.

Our study began by identifying the *aidōs* as a prospective, inhibitory emotion focusing on one's idea of oneself, especially as that idea is affected by or comes into contact with others, and, despite the changes which take place in usage, in values, and in social forms, this focus on self *vis-à-vis* others remains constant. From the earliest period, too, Greek ideas of selfhood are mediated through the concept of honour, and at every stage development of the sense of self on which *aidōs* rests is promoted and maintained by focus on the status of self and others as bearers of honour. Thus I think it is true to say that study of *aidōs* is a study in the psychology and ethics of honour; but this statement would be misleading if it suggested that *aidōs* is concerned with nothing more than that concept of prestige, of external validation of one's own status and achievements, which is conveyed in Greek by the concepts of *timē*, *kleos*, *eukleia*, and so on. The link between *aidōs* and *timē* is, of course, fundamental, but the crucial point is that *aidōs* includes concern both for one's own *timē* and for that of others. As a result, part of the function of *aidōs* is to recognize the point at which self-assertion encroaches illegitimately upon the *timē* of others, and this means that *aidōs*, while always responding to a situation in which *timē* is relevant, is concerned not only with one's own prestige, but also with the concepts of moderation and appropriateness in the pursuit of prestige.

Behind the idea of one's own *timē*, moreover, lies a subjective claim to honour and an internalized self-image that is not wholly dependent on the opinions of others; to be concerned for one's self-image in Greek is to be concerned for one's *timē*, but at no stage does this necessarily imply concern for one's outward reputation to the exclusion of one's image in one's own eyes. The code of honour to which *aidōs* relates demands individual determination actually to possess an excellence, not merely that one should seem to others to possess it.

The code of honour studied in this book is also a code of appropriateness, and thus the concept of *to aischron* (and the complex of
quasi-aesthetic terms which belong with it) is as central to *aidōs* as is
that of *timē*. The quasi-aesthetic standard of appropriateness is
absolutely inseparable from the concept of honour; competitive
failure (failure to meet a self-assertive goal) is *aischron*, unseemly, or
inappropriate, both in one's own eyes and in those of others, and the
same is true of co-operative failure (pursuit of self-assertive goals
without due regard for the honour of others). Thus, in the Greek
context, it does no good at all to limit the application of the term
'honour' to self-assertive, agonistic behaviour, or to consider the
standard of appropriateness as somehow distinct from the complex
of terms based on honour. The values are all of a piece, and reflect
the fact that the honour of self is intricately bound up with that of
others.

These categories of appropriateness and 'how things look' persist
throughout the period which we have studied, and with them persist
the conceptual associations of the terms involved. These associations
of *aidōs* and of the categories of value with which it belongs do much
to constitute the distinctness of the concept, as well as of the moral,
social, and psychological outlook in which it is at home. That such a
central term of Greek moral and social discourse should carry such
close associations with 'face' and facial or ocular interaction (blushing, the lowering of one's eyes, etc.) and with terms of value which
are fundamentally aesthetic in nature (*kalon*, *aischron*, *aeikes*, etc.)
provides some indication that the conceptualization of experience
entailed by *aidōs* and related concepts is not our own. But this sense
of distinctness should not be allowed to dispel a corresponding sense
of familiarity, first of all because, to a large extent, the concept of
aidōs covers aspects of the emotional life of human beings which can
be readily recast in our own (more differentiated and less inclusive)
terms, and secondly because the conceptual uniqueness of *aidōs* and
of the categories of value with which it belongs does not preclude
such familiar features of our moral and emotional life as conscience,
the possession of internalized standards, or concern for the character
of our actions as such. There is, in these respects, no easy dichotomy
between 'us' and 'them'.

Concerning the standards of the honourable, the fine, or the
appropriate as discussed above, one major argument of this work
is that there is no case for sharp distinctions between self- and

other-regarding motives, competitive and co-operative values, non-moral and moral responses. These are the categories of our moral thinking, not those of the Greeks, and the Greek categories in which *aidōs* belongs can cover both sides of these modern disjunctions with no implication that either is to be reduced to the terms of the other. The other major theme, that *aidōs* does involve internalized standards, has been sufficiently elaborated above, and needs no restatement. These two positions, in themselves, are simple and unpretentious, yet they contradict many of the most significant and most widely accepted modern assumptions regarding the nature of *aidōs* and the values to which it relates. Obviously, I hope others will agree with me; but if forthcoming disagreement rests, as I have tried to make this work rest, on consideration of the entire range over which the relevant terms are used and on an appreciation of the inclusivity of the relevant moral and social attitudes, then the book will have done its job.

REFERENCES

Abbreviations used in this list

Abbreviations for several of the most frequently cited periodicals are given below. Other, less familiar titles, are given in full or with only slight abbreviation.

A und A	*Antike und Abendland*
AJP	*American Journal of Philology*
APQ	*American Philosophical Quarterly*
BICS	*Bulletin of the Institute of Classical Studies*
CP	*Classical Philology*
CQ	*Classical Quarterly*
CR	*Classical Review*
Entr. Fond. Hardt	Fondation Hardt: Entretiens sur l'antiquité classique
GR	*Greece and Rome*
GRBS	*Greek, Roman, and Byzantine Studies*
HSCP	*Harvard Studies in Classical Philology*
ICS	*Illinois Classical Studies*
JHS	*Journal of Hellenic Studies*
LCM	*Liverpool Classical Monthly*
MH	*Museum Helveticum*
Mnem.	*Mnemosyne*
PAS	*Proceedings of the Aristotelian Society*
PCPS	*Proceedings of the Cambridge Philological Society*
REG	*Revue des études grecs*
Rev. Phil.	*Revue de philologie*
RM	*Rheinisches Museum für Philologie*
TAPA	*American Philological Association: Transactions and Proceedings*
WdF	Wege der Forschung
WS	*Wiener Studien*
YCS	*Yale Classical Studies*

Dates of publication refer, as do page references in the notes above, to the edition (usually the latest or most authoritative) actually consulted. Date of first publication, for books, is usually given in parentheses, but, in order to avoid cluttering the bibliography, articles appearing in collections are normally designated by the date of the collection alone. In a few cases, however, I have referred to the article as originally published, and added references to an anthologized version.

ABOU-ZEID, A. (1965), 'Honour and Shame among the Bedouins of Egypt', in Peristiany (1965), 243–59.

ABU-LUGHOD, L. (1986), *Veiled Sentiments: Honor and Poetry in a Bedouin Society* (Berkeley and Los Angeles).

ACKRILL, J. L. (1963) (ed.), *Aristotle's Categories and De Interpretatione* (Oxford).

ADKINS, A. W. H. (1960*a*), *Merit and Responsibility* (Oxford).

—— (1960*b*), '"Honour" and "Punishment" in the Homeric Poems', *BICS* 7: 23–32.

—— (1963), '"Friendship" and "Self-Sufficiency" in Homer and Aristotle', *CQ* 13: 30–45.

—— (1966), 'Basic Greek Values in Euripides' *Hecuba* and *Hercules Furens*', *CQ* 16: 193–219.

—— (1970), *From the Many to the One* (London).

—— (1971), 'Homeric Values and Homeric Society', *JHS* 91: 1–14.

—— (1973), "ἀρετή, τέχνη, Democracy, and Sophists", *JHS* 93: 3–12.

—— (1975), 'Merit, Responsibility, and Thucydides', *CQ* 25: 208–20.

—— (1982*a*), 'Values, Goals, and Emotions in the *Iliad*', *CP* 77: 292–326.

—— (1982*b*), 'Divine and Human Values in Aeschylus: *Seven against Thebes*', *A und A* 28: 32–68.

—— (1982*c*), 'Law versus Claims in Early Greek Religious Ethics', *History of Religions* 21: 222–39.

—— (1987), 'Gagarin and the Morality of Homer', *CP* 82: 311–22.

ALLAN, D. J. (1971), 'The Fine and the Good in the *Eudemian Ethics*', in P. Moreaux and D. Harlfinger (edd.), *Untersuchungen zur* Eudemischen Ethik (Proc. 5th Symp. Arist.; Berlin), 63–72.

ALT, K. (1961), 'Schicksal und φύσις im Philoktet des Sophokles', *Hermes* 89: 141–74.

ANNAS, J. (1981), *An Introduction to Plato's* Republic (Oxford).

ARNOLD, M. (1970) (ed.), *Feelings and Emotions: The Loyola Symposium* (New York).

ARNOTT, W. G. (1981), 'Double the Vision: A Reading of Euripides' *Electra*', *GR* 28: 179–92.

ARROWSMITH, W. (1959), 'The Criticism of Greek Tragedy', *Tulane Drama Review* 3. 3: 31–57.

AUSUBEL, D. P. (1955), 'Relationships between Shame and Guilt in the Socializing Process', *Psychological Review* 62: 379–90.

AVERILL, J. R. (1980*a*), 'Emotion and Anxiety: Sociocultural, Biological, and Psychological Determinants', in Rorty (1980*a*), 37–72.

—— (1980*b*), 'A Constructivist View of Emotion', in Plutchik and Kellerman (1980), 305–39.

AVERY, H. C. (1965), 'Heracles, Philoctetes, Neoptolemus', *Hermes* 93: 279–97.

—— (1982), 'One Antiphon or Two?', *Hermes* 110: 145–58.

BARKER, E. (1960), *Greek Political Theory: Plato and his Predecessors* (repr., London; 1st edn., 1918).

BARNES, J. (1979), 'Aristotle's Concept of Mind', in J. Barnes, M. Schofield, and R. Sorabji (edd.), *Articles on Aristotle*, iv. (London), 32–41.

— (1982), *The Presocratic Philosophers*² (London; 1st edn., 1979).

BARRETT, W. S. (1964) (ed.), *Euripides: Hippolytos* (Oxford).

BARTHOLD, T. (1880) (ed.), *Euripides: Hippolytos* (Berlin).

BEDFORD, E. (1956–7), 'Emotions', *PAS* 57: 281–304.

BEIL, A. (1961), "αἰδώς bei Homer", *Der Altsprachliche Unterricht* 5. 1: 51–64.

BENEDICT, R. (1934), *Patterns of Culture* (Boston and New York).

— (1947), *The Chrysanthemum and the Sword: Patterns of Japanese Culture* (London).

BENVENISTE, E. (1973), *Indo-European Language and Society*, ET (London; orig. pub. 1969).

BERNS, G. (1973), 'Nomos and Physis: An Interpretation of Euripides' *Hippolytos*', *Hermes* 101: 165–87.

BESSLICH, S. (1981), 'Nausikaa und Telemach, Dichterische Funktion und Eigenwert der Person bei der Darstellung des jungen Menschen in der Odyssee', in G. Kurz, D. Müller, and W. Nicolai (edd.), *Gnomosyne, Festschrift W. Marg* (Munich), 103–16.

BIGNONE, E. (1938), *Studi sul pensiero antico* (Naples).

BLAIKLOCK, E. M. (1952), *The Male Characters of Euripides* (Wellington).

BLUNDELL, M. W. (1988), 'The *Phusis* of Neoptolemus in Sophocles' *Philoctetes*', *GR* 35: 137–48.

— (1989), *Helping Friends and Harming Enemies: A Study in Sophocles and Greek Ethics* (Cambridge).

BOARDMAN, J. (1975), *Athenian Red-Figure Vases: The Archaic Period* (London).

BOND, G. W. (1981) (ed.), *Euripides: Heracles* (Oxford).

BOWIE, E. (1986), 'Early Greek Elegy, Symposium, and Public Festival', *JHS* 106: 13–35.

— (1990), '*Miles Ludens*? The Problem of Martial Exhortation in Early Greek Elegy', in O. Murray (1990), 222–9.

BRAUND, D. C. (1980), 'Artemis Eukleia and Euripides' *Hippolytus*', *JHS* 100: 184–5.

BREMER, J. M. (1969), *Hamartia* (Amsterdam).

— (1975), 'The Meadow of Love and Two Passages in Euripides' *Hippolytos*', *Mnem.* 4. 28: 268–80.

BREMMER, J. N. (1990), 'Adolescents, *Symposion*, and Pederasty', in O. Murray (1990), 135–48.

BROADHEAD, H. D. (1960) (ed.), *The Persae of Aeschylus* (Cambridge).

BROWN, N. O. (1969), *Hermes the Thief: The Evolution of a Myth* (repr., New York; 1st edn., 1947).

BURIAN, P. H. (1971), 'Suppliant Drama' (Diss., Princeton).

— (1974*a*), 'Pelasgus and Politics in Aeschylus' Danaid Trilogy', *WS* 87: 5–14.

— (1947*b*), 'Suppliant and Saviour: Oedipus at Colonus', *Phoenix* 28: 408–29.

BURIAN, P. H. (1985), '*Logos* and *Pathos*: The Politics of the *Suppliant Women*', in P. H. Burian (ed.), *Directions in Euripidean Criticism* (Durham, NC), 129-55.

BURKERT, W. (1983), *Homo Necans: The Anthropology of Ancient Greek Sacrificial Ritual and Myth*, ET (Berkeley and Los Angeles; orig. pub. 1972).

—— (1985), *Greek Religion*, ET (Oxford; orig. pub. 1977).

BURNETT, A. P. (1983), *Three Archaic Poets: Archilochus, Alcaeus, Sappho* (London).

—— (1986), 'Hunt and Hearth in *Hippolytus*', in M. J. Cropp, E. Fantham, and S. E. Scully (edd.), *Greek Tragedy and its Legacy: Essays Presented to D. J. Conacher* (Calgary), 167-85.

BURNYEAT, M. F. (1980), 'Aristotle on Learning to Be Good', in Rorty (1980*b*), 69-92.

CAIRNS, D. L. (1989), 'Problems in *Aristotle's Philosophy of Action*', LCM 14. 6: 86-9.

—— (1990), 'Mixing with Men and Nausicaa's Nemesis', *CQ* 40: 263-6.

CAMPBELL, J. K. (1964), *Honour, Family, and Patronage: A Study of Institutions and Moral Values in a Greek Mountain Community* (Oxford).

—— (1965), 'Honour and the Devil', in Peristiany (1965), 139-70.

CANTARELLA, E. (1981), 'Spunti di riflessione critica su ὕβρις e τιμή in Omero', in *Symposium 1979: Actes du IVe colloque international de droit grec et hellenistique* (Athens), 85-96.

—— (1982), 'Studi sul lessico giuridico greco: ὕβρις in Omero', *Incontri Linguistici* 7: 19-30.

CARTER, L. B. (1986), *The Quiet Athenian* (Oxford).

CERRI, G. (1979), *Legislazione orale e tragedia greca* (Naples).

CHALK, H. H. O. (1962), "ἀρετή and βία in Euripides' *Herakles*", JHS 82: 7-18.

CHARLES, D. (1984), *Aristotle's Philosophy of Action* (London).

CHEYNS, A. (1967), *Sens et valeurs du mot aidōs dans les contextes homériques* (Travaux de la Faculté de Philosophie et Lettres, Louvain, ii. Section de Philol. Class. i. Rech. de Philol. et de Linguistique).

CLASS, M. (1964), *Gewissensregungen in der griechischen Tragödie* (Spudasmata 3; Hildesheim).

CLAUS, D. B. (1972), 'Phaedra and the Socratic Paradox', YCS 22: 223-38.

—— (1974), '*Aidōs* in the Language of Achilles', TAPA 105: 13-28.

—— (1977), 'Defining Moral Terms in *Works and Days*', TAPA 107: 73-84.

COBB-STEVENS, V. (1985), 'Opposites, Reversals, and Ambiguities: The Unsettled World of Theognis', in Figueira and Nagy (1985), 159-75.

COLLARD, C. (1972), 'The Funeral Oration in Euripides' *Supplices*', BICS 19: 39-53.

—— (1975) (ed.), *Euripides: Supplices* (Groningen).

CONACHER, D. J. (1967), *Euripidean Drama: Myth, Theme, and Structure* (Toronto).

—— (1980), *Aeschylus, Prometheus Bound: A Literary Commentary* (Toronto).

—— (1981), 'Rhetoric and Relevance in Euripidean Drama', AJP 102: 3-25.

COOK, A. B. (1901), 'Associated Reminiscences', CR 15: 338-45.

COOPER, J. M. (1973), 'The *Magna Moralia* and Aristotle's Moral Philosophy', *AJP* 94: 327–49.

—— (1975), *Reason and Human Good in Aristotle* (Cambridge, Mass.).

—— (1984), 'Plato's Theory of Human Motivation', *History of Philosophy Quarterly* 1: 3–21.

COPE, E. M. (1877) (ed.), *Aristotle's Rhetoric* (Cambridge).

CORNFORD, F. M. (1912), 'Psychology and Social Structure in the *Republic* of Plato', *CQ* 6: 246–65.

CRAIK, E. M. (1987), 'The First *Hippolytus*', *Mnem.* 4. 40: 143–8.

CREED, J. L. (1973), 'Moral Values in the Age of Thucydides', *CQ* 23: 213–31.

CROMBIE, I. M. (1962), *An Examination of Plato's Doctrines*, i (London).

CROSS, R. C., and WOOZLEY, A. D. (1966), *Plato's Republic: A Philosophical Commentary* (London).

DAHL, N. O. (1984), *Practical Reason, Aristotle, and Weakness of the Will* (Minneapolis).

DALE, A. M. (1954) (ed.), *Euripides: Alcestis* (Oxford).

DALFEN, J. (1984), 'Ist Kreon ein Mann ohne Arme? Das Problematische an der aidos in Tragödien des Euripides', in D. Ahrens (ed.), Θίασος τῶν Μουσῶν: *Festschrift J. Fink* (Cologne), 67–75.

DAWE, R. D. (1963), 'Inconsistency of Plot and Character in Aeschylus', *PCPS* 9: 21–62.

DENNISTON, J. D. (1939) (ed.), *Euripides: Electra* (Oxford).

—— (1954), *The Greek Particles²* (Oxford).

—— and PAGE, D. L. (1957) (edd.), *Aeschylus: Agamemnon* (Oxford).

DETIENNE, M., and VERNANT, J.-P. (1978), *Cunning Intelligence in Greek Culture and Society*, ET (Sussex; orig. pub. 1974).

DEVEREUX, G. (1985), *The Character of the Euripidean Hippolytos: An Ethnopsychoanalytical Study* (Chico, Calif.).

DICKIE, M. W. (1978), '*Dikē* as a Moral Term in Homer and Hesiod', *CP* 73: 91–101.

DIHLE, A. (1977), 'Das Satyrspiel "Sisyphus"', *Hermes* 105: 28–42.

DILLER, H. (1956), 'Über das Selbstbewußtsein der sophokleischen Personen', *WS* 66: 70–85.

DIMOCK, G. E. (1977), 'Euripides' *Hippolytus*, or Virtue Rewarded', *YCS* 25: 239–58.

DIRLMEIER, F. (1956) (ed.), *Aristoteles, Nikomachische Ethik* (Berlin).

—— (1962), *Merkwürdige Zitate in der* Eudemischen Ethik *des Aristoteles* (SB Heidelberger Ak. Wiss., Phil.-hist Kl., 1962. 2).

—— (1963) (ed.), *Aristoteles, Eudemische Ethik* (Berlin).

—— (1964) (ed.), *Aristoteles, Magna Moralia* (Berlin).

DODDS, E. R. (1925), 'The αἰδώς of Phaedra', *CR* 39: 102–4.

—— (1951), *The Greeks and the Irrational* (Berkeley and Los Angeles).

DÖRING, K. (1981), 'Die politische Theorie des Protagoras', in Kerferd (1981*b*), 109–15.

DOVER, K. J. (1964), 'The Poetry of Archilochus', in *Archiloque* (Entr. Fond. Hardt 10; Geneva), 181–222.

—— (1973), 'Some Neglected Aspects of Agamemnon's Dilemma', *JHS* 93: 58–69.

—— (1974), *Greek Popular Morality in the Time of Plato and Aristotle* (Oxford).

—— (1978), *Greek Homosexuality* (London).

—— (1983), 'The Portrayal of Moral Evaluation in Greek Poetry', *JHS* 103: 35–48.

DÜRING, I. (1968), 'Aristotle's Use of Examples in the *Topics*', in G. E. L. Owen (ed.), *Aristotle on Dialectic: The* Topics (Proc. 3rd Symp. Arist.; Oxford), 202–29.

EASTERLING, P. E. (1973), 'Presentation of Character in Aeschylus', *GR* 20: 3–19.

—— (1977), 'Characterization in Sophocles', *GR* 24: 121–9.

—— (1978), 'Sophocles' *Philoctetes* and Recent Criticism', *ICS* 3: 27–39.

—— (1984), 'The Tragic Homer', *BICS* 31: 1–8.

—— (1990), 'Constructing Character in Greek Tragedy', in Pelling (1990), 83–99.

EDWARDS, G. P. (1971), *The Language of Hesiod* (Oxford).

EKMAN, P. (1980), 'Biological and Cultural Contributions to Body and Facial Movement in the Expression of Emotions', in Rorty (1980*a*), 73–101.

ENGBERG-PEDERSEN, T. (1983), *Aristotle's Theory of Moral Insight* (Oxford).

ENGLAND, E. B. (1921) (ed.), *The Laws of Plato* (Manchester).

ERBSE, H. (1966), 'Neoptolemos und Philoktet bei Sophokles', *Hermes* 94: 177–201.

ERFFA, C. E. VON (1937), αἰδώς *und verwandte Begriffe in ihrer Entwicklung von Homer bis Demokrit* (*Philologus* Suppl. 30. 2; Leipzig).

EWING, A. C. (1957), reply to Warnock (1957) in 'Symposium: The Justification of Emotions' (*PAS* Suppl. 31), 59–74.

FARRAR, C. (1988), *The Origins of Democratic Thinking: The Invention of Politics in Classical Athens* (Cambridge).

FARRON, S. (1979), 'The Portrayal of Women in the *Iliad*', *Acta Classica* 22: 15–31.

FERGUSON, J. (1979), *Moral Values in the Ancient World* (New York).

FIGUEIRA, T. J., and NAGY, G. (1985) (edd.), *Theognis of Megara: Poetry and the Polis* (Baltimore).

FINLEY, M. I. (1956), *The World of Odysseus* (London).

FISHER, N. R. E. (1976), '*Hybris* and Dishonour: i', *GR* 23: 177–93.

—— (1979), '*Hybris* and Dishonour: ii', *GR* 26: 32–47.

FITTON, J. W. (1961), 'The *Suppliant Women* and the *Herakleidai* of Euripides', *Hermes* 89: 430–61.

FOLEY, H. P. (1985), *Ritual Irony: Poetry and Sacrifice in Euripides* (Ithaca, NY).

FORTENBAUGH, W. W. (1968), 'Aristotle and the Questionable Mean-Dispositions', *TAPA* 99: 203–31.

—— (1970), 'On the Antecedents of Aristotle's Bipartite Psychology', *GRBS* 11: 233–50.

—— (1975), *Aristotle on Emotion* (London).

—— (1977), 'Aristotle on Slaves and Women', in J. Barnes, M. Schofield, and R. Sorabji (edd.), *Articles on Aristotle*, ii. *Ethics and Politics* (London), 135–49.

—— (1979), 'Aristotle's *Rhetoric* on Emotions', in J. Barnes, M. Schofield, and R. Sorabji (edd.), *Articles on Aristotle*, iv. *Psychology and Aesthetics* (London), 133–53.

FOWLER, R. L. (1987), *The Nature of Early Greek Lyric: Three Preliminary Studies* (*Phoenix* Suppl. 21; Toronto).

FRAENKEL, E. (1950) (ed.), *Aeschylus: Agamemnon* (Oxford).

FRAISSE, J.-C. (1974), *Philia: La Notion d'amitié dans la philosophie antique* (Paris).

FRÄNKEL, H. (1921), *Die homerischen Gleichnisse* (Göttingen).

—— (1975), *Early Greek Poetry and Philosophy*, ET (Oxford; orig. pub. 1962).

FREEMAN, D. (1983), *Margaret Mead and Samoa: The Making and Unmaking of an Anthropological Myth* (Canberra).

FREUD, S. (1961*a*), *The Ego and the Id* (1923), in *Works*, xix, ed. J. Strachey (London).

—— (1961*b*), *Civilization and its Discontents* (1930 [1929]), in *Works*, xxi, ed. J. Strachey (London).

—— (1964), *New Introductory Lectures on Psychoanalysis* (1933 [1932]), in *Works*, xxii, ed. J. Strachey (London).

FRIIS JOHANSEN, H., and WHITTLE, E. W. (1980) (edd.), *Aeschylus: The Suppliants* (Copenhagen).

FURLEY, D. J. (1977), 'Aristotle on the Voluntary', in J. Barnes, M. Schofield, and R. Sorabji (edd.), *Articles on Aristotle*, ii. *Ethics and Politics* (London), 47–60.

—— (1981), 'Antiphon's Case against Justice', in Kerferd (1981*b*), 81–91.

GAGARIN, M. (1969), 'The Purpose of Plato's *Protagoras*', *TAPA* 100: 133–62.

—— (1973), '*Dikē* in the *Works and Days*', *CP* 68: 81–94.

—— (1974), '*Dikē* in Archaic Greek Thought', *CP* 69: 186–97.

—— (1976), *Aeschylean Drama* (Berkeley and Los Angeles).

—— (1981), *Drakon and Early Athenian Homicide Law* (New Haven, Conn.).

—— (1986), *Early Greek Law* (Berkeley and Los Angeles).

—— (1987), 'Morality in Homer', *CP* 82: 285–306.

GANTZ, T. N. (1977), 'The Fires of the *Oresteia*', *JHS* 97: 28–38.

GARLAND, R. (1990), *The Greek Way of Life* (London).

GARNER, R. (1987), *Law and Society in Classical Athens* (London).

—— (1990), *From Homer to Tragedy: The Art of Allusion in Greek Poetry* (London).

GARVIE, A. F. (1986) (ed.), *Aeschylus: Choephori* (Oxford).

GASKIN, R. (1990), 'Do Homeric Heroes Make Real Decisions?', *CQ* 40: 1–15.

GAUTHIER, R.-A. (1951), *Magnanimité: L'Idéal de la grandeur dans la philosophie païenne et dans la théologie chrétienne* (Paris).

GELLIE, G. H. (1972), *Sophocles: A Reading* (Melbourne).

—— (1981), 'Tragedy and Euripides' *Electra*', *BICS* 28: 1–12.

GERNET, L. (1981) *The Anthropology of Ancient Greece*, ET (Baltimore; orig. pub. 1968).

GIGANTE, M. (1956), *Nomos Basileus* (Naples).

GIGON, O. (1975), 'Die Selbstliebe in der Nikomachische Ethik des Aristoteles', in Δώρημα: *Festschrift H. Diller* (Athens), 77-113.

GILDERSLEEVE, B. L. (1890) (ed.), *Pindar, the Olympian and Pythian Odes* (New York).

—— (1980), *Syntax of Classical Greek from Homer to Demosthenes* (Groningen; 1st edn., New York, 1900).

GILL, C. (1990), 'The Articulation of the Self in the *Hippolytus*', in A. Powell (ed.), *Euripides, Women, and Sexuality* (London), 76-107.

GOHEEN, R. F. (1951), *The Imagery of Sophocles'* Antigone (Princeton).

GOLDHILL, S. (1984), *Language, Sexuality, Narrative: The* Oresteia (Cambridge).

—— (1986), *Reading Greek Tragedy* (Cambridge).

—— (1987), 'The Great Dionysia and Civic Ideology', *JHS* 107: 58-76.

—— (1990), 'Character and Action, Representation and Reading: Greek Tragedy and its Critics', in Pelling (1990), 100-27.

GOMME, A. W. (1956), *A Historical Commentary on Thucydides*, ii (Oxford).

GORDON, R. L. (1981) (ed.), *Myth, Religion, and Society: Structuralist Essays by M. Detienne, L. Gernet, J.-P. Vernant, and P. Vidal-Naquet* (Cambridge).

GÖRGEMANNS, H. (1960), *Beiträge zur Interpretation von Platons Nomoi* (Zetemata 25; Munich).

GOSLING, J. C. B. (1973), *Plato* (London).

GOULD, J. P. A. (1955), *The Development of Plato's Ethics* (Cambridge).

—— (1973), 'Hiketeia', *JHS* 93: 74-103.

—— (1978*a*), review of Dover (1974), *CR* 28: 285-7.

—— (1978*b*), 'Dramatic Character and "Human Intelligibility" in Greek Tragedy', *PCPS* 24: 43-67.

—— (1980), 'Law, Custom, and Myth: Aspects of the Social Position of Women in Classical Athens', *JHS* 100: 38-59.

GOULDNER, A. W. (1965), *Enter Plato: Classical Greece and the Origins of Social Theory* (London).

GRAESER, A. (1969), *Probleme der platonischen Seelenteilungslehre* (Zetemata 47; Munich).

GREENE, W. C. (1944), *Moira: Fate, Good, and Evil in Greek Thought* (Cambridge, Mass.).

GREENWOOD, L. H. G. (1953), *Aspects of Euripidean Tragedy* (Cambridge).

GRIFFIN, J. (1980), *Homer on Life and Death* (Oxford).

—— (1986), 'Homeric Words and Speakers', *JHS* 106: 36-57.

GRIFFITH, M. (1977), *The Authenticity of the* Prometheus Bound (Cambridge).

—— (1983) (ed.), *Aeschylus: Prometheus Bound* (Cambridge).

GRUBE, G. M. A. (1961), *The Drama of Euripides*² (London: 1st edn., 1941)

GUNDERT, H. (1972), 'Archilochos und Solon', in G. Pfohl (ed.), *Die griechische Elegie* (WdF 129; Darmstadt), 75-102.

HALDANE, J. A. (1965), 'Musical Themes and Imagery in Aeschylus', *JHS* 85: 33–41.

HALLIWELL, F. S. (1986), *Aristotle's Poetics* (London).

—— (1990), 'Traditional Greek Conceptions of Character', in Pelling (1990), 32–59.

HAMMOND, N. G. L. (1965), 'Personal Freedom and its Limitations in the *Oresteia*', *JHS* 85: 42–55.

HANKEY, R. N. A. (1990), '"Evil" in the *Odyssey*', in E. M. Craik (ed.), *'Owls to Athens': Essays . . . for Sir Kenneth Dover* (Oxford), 87–95.

HARDER, A. (1985) (ed.), *Euripides' Kresphontes and Archelaos* (*Mnem.* Suppl. 87; Leiden).

HARDER, R. (1972), 'Die geschichtliche Stellung des Tyrtaios', in G. Pfohl (ed.), *Die griechische Elegie* (WdF 129; Darmstadt), 146–73.

HARDIE, W. F. R. (1978), '"Magnanimity" in Aristotle's Ethics', *Phronesis* 23: 63–79.

—— (1980), *Aristotle's Ethical Theory*² (Oxford; 1st edn., 1968).

HARRISON, A. R. W. (1968), *The Law of Athens*, i. *The Family and Property* (Oxford).

HARRISON, E. L. (1960), 'Notes on Homeric Psychology', *Phoenix* 14: 63–80.

HAVELOCK, E. A. (1957), *The Liberal Temper in Greek Politics* (New Haven, Conn.).

—— (1978), *The Greek Concept of Justice: From its Shadow in Homer to its Substance in Plato* (Cambridge, Mass.).

HEATH, M. (1987), *The Poetics of Greek Tragedy* (London).

HEINIMANN, F. (1945), *Nomos und Phusis: Herkunft und Bedeutung einer Antithese im griechischen Denken des 5. Jahrhunderts* (Basle).

HEITSCH, E. (1948), *Aidesis im attischen Strafrecht* (Ak. Wiss. Lit., Mainz, Abh. der geistes- u. sozialwiss. Klasse, 1984. 1).

HENDERSON, J. (1973), *The Maculate Muse: Obscene Language in Attic Comedy* (New Haven, Conn.).

HERZFELD, M. (1985), *The Poetics of Manhood: Contest and Identity in a Cretan Mountain Village* (Princeton).

HEUBECK, A., WEST, S., and HAINSWORTH, J. B. (1988) (edd.), *A Commentary on Homer's* Odyssey, i (Oxford).

HIRZEL, R. (1902), *Der Eid* (Leipzig).

HOEKSTRA, A. (1950), 'Hésiode: *Les Travaux et les jours*, 404–7, 317–19, 21–24', *Mnem.* 4. 3: 404–7.

HOHENDAHL-ZOETELIEF, I. M. (1980), *Manners in the Homeric Epic* (*Mnem.* Suppl. 63; Leiden).

HOOKER, J. T. (1975), 'The Original Meaning of ὕβρις', *Archiv für Begriffsgeschichte* 19: 125–37.

—— (1987), 'Homeric Society: A Shame-Culture?', *GR* 34: 121–5.

HOPPIN, J. C. (1919), *A Handbook of Attic Red-Figured Vases* (Cambridge, Mass.).

HUSSEY, E. (1985), 'Thucydidean History and Democritean Theory', in P. Cartledge and F. D. Harvey (edd.), *Crux: Essays Presented to G. E. M. de Ste. Croix* (Exeter), 118–38.

HUTCHINSON, D. S. (1986), *The Virtues of Aristotle* (London).

HUTCHINSON, G. O. (1985) (ed.), *Aeschylus: Septem contra Thebas* (Oxford).

INGENKAMP, H.-G. (1967), *Untersuchungen zu den pseudo-platonischen Definitionen* (Wiesbaden).

IRWIN, T. H. (1977), *Plato's Moral Theory* (Oxford).

—— (1983), 'Euripides and Socrates', *CP* 78: 183–97.

—— (1985*a*) (ed.), *Aristotle: Nicomachean Ethics* (Indianapolis).

—— (1985*b*), 'Aristotle's Concept of Morality', in J. J. Cleary (ed.), *Proceedings of the Boston Area Colloq. in Anc. Phil.* 1 (Lanham, Md.), 115–43.

—— (1988), *Aristotle's First Principles* (Oxford).

ISENBERG, A. (1980), 'Natural Pride and Natural Shame', in Rorty (1980*a*), 355–83.

IZARD, C. E. (1977), *Human Emotions* (New York).

JAEGER, W. (1939), *Paideia*, i, ET (Oxford; orig. pub. 1933).

—— (1972), "Tyrtaios. Über die wahre ἀρετή", in G. Piohl (ed.), *Die griechische Elegie* (WdF 129; Darmstadt), 103–45.

JÄKEL, S. (1972), "φόβος und σέβας im frühen Griechischen", *Archiv für Begriffsgeschichte* 16: 141–65.

—— (1975), "φόβος und σέβας, πάθος und μάθος im Drama des Aischylos", *Eirene* 13: 43–76.

—— (1979), "φόβος und σέβας bei Sophokles", *Arctos* 13: 31–41.

—— (1980), "φόβος, σέβας, und αἰδώς in den Dramen des Euripides", *Arctos* 14: 15–30.

JEBB, R. C. (1882), 'Pindar', *JHS* 3: 144–83.

—— (1890) (ed.), *Sophocles: The Plays and Fragments*, iv. *Philoctetes* (Cambridge).

—— (1896), *Sophocles . . .*, vii. *Ajax* (Cambridge).

JONES, J. (1962), *On Aristotle and Greek Tragedy* (London).

JUST, R. (1975), 'Conceptions of Women in Classical Athens', *J. Anthr. Soc. Oxford*, 6. 1: 153–70.

—— (1985), 'Freedom, Slavery, and the Female Psyche', in P. Cartledge and F. D. Harvey (edd.), *Crux: Essays Presented to G. E. M. de Ste. Croix* (Exeter), 169–88.

—— (1989), *Women in Athenian Law and Life* (London).

KAHN, C. H. (1979), 'Sensation and Consciousness in Aristotle's Psychology', in J. Barnes, M. Schofield, and R. Sorabji (edd.), *Articles on Aristotle*, iv. *Psychology and Aesthetics* (London), 1–31.

—— (1981), 'The Origins of Social Contract Theory', in Kerferd (1981*b*), 92–108.

—— (1985), 'Democritus and the Origins of Moral Psychology', *AJP* 106: 1–31.

KAKRIDIS, H. J. (1963), *La Notion de l'amitié et de l'hospitalité chez Homère* (Thessaloniki).

KAMERBEEK, J. C. (1980) (ed.), *The Plays of Sophocles*, vi. *Philoctetes* (Leiden).

KANNICHT, R. (1969) (ed.), *Euripides: Helena*, 2 vols. (Heidelberg).

KELLS, J. H. (1973) (ed.), *Sophocles: Electra* (Cambridge).

KEMPER, T. D. (1978), *A Social Interactional Theory of Emotions* (New York).

KENNY, A. J. P. (1963), *Action, Emotion, and Will* (London).

— (1978), *The Aristotelian Ethics* (Oxford).

KERFERD, G. B. (1953), 'Protagoras' Doctrine of Justice and Virtue in the *Protagoras* of Plato', *JHS* 73: 42–5.

— (1956–7), 'The Moral and Political Doctrines of Antiphon the Sophist. A Reconsideration', *PCPS* 4: 26–32.

— (1981*a*), *The Sophistic Movement* (Cambridge).

— (1981*b*) (ed.), *The Sophists and their Legacy* (*Hermes* Einz. 44; Wiesbaden).

KIRK, G. S. (1985) (ed.), *The Iliad: A Commentary*, i (Cambridge).

KIRKWOOD, G. M. (1958), *A Study of Sophoclean Drama* (Ithaca, NY).

— (1965), 'Homer and Sophocles' *Ajax*', in M. J. Anderson (ed.), *Classical Drama and its Influence: Studies Presented to H. D. F. Kitto* (London), 51–70.

KLOSKO, G. (1982), '*Demotikē Aretē* in the *Republic*', *History of Political Thought* 3: 362–81.

— (1986), *The Development of Plato's Political Theory* (New York).

KNOX, B. M. W. (1964), *The Heroic Temper: Studies in Sophoclean Tragedy* (Berkeley and Los Angeles).

— (1979), *Word and Action. Essays on the Ancient Theatre* (Baltimore).

KOHLBERG, L. (1981), *Essays on Moral Development*, i. *The Philosophy of Moral Development* (San Francisco).

KONSTAN, D. (1988), 'Democrito sulla responsabilità dell' agente', *Quad. dell' Ist. di Filos.* (Perugia) 6: 11–27.

KOPPERSCHMIDT, J. (1967), *Die Hikesie als dramatische Form* (Diss., Tübingen).

KOSMAN, L. A. (1980), 'Being Properly Affected: Virtues and Feelings in Aristotle's Ethics', in Rorty (1980*b*), 103–16.

KOVACS, P. D. (1980), 'Shame, Pleasure, and Honor in Phaedra's Great Speech (Euripides, *Hippolytus* 375–87)', *AJP* 101: 287–303.

— (1987), *The Heroic Muse: Studies in the* Hippolytus *and the* Hecuba *of Euripides* (Baltimore).

KRAUT, R. (1973), 'Reason and Justice in Plato's *Republic*', in E. N. Lee, A. P. D. Mourelatos, and R. M. Rorty (edd.), *Exegesis and Argument* (*Phronesis* Suppl. 1; Assen), 207–24.

KRETSCHMER, P. (1894), *Die griechischen Vaseninschriften* (Berlin).

LACEY, W. K. (1968), *The Family in Classical Greece* (London).

LAZARUS, R. S., AVERILL, J. R., and OPTON, E. M. (1970), 'Towards a Cognitive Theory of Emotion', in Arnold (1970), 207–32.

— KANNER, A. D., and FOLKMAN, S. (1980), 'Emotions: A Cognitive-Phenomenological Analysis', in Plutchik and Kellerman (1980), 189–217.

LEAF, W. (1900–2) (ed.), *Homer: The Iliad* ², 2 vols. (London).

LEAR, J. (1988), *Aristotle: The Desire to Understand* (Cambridge).

LEIGHTON, D., and KLUCKHOHN, K. (1948), *Children of the People: The Navaho Individual and his Development* (Cambridge, Mass.).

LESKY, A. (1961), 'Eteokles in den Sieben gegen Theben', *WS* 74: 5–17.

— (1966), 'Decision and Responsibility in the Tragedy of Aeschylus', *JHS* 86: 78–85.

LESKY, A. (1983), *Greek Tragic Poetry*, ET (New Haven, Conn.; orig. pub. 1972).

LEVINE, D. B. (1985), 'Symposium and the Polis', in Figueira and Nagy (1985), 176–96.

LEWIS, H. B. (1971), *Shame and Guilt in Neurosis* (New York).

LEWIS, J. M. (1985), 'Eros and the Polis in Theognis Book II', in Figueira and Nagy (1985), 197–222.

LINFORTH, I. M. (1956), 'Philoctetes: The Play and the Man', *U. Cal. Pub. Class. Phil.* 15. 3: 95–156.

—— (1963), 'Electra's Day in the Tragedy of Sophocles', *U. Cal. Pub. Class. Phil.* 19. 2: 89–126.

LLOYD-JONES, H. (1957), Appendix to Loeb Aeschylus, ii², ed. H. Weir Smyth (London).

—— (1959), 'The End of the *Seven against Thebes*', *CQ* 9: 80–115.

—— (1962), 'The Guilt of Agamemnon', *CQ* 12: 187–99 [now in *Greek Epic, Lyric, and Tragedy* (Oxford, 1990)].

—— (1965), review of Barrett (1964), *JHS* 85: 164–71 [now in *Greek Epic, Lyric, and Tragedy* (Oxford, 1990)].

—— (1971), *The Justice of Zeus* (Berkeley and Los Angeles).

—— (1973), review of B. Snell, *Szenen aus den griechischen Dramen*, *CR* 87: 192–4 [now in *Greek Epic, Lyric, and Tragedy* (Oxford, 1990)].

—— (1983), 'Artemis and Iphigeneia', *JHS* 103: 87–102 [now in *Greek Comedy, Hellenistic Literature, Greek Religion, and Miscellanea* (Oxford, 1990)].

—— (1987), 'Ehre und Schande in der griechischen Kultur', *A und A* 33: 1–28 [now in *Greek Comedy, Hellenistic Literature, Greek Religion, and Miscellanea* (Oxford, 1990)].

LOMBARD, D. B. (1985), 'Aspects of αἰδώς in Euripides', *Acta Classica* 28: 5–12.

LONG, A. A. (1970), 'Morals and Values in Homer', *JHS* 90: 121–39.

LURIA, S. (1963), 'Antiphon der Sophist', *Eos* 53: 63–7 [also in C. J. Classen (ed.), *Sophistik* (WdF 187; Darmstadt, 1976)].

LUSCHNIG, C. A. E. (1988), *Time Holds the Mirror: A Study of Knowledge in Euripides' Hippolytus* (*Mnem.* Suppl. 102; Leiden).

LYND, H. M. (1958), *On Shame and the Search for Identity* (New York).

LYONS, W. (1980), *Emotion* (Cambridge).

MacDOWELL, D. M. (1963*a*), *Athenian Homicide Law in the Age of the Orators* (Manchester).

—— (1963*b*), "ἀρετή and Generosity", *Mnem.* 4. 16: 127–34.

—— (1976), '*Hybris* in Athens', *GR* 23: 14–31.

—— (1978), *The Law in Classical Athens* (London).

—— (1986), *Spartan Law* (Edinburgh).

—— (1990) (ed.), *Demosthenes: Against Meidias* (*Oration 21*) (Oxford).

McKAY, K. J. (1963), 'Ambivalent αἰδώς in Hesiod', *AJP* 84: 17–27.

MACKENZIE, M. M. (1981), *Plato on Punishment* (Berkeley and Los Angeles).

MACLEOD, C. W. (1982*a*) (ed.), *Homer: Iliad XXIV* (Cambridge).

—— (1982*b*), 'Politics and the *Oresteia*', *JHS* 102: 124–44 [also in *Collected Essays* (Oxford, 1983)].

MAGUIRE, J. P. (1977), 'Protagoras . . . or Plato, ii—The *Protagoras*', *Phronesis* 22: 103–22.

MANUWALD, B. (1979), 'Phaidra's tragischer Irrtum: Zur Rede Phaidras in Euripides' Hippolytos (vv. 373–430)', *RM* 122: 134–48.

MEAD, M. (1937) (ed.), *Cooperation and Competition among Primitive Peoples* (New York).

— (1948*a*), 'Social Change and Cultural Surrogates', in C. Kluckhohn and H. A. Murray (edd.), *Personality in Nature, Society, and Culture* (New York), 511–22.

— (1948*b*), 'Administrative Contributions to Democratic Character Formation at the Adolescent Level', in C. Kluckhohn and H. A. Murray (edd.), *Personality in Nature, Society, and Culture* (New York), 523–30.

— (1950), 'Some Anthropological Considerations concerning Guilt', in M. L. Reymert (ed.), *Feelings and Emotions: The Mooseheart Symposium* (New York), 362–73.

MERIDOR, R. (1987), 'Aeschylus' *Agamemnon* 944–57: Why Does Agamemnon Give in?', *CP* 82: 38–43.

MICHELINI, A. N. (1987), *Euripides and the Tragic Tradition* (Madison, Wis.).

MOLINE, J. (1975), 'Euripides, Socrates, and Virtue', *Hermes* 103: 45–67.

— (1978), 'Plato on the Complexity of the Psyche', *Archiv f. Gesch. d. Philosophie* 60: 1–26.

MONAN, J. D. (1968), *Moral Knowledge and its Methodology in Aristotle* (Oxford).

MORRIS, H. (1987), 'Nonmoral Guilt', in F. Schoeman (ed.), *Responsibility, Character, and the Emotions* (Cambridge), 220–40.

MORRISON, J. S. (1961), 'Antiphon', *PCPS* 7: 49–58 [also in C. J. Classen (ed.), *Sophistik* (WdF 187; Darmstadt, 1976)].

MORROW, G. R. (1960), *Plato's Cretan City* (Princeton).

MOTTE, A. (1973), *Prairies et jardins de la Grèce antique: De la religion à la philosophie* (Ac. Roy. Belg. Mém. Classe des Lettres 2. 61, fasc. 5; Brussels).

MOULTON, C. (1972), 'Antiphon the Sophist: On Truth', *TAPA* 103: 329–66.

— (1974), 'Antiphon the Sophist and Democritus', *MH* 31: 129–39.

MÜLLER, C. W. (1984), *Zur Datierung des sophokleischen Ödipus* (Ak. Wiss. Lit., Mainz, Abh. der geistes- u. sozialwiss. Klasse, 1984. 5).

MURRAY, G. G. A. (1913), *Euripides and his Age* (London).

— (1924), *The Rise of the Greek Epic* (Oxford).

MURRAY, O. (1980), *Early Greece* (London).

— (1983*a*), 'The Symposion as Social Organization', in R. Hägg (ed.), *The Greek Renaissance of the Eighth Century BC: Tradition and Innovation* (Stockholm), 195–9.

— (1983*b*), 'The Greek Symposion in History', in E. Gabba (ed.), *Tria Corda. Scritti in onore di A. Momigliano* (Como), 257–72.

— (1990) (ed.), *Sympotica: A Symposium on the Symposion* (Oxford).

NAGY, G. (1985), 'Theognis and Megara: A Poet's Vision of his City', in Figueira and Nagy (1985), 22–81.

NEIL, R. A. (1901) (ed.), *Aristophanes: Knights* (Cambridge).

NILL, M. (1985), *Morality and Self-Interest in Protagoras, Antiphon, and Democritus* (Philosophia Antiqua 43; Leiden).

NILSSON, M. P. (1955), *Geschichte der griechischen Religion*, i² (*Handbuch der Altertumswissenschaft* 5. 2. 1; Munich; 1st edn., 1941).

NORTH, H. F. (1966), *Sophrosyne: Self-Knowledge and Self-Restraint in Greek Literature* (Ithaca, NY).

NUSSBAUM, G. (1960), 'Labour and Status in the *Works and Days*', *CQ* 10: 213–20.

NUSSBAUM, M. C. (1976–7), 'Consequences and Character in Sophocles' *Philoctetes*', *Philosophy and Literature* 1: 26–53.

—— (1978) (ed.), *Aristotle's De Motu Animalium* (Princeton).

—— (1980), 'Shame, Separateness, and Political Unity: Aristotle's Criticism of Plato', in Rorty (1980*b*), 395–435.

O'BRIEN, M. J. (1957), 'Plato and the "Good Conscience": *Laws* 863e5–864b7', *TAPA* 88: 81–7.

—— (1967), *The Socratic Paradoxes and the Greek Mind* (Chapel Hill).

ORTONY, A. (1987), 'Is Guilt an Emotion?', *Cognition and Emotion* 1: 283–98.

—— CLORE, G. L., and COLLINS, A. (1988), *The Cognitive Structure of Emotions* (Cambridge).

OSTWALD, M. (1973), 'Was There a Concept ἄγραφος νόμος in Classical Greece?', in E. N. Lee, A. P. D. Mourelatos, and R. M. Rorty (edd.), *Exegesis and Argument* (*Phronesis* Suppl. 1; Assen), 70–104.

OWENS, J. (1981), 'The καλόν in Aristotelian Ethics', in D. J. O'Meara (ed.), *Studies in Aristotle* (Washington, DC), 261–78.

PAGE, D. L. (1941) (ed.), *Greek Literary Papyri*, i. *Poetry* (Loeb; Cambridge, Mass. and London).

PARKER, R. C. T. (1983), *Miasma: Pollution and Purification in Early Greek Religion* (Oxford).

PATZER, H. (1981), 'Der archaische Aretē-Kanon im Corpus Theognideum', in G. Kurz, D. Müller, and W. Nicolai (edd.), *Gnomosyne, Festschrift W. Marg* (Munich), 197–226.

PEARSON, L. (1962), *Popular Ethics in Ancient Greece* (Stanford).

PEDRICK, V. (1982), 'Supplication in the *Iliad* and the *Odyssey*', *TAPA* 112: 125–40.

PELLING, C. B. R. (1990) (ed.), *Characterization and Individuality in Greek Literature* (Oxford).

PENDRICK, G. (1987), 'Once Again Antiphon the Sophist and Antiphon of Rhamnus', *Hermes* 115: 47–60.

PENNER, T. (1971), 'Thought and Desire in Plato', in G. Vlastos (ed.), *Plato: A Collection of Critical Essays*, ii (Garden City, NY), 96–118.

PERADOTTO, J. J. (1964), 'Some Patterns of Nature Imagery in the *Oresteia*', *AJP* 85: 378–93.

PERISTIANY, J. G. (1965) (ed.), *Honour and Shame: The Values of Mediterranean Society* (London).

PETERS, R. S. (1970), 'The Education of the Emotions', in Arnold (1970), 187–204.

PIERS, G., and SINGER, M. B. (1953), *Shame and Guilt: A Psychoanalytic and a Cultural Study* (Springfield, Ill.).

PIPPIN, A. N. (1960), 'Euripides' *Helen*: A Comedy of Ideas', *CP* 55: 151–63.

PITCHER, G. (1965), 'Emotion', *Mind* 74: 326–46.

PITT-RIVERS, J. (1965), 'Honour and Social Status', in Peristiany (1965), 19–78.

PLESCIA, J. (1970), *The Oath and Perjury in Ancient Greece* (Tallahasee).

PLUTCHIK, R., and KELLERMAN, H. (1980) (edd.), *Emotion: Theory, Research, and Experience*, i. *Theories of Emotion* (New York).

PODLECKI, A. J. (1984), *The Early Greek Poets and their Times* (Vancouver).

POE, J. P. (1974), *Heroism and Divine Justice in Sophocles' Philoctetes* (*Mnem.* Suppl. 34; Leiden).

POMEROY, S. B. (1975), *Goddesses, Whores, Wives, and Slaves* (New York).

PRICE, A. W. (1990), 'Plato and Freud', in C. Gill (ed.), *The Person and the Human Mind: Issues in Ancient and Modern Philosophy* (Oxford), 247–70.

PROCOPÉ, J. F. (1989), 'Democritus on Politics and the Care of the Soul', *CQ* 39: 307–31.

RANKIN, H. D. (1983), *Sophists, Socratics, and Cynics* (London).

RAWLS, J. (1973), *A Theory of Justice* (Oxford).

RECKFORD, K. J. (1972), 'Phaethon, Hippolytus, Aphrodite', *TAPA* 103: 405–32.

REDFIELD, J. M. (1975), *Nature and Culture in the* Iliad (Chicago).

REES, D. A. (1957), 'Bipartition of the Soul in the Early Academy', *JHS* 77: 112–18.

—— (1971), '"Magnanimity" in the *Eudemian* and *Nicomachean Ethics*', in P. Moraux, and D. Harlfinger (edd.), *Untersuchungen zur Eudemischen Ethik* (Proc. 5th Symp. Arist.; Berlin), 231–43.

REINHARDT, K. (1979), *Sophocles*, ET (Oxford; orig. pub. 1933).

RICHARDSON, N. J. (1974) (ed.), *The Homeric Hymn to Demeter* (Oxford).

RIEDINGER, J.-C. (1976), 'Remarques sur la τιμή chez Homère', *REG* 89: 244–64.

—— (1980), 'Les Deux αἰδώς chez Homère', *Rev. Phil.* 54: 62–79.

RIVIER, A. (1968), 'Remarques sur le "nécessaire" et la "nécessité" chez Eschyle', *REG* 81: 5–39.

ROBINSON, D. B. (1969), 'Topics in Sophocles' *Philoctetes*', *CQ* 19: 34–56.

—— (1990), "Homeric φίλος: Love of Life and Limbs, Friendship with one's θυμός", in E. M. Craik (ed.), *'Owls to Athens': Essays . . . for Sir Kenneth Dover* (Oxford), 97–108.

ROBINSON, R. (1971), 'Plato's Separation of Reason from Desire', *Phronesis* 16: 38–48.

ROBINSON, T. M. (1970), *Plato's Psychology* (Toronto).

RODGERS, V. A. (1969), "σύνεσις and the Expression of Conscience", *GRBS* 10: 241–54.

—— (1971), "Some Thoughts on δίκη", *CQ* 21: 289–301.

ROISMAN, H. (1984), *Loyalty in Early Greek Epic and Tragedy* (Beiträge zur klassischen Philologie 155; Meisenheim am Glan).

ROMILLY, J. DE (1958), *La Crainte et l'angoisse dans le théâtre d'Eschyle* (Paris).

RORTY, A. O. (1980*a*) (ed.), *Explaining Emotions* (Berkeley and Los Angeles).

—— (1980*b*) (ed.), *Essays on Aristotle's Ethics* (Berkeley and Los Angeles).

ROSE, P. W. (1976), 'Sophocles' *Philoctetes* and the Teachings of the Sophists', *HSCP* 80: 49–105.

ROWE, C. J. (1971), *The* Eudemian *and* Nicomachean Ethics: *A Study in the Development of Aristotle's Thought* (*PCPS* Suppl. 3; Cambridge).

SAUNDERS, T. J. (1962), 'The Structure of the Soul and the State in Plato's *Laws*', *Eranos* 60: 37–55.

—— (1977–8), 'Antiphon the Sophist on Natural Laws', *PAS* 78: 215–36.

SAXONHOUSE, A. W. (1986), 'Myths and the Origins of Cities: Reflections on the Autochthony Theme in Euripides' *Ion*', in J. P. Euben (ed.), *Greek Tragedy and Political Theory* (Berkeley and Los Angeles), 252–73.

SCHEFOLD, K. (1978), *Götter- und Heldensagen der Griechen in der spätarchaischen Kunst* (Munich).

SCHEIN, S. L. (1984), *The Mortal Hero: An Introduction to Homer's* Iliad (Berkeley and Los Angeles).

SCHMITT, A. (1990), *Selbständigkeit und Abhängigkeit menschlichen Handelns bei Homer: Hermeneutische Untersuchungen zur Psychologie Homers* (Ak. Wiss. Lit., Mainz, Abh. der geistes- u. sozialwiss. Klasse, 1990. 5).

SCHOFIELD, M. (1986), '*Euboulia* in the *Iliad*', *CQ* 36: 6–31.

SCOTT, M. (1979), 'Pity and Pathos in Homer', *Acta Classica* 22: 1–14.

—— (1980), '*Aidōs* and *Nemesis* in the Works of Homer, and their Relevance to Social or Co-operative Values', *Acta Classica* 23: 13–35.

—— (1982), '*Philos, Philotēs*, and *Xenia*', *Acta Classica* 25: 1–19.

SEAFORD, R. A. S. (1987), 'The Tragic Wedding', *JHS* 107: 106–30.

—— (1990), 'The Structural Problems of Marriage in Euripides', in A. Powell (ed.), *Euripides, Women, and Sexuality* (London), 151–76.

SEALE, D. (1972), 'The Element of Surprise in Sophocles' *Philoctetes*', *BICS* 19: 94–102.

SEEL, O. (1953), 'Zur Vorgeschichte des Gewissens-Begriffs im altgriechischen Denken', in H. Kusch (ed.), *Festschrift Franz Dornseiff* (Leipzig), 291–319.

SEGAL, C. P. (1966), 'The *Electra* of Sophocles', *TAPA* 97: 473–545.

—— (1970), 'Shame and Purity in Euripides' *Hippolytus*', *Hermes* 98: 288–99.

—— (1981), *Tragedy and Civilisation: An Interpretation of Sophocles* (Cambridge, Mass.).

—— (1986), 'Greek Tragedy and Society: A Structuralist Perspective', in J. P. Euben (ed.), *Greek Tragedy and Political Theory* (Berkeley and Los Angeles), 43–75.

SHARPLES, R. W. (1983), '"But why has my spirit spoken with me thus?": Homeric Decision-Making', *GR* 30: 1–7.

—— (1990) (ed.), *Alexander of Aphrodisias: Ethical Problems* (London).

SHAW, M. H. (1982), 'The ἦθος of Theseus in "The Suppliant Women"', *Hermes* 110: 3–19.

SHEPPARD, J. T. (1918*a*), 'The *Electra* of Euripides', *CR* 32: 137–41.

—— (1918*b*), 'The Tragedy of Electra, according to Sophocles', *CQ* 12: 80–8.

SHERMAN, N. (1989), *The Fabric of Character: Aristotle's Theory of Virtue* (Oxford).

SICHERL, M. (1977), 'The Tragic Issue in Sophocles' *Ajax*', *YCS* 25: 67–98.

SIMMONS, G. C. (1972), 'Protagoras on Education and Society', *Paedagogica Historica* 12: 518–37.

SINCLAIR, T. A. (1925), 'On αἰδώς in Hesiod', *CR* 39: 147–8.

—— (1967), *A History of Greek Political Thought*² (London; 1st edn., 1951).

SLATER, W. J. (1990), 'Sympotic Ethics in the *Odyssey*', in O. Murray (1990), 213–20.

SNELL, B. (1928), *Aischylos und das Handeln im Drama* (*Philologus* Suppl. 20. 1; Leipzig).

—— (1930*a*), 'Das Bewußtsein von eigenen Entscheidungen im frühen Griechentum', *Philologus* 85: 141–58 [also in *Gesammelte Schriften* (Göttingen, 1966)].

—— (1930*b*), review of Zucker (1928), *Gnomon* 6: 21–30 [also in *Gesammelte Schriften* (Göttingen, 1966)].

—— (1948), 'Das früheste Zeugnis über Sokrates', *Philologus* 97: 125–34.

—— (1961), *Poetry and Society* (Bloomington, Ind.).

—— (1964), *Scenes from Greek Drama* (Berkeley and Los Angeles).

—— (1975), *Die Entdeckung des Geistes*⁴ (Göttingen; 1st edn., 1946).

SOLMSEN, F. (1962), 'Hesiodic Motifs in Plato', in *Hésiode et son influence* (Entr. Fond. Hardt 7; Geneva), 173–211.

—— (1973), '"Bad Shame" and Related Problems in Phaedra's Speech (Euripides, *Hippolytus* 380–388)', *Hermes* 101: 420–5.

SOLOMON, R. C. (1980), 'Emotions and Choice', in Rorty (1980*a*), 251–81.

SORABJI, R. R. K. (1979), 'Body and Soul in Aristotle', in J. Barnes, M. Schofield, and R. Sorabji (edd), *Articles on Aristotle*, iv. *Psychology and Aesthetics* (London), 42–64.

—— (1980), 'Aristotle on the Role of Intellect in Virtue', in Rorty (1980*b*), 201–20.

SOUSA, R. DE (1980*a*), 'The Rationality of Emotions', in Rorty (1980*a*), 127–51.

—— (1980*b*), 'Self-Deceptive Emotions', in Rorty (1980*a*), 283–97.

—— (1987), *The Rationality of Emotion* (Cambridge, Mass.).

SPRAGUE, R. K. (1972) (ed.), *The Older Sophists* (Columbia, SC).

STAGAKIS, G. (1975), *Studies in the Homeric Society* (*Hermes* Einz. 26; Wiesbaden).

STALLEY, R. F. (1975), 'Plato's Arguments for the Division of the Reasoning and Appetitive Elements within the Soul', *Phronesis* 20: 110–28.

—— (1983), *An Introduction to Plato's Laws* (Oxford).

STANFORD, W. B. (1968), *The Ulysses Theme: A Study in the Adaptability of a Traditional Hero*² (Ann Arbor; 1st edn., 1954).

—— (1983), *Greek Tragedy and the Emotions* (London).

STANTON, J. M. (1983), 'An Application of Moral Development Theory to Homer' (Diss., Boston College).

STARK, R. (1972), *Aristotelesstudien*² (Zetemata 8; Munich).

STEBLER, U. (1971), *Entstehung und Entwicklung des Gewissens im Spiegel der griechischen Tragödie* (Berne and Frankfurt).

STOCKS, J. L. (1915), 'Plato and the Tripartite Soul', *Mind* 24: 207–21.

STROUD, R. S. (1968), *Drakon's Law on Homicide* (Berkeley and Los Angeles).

SZLEZAK, T. A. (1986), 'Mania und Aidos: Bemerkungen zur Ethik und Anthropologie des Euripides', *A und A* 32: 46–59.

TAPLIN, O. (1971), 'Significant Actions in Sophocles' *Philoctetes*', *GRBS* 12: 25–44.

—— (1978), *Greek Tragedy in Action* (London).

—— (1979), 'Yielding to Forethought: Sophocles' *Ajax*', in G. W. Bowersock, W. Burkert, and M. C. J. Putnam (edd.), *Arktouros. Hellenic Studies Presented to B. M. W. Knox* (Berlin and New York), 122–9.

—— (1990), 'Agamemnon's Role in the *Iliad*', in Pelling (1990), 60–82.

TAYLOR, C. C. W. (1967), 'Pleasure, Knowledge, and Sensation in Democritus', *Phronesis* 12: 6–27.

TAYLOR, G. (1985), *Pride, Shame, and Guilt: Emotions of Self-Assessment* (Oxford).

THALBERG, I. (1964), 'Emotion and Thought', *APQ* 1: 45–55.

THORNTON, A. H. F. (1970), *People and Themes in Homer's* Odyssey (London).

—— (1984), *Homer's* Iliad: *Its Composition and the Motif of Supplication* (Hypomnemata 81; Göttingen).

TOMKINS, S. (1970), 'Affect as the Primary Motivational System', in Arnold (1970), 101–10.

TSAGARAKIS, O. (1977), *Self-Expression in Early Greek Lyric, Elegiac, and Iambic Poetry* (Palingenesia 11; Wiesbaden).

UNTERSTEINER, M. (1954), *The Sophists*, ET (Oxford; orig. pub. 1949).

VALGIGLIO, E. (1969), 'Interpretazioni Esiodee', *Maia* 21: 161–74.

VENSKE, W. (1938), *Platon und der Ruhm* (Kieler Arbeiten zur kl. Philol. 4; Würzburg).

VERDENIUS, W. J. (1944–5), "αἰδώς bei Homer", *Mnem.* 3. 12: 47–60.

—— (1962), 'Aufbau und Absicht der Erga', in *Hésiode et son influence* (Entr. Fond. Hardt 7; Geneva), 109–70.

—— (1985), *A Commentary on Hesiod*, Works and Days, *1–382* (*Mnem.* Suppl. 68; Leiden).

VERNANT, J.-P. (1980), *Myth and Society in Ancient Greece*, ET (Sussex; orig. pub. 1974).

—— and VIDAL-NAQUET, P. (1981), *Myth and Tragedy in Ancient Greece*, ET (Sussex; orig. pub. 1972).

VERRALL, A. W. (1908) (ed.), *Aeschylus: Eumenides* (Cambridge).

VICKERS, B. (1973), *Towards Greek Tragedy* (London).

VIDAL-NAQUET, P. (1986), *The Black Hunter: Forms of Thought and Forms of Society in the Greek World*, ET (Baltimore; orig. pub. 1981).

VLASTOS, G. (1973), *Platonic Studies* (Princeton).

— (1975*a*), *Plato's Universe* (Oxford).

— (1975*b*), 'Ethics and Physics in Democritus', in R. E. Allen and D. J. Furley (edd.), *Studies in Presocratic Philosophy*, ii (London), 381–408.

VOIGT, C. (1972), *Überlegung und Entscheidung: Studien zur Selbstauffassung des Menschen bei Homer* (Beiträge zur klassischen Philologie 48, Meisenheim am Glan; orig. pub. 1934).

VOROS, F. K. (1974), 'The Ethical Theory of Democritus: On Duty', *Platon* 26: 113–22.

WALCOT, P. (1970), *Greek Peasants, Ancient and Modern* (Manchester).

— (1976), *Greek Drama in its Theatrical and Social Context* (Cardiff).

— (1977), 'Odysseus and the Art of Lying', *Ancient Society* 8: 1–19.

— (1978), *Envy and the Greeks* (Warminster).

— (1979), 'Cattle Raiding, Heroic Tradition, and Ritual: The Greek Evidence', *History of Religions* 18: 326–51.

WALSH, J. J. (1963), *Aristotle's Conception of Moral Weakness* (New York).

WARNOCK, M. (1957), 'Symposium: The Justification of Emotions' (*PAS* Suppl. 31), 43–58 [see also Ewing (1957)].

WEBSTER, T. B. L. (1967), *The Tragedies of Euripides* (London).

— (1970) (ed.), *Sophocles: Philoctetes* (Cambridge).

WECKLEIN, N. (1885) (ed.), *Euripides: Hippolytos* (Leipzig).

WEST, M. L. (1966) (ed.), *Hesiod: Theogony* (Oxford).

— (1974), *Studies in Greek Elegy and Iambus* (Berlin).

— (1978) (ed.), *Hesiod: Works and Days* (Oxford).

— (1979), 'The Prometheus Trilogy', *JHS* 99: 130–48.

WHITE, N. P. (1979), *A Companion to Plato's* Republic (Oxford).

WHITMAN, C. H. (1951), *Sophocles: A Study of Heroic Humanism* (Cambridge, Mass.).

— (1964), *Aristophanes and the Comic Hero* (Cambridge, Mass.).

WICKER, F. W., PAYNE, G. C., and MORGAN, R. M. (1983), 'Participant Descriptions of Guilt and Shame', *Motivation and Emotion* 7: 25–39.

WIERZBICKA, A. (1986), 'Human Emotions: Universal or Culture-Specific?', *American Anthropologist* 88: 584–94.

WILAMOWITZ-MOELLENDORF, U. VON (1895) (ed.), *Euripides: Herakles* (Berlin).

— (1926) (ed.), *Euripides: Ion* (Berlin).

— (1927) (ed.), *Aristophanes: Lysistrata* (Berlin).

— (1959), *Der Glaube der Hellenen*[3], 2 vols. (Darmstadt; 1st edn., Berlin, 1931–2).

WILLIAMS, B. (1973), 'The Analogy of City and Soul in Plato's *Republic*', in E. N. Lee, A. P. D. Mourelatos, and R. M. Rorty (edd.), *Exegesis and Argument* (*Phronesis* Suppl. 1; Assen), 196–206.

WILLINK, C. W. (1968), 'Some Problems of Text and Interpretation in the *Hippolytus*', *CQ* 18: 11–43.

— (1986) (ed.), *Euripides: Orestes* (Oxford).

WINNINGTON-INGRAM, R. P. (1960), '*Hippolytus*: A Study in Causation', in *Euripide* (Entr. Fond. Hardt 6; Geneva), 167-97.

—— (1965), 'Tragedy and Greek Archaic Thought', in M. J. Anderson (ed.), *Classical Drama and its Influence: Studies Presented to H. D. F. Kitto* (London), 29-50.

—— (1980), *Sophocles: An Interpretation* (Cambridge).

—— (1983), *Studies in Aeschylus* (Cambridge).

WOLFF, E. (1929), review of Snell (1928), *Gnomon* 5: 386-40.

WOODS, M. (1982) (ed.), *Aristotle's Eudemian Ethics, Books I, II, and VIII* (Oxford).

ZEITLIN, F. I. (1965), 'The Motif of the Corrupted Sacrifice in Aeschylus' *Oresteia*', *TAPA* 96: 463-508.

—— (1966), 'Postscript to Sacrificial Imagery in the *Oresteia*', *TAPA* 97: 645-53.

—— (1985), 'The Power of Aphrodite: Eros and the Boundaries of the Self in the *Hippolytus*', in P. H. Burian (ed.), *Directions in Euripidean Criticism* (Durham, NC), 112-28.

ZUCKER, F. (1928), *Syneidesis-Conscientia* (Jenaer akademische Reden, Heft 6).

ZUNTZ, G. (1963), *The Political Plays of Euripides*[2] (Manchester).

ZÜRCHER, W. (1947), *Die Darstellung des Menschen im Drama des Euripides* (Basle).

GLOSSARY

Transliterated Greek terms are translated and explained on first occurrence in the text; this glossary is therefore intended simply as an *aide-mémoire* to the Greekless reader. Hence the English equivalents given are of the stock, class-room variety, and make no claim to convey either the essence or the range of the terms translated. Nouns and adjectives are given in the nominative singular (nominative singular masculine, in the case of adjectives), and so those who do not know Greek should be aware that the endings of these terms may appear differently in the text, since nouns can vary in number and adjectives in number and gender (I do not normally transliterate the oblique cases). Verbs, moreover, may sometimes have prefixes. Those who know no Greek are urged to acquire the habit of recognizing key clusters by their stem; they may, however, care to note the following very typical changes of ending. Verbs: first persons in *-ō*, *-omai* give infinitives in *-ein* (*-an*, *-oun*), *-esthai* (*-asthai*, *-eisthai*, *-ousthai*). Nouns: sing. *-os* generally has pl. *-oi* (or else *-ea* or *-ē*); sing. *-ē* has pl. *-ai*; fem. sing. *-a* has pl. *-ai* (but neut. sing. *-ma* has pl. *-mata*); sing. *-on* has pl. *-a*. Adjectives whose masc. sing. ends in *-os* have (sing.) *-os*, *-ē* (or *-a*), *-on* (pl.) *-oi*, *-ai*, *-a*. Adjectives in *-ēs* have neut. sing. in *es* (pl. *-eis*, *-ē*). Some masc. and fem. nouns have plurals in *-es* or *-eis*. Adjectives ending in *-os* form adverbs in *-ōs*.

adikeō: (v.) I do wrong, I harm, I treat unjustly
adikia: (n.) injustice, wrong
adikos: (adj.) unjust
aidēmōn: (adj.) prone to *aidōs*
aideomai: (v.) I am ashamed, I respect
aidesis: (n.) pardon
aidoios: (adj.) reverend, deserving *aidōs* (less often: reverent, showing *aidōs*)
aidophrōn: (adj.) reverent-minded, prone to *aidōs*
aidōs: (n.) shame, respect, sense of honour, modesty
aeikelios: (adj.) unseemly
aeikēs: (adj.) unseemly
aeikizō, aeikizomai: (v.) I disfigure
agathos: (adj. and subst.) good (at/for), noble
agōn: (n.) contest
aischos: (n.) ugliness, disgrace; pl. (*aischea*) insults
aischrokerdeia: (n.) base gain
aischros: (adj.) ugly, disgraceful
aischunē: (n.) (objective) disgrace; (subjective) shame
aischunō: (v.) I make ugly, I dishonour
aischunomai: (v.) I am ashamed (sometimes: I respect)
aischuntēlos: (adj.) prone to *aischunē/aidōs*

akolasia: (n.) licentiousness

akolastos: (adj. and subst.) wanton, licentious

akrasia: (n.) weakness of will

akratēs: (adj. and subst.) weak-willed, incontinent

anaideïē, anaideia: (n.) shamelessness, ruthlessness, impudence

anaidēs: (adj.) shameless, ruthless, impudent

anaischuntia: (n.) shamelessness

anaischuntos: (adj.) shameless

andreia: (n.) bravery (cognate with *anēr*, man)

anosios: (adj.) unholy

aretē: (n.) excellence

asebeia: (n.) impiety

asebēs: (adj.) impious

atasthaliē: (n.) reckless folly

atasthalos: (adj.) reckless

atimiē, atimia: (n.) dishonour, disfranchisement

charis: (n.) grace, gratitude, reciprocity

chrēstos: (adj.) good, useful

deilia: (n.) cowardice

deilos: (adj.) cowardly, base

deinos: (adj.) formidable, terrible, clever

deos: (n.) fear

diathesis: (n.) disposition

dikaios: (adj.) just

dikaiosunē: (n.) justice

dikē: (n.) suit, settlement, penalty, justice

dunamis: (n.) capacity

duskleia: (n.) ill-repute

dussebeia: (n.) impiety, lack of reverence

dussebēs: (adj.) impious, lacking reverence

echthros: (adj. and subst.) enemy

eidos: (n.) form

elencheïē (n.) showing up, disgrace

elenchō: (v.) I show up, refute, prove, put to shame

elenchos: (n.) showing up, disgrace (neut. in Homer); showing up, examination, proof, refutation (masc., class.)

eleos: (n.) pity

enkrateia: (n.) self-control

enkratēs: (adj.) self-controlled

epistēmē: (n.) knowledge, science

epithumia: (n.) appetite, desire (cf. *to epithumētikon* in Plato)

ergon: (n.) deed, work, function, product

esthlos: (adj.) good, noble

ethos: (n.) habit

ēthos: (n.) character

eugeneia: (n.) nobility of birth

eugenēs: (adj.) well-born

eukleia: (n.) good reputation

eukleēs: (adj.) of good repute

eusebeia: (n.) piety, reverence

eusebēs: (adj.) pious, reverent, righteous

gennaios: (adj.) well-born (true to one's inherited nature)

gnōmē: (n.) knowledge, intelligence, judgement; aphorism, proverb

habrotēs: (n.) softness, delicacy

hamartia: (n.) error, offence

hazomai: (v.) I experience religious scruple

hetairos: (n.) comrade, companion

hexis: (n.) settled state

hiketēs: (n.) suppliant

hosios: (adj.) holy, ritually pure

hosiotēs: (n.) religiosity, piety

hubris: (n.) insolence, arrogance

kakia: (n.) 'badness', cowardice, baseness, defect, vice

kakos: (adj., often subst.) bad, base, cowardly

kakotēs: (n.) 'badness', baseness

kalos: (adj.) beautiful, noble, fine

kerdos: (n.) gain, profit

kinēsis: (n.) movement, change

kleos: (n.) fame, reputation

kudos: (n.) glory

kurios: (as subst., Ath. law) guardian of a woman

lōbē: (n.) disfigurement, disgrace

logos: (n.) word, speech, account, reason, ratio (cf. *to logistikon*: the rational (faculty))

mania: (n.) madness

miasma: (n.) pollution

nemesaō, nemesaomai, nemesizomai: (v.) I am (justly) indignant

nemessētos: (adj.) such as to arouse righteous indignation

nemesis: (n.) righteous indignation

nomos: (n.) law, custom

oiktos: (n.) pity

oiktros: (adj.) pitiful

oneidizō: (v.) I reproach

oneidos: (n.) reproach

opizomai: (v.) I fear divine anger

parthenos: (n.) maiden

pathos: (n.) affect, experience, attribute, suffering

philautia: (n.) self-love

philia: (n.) friendship
philos: (adj. and subst.) dear; friend
philotēs: (n.) friendship; (Homer) love, sex
philotimia: (n.) love of honour, ambition
phrēn, phrenes: (n.) diaphragm (?), mind
phronēsis: (n.) intelligence, (practical) wisdom
phthonos: (n.) envy, malice
phusis: (n.) nature
polis: (n.) city(-state)
proairesis: (n.) deliberative choice
saophrōn: see *sōphrōn*
sebas: (n.) (objective) majesty; (subjective) awe, reverence
sebazomai, sebizō, sebō, sebomai: (v.) I revere, I honour
semnos: (adj.) reverend, august, awesome, haughty
semnotēs: (n.) dignity, haughtiness, self-importance
semnunomai: (v.) I behave with dignity, *or* with self-importance
sophia: (n.) wisdom
sophos: (adj.) wise
sōphrōn: (adj.) sensible, self-controlled, moderate, modest, chaste, sober, etc.
sōphrosunē: (n.) good sense, self-control, moderation, modesty, chastity, sobriety, etc.
sōtēr: (n.) saviour
sōtēria: (n.) safety
suneidēsis (n.) consciousness, conscience
sunoida (inf. *suneidenai*): (v.) I am aware; (reflex.) I have on my conscience
tharsos: (n.) boldness, confidence
thumos: (n.) spirit (cf. *to thumoeides* in Plato)
timaō: (v.) I honour
timē (n.) honour, prestige, worth
xenia: (n.) guest-friendship
xenos/xeinos: (n.) guest, host, guest-friend

INDEX OF PRINCIPAL PASSAGES

This index contains passages discussed (rather than merely cited) in the text or notes. Doubtful or spurious works appear under the name of the author to whom they are traditionally ascribed, with no implications regarding their authenticity or otherwise.

AESCHINES

1.24	372 n.84
1.26	293 n.100
1.180	372 n.84

AESCHYLUS

Agamemnon

179–81	347 n.10
206–23	198–200
258–60	207–8
362–6	181 n.5
362–4	208
399–401	181 n.5
613–14	204
779–80	207
855–8	204–5
905–57	194–8
1203–5	186–7
1363	181
1372–6	205
1612	207
1626	181

Choephori

55–7	207, 212 n.137
106–8	209 n.118
140–1	249 n.121
301–4	180 n.3
407–9	180 n.3
444–50	180 n.3
494–5	180
663–7	188 n.34
896–903	200–2
899	244
917	188
930	200 n.79
973–4	180 n.3
990	181

Eumenides

92	211
95–8	180

269–72	211
483–4	209
545–9	209, 214
640	208
680	209
696–7	214
710	209
715	209
739–40	208
749	209
760	208–9

Persae

694–703	206–7
694–6	212
809–10	198

Prometheus Bound (PV)

133–4	185–6
266	206 n.105
937	207 n.109

Seven against Thebes (Sept.)

409–11	182 n.11
683–5	181–3
831	183, 211
1029–30	206 n.105

Supplices

27–9	183
191–202	183–4
333–454	189–91
345–6	189–90, 193
387–91	190–1 n.39
397–401	191
455	192
478–9	192–3
490–1	185 n.20
578–9	187–8
641	185 n.20
707–9	211
991–1009	186

Fragments (Radt)
132c   202–4
135   211
168.21–4   186 n.26

ALEXANDER OF APHRODISIAS
Ethical Problems 21   428 n.255

AMMONIUS
De adfinium vocabulorum differentia
(Nickau)
17   300–1 n.129

ANTIPHON 'THE ORATOR'
2. d. 11–12   345–7
3. b. 12   346
5. 18   350 n.24
5. 88–9   347
5. 91–3   347–9
6. 1   349–50
6. 4   350
6. 23   351 n.27

ANTIPHON 'THE SOPHIST' (DK)
B44A   361–3
B44B   362 n.58

ARCHILOCHUS (West)
5   167 n.64, 203
14   167 n.64
133   167 n.64

ARISTOPHANES
Archarnians
289–91   352 n.28

Clouds
995   301 n.131

Frogs
1474   352 n.28

Knights
182–5   353
298   159 n.45, 210 n.124

1239   159 n.45, 210 n.124, 352 n.28
1354–7   352

Thesmophoriazusae
902   352 n.28

Wasps
447   301 n.131, 352 n.28
743–9   352
999–1002   352

Wealth
367–8   352 n.28
774–8   353 n.31

ARISTOTLE
Categories
8b25–10a10   398 n.165, 409 n.204
8b27–9a13   398
8b27–8   428 n.255
8b36–7   409 n.204
9a8–13   428 n.255
9a15   409 n.204
9a19–21   409 n.204
9a21–3   409 n.204
9a28–10a10   393 n.152
9b3   409 n.204
9b35–10a2   409 n.204
15b11–12   393 n.152

De Anima (*DA*)
403a16–b3   394
403a25–7   393 n.152
412a10–11   401–2, 406
412a22–8   401–2, 406
417a21–b7   401–2, 406
417b16   402
429a24–430a25   394 n.155
432b26–433a1   395 n.156

De Motu Animalium (*MA*)
701b16–22   395 n.156
703b18–20   395 n.156

Eudemian Ethics (*EE*)
1218b37–1219a8   399–400 n.174
1219a32–3   400 n.174
1220a19–29   409 n.206
1220a39–b3   426–7 n.253
1220b5–7   409
1220b6–20   402–10

1220b7–10	402
1220b12–20	393, 404 n.193
1220b12–14	396 n.158
1220b13	394 n.154, 412 n.214
1220b14–15	409, 412 n.212
1220b16–20	402
1220b16–18	413
1220b17	409 n.205, 413
1220b35–7	411 n.208
1220b38	409 n.205
1221a1	411–12
1221a15–16	409 n.205
1223a36–7	419 n.229
1223b11–12	400 n.174, 419 n.229
1227b15–17	419 n.229
1229a1–2	420
1229a13	420
1229a29–30	420 n.234
1230a16–21	420
1230b23–4	421 n.235
1231b5–26	409 n.205, 428 n.256
1233b18	412 n.214
1233b26–9	411, 422 n.240
1234a23–33	412 n.214, 429 n.256
1234a26–8	405 n.197
1234a26–33	411 n.208
1234a27–32	404
1234a27–8	424 n.245
1234a32	429
1248b19–20	421 n.239, 422 n.241
1248b34–7	421 n.239
1249a14–17	421 n.239

Historia Animalium

588a17–b3	407 n.201

Magna Moralia

1184b4	421 n.236
1186a14–17	402, 403
1191a4	420 n.234
1191a5–13	420
1191a18–21	421 n.235
1191a21–3	420 n.234
1191a22–5	420
1191b23–38	428 n.256
1193a1–10	411–12, 423 n.244, 429
1197a39	407
1200a37–b2	400 n.174
1212b3–23	421 n.239

Metaphysics

1022b1–2	409 n.204
1022b10–12	428 n.255
1022b15–19	393 n.152
1047b31–5	401, 406

Nicomachean Ethics (EN)

1095b6–7	425
1095b22–30	421 n.236
1098a33–b4	425
1103a14–b25	426–7 n.253
1103a18–b25	407 n.199
1103a26–34	402 n.183
1103b17–21	409
1105b19–28	398 n.165
1105b21–3	396 n.158
1105b21	394 n.154
1105b23–5	403
1105b28–1106a13	412, 414 n.220
1106a2–4	429 n.256
1106a6–12	402
1106a7–9	412
1106a7–8	403 n.190, 407
1106a9–10	403
1108a30–5	411–13
1108a31–4	423 n.244
1115a12–14	422 n.240
1115b11–13	420
1115b12–13	421 n.239
1116a17–29	420
1116a18–19	420 n.235
1116a28–9	411 n.208, 420 n.235
1117a9–22	426
1123b35	421 n.236
1125b26–1126b10	428 n.256
1128b10–35	414–30
1128b10–15	393, 412 n.213, 413 n.216
1128b11–12	422
1128b23–5	423
1128b33–4	400 n.174, 429
1139a15–17	400 n.174
1144a14–1145a12	426
1144b1–17	404
1144b4–9	405
1145a18	400 n.174
1149a25–b2	426 n.251
1151a5–11	400 n.174, 419 n.229
1151a27–8	400 n.174, 419 n.229, 429
1151b28–9	400 n.174, 419 n.229, 429
1168b25–31	421 n.239
1169a8–13	421 n.239
1169a11–15	427 n.254
1169a18–22	427 n.254
1169a25–b1	421 n.239
1179b4–20	423–5

1179b20–1180a32   426 n.253
1179b24–1180a1   424 n.245

Physics
201a19–22   401
226a27–9   393 n.152
226b26–7   393 n.152
245b3–5   396 n.158
246a11–17   399, 412 n.213, 429
247a7–18   396 n.158
248a6–9   386 n.158

Politics
1260a13   338
1270b34–5   390 n.144
1331a39–b1   416 n.223, 422 n.240
1335a2–4   416 n.223

Rhetoric
1360b28   421 n.236
1366a33–4   421 n.239, 422 n.241
1366a36–1367a6   427 n.254
1366b18–19   427 n.254
1366b34–5   426 n.252
1367a6–14   426 n.252
1378a19–26   396
1378a20–3   393 n.152
1378a30–2   395 n.156, 396
1380a19–21   159–60 n.45
1381b19–21   423
1381b29–32   423
1382b8–9   422 n.240
1383b12–1384a23   415 n.222
1383b12–1385a13   396–7
1383b13–15   422
1383b15–17   212 n.138
1383b15   417 n.226
1383b17–1384a23   423 n.242
1384a23–1385a15   422 n.240
1384a24–5   422
1389a3–b12   416 n.223

Topics
126a6–12   385 n.123
151a16–17   395 n.156

ARISTOXENUS (Wehrli)
42a–c   300 n.129

BACCHYLIDES (Snell-Maehler)
5.104–7   155 n.29

CALLINUS (West)
1.1–4   160–1

CRITIAS (DK)
B25   29 n.68, 360–1 n.52
B44   167 n.64

DEMOCRITUS (DK)
B33   258 n.157, 342 n.275
B41   364
B42   364 n.64
B43   367
B45   367 n.72
B48   369 n.77
B83   364 n.64
B84   365–70
B174   366
B179   365
B181   364
B182   365
B191   367 n.72
B244   365–70
B262   366–7
B264   282, 365–70

DEMOSTHENES
Orationes
25.35   282 n.58
27.65   372 n.84
54.22   372 n.84

Epistulae
3.37   369 n.78
48.2   369 n.78

DISSOI LOGOI (DK)
2.5   181 n.5

Epicorum Graecorum Fragmenta (ed. Davies)
Cypria fr.24   372

EURIPIDES
Alcestis
155   274 n.34
279   274

282	274
433–4	274 n.34
542	288
544	289
549–50	288
553–60	288
563–7	289
597–601	289
658–61	269
694–702	269
725–8	268
823	289
855–60	289
857	289
950–3	270 n.16
954–7	270
1057–61	270 n.16, 274

Andromache

451–2	335 n.254
804–15	304–5
833–5	305
859	279 n.52
918	305 n.144
919–20	305

Electra

32–49	271–2
253–4	272
261–2	272
274	268 n.10
303–13	271
364–5	272 n.25
367–90	272
367–70	342 n.273
404–5	271 n.23
658	271 n.23

Hecuba

251–3	274 n.35
310–11	274 n.35
515	290–1 n.88
599–602	342 n.275
787–856	280 n.52
806	280 n.53
968–73	268 n.10
974–5	306 n.146
1247–8	288 n.82

Helen

414–17	268 n.10
415–17	302 n.134
790–1	268 n.10

845–6	268 n.10
884–6	302 n.135
947–53	284 n.68
947–9	276 n.41
998–1004	280–2
999	369 n.79

Heracles

284–94	268 n.9
299–301	342 n.276
557	281 n.58
1146–62	291–2
1160	296–7
1199–1201	295, 297
1214–54	293–4
1286–90	294
1347–8	295
1378–85	294, 296
1423	297 n.111

Heraclidae

6–9	273 n.30
41–4	306 n.146
101–3	276–7
181–246	278–9
255–6	279 n.51
315	279 n.51
450	279 n.51
458–60	342 n.276
541–2	297
567–71	269 n.15
813–16	299–300
839–40	265 n.1

Hippolytus

73–87	314–19, 329
78–80	342 n.277
93–6	282 n.59
210	318 n.201
243–6	293, 302, 329, 331, 333
317	293 n.99
325–35	330–2
352–61	332
373–430	322–39
375–87	322–9
391–402	322 n.214
391–9	331
403–30	333–4
403–4	334 n.250, 336, 360 n.52
462–524	335–6
462–6	321 n.207
466	335–6
487–9	336–7

Hippolytus (*cont.*):

499	336
503–6	336–7
596	337
612	320, 335
653–5	293 n.99
656	320
656–8	335
686–8	337
715–21	337
717–21	335
944–6	321 n.207
945	319
948–99	319
993–1001	320
1035	321, 339
1078–81	281–2 n.59
1258–60	273 n.30

Hypsipyle (Bond)

60.58–9	335 n.258

Ion

288	307 n.151
336–7	281 n.58, 307 n.151
341	302 n.134, 307
367	302, 308
392–400	308
589–601	308
636–7	270 n.17
719–22	270
977	273 n.30
1074–5	270
1266	318 n.201
1312–19	279–80 n.52
1382	271
1526	271
1557–8	302 n.135

Iphigeneia at Aulis

185–91	309
378–80	273 n.30, 284
446–53	284
558–72	309, 340–1
678–9	309
735	309
819–24	310
829–34	310
833–4	310 n.162
839–40	310
847–52	311
848	302 n.134, 311
858	313 n.175

900–2	276 n.41
902–16	282–3
919–74	283–4
992–7	312
1028–32	310 n.162
1089–97	340
1144–5	335 n.254
1338–44	313
1463	316

Iphigeneia among the Taurians

372–6	307 n.150, 310, 318 n.201
605–8	275
606	274
674–86	274–5
689–91	275
713	302 n.135
947–54	290

Medea

85–6	281 n.59
324–51	277–8
439–40	273 n.30, 340
465–6	275 n.37
469–72	273 n.30

Orestes

43	304
97–105	298–9
280	304 n.140
396	303–4
459–61	293
459–69	304
460–7	274 n.36, 298
544–5	304
557–60	304 n.140

Phoenissae

93–4	306 n.146
509–14	266
510–12	266 n.3
994–1005	267
1015–18	267
1485–92	306 n.147
1622–4	276 n.41

Rhesus

926–7	299 n.124

Supplices

34–41	285
34–6	278 n.46
161	285

163–92	285	Fragments (MW)	
164–5	276	204.81–4	151 n.16, 210 n.124
219–49	285		
301–31	285		
337–46	285–6	**HOMER**	
767–8	266 n.1	Epigrams	
909–17	342	8.3–4	157 n.36

Troades

401–2	266 n.1	*Iliad*	
717–18	290 n.88	1.22–5	115
786–9	290 n.88	1.101–303	98–103
1025–8	298	1.149	98–9
1027	306 n.147	1.158	98–9
		1.275–84	99–101
Fragments (N²)		1.293–4	100
109	273 n.30	1.331	88, 95
285	150 n.9	2.119–22	59
365	324 n.222	2.216	58
436	293 n.100	2.262	57 n.44, 125
452	281 n.59	2.298	59
460	268 n.12	2.377	99
593	273 n.30	3.38	58
1027	342 n.275	3.172	89
		3.410	54
		3.410–12	123
HERODOTUS		4.171–81	74
		4.242	137–8
5.75.1	354 n.34	4.339	171 n.84
7.104.4–5	375 n.94	4.368–418	95–6
9.53	165 n.60	5.529–32 (~ 15.561–4)	68
		5.529–30	161
		5.787	65, 68
HESIOD		6.161–2	129
		6.167	137
Theogony		6.209	20 n.46, 57, 71
80–93	148 n.3	6.266–7	136
312	155 n.29	6.325–41	76–7
833	155 n.29	6.325	58
		6.344–8	145 n.293
Works and Days		6.350–1	71, 77, 126–7 n.239
11–41	327	6.416–17	137
185–201	152	6.418–19	240 n.85
193	152 n.18	6.431–2	71
225–6	153	6.441–6	80–1, 143, 281
270–3	153 n.22	6.521–5	77–8
276–80	155	7.93	48
280–5	155	8.139–56	72–4
311	150	8.228	65, 68
317–19	148–51	9.33–49	96 n.105
317	149 n.6	9.302	132
320–4	151	9.312–13	171 n.84
327–34	151–2, 154	9.348–55	203
330	152 n.17	9.372–3	98 n.151
353–8	174		

Iliad (*cont.*):

9.459–61	51
9.497	93–4
9.508	93
9.522	67 n.72
9.523	54, 93, 99, 132
9.630–2	93
9.632–3	94
9.640	93, 108 n.181, 132
10.114–15	97
10.129–30	97
10.237–9	49, 96–7
11.314–15	65
11.404–10	81 n.113, 114 n.290
11.649	54 n.34
13.121–2	52
13.222–34	75
13.568	57 n.44,126
13.622	55
13.768	58
14.80–1	74, 144
14.84	61, 75
14.210	90
14.330–40	123
14.336	54
15.128–9	126–7 n.129
15.496	62
15.502–3	83
15.655–8	69
15.661–6	69–70
16.538–40	84
16.544–6	84
17.91–105	75, 85
17.91–5	52
17.142–50	86–7
17.254–5	85
17.336–7	71–2
18.98–126	145 n.293
18.178–80	137
18.386	90
18.394	88, 90
18.425	90
19.86	99
19.182	54
21.71–135	116–17
21.436–8	59–60
21.468–9	60 n.47, 92
22.75	57 n.44, 125
22.82	141
22.82–4	71
22.82–9	91
22.100	81
22.104–7	81–2, 166, 298
22.105–7	50
22.123–4	116
22.256	61 n.53
22.332	136–7
22.418	132
22.419–20	89 n.129
22.482–507	71
23.473	58–9
23.473–94	98
23.494	76 n.107
23.571	57, 96 n.144
23.585	96 n.144
24.19	61
24.40–5	132, 155
24.52–4	132
24.56–63	132 n.257
24.90–1	112
24.110–11	92
24.133–7	118
24.238	58
24.418–22	119 n.214
24.463	54
24.480–4	119
24.486–570	118–19
24.571–90	240 n.85

Odyssey

1.35–43	181 n.5
1.43	128
1.119–20	110
1.227–9	56, 131
1.263	85 n.120
2.64–7	134
2.64–6	52, 53
2.64	85 n.120
2.65–6	161
2.67	129
2.85–6	57
2.131	91
2.134–7	91
2.136–7	52
3.14	48, 104, 141
3.24	73 n.94, 89 n.129, 104, 141
3.76	104 n.167
3.96 (= 4.326)	48, 105, 141
3.250	171 n.84
3.265	63
4.158–9	85 n.120
4.158–60	104, 127
4.195–6	111
4.533	63
5.447–50	114
6.66–70	123

6.66-7	121	17.347	49, 106
6.135-6	126	17.352	106
6.221-2	125-6	17.415-18	112 n.194
6.242	61	17.449	106
6.274-88	73 n.94, 121-3	17.454	127
6.286	76 n.107, 81 n.113	17.475-87	106-8
6.329-30	92	17.578	106 n.177
7.299-301	122	18.12	139
7.305-6	138-9	18.184	123
8.18-23	158 n.38	18.220-5	110
8.21-2	89	18.222	61
8.85-6	111	18.225	55
8.169-77	158 n.38, 148 n.3	18.228-32	128
8.180	4 n.5	18.321	58-9
8.324	123	18.383	127
8.522-43	111 n.193	19.118-21	112
9.175-6	113	19.124-6	101 n.161
9.188-9	112	19.243	106 n.177
9.189	130	19.272-4	113
9.248	130	19.329-34	112
9.268	113	19.373	57 n.43
9.269-71	114	20.169-71	131
9.270	105	20.227-8	127
9.478-9	136	20.316-19	63-4
9.503	61	20.343-4	48, 52, 91
10.72	66	20.366	61
11.360	90, 113	21.28-9	108 n.181
11.412	63 n.61	21.28	136
11.424	124	21.323-9	139
11.429	63	21.329, 331-3	65
11.432-4	124, 244	21.424	67 n.72
11.433	55, 63	22.38-40	134
11.445-6	124, 126	22.59	54
13.213	114	22.310-29	116
13.402	61	22.344-77	116
14.32	61	22.351	96 n.144
14.37-8	109	22.372-4	129
14.38	66	22.413-15	133
14.56-8	109 n.185	22.414-15	103
14.83-4	133	22.418	125
14.145-65	88	22.424-5	124-5
14.234	88, 90	22.463-4	125
14.283-4	136	22.489	54
14.284	133	23.63-7	133
14.386-9	108	23.65-6	103
15.69-71	111		
15.69	76 n.107, 81 n.113		
15.373	109 n.185, 141	**HOMERIC HYMNS**	
16.75 (= 19.527)	124	*To Demeter (h. Hom. Cer.)*	
16.106-9	63-4	1	157 n.36
17.188-9	89	10-11	157 n.36, 212 n.137
17.216	62	64-5	156
17.322-3	101 n.161, 164 n.57	76	157

To Demeter (cont.):
190	157
213–15	157–8
478–9	157 n.36
485–6	157 n.36

To Hermes (*h. Hom. Merc.*)
156	159
172–3	159 n.44
381–2	159
552	157 n.36

IBYCUS (*PMG = PMGF* (Davies)):
286	316

LUCIAN

De Syria Dea
60	318 n.200

LYSIAS
1.32–3	309 n.155

PINDAR

Isthmian Odes
2.37	176, 183 n.16

Nemean Odes
5.14–18	177
9.33–4	177 n.108
9.34–7	176
11.45–6	176–7

Olympian Odes
7.43–7	176
7.89	176
10.105	155 n.29
13.115	177 n.108

Pythian Odes
4.145–6	177
4.174	177
4.218	177
9.12	177
9.40–1	177

PLATO

Apology
28be	379 n.105

Charmides
157d	373
158cd	373
158c	314 n.180
160c	314 n.180
160e–161b	339 n.264, 373

Crito
46c–48a	379

Definitiones
412c	104 n.167, 373 n.88, 411 n.211
416a	385 n.123

Epistulae
6.323b	376 n.97
7.328c	380
7.337a	372

Euthyphro
12ac	371–2

Gorgias
474c–475e	367 n.73
507d–508a	376 n.97
522d	379–80

Hippias Major
298b	380
304cd	380

Laches
184d–185e	379 n.106

Laws
632c	377 n.101
661e–662a	367 n.73
646e–647b	374
648bc	374
649b–650b	374
666bc	374 n.91
671ce	374
672d	374 n.92
699c–701e	375–6
700a	377
713e	375 n.95
727a–728c	377 n.101
729bc	377 n.100
738e	376 n.98
813cd	377–8
832c	377
837c	378 n.103
841ac	376 n.98

841e	376 n.98	548c	383
845bc	376 n.98	550b	385, 387 n.132
863e–864b	377 n.99	553d	384 n.120, 386 n.129
875cd	377 n.101	560a	389 n.141, 391 n.146
886a	379	560de	375 n.75
		562e	375 n.75
Phaedrus		571c	382
251a	384 n.121	581ab	386–7
253c–254e	384	581b	386 n.129
256a	383 n.117, 384 n.121	587a	385
256c	391 n.147	590d–591a	386 n.129, 391 n.145
		602c–609b	389 n.140
Politicus		604a	389 n.143
310de	374 n.90	605e–606c	382–3
		606a	384 n.120
Protagoras			
320c–328c	355–60	*Symposium*	
320c–322d	356	178d–179a	378
324e–325a	358	180c–185c	378
325cd	357	194c	379
325d–326c	358 n.43	204d–212a	378
326d	358 n.46	218d	379
327bd	357 n.40		
327b	358	*Theaetetus*	
327e	342 n.274	167c	358 n.43, 361 n.53
329c	356 n.39		
333bc	373 n.88	*Timaeus*	
		49cd	380
Republic			
330e–331a	353 n.32		
344ac	361 n.52, 362 n.57, 381 n.110	**PLUTARCH**	
351ce	376 n.97	*Vita Aristidis*	
358e–360d	361 n.55, 381 n.110	20.6	318 n.200
362e–367e	381 n.110		
365cd	363 n.59		
400c–403e	387	**PROTAGORAS (DK)**	
430ab	384 n.120		
436b–441c	382 n.112	3	357 n.40
439e–440a	383		
440ad	385		
440b	385 n.124	**SOLON (West)**	
440cd	383, 384 n.120	32	164–7, 204
441ab	386		
441a	383, 388 n.135		
441e–442c	385	**SOPHOCLES**	
441e–442a	387 n.134	*Ajax*	
442ab	385	79	228
442bc	384 n.120	96–8	228
443de	385	105–17	229–30
465ab	372	121–6	240 n.87
496c	381 n.109	141–3	229
522ab	387 n.134	150–7	229
548b	389	174	229

Ajax (*cont.*):

344–5	230
364–7	230
382	230
418–27	230
430–80	231
485–524	231–4
550–77	234
651–3	234
666–7	234 n.63
678–83	234
954–60	235
961–71	235 n.64
988–9	235
1042–3	235
1057–9	235
1061	229 n.44, 235
1062–5	235
1067–70	236
1071–86	235–6
1085–90	236–7
1091–2	237
1151	237
1159–62	237
1258–63	237
1291–8	237
1305–7	237
1320–4	238
1332–45	238
1347	239
1349	239
1356–7	238–9
1365–7	240 n.87
1370–1	239
1393–1401	240

Antigone

502–11	219–20

Electra

57–63	250 n.123
245–50	247–8
254–60	248
271–4	241
278–93	242
307–9	248–9
351	241
355–6	241
516–18	242
520–4	242
525–621	242–7
552–3	242 n.95
556–7	242 n.95

558–60	243–5
577–83	245
586	241 n.93
596–7	242 n.95
605–7	242 n.95
605–9	246, 247
612–15	246
616	301 n.133
616–21	246–7

Oedipus Coloneus

237–53	221–2
258–91	222 n.19
266–7	222 n.19
567–9	222
636	222
863	223
902–3	222–3
960–1	223
978–80	223 n.25
1189–91	224
1267–9	224
1375–82	225
1399–1423	226

Oedipus Tyrannus

647	209 n.121
652–3	210 n.125
830–3	217
1079	301
1287–9	217 n.8
1318	218
1337–46	218
1347	218
1357–61	218
1384–5	217
1398–1408	218
1407–12	216–17
1409–15	218
1419–21	218
1423–8	216
1486–1502	216

Philoctetes

50–69	250
79–85	250–1
83–4	251 n.127
86–9	252
93–5	252
100	252
108–20	252
468–506	253–4
473–9	254

424–5	255–6	399	174
841–2	256	409–10	173, 342
874–6	257	465–6	171 n.84
900–9	257–9	479–83	168
929–30	259	607–10	171 n.84
934–5	259	627–8	169
967–70	259–60	635–6	172
1011–12	260	1082a	172 n.90
1068	260 n.165	1135–50	172 n.90
1222–49	260–2	1147–50	171 n.84
1250–1	261	1161–2	173 n.92
		1181–2	172 n.90
Trachiniae		1272	175
596–7	360 n.52, 363 n.59	1263–6	174
721–2	363 n.59	1297–8	175
		1329–34	174–5

Fragments (Radt)
352   243

Stoicorum Veterum Fragmenta (von Arnim)

iii.407   301 n.129
iii.409   301 n.129
iii.416   301 n.129

THUCYDIDES

1.37.2	360 n.52
1.49.4	350 n.25
1.84.3	358 n.44
2.11.4–5	350 n.25
2.37.3	350 n.25, 359 n.47
2.51.5	290 n.87
6.13.1	350 n.25
6.24.4	350 n.25
8.27.2–3	165 n.60

THEOGNIS

27–30	170–1, 172 n.91
41	172 n.90
53–68	169–70
58–68	174
83–6	171
101–12	174
207	155 n.29
253	3–4
253–4	174
289–92	172
292	172 n.91
379	172 n.90
383–92	171 n.86
393–400	171 n.86

TYRTAEUS (West)

10.1–12	162
10.15–26	161–2
11.14–16	162
12.1–42	162–3
12.40	4 n.5

XENOPHON

Memorabilia Socratis
4.4.24   362 n.58

GENERAL INDEX

Adkins, A. W. H. 50-1, 55, 56, 62, 65,
  72-4, 101-3, 127-8, 243-5
adultery (*moicheia*) 181, 308-9 n.155,
  321, 328, 337
'affective quality' (Arist.) 393 n.152, 409
aieikēs/aeikelios 60-4
aideomai:
  reflexive 365-70
  usage of 2-4, 13-14, 48-50, 140, 264,
    299-301, 372 n.84
aidesis 224-5
aidoios, usage of 106 n.177, 183-4, 192
aidophrōn 221
aidōs:
  ambivalence of 48-9, 106, 149-51, 284,
    313-14, 324-40
  in battle 68-87, 265-8, 375, 420-2
  and conscience 82, 141-6, 297, 301-3,
    304, 367-70, 376-8, 379-81, 430-1
  denial of 166-7, 202-6
  departure of 152, 172-3, 247, 273
    n.30, 340, 356 n.38, 375-6
  and the eyes 98-9 n.151, 158, 184,
    217-18, 231, 292-3, 312, 352
  and fear 49, 50, 69, 88-9, 157, 236,
    372-3, 374-6
  for the gods 135, 156-7, 172 n.90,
    197-8, 208
  and good sense 126-30
  other-regarding 13, 70, 87-119, 141,
    208-9, 226-7, 232-3, 238-9, 266,
    271, 272-87, 433-4
  personified 152, 155 n.29, 224, 281
    n.58, 307 n.151
  and pity 49, 92-3, 157
  reciprocity of 158-9, 184-5
  retrospective 166, 187-8, 295-303, 352
  self-regarding 13, 68-9, 71-4, 96, 100,
    182-3, 226-7, 230-1, 232, 265, 270,
    272, 283-4, 433-4
  and sexuality 121-6, 185-8, 305-40,
    384
  utility of in community 214, 235-6,
    356-8
  and young people 73, 103-4, 121-3,
    185-6, 306-7, 309, 310-11, 312, 314-
    15, 318, 415-16, 424-5

aischos 54-7
aischron 59-60, 243-5
aischros 58-9
aischunē 175, 182 n.11, 415
aischunō 57-8
aischunomai:
  reflexive 365-70, 380
  synonymous with *aideomai* 138-9, 205
    n.102, 216 n.4, 299 n.121, 301, 373
    n.84, 415
  usage of 264
aischuntēlos 373 n.87, 403-4, 411
akolasia 420
akrasia 322-3 n.214, 338, 400 n.174, 420
anaideia 98-9, 125, 151-2, 155, 159-60,
  210 n.124, 212, 268-9
anaischuntia 408
anger 383, 388, 395-6, 409, 429 n.256
  see also *nemesis*
appropriateness, standards of 54-68,
  130-5, 198, 239, 433
aretē 101, 127-8, 162-4, 169-75, 340-2,
  399-401, 404, 418, 419-20, 426-7,
  428-30
Artemis 316-18
atasthaliē 131-3

Bali 38-9
Benedict, R. 27-8

change, Aristotle's analysis of 393-5
chastity 314-18
  see also *aidōs*, and sexuality
competition, *see* values, co-operative/
  competitive
conformity (versus commitment) 143-5,
  220-1, 376-7, 379-80
conscience 28-42, 44 n.105, 142-4, 166-
  7, 203-4, 220-1, 230 n.48, 240, 257-
  9, 261-3, 281-2, 297, 303-5, 343-54,
  366-7, 381 n.109, 388, 391-2
co-operation, *see* values, co-operative/
  competitive

decisions 192-3, 199-200, 201
diathesis 398, 409 nn.204, 206, 428 n.255
dikaiosunē, *see* justice

dikē, see justice; retaliation
dunamis 398, 401–11
duty 364–5, 367–8

education 80–1, 173, 341–2, 356–8, 365, 368, 374–5, 377, 387–8, 389–90, 423–4, 429–30
    see also socialization
ego-ideal 18–20, 383–4
    see also superego
elegy 168
elenchos 65–7
emotion 5–14, 72–3, 385–9, 393–8, 405
    and *aidōs* 9–14, 104, 108–9, 115, 398, 405
    occurrent/non-occurrent 11, 115, 177, 188, 397–8, 400–1
enkardion 366–7
enkrateia 338, 400 n.174, 419–20
enmity, *see* friends and enemies
ephēbeia 317–18
eusebeia 208 n.111, 220 n.13
euthumia 366–7

Fortenbaugh, W. W. 382–3
Freud, S. 19, 34
friends and enemies 228–9, 234–40, 241
friendship, *see philia*

guest-friendship 105–13, 288–90
guilt 17, 18–47, 145, 218–19, 296, 365–6
    see also shame
guilt-culture 27–47
    see also shame-culture

hamartia 260–1
hazomai 136
Hector, attitude to *aidōs* of 78–83
hexis 398–401, 402, 405, 414, 418, 428–9
honour 13–14, 52, 94–5, 432–4
    of civic institutions 213–14, 376
    community of 70–1, 85–6, 125, 160–1, 164–5
    conflicts over 95–103
    and female sexuality 120, 124–5, 186, 310, 327–8
    inclusive code of 95, 99 n.154, 139–40, 154–6, 180–1, 227, 231–3, 238–41, 249, 269, 275–6, 289–90, 432–3
    invested in objects 210–11 n.129
    and the oath 209–10
    and supplication 115, 185, 189, 209–10, 223, 254, 276, 280, 285, 312
    and the *thumoeides* 383, 386–91

hubris 56, 131, 154, 229–30, 235, 236–7
hylomorphism 394–6

initiation 317–18
internalization, *see* conscience; sanctions, internal/external

Japan 27–8
Jung, C. G. 143
justice 152–6, 172–3, 238–9, 356, 361–3

kalon 147, 243, 329–38, 378–9, 418, 420–2, 425–7
kataplēxis 411
kerdos, in pejorative sense 171, 219 n.11

Leighton, D., and Kluckhohn, C. 28, 32
Lewis, H. B. 19–20, 21
lies 171 n.84, 205, 250, 335
logos, see reason
Lombard, D. B. 311–12
loyalty, see *philia*; honour and female sexuality; honour, community of

marriage 316–18
Mead, M. 29–32, 33–7
meadow, symbolism of 315–16
miasma, see pollution

Navaho 28, 32
nemesis 51–4, 56, 84–6, 98, 133, 143
nomos 362, 364

oaths 209–10, 320–1
opizomai 136–7

Paris, lack of *aidōs* in 76–7
paternal model 44 n.105, 218, 231, 280–1
pathos 393–7, 402–5
pederasty 174–5, 211, 378
philautia 280–2, 369 n.79, 377 n.101, 421 n.239, 430
philia (*philotēs*) 87, 89–100, 174–5, 211, 228, 242–3, 273–6, 340
phronēsis 425–7, 429–30
phthonos 194–5
phusis 258–9, 362
Piers, G. 18–20
pollution 216, 222 n.19, 291–4, 346–8, 350
potential(ity), see *dunamis*
proairesis 426

Protagoras 355-6
psuchē, *see* soul; *see also* tripartite soul
punishment 213-14, 235-6, 357, 362,
      389-90

rape 307-8
reason 382-3, 386-7, 388, 420, 425
Redfield, J. M. 141-3
relativism 195-6, 215, 267-8, 284, 287,
      313-14, 327, 332
remorse 21-2 nn.47-8, 145, 304-5, 346-
      7, 352, 369
reputation, *see* sanctions, internal/
      external
'results culture' 71-9
retaliation 225-7, 237, 241-9

Samoa 38
sanctions:
   divine 29, 107, 209, 350
   internal/external 27-33, 35, 36-7, 39-
      40, 107, 141-3, 275, 333-4, 350-1,
      354, 358-60, 361-70, 381-2, 389-91,
      421-5, 427-8
sebas 137-8, 157, 206-14
self-interest 107-8, 112, 128-9, 275-6,
      279-87, 359-60, 361-2, 367-9
selfishness 266, 281 n.59
semnos 157 n.36, 281-2 n.59, 313
shame 14-47, 218-19
   and *aidōs* 14-15, 26

phenomenology of 15, 73, 158, 207,
      217, 292-3
   see also guilt
shame-culture 27-47, 140, 392
   see also guilt-culture
Snell, B. 202-6
socialization 28, 32-42, 143-4, 358-9,
      388, 426-7
Socrates 322-3 n.214, 339, 381
sōphrosunē 104, 127, 168, 234 n.63, 249,
      272, 306, 314-15, 339, 373, 404,
      419-20
soul 394
superego 18-20, 34, 384 n.120
   see also ego-ideal
supplication 113-19, 183-5, 189-93, 209-
      10, 221-7, 253-4, 276-87, 330-1
symposium 168-9, 174-5, 374-5

Taylor, G. 15-18
theft 151, 159-60
thumoeides 383-92
time, *see* honour
tripartite soul 381-92

values 100-3
   co-operative/competitive 50-1, 53, 60,
      66-8, 83-7, 100-2, 127-8, 140, 232-
      3, 252, 390, 434

weakness of the will, see *akrasia*
women 120-5, 185-8, 205, 305-40